Mphanga Anthony Ngwatu
20/1/1990 - home.

CHRISTIAN ETHICS

Moral Theology
in the Light of Vatican II

Volume II: Special Moral Theology

D1189537

CHRISTIAN ETHICS

Moral Theology
in the Light of Vatican II

Volume II: Special Moral Theology

Karl H. Peschke, S.V.D.

C. GOODLIFFE NEALE
Alcester B49 6ER
1985

BJ1249
P39
.1986†
vol 2
0168307739

Copyright © 1985 by Karl H. Peschke

Nihil Obstat: Kevin J. McDonald STL.

Imprimatur: Mgr. D. Leonard VG.

Birmingham, 23rd August 1985.

First printing 1978
Fourth printing, adapted
  to the new Code, 1985
Fifth printing 1986

LC Class No: BJ 1251
Dewey: 241.19 (Old Dewey: 241.18)
ISBN: 0 948169 01 X

Printed by
Presscraft, Hartlebury, West Midlands

Published by
C. Goodliffe Neale Ltd., Arden Forest Industrial Estate, Alcester,
Warwickshire B49 6ER, England

CONTENTS

Abbreviations   xi

Introduction   xiii

PART I

CHRISTIAN RESPONSIBILITY IN THE RELIGIOUS REALM

The theological virtues in general   1

Chapter I: THE VIRTUE OF FAITH

A.   Essence of theological faith   7
   I.   Concept of faith   7
     1.   Faith as personal encounter with God   9
     2.   Faith as assent to revealed truths   11
   II.   Knowledge of faith necessary for salvation   14

B.   Man under the obedience of faith   16

C.   Duties with regard to faith   19
   I.   Duty of knowing the truths of faith   19
   II.   Obligation to profess the faith   21
   III.   Duty of spreading the faith   24
   IV.   Obligation to safeguard the faith   27
   V.   Promotion of unity of faith   29
     1.   Nature and motivation of the ecumenical movement   29
     2.   Practical demands regarding the fostering of unity   31
     Appendix: Guidelines on the sharing of spiritual resources   34
   VI.   Duty of submission to the teaching authority of the Church   39

D.   Sins against faith   44
   I.   Pride   45
   II.   Unbelief   45
   III.   Sins against the Christian faith   47

Chapter II: THE VIRTUE OF HOPE   51

A.   Essence of theological hope   52
   I.   Hope in Holy Scripture   52
   II.   Concept of hope in theology   55

B.	Fruits and challenges of hope	57
	1. Endurance in suffering	57
	2. Openness for the future	58
	3. Summons to transform the world	59
C.	Sins against hope	60
	1. Presumption	60
	2. Despair	61
	3. Resignation	62

Chapter III: THE VIRTUE OF DIVINE LOVE   64

A.	Essence of divine love	65
	I. Nature of divine love in Holy Scripture	65
	II. Concept of divine love in theology	71
	III. Qualities of divine love	73
B.	Realization of divine love in prayer and deed	75
C.	Sins against the love of God	78
	1. Indifference	79
	2. Hatred of God	79

Chapter IV: NATURE OF DIVINE WORSHIP   81

A.	Notion and object of divine worship	82
	I. Concept of divine worship	82
	II. Different forms of worship	83
	III. Worship of God and veneration of saints	86
B.	Foundation of divine worship	87
	I. Duty to worship in general	88
	II. Necessity of external and corporate worship	89
C.	Sins contrary to the nature of worship: false cult	93
	I. False worship of the true God	93
	II. Worship of false gods (idolatry)	95
	III. Superstition	97
	1. Vain observances	99
	2. Divination	101
	3. Magic	104

Chapter V: SPECIFIC MANIFESTATIONS AND DUTIES OF WORSHIP   107

A.	Prayer	107
	I. Nature of prayer	108
	II. Necessity of prayer	111
	III. Conditions of prayer	113
B.	Consecration of human life by the sacraments	116
	I. Notion and function of the sacraments	116
	II. Necessity and obligation of sacramental worship	118
	III. Dispositions for valid and fruitful reception	122
	IV. Requirements for valid and worthy administration	126

C. Consecration of time by holy days 129
    I. The celebration of Sunday and holy seasons 130
        1. Biblical origin of the Sunday celebration 131
        2. The binding authority of the Sunday precept 135
        3. The Sunday Mass 137
        4. The Sunday rest 145
    II. Days of religious fast and abstinence 151

D. Vows 154
    I. Meaning of the vow 154
    II. Conditions for validity 155
    III. Binding force and fulfillment 157
    IV. Release from vows 159

E. Duties of reverence for the sacred 162
    I. Reverence for God's name 162
    II. Reverence for consecrated persons 164
    III. Reverence for sacred places 165
    IV. Reverence for sacred objects and things 166

PART II

CHRISTIAN RESPONSIBILITY TOWARDS THE CREATED WORLD

170

Chapter I: FRATERNAL LOVE AND JUSTICE 172

A. Nature and order of fraternal love 172
    I. The commandment of fraternal love according to Holy Scripture 173
    II. Nature of fraternal love 178
        1. Notion of fraternal love 178
        2. Qualities of fraternal love 182
    III. Universality and order of fraternal love 184
        1. Order of love with regard to persons 184
           a) Well-ordered love of self 184
           b) Well-ordered love of neighbours 186
        2. Order of love in relation to the gravity of needs 187
        3. Love of enemies 189

B. Primary manifestations of fraternal love 194
    I. Corporal works of charity 195
        1. The corporal works of charity in general 195
        2. Principles concerning material assistance 198
    II. Spiritual works of charity 201
        1. The spiritual works of charity in general 202
        2. Fraternal correction 206

C. The virtue of justice   210
    I.   Virtue of justice in Holy Scripture   210
    II.   Nature of justice   212
          1. Concept of justice   212
          2. Properties of justice   215
    III. Classifications of justice   216
    IV.   Justice and love   219

Chapter II: MORAL RESPONSIBILITY IN COMMUNITY LIFE   221

A. Nature and order of society in general   222
    I.   Nature of society   222
          1. Notion of society   222
          2. The common good: aim and function of society   223
          3. The complementary function of society
              (principle of subsidiarity)   224
    II.   Responsible use of authority   227
          1. Authority in Holy Scripture   228
          2. Reason and function of authority   229
          3. Exercise of authority in a spirit of service   231
    III. The virtue of obedience   232
          1. Obedience in Holy Scripture   233
          2. Need and value of obedience   236
          3. Practice of obedience in a spirit of
              co-responsibility   239

B. The family   242
    I.   Nature and functions of the family   243
    II.   Mutual obligations of spouses   245
    III. Parental duties and rights   246
    IV.   Duties of children towards parents   256
    V.   The wider family   258

C. The state   260
    I.   Nature and origin of the state   260
    II.   Tasks and moral duties of state authority   265
          1. Tasks of state authority in general   267
              a) Legislation and administration of justice   267
              b) Promotion of socio-economic welfare and
                 public health   269
          2. Criminal jurisdiction of the state   271
              a) Punitive right of the state in general   271
              b) Right of the state to death penalty   272
          3. Requirements of a just fiscal policy   274
    III. The national right to self-defence by war   275
          1. Moral admissibility of war   276
          2. Conditions of a just war   277
          3. Means and methods of warfare   279
          4. Problem of atomic warfare   280
          5. Participation in war   281

IV.	Duties of citizens	283
	1. Civil obedience and respect	283
	2. Obligation to pay taxes	284
	3. Civic responsibility and participation	287
V.	The right of resistance against unjust state authority	288
	1. Resistance against illegitimate rulers	289
	2. Resistance against legitimate rulers	290

D. The Church   294

I.	The Church authority	295
	1. Mediator between God and men	295
	2. Teacher of the divine truth and the moral law	297
	3. The Church as servant in her ministry	298
II.	Duties of believers	299
III.	Church and state	301
	1. Guidelines for the relation between Church and state	301
	2. Religious tolerance	305

Chapter III: BODILY LIFE AND HEALTH   307

A.	Christian view of body and bodily life	307
B.	Responsibility for health	308
	1. Nourishment	310
	2. Clothing and housing	311
	3. Recreation and sports	311
	4. Stimulants and drugs	312
C.	Medical treatments and operations	316
I.	Medical and surgical treatments in general	317
	1. Moral rights and duties of the physician	317
	2. Ordinary and extraordinary treatments	318
	3. The duty to preserve life	321
	4. Cooperation in illicit operations	324
II.	Particular surgeries	325
	1. Cosmetic surgery	325
	2. Transplantation of organs	325
	3. Sterilization and castration	329
	4. Operations in cases of difficult pregnancy	333
III.	Psychotherapeutic treatments	337
IV.	Experimentation on human beings	340
D.	Endangering of health and life	341
I.	Permissible endangering of health and life	342
II.	Sinful endangering of health and life	343
E.	Destruction of human life	344
I.	Suicide and indirect killing of oneself	345
II.	Murder and indirect killing of fellowman	348
	1. Murder and indirect killing in general	348

vii

2.	Euthanasia	351
3.	Abortion	353
III.	Self-defence	365
	1. Concept and conditions of self-defence	365
	2. Arguments in justification of self-defence	366
F.	Acceptance of suffering and death	368

Chapter IV: SEXUALITY AND MARRIAGE — 371

A. Nature and meaning of human sexuality — 372

   1. Biblical view of sexuality — 373
   2. Man's sexual constitution in general — 376
   3. Nature and purpose of sexual love — 378
   4. Social dependence of sexual actuation — 381
   5. Christian reverence for the dignity of woman — 382

B. Mastery of sexuality and failures in it — 386

   I. Virtues of modesty and chastity — 386
      1. The virtue of modesty and its offences — 386
      2. The virtue of chastity — 392
         a) Nature of the virtue — 392
         b) Questions of imputability — 394
   II. Sexual fantasies and impure thoughts — 396
   III. Moral perspectives of masturbation — 401
      1. Occurrence, causes and effects — 401
      2. Moral evaluation — 403
   IV. Encounter of the sexes — 408
      1. Genuine growth in human love — 408
      2. Necking and petting — 412
      3. The problem of premarital intercourse — 416
      4. Other sins of heterosexual nature — 426
   V. Sexual deviations and the problem of homosexuality — 431

C. Moral responsibility in the marriage state — 440

   I. The time of engagement — 440
      1. Meaning of the engagement time — 440
      2. Rights, duties and chastity of the engaged — 441
   II. Nature of marriage — 443
      1. The ends of marriage — 443
         a) Procreation and education of children — 443
         b) Mutual assistance and completion in love — 444
      2. Unity of marriage (monogamy) — 446
      3. Indissolubility of marriage — 448
      4. Marriage as a public act — 460
      5. Marriage as a sacrament — 461
         a) Sacramental sign and grace — 461

	covenant	462
	c) Mixed marriages	463
III.	Responsible parenthood and regulation of birth	465
	1. Justification and limits of birth control	466
	2. Natural family planning	469
	3. Unlawful means of birth control according to *Humanae Vitae*	471
	4. Echo on *Humanae Vitae* and interpretations	475
	5. Artificial insemination	479
IV.	Marital love and conjugal intimacies	481
	1. The right to the conjugal act	481
	2. Causes excusing from the marriage debt	482
	3. Care for affectionate love	483

Chapter V: WORK AND PROPERTY   485

A.	The moral order of work	487
I.	Christian evaluation of work	487
	1. Work in Holy Scripture	487
	2. Theology of work	490
II.	Moral duties in work and profession	494
III.	The right to work and to just compensation	496
	1. The right to work	496
	2. The right to a just wage	497
	3. The right to protection and social security	501
IV.	The right to organize and to strike	504
V.	Promotion of worker participation	510
B.	The moral order of property	513
I.	Meaning and basis of private property	514
	1. Holy Scripture on the value of material goods	514
	2. Moral basis for the right to private property	518
	3. The universal purpose of created things	521
II.	Acquisition of proprietary rights	523
	1. Work and accession	523
	2. Occupancy	525
	3. Contracts	527
	A' Contracts in general	527
	B' Contracts of sale	532
	C' Last will or testament	535
	4. Prescription	538
III.	Moral duties concerning property	541
	1. Property as stewardship	541
	2. Social obligations concerning property	543
	3. Unaccountable use of property: avarice and waste	544
IV.	Violation of proprietary rights	546
	1. Unjust damage	547
	2. Fraud	548

		3.	Usury and profiteering	549
		4.	Theft	551
		5.	Reasons which permit appropriation of another's goods	555
			a) Appropriation in necessity (food theft)	555
			b) Occult compensation	556
	V.	Restitution for violation of proprietary rights		557
		1.	Restitution on grounds of unjust possession	559
		2.	Restitution for tax evasions	562
		3.	Restitution for unjust damage	563
		4.	Restitution for culpable cooperation in damage	565
		5.	Recipient of restitution, manner and excuses	568
	VI.	Socialization and land reform		570

Chapter VI: **TRUTH, FIDELITY AND HONOUR**   574

A. Truthfulness   574
   I. Truthfulness in Holy Scripture   574
   II. The virtue of truthfulness and its duties   577
      1. Truthfulness in thought   578
      2. Truthfulness in conduct   579
      3. Truthfulness in words   581
   III. The lie and lawful concealment of the truth   582
   IV. The oath   594

B. Fidelity   597
   I. Nature and foundation of fidelity   597
   II. The promise   598

C. The secret   599

D. The moral good of honour   603
   I. Nature and foundation of honour   603
   II. Principal duties of honour   604
      1. Regard for one's own honour   604
      2. Respect for one's neighbour   606
   III. Offences against the honour of others   607
      1. Contumely   608
      2. Detraction and calumny   609

Bibliography   615
Index

ABBREVIATIONS

I. *Documents of Vatican II.*

AA = Apostolicam Actuositatem: Decree on the Apostolate of the Laity.

AG = Ad Gentes: Decree on the Church's Missionary Activity.

CD = Christus Dominus: Decree on the Bishop's Pastoral Office in the Church.

DH = Dignitatis Humanae: Declaration on Religious Freedom.

DV = Dei Verbum: Dogmatic Constitution on Divine Revelation.

GE = Gravissimum Educationis: Declaration on Christian Education.

GS = Gaudium et Spes: Pastoral Constitution on the Church in the Modern World.

IM = Inter Mirifica: Decree on the Instruments of Social Communication.

LG = Lumen Gentium: Dogmatic Constitution on the Church.

NA = Nostra Aetate: Declaration on the Relationship of the Church to Non-Christian Religions.

OE = Orientalium Ecclesiarum: Decree on Eastern Catholic Churches.

OT = Optatam Totius: Decree on Priestly Formation.

PC = Perfectae Caritatis: Decree on the Appropriate Renewal of the Religious Life.

PO = Presbyterorum Ordinis: Decree on the Ministry and Life of Priests.

SC = Sacrosanctum Concilium: Constitution on the Sacred Liturgy.

UR = Unitatis Redintegratio: Decree on Ecumenism.

II. *Social Encyclicals*

RN = Rerum Novarum: Encyclical Letter of Pope Leo XIII on the Condition of Workers (1891).

QA = Quadragesimo Anno: Encyclical Letter of Pope Pius XI on Social Reconstruction (1931).

MM = Mater et Magistra: Encyclical Letter of Pope John XXIII on Recent Developments of the Social Question (1961).

PT = Pacem in Terris: Encyclical Letter of Pope John XXIII on His Program for World Peace (1963).

PP = Populorum Progressio: Encyclical Letter of Pope Paul VI on the Development of Peoples (1967).

Acknowledgements

The author sincerely thanks his confreres Father Thomas Cassidy, Peter McHugh, Michael Murphy, John McSherry and Stanley Plutz for checking his writings, throughout the many years during which the text of this book was formulated and reformulated, and for their welcome suggestions.

He likewise thanks Fathers Constante Floresca and Alois Lehberger for helping him in the reading of the proofs.

INTRODUCTION

Special moral theology treats of human behaviour in the different spheres and situations of human life. It presupposes the principles of general moral theology, upon which it builds and which it applies to the particular fields of human actions. This book therefore finds its necessary completion in the first volume of Christian Ethics, the presentation of general moral theology.[1]

Among the topics of general moral theology the question after the ultimate purpose of the moral demand and the problem of natural law are of particular moment for special moral theology. Traditional moral teaching has very much emphasized the importance of natural law for the finding of the moral norm. According to the principle "action follows being", the moral obligation is to be derived from the nature of man and of the beings to which his action is related. This doctrine certainly retains its importance also today. But it is also the cause of many controversies. Differences in the understanding of human nature naturally result in differences of opinion concerning the moral obligation. This is a permanent challenge to understand human nature always better and more correctly. Scholars of our time stress the need to listen to the empirical sciences, especially to psychology and sociology, in order to complete the knowledge of man's nature. Moral theology cannot dispense with this effort. Special moral theology in particular stands in need of this knowledge. In order, for example, to evaluate superstition correctly, the moral theologian must know of the phenomena of parapsychology; in order to evaluate sexual behaviour, he must have a correct grasp of the social and personal implications of sexuality; in order to discuss the socio-economic order, he must be informed about the laws of labour relations and economic development.

In spite of the great reservations of many theologians of our time against the traditional natural law theory, this approach to the moral norm in a last analysis leans upon the same basic

---

[1] Karl H. Peschke: Christian Ethics. Moral Theology in the Light of Vatican II. Vol. I: General Moral Theology. — Alcester: C. Goodliffe Neale, 1987, revised edition

principles as those of natural law ethics. The moral order is derived from man's nature, only that the knowledge of this nature is completed by the new insights of psychology, the social sciences and other similar disciplines. The approach is basically ontologic, i.e. from man's being conclusions are drawn to the moral ought.

But acquaintance with the anthropological sciences is not the only presupposition for the elaboration of the moral norm. Of equal importance for the determination of the moral law is the goal and purpose for which man and the world are created. The goal to be achieved is a most decisive criterion for the decision of what is to be approved as morally good and what is to be rejected as morally evil. The Protestant theologian H.-D. Wendland demands the development of an eschatological ethics and an eschatological natural law.[1] By this he understands an ethics and natural law which receive their orientation and norms not only from the nature of the created beings as they exist at present (ontological point of departure), but at least to an equal extent from the new creation which is to come and the perfection of the kingdom which God has planned for the end of time (eschatological point of departure). He feels that not only Protestant ethics is in need of this eschatological orientation, but also Catholic moral theology and natural law doctrine.

One may object that Thomistic and scholastic theology has always pointed out God's glory as the ultimate end of man, which he has to keep in mind in whatever he does. This is certainly true. Nevertheless God's glory remained a rather abstract notion in this system. It did not influence much the content of the moral norm. For all practical purposes the moral law was derived from the concrete nature of man and creation. This is the ontological point of departure.

The ultimate goal of creation and the purpose of God with man and the world have to receive greater attention also in Catholic moral theology. The goal is briefly defined as God's glory through establishment of his kingdom. This is further explained in the first volume of this ethics. A very valuable and basic

---

[1] "A critical, eschatological 'natural law'..., this is the theological task whose solution is necessary for the theology of society and the Christian image of the responsible society in social ethics" (Heinz-Dietrich Wendland: Die Kirche in der modernen Gesellschaft. — Hamburg: Furche, 1956, 145; see also the article "Eschatologie" by the same author in: Evangelisches Soziallexikon, ed. by F. Karrenberg. — Stuttgart: Kreuz-Verlag, 1965, 358-362). Confer the study "Eschatologisches Naturrecht", in: Naturrecht in der Kontroverse. Kritik evangelischer Theologie an der katholischen Lehre von Naturrecht und natürlicher Sittlichkeit, by Karlheinz Peschke. — Salzburg: Otto Müller, 1967, 127-141.

contribution to the question is given by the Second Vatican Council. It explains that "Christians, on pilgrimage toward the heavenly city, should seek and savour the things which are above. This duty in no way decreases, but rather increases, the weight of their obligation to work with all men in constructing a more human world... Manifested at the beginning of time, the divine plan is that man should subdue the earth, bring creation to perfection, and develop himself. When a man so acts he simultaneously obeys the great Christian commandment that he place himself at the service of his brother men" (GS 57). Man is called to "be a partner in the work of bringing God's creation to perfection" (GS 67; cf. 34). In all his actions he has to keep this goal in mind and to serve it. This point of departure for the moral norm can truly be termed eschatological.

The eschatological orientation is essential for Christian ethics. The calling of man to cooperate with God in the unfolding of his creation with everything that it implies must be present as a final criterion in all moral deliberations. Christian ethics is theonomous not only because the word of God in Holy Scripture is always a basic source of moral inspiration for it, but also because it finds its centre in the plan of God with this world and in his glory.

Man's relation to God is the most basic factor in his moral life. It is therefore proper that the study of man's responsibility in the religious realm precede the study of his responsibility towards the created world. Holy Scripture takes it for granted that this should be the order. It places the commandments of the decalogue concerned with the worship of God in front of the other commandments concerned with man's obligations towards his fellowmen, and always ranks love of God before love of neighbour.

This presentation of special moral theology is accordingly divided in two parts. Each part is introduced by the study of some fundamental virtues which are of particular importance for the respective sections. The other chapters basically follow the order of the ten commandments. Part one on the religious realm deals with the theological virtues of faith, hope and charity; the nature of divine worship; the sins of false cult; the specific manifestations and duties of divine worship. Part two on the created world deals with the virtues of fraternal love and justice; community life in family, state and Church; bodily life and health; sexuality and marriage; work and property; truth, fidelity and honour.

References to canon law relate to the new *Codex Iuris Canonici* (CIC), promulgated by Pope John Paul II in 1983.

PART I

CHRISTIAN RESPONSIBILITY
IN THE RELIGIOUS REALM

The Theological Virtues in General

The religious life manifests itself above all in the acts of worship, such as prayer, sacrifices, sacramental rites, cultic celebrations. But the soul of all worship is the divine or theological virtues, which open man's heart for God and unite man with God. They kindle and inspire the religious life and are the basic endowments for it. The recitation of prayers and the performance of cultic acts are empty shells without the spirit of these virtues. On the other hand the divine virtues also stand in need of the external expression by prayers, liturgical services and sacraments. Through the external acts they are sustained, formed and strengthened.[1]

The theological virtues are three according to the consistent teaching of Christian theology: faith, hope and charity. The reason for this triad is the teaching of the New Testament letters, which do not only emphasize the value of these three virtues individually, but repeatedly combine them in one group. St. Paul remembers the "work of faith and labour of love and steadfastness of hope" of the Thessalonians (1 Thess 1:3). He places these three virtues at the summit of all the others. "So faith, hope, love abide, these three; but greatest of these is love" (1 Cor 13:13; cf. Rom 5:1-5; Gal 5:5f; Col 1:4f; 1 Thess 5:8; Heb 10:22-24; 1 Pet 1:21f). The threefold number gained a firm place in the tradition of the Church. The Council of Trent takes up the doctrine of the three theological virtues,

---

[1] Theological or divine virtues are virtues which have God as their immediate object and motive. In contradistinction, the moral virtues have created values as their immediate object. Only mediately, insofar as God himself is obeyed in every authentic moral law, do moral virtues include a relation to God. The theological virtues, on the contrary, elevate the soul without any mediating link to God.

1

declaring that in the act of justification they are infused together with the other gifts of grace into man's soul.[1]

A speculative, compelling inference of faith, hope and charity as the only theological virtues from the essence of man and of the religious-moral life is however not possible. St. Thomas only gives a reason of suitability. In fact Scripture itself frequently mentions other theological virtues, like fear of the Lord, trust in God, piety. The proposition therefore that there are three theological virtues must be taken in the affirmative and not in the exclusive sense. But it remains most true that faith, hope and charity are three principal virtues of man's inner religious life.

The primary purpose of the divine virtues is to equip man for the sacred dialogue with God. Through faith, hope and love man is able to understand the salvific word of God, to receive it in his heart and to respond to it. The divine virtues are the foundations of man's religious existence and life with God. They relate man and his entire activity, and together with it the whole world, to the divine service and to Christ's kingdom. In line with this fundamental importance of the divine virtues, Holy Scripture and tradition consider them as necessary means of salvation.

According to the teaching of Holy Scripture a man cannot be justified and saved without the virtues of faith, hope and charity. Faith is the primary condition for salvation. "He who believes and is baptized will be saved; but he who does not believe will be condemned" (Mk 16:16). St. Paul repeatedly and forcibly asserts that man is justified and lives through faith (Rom 1:17; 3:28-30; Gal 2:20f; 3:11; Phil 3:9). Whoever wants to draw near to God, so we read in the letter to the Hebrews, must believe in him, for "without faith it is impossible to please him" (Heb 11:6). Therefore faith is enjoined as a commandment: "This is his commandment, that we should believe in the name of his Son Jesus Christ" (1 Jn 3:23; cf. 1 Tim 1:18f).[2]

The necessity of hope is stated in the letter to the Romans, where St. Paul explains that Christians wait with eager longing for the future glory and redemption, and that "in this hope we were saved" (Rom 8:18-24; cf. 1 Tim 6:17). Again, the letter

---

[1] DS 1530.

[2] The magisterium of the Church has repeatedly declared that faith falls under the precept: DS 2021; 2116; 2165; 3008.

to the Hebrews expresses the same thought; it says that we belong to God and "are his house if we hold fast our confidence and pride in our hope" (Heb 3:6).

The absolute need of love is most emphatically stated by Paul's enthusiastic praise of charity in 1 Cor 13: If a man speaks in the tongues of angels, if he has prophetic powers and understands all mysteries and all knowledge, if he has all faith so as to remove mountains, and if he gives away all he has, but has no love, he is nothing. No less clear is St. John, who makes plain that "he who does not love remains in death" (1 Jn 3:14); while "he who abides in love abides in God, and God abides in him" (1 Jn 4:16). With this intrinsic need of love corresponds the express commandment of Christ. "You shall love the Lord your God with all your heart, and with all your soul, and with all your mind. This is the great and first commandment. And a second is like it. You shall love your neighbour as yourself" (Mt 22:37-39 par).

On the basis of the scriptural teaching the Council of Trent pronounces the strict necessity of the three theological virtues for justification and eternal life. It declares that faith is the beginning, fundament and root of all justification and that without faith one cannot please God;[1] that besides faith also hope and charity are necessary to become a living member of Christ and to attain eternal life.[2] The absolute necessity of charity for justification constitutes one of the definitions of the Tridentine Council.[3]

Reason confirms the necessity of the three virtues for man's salvation. In the concrete order of salvation man's ultimate end is supernatural and divine. It consists in the community with God and in participation in his reign. The vocation to such an end presupposes some access to the mystery of the divine persons and sufficient knowledge of the nature of God's reign. This requires a corresponding supernatural light, which is the light of faith. Furthermore man will not strive after an end which he does not love and does not hope to attain. Hence he must love God and his reign, and he must hope to be admitted into his community. Besides, hope alone will move a man to pray and thus to fulfill another condition of his salvation. For a safe theological doctrine says that without prayer no man can be saved.[4]

---

[1] DS 1532; cf. 3012.
[2] DS 1531.
[3] DS 1561.
[4] Cf. Noldin II, 1959, nr. 146.

According to traditional doctrine the divine virtues are intrinsically supernatural and therefore always necessarily infused. They are imparted together with sanctifying grace. Yet since in the understanding of hitherto theological teaching the life of grace is usually only gained by means of the sacraments and fundamentally through baptism, only Christians were considered capable of the theological virtues. Although it is obvious that non-Christians also possess religion, their religious life was subsumed under the virtue of religion. This virtue has according to St. Thomas Aquinas not God himself as its object, but only the acts of cult. Therefore he did not regard it as a theological virtue.

This doctrine has however justly been contested by recent theologians. Richard Egenter shows that the argument of St. Thomas on the object of the virtue of religion is not consistent, since in his other teachings a habit is never specified by its acts, but rather by the object of its acts. Now the object of the acts of cult is God: God is adored, God is worshipped, to God are offered prayers and sacrifices. Hence God is the object of the virtue of religion, and the existence of a natural theological virtue must be granted.[1] G. Ermecke[2] and A. Auer[3] regard Egenter's comment as valid and agree with him in the admission of a natural theological virtue.

The question of theological virtues in the non-Christian world receives further light by the new understanding theology has gained of the universal presence of the salvific grace of Christ and of the Holy Spirit in the world. Vatican II itself made this understanding its own and forwards it. It teaches that grace works in the hearts of all men in an unseen way and that the Holy Spirit offers to every man the possibility of being associated with the paschal mystery (GS 22; LG 16). Hence in the present supernatural order all men of good will receive the graces necessary to become citizens of the kingdom of Christ. Accordingly everybody is also in the condition to obtain the divine

[1] Richard Egenter: Das Wesen der religio und ihre Stellung im Tugendsystem nach dem heiligen Thomas von Aquin; in: Der Mensch vor Gott, Festschrift für Th. Steinbüchel; ed. by Ph. Weindel and R. Hofmann. — Düsseldorf: Patmos, 1948, 55-65. The same publication contains an article by Rudolf Hofmann: Gottesverehrung als moraltheologisches Problem (pp. 399-416), who equally defines God as the object of the virtue of religion.

[2] Mausbach/Ermecke: Katholische Moraltheologie, vol. 2. — Münster: Aschendorff, 1954, 166.

[3] Alfons Auer, article "Gottesverehrung" in: Lexikon für Theologie und Kirche, vol. 4, 1960, column 1135.

virtues and to practise them, even under the presupposition that they are intrinsically supernatural and always infused.

Actually, since all men are destined for the same ultimate goal (cf. GS 22; 24; NA 1), which is a supernatural one, all must also receive the corresponding supernatural powers and qualifications for this vocation and for their task as cooperators in God's salvific plan. The theological virtues love and hope are after all expressly mentioned by the Council as part of the spiritual outfit of all men of good will. After having explained that the Christian "receives 'the first-fruits of the Spirit' (Rom 8:23) by which he becomes capable of discharging the new law of love", and that he hastens "forward to resurrection in the strength which comes from hope", the same text immediately continues with the comment that "all this holds true not only for Christians, but for all men of good will" (GS 22). To the degree therefore to which non-Christians are capable of sharing in the grace of Christ and in his Holy Spirit, to the same degree they also participate in the gift of the infused divine virtues and are able to practise them.

In the acts of worship, especially in the liturgy, the divine virtues tend to give expression to the devotion, hope and love which they cherish. Man's prayers give voice to his adoration, and the liturgical actions, symbols and sacraments are signs which announce the faith of the heart and express its hope and love.

Through prayer and cult the divine virtues are inversely also nourished and formed. Especially the celebration of the liturgy and of the sacraments gives nourishment to the virtues and contributes to their formation. What the Constitution on the Sacred Liturgy of Vatican II writes in this regard of faith, can be equally applied to hope and love: "When the Church prays or sings or acts, the faith of those taking part is nourished and their minds are raised to God, so that they may offer Him the worship which reason requires and more copiously receive His grace" (SC 33; cf. 59).

Hence the celebration of the liturgy announces the Christian faith and gives nourishment to it, more so than individual contemplation. The liturgy is equally a promise of salvation and a pledge of hope. Our hope in the future perfection of all things in Christ is sustained by the visible manifestation of the paschal

love between Christ and the Church. It belongs to the present
order of salvation that men cannot experience, without the visible
signs of the sacred cult and the liturgy, the richness of the
salvation God has prepared for his children and the bond of
love that unites them with their Father in heaven.

Chapter 1

THE VIRTUE OF FAITH[1]

A. Essence of theological faith

I. Concept of faith

Theological faith is usually conceived of as assent to truths contained in biblical revelation and to doctrines proposed by the Church as dogmas of faith. Yet faith is not primarily assent to a specific set of propositions. It is a personal encounter with God, a self-disclosure of the divine Father and a personal adherence to him.

Faith opens the way to knowledge of a person. The one who believes shares in the being and world of another, in his thought, in his knowledge, understanding, love and desire. "To believe something is but the secondary form of this. From this it is clear that faith is primarily and properly not a relation of man to things, propositions, or formulas, but a relation to persons. And this relation is directed in particular to knowledge of the person. Faith is the manner and means by which we gain an understanding approach to a person. This is so true that without faith the reality and the mystery of the person remains closed in its most profound and real sense. A person is not really known as he is by being taken under control and analysed by tests or experiments... Knowledge of a person on the lines of mathematics or the natural sciences is inappropriate because such methods are inapplicable. A person in his true nature, in his

---

[1] References: Jean Mouroux: I Believe. The Personal Structure of Faith. — London: G. Chapman, 1959. Josef Pieper: Belief and Faith. — London: Faber and Faber, 1963. S. J. Heijke: The Bible on Faith. — De Pere, Wisc.: St. Norbert Abbey Press, 1966. Ingo Hermann: The Experience of Faith. — New York: P. J. Kenedy and Sons, 1966. Gerhard Ebeling: The Nature of Faith. — Wm. Collins Fontana Library, 1967. Heinrich Fries: Faith Under Challenge. — New York: Herder and Herder, 1969. Jean Danielou: The Faith Eternal and the Man of Today. — Chicago: Franciscan Herald Press, 1970. John Powell: A Reason to Live! A Reason to Die! — Niles, Ill.: Argus Communications, 1972. Paul Surlis (ed.): Faith: Its Nature and Meaning. — Dublin: Gill and Macmillan, 1972. Robert Ackermann: Belief and Knowledge. — London: Macmillan, 1973.

very self, is only known if he allows himself to be known, if he discloses himself."[1]

Faith necessarily includes certain particulars, in the form of: I believe what you say, what you ask, what you promise. Thus faith implies also a faith in assertions. But this belief in propositions and statements is related to the person who is believed and primarily a participation in his thoughts and world. These thoughts, in the case of human beings, must not necessarily correspond with outside reality. They must only represent his inner convictions and feelings. Faith guarantees this correspondence of a person's utterances with his inner insights, experiences and convictions. The correctness of statements concerning outside reality however is guaranteed to the extent of the trusted person's competence and knowledge.

"Faith is therefore not a preliminary, partial, or approximate type of knowledge. It is authentic knowledge; it is understanding in that realm which is primarily not concerned with world, things and objects, but with the person."[2] Faith alone admits to deeper knowledge of a person. From this it is clear how one-sided it is to consider knowledge as genuine only where one's own experimental insight can reach. With such a limitation important areas of reality would be closed to our knowledge: the sphere of the person.

Holy Scripture is in basic agreement with the insight that faith is primarily a personal encounter and relation. In the understanding of the OT faith is a total bond with God. Its most obvious features are "trust in the God of the Covenant, the expectation and hope of his help, the taking refuge in his love, and an absolute holding fast to him and his words."[3] Knowledge of God's salvific intervention in history is usually implied, though not stressed as the predominant aspect of faith. The NT, it is true, rather strongly emphasizes the knowledge of faith, which consists in the recognition of Christ as the Messiah and Son of God, and in the assent to his message of salvation. But faith is not less man's humble submission and personal selfsurrender to God, trust and confidence in him, and readiness to obey his commandments. In the OT as well as in the NT faith is man's comprehensive "Yes" to God.

[1] Heinrich Fries, article "Faith and Knowledge" in: Sacramentum Mundi, vol. II. — London: Burns and Oates, 1968, 331.

[2] H. Fries, l. c. 331.

[3] R. Schnackenburg: The Moral Teaching of the New Testament. — London: Burns and Oates, 1967, 35.

The magisterium of the Church teaches that the act of faith is a complete surrender of man to God, one which includes acceptance of revealed doctrine, voluntary submission to grace and trust in God's promises.[1]

Theologians, recognizing the complexity of faith, distinguish the following basic dimensions in theological faith: faith as knowledge of revealed truth (fides quae creditur); and faith as trusting obedience to God and as a personal encounter with him (fides qua creditur). "In this sense faith is the disposition for justification and ordination to final salvation in the beatific vision, that is, to participation in the life of the glorious Christ."[2]

1. *Faith as personal encounter with God*

Faith in its primary sense is man's trusting, humble sub-mission and personal self-surrender to God, which includes acceptance of God's will and word; or shorter: it is trusting self-surrender to God. Faith in this sense is the most fundamental attitude of man before God. Its object is God and its motive God's supreme sovereignty and trustworthiness.

Christian faith, just as much as faith in general, "is not primarily and originally a relation to things and propositions, but a personal act, a confrontation between the human 'I' and the divine 'You'."[3] This encounter does not depend on positive revelation, although in the present order of salvation grace always elevates the bond to an entirely new, personal immediacy and even converts it into a relation of friendship by a new spiritual light and subsistence.

The confrontation with his own being and free, responsible nature confronts man necessarily with the incomprehensible ground of his existence, called God. He cannot escape this confrontation nor evade the request of the divine absolute to total commitment. "God is not an object among other objects of experience which under certain circumstances one may fail to discover, but is necessarily affirmed in the accomplishment of man's intellectual and moral activity, even if he is explicitly

---

[1] DS 1527; 3008; 3010; DV 5. Cf. Juan Alfaro, art. "Faith" (II) in: *Sacramentum Mundi*, vol. II, 314.

[2] J. Alfaro, 1. c. 314.

[3] H. Fries, art. "Faith and Knowledge" in: *Sacramentum Mundi*, vol. II, 331f.

denied, or not named, or is met with under quite different conceptual modes of expression."[1]

Of course man ought to ask himself whether he interprets this reality accurately and whether it should not rightly be construed as a supreme, most radical, saving and forgiving presence of the mystery of God. He is urged to inquire after that historical and social form of religion to which he must trust himself as the correct substantiation and true fulfillment of his deepest faith. The first beginnings of faith must thus increasingly develop into a more conscious, explicit belief.

Faith as the personal encounter between God and man presupposes a self-disclosure of God and of the mystery of his inner being. In one way or the other — as has already been said — God makes his presence felt to every man and reveals himself in the ground of the human soul and person. Yet God has besides manifested himself in a most direct and explicit way. He has made known himself and speaks to man in biblical revelation. In the person and message of Jesus Christ it has found its culmination and completion. It stands to reason that man has to take seriously God's external word and self-manifestation, and that he has to confront himself with it in great sincerity and probity.

Nevertheless it remains true that even previous to the explicit preaching of the Christian message every human being "is always potentially a believer and already in possession, in the grace that is prior to his freedom, of what he is to believe (i.e., freely accepted): God's direct self-communication in Christ. It is quite possible, in fact, that the person whom the preacher of the faith encounters is already justified (because he was obedient to the dictates of his conscience, to the extent this had made itself heard), and therefore already believes, in the theological sense... Bringing someone to the faith will mean the endeavour to develop this already existing faith into its full Christological and ecclesiastical, explicit, social, consciously professed form."[2]

If in Holy Scripture man's faith is repeatedly exemplified by Abraham's believing and faithful self-abandonment to God, in the OT (Gen 12:1-4; 15:1-6) as well as in the NT (Rom 4; Heb 11:8-11.17-19), then this is proof that the revealed books too consider faith primarily as man's attitude of trusting self-surrender before God and only in a second instance as assent

---

[1] K. Rahner, art. "Faith" (I) in: Sacramentum Mundi, vol. II, 311.
[2] K. Rahner, 1. c. 310.

to revealed doctrines. For Abraham's faith did not include God's covenant with the chosen people at Sinai nor all the following revelations by the sacred authors of the OT, because he lived before them. Much less did his faith include the revelation of the NT or any explicit belief in Christ. Nevertheless his faith was truly divine and salvific so that it justified him before God, as St. Paul agrees (Rom 4). "No distrust made him waver concerning the promise of God, but he grew strong in his faith as he gave glory to God, fully convinced that God was able to do what he had promised. That is why his faith was 'reckoned to him as righteousness' " (Rom 4:20-22).

Naturally, if the revelation of God culminates in Christ, then those who hear and receive this word of God must respond to it in reverent openness to the divine mystery as made manifest in his Son. Christian faith is an entrance into the history of salvation, which God initiated with Abraham, continued with his posterity and brought to fulfillment in Jesus Christ. It is response to the God of the covenant in fellowship with the person and in the knowledge of Christ. The Christian makes the áttitudes and thoughts of Jesus and the secrets of his doctrine his own and joins in ·Christ's perfect response to the Father. The believer becomes so much one with Christ that St. Paul can say: "It is no longer I who live, but Christ who lives in me" (Gal 2:20). For the New Testament, "faith and communion with Christ belong so closely together that it is possible to say that faith in Christ means that faith is brought about through a life-relationship with Christ."[1]

2. *Faith as assent to revealed truths*

Faith in its second sense as "fides quae creditur" is the firm assent on the authority of God to whatever he has revealed in Christ. Faith in a person necessarily includes — as has been explained — faith in the word and assertions made by the person who is believed in. This is especially true with reference to faith in God. Wherever it becomes clear that he has revealed himself in deeds or words. man is bound to accept the divine message in "obedience of faith" (Rom 1:5; 16:26).

a) *Object of faith* in this second sense is the truths revealed by God in positive, historical revelation, in particular in the Holy Scriptures of the Old and New Testament.

---

[1] Heinrich Zimmermann. art. "Faith in the New Testament" in: Encyclopedia of Biblical Theology, ed by J. Bauer, vol. I, 1969, 252f.

"Trust in God's promises and obedience to his command-ments are the most obvious features of faith in the OT, but it usually implies knowledge of God's salvific intervention in history, whether this has already happened or is yet to come."[1] The fundamental article of Israel's faith is the dogma that Yahweh is the only God and Saviour. "I, I am the Lord, and besides me there is no saviour" (Is 43:11). The entire Old Testament reveals Yahweh as the God of the covenant who intervened in history for the salvation of his people.

In the New Testament the aspect of knowledge is particularly stressed. "The acceptance of the message of Christ makes one a 'believer'."[2] To believe is to recognize Jesus as him whom the Father has sent; to confess that he is the Son of God; to accept the mystery of his death and resurrection and its meaning for salvation; to profess his doctrine as the word of truth and to persevere in it; and to submit to the Church as the guardian of the divine mysteries and the custodian of the gospel. Pro-fession of faith in Christ and the Trinity was of basic importance in the baptismal liturgy. From the very beginning the Church has expressed this faith in special formulas which those who wanted to become Christians had to avow and to believe (Acts 8:37; Rom 1:2-4; 10:9; Phil 2:5-11; 1 Thess 4:14; 1 Jn 4:2.15).

b)   *Motive of faith* is the authority of God who speaks to man in the word of revelation, his truthfulness and infal-libility.[3]

Naturally this motive can only become effective if a man is assured of the divine authorship of the facts and words of positive revelation. Faith in Christian revelation, as well as in any other divine revelation, therefore presupposes certainty of its divine origin. Although the signs of credibility, like miracles and prophecies, contribute to the acquisition of this certainty, it is lastly by the grace of God that a man can believe. God's self-manifestation in the history of the chosen people and in his Son Jesus Christ can only be realized and known as of divine origin if God gives testimony to himself on this account in the heart of man.

The prophets describe what God does to the believer as creating a "new heart", as infusing a "new spirit", that is, as a spiritual transformation in man's inmost thoughts, feelings and

---

[1] Juan Alfaro, art. "Faith" (II) in: Sacramentum Mundi, vol. II. 1968, 314.

[2] Encyclopedia of Bibl. Theol., 1. c. 254.

[3] DS 3008; 3032; 3542.

purposes (Jer 24:7; Ezek 36:26-28). For St. Paul the Spirit inwardly enlightens the heart of the believer with a new knowledge and filial love of God (1 Cor 2:10-16; 12:3, 2 Cor 4:4-6; Gal 4:6; Eph 1:16-19; Acts 16:14). According to Mt 11:25-27 and Jn 6:44-45 the preaching and miracles of Christ do not of themselves enable a man to believe in him. God must also draw the man to himself by an interior revelation.[1]

This is confirmed by the magisterium of the Church. The Dogmatic Constitution on Divine Revelation of Vatican II states that, if "faith is to be shown, the grace of God and the help of the Holy Spirit must precede and assist, moving the heart and turning it to God, opening the eyes of the mind, and giving 'joy and ease to everyone in assenting to the truth and believing it.' To bring about an ever deeper understanding of revelation, the same Holy Spirit constantly brings faith to completion by His gifts" (DV 5).[2]

Since grace is a free gift of God, the preacher of the gospel cannot force it nor can the listener of the word. Conversion to faith is always a process with many stages. The one preacher plants, the other waters, but God gives the growth (1 Cor 3:6f). It cannot even "be presumed that if the whole explicit content of the faith is presented in an objectively sufficient way, it can only be due to personal (subjective) guilt in every individual case, whatever the particular situation and limits of time, if in fact all these stages in the genesis of faith are not accomplished. The messenger of the gospel can therefore rightly ask himself what stage in a gradual history of faith has been reached by the collective or individual kairos. He can then try to lead as far as that point, i.e., to indicate the ways of access and for the rest patiently leave God to bring about a situation where further progress will be possible. Otherwise he would perhaps waste too much human and ecclesiastical effort."[3]

Nevertheless the fact that faith in Christ is lastly a gift of grace does not preclude the need of humble, self-forgetful openness to the word of revelation from the side of man. The act of faith always remains a free decision. The person who is on the way to faith must possess a sincere will for the truth, even if the truth he comes to know should require renunciations and a change of life from him. Already for pre-Christian philosophers the attainment of the highest truth was dependent upon a moral

---

[1] Cf. J. Alfaro, 1. c. 316f.
[2] Cf. also DS 3010.
[3] Karl Rahner, art. "Faith" (I), in: Sacramentum Mundi, vol. II, 310.

eros. Only a pure aspiration, according to Plato, can conduct the soul to the supreme beauty and goodness, the divine wisdom.

A humble, reverent attitude and disposition alone are admitted to the sanctuary of religious knowledge. "Since human pride rebels against this humility, faith is not just an obvious and untroubled possession of truth, but something which — more or less according to the individual — must be wrested from doubt by a struggle and is to that extent not theoretical but practical, a decision of the personality as a whole. Already in the Old Testament religious vision is bound up inseparably with a readiness and inclination of the will. 'Wisdom' cannot enter an evil soul and a polluted body. And Our Lord declares that he alone comes to the light who loves and performs truth."[1]

II. Knowledge of faith necessary for salvation

The question arises which knowledge of God and the divine mysteries is necessary in order that a man can put an act of salvific faith. The opinions of theologians on the matter have differed in the course of history, but a decisive word has been said by Vatican II.

According to the opinion of older theologians, who quote in their favour St. Augustine and St. Thomas Aquinas, a man must know and believe by necessity of means four fundamental truths about God: the existence of God, the retribution of good and evil by God, the mystery of the Blessed Trinity, and the mystery of Incarnation. Another group of more recent theologians maintain that it is sufficient to believe in the existence of a personal God who rewards the good and punishes the wicked. They point out that for many pagans it is impossible ever to know the mysteries of the Trinity and of Incarnation. They base themselves on Hebrew 11:6, which states that "whoever would draw near to God must believe that he exists and that he rewards those who seek him."[2] Yet a third group of theologians object that even this second opinion does not do justice to those numerous pagans of good will who have no clear concept of God, since "the conception of Deity is very often no more

---

[1] Otto Karrer: Religions of Mankind. — New York: Sheed and Ward, 1945, 238.

[2] Häring writes: "According to the more probable teaching, which today is the view more commonly held, only faith in the existence of God who is our salvation (this means faith in God who mercifully rewards, who justly punishes) is absolutely and indispensably necessary for salvation" (II, 1963, 30).

than a vague notion of 'Heaven' — a pantheon of divine figures or a mere consciousness of the Holy, the apprehension of an eternal law to which man is subject."[1] Millions of Buddhists, Confucians and other pagans lack the knowledge of a personal God and Creator without any guilt of theirs. Hence these theologians conclude — among them Ripalda, Scheeben, Mausbach and Karrer[2] — that an implicit faith in God and final retribution is sufficient, such as contained in the acknowledgement of an inviolable moral order and in the submission to its demands, as perceived in the voice of one's conscience.

Some further explanations are necessary with regard to the problem how the demands of Hebrew 11:6 are verified in the theory of this latter group. As point of departure serves the fact that all men, even the primitives, are aware of a moral order and duty which holds them responsible for their conduct. "All men, whatever their level of culture and whatever their religion, so far as they are truly men and not human beings subject to some psychological abnormality which excludes them from the religious and moral sphere, possess a moral consciousness. They distinguish between good and evil. As moral beings they are aware of the 'obligation' of goodness as essentially holy and at bottom religious. This recognition does not depend upon an explicit belief in God. The man who is ignorant of God's existence or who questions it will not therefore murder his parents, betray his friends or country, embezzle or slander. Or at least he is aware that such conduct is wrong and will be ashamed of it."[3] The consciousness of truth and moral values belongs to the essence of humanity.

The notion of moral good and evil, however, and the recognition of the binding character of morality implicitly contains a metaphysical and religious element. "Man may call this transcendent order to which he feels himself bound in conscience by whatever name he pleases, Tao, Karma, cosmic law or categorical imperative; it is always a super-personal power which

---

[1] Otto Karrer: Religions of Mankind. — New York: Sheed and Ward, 1945, 231.

[2] The opinion of Ripalda, Gutberlet, Scheeben, Mausbach, and Karrer maintains "that invincible ignorance or honest doubt of God's existence does not exclude a heathen from receiving God's grace, provided he lives according to his conscience, is repentant for faults committed against it and in his entire disposition is a 'seeker' for truth" (O. Karrer, 1. c. 236).

[3] Otto Karrer, 1. c. 233f.

exacts his homage, 'something that demands reverence, is adorable, evokes desire and effort' (Augustine). That is to say, it is 'numinous.' The recognition of this holy object implies a practical reference to God. The struggle for purification, righteousness and goodness involves a recognition of God" and of a final retribution for good and evil.[1]

The man who surrenders himself to the demands of the moral law in his heart because he realizes its absolute and sacred character, sets by his submission to this superior, holy reality implicitly an act of faith. In the opinion of Scheeben, Mausbach and Karrer, there is theological faith wherever the soul is prepared to correspond with the truth and holiness perceived, and to follow "the true light that enlightens every man" (Jn 1:9). "If in practice the man enlightened by such a revelation surrenders himself to the Holy One of whom the perception and notion have thus come to birth in his intellect and follows that inner light with an upright will, he elicits an act of faith in the strict sense."[2]

The Dogmatic Constitution on the Church of Vatican II dedicates article 16 to the question who else besides Christians is included in the plan of salvation. First are listed the Jews, second those who acknowledge the Creator, third those who seek the unknown God in images and shadows, and finally all those who strive by their deeds to do God's will as it is known to them. Divine Providence does not "deny the help necessary for salvation to those who, without blame on their part, have not yet arrived at an explicit knowledge of God, but who strive to live a good life, thanks to His grace" (LG 16). Hence the most elementary, but still sufficient knowledge of faith is the recognition of the moral obligation to goodness and holiness. Therewith the question on the knowledge of faith necessary for salvation has been answered by Vatican II in the sense of those theologians who hold the third opinion.

B.   Man under the obedience of faith

Faith, so it has been pointed out, is first of all a personal relationship between God and man. It is man's trusting self-surrender to God. The man of faith does not reserve anything to his own, self-asserting will. He unconditionally commits himself to the holy will of God. In this sense the letter to the Hebrews

---

[1] Ib. 234.
[2] Ib. 243.

can speak of Jesus as "the pioneer and perfecter of our faith" (Heb 12:2). For Christ showed through his unreserved submission to the Father's will the true and perfect realization of the obedience of faith. He is "the absolute fulfillment of what faith most radically means."[1]

The call to the obedience of faith engages every man. Every man is subject to its claims. Because as a creature of God, every man is confronted with the will of his Creator in the depth of his being. He cannot escape the ultimate decision for or against God. Either he surrenders himself to him through faith, or he refuses submission by asserting his own will. It is the choice between obedience or pride, harmony or discord, salvation or perdition.

For the sake of his own salvation as much as for the sake of the true good of his fellowmen and of the world at large, every man is bound to the obedience of faith. This is a most basic, existential duty. Certainly, the perfection of the virtue of faith is not the matter of one decision only. It is a lifelong task. A man is not expected to possess a perfect faith from the beginning of his religious life. But he is expected to renounce his self-assertion more and more and to strive after a sincere commitment to God.

"Faith signifies the daily turning away from the danger and temptation to refuse faith and its word, and therewith God — to close ourselves in ourselves in a mistaken autonomy, anthropocentrism, and worldliness. Faith means to beg each day, 'Lord, I believe; help my unbelief' (Mark 9:24), for in the believer belief and unbelief run together. Faith means to imitate Jesus Christ, to be ready to assume his fate: the cross and resurrection. Belief means to have the mind and spirit of Jesus Christ (see 1 Corinthians 2:16), to mold one's life and all that it contains in such a way that faith becomes the light that enlightens the believer, that illuminates the ways of existence, that frees the energies and vital forces that our life requires each day."[2]

In order to maintain the faith and to grow in it, a man must care for it and nourish it. Like the roots of a plant, faith must seek greater depth. Otherwise it will wither away and die. A living faith will largely depend on what is called a life of prayer. If a person does not open up to God in prayer, he will not be able to develop a strong and vigorous faith.

---

[1] Heinrich Fries: Faith Under Challenge. — New York: Herder and Herder, 1969, 18.

[2] H. Fries, 1. c. 19f.

It is not an easy matter to surrender oneself to God without reservations. For one really does not know what this may involve in baptisms of fire, sacrifices, loneliness and struggles. Certainly, one equally does not know what it may bring about in new life, worthy fruits, conquests and joys. This condition of darkness and hesitation finds expression in a prayer by Michel Quoist:

> I am afraid of saying "Yes", Lord.
> Where will you take me?
> I am afraid of drawing the longer straw,
> I am afraid of signing my name to an unread agree-
> ment,
> I am afraid of the "yes" that entails other "yeses".[1]

The obedience of faith ruthlessly asks the adherence of the whole person and the commitment of his whole life. It supposes continual departures from old stages and ventures into new ones. Man shrinks back from such an unconditional surrender to the unknown will of God. But at stake is his relationship to God, the source of his being. At stake is the meaning and fulfillment of his life.

The fruits of a deep faith can best be seen in the saints. "They seem to be living suggestions of what a persevering God can do in a faithful human being. It is strengthening for us to see the miracles that God has worked in them, the miracles of gentleness, faithfulness, unselfishness, innocence, joy and peace. It seems more natural for them to act like God, who is love, than to act like men. The long and slow process of faith has transfigured them. They seem attuned to God in a way that makes most of us envious... As the French author, Leon Bloy, once wrote: 'Only the saints are truly happy. The pity of our lives is that we are not all saints.' "[2]

Outstanding example of an unreserved trusting submission to God's will is Mary, the mother of our Lord. Her faith is summed up in the answer she gave to the angel Gabriel when he disclosed God's plan with her: "Behold, I am the handmaid of the Lord; let it be to me according to your word" (Lk 1:38).

This radical faith is not dependent on signs and wonders; it is prior to them. Indeed it is able to work signs and wonders

---

[1] Quoted by John Powell: A Reason to Live! A Reason to Die! — Niles, Ill.: Argus Communications, 1972, 122.

[2] John Powell, 1. c. 136.

itself. This is the faith of which Christ assures that it can move mountains and nothing is impossible to it (Mt 17:20; 21: 21f). But it surely needs a wholly unselfish will, ready to be used by God in the service of his great concerns, and of his kingdom.

C. Duties with regard to the faith of Christian revelation

The most universal demand of Christian faith is a life in accordance with the teaching of Christ and Holy Scripture. "Faith needs to prove its fruitfulness by penetrating the believer's entire life, including its worldly dimensions, and by activating him toward justice and love" (GS 21). From this point of view the entire Christian life can be regarded as flowing from faith. In the following, however, only those duties shall be dealt with which have faith itself as their object, its knowledge, profession, promotion and defence.

I. Duty of knowing the truths of faith

Since Christian revelation is the self-communication of God in history and the source from which the believer's life is nourished, the Christian has the serious obligation to acquire a sufficient knowledge of his faith. He must at least have so much knowledge of his faith as is necessary for a good Christian life in accordance with his age and position. The conditions of time must be taken into consideration too. What might have been sufficient knowledge in former times when most men could not read and write, is no longer adequate in our time when the general educational level is so much higher and every conceivable error propagated among the masses through the media of mass communication.

The most fundamental knowledge required from all Catholics who have the use of reason and are of sufficient age comprises, according to the common teaching of the handbooks of Catholic moral theology, the Apostles' Creed (at least in its essential truths), the Our Father, the Ten Commandments, the chief precepts of the Church (the obligations to annual Communion, annual confession and weekly Sunday Mass),[1] and the necessary

---

[1] Other precepts of the Church listed by the catechisms are the obligations to Sunday rest, to fast and abstinence on the days appointed by the Church, to material support of the Church, and to observance of the laws of the Church concerning matrimony.

sacraments (baptism, penance and holy Eucharist). Knowledge of the other sacraments is required of the person who wants to or must receive them, in that this is necessary for a worthy reception. There is no grave obligation to know these truths by heart, unless this is the only means to appropriate them. Far more important than knowledge by heart is a true penetration into the meaning of the divine truths.

In cases of emergency, when a dying person is to be baptized or absolved, faith in God who retributes according to one's works and who has redeemed us through his Son Jesus Christ is sufficient. Although implicit faith in the personal God who rewards and punishes is sufficient for salvation, it does not seem to be sufficient for baptism which admits one into the visible Church. One cannot be a member of the visible Church without faith in Christ. Furthermore one can hardly imagine that a person who has attained the use of reason has the judicious wish to be baptized without any knowledge of Christian religion and without any faith in Christ.

Besides the acquisition of the most fundamental truths of faith, the constant deepening of the knowledge and understanding of faith is among the basic duties of a Christian. For faith can only enlighten and transform the Christian's life if it penetrates into his thoughts and heart. The way to a better knowledge of faith is certainly further study and information, but prayer and meditation on the truths of faith are even more important. A non-praying faith is a material, impersonal faith and not the life-giving relationship with God which it should be.

Life in and with the Church is another, most important means to provide nourishment and growth to faith and therefore an obligation. Profound insight into the world of faith is assured only by participation in the faith of the Church, which is above all realized in the celebration of the liturgy and the sacraments. This is all the more the case since the liturgical services offer to all believers further instruction in the form of sermons and explanations. Christians may not fail to avail themselves of these opportunities to unfold their faith and to mature in it. "Habitual neglect of the Sunday sermon by those who have no other means of instruction in such matters is surely a mortal sin, for they neglect the one source of alerting and deepening the knowledge of their faith."[1]

---

[1] Häring II, 1963, 33.

With the obligation to learn and to know the faith corresponds the obligation of priests, parents, teachers and other educators to provide efficiently for the religious education of those who are entrusted to their care. After the priest, parents are particularly responsible for the faith of their children. Parents are the first ones to introduce their children into the world of religion, and without their cooperation the priest's educational efforts are hampered, if not frustrated. Therefore the priest may rightly refuse to absolve in confession parents who fail to provide that their children obtain the necessary catechetical and religious instruction.

II. Obligation to profess one's faith

There is a kind of profession of faith, and indeed one that is very important, which consists in the practical witness of a faithful Christian life of love of God and neighbour. To this we are always bound. But over and above this there are times when a Christian must explicitly profess his faith, namely whenever the divine honour and the salvation of our neighbour call for it.

Christ demands of his disciples the positive readiness to acknowledge him before men and the negative determination not to deny the faith in him. "Every one who acknowledges me before men, I also will acknowledge before my Father who is in heaven; but whoever denies me before men, I also will deny before my Father who is in heaven" (Mt 10:32f; cf. Mk 8:38; Lk 9:26; 2 Tim 2:12). The disciples must even be prepared to separate all natural bonds for Jesus' sake and to sacrifice their lives for their belief (Mt 10:34-39).

The suffering and death of so many Christian martyrs up to the present time in confession of their religion is the most eloquent witness for the conviction of the Church that the faith must be confessed before the world. Against heretic contestation of the duty to profess the faith even by martyrdom, the Fathers of the Church refer precisely to this example of Christian martyrs (Irenaeus, Tertullian, Augustine).

External profession of faith is a demand of love of God and neighbour. Since the truths of faith are of the highest value, a man is bound to share them with others for the sake of the growth of God's kingdom and of the salvation of his fellowmen. Above all a man is bound to defend the faith against suppression and extinction by those who oppose it because they do not know or hate the truth.[1]

1. *The duty not to deny the faith*

Denial of faith is the mere external negation of it. Internal renouncing of the faith is apostasy, which is dealt with at a later occasion.

To deny one's faith, whether directly or indirectly, is never allowed. For such denial is a falsehood which results to the detriment of God's honour and of the eternal welfare of one's fellowmen.

He directly denies his faith who declares that he is not a Christian, or that he is an atheist or Moslem, or who sacrifices to idols. Hence direct denial of faith consists in words or actions which by their nature contain a denial of the true faith or a profession of a false one.

He indirectly denies his faith who, when asked about it, remains silent, while another replies that the person questioned is not a Christian or not a Catholic. The same holds if one frequents only non-Catholic services to make others believe he has fallen away from his faith. Hence indirect denial of the faith is any action or omission which contains a denial of the faith, not in itself, but under the given circumstances. Omission of the sign of the cross, however, or even of the genuflection before the Blessed Sacrament are in themselves no denial of faith, since such omissions do not justly permit the conclusion that one is not a Christian or Catholic.[2]

2. *The duty to profess the faith*

Christians are required to profess their faith in word and deed before the world in order to promote the kingdom of

---

[1] If there is a faith, we must persist in its profession. "The profession of faith signifies and requires that it must address itself to, and defend itself before, the public, the neutral as well as the hostile, the scientific as well as the social and political. Profession of the faith signifies that the one who so professes can be put on trial, that he must profess his profession of faith in the open, that he who professes his faith may have to endure ridicule, mockery, obstacles, injury, and, in extreme cases, punishment, persecution, and finally death, for the sake of this profession of faith. It signifies, then, that the believer becomes an open professor of the faith — that he reaches martyrdom" (Heinrich Fries: Faith Under Challenge. — New York: Herder and Herder, 1969, 67; cf. the whole chapter III: "Faith and Conviction", 54-70).

[2] Cf. Jone 1963, nr. 120.

God and the salvation of men. For serious motives, however, it can be lawful and sometimes even obligatory to conceal one's faith, e.g. if one can thus escape imprisonment, torture or death and preserve one's freedom and life for the best of those entrusted to one's care in family, Church or state. Flight, too, is permissible in times of persecution. Christ himself instructs his disciples: "When they persecute you in one town, flee to the next" (Mt 10:23; cf. Acts 9:23-25). Yet if the presence of a priest is necessary for the welfare of the faithful, he may not flee.

Public defence of the faith is necessary if one can thereby avoid mocking and contempt of the faith. One must equally profess one's faith and may not hide it if its concealment is prejudicial to the cause of Christian religion or to the faith of others. When questioned by the proper authority, one must confess one's faith at the risk of one's life and cannot decline to answer.[1] It is however not a denial of faith to conceal one's state as a priest or religious in the same circumstances. Private or unauthorized questioners may be given evasive or equivocal answers or no answer at all, provided this is not equivalent to a denial of faith. If a state authority, which persecutes religion, orders by general edict that all believers have to present themselves before the public officials or to carry certain signs, nobody is bound to obey, since such a law is unjust.

When certain "rites" prescribed by civil authorities are in themselves ambiguous, so that they can be considered an expression of a false cult or of a morally unobjectionable civil homage, the believer may participate in the exercise of such rites. But he must have a serious reason for doing so and manifest clearly by his behaviour or even by means of an express declaration that he is taking part not in a religious rite, but only in a purely civil ceremony. In accordance with this principle the Church has permitted the veneration of the statues of Confucius, the tablets of ancestors and the sacred shrines in China, Japan, Siam and other countries.[2]

The positive law of the Church furthermore demands a public profession of faith before the Church authority at certain times. Thus the Church demands a profession of faith from every adult about to be baptized, from every convert from another Christian denomination or Church, and from apostates who return to their original faith. An exception is made if the danger of death

---

[1] Cf. DS 2118.
[2] Cf. AAS 32 (1940), 24-26; 379.

leaves no time for this. The conversion need not be made generally known. For some good reason one may keep it secret for some time.[1]

III.   Duty of spreading the faith

The Second Vatican Council repeatedly asserts the duty of all Christians to spread the faith. "The obligation of spreading the faith is imposed on every disciple of Christ, according to his ability" (LG 17; AG 23). Every Christian must be filled with zeal to communicate to others the great blessing of the true faith wherever there is need. "Indeed, the law of love, which is the Lord's greatest commandment, impels all the faithful to promote God's glory through the spread of His kingdom and to obtain for all men that eternal life which consists in knowing the only true God and Him whom He sent, Jesus Christ (cf. Jn 17:3). On all Christians therefore is laid the splendid burden of working to make the divine message of salvation known and accepted by all men throughout the world" (AA 3).

Zeal for the spread of the faith may not be based on the false assumption that all those who do not explicitly profess the faith and acknowledge the Church's authority will be lost. God's saving grace is in an unseen way at work in the hearts of all men and offers them the possibility of salvation. But those ignorant of God's revelation in Christ do not have the free access to the abundant treasures of grace and truth found in the Church as believers have. True zeal for God's reign, therefore, and love for neighbour seeks to open to all men this infinite treasure of divine revelation and love.

The need to communicate the redemptive truth of faith and the fulness of salvation exists wherever, also in Christian countries, people lack the true faith or reject it. Yet the need is especially great in countries which are missions or are still in want of missionary help. With them in particular the "Decree on the Missionary Activity of the Church" (AG) of Vatican II is concerned.

---

[1] In order to avoid serious hardships which for a certain convert would result if his conversion becomes known, he can be excused from the observance of the positive divine and ecclesiastic precepts, e.g. the weekly attendance at Sunday Mass. He can also be allowed to continue in the attendance at religious services of his former religion, as long as the reasons persist which dissuade from the publication of the conversion. But in no instance can he actively participate in those distinctive functions of his former faith which contain an approbation of heresy or unbelief.

According to the Decree, missionary activity consists in the evangelization and the planting of the Church among those peoples and groups where she has not yet taken root (AG 6). Mission fields are consequently those countries or regions where these peoples and groups live. If the congregation of the faithful in a country already enjoys a certain stability and is to a certain degree equipped, insufficient though it be, with its own local priests, religious and laymen, it is no longer mission in the strict sense. But as long as the new congregation suffers from a very serious lack of priests and of material support, it still needs missionary help, and the Church has a missionary task with regard to it (AG ·19).

1. *Motivation of the missionary activity*

Before Christ was taken up into heaven, he founded his Church as the sacrament of salvation and sent his apostles into all the world, just as he himself had been sent by his Father. He gave them this command: "Go therefore and make disciples of all nations, baptizing them in the name of the Father and of the Son and of the Holy Spirit, teaching them to observe all that I have commanded you" (Mt 28:19f; cf. Mk 16:15f).

Yet not only in virtue of this express command does the duty to spread the faith and the saving work of Christ exist, but also "by reason of the love with which they love God and by which they desire to share with all men in the spiritual goods of both this life and the life to come" (AG 7).

Besides, by means of the missionary activity the plan of God is fulfilled to which Christ was devoted for the glory of the Father. "According to this plan, the whole human race is to form one people of God... Since it concerns brotherly concord, this design surely corresponds with the inmost wishes of all men" (AG 7). Thus, by manifesting Christ, the Church reveals to men the real truth about their condition and their vocation. For Christ is the source and model of that renewed humanity, penetrated with brotherly love, sincerity and a peaceful spirit, to which all aspire.

2. *Practical demands*

Every disciple of Christ has the obligation to do his part in spreading the faith. Yet since Christians have different gifts, each one must collaborate in the work of the gospel according to his own opportunities, abilities, charismatic gifts and vocation.

"The responsibility to proclaim the gospel throughout the world falls primarily on the body of bishops" (AG 29). Hence among their affairs of general concern, special consideration should be given to the missionary activity. The bishops' task is to raise up from among their people those who will offer prayers and penance to God for the evangelization of the world; to foster willingly vocations to mission communities among young people and clerics; to promote the works of mission institutes among their faithful; to release means and to collect offerings by which the missions receive direct help; to promote projects for providing a brotherly welcome and due pastoral care for those who immigrate from mission lands for the sake of studying or working (AG 38).

Religious communities have always played a very great and praiseworthy role in the evangelization of the world. Yet still, they as well as the more recent secular institutes should sincerely ask themselves whether they are conscious enough of their duty to take their part in the propagation of the faith and whether their members are involved as much as possible in the missionary activities.

Priests too, as the collaborators of the bishops, are responsible for the missionary work of the Church in a special way. In their pastoral activity they should stir up and preserve amid the faithful a zeal for the evangelization of the world and thus help their bishops in the fulfillment of their missionary tasks.

In those lands which are already Christian, laymen cooperate in the work of evangelization by nurturing in themselves and in others a knowledge and love of the missions (e.g. by means of mission magazines); by stimulating vocations in their own families, in Catholic organizations and in schools; by providing subsidies of various kinds. Laymen should also willingly offer socio-economic cooperation to peoples undergoing development.

Those who feel a divine call to the missionary vocation — be it as a priest, a brother, a sister or a lay missionary, be it for a limited period or permanently — should generously follow this call of grace for the love of God and their brethren. If any one, prompted by unworthy motives such as private or group egotism, should dissuade others from following the call to the mission field, he can scarcely be excused from the guilt of serious sin.

In mission lands the main duty of those who are already

baptized is the witness of their Christian life in the home, in their social group and in their professional circle. "For in them there must appear the new man created according to God in justice and true holiness (cf. Eph 4:24). But they must give expression to this newness of life in the social and cultural framework of their own homeland, according to their own national traditions." They must develop their traditions in accordance with modern conditions and finally perfect them in Christ (AG 21). Finally from the beginning of missionary activity special attention is to be given to the fostering of religious vocations among the indigenous and to the formation of a native clergy and later on a native hierarchy. By this means the new plant of the Church must be enabled to take firmer root and become slowly able to support itself and eventually achieve full autonomy.

IV. Obligation to safeguard the faith

The Christian has the duty to protect himself against dangers which threaten his faith and to defend the rights of his belief and religion in society. Of course the present conditions of life make it impossible to avoid all challenges and threats to one's faith. All the more the Christian is required to prove ardent in his prayers, to strengthen his solidarity with the community of believers, and to become ever more acquainted with the truth and values of faith. Defective understanding of the truths of faith leaves one defenceless against the many objections arising from an anti-religious environment.

Nevertheless certain dangers can and must be avoided also in our times. The Christian has the obligation to be selective in the films he attends and in the radio and television programs he dials. "It is surely a mortal sin to attend any and every movie indiscriminately without any previous inquiry regarding its religious or moral nature."[1] This is not much less true with regard to radio and television.

Similarly one must be selective in one's literature, and this the more the less one is able to confront the aggressions against faith and the ideological errors because of lack of time or insight. Although the Index of books forbidden by the Church has been abrogated,[2] the demand of the natural law remains in

---

[1] B. Häring II, 1963, 41.
[2] According to a notification of the Sacred Congr. for the Doctrine of the Faith, published in AAS 58 (1966), 445, the Index of forbidden books no longer has the force of law.

force not to read books which endanger one's spiritual life and sound moral outlook (nor to publish or sell them), just as one is not allowed to take noxious food or dangerous drugs. A person who repeatedly reads books and sees motion pictures that glorify war and crime may finally be keen on the "adventure" of another war or of some crime. This holds good for depreciation of faith and promotion of anti-religious ideologies as well and for many other spheres of life. One may equally not subscribe to newspapers or magazines hostile to faith and morals and support them.

A very sensitive area is that of close personal friendships between people of different Christian convictions and religious beliefs. Such close friendships may be permitted for mature Christians who are firmly grounded in their faith and with a partner who has sincere respect for true values and also for the values of faith. But if a friendship should prove a hazard for the faith, one must be ready to renounce it. The same holds true for employments and especially for marriages detrimental to faith. The thorny problem of mixed marriages is more amply discussed in the section on the moral responsibility in the marriage state.

Concern for the faith will further strive to protect the faith of others and to promote its rights in society. Parents and educators have the obligation to guide those entrusted to their care with regard to literature, movies, television, etc. Parents must also beware of exposing their children to television programs which may be innoxious for adults, but which do spiritual harm to children. Positively, the duty to guidance includes the procurement and recommendation of good readings and wholesome entertainment. The instruction and exhortation of the Christian faithful by the pastors of the flock concerning literature, radio, film and television is an important task of the pastoral care.

Prominent in the struggle with present-day dangers to faith, in nearly every country, is the concern for the Christian schools or at least religious instruction in public schools. Every Christian child has a divine right to an education that is Christian. The state has no right to tax Catholic and other Christian parents for support of non-religious schools and at the same time compel the same people to bear the entire burden of support for the Christian schools of their choice. Much less has it the right to interfere with the establishment of confessional schools. The state must support every legitimate type of school demanded by the parents or none at all (see also pp. 252f).

The joining to political parties with programs hostile to faith is obviously a grave sin against the obligation to protect one's faith and to defend the rights of one's religion in society. Such a step could only be justified if all the other parties are even more hostile to the good cause and to faith.

As to Freemasonry, the new Code no longer contains an explicit condemnation. An implicit condemnation of certain militant forms is contained in can. 1374. But a recent Declaration of the Congr. for the Doctrine of Faith on Masonic associations makes plain that also today membership remains forbidden to Catholics. Their principles continue to be irreconcilable with the doctrine of the Church. "Christian believers who become members of Masonic associations live in grave sin and cannot receive Holy Communion". Local eccl. authorities cannot pronounce judgements which derogate from the Roman verdict (AAS 76, 1984, p. 300).

Against the ever increasing danger to divorce religion and life, the Christian has the pressing obligation to christianize all areas of human life. Above all he has the duty to defend the rights of religion in pulic institutions, places of work and in the entire life of society (cf. AA 13f).

V. Promotion of unity of faith

The Church established by Christ is one and unique. Yet this unity is impaired. There exist many Christian communions separated from each other. They all proclaim themselves to be the true disciples of the Lord, but their convictions clash and diverge. This discord openly contradicts the will of Christ and inflicts great damage on the cause of proclaiming the good news to every creature. Thus a growing remorse among Christians over their division is emerging and from day to day an increased longing for unity is felt. From the Catholic side the Decree of Ecumenism (UR) of Vatican II is a very important step towards better relations between the various Christian Communions. Justly this decree is said to mark a new era in the ecumenical movement.

1. *Nature and motivation of the ecumenical movement*

In the course of history various schisms have divided the one Church. Churches and Communities different from the

Catholic Church formed themselves, such as the Nestorians (431), Monophysites (541), Eastern Orthodox Churches (1054), Lutherans and different Protestant denominations (1517), Anglicans (1532) and others. The reasons for these separations are of different nature, and the fault is not always to be attributed to one side only. In humble acknowledgement of deficiencies also on the part of the Catholic Church, Vatican II states that for the divisions, "at times, men of both sides were to blame" (UR 3).

Yet whatever the reasons for the divisions in the past, "one cannot impute the sin of separation to those who at present are born into these Communities and are instilled therein with Christ's faith." To the extent that they believe in Christ, strive to live as his disciples and are properly baptized, they ought to accept each other as brothers in the Lord (UR 3).

In spite of the differences which separate the Christian Communities and have caused detriment to the common faith, there are some and at times very many significant elements of the Christian religion which the Churches and Communities have in common. Among them are such endowments as the written word of God; the life of grace; faith, hope and charity; and other interior gifts of the Holy Spirit and visible elements. In virtue of these elements the different Communities are enabled to contribute to the realization of the mystery of salvation (UR 3).

Nevertheless the Christian creed has not been preserved by all Communities with equal integrity and completeness. And the fullness of unity with the apostolic college is lacking. Moreover the differences of convictions led to opposition and discord among the Christian Communities. This openly contradicts the will of Christ. For he prayed on the eve of his passion to his Father: "That they may all be one; even as thou, Father, art in me, and I in thee; that they also may be one is us, so that the world may believe that thou hast sent me" (Jn 17:21). According to the teaching of the apostle Paul the Church is "one body and one Spirit, just as you were called to the one hope that belongs to your call, one Lord, one faith, one baptism" (Eph 4:4f; cf. Gal 3:27f).

The existing separation scandalizes the world. For Christ also gave his followers a new commandment of mutual love (Jn 13:34). All messengers of the gospel preach it as the substance of Christ's teaching. Yet at the same time they fight each other. Many different doctrines present themselves as the true one, and yet the truth cannot be but one. The credibility of the Christian message is called into question.

The Christians themselves suffer all together from this separation, because the fullness of catholicity cannot be effected among them. And this to a certain extent also holds for the Catholic Church. True, Vatican II expresses the conviction that "it is through Christ's Catholic Church alone, which is the all-embracing means of salvation, that the fullness of the means of salvation can be obtained. It was to the apostolic college alone, of which Peter is the head, that we believe our Lord entrusted all the blessings of the New Covenant, in order to establish on earth the one body of Christ" (UR 3). But because of the divisions the Catholic Church herself finds it more difficult to express in actual life her full catholicity in all aspects (cf. UR 4).

2. *Practical demands regarding the fostering of unity*

Concern for restoring unity pertains to the whole Church. It extends to faithful and clergy alike, according to the potential of each, whether it be exercised in daily Christian living or in theological and historical studies (UR 5).

a) *Church renewal.* It essentially consists in an increase of fidelity to the Church's own calling. Therefore, if the influence of events has led to deficiencies in conduct, in Church discipline, or also in the formulation of doctrine, these should be appropriately rectified at the proper moment.

The ecumenical spirit demands of the faithful to be genuinely self-denying, humble, gentle in the service of others, and to have an attitude of brotherly generosity towards them. The more purely they strive to live according to the gospel, the more they are fostering and even practicing Christian unity (UR 7).

b) *Ecumenical education.* Since all Christians should be of an ecumenical mind, the Secretariat for Promoting Christian Unity urges in special guidelines[1] that the principles of ecumenism should be appropriately introduced in all institutions of advanced learning. Bishops and episcopal conferences have the task to translate the general principles into practice according to the requirements of concrete conditions and circumstances.

---

[1] Directorium ad ea quae a Concilio Vaticano Secundo de re oecumenica promulgata sunt exsequenda, pars altera; AAS 62 (1970), 705-724. Cf. The Pope Speaks 15 (1970), 172-185.

The guidelines express the wish that teachers and students should learn more about other Churches and Communities, and so assess more correctly what unites Christians and what divides them. For this reason courses of philosophy ought to take into account the philosophical principles which often underlie existing theological and exegetical views among the various Christian Communities. In the exposition of history due consideration is to be given to the different Christian Churches. Events and personalities involved in the various religious divisions should be dealt with fairly. In other subjects attention can be paid to those spiritual elements which are part of the common Christian inheritance, e.g. in the field of literature, the arts and music. Finally space may be assigned in university journals and reviews for ecumenical news and articles on ecumenical subjects.

On the one hand, so the guidelines exhort Catholics, ecumenical action must be absolutely faithful to the truth which they have received from the Apostles and Fathers. But on the other hand the truths of Catholic doctrine "do not all occupy the same principal or central place in the mystery revealed in Jesus Christ."[1]   Furthermore there is a legitimate diversity in the manner of expressing things in theology, which students should be prepared to recognize.   The various theological formulations are often complementary rather than conflicting.

c) *Dialogue.* Ecumenical dialogue presupposes a solid knowledge of one's own faith and a firm fidelity to it, without which dialogue is reduced to a conversation in which neither side achieves genuine progress in the understanding of the religious truths. But such dialogue also requires a mind that is open for new insights, and all effort should be made to eliminate words, judgments and actions which do not respond to the condition of separated brethren with truth and fairness.

The purpose of ecumenical discussion meetings is that everyone may gain a better knowledge and more just appreciation of the teaching and religious life of both Communions. This demands that those who take part in such meetings do so under authoritative guidance and with true competence. The representatives of the Christian Communions must possess the "readiness to acknowledge that not everyone is equally equipped for dialogue because there are differences of intellectual training, maturity of mind and spiritual development."[2]   Nothing would be so

[1] Guidelines II, in: The Pope Speaks, 15 (1970), 177.
[2] Guidelines II, 1. c. 179.

foreign to the spirit of ecumenism as a false conciliatory approach which obscures the genuine meaning of the dogmatic and theological doctrines and disregards the truth.

d) *Cooperation in social matters.* Such cooperation should be ever increasingly developed. "It should contribute to a just appreciation of the dignity of the human person, the promotion of the blessings of peace, the application of gospel principles to social life, and the advancement of the arts and sciences in a Christian spirit. Christians should also work together in the use of every possible means to relieve the afflictions of our times, such as famine and natural disasters, illiteracy and poverty, lack of housing, and the unequal distribution of wealth. Through such cooperation, all believers in Christ are able to learn easily how they can understand each other better and esteem each other more" (UR 12).

e) *Public and private prayer* for the unity of Christians. Prayers are certainly among the most prominent means of petitioning for the grace of unity. Hence Christians are urged to offer frequently prayers for unity of the Church in private and in public. The guidelines of the Secretariat for Promoting Christian Unity request Catholics to nourish their ecumenical piety not only from the sources of their own spirituality, but also "from the treasures of the many traditions, past and present, which are alive in other Churches and ecclesial Communities. Such are the treasures found in the liturgy, monasticism and mystical tradition of the Christian East; in Anglican worship and piety; in the evangelical prayer and spirituality of Protestants."[1] Besides, it is desirable that in certain special circumstances Christians should join together in common prayers. Such prayers are a genuine expression of the ties which even now bind the different Christian groups to each other.

As for common worship however the Second Vatican Council cautions that "it may not be regarded as a means to be used indiscriminately for the restoration of unity among Christians." For common worship signifies the unity of the belief of those who worship together (1st principle), and this generally rules out common worship of different Christian Churches or Communities. Yet common worship would also provide a sharing in the means of grace (2nd principle), and this sometimes commends it (UR 8).

---

[1] Guidelines II, 1. c. 176.

The practical course to be adopted by Catholics has received further determination by guidelines of the Secretariat of Promoting Christian Unity. They shall be added below for reference as an appendix.

Appendix

Guidelines on the sharing of spiritual resources[1]

The Decree on Ecumenism states that from the elements and endowments "which go together to build up and give life to the Church itself, some, even many, can exist outside the visible boundaries of the Catholic Church" (UR 3). These common elements offer the basis for a certain "*communicatio in spiritualibus*". But as the spiritual endowments are found in different ways in the several Christian Communities, the sharing in spiritual activity and resources must vary according to the conditions of the people, Churches and Communities involved.

As a general principle there should be regard for a certain give-and-take ("reciprocity"), if sharing in spiritual activity and resources, even within defined limits, is to contribute to the growth of harmony among Christians. The local Ordinary or, if need be, the episcopal conference may indicate suitable measures for preventing the dangers of indifferentism and proselytism.

Before giving some more detailed rules, a definition of a few expressions is in place.

(1) The term "sharing of spiritual activity and resources" (*communicatio in spiritualibus*) is used to cover all prayer offered in common, common use of sacred places and objects, as well as all sharing in liturgical worship (*communicatio in sacris*) in the strict sense.

(2) There is *communicatio in sacris* when anyone takes part in the liturgical worship or in the sacraments of another Church or ecclesial Community. It is one special type of *communicatio in spiritualibus,* as explained under (1).

(3) By "liturgical worship" is meant worship carried out according to the books, prescriptions or customs of a Church Community, celebrated by a minister or delegate of such Church or Community, in his capacity as minister of that Community.

---

[1] Directorium ad ea quae a Concilio Vaticano Secundo de re oecumenica promulgata sunt exsequenda, pars prima; AAS 59 (1967), 574–592. Cf. The Pope Speaks 12 (1967), 250–263. See also CJC 844, 874 § 2 and 908.

a) Prayer in common

(1) Occasions. Occasion for common prayer could be any common concern, in which Catholics and their separated brethren can and should cooperate, for example: peace, social justice, mutual charity among men, the dignity of the family, and so on. The same may be said of occasions when a nation or community wishes to make a common act of thanksgiving or petition to God, as on a national feast day, at a time of public disaster or mourning. It is also recommended at times when Christians hold meetings for study or common action. However common prayer should particularly be concerned with the restoration of Christian unity. As far as the participation of Catholics is concerned, it is committed to the guidance and encouragement of local Ordinaries.

(2) Form of services. In such services there is room for any readings, prayers and hymns which manifest the faith or spiritual life shared by all Christians. There is a place for an exhortation, address or biblical meditation. Representatives of the Churches or Communities concerned should agree and cooperate in arranging such prayer.

It is desirable that the structure of services of this kind should conform to the pattern of community prayer recommended by the liturgical revival. Particular consideration should be given to the liturgical order of Eastern Churches, if services are arranged to take place in their church building.

(3) Place. When arranging prayer services with the Eastern brethren, the church is to be regarded as by far the most suitable place. In case of such services with the other separated brethren, a place should be chosen acceptable to all those taking part. In itself nothing prevents holding the common service in the church of one or other of the Communities, if there is need for this and the local Ordinary approves.

(4) Dress. Choir dress may be used where circumstances indicate this and there is common agreement among the participants.

b) Sharing in sacramental worship

(I) WITH THE SEPARATED EASTERN BRETHREN

Since the Eastern Churches, although they are separated from the Catholic Church, possess true sacraments and especially the priesthood and the Eucharist, some worship in common is possible and even advisable. Pastors however should carefully instruct the faithful, so that they will be clearly aware of the correct manner of acting in regard to this sharing.

In granting permission for sharing in the sacraments of penance, holy Eucharist or anointing of the sick, it is fitting that the greatest possible attention be given to reciprocity and that the Catholic authority, whether the local one, the synod or the episcopal conference, does not extend these permissions except after satisfactory consultations with the competent authorities of the separated Eastern Church.

Besides cases of necessity, there would be just cause for sharing in each other's sacraments if special circumstances make it materially or morally impossible over a long period for one of the faithful to receive the sacraments in his own Church. In these cases Catholics must observe the discipline of the separated Eastern Church as much as they can. The absence of available confessors justifies a sharing in the sacrament of confession.

In addition to the just mentioned cases, Catholics may be allowed to attend liturgical services of the separated Eastern brothers if they have a just cause, for example for reasons arising out of a public office or function, blood relationships, friendships, desire to be better informed, etc. In such cases there is nothing against their taking part in the common responses, hymns and actions of the Church in which they are guests. If the Holy Liturgy (Mass) is attended on a Sunday or holy day of obligation, Catholics are not then bound to assist at Mass in a Catholic church. It is likewise a good thing if on such days Catholics who for just reasons cannot go to the Holy Liturgy of their own Church, attend the Holy Liturgy of their separated Eastern brethren, if this is possible. Reception of Holy Communion in all these latter cases is only allowed with the (individual or general) permission of the competent Catholic authority.

Local Ordinaries can also give permission for a Catholic to read lessons at a liturgical service, if he is invited. These same principles govern the manner in which a separated Eastern Christian may assist at services in Catholic churches.

(II)   WITH OTHER SEPARATED BRETHREN
(PROTESTANTS AND ANGLICANS)

Since the unity of sacramental faith between Catholics and the other separated brethren is deficient, the participation of the separated brethren with Catholics, especially in the sacraments of the Eucharist, penance, and anointing of the sick, is forbidden.

Nevertheless, since the sacraments are both signs of unity and sources of grace, the Church can for adequate reasons allow access to those sacraments to a separated brother. This may be permitted in danger of death or in urgent need (during persecution, in prisons), if the separated brother has no access to a minister of his own Communion and spontaneously asks a Catholic priest for the sacraments — so long as he declares a faith in these sacraments in harmony with that of the Church, and is rightly disposed. In other cases the judge of this urgent necessity must be the diocesan bishop or the episcopal conference.[1] A Catholic in similar circumstances may not ask for these sacraments except from a minister who has validly received the sacrament of orders.

A Protestant is not to act as a Scripture reader or to preach during the celebration of the Eucharist. The same is to be said of a Catholic at the celebration of the Lord's Supper or at the principal liturgical service held by the Protestant Christians.

c) Sharing in other liturgical services

When taking part in services which do not call for sacramental sharing, ministers of other Churches or Communities may, by mutual consent, take a place suitable to their dignity. An Eastern clergyman who is representing his Church should have the place and the liturgical honours which Catholics of equal rank and dignity have in the Catholic Church.

Catholic ministers who are present at ceremonies celebrated by other Churches and Communities may, with due regard for local customs, wear choir dress or — at an Orthodox service — the insignia of their ecclesiastical rank.

At these non-sacramental services it is allowable for both to exercise some functions, with the previous permission of the

---

[1] A special instruction on the admission of non-Catholic Christians to the Eucharist of June 1, 1972, explains that such urgent necessity is "not confined to situations of oppression and danger. Christians may find themselves in grave spiritual necessity and with no chance of recourse to their own communities. In our time, for example, which is one of large-scale migration, it happens much more often than before that non-Catholic Christians are scattered in Catholic regions. They are often deprived of the help of their own community and are unable to seek its assistance except at great trouble and expense. If the other conditions set forth in the Handbook are verified, these persons may be admitted to Eucharistic communion, but it rests with the local bishop to consider each case" (AAS 64, 1972, 524f; cf. The Pope Speaks 17, 1972/3, 179).

local Ordinary and the consent of the authorities of the Church or Community concerned.

d)   Norms regarding godparents and marriage witnesses

It is permissible for a just cause for a member of the separated Eastern Churches to act as godparent, together with a Catholic godparent, at a Catholic baptism and vice versa. In this case the duty of providing for the Christian education of the baptized person binds in the first place the godparent who belongs to the Church in which the child is baptized.

For the other separated brethren it is not permissible to act as godparent at a Catholic baptism and vice versa. The reason is that a godparent is also, as a representative of a community of faith, standing as sponsor for the faith of the candidate. However, because of ties of blood or friendship, a Christian of another Community, since he has faith in Christ, can be admitted with a Catholic godparent as a Christian witness of the baptism. In comparable circumstances a Catholic can do the same for a member of a separated Community. In these cases the responsibility for the Christian education of the candidate belongs of itself to the godparent who is a member of the Church in which the candidate is baptized. Pastors should carefully explain to the faithful the reasons for this regulation.

The separated brethren may act as official witnesses (bridesmaid or best man) at a Catholic marriage, and Catholics at a marriage which is properly celebrated between separated brethren.

e)   Common use of sacred places and objects

If the separated brethren have no place in which to carry out their religious rites properly and with dignity, the local Ordinary may allow them the use of a Catholic building, cemetery or church. To members of the separated Eastern Churches also the use of other sacred things necessary for their religious rites may be allowed, if they ask for it.

f)   Admission of non-Catholic ministers in Catholic schools and hospitals

The authorities of Catholic schools and institutions should take care to offer to ministers of other Churches and Communities every facility for giving spiritual and sacramental ministration to their own communicants who attend Catholic institutions. As far as circumstances allow, and with the local Ordinary's permission, these facilities can be offered on the Catholic premises, including the church.

In hospitals and similar institutions conducted by Catholics, the authorities in charge should promptly advise ministers of other Churches and Communities of the presence of their communicants and afford them every facility for visiting the sick and giving them spiritual and sacramental ministrations.

VI.   Duty of submission to the teaching authority of the Church

The custody and proclamation of the word of revelation has been entrusted by Christ to the Church, so that the salutary truths of his life, death and resurrection would remain historically present in the world. This implies that the believer must accept the teaching of the Church and submit to it where she proposes and expounds the revealed truth authentically. "He who hears you hears me, and he who rejects you rejects me, and he who rejects me rejects him who sent me" (Lk 10:16).

The concrete bearer of the supreme doctrinal authority in the Church is the college of the bishops with and under the pope. Already from a natural point of view this magisterium can claim greater competence in doctrinal matters than the individual believer. It has been established precisely for the transmission, study and explanation of the religious truths of divine faith and possesses expert knowledge in this field. Hence its decisions in doctrinal matters have special weight and merit particular assent. Furthermore Christ assured Peter of a special assistance against error and the forces of darkness (Mt 16:18f) and promised and sent the apostles the Holy Spirit to bear witness to him and to introduce them in all the truth (Jn 14:16f; 15:26; 16:13; Acts 1:8; 2:2-4).

The teaching authority of the Church reaches forth to the whole content of Christian revelation and to other truths which touch matters of faith and morals directly or indirectly. Besides the ordinary teaching authority, which the Church normally exercises in her pronouncements regarding faith and morals, she also possesses infallible teaching power, that "extends as far as extends the deposit of divine revelation, which must be religiously guarded and faithfully expounded" (LG 25). This latter power naturally is much less frequently brought into play. For the detailed exposition on the object of the doctrinal and infallible authority of the Church see fundamental and dogmatic theology.

The assent to the teachings of the magisterium in faith and morals is of an essentially different quality according as a doctrine is proposed by the magisterium as infallibly true or not. In the past this separation was frequently not carried through with sufficient clarity, and theologians were inclined to require in a last analysis an absolute assent to the non-infallible pronouncements of the Holy See too. "It cannot be denied that the practical preaching of Church doctrine often unduly blurred the basic and acknowledged differences between doctrinal utterances, as regards their binding force. In the preaching of doctrine in the Church today this distinction must be clearly brought out. The normal duty of inner assent to non-defined doctrinal pronouncements of the magisterium (LG 25) is not to be propounded in such a way that in practice an absolute assent is still demanded, or as if there were no instance in which one of the faithful might withhold his assent."[1]

Absolute assent of divine faith (assensus fidei) is only demanded for doctrines which the ordinary or extraordinary magisterium propose as infallibly true (or which an individual believer personally recognizes as certainly revealed). Only this absolute assent is ascribed to the theological virtue of faith. What regards the infallibility of doctrines taught by the ordinary magisterium of the whole episcopate, without conciliary or papal definition, it must be noted that "it is not enough that a doctrine be propounded with moral unanimity by the whole episcopate. It is further required that the doctrine be explicitly propounded 'tamquam definitive tenenda' (LG 25). Hence mere *de facto* universality of Church doctrine related to the faith is not enough. It has often been assumed in the past, with practical effects, that a doctrine is irreformable in the Church simply because it has been generally taught without clearly notable contradiction over a considerable period of time. This view runs counter to the facts, because many doctrines which were once universally held have proved to be problematic or erroneous, and is fundamentally unsound."[2]

Religious assent (assensus religiosus) or reverential and filial adherence is called for to the teachings of the authoritative, non-infallible magisterium. Vatican II states in this regard that "in matters of faith and morals, the bishops speak in the name of Christ and the faithful are to accept their teaching and adhere

[1] Karl Rahner, art. "Magisterium" in: Sacramentum Mundi, vol. 3, 1969, 356.

[2] K. Rahner, 1. c. 356.

to it with a religious assent of soul. This religious submission of will and of mind must be shown in a special way to the authentic teaching authority of the Roman Pontiff, even when he is not speaking ex cathedra. That is, it must be shown in such a way that his supreme magisterium is acknowledged with reverence, the judgments made by him are sincerely adhered to, according to his manifest mind and will" (LG 25; cf. GS 50; DH 14). This assent to the non-infallible teaching of the magisterium is ascribed to the virtue of submission to competent authority, which submission, insofar as it is rendered to the Church authority, could also be termed ecclesiastical faith. Yet it must be born in mind that this faith is basically human, though reverential and filial faith, not divine faith.

The text quoted from Vatican II in principle requires "religious assent of soul" and "religious submission of will and mind" to the teachings of the bishops in general and of the Roman Pontiff in particular, even when they do not intend to propound doctrines infallibly. Yet Rahner, commenting on this text, rightly remarks that this does not preclude the possibility of a reverential silence (silentium obsequiosum) in instances where somebody's inner convictions do not permit a perfect internal assent, for this is the common teaching.[1]

It lies in the nature of non-infallible doctrines that they can be fallible and are not irreformable. Hence assent to these doctrines is not an unconditional acceptance of the same. It is made with at least two conditions: "unless the Church decides otherwise at some time", and "unless the contrary becomes evident."[2] In a pastoral letter of 1967 the German bishops state "the fact that in the exercise of its office, the doctrinal authority of the Church can be subject to error and has in fact erred."[3] This is not reason for the believer to refuse due respect and submission to non-infallible doctrines of the Church magisterium.

---

[1] Commentary on the Documents of Vatican II, ed. by H. Vorgrimler, vol. 1. — Burns and Oates/Herder and Herder, 1967, 209. The right to reverential silence is, e.g., defended by F. M. Gallati: Wenn die Päpste sprechen. — Wien: Herder, 1960, 173-175.

[2] Cf. Francis Sullivan: De Ecclesia (Rome, 1963, 348); quoted by David Leigh: The Church as a Moral Guide. — AmEcRev 158 (1968) 390. Leigh explains among others that "a few thinkers recently, e.g. Baum and Kevin Kelly, assert that much of the natural law lies outside the competence of the indefectible teaching role of the Christian community. The others, however, affirm that the entire moral law is 'implicitly' contained within revelation or 'intrinsically connected' with revelation and thus within the scope of infallibility (Fuchs, Ford, McCormick, Reed, Schüller)" (ib. 397).

[3] Quoted by Rahner, art. Magisterium, 1. c. 356.

But it is reason to sober appraisal of its teachings. "The Church too, in its doctrine and practice, cannot always allow itself to be faced by the dilemma of either giving an absolutely binding doctrinal decision or simply remaining silent and leaving everything to the personal opinion of the individual. To safeguard the real substance of the faith, the Church must give doctrinal instructions, which have a certain degree of obligation but not being definitions of the faith, have a certain provisional character, even to the extent of possible error. This is a risk which must be taken, since otherwise the Church would find it quite impossible to preach its faith as the decisive reality of life."[1]

There can be no doubt that the Church magisterium is the most competent authority in matters of faith and morals and that its corresponding decisions are reliable and trustworthy. For this reason the believer is bound to submit and to adhere to them sincerely. But on the other hand the decisions of the Holy See, of the bishops and the Roman congregations do not demand a firmness of assent out of proportion to their degree of certainty. And it is thinkable that a believer occasionally feels in conscience justified or even obliged to question and to disagree with a particular decision of the magisterium. But he is never allowed to be self-assertive and arrogant in his refusal, and he must always remain discreet and reverential in his critical inquiry and judgment. "The Christian who believes he has a right to his private opinion, that he already knows what the Church will only come to grasp later, must ask himself in sober self-criticism before God and his conscience, whether he has the necessary depth and breadth of theological expertise to allow his private theory and practice to depart from the present doctrine of the ecclesiastical authorities. The case is in principle admissible. But conceit and presumption will have to answer for their wilfulness before the judgment-seat of God."[2]

In instances of such disagreement at least external submission to the decisions of the magisterium in public comments is always required. There is no place in sermons and religious instruction for opinions contrary to the provisional doctrinal pronouncements of the Church, even though in certain circumstances the faithful should have the nature and the limited scope of such provisional pronouncements explained to them. This does not preclude the right to further investigations in the

---

[1] Pastoral Letter of the German bishops 1967, 1. c. 357.
[2] Ib. 357.

truth and to presentation of contrary arguments in competent quarters through the written or spoken word.[1]

It should finally be noted that the decisions of the Church by comparison with the judgment of any individual scholar must certainly be considered as weightier and more probable. That is to say, presumption stands in favour of the magisterium against the individual opinions of the faithful and theologians. No opinion against an authoritative teaching can by itself gain the status of "safe probability", if external authorities are weighed against each other. Furthermore the assent to the teachings of the magisterium has moral certitude, that is, a surety that excludes the prudent fear of error and provides a justifiable basis for action.

In order to avoid wrong antagonisms, attention should at length be given to the distinction between *theoretical and practical authority* of the Church. The theoretical authority of the Church is concerned with truth or falsity of religious and moral doctrines, and only in this realm the question of infallible or non-infallible pronouncements arises and has meaning. That precisely is the authority which appeals to religious assent of mind and, in the case of infallible statements, to submission of faith. The practical authority of the Church on the other hand is concerned with ecclesiastical discipline, liturgical prescriptions, administrative measures and ecclesiastical laws. This authority appeals to obedience and submission of the will, but not to intellectual assent or faith, since no question of truth is involved, but only the question of usefulness, judiciousness and sound policy. When a pope permits children to receive Communion at an early age, or introduces vernacular language in the liturgy, or when he splits one diocese into two, or introduces changes in canon law, it may be felicitous or unfortunate, it may be more adequate than a former law or less adequate — but questions of infallibility and truth are irrelevant in these cases. The Catholic is bound to obey the prescription or commandment, but he is not obliged to find it felicitous. Naturally the Church can rightly expect her believers to accept also these practical decisions with the respect due to them.[2]

---

[1] Cf. Häring II, 1963, 52. This is also the opinion of Gregory Baum: Teaching of Vatican II. — The Ecumenist 3 (1965), 92f (quoted by D. Leigh, 1. c. 391) and John J. Reed: Natural Law, Theology, and the Church. — Theol. Studies 26 (1965), 59f.

[2] Cf. Dietrich von Hildebrand: Belief and obedience. The critical difference. — Triumph, March, 1970.

D.   Sins against faith

The most radical denial of faith is the refusal to submit to God's sovereignty and will. Either man does not trust that God really wants the best of his creatures or, worse, he is too proud to acknowledge any authority higher than his own will. Although at one time the stress may lie more on distrust and at another time more on pride, both sins are usually related and go hand in hand. They are directly opposed to the deepest source of all faith, the trusting self-surrender to God.

Frequent result of the sin of pride is the sin of unbelief. The existence of God is denied because man wants to shape his life according to his own will. He acknowledges no law beyond the law he gives to himself. Since the existence of God would interfere with this autonomy, man rejects it as inadmissible. This is the sin of atheism.

At other times God's existence is not so much theoretically denied as practically ignored. Fulfillment and happiness are exclusively sought in the promotion of the values of this world. Faith and religion are considered as unprofitable. The term secularism has been coined for this form of unbelief.

There are also those sins which are directed against the faith of Christian revelation. The Christian believer may sin by neglecting the duties with regard to his faith. Whoever neglects his duty to know the faith, to profess, spread and safeguard it, and to promote the unity of faith according to his possibilities, he sins against faith to the degree of his negligence. These sins of omission are the most common offences against the Christian faith. The believer must be on guard particularly against them.

The divine virtue of faith can likewise be violated by credulity. The credulous person accepts and defends doctrines as of divine faith which are of mere human origin. All kinds of private revelations are readily accepted because of a desire for the extraordinary and sensational, or because of a longing for palpable assurances.[1]

Finally there are those sins which violate the Christian faith by direct opposition and destroy it, such as infidelity, apostasy and heresy. In the following some closer attention shall still be

---

[1] The Church's approbation of private revelations merely means that they contain nothing against faith and morals. He never sins against divine faith who denies them because he is not convinced that they are from God.

given to the sins of pride, unbelief and disregard for the Christian faith.

I. Pride

There is a root of evil which Scripture describes as "Satan" (the one who obstructs, opposes), "the father of lies", "the prince of this world", "the power of death". These expressions indicate the presence of a force in creation that resists God. It is characterized by the refusal to submit to God and to serve him. Its sin is the disobedience of pride.

Self-assertive pride is the sin most diametrically opposed to the obedience of faith. The proud man wants to organize his life according to his own plan and not according to a plan designed by somebody else. He wills to be autonomous and self-sufficient. But since man by his nature is a creature dependent on God's will, this prideful autonomy is ultimately a contradiction and perversion. It must end up in a lie. In order to free himself from this lie, man would have to turn to the truth. But pride again prevents him to accept the truth. Because the truth which comes from God would expose his misshapen sinfulness. It would compromise him. It would demand a change of life. Man would have to surrender to God.

Christ has this infidelity in mind when he speaks of the man who "hates the light, and does not come to the light, lest his deeds should be exposed" (Jn 3:20). It is upon him that he passes the sentence: "He who does not believe will be condemned" (Mk 16:16). Although such a man sees the truth, he cannot endure it. It interferes with his desires. He is an enemy of God in the strict sense, because he is an enemy of goodness. He does not want to know of holiness, because it would oblige him to surrender his arrogant and ruthless egoism. If the sin of pride is complete, it is a fundamental option in radical opposition to God's will. Where this is the case, the divine anathema is naturally incurred.

II. Unbelief

The sin of pride can have many different degrees. In its imperfect forms it can coexist with some faith in God. Even a deep-rooted pride can coexist with the theoretical admission of the existence of God (cf. the Pharisees and scribes in the gospels). Nevertheless the more determined a person is in his refusal of God's sovereignty, the more he will be inclined to deny the existence of God altogether. Also a total distrust in God's goodness, caused by great disillusions, may finally result in the theoretical refusal to accord him any place in one's life. From among the different manifestations of unbelief, atheism and secularism stand out as the more important ones.

In the past also paganism has very often been identified with unbelief. But this is not precise. At least a distinction must be made. As far as the faith in Christ is concerned, pagans do indeed not believe in Christ. In this regard they can be called unbelievers. But as to the faith in God and the acceptance of his will, they are by no means unbelievers. There is much genuine faith in God among them (cf. LG 16; GS 22). In this sense the paganism of the non-Christian religions is the opposite of unbelief, atheism and secularism.

1. *Atheism* is a complex phenomenon. "The word atheism is applied to phenomena which are quite distinct from one another. For while God is expressly denied by some, others believe that man can assert absolutely nothing about Him.... Again some form for themselves such a fallacious idea of God that when they repudiate this figment they are by no means rejecting the God of the gospel. Some never get to the point of raising questions about God" (GS 19).

Hence atheism is not necessarily the denial of the absolute as such, but not seldom a protest against the form with which the absolute is identified. There is "good reason to suppose that many an 'atheist' is not an atheist in reality and in his fundamental intuition; that, as Eckhart said, many a man who blasphemes God loves Him. He is scoffing at a presentment of God which appears to him unworthy. And it may well be that his environment has given occasion to the misunderstanding and makes it impossible for him to replace the 'caricature' by a worthier conception. If such a man sincerely loves the goodness and the holiness which his own heart reveals to him, he can scarcely be termed a man 'who hates the light.' On the contrary, he 'is not far from the kingdom of God'."[1]

Atheism as the sin of unbelief is more than merely the conceptual denial of God; it is at the same time the refusal to submit to the claims of the absolute which manifest themselves in man's conscience. Man refuses to place himself at the service of a superior will. He arrogantly acknowledges nothing but the

---

[1] Otto Karrer: Religions of Mankind.—New York: Sheed and Ward, 1945, 244f.

goals of his own, self-seeking will. There is an ultimate "no" to the divine ground of reality, the source of all goodness and holiness. God and religion are not opposed because they are presented in caricatures. They are rejected and suppressed because they are obstacles to man's selfish desire for unrestrained freedom and absolute power.

2. *Secularism* is a world view which allows for nothing but a wordly world which is totally autonomous and self-sufficient. The shaping of this world is considered the only profitable task. This alone is worthy of man's effort and dedication. God is not needed in this task. He is irrelevant. Religion is consequently likewise superfluous, if not rather an obstacle to man's secular goals. Secularism does not seek the kingdom of God, but the kingdom of mankind. It extols not 'eternal glory', but the glory of the present time.

To be sure, secularism must be distinguished from the legitimate phenomenon of secularization. The realities of this world, like science, techniques, economy, arts, can claim an independence of their own. They are values in their own right. They are worthy of man's creative effort to develop them to the full. The secular world obeys its own laws, which are not subject to the norms of faith and religion. This however does not preclude that man has the responsibility to use the secular realities in harmony with the plan of their Creator. For the truth is that neither the secular world nor secular man created themselves. Their existence depends on the will of a superior being. Therefore their autonomy is only a relative one and by no means absolute (cf. GS 36).

The error and sin of secularism lies in this that it sets the secular world absolute. Man disregards the truth that he is created and therefore dependent on the will of his Creator. In arrogant self-assertion he falsifies the fact of a relative independence of worldly affairs in an absolute autonomy. Any claims of a divine authority to which he should submit are considered an intolerable interference with his creative freedom to build a world according to his own design. Therefore God is set aside. Therefore religion is defied. But a worldly world without God is a chimera. It is an illusion. It cannot be a human world. Secularism is yet another form of unbelief and pride which deeply contradicts human nature and scorns the image of the child of God in man.

III. Sins against the Christian faith

The sins which most directly offend against the Christian faith are infidelity, heresy, schism and apostasy. Infidelity is the culpable neglect of one who is not baptized to inquire into the true faith or his conscious resistance against it. Heresy is the obstinate (conscious and wilful) adherence of a Christian to an error that contradicts a divinely revealed truth.[1] Schism is the obstinate refusal to submit to the primacy of the pope without otherwise rejecting the teaching of the Church. Apostasy is complete defection from the faith on the part of one who received the true faith in baptism.[2]

In the course of the centuries several great schisms took place and heresies rose up which divided the Church. Vatican II judges that for these divisions, "at times, men of both sides were to blame. However, one cannot impute the sin of separation to those who at present are born into these Communities and are instilled therein with Christ's faith" (DH 3). Hence those who are at present born into the different, separated Christian Communities are not for that reason guilty of the sin of schism or heresy.

But this does not mean that the whole issue of heresy and sinful refusal of the truth of Christian faith is irrelevant today. Intellectual pride, self-complacent vanity, recalcitrant egoism, refusal to adjust to the new demands of faith can all give rise to sinful slight and disregard of the truths of faith. "Pride is at work in all heretics, who presume that their errors come directly from God, directly from Christ, in order to be able to close their ears to the voice of the Church."[3]

---

[1] This definition holds for the culpable, formal heresy. Not seldom however the heresy is material only and hence inculpale because of ignorance of the truth and of invincible error. In speaking of heresy, ecclesiastical law has always formal heresy in mind.

[2] The question is discussed whether a Catholic could desert the Church and her faith without necessarily incurring the subjective guilt of heresy. The First Vatican Council defines that a Catholic "never can possess a valid reason for changing this faith or calling it into doubt" (DS 3014; 3036). Mausbach II, 1954, p. 71 holds that the Council only speaks of an objectively valid reason, while Häring II, 1963, p. 55 takes the view that the Council refers to subjective reasons and subjective guilt. However Häring adds that the situation of the poorly instructed Catholic is different, and that he could doubt the Catholic truth without committing grave sin and even join a heretical sect without formal sin against faith (ib. 56).

[3] B. Häring I, 1966, 557.

To the extent that doubts against faith have similar reasons and stem from pride or also discontent resentment at divine providence, they are likewise sins against faith. But doubts which turn up in the course of an honest search for truth could not be qualified as sinful. This kind of doubt "is often rather an unwelcome companion than a foe of religion. . . . it often signifies a concern, anxiety and trouble about religion, some degree of which we might well desiderate for many others."[1]

As regards the sinful refusal to submit to the decisions of the magisterium of the Church in matters of faith and morals, it amounts to the sin of heresy only if infallible decisions are concerned. Refusal to accept the non-infallible teachings of the magisterium is not a sin against faith, but against the obedience and reverence due to the Church,[2] unless this refusal is in some exceptional case justified by serious reasons, as has been explained.

Finally the Church herself has the grave obligation to remain faithful to the Christian message in every regard, not only on the doctrinal level, but also on the level of practical policies. The message of faith may never be placed in the service of vested interests of a religious institution. Quite on the contrary, every religious institution must place itself in the unconditional service of the proclamation of the gospel.

"Faith has often been misused in an ideological manner in the course of history. Moreover, the ideological alienation of faith is a constant possibility. This alienation is always present when faith fails to strive after its own clear representation and irreplaceable realization, fails to live from its innermost motives, and enters into the service of particular interests, aims, and goals, which are then presented as the necessary consequences of faith, and are attributed a validity equal to that of faith itself. . . . Insight into this differentiation of faith and its protection against ideological falsification is, today, the task and the duty of the believer, and of the believing community. They must undergo a constant, self-critical examination of whether they believe, unconditionally and undisguisedly, and live in the faith, or whether they place faith in the egoistical service of their interests in the will to power, success, and prestige. They must decide whether

---

1 Otto Karrer: Religions of Mankind. — New York: Sheed and Ward, 1945, 245.

2 Cf. Jone, 1963, 123.

they live from the faith, or from other sources and motives, which they garnish and conceal with faith and religion."[1]

Faith is not an ideology, but the selfless, thankful, loving acceptance of God, his will, his words and deeds. Its doctrines and basic structures do not stand in the service of human domination and personal interests. Faith follows the sign of love, which apprehends its way in the example of Christ. It is characterized by the norm: "He who is greatest among you shall be your servant" (Mt 23:11).

---

[1] Heinrich Fries: Faith Under Challenge. — New York: Herder and Herder, 1969, 132f.

Chapter II

THE VIRTUE OF HOPE[1]

Hope is a vital condition of human life. Without hope a man cannot exist. Man experiences his existence as longing and striving, as a dynamism proceeding from a hidden impulse and aspiring for a better, more perfect life. Man cannot disregard his desire for perfection and lasting, untroubled happiness. But since this desire is never completely fulfilled in his earthly existence, he hopes for fulfillment always again from the future. Hence hope remains a permanent companion of temporal life. Hope for a better future is ineradicably grounded in the limitation of man's finiteness and his longing for perfect goodness and completion. Man also observes something similar in the external world. What has been attained is nowhere sufficient. All beings strive after liberation from restrictions and press towards greater perfection. Yet in man the immense longing of the universe for what is better and more perfect concentrates and culminates.

There are many things for which a man may hope: his health and that of his children, his freedom and that of his country, the triumph of what he believes to be right ideas, the relief of the needy and oppressed. Yet a gambler may also hope for winnings and a counterfeiter for success of his forgery. Taken in this most general sense, hope is not a virtue but an affection. Thomas Aquinas defines it as a desire of a good which is hard but not impossible to attain (desiderium boni possibilis ardui). Since it is essential for this desire to confide in fulfillment, hope may further be specified as a desire accompanied by expectation of fulfillment.

---

[1] References: C. F. D. Moule: The Meaning of Hope.—Philadelphia: Fortress Press, 1963. Jürgen Moltmann: Theology of Hope. — London: SCM Press, 1967. Josef Pieper: Hope and History. — New York: Herder and Herder, 1969. Studia Moralia, vol. VII: Contributiones ad problema spei. — Roma: Desclée, 1969. J. Moltmann: The Future of Hope. — New York: Herder and Herder, 1970. Concilium, Nov. 1970, vol. 9, nr. 6: Hope. Bernard Häring: Hope is the Remedy. — Garden City, N.Y.: Image Books, 1972. Paul Tihon: Lived Hope and Freedom in the Face of Death; idem: Hope and Action. — Lumen Vitae 28 (1973), 296-320; 373-397.

Though it is not of the essence of hope that its object be morally good, it is of the essence of the virtue of hope. Hope becomes virtue only if it is unwaveringly directed towards what is morally good and lovable. Christian hope is of this nature.

A.   Essence of theological hope

I.   Hope in Holy Scripture

1.   *The Old Testament*. The entire Old Testament is like an incarnation of hope from beginning to end. The history of Israel is the history of an immense longing, which wells up always again and again. It reaches out to always new goals until it finds its final goal in the reign of the messianic times.

Ever since the fundamental event in Israel's history, the calling of Abraham, this atmosphere of hope is characteristic for the chosen people. The hope of the patriarchs, based on God's promise, had as its object the growth to a great nation, through which also the other nations would be blessed, and the promised land. "Go from your country", God bids Abraham, "to the land that I will show you. And I will make of you a great nation, and I will bless you...; and by you all the families of the earth shall bless themselves" (Gen 12:1-3; cf. 13:14-17; 15:1-6; etc.). The great events of Israel's early history are nothing else than stages in the realization of this promise: the exodus from Egypt, the march through the desert, the crossing of the Jordan, and the progressive conquest of the towns of Canaan. Later, during the time of the exile, Israel will hope for liberation from the oppressor and for return to the Land of Promise.

Foreshadowed in these hopes, the final object of Israel's longing gradually becomes more explicit: the messianic reign. Starting with Jacob's prophecy about Juda (Gen 49:10), the messianic hope is constantly growing, although it was only from the time of the prophets that he who was to be the Christ was clearly foretold. The messianic era is most beautifully described by Isaiah: "The people who walked in darkness have seen a great light; those who dwelt in a land of deep darkness, on them has light shined... For to us a child is born, to us a son is given; and the government will be upon his shoulder, and his name will be called 'Wonderful Counsellor, Mighty God, Everlasting Father, Prince of Peace.' Of the increase of his government and of peace there will be no end, upon the throne of David, and over his kingdom, to establish it, and to uphold it with justice and righteousness from this time forth and for evermore" (Is 9:2.6f; cf. 2:2-5). The expectation of the whole people is directed towards this happy, blessed future, and the Israelites long for its appearance.

Often contained in this hope and sometimes added to it are such objects of Israel's prayer and longing as blessing, mercy, help, just judgment, forgiveness and salvation from Yahweh. False and empty hope builds on idols made with hands, on men, riches, power, certain religious practices. The true, devout Israelite puts his trust in Yahweh. "And now, Lord, for what do I wait? My hope is in thee" (Ps 39:7; 70:5; Jer 17:7). Fellowship with the Lord matters more than anything else.

Motive of Israel's hope is the promises of Yahweh. "I will fulfill the oath which I swore to Abraham your father," assures the Lord to Isaac (Gen 26:3; cf. 17:1f; 28:13-15; 48:3f; etc.). Yahweh is faithful to the covenant which he entered with the chosen people and to the promises it implies. "Know therefore that the Lord your God is God, the faithful God who keeps covenant and steadfast love with those who love him and keep his commandments, to a thousand generations" (Deut 7:9). The fidelity of Yahweh has been proven by many interventions in favour of his people, whom he had repeatedly saved "with a mighty hand and an outstretched arm" (Deut 5:15). Israel recalled these great deeds, the *"magnalia* in its liturgy, to reinforce its pleas for help and to strengthen its own hope. Thanksgiving for the mighty works of Yahweh which Israel has experienced becomes a confession of hope."[1] Fruit of this hope is endurance in affliction and the strength to confident, resolute action in world and history.

Closely linked to hope and equally founded in the fidelity of Yahweh is a spiritual doctrine of trust in God alone, which is latent everywhere in the OT. It is most forcibly and magnificently expressed in the Psalms: God is the shelter, the rock, the stronghold.

The bearer of the promises is not primarily the individual Israelite but the people as a whole which is the immediate partner in the covenant. Only in a second instance the promises address the loyal individual.

2. *The New Testament.* In John hope coincides with faith, and in the gospels it is so closely linked with faith that they become indistinguishable. Yet an attentive listening to the

---

[1] Ferdinand Kerstien, art. "Hope" in: Sacramentum Mundi, vol. III, 1969, 61.

texts and to the entire message of the gospels nonetheless reveals much about Christian hope.

Jesus announces himself as the Messiah. Hence he is the fulfillment of Israel's expectation of long centuries. One therefore sometimes gets the impression as if by Christ's coming history has been completed, since the promise is there. But such a summary impression is altered by the parables of the kingdom, by Christ's eschatological discourses, and most of all by his resurrection. No doubt, the kingdom is already there, it has arrived (Mt 12:28; Lk 11:20). But it must nevertheless still grow, as is made plain by the parables of the seed that has to grow until harvest time (Mk 4:26-29), of the grain of mustard (Mt 13:31f par), and of the leaven (Mt 13:33 par). There is still much room for hope, since another coming of the Lord at the end of time is to be expected, where all the peoples will be judged and the perfect reign of God will finally be established (cf. the eschatological discourse Mt 25 and 26 par). Hence Christians wait with longing for the completion of the salvific work which God has begun (cf. Phil 1:6).

The theology of hope is especially unfolded by St. Paul, who clearly sets hope off against faith and unites it with faith and charity to the triad of the theological virtues. The hope of Christians is of divine origin and its fruits are joy and peace. "May the God of hope fill you with all joy and peace in believing, so that by the power of the Holy Spirit you may abound in hope" (Rom 15:13; cf. 12:12).

The object of hope is described by the NT in many different ways, but they have this in common that they almost always indicate an object of eschatological nature. Thus the object of hope is described as life everlasting, resurrection, conquest of suffering and death, inheritance, the kingdom, the heavenly Jerusalem, the new heavens and the new earth, forgiveness, justice, peace, salvation. A thought dear to Paul is the idea of the *doxa,* the glory of God and Christ, in which the Christian is supposed to share. Christians "rejoice in the hope of sharing the glory of God" (Rom 5:2; cf. 8:18; Eph 1:18; Col 1:27; Tit 2:13).

The main motive of hope is God's promise and faithfulness. "Let us hold fast the confession of our hope without wavering, for he who promised is faithful" (Heb 10:23; cf. Gal 3:29; Tit 1:2; Heb 6:11-20). Connected with this, as another motive, are the great works of God already performed on our behalf. Just as the OT hope was anchored in Yahweh's mighty deeds of the past, so Christian hope has its anchor in the revelation of God's love in the mission, death and resurrection of Jesus Christ and in the gift of the Holy Spirit (cf. Rom 5:1-11; Eph 1:3-14; 1 Tim 1:1; Heb 9:11-15). By this a beginning has already been made in the divine work of salvation. Christ's resurrection in particular is the pledge of Christian hope. What happened to Christ is understood as the assurance of the coming glory of God and of the final victory of life from God over death. This hope characterizes the Christians and distinguishes them from the pagans, who are without hope (Eph 2:12; 1 Thess 4:13).

The gospel call is addressed to all mankind. It summons every man to the hope whose foundation has been laid in Christ and promises a universal, eschatological salvation. Consequently Christian hope must reach out to all men and assume responsibility for the future of the entire human race and even of the whole creation (cf. Rom 8:18-25).

II. Concept of hope in theology

Theology defines hope as that virtue, made possible by the grace of God, by which man expects the fulness of salvation and the means to attain it, confident of the omnipotent aid of God.[1]

Object of the virtue of hope is according to the definition the fulness of salvation, which of course in a last analysis consists in the blessed community with God, so that the object is ultimately God himself. Traditional theology usually specifies the object as eternal salvation, eternal happiness, eternal life or beatifying possession of God. Recent theological reflection strives to overcome the somewhat individualistic understanding of the object of hope and to bring its universal and also cosmic character more to the foreground. Hence the object of hope is defined as the consummation of the messianic reign, or the completion of creation in Christ as the head of the universe, or the universal consummation of all things prefigured in Christ's resurrection.

Yet Christian hope does not only expect a new creation at the end of time. The Spirit of the Lord is sent to renew

---

[1] Some authors define hope as a "certain expectation" (Noldin) or "certain confidence" (Marc, Prümmer, Zalba). Others like Mausbach, Schilling, Jone, Alfaro omit the word "certain" in the definition. Hope should of course not be defined in such a way that it becomes a sure expectation. There remains always an element of uncertainty in it. The reason for the uncertainty however lies alone in man's moral insufficiency, while the trust in God's infinite power, goodness and fidelity ought certainly to be unconditional.

the face of the earth. The kingdom of God is to grow already
now among men. The renewal of the human heart in justice
and holiness, the better ordering of the present world, the
establishment of peace among men and nations likewise pertain
to the object of hope. Hence Christian hope may not consider
itself as merely eschatological and "distinct from the minor
hopes that are directed towards attainable goals and visible
changes in human life, neither can it as a result dissociate itself
from such hopes by relegating them to a different sphere while
considering its own future to be supra-worldly and purely spiritual
in character. The Christian hope is directed towards a *novum
ultimum,* towards a new creation of all things by the God of
the resurrection of Jesus Christ. It thereby opens a future outlook that embraces all things, including also death, and into
this it can and must also take the limited hopes of a renewal
of life, stimulating them, relativizing them, giving them
direction."[1]

Certainly these minor hopes are only precursory and therewith provisional movements. But they have an intrinsic relation
to the final, eschatological hope and stand in its service. Traditional theology expresses this truth in the doctrine of the
secondary object of hope, which consists in all the spiritual and
temporal means necessary for the attainment of the ultimate
goal of hope. The question is only to determine sufficiently
well which minor hopes fall within the scope of these spiritual
and temporal means. The liturgy asks for "health of body
and soul". And Christ restored the use of eyes, ears, tongue
and limbs to numbers of sick people who had hoped in him.
Those who hope in Christ can but contradict the unredeemed
world, the sorrow and suffering caused by it, the injustice and
wickedness present in it. Hence, although the final object of
hope is the consummation of God's glory, Christ's kingdom and
the universal salvation, all that which contributes to the realization
of this universal, ultimate goal, here and now in man's earthly
existence, is equally and with full right part of the confidence
of hope.

Motive of hope is primarily God's omnipotent aid, i.e. God's
readiness to help and his absolute power to do so. Often the
motive is formulated in a more biblical language as God's fidelity
to his promises. But it can be said that God's promises and

---

[1] Jürgen Moltmann: Theology of Hope. — London: SCM Press, 1970,
33f.

fidelity to them lastly result from his will to help; and further-more that even without express promises men have sufficient motive to hope in God. Supreme pledge of the Christian hope is the revelation of God's love in Jesus Christ. Christ's incarnation, life and redemptive suffering manifest and prove the infinite mercy of God. His resurrection is the supreme testimony of his omnipotence and steadfast faithfulness to those who love him. This primary motive of hope is supplemented by secondary motives. They are the sacraments and all the means of grace offered through the Church, which constitute the visible assurance of God's presence among men and of his saving will; the merits and intercession of the Blessed Virgin and the saints; and finally man's own faithfulness and sincere will, his good efforts and works of love. Just as a sinful, wicked life is a danger to hope, so it is easier to confide in God and to hope in acceptance by him for those who have always striven to merit his friendship and to live close to him.

B. Fruits and challenges of hope

1. *Endurance in suffering*

The Christian finds himself in the same world as everyone else. He suffers, struggles and dies like any other man. His Christian vocation does not release him from pain and sorrows, and he has to confront the problem of suffering as much as others who are of different belief. Yet although the ultimate meaning of suffering, particularly in its extreme forms, does not lie open at hand to the Christian either, his hope gives him strength and courage to hold out even in the profoundest darkness, without despairing or giving up. The fundamental Christian attitude to suffering is indeed hope. "We know that in everything God works for good with those who love him" (Rom 8:28), St. Paul comforts the Roman Christians. He reckons that the sufferings of the present time are not worthy to be compared with the glory to come (Rom 8:18). And besides, Christians have an example in Christ himself. "Was it not necessary that the Christ should suffer these things and enter into his glory?" (Lk 24:26). Thus Christians are taught and helped to carry their cross in patient endurance with Christ, confident that God's faithfulness will not derelict them and expose their suffering to futility, but transmute it together with the cross of Christ into glory. The star of hope sends its rays even in the deepest darkness of suffering as an everlasting source of comfort and joy, which nothing could replace.

Hope even gives strength to look at the bitterest thing of all: the remorse that we feel, when true penitence is aroused in us, for all the injury which our selfishness has caused to God and to others.[1] If there were only the fear of condemnation, man would have reason to escape the memory and admission of his guilt. But hope in the mercy of God and his promise of forgiveness for those who sincerely convert, gives the sinner courage to accept the remorse over his sins and the reprehension for it. Hope grants him the possibility of a new life and of a return to the love of God and the community with him.

While hope gives the Christian fortitude to endure in suffering, his patient bearing in distress also becomes a witness for the strength of the hope he possesses. By accepting the cross, suffering and death, by taking upon himself the trials and struggles of obedience in the body and surrendering himself to the pain of love, he "proclaims in the every-day world the future of the resurrection, of life and the righteousness of God."[2]

2.   *Openness for the future*

Because of its hope Christian life is essentially prospective, forward-looking, a departure into the unknown. In the encounter with the God of hope, man perpetually finds himself in what is new, surprising, unique and full of mystery. Christian life is consequently a life of ever new beginnings and of a searching heart. This prevents his thoughts, traditions and doctrines from hardening into ideologies. Faith and Christian life are not closed systems, marked out once and for all. They are open for further development and perfection, and even in need of it. For this reason, because the believer recognizes that he himself is still on the way to the fulness of truth, he is accessible to dialogue with all men of good will. He can make room for the good insights and findings of Christians and non-Christians alike. Hope is the mark of the pilgrim status of man, whose characteristic is

---

[1] Cf. C.F.D. Moule: The Meaning of Hope. — Philadelphia: Fortress Press, 1963, 31.

[2] J. Moltmann, 1. c. 163.

imperfection and therefore receptivity for future completion and readiness to give himself to the ever greater God.

3. *Summons to transform the world*

Christian hope does not render effort superfluous but demands it. Man hopes for God's justice and peace by striving now for their progressive realization. The "hope of our calling" (Eph 1:18; 4:4) is a summons to be mediators in that process by which all things should be brought home into the kingdom of Christ and submitted to his salvific lordship.

Vatican II teaches "that a hope related to the end of time does not diminish the importance of intervening duties, but rather undergirds the acquittal of them with fresh incentives" (GS 21). It claims the believer's active engagement in the progress of this world. For Christians, together with all men, are called to cooperate in the unfolding and completion of the divine work of creation (GS 34; 57; 67), which constitutes an important aspect of their final hope. And secondly, by the better ordering of society they contribute to the consummation of Christ's kingdom, which they are hoping for. Because here on this earth "grows the body of a new human family, a body which even now is able to give some kind of foreshadowing of the new age. Earthly progress must be carefully distinguished from the growth of Christ's kingdom. Nevertheless, to the extent that the former can contribute to the better ordering of human society, it is of vital concern to the kingdom of God" (GS 39).

Christian hope is the impulse to change the world in the perspective of God's creative plans and salvific goals. This is, or at least should be, the driving force behind all innerworldly hopes. "The horizon of expectation within which a Christian doctrine of conduct must be developed is the eschatological horizon of expectation of the kingdom of God, of his righteousness and his peace with a new creation, of his freedom and his humanity for all men. This horizon alone, with its formative effect on the present, leads a man in missionary hope to oppose and suffer under the inadequacies of the present, brings him into conflict with the present form of society... Only Christians who no longer understand their eschatological mission as a mission for the future of the world and of man can identify their call with the existing circumstances in the social roles of their callings and be content to fit in with these. But where the call is seen within the horizon of expectation proper to it, there our believing obedience, our discipleship and our love must be understood as 'creative discipleship' and 'creative love'."[1]

Creative discipleship sets things right and puts them in order. It sets about criticizing and transforming the present, because it is open and geared towards the universal future of the kingdom. Its expectation makes man ready to expend himself unreservedly in love and in the work of the reconciliation of the world with God and his future. Christians will often have to call into question things as they are, because of their hope, in order to renew and to transform them. This is implied when they are asked by St. Paul not to conform to this world. The hope of the gospel has a polemic and liberating effect with regard to the forces of lie, error, serfdom and injustice. Christians are demanded to transform the face of the world in which they live, in opposition to the forces of darkness and in creative expectation.[2]

C. Sins against hope

Hope can be abandoned basically in two ways: by presumption and by despair. Presumption expects in premature anticipation and certainty fulfillment of what is hoped for. Despair is the premature anticipation of non-fulfillment of the same hope. Despair may appear in the extreme form of a complete dereliction of hope or in the milder, more frequent form of resignation, which is a weak, timid, weary hope, called by the Middle Ages 'acedia' or 'tristitia' and reckoned among the capital sins.

1. *Presumption*

Presumption is the unwarrantable expectation of goods or helps of divine order. It rashly assumes that fulfillment will be obtained. Presumption is directly opposed to the fear of God, which is an essential element of theological hope.

Presumption can result from different causes and present itself in different ways. (a) A first form of presumption expects eternal salvation from man's own efforts alone. This attitude

---

[1] J. Moltmann, 1. c. 334.
[2] Cf. Moltmann, 1. c. 330.

offends against the dogma of the gratuitous character of grace and final salvation. At its root is the pride and heresy of Pelagianism, which exalts man's natural powers and undertakes to attain eternal happiness through mere moral achievements. (b) Another form of presumption expects eternal salvation from the merits of Christ alone. In a wanton and frivolous way man dispenses himself of his personal efforts in the work of salvation. He does not take pains to turn to God with all his heart and to obey his will faithfully, because he thinks himself certain of salvation if only he has faith in the merits of Christ. (c) Presumptuous is finally also the expectation of divine helps for sinful or improper objects. Expectation of God's aid for sinful intents is called blasphemous presumption. The reckoning with God's intervention or aid as substitute for human diligence and effort is temptation of God; e.g. ordeals as substitute for sober human trials, or hope for divine assistance in examinations as compensation for neglected studies. Multiplication of sins on the grounds that God forgives serious and numerous sins as readily as less serious and occasional offences is a grave sin of presumption of the same type. Of course God will pardon even the most heinous sin to the truly repentant sinner. But the point at issue is whether postponement of conversion and accumulation of sins will so readily be followed by a sincere repentance, or not rather by a hardening of the heart. The longer one has continued in sin, the more numerous the sins, the more difficult and improbable the conversion.

It is however not a sin of presumption if somebody commits a sinful action merely accompanied by the hope of forgiveness, but caused by human weakness.

2. *Despair*

Despair is the voluntary distrust of obtaining from God eternal salvation and the means necessary for it. It is the loss of confidence in the goodness and mercy of God and his divine assistance.

Despair can be caused by great sinfulness and severe remorse of conscience, which lead the sinner to believe that his sins are too heinous for the mercy of God. Yet heavy buffets of fate or continued failures, too, can cause a man to lose trust in God and to despair of his goodness. Not seldom these causes may work together.

Since in despair man relinquishes the hope of obtaining perfection and salvation, he will by consequence no longer care for his duty to strive after them. Either he will totally turn to the goods of this world and seek some kind of satisfaction in forms of hedonism or pseudo-heroic nihilism (not seldom glorified in contemporary literature), or he may lose the will to work and to live and eventually end in suicide. In all these attitudes man cuts off the bond which binds him to God and his will. He lastly also abandons the ties which join him to his fellowmen, together with whom he is supposed to labour for salvation. Fear of God may hold acts of despair in check, but only the virtue of hope can truly overcome them.

Despair must however not be confused with certain forms of depression, anxiety, melancholy and scruples, which are due to psychic stresses, emotional disturbances and mental illnesses. They induce feelings of discouragement and despair. But God's goodness is not questioned voluntarily. This is especially clear if such people continue in their religious life and prayer. In extreme cases mental illnesses may even lead to suicide, which is not completely or not at all imputable because of lack of inner freedom. — Equally habitual sinners who 'despair' of their betterment are often only pusillanimous souls, who rather despair of their own cooperation with grace than of divine assistance itself.

It is moreover not a sin against hope if one who is weary of life or has to suffer much, wishes that he were dead. Such a wish is lawful if made with resignation to God's will. A desire of this kind is expressed by St. Paul in the letter to the Philippians: "For to me to live is Christ, and to die is gain. If it is to be life in the flesh, that means fruitful labour for me. Yet which I shall choose I cannot tell. I am hard pressed between the two. My desire is to depart and be with Christ, for that is far better" (Phil 1:21-23).

3.   *Resignation*

Resignation passively submits to the insufficiency of existing conditions, distrustful of God's help to change them. It is not constituted by a complete loss of hope, but by a weak and weary hope. It still has faith in eternal salvation, but it does no longer believe in the possibility of a better world, because it doubts the interest of God in it and the necessary divine assistance.

Under the pretext of deficient help and grace of God man abdicates further striving and efforts. "God has exalted man and given him the prospect of a life that is wide and free, but man hangs back and lets himself down. God promises a new creation of all things in righteousness and peace, but man acts as if everything were as before and remained as before. God honours him with his promises, but man does not believe himself capable of what is required of him. That is the sin which most profoundly threatens the believer. It is not the evil he does, but the good he does not do, not his misdeeds but his omissions, that accuse him. They accuse him of lack of hope."[1]

Such resignation may have its cause in timidity that lacks confidence in God. It may result from disappointments and unsuccessful work. What remains is weariness without the courage and will to further engagement and efforts. Such withdrawal claims to preserve the soul from disappointments. It means to remain on the solid ground of reality, "to think clearly and not hope any more" (Camus). Man adopts a positivistic realism with no prospects for the future. The active interest in the great concerns of God, the unfolding of creation and the growth of his kingdom, is abandoned. There is no way to new, unknown possibilities, but only the trifling play with the existing possibilities, which finally ends in boredom, in outbreaks of absurdity, in a life without future and meaning.[2]

Neither in presumption nor in despair or resignation lies the answer to the questions and problems of life, but only in hope that is patient and enduring. "This world is not the heaven of self-realization, as it was said to be in Idealism. This world is not the hell of self-estrangement, as it is said to be in romanticist and existentialist writing. The world is not yet finished, but is understood as engaged in a history. It is therefore the world of possibilities, the world in which we can serve the future, promised truth and righteousness and peace. This is an age of diaspora, of sowing in hope, of self-surrender and sacrifice, for it is an age which stands within the horizon of a new future. Thus, self-expenditure in this world, day-to-day love in hope, becomes possible and becomes human within that horizon of expectation which transcends this world."[3]

---

[1] Jürgen Moltmann: Theology of Hope. — London: SCM Press, 1970, 22f.

[2] Cf. J. Moltmann, 1. c. 23f.

[3] Ib. 338.

Chapter III

THE VIRTUE OF DIVINE LOVE[1]

Love in the widest sense is any affection for some good. It is called forth by the experience of an object as a value, i.e. as something whose existence, preservation, acquisition or furtherance is good and desirable. Love is the most fundamental emotion of man, which is at the basis and origin of all the others. The immediate effect of the value-experience is pleasure in the object (*amor complacentiae*). Love may rest and terminate in this pleasure. Then it is an appreciative love, which does not attempt to acquire the object nor place itself at its service. Often however the pleasure in the object leads to the wish and determination to acquire the value, to enhance it, to become one with it.

If love is mainly concerned with the acquisition of the good for the one who loves, then it is called love of desire (*amor concupiscentiae*). Man seeks in this love essentially his own good, his personal enrichment, his perfection. The beloved value is not loved for its own sake, but for the benefit that a man derives from it for himself. If love aims at the preservation and promotion of the good of another person or being, it is called love of benevolence (*amor benevolentiae*) or also agape. This is the love which wills the good of another. The object appears as a value in itself, worthy of being supported and advanced for its own sake, and not only as a means for the perfection of the subject who loves. Notice must however be taken that these two forms of love, designate different prevalences in the expression of love, but not totally independent kinds of love.

---

[1] Louis Colin: Love the Lord Thy God. — Covent Garden/Glasgow: Sands and Co., 1956. Ceslaus Spicq: Agape in the New Testament, 3 volumes. — St. Louis/London: B. Herder Book Co., 1963-66. Thomas Barrosse: Christianity: Mystery of Love. An Essay in Biblical Theology. — Notre Dame, Ind.: Fides Publishers, 1964. D. Deden: The Bible on Love. — De Pere, Wisc.: St. Norbert Abbey Press, 1966. Hans Urs von Balthasar: Love Alone. — New York: Herder and Herder, 1969. Victor Paul Furnish: The Love Command in the New Testament. — Nashville and New York: Abingdon Press, 1972. Gene Outka: Agape: An Ethical Analysis. — New Haven: Yale University, 1973.

Love of desire may have as its object sensual, material or spiritual values, such as pleasant sensations, possessions, power, values of knowledge and beauty. Love of benevolence may be charitable love, concerned with the welfare of another person who is in material or spiritual need; love of friendship, which is the mutual love of two persons who want to share with each other their spiritual riches, their aspirations and the best they have; or devotional, mystical love (*amor devotionis*), in which a person gives himself up to the divine and aspires at communion and union with it. It is this latter love with which this chapter is concerned.

A. Essence of divine love

I. Nature of divine love in Holy Scripture

The terms almost universally used for love by the Greek bible are *agapan, agapesis* and *agape*. The substantive agape was introduced by the Septuagint in literature and hardly used in earlier writings, which is a noteworthy linguistic incident. These words are less emotionally charged than the current terms for love in Greek: *erasthai* and *eros,* which are the words most frequently used in classical and hellenistic Greek, and *philein* and *philis*. The agape group, as used outside the bible, designates a sober kind of love. It denotes a love which places a high value upon some person or thing, or which receives them with favour. In Sacred Scripture it acquires in addition a religious content which is, in many respects, new. These linguistic facts already indicate "that the biblical doctrine of love differs essentially from pagan ideas on the subject."[1]

1. *The Old Testament*

God's love for men is attested to everywhere in the OT. "True it is seldom mentioned *expressis verbis*, but nonetheless it is expressed clearly, though indirectly, in the numerous *narratives* of how he acted towards men."[2] Of its nature the love of God is spontaneous and free. But in accordance with the nature of the covenant, on which Israel's relationship to Yahweh is

---

[1] Viktor Warnach, art. "Love" in: Encyclopedia of Biblical Theology, ed. by Joh. Bauer, London, 1970, 518.
[2] V. Warnach, 1. c. 519.

founded, God expects and requires that men shall love him in return.

a) *Israel's love for Yahweh in the context of the covenant* (historical books). While in the book of Exodus Israel's covenant obligations are primarily motivated by fear of God, they find in the book of Deuteronomy their primary motive in the love of God. Deuteronomy speaks of man's love for God more often than any other of the historical books.

Love of God is for the most part understood as faithfulness to the covenant, and therefore essentially conceived as an obligation and commandment which is most intimately connected with the service of God and the keeping of the rest of the clauses of the covenant law. Yet this does not mean that Israel's love of God is a mere legal duty. "Man's love for God is far from being expressed in sheer legalism or external observance of the cult; on the contrary, it engages the whole of man, with all his powers; it must come from 'his whole heart' and must lead to a 'cleaving to' God that is living and dynamic."[1]

Deut 6:5 formulates the great commandment of love of God as a central theme of the covenant: "You shall love the Lord your God with all your heart, and with all your soul, and with all your might" (cf. Josh 22:5). The commandment expresses a threefold, total dedication of man to God. Man is required to love the Lord with all his heart, i.e. with all his spiritual and affective forces; with all his soul, i.e. with his entire existence and life; with all his might, i.e. in readiness to active, wholehearted service.[2]

The wholehearted love of God is realized through observance of Yahweh's commandments and statutes. It attests itself if a man fears the Lord, listens to his voice and serves him, walks in his ways and cleaves to him (Deut 5:9f; 7:9; 11:1.13.22; 13:3f; 19:9; 30:15ff; Josh 22:5; Neh 1:5; Dan 9:4). "What does the Lord your God require of you, but to fear the Lord your God, to walk in all his ways, to love him, to serve the Lord your God with all your heart and with all your soul, and

---

[1] V. Warnach, 1. c. 523.

[2] Rabbi Akiba gives an impressive explanation and witness of what it means to love God with all one's heart and soul. When about to suffer the martyrdom for his faith 135 A.D., he said: "I have loved Him with my whole heart, He will say, and with all my fortune; I had not yet had the occasion to love Him with my whole soul. The moment has arrived" (quoted in Dictionary of Biblical Theology, art. "Love", 285).

to keep the commandments and statutes of the Lord, which I command you this day for your good" (Deut 10:12f).

The commandment of love is accompanied by the promise of blessings for those who keep it and by the threat of chastisements for those who desert it (Ex 20:5f; Deut 11:13-17. 22-28; 30:15-20). "Know therefore that the Lord your God is God, the faithful God who keeps covenant and steadfast love with those who love him and keep his commandments, to a thousand generations, and requites to their face those who hate him, by destroying them" (Deut 7:9f). During her history Israel would not seldom suffer the sad consequences of her unfaithfulness to God's love, but also receive God's mercy again and again when returning to him anew (cf. Neh 1:5ff; Dan 9:4ff). "How blessed are those who love you! They will rejoice in your peace" (Tob 13:14).

b) *Love as bond of affection between Yahweh and Israel* (prophetic books). The prophets like to describe the love between Yahweh and Israel in pictures which express a mutual relation of affection. Although the prophets are rather reluctant in using the term "love" when speaking of Israel's dedication to Yahweh, they avail themselves of comparisons which strongly imply such a relationship.

The love of God for man is basically the love of a father for his child (Hos 11:1-4; Jer 31:20-22). Indeed it is greater than the love of a mother (Is 49:15, 66:13). The mutual bond between Yahweh and Israel finds expression above all in the metaphor of the marriage covenant between husband and wife. Jer 2:2f is the oldest text to use this comparison, and this in a formulation of great tenderness: "Thus says the Lord, I remember the devotion of your youth, your love as a bride, how you followed me in the wilderness, in a land not sown. Israel was holy to the Lord the first fruits of his harvest." Though Israel at times faithlessly derelicted her former love, the Lord always searches for her again in order to restore the broken union. "I have loved you with an everlasting love; therefore I have continued my faithfulness to you. Again I will build you, and you shall be built, O virgin Israel!" (Jer 31:3f; cf. Hos 2:14-20; Is 54:1-10; Ezek 16). At other times the affectionate regard between God and man is rendered in the relation between master and close servant or even friend (Is 41:8-10) or also between shepherd and sheep (Ezek 34:11-24; cf. Ps 23).

This love of affection constitutes the lasting ground for the never ceasing care and concern Yahweh has for his people, and therefore is a most strong motive of Israel's trust in God. Yet it likewise motivates God's imperative demand of faithful adherence to him and to his commandments.

c) *Unfaltering love as the virtue of the just* (didactic-sapient literature). The God-fearing Jew unceasingly expresses his grateful, trusting, loyal love for God in his prayers and hymns (Ps 40:16; 31:23; 116:1; 119:132; 145:20). This love extends to all that belongs to Yahweh: his name (Ps 119:132), his testimonies and promises (Ps 119:119.140.167), his law and commandments (Ps 119:47f.97. etc.), the holy temple where his "glory dwells" (Ps 26:8). Salvation is for those who love the Lord (Ps 69:36; 122:6). Therefore the pious Jew is invited to love the Lord, for he is faithful (Ps 31:23).

In Wisdom literature we also encounter a mystical attitude, e.g. in Wis 3:9: "Those who trust in him will understand truth, and the faithful will abide with him in love because grace and mercy are upon his elect." Through love a man is mystically united with God in close communion. "The love of wisdom, which is, in the last analysis, essentially love of the Creator (Sir 7:30; 47:8), leads to 'nearness to God' (Wis 6:19) and to 'friendship with God' (Wis 7:14), as also to 'living with' him (Wis 8:3)."[1]

2. *The New Testament*

a) The God of the NT is simply "the God of love" (2 Cor 13:11; 1 Jn 4:16). *God's love for men* and all creation finds its most eloquent expression in the unique fact of the incarnation of his only begotten Son, Jesus Christ. The dramatic dialogue of love between God and man centres and culminates in him. "Being mindful of his mercy" (Lk 1:54f), God manifested his love in Christ (1 Jn 4:9f; Rom 8:39). In Jesus Christ the perfect bond of unity between God and mankind has been effected and the new covenant concluded. Men have been drawn into the divine love to the extent that they are God's children and sons (1 Jn 3:1f; Gal 4:4-7). Therefore the love of God is primarily a father's love (Mt 5:45; Lk 15:11-32; 1 Jn 3:1). His love, which is a saving love, extends to all men (1 Tim 2:3f; 4:10; 2 Pet 3:9) and to the whole world. "For God

---

[1] V. Warnach, art. "Love", 1. c. 523f.

so loved the world that he gave his only Son, that whoever believes in him should not perish but have eternal life" (Jn 3:16). Although this love particularly applies to those who believe (Jn 17:20-26; 2 Thess 2:13) and who faithfully observe God's commandments (Jn 14:21.23), it also reaches out to sinners, who are as such his enemies (Mt 5:44f; Lk 6:35; Rom 5:8-10).

b) *Man's love for God* is response to the prior love of God. The divine love calls for reciprocity. The commandment of Deuteronomy is still in force. "You shall love the Lord your God with all your heart, and with all your soul, and with all your mind. This is the great and first commandment" (Mt 22: 37f par; cf. 1 Jn 4:19-21; 5:2f). Together with 'he other commandment of love of neighbour, which is of equal importance, it sums up the whole law and the prophets. No other love is compatible with the love of God. It demands a man's entire devotion and service (Mt 6:24 par).

The divine love in man is not one virtue set over against others on the same level. Agape is generated as a new form or sphere of existence from God. "God is love, and he who abides in love abides in God, and God abides in him" (1 Jn 4:16; cf. 3:1f). Love is a basic condition in which the Christian's entire being is grounded and founded (Eph 3:17-19). It is divine not only because it has God as its object, but above all because it proceeds from God and is ultimately a participation in his own eternal love. "For God's love has been poured into our hearts through the Holy Spirit who has been given to us" (Rom 5:5; cf. Jn 17:26). From this root all the good actions of a man must flow, and separated from this root they are nothing (1 Cor 13). Love is the greatest among all the moral as well as theological virtues. "So faith, hope, love abide, these three; but the greatest of these is love" (1 Cor 13:13).

Love for God proves itself in a total assent to the divine will and in the ready performance of his commands. "For this is the love of God, that we keep his commandments" (1 Jn 5:3; cf. Jn 14:15.21; 15:10; 1 Jn 2:4-6). "If a man loves me, he will keep my word; and my Father will love him, and we will come to him and make our home with him. He who does not love me does not keep my words; and the word which you hear is not mine but the Father's who sent me" (Jn 14:23f).

Although man's love for God is already the answer to God's love, the loving human response to the graceful offer of God calls forth a further response from God. With a father's love he

will guard those who love him and watch over their welfare.
"We know that everything works for good with those who love
him" (Rom 8:28). He makes them share in his unfathomable,
divine riches (1 Cor 2:9) and admits them to the innermost
communion with him (Jn 14:23; 15:10; 1 Jn 2:5f; 4:16). A
mystical bond of mutual love is established which can even be
called friendship (Jn 15:14f).

c)   Also in the NT the bond of love between God and men
finds expression in different *images and portayals* which imply a
relationship of affection and love. The image most frequently
used for the relation between God in heaven and men on earth
is the father-son relationship. Jesus himself not only addresses
God simply as "Father", but often refers to him as the Father
of his disciples and hearers. He speaks to them of God as their
Father in heaven who loves them, cares for them (Mt 5:45;
6:25-32; 7:11; Lk 12:28-30), and who is ready to forgive (Mt
6:14; Lk 15). Men on the other hand are expected to fulfill the
will of the Father (Mt 7:21), to imitate his love and mercy (Mt
5:48; 6:14f; Lk 6:36), and to seek ultimately him alone in
all things (Mt 5:16; 6:5f.16-18). In the writings of St. John
"Father" is the common designation for God. Through faith
(Jn 1:12f; 1 Jn 5:1) and the Spirit (Jn 3:3-6), through charity
(1 Jn 4:7) and a good life (1 Jn 2:29; 5:18), men are born
of God and become his children (Jn 1:12; 1 Jn 3:1f; 5:1).
According to St. Paul God is "our God and Father" (Gal 1:1;
1 Thess 1:3; etc.), through whom we receive grace, mercy and
peace (Rom 1:7; etc.; 1 Tim 1:2; 2 Tim 1:2). He is a Father
to us and we are his sons and daughters (2 Cor 6:18). God
offers to men the "spirit of sonship". Whoever "are led by the
Spirit of God are sons of God" and can call to him "Abba,
Father!" (Rom 8:14-17; Gal 4:6f).

The divine bond of love is still described by other images,
which however are only used for the relationship between
Christ and men. Christ is the good shepherd, who has compassion for the crowds which are like sheep without guidance
(Mt 9:36; Mk 6:34; 1 Pet 2:25). He goes before the sheep,
he knows them, and even lays down his life for them. And the
sheep hear his voice and follow him (Jn 10:1-18). Again, Christ
is the master who came to serve men even unto the sacrifice of
his life. He illustrates this self-giving love by the washing of his
disciples' feet (Jn 13:1-17). But he also expects from his
disciples a loving dedication to him, which must be ready to

renounce everything for the sake of his fellowship (Lk 14:26f.33; Jn 8:31; 13:35; 14:21; 15:8-10). Precisely because the relationship to his disciples is so much characterised by dedication and love, he can also call them his brethren (Mt 28:10; Jn 20:17, cf. Mt 25:40; Rom 8:29; Heb 2:11f.17) and even friends. "You are my friends if you do what I command you. No longer do I call you servants....; but I have called you friends, for all that I have heard from my Father I have made known to you" (Jn 15:14f; cf. Lk 12:4).

The apostolic writings finally compare the relation between Christ and the Church or the believer to the relationships between bridegroom and bride, husband and wife. Already John the Baptist likens Christ to a bridegroom, who comes to lead home his bride, which is the people of God (Jn 3:29). Paul feels a divine jealousy for the Christians of Corinth, who should reserve their sincere and pure devotion for Christ and for nobody else. "For I betrothed you to Christ to present you as a pure bride to her one husband" (2 Cor 11:2). He motivates the love between husband and wife by the love between Christ and the Church (Eph 5:21-33). And the Apocalypse joyfully exults in the marriage between the Lamb and his bride, which is the new Jerusalem or the people of God. The marriage signifies the consummation of all things at the end of time (Rev 19:7; 21:9; 22:17). "And I saw the holy city, new Jerusalem, coming down out of heaven from God, prepared as a bride adorned for her husband; and I heard a great voice from the throne saying, 'Behold, the dwelling of God is with men. He will dwell with them, and they shall be his people, and God himself will be with them' " (Rev 21:2f).

II. Concept of divine love in theology

The theological virtue of love is usually defined as that supernatural virtue by which we love God as the highest good for his own sake and all creation for God's sake. It is supernatural because it presupposes the prior gift of grace and divine life as the existential precondition for its being and exercise. The qualification "supernatural virtue" can therefore also be paraphrased as "virtue made possible by the grace of God".

The definition pinpoints the object and motive of the virtue. Its primary object is God as the highest, most perfect, most comprehensive good. Its secondary object are all beings and creatures which God loves and wills. This includes the animated nature: angels and men, our neighbours as well as ourselves; and the inanimate nature: the entire world and cosmos. The motive of divine love is always God himself: the infinite goodness and beauty which he possesses in himself and which is reflected in whatever he has created, and his love of friendship which he extends as the gift of his all surpassing kindness to the spiritual beings capable of this personal relation of mutual love.

The above definition however proves to be deficient in an important regard. It does not define divine love in itself, for the principal term in the definition is again love: the theological virtue of love is "that virtue by which we love..." An attempt must be made to define the content of divine love.

Man's love for God essentially belongs to the category of benevolent love, whose characteristic it is to will the good of another. But what good can a man will for God? To will the good of another can mean two things: first, the simple approval of the good he possesses and the esteem for it; and second, the wish and determination to protect and further the good of another and to add what is lacking in goodness. There is no doubt that man can and should love God in the first sense of benevolent love. Charity "means that we delight in God, in His perfection and blessedness; that we are glad and 'dance with joy' at the thought that God is what He is, infinitely good, beautiful, mighty and blissful."[1] Love of God is delight in his unfathomable holiness and infinite goodness, and joy in his eternal blessedness.

But to a certain extent also the second intent of benevolent love can be realized in the love of God. Though man cannot add anything to God's internal perfection, he can add to his external glory and praise. In this sense charity means to wish for the establishment of God's governance and to desire it really and effectively with all one's strength and in every possible way. This desire of divine love is expressed in the first petitions of the Our Father: "Hallowed be thy name. Thy kingdom come, Thy will be done, on earth as it is in heaven."

Finally, inasmuch as love of God is akin to love of friendship, it tends towards union with God. But it transcends human friendship insofar as this union is not only a union of affection and mutual sharing of spiritual values, but a total self-giving and abandonment to God. "To love God is to give oneself, body and soul, senses and faculties, wholly, irrevocably and forever, so that one ceases to belong to oneself and becomes the absolute property

[1] Louis Colin: Love the Lord Thy God. — Covent Garden/Glasgow: Sands and Co., 1956, 17.

of God."[1] Divine love is, at least in its perfection, innermost communion and mystical unity with God, a compenetration of God and man and mutual abiding one in the other.

Taking into consideration these different aspects of divine love, it can be defined as the joyful approval of God's infinite goodness and the desire to further his external glory and to be united with him; or shorter: the joyful, dedicated approval of everything that God is and wills.

God's goodness and beauty is manifested in many ways. All creation and all the beauty of nature is an expression of God's excellence and glory. Religious men of all times were aware that the contemplation of the wonders of nature is most apt to lead men to the praise and love of God. St. Francis of Assisi saw and loved God in Brother Fire and Sister Water. St. John of the Cross observes: "The soul is greatly moved to love her Beloved, God, by the consideration of the creatures, seeing that these are things that have been made by His own hand."[2] The sublimity of mountains, the immensity of the sea, the majesty of the starry sky, the silence of a lonely valley, the murmuring of a spring, the song of a bird, the charm of a rose or even of a simple daisy are all the echo and radiance of the unseen beauty. As reflecting God, they call men to love of him, to his worship and praise.

The divine, its superiority and its unfathomable goodness, can also be sensed and experienced in great ideals. Love of God can therefore also realize itself in the dedication to truth, goodness and beauty, e.g. in the dedication to arts, science, one's country, or to fellowmen in general. Even though these expressions of divine love will often need further purification, a man can still reach and love God and his absolute goodness through them.

III. Qualities of divine love

a) Love must be *sovereign*. Man must love God above all things and more than any creature. This is expressed by Holy Scripture in the request to love God with all one's heart, and with all one's soul, and with all one's strength (Deut 6:5; Mt 22:36-38; Mk 12:30; Lk 10:27) and in calling this the first and

---

[1] L. Colin, 1. c. 19.

[2] The Complete Works, ed. by E. Allison Peers, vol. II, Spiritual Canticle. — London: Burns Oates and Washbourne, 1953, 46.

greatest commandment. The love of God must be greater than the love of father and mother, brother and sister, wife and children, greater even than the love of one's own life (cf. Mt 10:37; Lk 14:26).

Only a supreme love is worthy of God. For the more perfect a being is, the more loveworthy he is, and the more right he has to be loved. God is infinite holiness, wisdom, goodness and beauty. Therefore he is infinitely lovable and infinitely worthy of being loved. Besides, God is the first principle and final cause of all things, and also as such he is entitled to our wholehearted love. Whatever a man is and has, he owes it to God, and it is to be placed in the service of his glory. Finally God's all-surpassing love for men as manifested in his Son Jesus Christ, in his incarnation, suffering and death, and in the Eucharist, calls for a love of equal dedication and total self-abandonment.

It is not required that our love for God be affectionately supreme (*affective summus*), i.e. that it surpasses in emotional warmth and tenderness every other love, e.g. the love of a mother for her child. Although such an ideal is worth striving for, it does not belong to the essence of divine love. Love of God is primarily of spiritual and not of emotional nature. Essential in the love for God is the supreme esteem for God and his will. Hence divine love must be sovereign in appreciation (*appretiative summus*), i.e. God must be appreciated above all other goods, and no other love may be placed above the love for him. Love of God is "a matter of will, not of feeling. To pray that the name of our Father in Heaven be hallowed, that His kingdom shall come, that His will may be done; to rejoice with Him in His infinite perfections; to fear...the forgetfulness that dishonors Him, the denial that blasphemes Him, the sin that strikes at Him; to have heartfelt sorrow at everything that violates what is due to Him and that bruises the Sacred Heart, and to atone for them by penance — these are all acts of will, and each is an act of love."[1]

If a man is requested to deny God or to act against the divine will, e.g. to kill an innocent man, he must rather sacrifice his own life than contradict the supreme claims of God upon him. The martyrdom, by which a man lays down his life for Christ and his brothers, as Christ did for us (1 Jn 3:16), is the highest proof of love. "Though few are presented with such an opportunity, nevertheless all must be prepared to confess Christ

---

[1] Louis Colin: Love the Lord Thy God. — Covent Garden/Glasgow: Sands and Co., 1956, 50.

before men, and to follow Him along the way of the cross through the persecutions which the Church will never fail to suffer" (LG 42).

b)   Love must be *interior and effective*. The Love of God may not stop short at a merely joyful appreciation of God's goodness and beauty or at an uncommitted approval of God's will, which prizes it as a value but does not mean to stand up for its realization. "Little children, let us not love in word or speech but in deed and in truth" (1 Jn 3:18). To love God with all one's heart and strength signifies to love his will in an efficacious way and to strive with all one's forces and means for its realization. This includes first of all the observance of God's commandments and the avoidance of sin. "He who has my commandments and keeps them, he it is who loves me" (Jn 14:21). "If any one says, 'I love God,' and hates his brother, he is a liar" (1 Jn 4:20). It further includes the positive, vigorous dedication to the cause of God's kingdom and glory. "To the carrying out of our hundred little daily duties, even the commonest ones, we should bring the magnanimity of a noble heart, a strong and ceaseless concern for God's greater glory and Christ's good pleasure."[1]

Sentiments and words of love without corresponding deeds are a spurious love, not worthy of the name. But conversely, external deeds and works of charity without the inner spirit of love are not authentic love either. External good works inspired by the desire of personal honour and glory are not expressions of the love of God or neighbour, but of improper self-love. Therefore Christ warns his disciples not to give alms for their own praise and glory, but for the sake of the Father in heaven (Mt 6:2-4). Even "if I give away all I have, and if I deliver my body to be burned, but have not love, I gain nothing" (1 Cor 13:3). The external good deed must flow from the inner love of God as its root and source. Only then is it acceptable before God, and even before men, and only then a man can be said to love God.

B.   Realization of divine love in prayer and deed

Love of God expresses itself in adoration, meditation, prayer and worship on the one hand, and in action and works of brotherly love on the other. At the same time these expressions

---

[1] L. Colin, 1. c. 57f.

of love also promote and deepen it. If the divine "love, as good seed, is to grow and bring forth fruit in the soul, each one of the faithful must willingly hear the Word of God and with the help of His grace act to fulfill His will. Each must share frequently in the sacraments, the Eucharist especially, and in liturgical rites. Each must apply himself constantly to prayer, self-denial, active brotherly service and the exercise of all the virtues" (LG 42).

There are tendencies today which are inclined to belittle and depreciate the role of prayer and contemplation in the exercise of the divine virtue of love. Prayer is rated by them as unprofitable activity and unavailing expenditure of time. Active love of the brother is underscored as the primary, if not the only serious way of loving God in a meaningful manner. Yet this is a blatant distortion of man's true relations to God and neighbour and a disregard of his real needs. Does not Holy Scripture invite man at every turn to prayer and to the praise of God? Did not Jesus commend Mary, who sat at his feet and listened to his teaching, and caution Martha, who was distracted with much serving and who complained over Mary's "inactivity" to the Lord? "Martha, Martha, you are anxious and troubled about many things; one thing is needful. Mary has chosen the good portion, which shall not be taken away from her" (Lk 10:41f).

Already human love and friendship want to enjoy the presence of the beloved or friend in mutual exchange of thoughts and ideas, of affection and personal dedication. A constant plunging into activity, even if undertaken in order to promote a cause of common concern and interest, will soon leave the longing for a real friendship unfulfilled and arouse in the other the feeling of being neglected in that sphere of personal rapport which matters most. Also in regard to divine love priority belongs to the total abandonment of the heart to God, to a pure glorifying thanksgiving, to the devotion which directly and solely centres and rests in God.

Religious traditions of mankind agree with Christianity in the conviction that the contemplative life precedes the active life, because it enables men to pursue a knowledge and devotion that sets free (cf. SC 2). "Prayer, ecclesiastical and personal, comes before action. It is not primarily a source of psychological strength, an opportunity for 'refuelling' as it were. It is an act in perfect harmony with love, an act of worship and glorification in which the person loved attempts to make a complete and selfless answer, in order to show that he has understood the divine message. The Old and New Testaments, the life of Christ, the theology of St. Paul and St. John, all testify to this precedence, and it is as ridiculous, as it is pathetic, to see contemporary Christians ignoring the fact and thinking that they only encounter Christ in their neighbour, or worse still imagining that their only task is to work in the (technological) world. They soon cease to be able to draw any distinction between worldly responsibility and the Christian mission. No one who does not know God in contemplation can recognize him in action, not even when he sees God reflected in 'the oppressed and humiliated'. The eucharistic celebration itself is an act of 'recollection', of contemplation and communion in love, and it is the only place from which the Christian can be sent out into the world: ite missa (missio) est. Only then can the 'unceasing prayer' that St. Paul prescribes (1 Thess 5:17) be performed in action."[1]

Man cannot truly love God without knowing him, for nothing is loved unless it is known. This knowledge must be correctly understood. It is not primarily a conceptual, scientific knowledge; it is primarily an existential knowledge, the knowledge gained in the personal encounter with God on the basis of faith, the practical knowledge flowing from the experience of the communion and unity with the divine. Meditation, contemplation, prayer is the only way to the personal knowledge of God and consequently also the way to an aboriginal, authentic understanding of the divine will and of his plan with the world. Without prayerful meditation man is in immediate danger to alienate himself from God and his true will. He conjures up the risk of losing the veritable goals out of sight, in whose service he is supposed to place his action and which alone make it an expression of love.

Naturally the divine love must also realize itself in work and deed. Only under this condition love can be called "the fulfilling of the law" (Rom 13:10; cf. Mt 22:40; Col 3:14). In plain and unequivocal words St. John exhorts his Christians not to "love in word or speech but in deed and in truth" (1 Jn 3:18).

In principle, it may be noted though, also prayer and meditation can be called a deed. In fact the attitude of concentrated meditation is the highest activity there is, a deed of the soul.[2] But usually love in work and deed denotes that activity by which a man exercises a transforming influence on the world that sur-

---

[1] Hans Urs von Balthasar: Love Alone. — New York: Herder and Herder, 1969, 88f.

[2] Cf. Erich Fromm: The Art of Loving. — New York: Bantam Books, 1970 (33rd printing), 18.

rounds him; in particular it means deeds of brotherly love. It is God's will that man cooperates in the work of creation and brings it to perfection; that he subjects the earth and harnesses its potentialities; that he promotes solidarity, justice and the union of love among mankind. Hence man's love for God must necessarily also express itself in the acceptance and realization of these tasks of the active life, which God has appointed to him.

Vatican II cautions that "there be no false opposition between professional and social activities on the one part, and religious life on the other" (GS 43). Works of brotherly love and active service cannot substitute for prayer and worship. On the other hand the devotional life may not be taken as an excuse for shirking from one's earthly responsibilities. The great commandment of love comprises the whole law: the devotion to God in prayer and cult, and the service of the Lord in works of active love.[1]

C. Sins against the love of God

Every sin offends against divine love. Sin and love contradict and exclude each other. Mortal sin destroys divine love radically, while venial sin diminishes it. Sins may contradict divine love directly, if they expressly turn against the primary object of divine love, God himself, by withholding or denying the love, praise and worship due to him. Or they may contradict divine love indirectly, if they offend against the rights of created beings and persons. These sins offend against the love of God insofar as they violate God's will that these rights be respected and also our brother be loved. The latter sins are dealt with, together with the respective moral virtues, in the different sections of special moral theology. The sins against divine worship are dealt with in the special section on the virtue of religion. In this context mention shall be made only of the sins of indifference and hatred against God.

---

[1] References concerning the relation between love of God and love of neighbour: Gaston Salet: Love of God, Love of Neighbor; in: Foundations of Biblical Spirituality. — Staten Island, N.Y.: Alba House, 1965, 37-64. Karl Rahner: Reflections on the Unity of the Love of Neighbour and the Love of God; in: Theological Investigations VI. — London: Darton, Longman and Todd, 1969, 231-249. Idem: Unity-Love-Mystery; in: Theological Investigations VIII, 1971, 229-247.

1. *Indifference* offends against the love of God, since God as the highest good merits to be loved with all our heart, and all our soul, and all our strength. It is sinful to the extent that it results from culpable negligence in acquiring a sufficient knowledge of God and in striving after communion and friendship with him. Often indifference against God and religious values results from deficient education and guidance in religious matters, which will excuse a man from culpable fault. Likewise it must be noted that not all men have an equal sense for the religious world. Some are by nature more predisposed to mystic experiences, some are naturally more attracted by religion and the life of prayer than others. These differences in inborn gifts and dispositions will result in different intensities of religious life. But the general neglect in the practice of the love of God is a defect and failing, and if resulting from laziness, disorderly love for creatures or similar sources subjectively sinful.

2. *Hatred* is the sin most directly opposed to charity. Hatred rejects and endeavours to destroy what is or seems to be an evil in itself or in some of its attributes and effects. Inasmuch as God is infinite goodness, it would seem impossible to hate him. Certainly for anyone who would see God as he is, the very essence of love and goodness, hate would be impossible. But in this earthly sojourn man knows God only obscurely and in imperfect images. Often this knowledge is not only deficient but even distorted. And above all man knows God more through the effects of his divine activity, through his decrees and laws, than in himself. God's laws however are for men not always desirable under every aspect, and his decrees are not seldom dark and painfully unintelligible, e.g. when his will inflicts upon men sickness, destitution, humiliation, unjust condemnation, etc.

Men who reject and hate God because of a wrong knowledge and picture they have of him cannot be called enemies of God in the strict sense, at least as long as this is the only source of their enmity. Ultimately their rejection is not directed against God himself, but against false presentations of God. Yet it must also be noted that human language about God is always imperfect. Deficiencies in the image of God may well serve as a pretext for refusing genuine claims of God upon man, because these claims appear uncomfortable and demand sacrifices from a self-centred human nature.

Men may revolt against God because of sufferings, miseries and various oppressions he sends upon them. In view of their distress it becomes too hard for them to believe in the love of

God. Although such revolt is humanly understandable, it must nevertheless be deemed as a lack of faith and love of God, which is not without sin. Often this is only a temporary desolation and despair, which a man will overcome after his emotions and depressions have calmed down.

The most frequent source of hatred of God is a sinful life in opposition to God's command. For the sinner who is completely drowned in his sin and who clings to his wrong aims and desires, God is no longer anything but an enemy. Such opposition against the true will of God was the reason for the hatred of the world against Christ. From his childhood he was destined to be "a sign that is spoken against" (Lk 2:34) and a stumbling block for those who disobey the word (Rom 9:32f; 1 Pet 2:8). Christ was persecuted and rejected by the world because the word he preached and the love he demanded stood in contradiction to the desires of men. "For every one who does evil hates the light" (Jn 3:20). Christ is the light of the world, yet darkness hates the light. And since the disciples and the Church share in the mission of Christ, their fate is alike. "If the world hates you, know that it has hated me before it hated you. If you were of the world, the world would love its own; but because you are not of the world, but I chose you out of the world, therefore the world hates you" (Jn 15:18f). The more sharply the revelation of the holy contradicts the wishes and ambitions of sinful men, the more is their hatred inflamed. The lives of many prophets and saints bear witness to this enmity.

It is to be admitted that the antireligious hostility against the ministers of Christ and the Church has at times been provoked by their frailty, by their lack of true brotherly concern, of humility and tolerance. But it is unjust to charge that all opposition to religion, to Christ and the Church is due to past and present weaknesses of its members and especially of the priests and religious. "There is a marked tendency in some quarters today, which is tantamount to a mania, to hold the Church responsible for all hostility against God. These sapient critics might well ponder that Christ, the holiest of men, ... was made the target of the most dreadful hatred of the enemies of God. And the reason was that they were already hostile in their hearts against His heavenly Father."[1] A Church that fulfills her mission in the world will be a stumbling block for it and a target of enmity just as Christ was.

---

[1] Häring II, 1963, 104.

Chapter IV

NATURE OF DIVINE WORSHIP[1]

The ultimate purpose of man and creation is God's glory. For this end they have been made. That is the reason of their existence. To this end they all have to contribute. "I am the Lord, that is my name; my glory I give to no other" (Is 42:8). Creation proclaims the praise of God by its very existence. Man as the crown of creation is to give glory to God also consciously with his mind and will. "Give glory to my name" (Mal 2:2; Is 42:12; Jer 13:16), demands the Lord from his people and from all the inhabitants of the earth.

In the present world of natural science and technology religion is not seldom dismissed as unscientific and unproductive. God is regarded as a personification of human wishes and religion as a euphoric opium for man's distress. It is contended that over against such figures of fantasy and illusion, man must devote himself in active assistance to his fellowmen and must solve his problems by the creation of better economic conditions. A materially prosperous society, which is free from all inequalities and offers economic and social welfare to everybody, is the end which alone merits man's total dedication. In the prophetic perspective of the Book of Revelation this "worship of the world" is contrasted under the imagery of the two beasts with the "worship of God".

The question of worship is intimately connected with the question of the nature and destiny of man. "If man is to be seen merely in the dimension of the economic and political, merely

---

[1] References: Otto Karrer: Religions of Mankind. — New York: Sheed and Ward, 1945. Charles M. Magsam: The Inner Life of Worship. — St. Meinrad, Ind.: Grail Publications, 1958. G. Delling: Worship in the New Testament. — Philadelphia: Westminster Press, 1962. Raymond Abba: Principles of Christian Worship. — New York/London: Oxford University Press, 1966. Wiebe Vos (ed.): Worship and Secularization. — Bossum, Holland: Brand, 1970. Henry E. Horn: Worship in Crisis. — Philadelphia: Fortress Press, 1972. Ninian Smart: The Concept of Worship. — London: Macmillan, 1972. Raimundo Panikkar: Worship and Secular Man. — London: Darton, Longman and Todd (Orbis Books), 1973.

as *homo faber* or as *animal sociale et politicum,* worship must be condemned as a useless waste of time or indeed as harmful preoccupation. But if real transcendence is the fundamental existential of human life, worship must be regarded as an essential act, without which a whole realm of human life would remain atrophied."[1] And for all religions and in particular for Christian theology man does have a transcendent destination. He does not find the ultimate meaning in himself and in the achievement of temporal welfare, but in the realization of God's eternal designs to God's greater glory and in communion with him.

A.   Notion and object of divine worship

I.   Concept of divine worhip

According to its etymological origin the term worship means "to ascribe worth". To worship God is to ascribe to him supreme worth. This is a self-evident conclusion from the very idea of God as "that than which nothing greater can be conceived" (Anselm). To have a God of necessity means to worship him.[2] The man who believes in God will most naturally revere and adore him: "Worthy art thou, our Lord and God, to receive glory and honour and power" (Rev 4:11).

The virtue of divine worship is often also designated as virtue of religion. Yet in the common usage of the word, religion has a wider and more basic meaning than worship. Religion is the fundamental faith in God. The essence of religion is constituted by the theological virtues, which are the soul of worship and which in the first place make religious life possible. Divine worship on the other hand flows from religion as its manifestation and expression. It designates the religious acts and the cult rendered to God, whether public or private. "The decisive element is the reverent homage paid to God or to the divine by means of outward signs, and the hope of life and salvation which goes with such homage."[3] Divine worship as virtue can be defined as that virtue by which man pays God the honour due to him.

The motive of worship is the sanctity, pre-eminence and

---

[1] Michael Schmaus, art. "Worship" in: Sacramentum Mundi, vol. VI, 1970, 390.

[2] "Habere Deum est colere Deum" (Luther in Tischreden, Kroker's ed. 1903, nr. 438).

[3] M. Schmaus, 1. c. 390.

magnificence of God. The splendour of God's holiness and glory is reflected in creation, in his epiphanies, and for Christians in a special way in Jesus Christ. Christ's life and death most strikingly reveal God's all-surpassing love and Christ's resurrection God's triumphant, radiant glory. Yet Christ not only manifests the holy majesty of God. He also shows man the true worship of the Father and renders this worship himself on behalf of mankind in the most perfect way. Christians are therefore called to worship God in unity with Christ as their head and mediator before God. Beyond this, Christ himself as the Son of God is the object of adoration. The New Testament gives honour and glory to Christ in a manner which the Old Testament reserves for the all-holy God (Mk 13:26; Jn 1:14; 17:1-5.24; 1 Cor 2:8; Tit 2:13; Heb 13:21; 1 Pet 4:11). Equal honour is given to the Lamb and to him who sits upon the throne. "Worthy is the Lamb who was slain, to receive power and wealth and wisdom and might and honour and glory and blessing.... To him who sits upon the throne and to the Lamb be blessing and honour and glory and might for ever and ever" (Rev 5:12f).

In religion and divine worship man affirms a twofold actuality: First, he accepts his own insignificance, nothingness and sinfulness as against the absolute fulness in being and the absolute worthiness of the holy. This results in reverence, which presses to distance (*mysterium tremendum*). Second, he acknowledges his dependence on the creator and his essential orientation towards God's beatifying fullness, which alone can give fulfillment to human indigence. The power of attraction which emanates from God calls forth longing and loving devotion, which press to union (*mysterium fascinosum*). This polarity of reverent distance and loving devotion permeates all religiosity as its elementary force.

What religiosity first experiences in the interiority of the heart, that it desires to express externally. The manifestation of the inner attitudes of reverence and pure devotion to God is the meaning and function of divine worship.

II. The different forms of worship

Every morally good act stands in the service of God's honour and glory and contains an acknowledgement of his absolute supremacy. "Whatever you do, do all to the glory of God" (1 Cor 10:31). Therefore every morally good act gives honour due to God and can be regarded as an act of divine worship. Yet acts of divine worship in the strict sense are those acts only which have God's adoration and praise as their explicit and immediate object. God is venerated not only implicitly and mediately in the faithful fulfillment of secular duties, but explicitly in acts which expressly intend his praise, veneration and recognition, and which aim at a personal encounter and at communion with him. This treatise is only concerned with the latter acts of explicit worship.

1. The forms of divine worship can be distinguished according to the different means and ways which man uses in order to give expression to his reverence for God and devotion to him. Prayer and sacrifice obtain the first place as the most fundamental expressions of religion. God is venerated through words directed to him or through gifts given away from man's possessions and somehow handed over to God. Added to this is in many religions the reading of the sacred books as the word that comes from God. In Christianity it is the proclamation of the good news of Jesus Christ and of the entire Holy Scriptures of the Old and New Testament (cf. SC 24). Especially in the liturgical worship man's prayer and divine praise are conceived as his answer to the word of God.

Among the acts of worship Christian religion accords a pre-eminent place to the sacred rites of the sacraments. They give expression to man's faith and love, reverence and adoration in external, liturgical actions enacted by the community of the believers under the leadership of an official minister. At the same time they are also means of grace for man, which lead him to closer communion with God. To the sacraments are still added the sacramentals as similar rites, but which are of lesser importance and of lesser efficacy in the bestowal of grace.

Other forms of worship are the sanctification of special days and seasons, the segregation of sacred places and objects, the veneration of God's name, of divine symbols and images. Reverence for God also expresses itself in the veneration of saints and in respect for consecrated persons who dedicate themselves in a special manner to the sacred service or ministry, such as priests and religious.

Vows are acts of worship in the line of a sacrifice. Handbooks usually list them among the extraordinary acts of worship together with oaths and adjuration. But since the sacraments and sacramentals are partially ordinary, partially extraordinary acts of worship, this division does not seem to be of great avail. Furthermore objections can be raised whether the oath is rightly numbered among the acts of divine worship. For the oath is not expressly intended as an act of worship; its immediate purpose is rather the social value of truthfulness and fidelity. Only mediately is the oath an act of worship, insofar as through it man acknowledges his faith in God and his responsibility before him. But every morally good act ought to be ordered towards God and performed in agreement with his will. The difference is only in this that in the oath man places himself more consciously before God and his divine command, which difference however is merely a gradual one. The oath shall therefore not be considered as an act of explicit worship, but be dealt with in the chapter on truth, honour and fidelity. Adjuration is a forcible prayer of petition. In the form of the exorcism it belongs to the sacramentals.

2. A further division distinguishes between liturgical and non-liturgical acts of worship. By liturgical worship is meant worship carried out according to the books, prescriptions or customs of a Church or Community, celebrated by a minister or delegate of such Church or Community, in his capacity as minister of that Community.[1] The liturgical worship is the official expression of the faith and religious convictions of a Church or Community.

The Catholic Church looks upon her liturgy as the divine service in which "full public worship is performed by the Mystical Body of Jesus Christ, that is, by the Head and His members. From this it follows that every liturgical celebration, because it is an action of Christ the priest and of His Body the Church, is a sacred action surpassing all others" (SC 7). The liturgical celebration enjoys pre-eminence over all the other acts of worship. Through the liturgy those within the Church are built up day by day into the Lord's holy temple, into a spiritual dwelling for God (SC 2). At the same time the faithful are fortified in their capacity to preach Christ and inspired to become of one heart in love. By means of the liturgy "the sanctification of men in Christ and the glorification of God, to which all other activities of the Church are directed as toward their goal, are most powerfully achieved" (SC 10).

Nevertheless the spiritual life is not confined to participation in the liturgy. Non-liturgical and extraliturgical worship too is

---

[1] Cf. the Guidelines of the Secretariat of Promoting Christian Unity, issued May 14, 1967, AAS 59 (1967), 584.

worthy to be cultivated and is indispensable. The Christian must also enter into his chamber to pray to the Father in secret (cf. Mt 6:6). And popular devotions are warmly recommended as an additional, though secondary source for Christian piety (SC 12f).

III.   Worship of God and veneration of saints

The supreme worship of adoration (cultus latriae) belongs to God alone. He alone is the All-Holy and Most High who merits total devotion and unconditional surrender. Because Jesus Christ is the Son of God and of one nature with the Father, equal worship is due to him as to the Father. Even the sacred humanity of Christ is to be honoured with latreutic cult, for through the hypostatic union it is filled with the majesty of God, as made evident above all in the glorious resurrection.

Yet since the motive of divine worship is the glory and holiness of God, and since this glory and holiness manifest themselves in a particular way in the saints, it follows that God must also be honoured in his elect. This is the basis for the veneration of the angels and saints (cultus duliae).

From the earliest times the Church venerated the apostles and Christian martyrs together with the Blessed Virgin Mary and the angels. To these were soon added those who had imitated Christ's virginity and poverty more perfectly, and finally others whom the outstanding practice of the Christian virtues and the divine charisms recommended to the pious devotion and imitation of the faithful. Yet already in antiquity there were also some individuals who rejected the veneration of the saints (e.g. Vigilantius); in the eighth century their cult was attacked by the Iconoclasts and again in the sixteenth century by the Reformers. On the other hand the veneration of saints is held in highest esteem in the Eastern Churches.

The Catholic Church has not commanded veneration of the saints, but strongly recommended it, for example at the Council of Trent[1] and again at the Second Vatican Council (LG 50f). Saints are creatures who are particularly close to God and therefore ought to be honoured. But inasmuch as they are creatures, the honour due to them is not adoration. Even though the Blessed Virgin Mary as the Mother of God and as the most perfect example of human holiness and love of God receives special veneration among all the other saints (cultus

---

[1] DS 1821; 1867; 2236.

hyperduliae; cf. LG 52ff), she is never adored nor should be adored. If occasionally Christians adopt the same outward signs of worship for God and for the saints, the inward attitude is still different. God is honoured in himself; the saints are not honoured in themselves, but because of the example they give us of devotion to God, because of their union with him in glory, and because of the intercession which they offer on our behalf. The devotion to them is ultimately directed to God.

It is supremely fittting "that we love those friends and fellow heirs of Jesus Christ, who are also our brothers and extraordinary benefactors, that we render due thanks to God for them and 'suppliantly invoke them and have recourse to their prayers, their power and help in obtaining benefits from God through His Son, Jesus Christ, our Lord, who is our sole Redeemer and Saviour.' For by its very nature every genuine testimony of love which we show to those in heaven tends toward and terminates in Christ, who is the 'crown of all saints.' Through Him it tends toward and terminates in God, who is wonderful in His saints and is magnified in them" (LG 50). For the same reason a want of reverence towards the saints is indirectly offensive to God (e.g. using their names in cursing or in blasphemous ways).

At times abuses and excesses may happen in the veneration of the Blessed Virgin and of the saints. Vatican II is aware of such danger and therefore requests all concerned to work hard to prevent or remedy possible defects. But such abuses cannot be an argument against the veneration of saints in principle. The faithful must only learn to place the accents correctly. They must understand "that the authentic cult of the saints consists not so much in the multiplying of external acts, but rather in the intensity of our active love. By such love, for our own greater good and that of the Church, we seek from the saints 'example in their way of life, fellowship in their communion, and aid by their intercession' " (LG 51).

B. Foundation of divine worship

The duty and necessity to express worship of God is at times denied altogether. Others approve of it in principle, but they disavow the need and obligation to external and particularly corporate worship. Therefore a first paragraph shall set forth the reasons for man's obligation to divine worship in general and a second paragraph the reasons for the need of external and corporate worship.

I. Duty to worship in general

Holy Scriptures assign to the duties of worship the first place in the decalogue. "I am the Lord your God... You shall have no other gods before me" (Ex 20:2f). It is revealing that the commandments of the first table do not concern themselves with the duty of worship generally speaking — this duty and need was for the ancient nations undisputed and self-evident — but only with the true worship of the only, true God. Adoration and worship is due to Yahweh alone. "To me every knee shall bow, every tongue shall swear," demands the Lord (Is 45:23; cf. 42:8; 48:11). Contemplating the greatness of God, the wonders of his creation and man's dependence on him, the psalmist calls upon the congregation: "O come, let us worship and bow down, let us kneel before the Lord, our Maker!" (Ps 95:6).

Christ reiterates this command of the decalogue: "You shall worship the Lord your God and him only shall you serve" (Mt 4:10). The obligation to adore God and to worship him is simply taken for granted, as is shown by Christ's frequent withdrawal to conversation with the Father in heaven, by his instructions on good prayer (Mt 6:7-13), by his participation and that of his disciples in the liturgical services of the synagogue, in the pilgrimages to the temple and in the celebration of sacred days. There was no need to emphasize this duty particularly, since the Jews did not show any negligence in this regard, but on the contrary were very conscientious.

For the early Church regular reunion in services of prayer and worship was a matter of course. "They devoted themselves to the apostles' teaching and fellowship, to the breaking of bread and the prayers" (Acts 2:42; cf. 20:7). St. Paul likewise takes the worship of the Christian communities for granted. He merely exhorts his Christians to let themselves be guided by the spirit and word of Christ as they "sing psalms and hymns and spiritual songs with thankfulness" (Col 3:16) and to celebrate the Lord's supper in a worthy way (1 Cor 11:17-34).

The *history of religion* shows that worship and cult are as old as mankind. Cultic religiosity is nowhere lacking entirely, neither among the primitive tribes nor among the higher cultures, even though the forms of worship can differ widely. Man is too much a creature whose only reason of existence is found in God; he is too essentially related to him, that he could ignore the fact that he totally depends on God's will and primarily exists for his glory.

Wherever people believe in a divinity, there *reason* tells them that they ought to incline in reverence before the infinite majesty of God. For since God is the supreme being, in whom all holiness and goodness and power dwells, and since on the other hand man is his creature, who possesses nothing from himself but everything from God, he can only fall down before God and give him all honour and glory and dominion. The refusal to give God supreme honour is the refusal to acknowledge one's true status and constitution. This means an existence in error, distortion and unreal fiction. It must leave a man spiritually diseased and unhappy, at least in the long run.

Psychology confirms man's need for a right relation to God in true submission and adoration. C. G. Jung finds a decisive source of psychological illness and neurosis of people, especially in the second half of their lives, in the lack of religious orientation. He regards religious belief as an essential precondition for psychological health. The human soul feels the urge towards an absolute. If a man gives absolute value to what is relative, he will remain unsatisfied and may eventually fall sick. "Only if man assumes an attitude towards the genuinely absolute which acknowledges it practically and concretely (in the chief commandment), will the deep anxiety and the last psychological compulsion be overcome. Only if the subjective order of experience is completely in keeping with the objective order of being (principle of reality), is the inner equilibrium of the soul assured."[1]

II. Necessity of external and corporate worship

The religion of the Old Testament was a religion of a strictly ordered, external cult, so much so that the prophets had repeatedly to reproach its externalization and to recall the fundamental need for inner devotion and love (Is 1:11-17; 29:13f; Jer 7:21-26; Amos 5:21-24). Christ wants a worship of the Father "in spirit and truth" (Jn 4:23f). The external offering without the devotion of the heart is worthless; but this does not mean that the external offering as such is objectionable. "If you are offering your gift at the altar, and there remember that

---

[1] Josef Rudin: Psychotherapie und Religion. — Olten: Walter Vlg., 1960, 127.

your brother has something against you, leave your gift there before the altar and go; first be reconciled to your brother, and then come and offer your gift" (Mt 5:23f). Christ approves of the external cult. He himself has participated in it (cf. Lk 4:16). Through the institution of the eucharistic sacrifice, the sacraments and the priesthood he laid the foundation for the liturgical, common worship of his Church. When celebrating the last supper with his disciples, in which he gave his body and blood to them for the first time under the species of bread and wine, he charged them: "Do this in remembrance of me" (Lk 22:19). The early Christians were only fulfilling the will of their master when they regularly came together for the breaking of the bread and the common praise of the Lord (Acts 2:42; 20:7).

1. *External cult* is a demand resulting from the very nature of man. Man as composed of body and soul must serve and glorify God with both, body and soul. For he must render service to God with his whole being. Therefore the interior sentiments of adoration must also be expressed exteriorly.

In fact man feels naturally and spontaneously urged to manifest his inner devotion for God in external acts of cult. Christ's saying "Out of the abundance of the heart the mouth speaks" (Mt 12:34) states a common experience. What moves a man in his soul, that he wants to embody in external words, signs and actions. Through visible things and external acts the heart is directed towards God, the attitudes of the mind are kept awake, intensified and deepened. While conversely the longer lasting neglect of the external signs and expressions brings about an increasing relaxation and chill of the inner attitudes.

"We moderns with our penchant for the technical and mechanical even in thought and sentiment are only too prone to underestimate the importance of sign and symbol in life. Our appreciation of the ritual and ceremonial symbol as an expression and demand of the psychic and spiritual is often too slight and has need for development through a conscious and earnest effort."[1] Just as the natural knowledge of God is gained via the visible creation, so the love of God and devotion to him are always kindled anew by the external worship of him.

2. External cult is furthermore an indispensable precondition for *corporate worship*, since external signs are the only way to communicate with a group and to unite it in one common

---
[1] Häring II, 1963, 130.

action. And as to the value and need of corporate worship, it is again confirmed by strong reasons.

Corporate worship "is demanded by the very essence of religion, insofar as religion is also social, and a necessary bond of the community in giving honour to God. Men must glorify God according to their whole nature, corporeal and spiritual. As individuals and as social beings they must pay honour to the source of their being, for not only the individual but also the community has been created by God for His own honour and glory. Both... are obliged to acknowledge Him and worship Him. It follows that not only external cult but also social cult, the cult offered by the community, is incumbent upon man."[1]

The common cult of the community is also a necessary complementation and corrective orientation for the private worship of the individual. In all realms of life the individual is greatly enriched by the community, and without the community his existence remains poor and inferior. This holds true for the life of worship too. The individual religiosity is fecundated by the worship of the community, kept in balance and protected against error. Besides, through this influence on the individual person the common cult promotes honest, virtuous living and peace and unity in the community.

When Christ laid the foundations for liturgical worship, especially in the sacraments of baptism, priesthood and the Eucharist, but also in the other sacraments, he was accounting for these demands and needs of human nature. In the liturgical service Christ associates himself with the Church "in the truly great work of giving perfect praise to God and making men holy." In the common service of the community before God "full public worship is performed by the Mystical Body of Jesus Christ, that is, by the Head and His members" (SC 7). Because of this importance of the liturgical cult, participation in it is the right and duty of all the believers (SC 14).

3. By way of a *practical conclusion,* Christians and in particular priests are required to attentive concern for the proper performance of the liturgical ceremonies in accordance with the rulings established by the community. For if corporate worship is a divine mandate, then the observance of the cultic laws, which found and guarantee the order of the common worship, is likewise a divine command. "Since the divine service is the worship of the entire Christian community, the Church, the

---

[1] Ib. 131.

individual is obliged to conform to the group as organized by the Church and submit to the forms and directives governing the whole body. Rather than subject the liturgy to his personal criticism, he should seek to profit by submissive use of what is at the service of all. As one individual member he does not have the right to make his personal likes or dislikes the standard for the community ceremonial, much less to revise or modify it according to his own whims. This is particularly true of the ceremonial intimately connected with the essentials of the sacrifice and the sacraments."[1] Although there should be sufficient room for all necessary adaptations of the liturgy to particular conditions and nations, even these adaptations cannot dispense with a certain order. The ministers of the Church must always let themselves be guided by a sense of responsibility for the greater community to which they belong and for the people to whom they serve as members of this community. It is quite obvious that for the sake of the well-conducted celebration of the liturgical services and for the unity of cult and faith there must always be a measure of conformity determined by common norms.

A second conclusion concerns the obligatory character of the participation in common worship. The chief end of worship is the glorification of God. In divine worship man renders unto the Lord the honour and glory due to his name. The worshipper's personal edification and inspiration is rather a second end. Hence the ultimate criterion for participation in the common cult cannot be a person's feeling and pleasure. A person is not dispensed from the sacred service for the simple reason that "he doesn't feel like it", and that he does not expect much spiritual elation from it. "Worship is a debt to be discharged independently of our feelings; it is giving unto the Lord the glory *due* unto His name; hence 'it is obligatory on Christians.' The primary purpose of worship is the glory of God, not the edification of man."[2] Worship is not merely a means to an end. There is no greater human activity than that of giving unto the Lord the glory due to his name. Hence any merely subjective evaluation of worship is misleading. God must come first, if man's edification is to follow. But man's edification does follow when worship is performed worthily and directed to its proper end.

---

[1] Ib. 133f.

[2] Raymond Abba: Principles of Christian Worship. With Special Reference to the Free Churches. — New York/London: Oxford University Press, 1966, 13.

C. Sins contrary to the nature of worship: false cult

The sins of false cult are most directly opposed to the nature of worship, insofar as they falsify the worship due to God at the root. Either the external acts of worship do not really render due honour to God, but instead attempt to place God in the service of man and are destitute of the spirit of devotion (false cult of the true God), or worship has as its object false gods (idolatry), or a resemblance of religious faith and trust is put on the devil and other dark and magic forces (superstition and magic).

I. False worship of the true God

True worship is centred in God's honour and glory. It is an expression of man's devotion and total submission to God. False worship on the contrary attempts to get hold of God by means of religious practices for man's utility; or it makes use of means which are unworthy of God, because they are not truly expression of man's inner devotion and oblation to God, but just an external surrogate for it; or the practices are even only an outlet for human passions and ambitions.

1. Quasi-magic practices of piety. Of this nature are certain rites and prayers to which special effects are attributed, if performed in rigid adherence to prescribed rituals and if repeated the required number of times. Such prayers and rites may for example be used against sicknesses of men and animals, or to bring about success in business, or to obtain a person's love, etc. The effects are no longer considered a gift of God's free, kind generosity, but they are regarded as the result of a secret force inherent in the rites and prayers. This force assures the desired success.

In the line of such practices are certain types of faith-healing. "Certain formulas, which are often ridiculous, must be repeated a specific number of times in order to prove infallibly effective against various maladies (to stop the flow of blood, to heal wounds, to destroy the venom of serpent bites, etc.). Guarding the secrecy of the formula from the uninitiated is usually considered a condition for its effectiveness."[1] To be distinguished from these

---

[1] Häring II, 1963, 218.

quasi-magic practices is the charism of healing through invocation of God's or Christ's name, which is already reported by St. Paul (1 Cor 12:28-30) and which flows from genuine trust in God.[1]

At times beneficiary effects for men are also expected from purely mechanical use of sacred objects, such as holy images or relics, which are touched by the faithful, imposed upon them, placed about the neck, sewn into the clothing. Sometimes threads of relics or other tiny religious objects are swallowed. A particular power is attributed to the image or relic as such without the necessary relation to God and the saints, to whom these objects point and for whom worship, faith and veneration ought ultimately to be intended. The aberration consists in the reliance on the effectiveness of the material object itself rather than on the interior devotion to God.

There is no doubt that such quasi-magic practices and methods are prejudicial to true worship and therefore sinful. They are illogical and confused and a source of much scandal. However in many instances the faithful are not aware of this disorder and hence more or less excused becaused of their ignorance. Besides, some genuine devotion is not seldom present in these practices after all. The wise director will therefore be careful not to eradicate the traces of genuine piety along with the abuse. Rather he will aim to instruct and enlighten those who cling to false forms and deepen the true piety present in their souls.

Priests on their part may at times fail in the opposite direction by too spiritualistic an approach to religion under neglect of man's justified longing and need for symbols and external rites. Thus they create a vacuum, which is all the more open for unrefined forms of piety.

2.   Vain worship by unworthy means.   Unworthy of God are those means and acts, employed in the service of the cult, which are not a genuine expression of man's devotion to God.

This is above all the case if external sacrifices and liturgical actions are employed as substitutes for man's personal obedience and devotion to God. The worshipper imagines God as a heavenly sovereign who claims his due from man in the form of sacrifices and other acts of worship. They are looked upon

---

[1] For a good information on the grace of healing through prayer cf. Francis Macnutt: Healing. — Notre Dame, Ind.: Ave Maria Press, 1974.

as a kind of taxes to be paid to God. For the rest, once the "taxes" are paid, man feels free to do what he wants.

This is the kind of ritualism so much criticized by the OT prophets. Speaking through his prophets, the Lord reproaches the chosen people: "I hate, I despise your feasts, and I take no delight in your solemn assemblies. Even though you offer me your burnt offerings and cereal offerings, I will not accept them, and the peace offerings of your fatted beasts I will not look upon. Take away from me the noise of your songs; to the melody of your harps I will not listen. But let justice roll down like waters, and righteousness like an ever-flowing stream" (Amos 5:21-24; cf. Is 1:11-17; Jer 7:21-26). Before anything else God wants the heart of man, his love and obedience. Without this soul the external offerings and rites are vain.

For similar reasons sacrifices of human beings are unworthy of God. Sacrifices must express a man's personal devotion; therefore the sacrifice must be something of his own. Yet the life of a human being belongs to no man, so that no man could offer a human person as expression of his devotion (cf. Deut 18:10; Jer 32:34f; Ezek 20:30f; 23:37-39).

Unworthy acts of cult are furthermore actions and rituals which constitute more an outlet for human passions and cater more to the satisfaction of human desires for pleasure, entertainment, prestige and the like, than that they give honour to God and are an expression of man's veneration for him. Examples of such forms of vain worship are sacred prostitution, which in ancient times was rather frequent, or certain processions of a more carnevalistic than religious nature, which were in use in some places until recently. But also arbitrary, capricious changes of liturgical ceremonies and functions according to one's whims fall in this category.

II. Worship of false Gods (idolatry)

The most extreme form of false cult is the worship and adoration of fictitious deities, mere creatures, demons and the devil. Against such preposterous abomination God commands in the first commandment of the decalogue the categorical rejection of any deity besides him. "You shall have no other gods before me" (Ex 20:3).

Worship of a whole heaven of deities of good and evil nature is a rather frequent religious phenomenon. The religions of the ancient Orient, of Greece and the Roman empire, with whom Scriptures of the Old and New Testament were confronted, were all polytheistic. The root for the worship of the many gods and goddesses was generally not willful apostasy from the true God but simple ignorance. This idolatry does therefore usually not involve personal guilt. Yet objectively polytheism is an error and aberration; it is to be rejected and must be overcome. Time and again Scriptures stand up against the threat of idolatry and fight against it vehemently (Gen 35:2-4; Josh 24:14-23; Judg 2:11-14; Jer 32:29-36; 1 Cor 10:14; 1 Jn 5:21; Rev 21:8; etc.).

Idolatry may be based on a dualistic concept of the world. Besides the good God there is also an evil spirit, the adversary of God. In order to appease the evil spirit and to win his favour, he too is paid tribute and offered sacrifices. Such kind of reasoning generally underlay the idolatrous inclinations of Israel. Although they still adhered to Yahweh, they cultivated at the same time the local deities, which might after all exist and possess power to harm them. But Holy Scripture denies the correctness of this logic. Although it admits of the existence of evil forces and in particular of the devil, they are completely under the domination of God. Even though some power has been given to them, the way to cope with these forces is absolutely not the offering of worship, but virtuous living.

Also earthly creatures have been made the object of idolatrous cult. Especially emperors have frequently been deified, yet also other outstanding personalities. Even creatures like animals, trees, stones, etc. have received sacred cult. It is often not easy to decide whether these creatures were considered real deities or only dwellings of gods or consecrated symbols and objects. However that may be, they constitute part of an idolatrous cult which is not worthy of man and ought to be abandoned.

In a wider, but truly significant sense Holy Scripture calls idolatry the elevation of created, temporal values to final goods. The Bible designates those as idolaters who enthrone money, pleasure and similar earthly things as their highest goods (Mt 6:24; Eph 5:5; Phil 3:19; Col 3:5). This kind of idolatry is a most real danger in our present civilization with its cult of wealth, material progress, state power, etc. When man deserts God and becomes totally immersed in the temporal, material and carnal, he ends up by investing with a divine halo the created values to whom he dedicates his life, thus betraying once more his essentially religious nature.

III. Superstition[1]

Superstition in the wide sense is the acceptance of beliefs and practices objectively groundless and therefore futile and absurd. This broad concept of superstition also includes the quasi-magic abuses of genuine religious beliefs and practices, which have been mentioned earlier as forms of false worship of the true God. In the narrower sense superstition consists in futile beliefs and practices occasioned by the credence in imaginary powers. Whilst the error of superstitious religious practices lies in the reliance on inappropriate, futile means, by which a man wants to obtain favours from truly existing, spiritual powers, namely from God and the saints, the error of superstition in the narrower sense primarily lies in the assumption of powers which have no existence at all.

Superstition must be distinguished from rites and customs which are not strictly rational, but which nevertheless possess meaning as symbols or conventional signs. The use of religious and liturgical symbols, which give visible expression to spiritual realities, has genuine meaning. They help man to approach the divine. Yet there is no compulsive ratiocination behind their choice. The use of holy water for the blessing of persons and objects expresses by a visible sign man's petition for God's help and protection; or it symbolizes their consecration to the service of God. The sign is truly meaningful, although there is no reason which would strictly require this sign. Other signs could do as well. The custom of shaking hands in order to greet a person, and of using the right (lucky) hand in doing so, is today an expression of mutual respect, politeness and friendship. As such it possesses true meaning, although it was in origin probably a magical gesture and does not necessarily possess the present significance.

---

[1] References: Fr. Reginald-Omez: Psychical Phenomena (Faith and Fact Books, 58). — London: Burns and Oates, 1963. Parapsychology Today; ed. by J. B. Rhine and R. Brier. — New York: Citadel, 1968. Parapsychologie. Entwicklung, Ergebnisse, Probleme; ed. by Hans Bender. — Darmstadt: Wissenschaftliche Buchgesellschaft, 1971. Gustav Jahoda: The Psychology of Superstition. — London: The Penguin Press, 1971. H. Boelaars: Riflessioni sulla Magia; in: Studia Moralia, vol. 10. — Roma: Academia Alfonsiana, 1972, 73-126.

Superstition must likewise be distinguished from the use of man's parapsychological abilities. Even though their nature and conditions are not yet fully known and explicable to the scientific reason, their existence is experimentally proven. The divining rod and the magic pendulum can doubtlessly be used by some persons to discover water, minerals, and at times even lost objects. Tableturning can reveal hidden facts, although experts usually assure that it can only reveal with certainty those facts which are known, at least unconsciously, to one of the participants. Faith healing is another phenomenon of parapsychological nature which is successfully applied, even though it finds its limits in organic sicknesses of a more severe nature. Of course the use of these extraordinary powers may at times be intermingled with superstitious practices or also be accompanied by imposition and fraud. To the extent to which this is the case, one could naturally not approve of these procedures and would have to object against them.

Among the sources of superstition ignorance certainly plays an important role. People who lack information about the scientific facts, who do not know the explanations for the phenomena of nature, who have not been taught the proper concept of God, fall more easily prey to superstition. Ignorant man comes to believe in mysterious forces because of his need to find an explanation for the unusual and fearful things he cannot understand. Besides, superstitious beliefs and practices are often handed down from the ancestors. They are taken for granted, and it is hard for the individual to escape them.

The deepest source of superstition is however the lack of true faith in God and of true religion. The lack of true faith explains why even among the educated many superstitions are still rampant. Inspite of all scientific progress and knowledge, man's existence remains insecure and threatened by many unpredictable sways. In his insecurity and anxiety man searches for safety and protection. If he is not able to take refuge in divine providence and to find trust in God, he will be prone to superstitious beliefs which offer an apparent security. Superstition "is one of man's despairing attempts to explain his baffling existence and escape its insecurity and anxiety. It can reveal an obscure knowledge of the numinous depths of existence and his ordination to transcendence. But primarily superstition distorts man's view of the absolute sovereignty of God, since it is inspired by the idea that by his own expert ritual words and acts he can propitiate the gods or forces on which he feels his enigmatic existence to depend."[1]

Superstition resulting from ignorance certainly excuses a man from personal fault, unless he has to blame himself for his lack of knowledge. But default of that basic faith which consists in man's trusting self-surrender to God must be reckoned as sin and guilt. Scriptures severely condemn the grave forms of superstition, such as divination, augury, necromancy, use of charms, magic, sorcery (Deut 18:9-14; Is 2:6; 8:19; Jer 27:9f; Acts 19:19) and even decree death penalty for sorcerers, mediums and wizards (Ex 22:18; Lev 20:27). Inasmuch as superstition results from lack of faith, it is indeed a serious sin of irreligion. Because instead of placing his faith and trust in God, man places it in imaginary powers and tries to find protection and help where there is none. Besides, superstition is often a sin of personal and social irresponsibility, at least objectively, since man bases his decisions on illusions instead of sound reason. Thus necessary decisions are not taken, resolute action is paralyzed, and the true demands of life are not faced.

One must however admit that there are many forces at work in this world which are unusual but still real, strange but still within the natural. They are of the nature of the mentioned parapsychological phenomena. Many of these phenomena were formerly listed among the superstitious and magic practices, but unjustly so. They are realities with which men have to reckon, and their use cannot simply and generally be qualified as sinful. The observation of such unusual parapsychological powers will often induce people to give some credit also to superstitious practices in the proper sense for the reason that there exist many things which are beyond our understanding. This must be considered as an excusing factor in the adherence to superstitions, which factor can lastly be reduced to ignorance. A certain cautious attitude is certainly in place. On the one hand unusual phenomena should not too globally be dismissed as magic and superstitious; and on the other hand one should also not credulously fall for them, whether they are of profane or religious character.

1. *Vain observances*

Vain observances consist in the observation of certain signs

---

[1] B. Kloppenburg, art. "Superstition" (I) in: Sacramentum Mundi, vol. VI, 1970, 194.

and conditions and in the use of certain things for no valid reason.

Examples for the vain observance of certain signs and conditions are the fear of black cats that cross one's way as a sign of bad luck; the dread of number 13 as a bad omen; the observation of lucky and unlucky days. Thus Monday is held to be an unlucky day. The Hindus regard Wednesday as the unluckiest of days. Friday passed among the ancients as the luckiest day. But in Christian times it became, as the day on which Christ died, a day of ill-omen. Tuesday and Thursday are supposed to be lucky days.

The vain use of certain things for protection or for good luck is equally common. To this category belong the talismans, amulets and mascots. Talismans are objects that are supposed to bring luck and to ensure fortune and success to their owner. Amulets are meant to ward off harmful influences. The two are not always sharply distinguished. Often they are worn around the neck, as bracelets and rings, or sewn into a person's clothing. Or they are fixed to doors, trees, boats, cars, etc. Sometimes they are symbols and figures bought in the jeweller's store; at other times they are such worthless and ludicrous items as lost trouser-buttons, hairs from black cats, elephant bristles, coins with holes in them or lucky pennies. Mascots are used as protection against misfortune. They are descendants of masks of hideous animals, of the devil or fearful human masks, intended to frighten away demons. Modern superstition has made stuffed dolls out of them, teddy-bears, tigers and other animals and puppets. For some these mascots may be only toys and entertainments. But others would not go on a journey without them. Among the bringers of luck is counted a horseshoe which one has found (i.e. it may not be bought), and which then is fastened to houses, cars, masts of ships, etc.

Moral theology must disapprove of any truly superstitious observances. The judgment of traditional handbooks is generally even very severe. All vain observances contradict in a greater or lesser degree the dignity of the divine faith and are opposed to right reason. Still it would be too severe a judgment to qualify them all as gravely sinful. Very often they only constitute venial sins or even merely imperfections. They are not seldom "due to an unreasoning timidity which cannot simply ignore foolish practices if they are widespread. They are rather the tribute weakness pays to conformity."[1] However if the observance of

---

[1] Häring II, 1963, 235.

all kinds of bad and good omens and the use of all sorts of amulets becomes a whole system that controls a person's entire life, with the consequence that trust in God and reliance on prayer and the sacraments are only granted a secondary role, if any important role at all, then such existence in superstition can no longer be excused from grave sin.

2. *Divination*

Divination is the attempt to foretell the future by certain means or to obtain other occult knowledge. Such other occult knowledge can concern the fate of a missing person, the whereabouts of lost things, the perpetrators of unsolved crimes, forgotten memories, the condition of absent persons, and the like. One cannot deny that some parapsychologically gifted persons can at times achieve surprisingly much in revealing hidden facts. Although it is equally true that not seldom some kind of fraud is used, especially if it comes to the foretelling of the future. Precognition of the future is a much rarer gift and is accompanied by many more uncertainties than the divination of occult present or past events.

A general moral qualification of divination will best distinguish between prediction of the future and the revelation of other occult knowledge. Not every belief in vaticinations is superstitious and hence sinful. Some people indeed possess a special gift of prophecy and foreboding. But sure reliance on vaticinations or fortune telling cannot be regarded as accountable, because of the too limited dependability of such predictions and because of the frequently involved fraud. It is certainly irresponsible to neglect any of one's duties because of prophecies (e.g. one's studies, one's profession, one's family). Consultation of fortune tellers is often also objectionable because of the methods used, e.g. if diviners give their soothsaying a pseudo-religious framing, as in spiritism, or if they (allegedly) derive their knowledge from a pact with the devil.

Divination of occult knowledge is a more frequent phenomenon. It cannot simply be dismissed as irresponsible and sinful. We find parapsychologically gifted people even among priests and religious, and their confreres do not find objections in consulting them in difficult situations, e.g. in order to find lost objects or to gain information about missing persons. Divination of occult knowledge seems admissible if one is entitled to the knowledge, if there is no danger of harmful errors, and if the methods used are inoffensive.

The medium and its consultants must be entitled to the knowledge. The general obligation to respect personal secrets also binds them. Even though a person might have access to personal secrets of other people, e.g. to their letters, he cannot snoop around in them. Thus, to give an especially prominent example, mediums would not be allowed to search for confessional matters that fall under the seal and to reveal them. Precaution must also be taken that harmful errors be avoided, e.g. in attempts to solve crimes. Any indications that point to a possible delinquent need full confirmation by the ordinary means of evidence.[1] Finally also this form of divination must refrain from offensive methods, such as spiritism or conjuration of the devil.

This judgment holds for occasional consultation. Objections must however be raised against regular participation in seances with mediums, even though these seances do not give themselves any kind of pseudo-religious varnish. Frequent indulgence in occultism constitutes a danger to faith and also to a person's psychological balance. Experience shows that much involvement in extra-sensorial practices can lead to mediumistic psychoses, which in extreme cases may even end in suicide attempts.[2] — Some of the specific forms of divination require an additional comment.

a) *Astrology.* It assumes that there is a regular connection between the position of the stars at the moment of a person's birth and that person's character and destiny. This leads to the attempt to read a person's future from the stars. Astrology is a very ancient form of divination, spread among many people, and also today widely practised.

A popular form of astrology are the horoscopes, which can be found in many newspapers and magazines. Yet even most professional astrologers dismiss them as worthless. Observance of horoscopes is a truly superstitious practice, not worthy of a responsible man. If they nevertheless enjoy so much popularity, so is this a sign that secularized man after all cannot

---

[1] Instructive cases for the use of parapsychological abilities in the solution of criminal cases are produced by H. C. Tenhaeff: Über die Anwendung paranormaler Fähigkeiten. Leistungen von Sensitiven für polizeiliche und andere Zwecke; in: Parapsychologie, ed. by Hans Bender. — Darmstadt: Wissenschaftliche Buchgesellschaft, 1971, 285-305.

[2] Hans Bender: Mediumistische Psychosen. Ein Beitrag zur Pathologie spiritistischer Praktiken; in Parapsychologie, l. c. 574-604.

escape the awareness of his being dependent on powers which transcend this world. But since his faith in God is languid or lost, he turns to substitutes in order to satisfy his feeling of contingency. "Instructions and advice that seem to come from the depths of the universe, guidance from this mysterious 'other world' to help one through life, inspire a fear which apes the reverential."[1] This precisely is the mark of the sin of superstition.

Yet also the so-called scientific astrology was not able to provide proof for the validity of its methods and conclusions. To a large extent it cannot escape the blame of superstition either. Astrology with its gross classifications according to constellations is never able to give a truly individual horoscope for every person. The constellation of stars is for all people born at approximately the same time the same, which must lead to the same horoscope and consequently to the same destiny for all of them. Dozens of people have the same horoscope as Napoleon, Goethe or Ghandi. But who of them was similarly talented or had a similar destiny? That is not even true of twins. Furthermore the laws of interpretation are so manifold that they admit of an endless number of possible combinations, and the methods of individual astrologers vary so widely that the different practitioners interpret a single horoscope in as many different ways. Therefore professional astrology too must be judged inept and baseless as a scientific way to a person's future.

This rejection does not preclude that the stars may have some influence on man's health and psychic activity, just as the moon has. But this influence, like that of climatic and meteorological conditions, is rather indirect and never predetermines the decision of the will. Besides, the radiation of the stars will not only influence a person at the moment of his birth, when his umbilicus is severed, but it will influence all people throughout all their lives.

Yet even though astrology cannot be accepted as a genuine science, the possibility cannot be totally excluded that the contemplation of the stars may serve as a means to spark parapsychological insights of sensitive persons. This would explain why astrologers are after all at times able to make some startling predictions, as even St. Thomas has observed.[2]

b) *Fortune telling* from cards, tea leaves, crystal balls,

---

[1] Art. "Superstition, III. Astrology" by Johannes Fassbender; in: Sacramentum Mundi VI, 1970, 198.

[2] St. Thomas Aquinas, II-II, q. 95, a. 5, ad 2.

etc. These means frequently constitute the equipment of the more popular fortune tellers. There is no doubt that very often such soothsaying is more an exploitation of the naive credulity of the customers, than an actual belief in occult powers and the use of paranormal abilities. Soothsayers have at times an organized system of espionage to supply them with information. And as professionals they may be masters of the art of association. On the other hand one cannot exclude that these aids may serve as a means of concentration to parapsychologically endowed mediums, just as the stars can do for sensitive persons. The same can hold for palmistry, which attempts to read the future from the lines of a man's hand. In addition, however, the lines of the hand give veritable clues to a person's character, just as a person's handwriting does.

c) *Necromancy and spiritism.* These forms of divination consist in the attempt to conjure up the spirits of the dead or the spirit world, and to obtain from them occult knowledge and insights into the future. The judgment of science is that until now all demonstrations of communications with spirits from the other world can without artificiality be explained by a combination of abilities of living persons.[1]

Spiritistic seances are a rather frequent occurence in certain countries. Spiritism has elaborated them in a religious cult, which above all attracts people from among the less educated sectors of society. The spiritistic gatherings make a real substitute for true religion and faith. They must therefore be classified as false worship and as such be rejected. The (former) Holy Office has forbidden attendance at and active participation in spiritistic seances because of the dangers to faith and good morals.[2] They even constitute a danger to a person's psychological health and balance. Occasional participation for the purpose of instruction and scientific inquiry is permissible, particularly if the medium refrains from any pseudo-religious framing. The participant ought to be aware that the spirits, which speak up, are personifications of the unconscious of the medium and its productions.

3. *Magic*

Magic is the attempt to bring about certain effects by mysterious powers in a preternatural way. Magic is divided into

---

[1] Cf. Joseph Rhine: Zum Problem der spiritistischen Hypothese; in: Parapsychologie, ed. by H. Bender, 1971, 568.

[2] ASS 30 (1897-98), 701, and AAS 9 (1917), 268.

white magic, which aims at helpful or at least permissible effects, and black magic, which seeks to inflict harm or strives after other sinful ends. Often the term magic is used to designate practices which undertake to attain certain effects with totally insufficient means, naturally in vain. Such practices are of course plain superstition. But also the use of really existing, though mysterious powers is called magic. Inasmuch as these powers are not purely imaginary, the belief in them and their use cannot be classified as superstition.

Scientists have been able to prove on an expirimental basis that some people possess the ability to influence objects and other persons physically and psychologically merely by means of their spiritual forces. For example the conviction of many dice-players that they can mentally influence the number they want to throw has been confirmed by experiments. The desired numbers occurred much more often than probability calculus would permit. Other experiments of psychokinesis have been conducted, and it seems with success, in which bigger objects like handkerchiefs, wastepaper baskets and even tables have been moved by the spiritual forces of mediums. Telehypnosis from distances of several hundred meters and even some kilometers has effectively been carried out.[1] Well known are the abilities of faith healers, who can heal sicknesses of men and even of animals by psychological influence. And one will have to conclude that a person who can heal by his psychological forces, will also be able to cause sickness by the same forces. The belief in the evil eye must not be mere phantasy; it merits to be taken more seriously.

It is to be noticed that people do not usually speak of magic but rather of miraculous powers if a person explicitly relates his extraordinary gifts to God, considers himself only as his instrument, and uses them exclusively for the benefit of others. Don Bosco may be the example of such an instance. The term magic is likewise hardly applied to faith healers who use their powers for the good of others. Magic, sorcery, witchcraft are words used to describe the activities of people who use their gift to influence the health of men and animals in a dubious or evil way. The term magic is also employed for any other good or evil use of mysterious forces, unless people discern an explicit relation to the power of the true God.

---

[1] Cf. Parapsychologie. Entwicklung, Ergebnisse, Probleme; ed. by Hans Bender, 1971.

The use of parapsychological powers is in principle subject to the same moral laws as any other human activity and any other influence exercised upon others. In themselves parapsychological abilities are not evil. They are gifts of the Creator as much as any other special qualities a man possesses. And it is man's obligation to make rightful and good use of them. To avail oneself of these powers for good or at least neutral effects is lawful and admissible; but to place them in the service of evil purposes and harmful effects is sinful and irresponsible.

The realization that certain people may possess unusual powers led at all times to many suspicions concerning the possible responsibility of strange people for sicknesses and any kind of misfortune. Credulous attribution of evil effects to peculiar persons is a grave sin of injustice and superstition. Even where a possible abuse of parapsychological powers might come into question, the common principle remains in force: Crime must be proven and cannot be presumed. The circumstance that such a proof is most difficult in the case of paranormal powers does not invalidate the principle. There is too great a danger that a person be unjustly accused for evil magic and be made the scapegoat for misfortune. One must also keep in mind that such paranormal endowments are most rare. Lastly, more than any measures of prosecution against evil magic men need a firm foundation in faith and love, a faithful life of prayer, devoted use of the sacraments and loyal adherence to Christ and the Church.[1]

---

[1] In his autobiography Mike Warnke, a former priest of a Satan's cult, says that spells had no effect on Christians if they had a living faith, while otherwise they were indeed able to cause harm (The Satan-Seller. — Plainfield, N.J.: Logos International, 1972). The same experience is reported in the autobiography of Doreen Irvine: From Witchcraft to Christ. — London: Concordia, 1973.

Chapter V

SPECIFIC MANIFESTATIONS AND DUTIES
OF WORSHIP

A. Prayer[1]

Prayer is the most elementary religious act. It is th
acceptance of the prime fact of being created, of being depender
on God and destined for him. It is likewise the expression c
man's faith in a loving Father who is good and merciful. Praye
can take many forms: from ardent supplication (Ps 74) t
despairing protest (Job 31), from almost disrespectful argumen
(Gen 18:23-33; Jer 14:11-22) to peaceful confidence in God'
providence (Ps 23; 27; 34), from adoration, praise and thanks
giving (1 Chron 29:10-19) to humble repentance (1 Chron 21
17; Ps 51). Yet beyond the diversity of forms, prayer is alway
characterized by an attitude of confidence in the divine goodnes
and a sense of awe before the divine majesty.

Absolute confidence in the Father in heaven is in particula:
the distinctive trait of Jesus' prayer. He converses with God a:
the child speaks to his father. This confidence in the goodnes:
and power of the heavenly Father was taken over by the Church
In addition the prayer of the New Testament is characterizec
by its close relation to Christ. Closeness to Jesus gives acces:
to prayer. The classic expression of this conviction is the
"through Christ" of the Pauline letters. The pneuma of Christ.
i.e. the closeness of the Lord, enables Christians to pray. It i:

---

[1] References: Maurice Nédoncelle: God's Encounter with Man. A
Contemporary Approach to Prayer. — New York: Sheed and Ward, 1964.
Paul Hinnebusch: Prayer, the Search for Authenticity. — New York: Sheed
and Ward, 1969. The Prayer Life; November issue of Concilium 1972,
vol. 9, nr. 8. Cahal Brendan Daly: Prayer in the Modern World. —
Review for Religious 31 (1972), 901-914. Jesus Solano: The Roots of
Christian Prayer. — Review for Religious 33 (1974), 553-564. Bernard
Häring: Prayer: The Integration of Faith and Life. — Notre Dame, Ind.:
Fides Publ., 1975.

the Spirit within us who cries, "Abba, Father!" (Rom 8:15; Gal 4:6).[1]

I. Nature of Prayer

1. *Concept of prayer.* A definition of prayer encounters the difficulty that prayer is of a very unique nature, which cannot be adequately described in concepts taken from other fields of reality. It is by personal experience that a man must come to know what prayer is and how to pray. Nevertheless a certain conceptual clarification of the notion of prayer is appropriate and also possible.

There are two classical definitions of prayer. "Speaking to God" has been the description of prayer since the Apostolic Fathers. The negotiations of Abraham with Yahweh, which strike us as rather anthropomorphic (Gen 18:23-33), the dialogue between the Lord and Job (Job 38-42), or Christ's wrestling with the will of the Father in Gethsemane (Lk 22:41-44) illustrate this notion. This definition above all stresses the truth that God has personal concern for man, that he is reached by man's prayers, that he hears man and listens to him.

The other definition is generally attributed to John Damascene: "raising of the soul to God."[2] Theologians commonly adopted this definition. Scripture speaks of "pouring out the soul before God" (1 Sam 1:15), of longing for God "as a hart longs for flowing streams" (Ps 42:1), of lifting up the soul (Ps 25:1), of taking refuge in the Lord (Ps 31:1f). The definition stresses more God's holiness and all-embracing perfection, with which man strives to unite himself. Prayer as elevation of the soul means that the whole person is set in motion towards God in acts of praise, devotion, hope, love. Therefore mere mental reflection on God is not yet prayer; it remains in the line of inquiry and study.

Recent theologians have made attempts at still another definition. Prayer is defined as the somehow formulated, loving

---

[1] Cf. art. "Prayer" by Josef Sudbrack, in: Sacramentum Mundi, vol. V, 1970, 74ff.

[2] "Oratio est ascensio mentis ad Deum" (De fide 1. 3, c. 24). Dominicus Prümmer modifies this definition into "pius motus mentis in Deum" (Manuale Theologiae Moralis II, 1958, nr. 332).

acceptance of the loving will of God.[1] This definition stresses the truth that prayer is abandonment to God's will and response to his love. Prayer in the strict sense must also in some way be formulated, if not in words, so at least conceptually. Loving union with God in pure contemplation without conceptual formulations is not prayer in the strict sense of the definition, although it can still be called prayer in a wider sense.

The last definition has the great merit that it points out an essential property of prayer, the abandonment to God's will, which the other definitions do not so clearly bring to the fore. Nevertheless some caution may be in place against attributing too exclusive a position to this abandonment in the notion of prayer. "The attempt to make abandonment to God's providence the quintessence of prayer ignores its character of dialogue. It stresses one truth, the immutability of God (which taken in isolation would mean that real prayer is impossible) and forgets the other, that God is 'personally' concerned with our affairs. The immutability of God must not be reduced to a proposition which can be manipulated in the usual categories of human thought. It must be kept open for the truth of the incarnation and crucifixion, for the truth that God 'changes' for the sake of man. This is the only possible source of the dialogical character of prayer."[2]

2. *Various kinds of prayer.* According to content, prayer is divided into prayer of adoration or praise, of thanksgiving, petition and propitiation. The prayer of adoration, praise and thanksgiving primarily centres in the glorification of God. It is expression of man's loving devotion to God (amor devotionis), and as such a mode of benevolent love. The prayer of petition, intercession and propitiation on the other hand more directly centres in the need of man, although it likewise gives honour to God. It is an expression of the other great category of love, of love of desire. Loving, beseeching hope in God prevails.

In itself the prayer of adoration and thanksgiving is a more

---

[1] Cf. K. Rahner/H. Vorgrimler: Kleines theologisches Wörterbuch (Herder-Bücherei, Band 108/109, 1961), where prayer is defined as "die in irgendeiner Weise 'formulierte' oder begrifflichgemachte liebend antwortende Entgegennahme des Liebeswillens Gottes" (p. 117). Luc. Verschueren finds the quintessence of prayer in the unconditional acceptance of the holy will of God (Het gebed; in: De Katholieke Kerk, II, Utrecht/Brussel, 1943, vol. 23 pp. 769-773). Another definition, already used by the Fathers, defines prayer as the abiding with God in love.

[2] Josef Sudbrack, art. "Prayer" in: Sacramentum Mundi, vol. V, 1970, 78f.

perfect act of worship than the prayer of petition, just as the love of benevolence is a more perfect love than the love of desire. Yet the same as love of benevolence and love of desire designate prevalences in the expression of love, but not totally independent forms of love, so are prayer of adoration and prayer of petition not totally independent forms of worship. Prayer of petition, intercession and propitiation remains most suited for man in his earthly existence. It focuses man's attention on his total dependence on God, the awareness of which constitutes an indispensable element of religion. Besides, the worth of a prayer also depends on its object. And from this point of view a prayer of petition may be of greater excellence than a prayer of praise. Petition for the gift of divine love, for the advent of the kingdom of God is a more excellent prayer than praise and thanksgiving for a successfully passed examination, a good meal, or similar temporal things.

According to form, prayer may be interior or exterior, individual or common, informal or formal, extra-liturgical or liturgical. Interior prayer or mental prayer is the encounter of the heart with God and the dwelling of the soul with him. Merely interior prayer prescinds from any external word, although it is in some manner associated with mental words and images. Meditation and contemplation are two prominent forms of interior prayer. Meditation proceeds from conceptual cognition and reasoning to spiritual affections. According as conceptual reasoning or affections prevail, meditation is called meditative or affective prayer. Contemplation is the simple perception, the loving, blissful intuition of a divine truth accompanied by love, admiration and other affections of the heart.

Exterior prayer expresses itself in external words and rites. If it is to be authentic, it must be sustained by interior prayer or at least by a desire to awaken interior prayer. Yet even though prayer is essentially devotion of the heart, exterior prayer is by no means to be slighted and to be left to one side. Since man is a unity of mind and body, the prayer of the heart spontaneously strives to express itself in external postures, formulas and rites; and vice versa, the exterior words and forms kindle the spirit of prayer anew.

Individual and common prayer must mutually complement each other. Each man is individual and social in being. God has called each one by his own name. Man's love for God is a personal decision. Every man has his own, individual needs and his own, distinctive calling, by which he is to glorify God.

Therefore Christ exhorts: "When you pray, go into your room and shut the door and pray to your Father who is in secret" (Mt 6:6). The prayer of the community cannot thrive without the personal meditation and prayer of its members. But conversely the individual also needs the support of the prayer of the community. He receives from it many impulses and spiritual enrichments, which prevent him from becoming narrow and one-sided in his religious thought and petitions. For this reason our Lord likewise directs his disciples to pray in common. "Where two or three are gathered in my name, there am I in the midst of them" (Mt 18:20).

Informal prayer gives spontaneous expression to the thoughts of the mind and the affections of the heart. It chooses its words under the inspiration of the concrete moment and after the manner of conversation, where men speak freely with their fellowmen. This free and informal prayer must be considered an important goal of every prayer formation. Of course formal prayer transmits the rich treasures of the religious experiences and insights of past generations, of the saints and other inspired people. It is most apt to stimulate and shape our personal prayer. Prayer life cannot do without fixed formulas. The dignity of the holy liturgy and the necessity for conformity in liturgical celebrations in particular make it imperative for the Church to require pre-formed prayers for official use in the divine worship. Liturgical prayer is therefore formal prayer. It may be destined for worship in common, as in the celebration of the sacraments, or intended for individual recitation, as is usually the case with the Divine Office of priests and clerics.

II. Necessity of prayer

Just as history shows that religion and worship are nowhere lacking entirely, so it also proves the fact that men of all nations and of all times have prayed and pray. Spontaneously and by interior inclination men feel urged to turn in prayer to God. The basic law for Christians is the example and word of Christ. He taught his disciples to pray, and his example is a call to constant prayer. Often he withdrew to lonely places in order to converse with his heavenly Father. Often he addressed his Father before the disciples and the crowds in prayers of thanksgiving and praise.

The intrinsic reason for the obligation to pray is first of all set by man's duty to love God. Prayer is the devoted, affectionate speech of the child with his Father, of the disciple with his master, of the friend with his divine brother. Prayer as conversation with God is the primary expression of man's love for him. Prayer is also the means to draw near to God and to know him, which is the pre-condition for love. For a man cannot love what he does not know. Although God makes his presence felt to every heart, man comes to know him better and more closely only through meditation and prayer. And once the love of God has been kindled in the soul through God's call of grace, prayer is the necessary means to keep the friendship with him alive and to maintain the communion with the Lord.

The necessity to pray secondly follows from man's duty to worship God. For prayer is the most elementary act of worship. Man cannot worship without praying to God. The primary expression of man's devotion and reverence for God is prayer, whether worship is internal or external, private or in common.

Prayer is thirdly also commanded by man's need for the other theological virtues, faith and hope, because prayer is the primary means to keep these virtues alive and to nurture them. In the treatise on the theological virtues it has been pointed out that precisely the need to practise these virtues obliges man to foster his life of prayer as the source of their nourishment.

Devotion to God and concern for man's spiritual welfare should spontaneously urge every Christian and God-fearing believer to pray frequently and regularly. Manuals of moral theology commonly consider the devout participation in holy Mass on Sundays and holy days of obligation as a minimum of prayer life which is expected from every Catholic. This demand is supported by the third commandment of the decalogue. Priests and deacons are besides obliged to the prayer of the Divine Office (breviary). They "are bound to pray the entire Office every day, either in common or individually." (SC 96; cf. PO 5).[1]   Also religious have additional duties with regard to prayer, which are specified by their rules and constitutions. Naturally, beyond any prescriptions of the positive law, every person is bound to pray as much as is required by his individual, spiritual needs.

----

[1] The General Instruction on the Liturgy of the Hours enjoins that particular importance be attached to Lauds and Vespers, which should not be omitted except for a grave reason (nr. 29).

The Christian moral spirit has created the custom of regular morning, evening and table prayers. Though not expressly commanded, these prayers are so intimately bound up with Christian piety that the Christian deems it a matter of course not to omit them. Even if an occasional omission is not sinful, one could not neglect them entirely or disregard them for a considerable time without hurt to one's inner life and consequently without sin. If the individual should have no quiet time and no suitable place for his morning and evening prayers, nothing prevents him from choosing other, more convenient times. But also then a certain regularity is necessary. "The normal and usual thing must be the prayer at specifically determined times, ordinarily in the morning and evening, for without such a program men would soon forget to pray altogether."[1] Families are called upon to maintain and foster the habits of common prayer. The custom of common morning and evening prayers with the children and of common prayers at meals is very praiseworthy. A family who no longer prays together will gradually become impoverished in Christian spirit and turn more and more profane.

III. Conditions of prayer

Handbooks list differently many conditions or qualities of prayer. At least three conditions are demanded for prayer in general: attention, reverence or (by other authors) humility, and trust. For prayer of petition a further condition is added: the petitions may only ask for what is conducive to salvation or for what is fitting. (Oratio est petitio decentium a Deo.) Frequently also perseverance is listed among the conditions of prayer. But this seems less correct, for even without this condition a prayer can be good in itself. Perseverance in prayer is however a condition for a good Christian life and for the surer granting of a prayer (cf. Lk 18:1-8).[2]

1. *Attention.* Attention is distinguished in external and internal, in actual and virtual attention. External attention consists in the avoidance of all disturbing activities which could hinder the occupation of the mind with God or make it impossible. Internal attention is the application of the mind to the

---

[1] Häring II, 1963, 269.

[2] The state of grace is not necessarily required for a worthy prayer, although it increases its value. Sufficient is actual grace, which is offered also to sinners.

meaning of the prayer text, to God's presence, or to a divine truth. The external attention is not attention in the proper sense of the word. Strictly speaking it is not attention itself, but only its preparation and protection. Actual attention is the factual application of the mind to the content of a prayer or to the presence of God; while virtual attention is the persisting intention to pray, although the mind is momentarily distracted by involuntary distractions.

As far as possible prayer ought to be performed with actual attention. This must always be the definite goal of every worshipper. As to oral prayer, however, it is not necessary that the meaning of every word or every sentence be attended to. It is sufficient if the attention is directed towards God in a general way.

Involuntary distractions do not destroy the value of internal or external prayer. The one who is involuntarily distracted still retains the intention to pray and is therefore not entirely lacking in devotion. Besides, the state of external composure and the continuation in the recitation of prayer texts are apt to lead the mind back to the meditation of the divine truths and to converse with God.

Yet the question may be asked whether an involuntarily distracted prayer can still be called prayer in a real sense. Some theologians hold that a distracted prayer is real prayer as long as the intention to pray persists. They consequently conclude that virtual attention is that degree of attention which is still sufficient for a real prayer.

Mere external attention and mere external recitation of prayer texts without the internal intention to pray is certainly not a sufficient condition for prayer. It is not the external posture and word that constitute the prayer, but the lifting of the heart to God. Therefore our Lord exhorts: "In praying do not heap up empty phrases as the Gentiles do; for they think that they will be heard for their many words. Do not be like them" (Mt 6:7f).

In regard to the prayer of the Divine Office, however, many authors consider external attention sufficient for the compliance with the precept of the law. Otherwise burdensome duties to repetitions would result and occasion to many scruples be given. The purpose of the law is sufficiently assured if external recitation of the canonical hours is guaranteed. For as a rule priests and clerics will strive to pray the Divine Office meaningfully once they say it. Naturally, if the breviary is recited without any internal attention and wilfully distracted, it does not meet with the necessary conditions for prayer either and is therefore no real prayer. Moreover also for the recitation of the breviary holds that voluntary distractions are sinful.

Involuntary distractions are not sinful. Voluntary distractions on the contrary are sinful or at least imperfections, because they imply an irreverence against God, unless there is a special reason which justifies such distractions, e.g. common prayers during work.

2. *Reverence.* Reverence is that fundamental attitude in worship which acknowledges God as the all-holy Lord and omnipotent Creator. It is man's answer to the *mysterium tremendum* in God. While Tillmann, Noldin, Häring, and others enumerate reverence as one of the conditions of prayer, Tanquerey, Prümmer, Marc, and others name humility instead. Yet it seems more appropriate to count reverence among the essential conditions of prayer, since reverence as one of the fundamental attitudes of worship must also be realized in prayer as its most elementary act. On the other hand that aspect of humility by which a man accepts his insignificance and sinfulness in the presence of the eternal and all-holy God appears to be included in the attitude of reverence before him.

Reverence first demands externally fitting comportment, which in part is already comprised in the demand of external attention. But above all prayer requires internal respect for God's holiness and sacred will, which is incompatible with voluntary adherence to the state of mortal sin. This does not mean that the sinner cannot pray. He can and even must pray. But in order that his prayer be valid and worthy, it must at least be accompanied by a desire for conversion and sanctification.

3. *Trust.* Confidence in the goodness and fidelity of God is indispensable for prayer, most especially for prayer of petition. A genuine prayer of petition is not possible without the hope of being heard. Trust in God furthermore disposes man to place his fate without any fear and reservations into the hands of God, convinced that he knows best what is good for his creatures. Trusting abandonment to God's will must be the characteristic of every prayer, because it forms the basis for the communion and friendship with God, which is the precondition for prayerful converse with him.

4. *Fittingness of petitions.* The fourth condition only applies to prayer of petition. The object of petitions to God

must be morally good and in some way related to man's salvation. It may never be of a sinful nature, e.g. aid in a robbery.
Since prayer of petition is an act of the virtue of hope, the
petitions can have as their object all the goods and at the same
time only the goods which are encompassed by the virtue of
hope: first the coming of God's kingdom and eternal salvation,
then all the spiritual and temporal goods in some way related to
and in the service of eternal values. These goods may be requested for oneself, for one's fellowmen here on earth, or also
for the souls in purgatory. The perfect model of the Christian
prayer is the Our Father, which Christ himself taught his disciples
(Mt 6:9-13; Lk 11:2-4).

A problem may result from the realization that prayers of
petition are not always heard, even if their object seems very
reasonable and good. But the true believer first of all seeks
God's favour, and anything else he only wishes if this is consistent with the holy will of God. Thus genuine prayer leaves
the manner in which it is to be answered to God's discretion,
trusting that God's unremitting care will not deliver up and
abandon his children.

B.   Consecration of human life by the sacraments

The sacraments, as defined in the theology of the Catholic
Church, are the seven vital actions of the Church in its liturgy
which are efficacious for salvation: Eucharist, baptism, confirmation, penance, anointing of the sick, holy orders and matrimony.[1]
Nature and mode of action, biblical foundation and institution,
external signs and ceremonies, minister and recipient of the
sacraments are explained by dogmatic theology and by liturgy
in detail. The reflections here will limit themselves to the moral
obligations connected with the sacramental worship. Some
remarks on the notion and function of the sacraments shall be
premised in order to elucidate their character as acts of divine
worship and the place they obtain in the divine service.

I.   Notion and function of the sacraments

In the past the sacraments were primarily and rather
unilaterally viewed as actions from the side of God through

---

[1] Cf. art. "Sacraments" by Raphael Schulte in: Sacramentum Mundi
V, 1970, 378-384.

the Church, by which God imparts grace to man and sanctifies him. Thus the sacraments were defined as signs imparting grace. The other, equally important aspect of the sacraments as acts of worship, by which man from his side renders praise and thanks to God, was largely left out of view. And yet there can be no doubt that the sacraments are the most outstanding acts of common worship in the Church.

The Second Vatican Council has remedied this deficiency when it declares that "the purpose of the sacraments is to sanctify men, to build up the body of Christ, and finally, to give worship to God" (SC 59). These functions of the sacraments agree with the functions of the liturgy in general, whose most prominent components are the sacraments. In the liturgy, thus the Council explains, "the sanctification of man is manifested by signs perceptible to the senses, and is effected in a way which is proper to each of these signs; in the liturgy full public worship is performed by the Mystical Body of Jesus Christ" (SC 7). Sanctification of men and public worship of God are the two most important functions of the sacraments, just as of the liturgy in general. Externally the sacraments are signs; as such they have universally been viewed by the theological definitions. More explicitly, they are symbolic actions composed of words and signs.

In consideration of the above reflections the sacraments may be characterized as symbolic actions performed by the Church which sanctify men and give worship to God. This definition does not expressly mention the up-building of the body of Christ, likewise referred to by SC 59. This purpose explicitates the social aspect of the sacraments. Still this can be considered as one particular aspect of the sanctification of men. The notion of sanctification must only be taken in its comprehensive meaning as individual and social together.

There are still other rites in the liturgy which resemble the sacraments, as denoted by their name: the sacramentals. They do not sanctify men in the same fundamental way as the sacraments do; but "by them men are disposed to receive the chief effect of the sacraments, and various occasions in life are rendered holy" (SC 60). The sacramentals may be characterized as symbolic actions which *dispose* men for God's grace and give worship to God. While the institution of the sacraments is directly traced back to Christ, the sacramentals owe their institution to the Church alone.

The sacraments and sacramentals sanctify almost every event

in the lives of the faithful (SC 61). The sacraments consecrate the major events and more important recurrences of human life, such as birth, entrance into the age of responsibility, marriage, grave sickness and death, daily life and work, self-examination and renewal. The sacramentals on the other hand prevalently bless the minor events of human life, the utensils and means of human living, such as fields and crops (often in the course of a procession), houses (often regularly at the beginning of the year), herbs, animals, cars, etc.; and of course sacramentals are used to bless all the buildings and items destined for religious purposes.

The sacraments and sacramentals give access to the streams of grace (SC 61) and consecrate man for a life of divine worship. The sacraments in particular impart an existential consecration by assimilating man to Christ and drawing him into his life of love, obedience, service and sacrifice. Through them man is not only designated to a life of divine cult, but assigned and sent out to consecrate the whole world by placing it into the service of its Creator and leading it back to him.

II. Necessity and obligation of sacramental worship

The general duty to reception of the sacraments and to participation in sacramental worship is based, first, on man's obligation to personal sanctification. If God makes his divine grace available to man by the special means of the sacraments, which Christ himself has instituted in order to impart divine life and to increase it, man cannot ignore them. His gratitude towards God and the discipleship with Christ oblige him to avail himself of them in conformity with the mind of Christ. Secondly, man has also a mission to sanctify the world, and the sacraments are means to equip him for this mission. Therefore he is bound to make use of them and to strengthen himself by their grace. Thirdly, man can nowhere follow his duty to external and communal worship better than in the celebration of the sacraments. They are the most distinguished liturgical services of the Christian community, enacted by the Church as the expression of her reverence and her devotion to God. The very essence of Christian worship and religion is pronounced in them.

The devout Christian will however not view the sacraments primarily in the light of obligation. Rather they are for him gifts from God and an invitation of his love. He will approach the sacraments in the spirit of loving and grateful response. His innermost devotion will impel him to receive them and, in the case of the holy Eucharist and of penance, to receive them frequently.

The obligation to the different sacraments is not the same for all of them, because not all of them are of equal importance and because they have different functions. Therefore some specifications are necessary as to the particular obligation of the individual sacraments.

Baptism is the sacrament by which a man is spiritually reborn and becomes a child of God. Its outward sign consists in the washing with water. Baptism is an absolutely necessary means of salvation. "Unless one is born of water and the Spirit, he cannot enter the kingdom of God" (Jn 3:5; cf. Mk 16:16). According to Christ's will a man can become a member of his Church only by means of this sacrament, and whoever wants to be his disciple must be ready to be baptized. Therefore he charges the apostles: "Go and make disciples of all nations, baptizing them in the name of the Father and of the Son and of the Holy Spirit" (Mt 28:19). Hence whoever has come to faith in Christ, has the grave obligation to receive baptism. This is the foundation of the fellowship with Christ and the precondition for all the other sacraments.

Christian parents have the grave obligation to have their children baptized. For it is their duty to provide their children with all material and spiritual needs and to give them the best they possess, especially in the realm of spiritual values.

Confirmation equips the Christian for his apostolic mission and for the public witness to Christ, to which he is obliged as his disciple. Under the outward signs of the imposition of hands and anointing with chrism the believer receives the Holy Spirit to assist and strengthen him in this task. The significance of the sacrament for the Christian apostolate is the reason why Christians are obliged to receive it. However since this sacrament only completes the grace of discipleship and does not found it, the obligation to it does not seem to be a grave one.

The holy Eucharist is the renewal of Christ's sacrifice and the sacred banquet in which Christians receive the body and blood of Christ under the species of bread and wine. It is the sacrament of love and unity which gives daily nourishment to the believer. Christians certainly have the grave obligation to avail themselves regularly of this most powerful and necessary means of grace. Because of the great importance of this sacrament for the divine worship and for man's sanctification, the Church has laid down some basic requirements as to the participation in the eucharistic sacrifice and the reception of Holy Communion.

Catholics are obliged to participate every Sunday and holy day of obligation in the sacrifice of the Mass. This obligation is based on man's need to regular spiritual nourishment, without which the divine life of grace cannot be preserved, and on the duty to common worship of God, which is most aptly rendered by regular participation in Mass. The duty to sanctification of Sundays and holy days will still be dealt with more in detail in a separate section.

As to the reception of the holy Eucharist, the faithful should ideally receive it whenever they go to Mass. It is Christ's express desire that Christians have communion with him in the eucharistic banquet. "Unless you eat the flesh of the Son of man and drink his blood, you have no life in you" (Jn 6:53). This command of Christ implies that Christians must at least sometimes receive him in Holy Communion, though not necessarily every Sunday. In order to assure that Catholics are not negligent in this regard, the law of the Catholic Church decreed that all the faithful who have attained the use of reason must receive Holy Communion at least once a year during Easter season (CIC 920). This obligation is a grave one. Holy Viaticum in danger of death is no longer a precept, though certainly still recommended. Even if Catholic believers have already received Holy Communion that same day, it is nevertheless strongly suggested that in danger of death they should communicate again (CIC 921).

From of old Catholics are accustomed to express their reverence for the holy Eucharist by a period of fast before reception of Holy Communion. Thus they give utterance to their conviction of faith that the consecrated bread and wine must be distinguished from ordinary food and drink. For many centuries the order of the Church provided that those who wanted to communicate in the morning had to abstain from every food and drink, water included, from midnight on. But in recent times this strict discipline has been mitigated considerably. The present discipline of the eucharistic fast provides that communicants must have fasted from solid food and from drink, with the exception of water and medicine, for the period of one hour before Holy Communion. Water never breaks the fast according to the new regulations. Furthermore the elderly and those who are suffering from some illness, as well as those who care for them, may receive the blessed Eucharist even if within the preceding hour they have consumed something.[1] A priest who, on the same day, celebrates the blessed Eucharist twice or three times may consume something before the second or third celebration, even though there is not an hour's interval (cf. CIC 919).

Penance is the sacrament in which sins committed after baptism are forgiven the repentant sinner by the absolution of a priest. For those who have fallen in grave sins it is the ordinary means of obtaining pardon from God's mercy and reconciliation with the Church. Therefore this sacrament is gravely obligatory for the sinner who has committed grave sins. In order that Catholics do not postpone the fulfillment of this obligation unduly, the law of the Church provides that all the faithful who have fallen into mortal sin must sincerely confess their sins at least once a year (CIC 989). Although it is not required that this be done during Easter season, the practice of the faithful to combine their yearly confession with Easter Communion is certainly to be welcomed.

The more frequent reception of the sacrament of penance, not only for the remission of grave but also of venial sins, is very much to be recommended. Confession is an act of genuine worship with sacramental efficacy. It fosters a more careful examination of conscience, counters spiritual negligence, provides spiritual direction and is a way to true, humble penance.

The anointing of the sick (by means of consecrated plant oil) is meant to implore God's blessing over the dangerously sick in order to restore their health, if this is God's will, and to strengthen their souls through the gift of divine grace. Since this sacrament is a means of grace and unites a Christian with Christ in his sickness and death, the faithful ought to appreciate it. They ought readily to make use of it for the best of their bodily health and particularly for their spiritual welfare. The obligation to avail oneself of this sacrament however cannot be

---

[1] This also applies to sick priests, even if they are not confined to bed, whether they are to celebrate Mass or to receive Communion.

called a grave one, since the sacrament is not indispensable for salvation.

Holy orders confer the powers of the priestly office in the Church. They are naturally gravely obligatory for those who want to perform the functions of deacons, priests or bishops. Holy orders are the basis for the valid administration of most of the sacraments, whose ministers priests and bishops are. Moreover it is irresponsible to exercise the grave duties of the priestly office without necessary qualification in training and ecclesiastical authorization.

Matrimony is the sacrament which Christian couples impart each other in a valid marriage bond. Only the sacramental marriage is acknowledged by the Church as valid for Catholics. Therefore Catholics who want to marry have the grave obligation to secure the validity of their marriage before the Church in order to receive this sacrament. Catholics must observe the canonical form demanded by the Church and obtain the necessary dispensations from ecclesiastical marriage impediments, if such impediments exist and dispensation is possible. Since Catholics may not exclude themselves from the Church community by an invalid marriage, and since they have the grave duty to give a Christian foundation to their marriage and future family, they are gravely obliged to receive this sacrament if they marry.

III. Dispositions for valid and fruitful reception

Precondition for the reception of the sacraments is that a man be in the wayfaring state; therefore the sacraments cannot be administered to the deceased. Furthermore baptism is presupposed for the reception of the other six sacraments.

1. *Faith*

According to the opinion of many older theologians, the valid reception of the sacraments does not require faith.[1] Vatican II however expresses a different view. It declares that the sacraments "presuppose faith", as they also nourish and express it. Therefore they are called "sacraments of faith" (SC 59; cf. 9). Although it is not specified whether faith is the condition

---

[1] Cf. Jone, 1963, nr. 462.

for valid or only for fruitful reception, the general character of the assertion suggests that faith is necessary for valid and not merely for fruitful reception. This is further confirmed by intrinsic reasons.

The sincere, judicious wish to receive the sacraments at least presupposes faith in God's existence and man's calling to serve him, and faith in the Christ of the New Testament, who is the Son of God and the Saviour of mankind. Faith in Christ is of the essence of Christian religion. By the sincere reception of the sacraments a man embraces the Christian religion and professes himself as it's follower. How could he do so without faith in God and Christ? It is not conceivable that a man could possess the veritable intention to receive the sacraments without this basic faith. In the absence of a veritable intention however the reception of a sacrament is invalid. Therefore faith is required as a condition not only for fruitful but also for valid reception of the sacraments. Not required however is that a person possess a complete knowledge of the Christian faith or a faith free from all error or doubt.

A difficulty arises for the baptism of infants who cannot yet elicit an act of faith. How can their baptism be valid if they are unable to fulfill the condition of a personal faith in God and Christ? The infant's person is still closely united with his parents or with those who take their place or are his educators. He is fully dependent on them and entirely confides himself to their decisions. Therefore the faith of the parents and educators also guarantees the faith of the child and is sufficient for the child's baptism. Even the Church, present in her minister, can pronounce the faith in the name of the babe, because every child is in some way entrusted to her care, and she has responsibility for him. Yet ecclesiastical law itself forbids that a child be baptized in the Catholic faith, without or even with the consent of the parents, if his Catholic education is not assured, unless one foresees that the child will die before attaining the use of reason (CIC 868 § 1).

2. *Right intention*

In order to receive a sacrament validly, the recipient must be disposed to it by a sufficient intention. The grace of God does not force itself upon anybody against his will. Much less is an act of worship possible without a person's consent. The personal encounter with God and Christ in the sacraments demands a readiness of the heart to meet and to receive the Lord. As to the baptism of infants, the infant is certainly unable to make a personal intention; but he also cannot place an obstacle preventing the grace of Christ. The parents and the Church substitute with their intention for the child as his representatives before God.

An intention may be actual, virtual or habitual. An actual intention is a determination of the will of which a person is conscious here and now and which gives rise to his present actions. A virtual intention is a determination of the will which is not consciously in the mind, but which nevertheless is the cause of a person's present activity. Thus a person who is about to be baptized will not all the time think of his intention to become a Christian. He must pay attention how to participate in the sacred rites; at times he may also be dissipated. But his present activity flows from the determination of the will to be baptized. His intention is virtual. A habitual intention is a lasting willingness or readiness for some matter, which however does not influence a person's present action. Thus Catholics generally have the intention to die with the sacred rites of the Church. But this does not influence the actions of their daily life.[1]

Inasmuch as the sacraments are acts of worship, at least a virtual intention of the recipient is necessary in order that a personal encounter with God can come about and a personal act of worship be paid. But inasmuch as the sacraments are also means of sanctification in the sense of objective consecration and communication of divine grace, a habitual intention is in principle sufficient for their valid reception.

An exception is made by those sacraments for which the acts of the recipient are a constitutive part or at least the indispensable condition of the valid reception. In these cases a virtual intention is always required. This holds for the sacrament of matrimony, since here the recipient is also the minister. It most probably also holds for the sacrament of penance, because many authors justly regard the acts of the penitent as the matter

---

[1] Another division distinguishes between an implicit and explicit intention. The implicit intention is a willingness for something which is contained in another, explicit intention; while the explicit intention is a willingness or determination for an object specifically known and consented to. Thus, e.g., the explicit intention to live as a Catholic Christian implicitly contains the intention to receive the last sacraments in danger of death, i.e. the anointing of the sick and the Viaticum.

of this sacrament or at least as a necessary condition for its reception.[1]

3. *Love of God*

The worthy and fruitful (not valid) reception of the sacraments always requires some love of God, at least that initial love by which a man is sincerely willing to obey God and to serve him. Distinction is made between the sacraments of the dead, baptism and penance, and the sacraments of the living, Eucharist, confirmation, anointing of the sick, holy orders and matrimony. Baptism and penance restore the divine life of grace to those who have been separated from God through sin. The two sacraments do not presuppose the state of grace for their reception, but they create or renew it. Their worthy reception at least demands the love of imperfect contrition and the earnest will to sin no more.

The sacraments of the living demand the state of grace for a worthy reception, i.e. the union with God through the divine life and love. (Note however that the state of grace is not required for their valid reception.) Therefore a Christian in grave sin who wants to receive a sacrament of the living must first recover the state of grace, either by perfect contrition or, preferably, by confession of his sins in the sacrament of penance. Confession of one's mortal sins is obligatory before the reception of Holy Communion, unless there is urgent necessity to receive Communion, and confession is morally impossible

---

[1] The intention necessary for the reception of the various sacraments is explained in detail by dogmatic theology. Only some brief comments shall be added here.

An explicit habitual intention is required for holy orders, since the intention to assume a new state and new burdens is not readily included in another act of the will. A similar intention is required for baptism, since by this sacrament a man accepts the Christian religion with the corresponding obligations, for which he must have made a specific option. Therefore the general intention to live according to God's will does not imply in a sufficiently explicit way the intention to be baptized. Baptism at least presupposes explicit faith in Christ. On the other hand, the intention to live as a Christian and to do whatever is necessary to follow Christ already ensues from faith and therefore implies a sufficient intention for baptism.

Implicit habitual intention suffices for the reception of confirmation and of the anointing of the sick. Therefore if a priest can presume that a person has not revoked his will to die as a Christian, the anointing of the sick may be given him, even though he be unconscious.

(CIC 916).[1] In this case an act of perfect contrition suffices. However a priest who has celebrated Mass or a believer who has received Communion under these conditions must receive the sacrament of penance as soon as this is possible (ib.).

IV.   Requirements for valid and worthy administration

A first condition for valid administration of the sacraments is the necessary power and authorization of the minister by Christ and the Church. Additional provisions have been laid down by the Church for the lawful use of the sacramental powers. A second condition for valid administration is the right intention of the minister. Further requirements for a worthy (not for a valid) dispensation of the sacraments are observance of the rites, devotion and state of grace.

1.   *Authorization by Christ and the Church*

The minister of the sacraments acts as representative of Christ, who is the ultimate source of the sacramental grace and who alone can confer the divine life which the sacraments effect in the recipient. Wherefore the sacraments can validly be administered only by those to whom the power has been granted by Christ. Since however Christ entrusted the sacraments to the Church, the power and authorization to the administration of the sacraments is proximately determined and confered by her. Besides, the sacraments are acts of the Church as the community of the believers. The minister celebrates the sacraments in the name of the Christian community and must therefore be authorized to it by the community. The sacraments also admit to communion with the Church and at times confer special functions in her, which again presupposes the right and the authority to such acts by the Church. Hence only a minister authorized by the Church can validly and lawfully administer the sacraments.

The further determination of who is empowered to the valid and lawful administration of the various sacraments belongs to dogmatic theology and to ecclesiastical law. Briefly the following provisions hold: Baptism can be validly administered by every

---

[1] Cf. also DS 1646f and 1661.

man; yet the ordinary ministers of the sacrament are priests and deacons; laymen can administer it lawfully only in case of urgent need. Matrimony is administered by the Christian bride and groom, presupposing the conditions set by the Church are fulfilled: firstly observance of the canonical form, which is required for the validity of the sacrament and which demands presence of an authorized priest and of two witnesses, or, if the canonical form cannot be observed, dispensation from it by the competent authority; and secondly absence of impediments, some of which invalidate the sacrament while others make its administration unlawful. The sacrament of holy orders is reserved to bishops. The other sacraments, Eucharist, penance, anointing of the sick and confirmation, require the power of the priesthood. In addition special jurisdiction is necessary for the administration of the sacraments of penance and confirmation, which jurisdiction is required in both cases for the validity of these sacraments (cf. CIC 966 and 822).

Validly ordained bishops and priests of Christian Churches and Communions which are separated from the Catholic Church can validly administer the sacraments to Catholics as well. For the norms concerning the lawful sharing in sacramental worship with the separated brethren, confer the section "Promotion of unity of faith" in the chapter on the divine virtue of faith.

2. *Right intention*

Inasmuch as the sacraments are entrusted to the Church and her ministers, the minister must need decide when and to whom he will dispense a sacrament. The administration of the sacraments therefore requires a specific decision of the minister to confer the sacramental grace to a particular recipient. Unintended administration by mere performance of the external rite, e.g. in a moment of mental disturbance or while intoxicated, contradicts the dignity of the sacraments. Accordingly the valid administration of the sacraments at least demands virtual intention. The intention need however not be explicit. Implicit virtual intention is sufficient, e.g. the intention to do what the Church does, or what Christ instituted, or what Christians believe in. Thus baptism is valid if administered by a Jewish physician to a dying baby with the intention of doing as Christians do.

Conditional administration is only valid if the condition refers to the past or present, but not if it refers to the uncertain future (except in the case of matrimony). The baptism of an infant in non-Christian countries under condition that he will stay in the Catholic orphanage and not be taken out by pagan relatives is invalid.

3. *Observance of the rite*

The minister of the sacraments is in conscience obliged to follow the rites prescribed by the Church and to observe the rubrics which order the celebration and administration of the sacraments. For the sacraments are entrusted to the care and authority of the Church. They pertain to the public and official cult of the community of believers, which must be performed according to the laws decreed by this community. The minister acts as representative of the Church and not in his own authority. Disregard of the prescribed rites in the celebration of the sacraments is therefore an offence against the Church community and violation of the duties the minister accepts when he is admitted to the ministry.

The minister is not permitted to modify the sacramental rites by any omission or addition according to his own whims. All modifications are within the competence of the ecclesiastic authority. Of gravest moment is the observance of the sacramental matter and form, since this is required for the validity of the sacraments. Private changes in this regard are a sacrilegious encroachment on the rights of Christ and the Church.

But also the other preceptive rubrics must be followed in conscience. The greater the symbolic significance of a rite, the greater its obligation. Deliberate disregard of important rites which causes scandal and disgust to the Christian faithful, or at least to the sounder and maturer part of them, is gravely sinful, especially if it happens repeatedly. Nevertheless apart from serious contempt, the neglect of a rubric should not easily be qualified as gravely sinful. Traditional handbooks certainly overdrew the moral weight of rubrics.[1] Disregard of the sacred rites for insufficient or even unworthy motives, e.g. carelessness,

---

[1] Cf. Karlheinz Peschke: Die Sünde in den Traktaten über die Sakramente; in: In Verbo Tuo. Festschrift zum 50-jährigen Bestehen des Missionspriesterseminars St. Augustin. — St. Augustin 1963, 235-246.

vainglory or idle show, must be disapproved. But it will generally
not be more than a venial sin.

Priests have the duty to be well acquainted with the rites
and rubrics, to keep themselves informed about any regulations
issued by the competent authorities, and to implement them.

4.   *Devotion and state of grace*

Devout celebration of the sacraments must be among the
minister's primary concerns. The religious ceremonies he
performs and the prayers he says must be a true and worthy
glorification of God and an incitement to the piety of the
faithful (cf. SC 11). "His every action should be animated with
concern for the faithful, whose sacred leader he is in the holy
word and chant of the liturgy. To fail in this spirit of reverence
for the sacred mysteries and to have no concern for the edification
of the faithful is often more regrettable than an occasional slip
in the less important rubrics due to inadvertence or thoughtlessness."[1]

The minister's entire life must correspond with his sacred
vocation and duties. He ought to live the Christian ideals he
preaches and proclaims in the celebration of the sacraments. At
least he must strive after realizing them in patient endeavour.
It is for this reason that theological manuals demand the state
of grace for the worthy (not for the valid) administration of the
sacraments. It is generally held that a layman administering a
sacrament (baptism or matrimony) in the state of mortal sin
commits only a venial sin. An ordained minister would sin
more seriously, unless he administers the sacrament in an urgent
necessity or merely distributes Holy Communion. The state of
grace may be recovered by perfect contrition or by confession.

C.   Consecration of time by holy days

The Christian community sanctifies time and daily life above
all by the weekly celebration of the Sunday, the Lord's day.
There are also a number of special feasts and holy seasons which
re-occur in an annual cycle, such as Advent and Christmas,
Lent and Eastertime, the other feasts of the Lord, Our Lady

---

[1] Häring II, 1963, 182,

and the saints, which consecrate the year. In addition the Catholic Church promotes the spirit of penance among her believers by the practice of certain days of fast and abstinence. The following considerations shall therefore concern themselves, first, with the celebration of Sundays and holy seasons and, second, with the days of fast and abstinence.

I. The celebration of Sunday and holy seasons[1]

The celebration of Sunday and holy days is at present the object of critical questioning and re-evaluation. Especially the obligatory character of the Sunday Mass and of course also the Sunday rest is challenged. The Sunday obligation is a positive law of the Church, so it is said, which obliges only those who have understood its inner value and meaning.[2] The Mass is not the only and not even the most comprehensive means to worship God; the entire life of a Christian ought to be worship and service of the Lord. The Spirit of God is not bound to certain times and places, but rather blows where it wills. And ultimately a man is judged according to the criterion and measure of his charity.

Some of these objections have already been examined and answered in the sections which discuss the duty to love God, to pray and to venerate God by external and common worship. But the obligation of the Sunday observance raises some questions of its own and requires a special justification. It can certainly not be said that the objective duty to the attendance at Sunday Mass depends on the subjective insight into its meaning, as little as the validity of traffic rules depends on the subjective insight into their meaning by the individual, or the objective right to equality of all men hinges on the subjective conviction of its justification. But the reasons which justify the obligation

---

[1] References: Hans Huber: Geist und Buchstabe der Sonntagsruhe. Eine historisch-kritische Untersuchung bis auf Thomas von Aquin. — Salzburg: Otto Müller, 1958. J. A. Jungmann: The Meaning of Sunday. — Notre Dame: Fides Publishers, 1961. Charles Curran: Catholic Convictions on Sunday Observance; in: Christian Morality Today. — Notre Dame, Ind.: Fides Publishers, 1966, 107-119. Willy Rordorf: Sunday, the history of the day of rest and worship in the earliest centuries of the Christian Church. — Philadelphia: Westminster Press, 1968. Paul K. Jewett: The Lord's Day. A Theological Guide to the Christian Day of Worship. — Grand Rapids: Erdmans, 1972.

[2] Cf. Georg Troxler: Das Kirchengebot der Sonntagsmesspflicht. — Universitätsverlag Freiburg Schweiz, 1971, 234ff; 245-249.

to the Sunday observance must be discernible. Their explanation can justly be expected.

1.   *Biblical origin of the Sunday celebration*

Even without revelation man feels the need for regular times of common worship and for a recurrent day of rest. "No matter what the cultural context, the regular recurrence of a day of rest is necessary for the physical and moral health of a man, for the productivity of his spirit, and the harmony of his life. For the believer there is also need for a regular day when he can devote himself to worship."[1] The duty to worship God individually as well as in common is part of being a creature. And as far as cultic acts of the community are concerned, they are possible only if certain regular times and days are set apart for them. Hence one can justly say that the reservation of certain times and days for common worship and rest is a demand of human nature.

Days of worship need not follow a weekly pattern, which pattern has actually been adopted by the Jewish and Christian religion as well as by Islamism. Nor is it necessary that the regular day of worship always fall together with the day of rest. The early Christians rested on the Sabbath, but worshipped on the following day. Nevertheless the ideal is that the two should coincide.

a)   The sanctification of the Sabbath in the OT

Even though the celebration of the Sunday began independently of the Sabbath, there are still some points of contact between the two. The Sabbath prefigures the Sunday and finds in it its fulfillment. "From the methodological point of view it is not only useful but necessary to consider the Sabbath as a prefiguration of Sunday in the history of salvation."[2]

The writer of the book of Exodus traces the origin of the Sabbath back to God's own example in the work of creation

---

[1] Ambrose Verheul: From the Sabbath to the day of the Lord. — Theology Digest 19 (1971), 58.

[2] Henri Oster, art. "Sunday" in: Sacramentum Mundi, vol. VI, 1970, 190; cf. also A. Verheul, l. c. 59.

(cf. Gen 1:1-2:3) and to an express command of Yahweh. "Remember the sabbath day, to keep it holy. Six days you shall labour and do all your work; but the seventh day is a sabbath to the Lord your God; in it you shall not do any work...; for in six days the Lord made heaven and earth, the sea and all that is in them, and rested the seventh day; therefore the Lord blessed the sabbath day and hallowed it" (Ex 20:8-11).

The Sabbath commemorates Israel's deliverance out of Egypt; the freedom from work on this day is symbolic for the freedom from the former slavery (Deut 5:15). It is also a sign of the covenant and of Israel's sanctification by the Lord. "You shall keep my sabbaths, for this is a sign between men and you throughout your generations, that you may know that I, the Lord, sanctify you" (Ex 31:12-17; cf. Ezek 20:12). It is finally a day when men should remember God and take time to honour him (Lev 23:3; Is 56:2-7; 66:23).

At first the Sabbath was only a day of rest. The oldest documents of Exodus do not mention prayer or sacrifice. But it soon developed into a day of worship on which additional sacrifices were offered (Num 28:9f), the loaves of proposition replaced (Lev 24:5-8), and the people assembled in a holy convocation (Lev 23:3.37f).

From the very beginning the Sabbath had a religious character. It is the day which Yahweh has made holy (Ex 20:11). It is a day for the Lord (Lev 23:3). "Just as the firstborn of the flock and the fruits of the field constituted a tithe representative of man's work, so the sabbath represented, as it were, a tithe of man's days."[1] Therefore the observance of the Sabbath is strictly binding. A violation could be punished by death (Ex 31:14f; Num 15:32-36). The prophets regard Sabbath observance as the condition for Yahweh's blessings (Is 58:13f; Jer 17:19-27; Ezek 20:13).

During the Babylonian captivity, when sacrifices could no longer be offered in the temple of Jerusalem, the importance of the Sabbath increased. The people gathered in the synagogues to pray and to read the Bible. The sanctification of the Sabbath was enforced and hedged in by ever more detailed prescriptions. The lists of forbidden works grew longer and longer. At the

---

[1] Walter Kornfeld, art. "Sabbath" in: Encyclopedia of Biblical Theology, ed. by J. Bauer, 1969, 799.

time of Christ the Pharisees said that on the Sabbath it was unlawful for a man to carry his bed (Jn 5:10), to care for the sick (Lk 13:14), to pluck ears of corn (Mt 12:1f), and to walk more than two thousand paces (cf. Acts 1:12). The observance of the Sabbath commandment had unfortunately resulted in a rigid, scrupulous legalism, which oppressed men rather than served them.

b)   The Day of the Lord in the NT

In the beginning of the Church the Sunday existed side by side with the Sabbath (Acts 2:42-47 etc.). Jesus himself respected the Sabbath (Lk 4:16), although he rejected its unduly narrow interpretation by the Jews of his time and put man before the Sabbath (Mk 2:23-28; 3:1-5; Lk 13:10-17; 14:1-6). To the early missionaries the reunions on the Sabbath in the synagogues served for preaching the gospel among the Jews (Acts 13:14; 16:13; 17:2; 18:4). For a long time there was no rest from work on Sunday. The Sabbath remained the day of rest, since this was also a public holiday in the Roman empire.

Yet from the very origins of the Church, the Sunday was singled out by the young Christian community as their own, proper day of worship. Soon the Sunday service replaced the worship on the Sabbath completely, and when three hundred years later Christianity was officially recognized by the state, the Sunday also became the public day of rest. The new covenant had brought the Sabbath of the old covenant to an end, but as a type it had its fulfillment in Christ (2 Cor 1:20).

The Christian Sunday celebration originates from the conviction that the risen Christ wants to meet his faithful on this day. All the evangelists attach importance to the fact that Christ rose from the dead and met his disciples "on the first day of the week" (Mk 16:2; Mt 28:1; Lk 24:1; Jn 20:1.19). It is again on a Sunday when he appears to them one week later (Jn 20:26). And St. Luke relates that the descent of the Holy Spirit, fifty days later, equally took place on a Sunday (Acts 2:1-4).

At the occasion of his appearances the Lord broke the bread to his apostles and disciples and ate with them (Lk 24:30; Jn 21:9-13). This recalls the eucharistic meal which Christ had instituted on the eve before his passion and which his disciples were supposed to perform in his memory. Christians therefore came together on Sundays to break the bread. St. Luke reports in one of his accounts that "on the first day of the week, we were gathered together to break bread" (Acts 20:7). The text connotes that this was not just an occasional gathering, but a custom which had become traditional (cf. also 1 Cor 16:1f).

The custom of the Sunday celebration, where the Christian community assembles to hear the word of God and to partake in the eucharistic meal, is confirmed by such early writers as the author of the Didache (about 100 A.D.), Ignatius of Antioch (died 107) and Justin the martyr (died about 160). Hippolyt, Tertullian, Origen and Cyprian take the divine service on Sundays for granted.[1]

The Sunday is characterized as "the first day", but also as "the eighth day" (cf. Jn 20:26) because it proclaims a day of rest and eternal worship. "According to the Fathers, the first day of the week is a sign of renewal, a sign of the Resurrection. But since it follows the seventh day, one can also call it the eighth day as a sign of the final end, of eternal fulfillment."[2] This eschatological aspect gives Sunday an air of waiting for the final redemption and the cosmic completion of all things.

The name "the Lord's day" is found as early as Rev 1:10. Ecclesiastical Latin and the Romanic languages have preserved this designation in their expressions for Sunday, e.g. dominica, domingo, dimanche.

The first Christian writer to use the term "the day of the sun" (dies solis) for the day of the Lord is Justin the martyr in his first Apology about 150. He adopted this term from the planetary week for the sake of his pagan readers to whom this name was more familiar.[3] He writes: "On the day called 'the day of the sun' all come from the city and the countryside to meet and partake of the eucharistic meal... (Sunday) is the day they gather because it is the first day when

---

[1] Cf. Georg Troxler: Das Kirchengebot der Sonntagsmesspflicht. — Universitätsverlag Freiburg Schweiz, 1971, 26-33.

[2] Ambrose Verheul: From the Sabbath to the day of the Lord. — Theology Digest 19 (1971), 65.

[3] The planetary week came from the Orient and gradually spread in the Hellenistic world, although it was not officially recognized in ancient Rome. The Sunday was the second day in the planetary week, while the first was the day of Saturn (cf. art. "Sonntag" in: Lexikon für Theologie und Kirche IX, 1964, 878).

God created the world and when Jesus Christ, our Saviour, rose from the dead" (I Apol 67:3).

2. *The binding authority of the Sunday precept*

Wherever Christian people have been taught the ten commandments, they have learned that the third commandment says: "Remember the Sabbath day, to keep it holy." So it is written in the catechisms from time immemorial. In the context of Christian religion Sabbath stands for Sunday. In this sense the third commandment has been universally explained to children and adults. It appeared as one of the commandments directly given by God himself. And even though it was clear that this was not an obligation of natural law, it was quite commonly regarded as the most typical example of a positive command of divine law. In short, the precept of Sunday sanctification was in the consciousness of Christian people very widely taken for a positive divine command.

But theologians are in this regard by no means of a common opinion. Many of them hold that the entire obligation of Sunday sanctification, which comprises the obligations to Mass attendance and to Sunday rest, is merely ecclesiastical law. The OT law of Sabbath sanctification has come to an end with Christ, and as to the Sunday observance in the new covenant, there is no express commandment given by the Lord.

Thomas Aquinas is usually quoted as a representative of this opinion. A closer look into his writings however reveals that he upholds this view expressly only for the precept of Sunday rest, while he is silent on the question as to whether the obligation to Mass attendance on Sundays is of positive divine or of ecclesiastical law.[1]

Some theologians hold the view that the obligation to keep one day of the week holy is divine law, while the choice of the particular day is ecclesiastical law.[2] The reason is that God himself followed such a rhythm in the work of creation, and in accordance with this also ordered man to work six days and reserve one day for sacred rest and divine cult (Cf. Gen

---

[1] Cf. Georg Troxler l. c. 136-139.

[2] Cf. Prümmer II, 1958, nr. 465; Tanquerey II, 1919, nr. 1011; Göpfert, Moraltheologie I, 1923, nr. 338; Zalba, Theol. Mor. Comp. I, 1958, nr. 1244 ("Quod aliquis cultus specialis Deo sit tribuendus per hebdomadam, cum abstentione aliqua ab actibus qui hunc cultum impediant, potest dici de iure divino").

1-2:3; Ex 20:8-11). The early Christians of course rejected the narrow interpretation of the Sabbath rest by the Jewish authorities in agreement with the mind of Christ. They did not feel bound by it. But a weekly day of rest was assured to them by the fact that the Sabbath or day of Saturn was a public holiday in the Roman empire. And as soon as the Church was officially recognized by the state, she did not abolish the weekly day of rest, but only transferred it to Sunday. One may conclude from this that the Church has always taken for granted that there should be one day of rest from work in a week, though not in the narrow interpretation of the Jews. This practice, it is true, has also been sanctioned by an ecclesiastical law. But one may still ask whether the ultimate source for this law is merely a positive order of the Church, or whether it is not after all the authority of Holy Scripture which has inspired this law, because Scripture teaches such a rhythm as instituted by God.

It must however be admitted that the majority of theologians regard the precept of Sunday rest as merely an ecclesiastical law. As to the precept of Mass attendance, the views are more divided. B. Häring writes: "As to the celebration of the cult on the first day of the week we are certain it was determined by an apostolic, perhaps even by a positive divine command. The Apostles who made the ruling were 'organs of revelation' in union with Christ and in subordination to Him."[1]

Vatican II does not solve the controversy. But it attributes to the obligation of Mass attendance on Sundays something more than a mere ecclesiastic authority. The precept is qualified as of apostolic origin. "By an apostolic tradition which took its origin from the very day of Christ's resurrection, the Church celebrates the paschal mystery every eighth day... on this day Christ's faithful should come together" to celebrate the Eucharist (SC 106). The Council apparently wants to say that the celebration of the Sunday is a tradition of particular dignity. The Church cannot alter this law in the same way as it can change such purely ecclesiastical legislations as the position of the altar

---

[1] Häring II, 1963, 333. Adolf Knauber points out that the events in connection with the resurrection themselves and not least the great sign of Pentecost distinguished the hitherto unheeded first day of the week. "This impression that the 'first day of the week' was his day had downright become a kind of revealed insight in the paschal mystery and henceforth belonged as a permanent constituent to the primitive kerygma and discipline" ("Aus apostolischer Überlieferung . . ." Zur Frühgeschichte der sonntäglichen Eucharistieverpflichtung. — Theologie und Glaube 63, 1973, 315).

and the priest in the church or the days of fast and abstinence.

All Catholic theologians agree that men have an obligation by natural divine law to worship God and to do so also in common as a community by public acts. Since such acts presuppose common times, places and rites, there must be a religious authority which is entitled to determine the time and other particulars of the public cult. This right of the religious authority is a demand of natural law as well, since without it the common cult could not be realized. It is left to the prudent judgment of the religious authorities to determine the precise time, place and rites of public worship. In this choice they possess freedom within the scope of what is to be achieved. But once the choice has been made and has been declared as the official ruling, it binds the community and its individual members. The obligation to comply with such positive laws of human authorities can be grave or light according to the importance of the matter. The obligation is not simply a light one for the reason that the determination does not directly come from God but from a human authority, as has occasionally been maintained in recent times.[1] Traffic laws are made by human authorities; but many of them oblige gravely, since they are the necessary means to secure health and life of the road user. Inasmuch as human and ecclesiastical laws are the necessary condition for the safeguard and realization of divine demands of natural law, they participate in the binding force of these demands.

The ecclesiastical law of the Catholic Church obliges Catholics to attend a holy Mass and to observe a sacred rest on Sundays and holidays of obligation (CIC 1247). The precepts bind in conscience. They require some further explanation and specification in the following.

3. *The Sunday Mass*

One of the most perfect expressions of religion besides prayer is the sacrifice. For Catholics and many other Christians the sacrifice in the noblest sense is the sacrifice of the Mass. Under the species of bread and wine Christ offers himself on the altar to the Father in heaven, and Christians unite themselves with him in this sacrifice as his members. By offering the Immaculate Victim, they offer themselves too and make the sacrifice an expression of their own, inner donation to God (cf. SC 48). But

---

[1] Cf. G. Troxler, l. c. 238f.

the Mass is also a fountain of grace and sanctification for those who participate in it. In the banquet of Holy Communion Christians partake in the body and blood of Christ. God bends down to man to draw him into the communion with him. As the memorial of Christ's life, death and resurrection, the Mass is furthermore the outstanding means to profess the common faith in Christ and to nourish and to deepen it (cf. SC 33). And not least the Eucharist inspires the faithful to become of one heart in love, to grow in charity, and to practise in deed what they profess by creed (cf. SC 10).

a)   Historical development

From the first beginnings of the primitive apostolic communities Christians used to come together on the first day of the week "to break bread" (Acts 20:7; cf. 1 Cor 16:2). Thus they fulfilled the request of the Lord at the last supper to celebrate the eucharistic meal in his memory. "Do this in remembrance of me" (Lk 22:19). This tradition was at that time not formulated in a positive precept of the Church. But participation in the common gatherings was considered as a matter of course and as an established discipline in the community. Negligence in the participation is reproached by the letter to the Hebrews as something which is deplorable and ought not to be (Heb 10:25).

The same attitude is found in the writings of the apostolic and early Fathers. "The participation in the common celebration of the Eucharist on Sundays is, wherever the possibility to it lends itself, the self-evident concrete expression of the faith in Christ of the community, an 'order' which is accepted by all and without discussion.... Without a formally pronounced positive law of the Church, solely enjoined by occasional reminders and renewed requests, all are conscious of the obligation. Symptoms of diminishing zeal or tendencies of segregation, as they are already indicated in the letter to the Hebrew (Heb 10:25), are intercepted by admonitions or also seriously reproaching exhortations."[1] Ignatius of Antioch (died about 110) gives very emphatic expression to the obligatory character of the assemblies when he writes: "Who does not appear in the congregation

---

[1] Adolf Knauber: "Aus apostolischer Überlieferung . . . ." Zur Frühgeschichte der sonntäglichen Eucharistieverpflichtung. — Theologie und Glaube 63 (1973), 318f. The article is a very valuable, careful contribution to the discussion of the obligation to attendance at Sunday Mass.

(*epi to auto*) is possessed by haughtiness and has already judged himself."[1]

The first synod to enjoin the obligation to participation in Sunday Mass is the Synod of Elvira, Spain (between 300 and 312). Soon other local synods follow, such as the Synods of Antioch in 341 and of Sardica in 343. Later synods define and unify the Sunday observance more and more. Participation in holy Mass on Sundays is everywhere regarded as one of the basic obligations of a Christian.

Regular participation of the believer in Sunday Mass is also for Vatican II an established order in the Church. Mass attendance on Sundays belongs to the basic religious duties of a Catholic. On Sundays "Christ's faithful should come together into one place" to celebrate the holy Eucharist (SC 106). Since this obtains so important a place in the life of the Church, the "sacred Synod strongly urges pastors of souls that, when instructing the faithful, they insistently teach them to take their part in the entire Mass, especially on Sundays and feasts of obligation" (SC 56).

b) Meaning and reason

The basic meaning of the Sunday celebration is summed up in the Constitution on the Sacred Liturgy: "On this day Christ's faithful should come together into one place so that, by hearing the word of God and taking part in the Eucharist, they may call to mind the passion, the resurrection, and the glorification of the Lord Jesus, and may thank God who 'has begotten us again, through the resurrection of Jesus Christ from the dead, unto a living hope' (1 Pet 1:13). Hence the Lord's day is the original feast day" (SC 106).

Accordingly the Sunday is first of all a day of common worship, where Christians come together to commemorate the passion and resurrection of their Lord. It is the day dedicated to the risen Lord.[2] Yet also all the other mysteries of the Christian faith and the entire work of redemption are recalled

---

[1] Ign. Eph. 5:3; similarly Eph. 13:1; Magn. 7:1; Philad. 6:2.

[2] The idea that the Sunday is the memorial of the Lord's resurrection is brought forth forcefully in the new Liturgy of the Hours not only in the Sunday Lauds, but equally in the other canonical Hours. The concluding prayer of Compline on Saturday night prays: "Be with us, O Lord, during this night, that rising at dawn, we may rejoice in the resurrection of Christ."

on this day. Since the single Sunday does not offer sufficient space to unfold all the mysteries of redemption in one celebration, the memorial of Christ's incarnation, life, passion and resurrection, of the mission of the Holy Spirit and the hoped-for return of the Lord is spread over the whole year. This has led to the liturgical year with its different readings from the holy books for each Sunday, which recall the various events of Christ's life and saving work (cf. SC 102). In short, the Sunday is in a most special and universal way the memorial of the Lord. Therefore it gives the believers the unique opportunity to express their common faith in Christ and to comply with the Lord's command: "Do this in remembrance of me" (Lk 22:19).

Besides, every Christian needs to be strengthened in his faith and to be renewed in his commitment to Christ. He finds this help in a very special and efficacious way in the holy Mass. There he receives the grace of Christ through the eucharistic banquet. There the mysteries of the faith are brought near to his heart through the words and sacred rites of the liturgy. The common profession of the faith and the experience of the community of like-minded brethren contribute much to strengthen the believer's faith and good will. This is why the individual faithful needs the community, but the community also needs the presence of its members.

Christians also sanctify the Sunday in order to give thanks and common praise to God. It has been shown earlier that men have the duty to offer God common worship. This presupposes certain times and days appointed for the common service of God. It is the right and obligation of the religious authority to provide for this need. From of old the Church has chosen the celebration of the holy Mass or Eucharist (which means "thanksgiving") as the appropriate form and time for this service. This order of the Church is not an arbitrary choice, as has been shown, but has its origin in an apostolic tradition.

Against a certain individualistic approach to the Sunday observance in the past, it must expressly be emphasized that the Sunday is a matter of the community. Not the individual but the community as a social body is to give praise and thanks to God on this day. God's people meet together in order to confess themselves as the community of those who belong to Christ and who constitute one body with him. Their assembly is an epiphany of the Church. Christians are also united among each other to a common fellowship in the breaking of the bread. The celebration of the Lord's sacrifice is perfected in the sacrificial meal, which symbolizes the unity of the faithful. Thus the Sunday is the day of unity and community in Christ.

The weekly regularity of the common gatherings is of so great importance because only by this means can the spirit of Christ be kept sufficiently alive in the community and become the transforming leaven for the world. Community is formed, lives and remains active not without a strong and lasting rhythm. The sacrifice of the Mass has been chosen as the sacramental rite for these assemblies because it is the deepest form of the proclamation of the death and resurrection of the Lord and the most comprehensive liturgical realization of the faith of the new covenant.[1]

In view of the strong roots of the Sunday obligation to Mass attendance in the constant practice of the Church and in view of the mentioned intrinsic reasons, it cannot legitimately be maintained — as this is sometimes done today — that the precept of Mass attendance is a legalistic usurpation of an authoritarian Church, which keeps her faithful on a string. It is rather the expression and further specification of an obligation which is inherent in human nature itself and particularly in the believer's commitment to Christ and to his faith.

The positive precept of Mass attendance on Sundays and holidays of obligation is first of all necessary in order to appoint a time and day where the community will come together to worship God in common and to celebrate the mysteries of the faith. It is secondly a protection of the faithful against spiritual negligence and weariness and a support in the care for their religious life. Mass attendance because of the pressure of a precept is not valueless as long as this pressure is accepted as legitimate and wholesome. The customary observance of the Sunday precept "had after all this in its favour that the community carried the individual through times of indifference and by this means preserved the point of contact for a new personal decision."[2]

c) Gravity of the obligation

According to universal interpretation the obligation to Mass attendance on Sundays and obligatory holidays is by its nature

---

[1] Cf. Wilhelm Thüsing: Eucharistiefeier und Sonntagspflicht im Neuen Testament. — Gottesdienst 1971, 10-12.

[2] Julius Cardinal Döpfner: Wir brauchen feste Zeiten. Zum Wert der "Sonntagspflicht". — Gottesdienst 1972, 21.

grave. The valuation already finds support in the strong words of Ignatius of Antioch who declares that a Christian who does not appear in the common gatherings is possessed by haughtiness and has judged himself (Eph 5:3). The synod of Elvira (about 300) deems participation in the Sunday Mass so important that it decrees: "Who stays in the town and does not come to church for three Sundays, shall be excluded for a time, so that he appears to be reprimanded" (can. 21).[1] This ruling found fast and wide acceptance in other parts of the Church and in regions as far away as Sardica (Sofia), as is shown by the decrees of the synod there in 343.[2]

Ecclesiastical law, which established itself as a separate discipline in the 12th century, developed a detailed casuistic as to when the conditions for the ex-communication provided for by the canons were fulfilled. From the middle of the 15th century on moral theologians regarded the culpable neglect of the Sunday Mass or of a notable part of it as gravely sinful.[3] This remained the universal teaching of moral theologians up to our times. In 1679 Innocent XI condemned the following proposition as scandalous and in practice detrimental: "The precept to observe the feast days does not oblige under mortal sin if scandal is excluded and there is absence of contempt."[1]

The precept of Mass attendance obliges Catholics in conscience. This must be upheld against occasional tendencies to deny any obligation of the precept under sin, which ultimately amounts to the dissolution of the precept. But one may still ask whether the neglectful omission of a Sunday Mass is in every single instance already gravely sinful. Does the occasional omission of a Sunday Mass really stand in such a radical contradiction to the salvific plan of God that it is generally the occasion for a fundamental option? Or would this not rather only hold for a more habitual neglect?

The early synods disciplined members of the community who

---

[1] Cf. C. Kirch: Enchiridion Fontium Historiae Ecclesiasticae Antiquae. Herder, 1956, nr. 334.

[2] Can. 11 of this synod says: "Remember also how in former times your fathers ordained that a laymen who stays in the town and does not participate in the congregation for three Sundays during three weeks should be expelled from the community."

[3] Cf. Georg Troxler: Das Kirchengebot der Sonntagsmesspflicht. — Universitätsverlag Freiburg Schweiz, 1971, 163ff.

[4] DS 2152.

missed Mass for three consecutive Sundays. Could this perhaps serve as a point of orientation for a more subtle distinction in the question of the gravity of the obligation to Mass attendance? Frequent neglect of Sunday Mass would have to be considered as gravely sinful, but not every occasional omission. The qualification that attendance at Sunday Mass is an obligation by its nature grave still allows for such an interpretation. Substantially the obligation is grave, but it admits of smallness of matter; i.e. an occasional omission is venially sinful.[1] A grave matter on the other hand would be had if a person misses Mass more often than he attends it.

d) Specific requirements and excuses

(1) Catholics are obliged to participate in an entire Mass on all Sundays and holidays of obligation. The holidays of obligation are at present appointed by the bishops' conferences for each country individually. Christmas is the holiday universally observed in the whole Church. Subjects of the obligation are all those who have attained the use of reason and have finished the seventh year (CIC 11).

More than in the past it is emphasized today that the two parts of the Mass inseparably belong together, namely the liturgy of the word and the liturgy of the Eucharist. "The two parts which, in a certain sense, go to make up the Mass, namely, the liturgy of the word and the Eucharistic liturgy, are so closely connected with each other that they form but one single act of worship." Therefore the Fathers of Vatican II strongly urge the faithful "to take their part in the entire Mass" (SC 56; cf. PO 4).

From ancient times the Church began the celebration of the Lord's day and of the great feasts on the afternoon of the day before.[2] It is in consideration of this old custom, but also of the fact that ever more people do not work on Saturday afternoon and experience it as a part of the Sunday, that the Church permits the celebration of the Saturday afternoon Masses. Catholics are allowed to fulfill their Sunday obligation by attending these Masses.

---

[1] This opinion is also held by François Reckinger: Wird man morgen wieder beichten?. — Kevelaer: Butzon und Bercker, 1974, 129-131.

[2] This custom has its origin in the Old Testament understanding of the natural day: it begins in the late afternoon with the appearance of the first star.

(2)   The faithful must be present bodily so as to celebrate the Mass together with the visible community of believers. The reason is that only in this way common external worship is possible and a common profession of the faith. The full participation in the Lord's banquet by Holy Communion naturally also demands personal presence.

Attendance at Mass by means of radio or television is only a substitute in cases where bodily presence is physically or morally impossible, e.g. in instances of sickness or old age. Otherwise it is not a sufficient participation in the celebration of the Sunday Mass. Apart from the fact that the community is then deprived of the presence of its members, the experience of the sacred atmosphere and of the common brotherhood in Christ is lacking. Besides, the surrounding in the private dwellings is in general much less conducive for spiritual recollection and more liable to disturbances, particularly during the time when Masses are broadcasted.

(3)   The faithful are bound to participate in the Mass with devotion and attention. Worship as an encounter with God is not possible without attention to what one is saying and doing and without internal devotion. "Mother Church earnestly desires that all the faithful be led to that full, conscious, and active participation in liturgical celebrations which is demanded by the very nature of the liturgy. Such participation.... is their right and duty by reason of their baptism" (SC 14; likewise 48).

Virtual attention is sufficient, i.e. the intention to pray persisting under involuntary distractions. Voluntary distractions however must be regarded as imputable defects. A mere external presence with total indifference to the sacred words and rites is no Mass attendance at all.

(4)   Excused from Mass attendance are those who are prevented from participation by a sufficiently grave reason, such as disproportionately great hardship or corporal or spiritual harm either to oneself or another. Difficulties sufficient to excuse on one or the other occasion may not be adequate reason for habitual or almost habitual absence.

In particular, the following are excused: the sick and convalescent for whom attendance at Mass involves possible harm; those who are a long distance from the church (possibly one hour for healthy people, less for the aged and weak); those who are too poor to have decent attire or to pay transportation; people hindered by their duties of state or profession, by duties of emergency help, or by urgent works of charity; children, women or employees who would incur serious disgrace of their parents, husbands or employers. One may occasionally miss Mass for the sake of necessary recreation or a pleasure trip if he has no other opportunity for such a trip (perhaps once in six weeks), or if this is the only opportunity he will have for a certain excursion. Possible defamation can excuse from going to Mass, e.g. unmarried women who are pregnant. Also local customs do excuse, e.g. women in the last months of pregnancy. But the customs must be reasonable and justified. Customs without sufficient justification should be discouraged. Thus it does not seem warranted that engaged couples whose marriage bans are published do not attend Mass on the respective Sundays. Dispensation from the observance of feast days can be granted by bishops (local Ordinaries) and parish priests (cf. CJC 1245).[1]

4. *The Sunday rest*

a) Historical development

The day of sacred rest for the Jews was the weekly Sabbath. The pagan feastdays and days of sacred rest were of a more irregular nature. But the day of Saturn, which coincided with the Sabbath as the first day of the planetary week, was distinguished by the mythical idea that one ought to abstain from business in order to avoid misfortune.[2]

Christians had to adapt themselves to their environment in regard to days of rest. The early Christians in Jewish surroundings rested on the Sabbath, but worshipped on the Sunday. This was certainly not the ideal condition. But the tiny persecuted Church did not possess the opportunity and power to transfer the day of rest to the Sunday. Nevertheless the choice of the Sunday as the day of worship by an inherent determination urged for abstention from work and for the transfer of the day of rest to this day.

---

[1] Local Ordinaries and pastors can dispense individual persons and families subject to them, even outside their territory, and in their territory also those domiciled elsewhere, in single cases and for a just cause. In a clerical exempt religious institute the same dispensing power is enjoyed by superiors in regard to their subjects and to those who reside in the religious house day and night.

[2] Cf. G. Troxler, 1. c. 35f.

Tertullian (died about 220) is the first to mention the Sunday rest. He considers it as the necessary consequence of an authentic Christian disposition.[1] Emperor Constantine, who granted the Christians complete freedom of religion and cult and built several splendid churches, decreed in 321 that in place of the Sabbath the Sunday should be the public day of worship and rest in the Roman Empire. In agreement with earlier legislations on public rest, working in the fields was not among the forbidden works.[2]

The first Church prescription concerning Sunday rest is found in the canons of ∶.∍ third synod of Orleans, 538. Wanting to bring some Christian values to the barbarians, it forbade work in the fields on Sunday "because it is easier then to go to church and devote oneself to prayer" (can. 28).[3] Martin of Braga (died 580) was the first to use the term "servile work" to denote the work a Christian should avoid on Sunday.

From the seventh century on the Sunday rest was commonly considered as a binding obligation for Christians. They are supposed to abstain from certain manual works and profane activities on Sundays. But the exact determination of the forbidden works is subject to variations, and the term "servile work" is not universally in use.[4] The term is definitively introduced in ecclesiastical legislation by the Decretals of Gregory IX (1234), an official collection of the laws of the Church.

But even after Gregory IX there was never a completely uniform interpretation of the forbidden "servile works". It is a relative concept, which is variously interpreted in the context of different times and places. According to Thomas Aquinas the prohibition to work on Sundays is not to be taken in as strict a

---

[1] Apologet. 16:11 (CCL I, 116); De orat. 23:2 (CCL I, 271); De idolatria 14:7 (CCL II, 1115).

[2] The Constantine law of Sunday rest, which appears in the Codex Justinianus, Liber 3, Title 12, runs as follows: "Let all judges, and all city people, and all occupied in trades, rest on revered Sunday. But let those dwelling in the country freely and with full liberty attend to the culture of their fields since it frequently happens that no other day is so fit for the sowing of grain or the culture of vines; hence the favorable time should not be allowed to pass lest provisions of heaven be lost" (quoted in: New Catholic Encyclopedia, vol. 13, 1967, 802).

[3] Cf. C. Kirch: Enchiridion Fontium Historiae Ecclesiasticae Antiquae. Herder, 1956, nr. 1038.

[4] The Decree of Gratian (1140), a private compilation of Church legislation, mentions the prohibition of work, but does not use the term servile work.

sense as the Jewish Sabbath observance. Therefore dispensation from certain forbidden works can more easily be granted.[1]

b) Meaning and reason

The Second Vatican Council desires that the Sunday should be a source of joy and relaxation for Christians. "The Lord's day is the original feast day, and it should be proposed to the piety of the faithful and taught to them in such a way that it may become in fact a day of joy and of freedom from work" (SC 106). The common worship itself should already contribute to this joy. But in order to achieve this purpose fully, people ought to be free from work. Even the divine worship of the Christian community can only fully unfold if people are free from work, and only under this condition can the Sunday become a feastday in the real sense.

The primary religious function of the Sunday rest is "to allow time for participating in the worship of the Mass and carrying out the spirit of worship throughout the day."[2] Man cannot dedicate himself with sufficient freedom to the actual worship of God if he is preoccupied with the demands of daily work and living. And acts of community worship inevitably require a common time of rest. (This is well illustrated by the religious feasts which are not public holidays and where the divine service is consequently poorly attended.) Also two hours freedom from work in the morning or evening would not fully suffice to create the atmosphere of repose, peace and festive mood which is desirable for the worship of the community. Moreover different circumstances prevent people from going to Mass all at the same time, so that with such a limited period of rest not all could participate in the divine service.

Besides the religious purpose the Sunday rest also serves other purposes of temporal and social nature. Viewed from this angle the Sunday rest has not a religious character, and its observance could not be urged in the name of divine worship. Nevertheless these temporal purposes are of great value as well. Thus the Sunday rest grants men a time of recreation and relaxation, which they need in order to restore their energy and

---

[1] S. Th. II-II, q. 122, a. 4, ad 4.
[2] Charles Curran: Christian Morality Today. — Notre Dame, Ind.: Fides Publishers, 1966, 117.

to dedicate themselves to work with new interest and joy. The common freedom from work permits a more intensive cultivation of the family ties and the fostering of community bonds. This is a social blessing of no little import. Finally the day of leisure spares out a time for the cultivation of spiritual and cultural values. Man must not be totally absorbed by the productive work with strictly economic output. There are still other values besides money and material gain which are necessary for a truly human life and without which the human personality cannot fully develop.

By freeing man from servile work, the Sunday allows him to dedicate himself to the activities of the spirit. Thus the Sunday rest provides for times of reflection and meditation and for the cultivation of the interior life. These latter values once more touch on the realm of religion and show the close relation between the day of rest and the worship of God, a relation which was strongly sensed by the Hebrews when they regarded the Sabbath rest as an obligation of an entirely religious nature.

In view of these purposes, the following general criterion can be established for the determination and interpretation of the forbidden works: Those works and activities are to be omitted which are incompatible with the requirements of common worship or obstruct it and, secondly, which frustrate the other temporal purposes of the Sunday rest. The feeling and common judgment of the well-disposed in the Christian community serve as a further orientation in the definition of the works which contradict the purpose of Sunday rest.

c)   Prohibited works in detail and gravity of the obligation

Ecclesiastical law obliges to abstain, on Sundays and holydays of obligation, "from those works and occupations which obstruct the worship to be rendered to God, the joy befitting the Lord's day, or the proper relaxation of mind and body" (CIC 1247). Traditionally the forbidden works have above all been described by the term "servile works" (cf. the former code, can. 1248). The definition of "servile work" always encountered some difficulties. Generally it has been understood as manual work of a heavier nature, such as mining, farming, fishing (primary sector of work), industrial labour, construction work, and the work of artisans (secondary sector of work). But it is justly argued that a limitation of servile work to this kind of manual labour is incomplete. As a further criterion the aspect of wage or hire has therefore been introduced. Servile works are those activities for which a fixed wage per hour or per day can be computed. (This also includes the very extensive third sector of work, that of services namely.) All these works contradict the spirit of Sunday rest, even if they are performed without payment, only for one's own utility and consumption or for some pious purpose.

The most decisive criterion for the determination of forbidden works however remains the factor whether a certain work disturbs the divine worship, festive mood and public sacred repose. It is on the basis of this criterion that the former eccl. law included among the forbidden activities public judicial acts and public commercial transactions.

The intrinsic reason of the law would also forbid all other professional occupations and even recreational or sportive activities which frustrate the purpose of the Sunday. If intellectual activities and liberal arts are pursued in such a way that they obstruct divine worship and foil the cultivation of a person's spiritual life and the necessary and wholesome care for the family bonds, then they too offend against the meaning of the Sunday rest.

Moral theologians generally hold that the obligation of sacred repose is by its nature grave, i.e. complete disregard of the obligation constitutes a grave sin. But the obligation admits of smallness of matter, e.g. if the work is of little disturbance to others, if it covers only a short period of time, etc. On the other hand the violation is the graver the longer the work lasts, the greater the public disturbance, and the more other people it involves (e.g. in a construction).

Very commonly about two to three hours of forbidden Sunday work were considered a grievous sin. But in this regard some further distinctions seem in place. The qualification may be valid for very disturbing, noisy activities, especially in the vicinity of the place of worship. But otherwise manual work of two hours and even half a day does not seem to be so profound a disturbance of the divine order that it could safely be qualified as a grave sin. True, such work is in conflict with the Sunday rest. But an occasional transgression is rather to be considered a venial sin. If however a person habitually performed forbidden works on Sundays for several hours, he would indeed be guilty of serious disregard for the concerns of God and the community of believers and therefore of a grave sin.

d)   Excuses from Sunday rest

All indispensable housework is legitimate on Sunday, such as cooking and necessary works in stables. Necessary laundry work, patching, sewing which cannot readily be done on weekdays are likewise permitted. Provided there is no occasion of scandal, the labourer who has worked elsewhere all week may cultivate his private garden on Sunday.

Urgent need and danger of serious harm or loss for oneself or for one's neighbour always excuse from the precept. The poor man who cannot support himself and his family unless he works on Sunday is excused from the law, as is the employee who is constrained to work in order not to lose his job. Farmers may harvest their grain, hay, etc., or gather fruit on Sunday if a storm threatens, or irrigate their fields in drought. The same holds for any necessary work in case of fire, flood, earthquake, etc.

Services which are necessary for the public welfare and the common good are equally allowed, such as public transportation, the work in gasoline stations, catering trades, hotels, hospitals, etc. Mechanics may repair vehicles for necessary travel or for journeys already begun, prepare tools and repair machineries which are needed on Monday. Workers may perform works and services which are necessary in order to prevent damages to industry.

At times it is argued that idleness of expensive machinery on Sundays is a loss and a disadvantage vis-a-vis those who work through. But abstention from Sunday work is always connected with sacrifices in material profit, whether one works as a farmer and craftsman or whether one operates an industrial enterprise. Besides, the pressure of the labour unions against Sunday work has shown that the industry is able to exist and to work profitably without Sunday work, even in competition with other countries which do not respect Sunday rest or respect it less.

There may be instances where continuous work cannot be totally avoided. But even then it is generally possible to stop work at least during the most important span of the Sunday for sixteen, twelve or eight hours.

Lawful custom may excuse from the observance of Sunday rest. This especially holds for markets and fairs, for public buying and selling. Stores in the town are often open on Sunday morning in consideration of those who come from the country-side to church and who have only then the opportunity to go shopping.

Dispensation from the observance of Sunday rest can be granted by bishops (local Ordinaries) and parish priests, in the same way as in the case of Mass attendance (cf. CJC 1245).

II. Days of religious fast and abstinence

All believers are bound to penance by a divine command.[1] "Repent, and believe in the gospel" (Mk 1:15). With these words our Lord himself demands penance from his disciples. Peter concludes his first sermon on Pentecost with a similar exhortation: "Repent, and be baptized every one of you in the name of Jesus Christ for the forgiveness of your sins" (Acts 2:38).

Already in the Old Testament works of penance were highly appreciated. Although the immediate motives for them are of varied nature, penance is essentially understood as "a pious action whose ultimate purpose is to enable us to love God and to commit ourselves to him. We should fast not for our own sake, but for our God."[2]

But penance also has a personal and social dimension. Penance was regarded as a sign and instrument of perfection and holiness, as Judith, Daniel, the prophetess Anna and other outstanding men and women testify, who worshipped God with fasting and prayer (Jud 8:6; Dan 10:3; Tob 12:8; Lk 2:37). Just and holy men also used their penance to atone for the sins of the whole community, such as Moses who fasted for 40 days to appease God because of the faults of a faithless people (Deut 9:18).

Christ himself spent 40 days and nights in prayer and fasting before he began his public ministry. He gave the greatest example of all penitents when he underwent sufferings not for his own sin but for the sins of others. Following in the footsteps of the divine master, anyone who calls himself a Christian must deny himself, take up his cross and follow the Lord (Mt 16:24

---

[1] Cf. the Apostolic Constitution "Paenitemini" of Pope Paul VI of Febr. 17, 1966; AAS 58 (1966), 177-198. The Constitution revises the legislation on the days of common penance in the Church. It also explains the biblical and theological background for these observances.

[2] Apost. Const. "Paenitemini", l. c. 179.

par; 1 Pet 2:21). Even though Christ rejects an externalized penance and fasting which is deprived of the soul of interior conversion and devotion, he does not dismiss these practices in themselves as worthless. He approves of them if performed in the right spirit (Mt 6:16-18).

With the great religious traditions and the example of the Lord Jesus himself before their eyes, Christians, from the beginning, observed days and seasons of fast and penance. Of the many penitential seasons which at one time or another have entered the liturgical calendar of the Church, the Lenten season is the most important. At all times it enjoyed the special appreciation of the Christian people. The Second Vatican Council expressly mentions it and recommends it to the piety of the faithful and to the special care of the priestly shepherds. "During Lent, penance should not be only internal and individual but also external and social. The practice of penance should be fostered according to the possibilities of the present day.... Such practice should be encouraged by the authorities" (SC 110). Another most ancient tradition is the practice of penitential works on Friday as the day of the Lord's passion.

The common practices of penance in the Church are primarily and essentially expressions of divine worship. They have much in common with the sacrifice. By denying himself some temporal satisfaction, man more vividly experiences the reality of still higher, eternal values which merit his attention and care. At times the religious practices of self-denial have more the character of an atonement for sins; at other times they are more expressions of gratitude and love for the Lord. At all times they serve the purification and sanctification of man and conform him to the image of Christ. Through the penitential observance, prays the Preface of Lent, "you correct our faults and raise our minds to you, you help us grow in holiness, and offer us the reward of everlasting life."

Ecclesiastical law, as revised by the Constitution "Paenitemini" of Pope Paul VI, provides the following norms concerning seasons and days of penance:

The days of penance to be observed as a matter of obligation throughout the Church are the individual Fridays and Ash Wednesday or the first day of Great Lent, according to the various rites. Substantial observance of these is a grave obligation.

Abstinence is to be observed on every Friday. On Ash Wednesday, or the first day of Great Lent in the various rites, and on Good Friday both fast and abstinence are to be observed. Episcopal conferences have the right to transfer days of penance for a just cause. But they should always take into account the special character of the Lenten season. They can also substitute other forms of penance, especially works of charity and devotional practices, in whole or in part, for fast and abstinence. (By way of information they should notify the Apostolic See of any regulations they make in this regard.)

Accordingly, if no other provisions are made by the local bishops' conferences, the obligatory days of fast and abstinence are Ash Wednesday and Good Friday (cf. also SC 110); days of abstinence only are all other Fridays.

Substantial observance of these norms is a grave obligation. This means to say that complete or almost complete disregard of the days of common penance without any excusing motive is a grave matter, while occasional neglect in individual instances is a venial sin, if not at times only an imperfection.[1]

Some further explanations must be given as to what the ecclesiastical precepts of fasting and abstinence require in detail.

1. *The precept of fasting.* The law of fasting prescribes that only one full meal may be taken in a day. A smaller amount of food may be taken in the morning and in the evening, as long as approved local custom on the quantity and nature of the food is observed. The two lighter meals together should not equal another full meal. Liquids, including milk and fruit juices, do not break the fast.

Subjects of the law of fast are those who have completed their 18th year and have not yet reached the age of 60 (CIC 1252; cf. 97 §1).

Former handbooks dwelt long on the reasons excusing from the precept of fasting. But since only two days of obligatory fasting are retained, every healthy person will be able to observe them. If however health or ability to work were to be seriously affected by the fast, the law would not bind. This also holds if a person is so poor that he generally suffers hunger.

2. *The precept of abstinence.* The law of abstinence forbids the eating of meat, but not eggs, foods prepared with milk, or seasonings made from animal fat. The forbidden meat is that of mammals and birds. The prohibition does not extend to fish

---

[1] Cf. Answer of the Sacred Congr. of Council to a "Dubium", Febr. 24. 1967; AAS 59 (1967), 229.

and other sea-food, amphibia and reptiles. Since the new legislation does no longer mention the prohibition of meat broth (as this was the case in the former code of canon law), it seems that it is no longer included in the law of abstinence.[1]

The law of abstinence obliges all who have completed their fourteenth year until the end of their life (CIC 1252). This modifies and abrogates the former legislation, which already obliged those who had completed their seventh year.

The obligation ceases if a holiday of obligation falls on a Friday. Furthermore those are excused whose health or ability to work (e.g. in mines, at furnaces) requires meat food; or whose masters do not permit any other food (e.g. servants, children, wives).

Dispensation from the law of fast and abstinence or also a commutation into another work of penance can be granted for a just cause by parish priests and superiors of clerical institutes to individual subjects or individual families (no mention is made that the clerical institute ought to be exempt); by bishops (local Ordinaries) also to entire towns or the entire diocese.

D.   Vows

Vows are often characterized as extraordinary acts of worship. Unless there is a special calling from God, people are not bound to worship him through vows. Vows constitute freely accepted obligations of divine homage. Best known, because publicly pronounced in the many different religious orders and congregations of the Catholic Church and also other Christian Churches, are the three vows of evangelical poverty, chastity and obedience. Their meaning and content is explained in many studies on the religious life. In this context here only the meaning of the vows in general shall be delineated, the conditions for them, their binding force and their cessation.

I.   Meaning of the vow

In the history of religion vows are a far-spread phenomenon. The motives for them are of different nature. They may be pronounced as a forceful prayer of petition in great need, or

---

[1] Cf. M. Zalba: Ad Const. Apost. "Paenitemini" adnotationes quaedam canonico-morales. — Periodica 55 (1966), 752.

also for reasons of moral purification, atonement, gratitude and dedication to God.

Vows have found a fruitful soil in the Jewish and Christian religion. They are highly thought of, and the obligation to fulfill them is taken very seriously (Deut 23:21-23; Ps 56:12; Mal 1:14). "When you vow a vow to God, do not delay paying it; for he has no pleasure in fools. Pay what you vow. It is better that you should not vow than that you should vow and not pay" (Eccl 5:4f).

Examples are the vow of Jacob, who promised to build God a house in Bethel and to give him the tenth, if the Lord grants him a safe return to his father's house (Gen 28:20-22), and the vow of Anna, who fervently prayed for a son and vowed to give him to the Lord, if her petition is fulfilled (1 Sam 1:10f). The Acts of the Apostles mention a vow of Paul (Acts 18:18), possibly made in thanksgiving for deliverance from great peril.

Moral theology defines the vow as a promise made to God by which a person voluntarily binds himself to the rendering of a good work which is possible and better than its opposite. It is a form of worship which is closely related to the sacrifice.

The value of the vow consists first of all in the homage paid to God. The offerings of the vow are an expression of man's devotion to God and love for him. Furthermore the vow confirms a person in the good which he has promised in dedication to God. Therefore every act in fulfillment of the vow becomes a special act of worship.

II. Conditions for validity

1. *Conditions on the part of the person making the vow*

a) Sufficient knowledge. The person who vows must possess clear insight into what he vows, i.e. he must have that knowledge which is required for a perfect human act. Therefore whoever does not have the full use of his reason, cannot make a valid vow, e.g. infants or intoxicated persons. In case of a well-founded doubt as to whether a vow was made with sufficient knowledge, it does not bind.

Ignorance and error invalidate a vow if they concern the essence of the thing vowed, an essential circumstance or the principal motive for vowing. Thus the vow of perfect chastity would be invalid if it were pronounced in the belief that this is only a renunciation of all sinful sexual pleasures. Likewise a vow to make a pilgrimage on foot would be invalid if the person believed that the distance to the sanctuary is 20 miles, while in reality it is 40 miles. Again, no vow is really made if one vows a donation for the recovery of his mother and it turns out that she was not ill.

b) Sufficient freedom. The vow must be pronounced with full consent of the will. Vows that are made under the influence of grave and unjustly inflicted fear are invalid. But if the fear is caused by some natural event, e.g. a thunderstorm, illness, etc., the vow is valid, unless the fear was so great that it disturbed the use of reason.

c) The serious will to bind oneself in conscience. A mere resolution is not a vow. In the case of a resolution a person does not intend to oblige himself under sin, while in the case of a vow he does. In instances of doubt one may presume that a resolution only was intended.

2. *Conditions on the part of the object*

a) The matter vowed must be possible, not only physically but also morally. If the vow turns out to be partly possible and partly impossible, it must be kept as far as it can be, provided the matter vowed is divisible. Thus if a person vowed to make a pilgrimage barefoot and realizes that he is unable to make it without shoes, he is still obliged to the pilgrimage itself. But if the matter of the vow is indivisible, nothing is to be observed. If one vows to make a pilgrimage to Rome, but is not permitted to leave the country, he is not obliged to any part of the pilgrimage. If a vow subsequently becomes impossible, e.g. because of sickness, its obligation ceases.

b) The matter vowed must be good and better than its opposite. The vow never to ride by car has as its object a matter which is indifferent and even useless. Therefore it is not valid. Again, the vow to marry is in itself not better than the vow not to marry and to enter the religious life. Therefore it is not valid. But if through the marriage a scandal could be removed or restitution be made for a serious offence, it would be a valid matter for a vow. In principle it holds that a vow which prevents a person from doing a greater good in the service of God is not valid. — Authors also commonly hold that one can make a vow to do something which is already obligatory.

3.   *Condition on the part of the Church*

Inasmuch as public vows are concerned, their acceptance by the Church is condition for their validity. That holds above all for the public vows in religious orders and institutes. Since public vows by their nature enjoy official approval by the Church, the Church has also the right to determine which vows are to be recognized as public and what are their legal effects.

III.   Binding force and fulfillment

The vow is a kind of self-imposed, personal law. As to its binding force, interpretation and fulfillment, the intention of the person who makes the vow is to be respected as a decisive criterion and norm. To the extent however that no particular intention exists, the general rule holds that the obligations arising from the vow are to be judged in accordance with the norms valid for human and in particular ecclesiastical laws.

1.   *Binding force of vows*

a)   Vows oblige gravely or venially according to the intention of the one who makes the vow and to the gravity of the matter. A matter which is insignificant can be vowed under venial obligation only, e.g. the vow to pray the litany of the Sacred Heart daily. A matter which is important can be vowed under venial or grave obligation, depending on the intention of the one who vows. In defect of a special intention a grave matter is supposed to oblige gravely, e.g. the vow to offer a considerable amount for a charitable purpose.[1]

b)   One can bind only himself by a vow, not others. A child is not bound by the vows of his parents, nor a community by the vows of its forefathers. Therefore if parents dedicate

---

[1] "Various insignificant matters will generally coalesce to form a 'materia gravis' if he (the person who vows) made a real vow; but not if his vow concerns some personal service. Thus, whoever vows to give a small alms daily will sin mortally if he neglects to do so for many successive days. But whoever vows to say an Our Father daily will sin only venially even by neglecting his vow for a long time" (Jone, Moral Theology, 1963, nr. 178).

their child to the religious life by a vow, the child is not obliged to fulfill the vow. Or if the forefathers of a community vow to hold a yearly procession, future members of the community are not obliged to observe it by virtue of the vow. (They may be obliged by virtue of legitimate custom which has obtained the force of a particular law.)

The obligation of a real vow however descends to the heirs. If a person dies without having dispensed an alms he vowed to give, the heirs must give the alms; otherwise they offend against an obligation which must be considered the will of the testator, and against the reverence due to God.

c) A conditional vow obliges after the condition has been fulfilled. Disjunctive vows leave a person free to opt for either part, even after a choice has already been made. Authors commonly hold that the vow would not oblige if, before one makes his choice, one of the parts becomes impossible through no fault of one's own. But this does not seem valid in an equal manner for all kinds of disjunctive vows. If a person vows to donate one out of two chalices to a needy church, and one chalice perishes before the vow is fulfilled, he may not be obliged to give the other. He may need it himself. But if a person vows either to go on a pilgrimage or to give an alms, and the pilgrimage becomes impossible for him, true piety still seems to oblige him to the possible part, i.e. to the alms. At any rate, authors agree that one cannot alter one's choice any more if, after one has opted for one part, the other then becomes impossible.

2. *Interpretation of vows*

The interpretation of vows is made according to the intention of the person vowing. If this is not clear, the vow is to be interpreted in the broad sense.

Hence he who vows in general to donate a chalice, need not give an expensive one. Or he who vows to fast for a month, need not fast on Sundays nor on days when he has to perform heavy work of such a nature which normally excuses from the obligation of fasting.

3. *Fulfillment of vows*

a) A vow is fulfilled by doing what one has vowed. The positive intention to fulfill the vow is not required, although it may often be desirable for a more perfect compliance with the same. He who vows to give a weekly alms and spontaneously helps a person in need without thinking of the vow, is not obliged to still another alms that same week in virtue of the vow.

b) A personal service vowed must be fulfilled in person, e.g. the vow to fast. Whereas a real vow can also be fulfilled by others, e.g. the donation of an alms. The person who made the vow need only give his approval.

c) As to time, the vow must be fulfilled without delay if no particular time has been determined. If the time is determined, the vow must be fulfilled within the period or at the date specified by the vow. In agreement with the norms ruling the observance of human laws, the obligation ceases after the time has elapsed if personal services are concerned; e.g. a day of fast on the Fridays of Lent is not to be fulfilled on another day. The obligation does however not cease if real works are concerned; e.g. the promise to give an alms during Lenten time still urges after Lent if it has not been fulfilled in time.

IV. Release from vows

1. *Cessation for intrinsic reasons*

A vow ceases to oblige if the final motive ceases, if the time for the fulfillment has elapsed, or if the matter vowed underwent substantial changes, e.g. if there is such a change of circumstances that the work promised either becomes impossible or ceases to be the better one. In instances in which the fulfillment of the vow would clearly prove an obstacle rather than a help to one's perfection or to the service of God, fulfillment of the vow would actually be forbidden.[1] Thus, for example, the vow of a woman to attend daily Mass may become incompatible with her duties as wife and mother, after she has married and given birth to several childern, if she is without help.

Should one culpably render the fulfillment of one's vow impossible, he has a special obligation to do penance for the sin he has thus committed. E.g., if somebody vows to support a needy student, but delays his aid for so long that it comes too late, he has to do penance by a similar work of charity.

---

[1] Cf. Häring II, 1963, 290.

2. *Suspension*

Private vows made before religious profession are suspended ipso iure upon profession (CIC 1198). No longer however does the new code of canon law mention a right of religious superiors to annul the private vows of their subjects made after religious profession, nor does it mention such a right for parents over the private vows of their children under age (as the former code of canon law did).

Suspension of the vow (indirect annulment) is possible by one who has power over the matter of the vow, for such a time as the matter vowed remains in his power (cf. CIC 1195). Thus a religious superior can suspend the private vows of a subject which interfere with the discipline of the community. Married partners have the right of suspension with regard to those vows of the other party which prejudice the mutual conjugal rights. A father can dissolve vows of his children which hinder him in the free government of his family.

The intrinsic reason for this right lies in this that the subject cannot vow something which is outside the area of his competence and within the competence of another. "The subject does not have the power to do what he chooses regarding the things in which he is subject to another, but he depends on the will of another. Therefore he cannot oblige himself strictly by vow regarding those things in which he is a subject without the consent of his superior."[1] The canonical details of the right to annulment however are positive ecclesiastical law.

3. *Dispensation*

Dispensation releases one from the obligation of a vow if it is granted by a competent superior for a just reason. The greater spiritual good of a person or also the good of a religious community and of the Church may at times recommend and even require a dispensation. The competent authority to judge the justification of a dispensation is the religious authority. Christ granted the right to loose and to bind to those who govern his Church (Mt 16:19; 18:18). Since dispensation is granted in the

---

[1] Thomas Aquinas, S. Th. II–II, q. 88, a. 8.

name of God, it is a vicarious power. For this reason every dispensation from a vow which is granted without sufficient reason is not merely illicit but also invalid.

According to ecclesiastical law the following persons can dispense from private vows, apart from the Holy Father: the local Ordinary, the parish priest and the superior of a religious, clerical institute of pontifical right with regard to their subjects, and those who have received delegated faculties from the Holy See or from the local Ordinary (CIC 1196). Dispensation from public, perpetual vows in a religious institute of pontifical right can only be granted by the Holy See; in an institute of diocesan right it can also be granted by the bishop of the diocese to which the professed person belongs (CIC 691 § 2).

At times the person asking for dispensation from his vows may have no valid reasons for being released from them as far as he personally is concerned. But especially in the case of the vows of religious profession, the Church herself may have reasons to release him from the vows for the sake of the common good and the welfare of the religious community to which he belongs. A member of a religious order may have lost all zeal for the spiritual life, be a perpetual malcontent, constantly stirring up disorder and dissatisfaction in the community, and be a source of scandal for outsiders. The ecclesiastical superior is permitted to grant dispensation in this case. Nevertheless one who is released from his vows for such reasons cannot be excused from the sin of disloyalty. The virtue of religion obliges him to do penance for his renunciation of the offering once made to God.

Dispensations from vows may not prejudice the acquired rights of others. This is the case if the vow was made primarily for the benefit of others and was accepted by them.

4. *Commutation*

Commutation of vows is the substitution of another work for the one vowed. Inasmuch as the work substituted is better or equivalent to the one vowed and as the vow is a private one, commutation can be made by the person who made the vow. Commutation into a less good work however can only be made by the one who has the power to dispense from a vow (CIC 1197).

Also in instances of commutation no acquired rights of others may be violated. Furthermore in order to commute a vow into something of lesser worth there must be a reason, which need not however be as grave as that required for a complete dispensation.

E. Duties of reverence for the sacred

I. Reverence for God's name

Among all peoples the name of the divinity is revered and kept sacred. Just as the name of a person is not an empty word but represents him, thus the name of God is a representation of his divine being.

The Israelites were very sensitive for the representative nature of a person's and in particular of God's name. To hallow Yahweh's name (Is 29:23), love it (Ps 5:11), praise it (Ps 7:17), exalt it (Ps 34:3) means nothing else than to hallow, love, praise and exalt Yahweh himself. It is an awesome name (Deut 28:58), a name that endures for ever (Ps 135:13). The sanctification of God's name is considered so important that it is included in the decalogue as one of its commandments: "You shall not take the name of the Lord your God in vain; for the Lord will not hold him guiltless who takes his name in vain" (Ex 20:7).[1]

The New Testament shows the same reverence for God's name and extends it to the name of his Son Jesus Christ. God's name must be hallowed, as the disciples are taught in the Lord's prayer, the "Our Father" (Mt 6:9). Christians have the duty of praising the name of God (Heb 13:15), and of being watchful lest their conduct cause it to be blasphemed (Rom 2:24; 2 Tim 6:1).

Because salvation is bound up with the name of Jesus (Mt 1:21; Acts 4:12; 10:43; Rom 10:13; 1 Cor 6:11), his name must likewise be revered and adored (Phil 2:9-11). Christians ought to conduct themselves in such a way that the name of the Lord Jesus be glorified (2 Thess 1:11f).

---

[1] "Through a respect ever more accentuated, Judaism will tend, in fact, no longer to venture to pronounce the name revealed at Horeb. In reading, it will be replaced by God (Elohim) or more often Adonai (my Lord). Thus the Jews will translate the Holy Scriptures from Hebrew into Greek, never writing down the name of Yahweh, but will render it by Kyrios (Lord)" (Dictionary of Biblical Theology, ed. by X. Léon-Dufour, 1967, art. "Name", 335).

Since then the name of God is an expression of his being and a symbol of his person, it must be used with reverence. To honour God's name is to honour God himself, and to dishonour his name is to dishonour the Lord. The same is true of the name of Jesus, of the pictures that represent him, and to a certain extent also of those who are particularly close to him, such as the Blessed Virgin Mary, the apostles and the saints.

Misuse of the name of God

The sacred name of God may be dishonoured in various ways and degrees. Distinction must be made between profane, vain use of God's name (profanity) and the sin of blasphemy.

1. *Profanity* is the disrespectful use of the holy name in thoughtlessness or anger. In itself it is a venial sin.

God's name may be profaned by unconcerned use of the same, i.e. by handling it as one deals with a profane subject. Theologians themselves must beware of speaking of God and the divine mysteries in the purely scientific manner in which the scientist discusses the phenomena of his discipline. The way how God's name is used in the catechetical and theological instruction must always betray the reverence and love for him.

Careless and frivolous use of God's name is "vain" use in the stricter sense of the term. The holy names are employed as means to express profane sentiments and emotions, such as surprise, excitement, fear. In an abusive way they serve as vehicles for worldly sentiments and excitements which have no relation to God.

Still a graver abuse is the profanation of God's name in sinful anger or in expression of other sinful emotions. Nevertheless the unreflecting utterance of holy names in moments of culpable excitement is not more than a venial sin. The habitual misuse of holy names in sinful anger however is a grave irreverence. The use of sacred names for hateful insults and for purposes of cursing is a grave sin.

2. *Blasphemy* is any speech or gesture that contains contempt for God or insults him. It is always gravely sinful.

The blasphemy is direct if God himself is insulted. It is blasphemous to curse God for being unjust or merciless, to shake one's fist towards heaven, to spit on his image or on the holy cross and to trample on them. Likewise blasphemous are mockery masses or processions with representations of God or Christ and similar actions in contempt of God.

The blasphemy is indirect if saints or sacred things are reviled. But such abuse is seriously sinful only if it implies real contempt for the sacred. To ridicule deficient forms of piety is not blasphemous, although it can easily be offensive in one way or the other.

N.B.: Expressions like: damn it!, hang it! bloody bastard!, etc. are also generally called curses. But inasmuch as they do not involve sacred names, they do not offend against the reverence for God and the sacred. The use of the expressions is often no sin at all, although it is frequently improper. But it may also easily offend against fraternal charity and constitute sins of anger.

II. Reverence for consecrated persons

Those persons are sacral who are devoted to the religious ministry by a special consecration or by public vows. This includes priests and deacons[1] and the members of religious communities. To the extent that they are signs of God's presence among men, reverence is due to them. For if sacred places and objects must be dealt with reverently because of their relation to God, religious respect must likewise be shown to consecrated persons. To the extent however that consecrated persons themselves ignore and forget their religious status, they will also be the cause of diminished reverence for them.

Unworthy treatment of consecrated persons is a personal sacrilege. This includes above all every physical violence inflicted upon them, such as beating, spitting upon, trampling, imprisonment and killing. A person who inflicts physical violence upon the Holy Father incurs an excommunication reserved to the Holy See. Who inflicts it upon a bishop incurs an interdict. Who inflicts it upon a cleric in contempt of the faith and of ecclesiastical authority shall be punished with a just punishment (CIC 1370). No longer does the new code of canon law insist on the "privilegium fori" and forbid the citation of clerics before secular courts (as defendants or accused). However their

---

[1] Those who have received ministries only (they now replace the minor orders), do no longer belong to the state of clerics. Entrance in the clerical state is brought about by the diaconate. (Cf. the two Motu Proprios of Aug. 15, 1972, "Ministeria Quaedam", AAS 64, 1972, 531. and "Ad Pascendam", ib. 540.)

unwarranted citation before such a court for the sake of defamation remains an offence and a personal sacrilege, independent of the silence of ecclesiastical law.

Sacrilege is furthermore the interference in the sacred preoccupations of consecrated persons, e.g. by forced employment in totally profane services which are incompatible with their religious vocation. Military service has always been regarded as an incompatible activity of this kind (cf. CJC 121).

The consecrated person can commit a personal sacrilege against himself by conduct which gravely offends against his religious vocation. Manuals commonly limit this form of sacrilege to graver sins against chastity. (Lay persons who participate in such sins would likewise commit a sacrilege.) But this does not mean that the sins against chastity are the gravest a consecrated person can commit, not even the gravest he can commit against his religious vocation. The profanization of a consecrated person's life by engrossment in totally profane business, habitual gambling, frequentation of taverns and the like, under grave neglect of the priestly duties, may well be a graver offence against the religious calling than an occasional fault in matters of chastity.

III. Reverence for sacred places

Places which have been set apart for the worship of God by a special dedication and in an exclusive way are considered holy. People universally feel impelled to show reverential behaviour in such places, because of the particular relation of the sites to the divine.

According to the law of the Church those places are sacred which through liturgical consecration or benediction have been set apart for the divine service or for the burial of the faithful (CJC 1154). This includes churches, public chapels and specially blessed cemeteries. The sacristy is not a sacred place if it is built on to a church, neither are the storage rooms, attic and basement of the church nor the church towers. Reverent behaviour is above all fitting in all churches and chapels where the Blessed Sacrament is kept, because of the special presence of God in it.

Gravely unworthy treatment of the sacred places is a local sacrilege. This includes: (1) profanation of the sacred places by activities and for purposes which gravely offend against their sacred character. This holds for profane shows, profane dances, marketing (cf. the expelling of the vendors from the temple by Jesus, Mk 11:15-17), judiciary acts, public banquets and fights;

(2) gravely sinful, notorious actions. According to canon law a church is desecrated by grievously injurious actions provoking the scandal of the faithful and, according to the judgement of the local Ordinary, so gravely opposed to the sanctity of the place that the sacred cult can no longer be performed in it, until reparation is made by liturgical reconciliation (CIC 1211).

The housing of refugees or the quartering of soldiers, particularly the sick and the wounded, in the sacred edifices in cases of urgent necessity is not a profanation of the sacred places. Private eating in church even without necessity is not a sacrilege, although it may be unbecoming. Occult grave sins are at least not grave sacrileges. Therefore there is no obligation to confess the fact that they were committed in a sacred place.

IV.   Reverence for sacred objects and things

Those things are sacred which are exclusively destined for the divine cult, either by their nature, as e.g. the sacraments and in particular the Blessed Sacrament of the Altar, or by a special consecration and benediction, as e.g. sacred vessels and vestments. Sacred are also relics and to a certain extent the words of Holy Scripture, because of their special relation to God and to Christ.

The more exclusively and directly an object or thing is ordered to the divine cult, the more it must be dealt with reverently. Greatest reverence is due to the holy Eucharist, because of Christ's special presence in this sacrament. Sacred vessels or vestments which have been consecrated or blessed for divine service may not be used for profane purposes. Other objects destined for the divine cult but not blessed for this purpose may also be used for profane purposes, e.g. carpets, lamps, candelabra, cruets, lavabo basins. The same holds for things that are blessed, but not for divine services. One may use blessed candles for studying, season his food with blessed salt, etc.

Unworthy use or treatment of sacred things is a "real" sacrilege. A particular abuse of sacred things is simony, the exploitation of the holy for temporal, material gain.

1.   *Real sacrilege*

A real sacrilege can be committed by the misuse of sacred things in the following ways:

a) Unworthy reception, celebration or treatment of the sacraments, especially of the holy Eucharist. Among the gravest forms of sacrilege is the deliberate desecration of the sacred species, e.g. in hatred of God, in contempt of the Christian religion, for superstitious purposes, etc. One guilty of this crime incurs an excommunication reserved to the Holy See. A cleric may still be punished by additional penalties (CIC 1367).

The holy Eucharist is treated in an unworthy way if the chalices, corporals, altar linen, etc., are quite soiled; if one does not care to renew the sacred species in due time; if one does not see to it that the sanctuary lamp burns before the Blessed Sacrament. If the negligence is great, it amounts to a sacrilege.

b) Unworthy treatment of sacred objects, e.g. of the sacred vessels, priestly vestments, holy oils, relics, the cross, other sacred images. Therefore he commits a sacrilege who scornfully treats the cross, sacred images, relics, etc. There is however no question of sin if one burns sacred objects when they become useless.

It is sacrilegious to use sacred vessels or vestments (which have been consecrated or blessed for divine service) for profane purposes, e.g. to use chalices at a drinking party. (Confer the chastisement of king Belshazzar who profaned the sacred vessels of the temple by using them in a banquet, Dan 5.) — If however such objects have lost their original form, e.g. if the chalices are melted down or the vestments taken apart, they may be used for secular purposes.

Theft or expropriation of sacred objects (including churches) and utensils directly destined for the divine service is likewise a sacrilege. Unjust acquisition of ordinary Church property, e.g. real estate, is however not a sacrilege. But naturally it is an offence against justice.

c) Abuse of the words of Holy Scripture for unholy and sinful purposes. Thus the use of Holy Scripture for superstitious and magic practices is gravely sinful and sacrilegious. The quotation of Scriptures for jokes is generally improper, but not ordinarily a sacrilege.

2. *Simony*

Material goods ought to be placed in the service of the holy, and not vice versa, the holy in the service of temporal, material profit. The offence of simony consists in the inversion of this true order. It is trade with holy things. (The term derives from Simon the magician, mentioned in Acts 8:18-24, who wanted to buy from the apostles for money the power to confer the Holy Spirit.)

Simony is the deliberate attempt to buy or sell a spiritual thing, or a temporal thing that is especially annexed to a spiritual thing, for a temporal price. The temporal price can consist in money or in other temporal goods and advantages.

The spiritual things which are not to be made objects of trade are the sacraments, prayers, indulgences, blessings and consecrations (sacramentals), exercise of ecclesiastical jurisdiction, admission into a religious community, reception of an ecclesiastical office. Temporal things especially annexed to a spiritual thing are benefices attached to an ecclesiastical office, consecrated chalices, indulgenced rosaries and similar items.

He commits simony who for a temporal price casts a vote for someone in an election to an ecclesiastical office; who bribes a competitor against accepting an appointment to such an office; who sells rosaries and similar objects at a higher price because they have been blessed.

No simony is however committed if sacred objects are sold for the price they are worth independently from any consecration or blessing; or if compensations are requested for expenses and special troubles. Thus it would not be simony to request some compensation for the expenses incurred in the procuration of relics, or for saying Mass at a late hour or in some distant place.

Simony is generally considered gravely sinful. Yet the possibility of venial sins is not totally to be excluded in this regard, e.g. if the temporal gain sought is only small and if no great injustice is committed. Thus a person will hardly sin gravely if he demands somewhat more for the procuration of relics than is strictly justified by the expenses he incurred; or if a priest requests a compensation for an extraordinary Mass slightly greater than is warranted by his special troubles. But a cleric would sin gravely if he made the administration of the sacraments or the

---

[1] No more mention is made in the new code of canon law that objects lose their indulgences by being sold or their blessings by being exposed for public sale.

exercise of his jurisdiction dependent upon even small remunerations.

According to the law of the Church, provision of an ecclesiastical office made in a simoniac manner is ipso iure void (CIC 149 § 3). Likewise ipso iure void is renunciation from an ecclesiastical office for simoniac reasons (CIC 188). It is understood that whatever is given or received through such a contract, and all income received from an office obtained in such a manner, must be restored, even prior to a judicial sentence. Furthermore whoever commits simony in the celebration or reception of a sacrament, shall be punished by interdict or suspension (CIC 1380).

PART II

CHRISTIAN RESPONSIBILITY TOWARDS
THE CREATED WORLD

All creatures are loved by God as manifestations of his divine goodness and beauty. All are called to contribute to his glory and to the realization of his kingdom. And all men are destined for the community of friendship with God. Hence if anyone loves God, he will also love those who are loved by God. He will respect the rights and freedom they need and can claim for the accomplishment of their divinely appointed task, and he will help them in the realization of their calling. This loving concern extends to all men and to all creation. It also includes the obligation to strive responsibly after the preservation and perfection of one's own self. All commandments and moral laws consequently flow from the love of God who calls creatures to serve him and to participate in his reign.

The precepts of the second table of the decalogue are therefore not of a merely profane nature, although their direct object is the love and justice due to men and creatures. Ultimate source of the commandments is the love of God. The context of the covenant makes it plain that they are given to man by divine will and authority. Their final objective is not self-glorification and not even human perfection, but the divine service and God's glory.

The disposition of the subject matter in this part follows for practical reasons the order of the second table of the decalogue. Yet premised is a chapter on the two fundamental virtues which ought to govern man's relation to the created world: love and justice. The other chapters deal with man's responsibility in community life (4th commandment), with the realms of health and bodily life (5th commandment), of sexuality and marriage (6th and 9th commandment), of work and property (7th and 10th commandment), and of truth, fidelity and honour (8th commandment). Here, as in the other parts of moral theology, the exposition intends to lay down the basic requirements for abiding

170

in the bond of grace, but also to show the dynamic character of Christian morality, "the nobility of the Christian vocation of the faithful, and their obligation to bring forth fruit in charity for the life of the world" (OT 16).

Chapter I

FRATERNAL LOVE AND JUSTICE

A. Nature and order of fraternal love[1]

Love is the unifying link between the realm of religious life and man's commitment in the world. Cognition of this unity, which unity has been taught ever since Jesus Christ by the New Testament, is a great gain for religion and morality. To believers in Christ the goal of religion could not be a merely visionary mysticism which withdraws from the world as an obstacle for communion with God. Love of God necessarily includes love of neighbour and of God's creation, and hence must prove itself in charitable action. The whole problem that people in modern times claim to find in loving God and in engaging resolutely in the world finds its basic answer here. Brotherly love affords love of God a decisive sphere of action. We cannot even love God without loving our neighbour. "For he who does not love his brother whom he has seen, cannot love God whom he has not seen" (1 Jn 4:20).

On the other hand love of God — and this is not often enough taken in account today — alone guarantees the unselfishness which is lacking to almost all human love. Only the "love grounded in God, becomes agape, which surpasses every natural eros, and the praise of which is sung at 1 Corinthians 13. It surpasses the love of friendship, for even without natural affinity

---

[1] References: François Cuttaz: Fraternal Charity. — Staten Island, N.Y.: Alba House, 1962. Ceslaus Spicq: Agape in the New Testament, 3 volumes. — St. Louis/London: B. Herder Book Co., 1963-66. Thomas Barrosse: Christianity: Mystery of Love. An Essay in Biblical Theology. — Notre Dame, Ind.: Fides Publishers, 1964. D. Deden: The Bible on Love. — De Pere, Wisc.: St. Norbert Abbey Press, 1966. M. J. Andre: As I loved you. — St. Louis/London: B. Herder Book Co., 1969. Marc Oraison: Being Together. Our Relationships with Other People. — New York: Doubleday, 1970. Victor Paul Furnish: The Love Command in the New Testament. — Nashville/New York: Abingdon Press, 1972. Gene Outka: Agape. An Ethical Analysis. — New Haven and London: Yale University Press, 1972.

it meets others with goodwill, readiness to help, understanding and forgiveness for the sake of God and Christ."[1]

Love of God and love of creatures are one and yet different. They are one in their common motive: God's amiability in himself and in his creatures. "With one unique love we love God and our neighbour; God for himself, ourselves and our neighbour for the sake of God."[2] But they are different because of their different object. God in his perfect holiness is the object of the love of God; and creatures, beings of limited goodness, are the object of love of neighbour, of self, and of the world. The fundamental difference of the object justifies and commends different treatises for the one and for the other.

Love of creatures comprehends love of neighbour, of self, and of the world. Yet love of neighbour poses by far most of the questions for moral theology. Less is to be said on love of self and love of nature. Therefore the necessary remarks with regard to the latter shall simply be included in the treatise on fraternal love.

I. The commandment of fraternal love according to Holy Scripture

1. *The Old Testament*

The commandment of *fraternal love* in the Old Testament has not the same, pre-eminent place as in the New Testament, but appears as one precept besides others (Lev 19:18). Actually it is even presented in a less solemn fashion than the other commandments. Nevertheless also the Israelite is asked to turn in loving concern to his fellowmen.

Love of neighbour is represented as due first and foremost to fellow Israelites, who have equally entered into the covenant with Yahweh (Lev 19:17f). In the background is the strong sense of solidarity as developed chiefly in the patriarchal system of society. The fact of being descended from the same ancestor makes a man regard those who belong to his people as "brothers". Under divine instruction, however, love of neighbour is secondarily also extended to aliens, i.e. to those foreigners who have settled down among the Israelites (Lev 19:33f; 24:22; Deut 10:18f). They are granted almost the same rights as the Israelites, although

---

[1] R. Schnackenburg: The Moral Teaching of the New Testament. — London: Burns and Oates, 1967, 107.

[2] Augustinus: De Trinitate, lib. VIII, n. IX (12) (CCL 50, 289).

there are some exceptions (Lev 25:39-46). The fraternal communion of love, thirdly, also comprises the slave, though to a rather limited degree (Ex 23:12; Deut 5:14f; Job 31:13f). Still, slaves enjoyed a more humane treatment in Israel than in any other nation of the Orient.

To a certain degree love of neighbour must even include the enemy (Ex 23:4f; Lev 19:17f; Prov 24:17f.29; 25:21f; Sir 28:1-9), though the "lex talionis" remains in force (Lev 24:17-21) and prayers for revenge and for punishment of the enemy are not seldom (Ps 35; 58; 69; 109; Jer 15:15; 18:19-23). There is no mention of love that is exercised towards non-Israelite foreigners and heathen nations until the rabbinical writings of the second century after Christ.[1] Insofar however as the messianic promises of a universal kingdom of justice and love also extend to the heathen nations, an attitude of benevolence towards them is not totally absent and is meant to grow (Is 2:2; 42:1-3.6f; Mic 4:1-4; Zech 9:9f).

Love of neighbour ought to be as great as love of self: "You shall love your neighbour as yourself" (Lev 19:18). This measure is equally contained in the negative form of the golden rule given by Tobit 4:15: "What you hate, do not do to any one." The content of love consists above all in just and upright conduct towards the neighbour. "Thus says the Lord of hosts, Render true judgments, show kindness and mercy each to his brother, do not oppress the widow, the fatherless, the sojourner, or the poor, and let none of you devise evil against his brother in your heart" (Zech 7:9f; cf. Sir 35:1-3; Mic 6:6-8). Practical help for the needy is the foremost positive task of fraternal love (Deut 15:11; Is 58:4-7). An example of this is the brief enumeration of some corporal works of mercy in the book of Tobit: "Give of your bread to the hungry, and of your clothing to the naked. Give all your surplus to charity, and do not let your eye begrudge the gift when you make it" (Tob 4:16; also 1:16-18). There are however also warnings not to give indiscriminately to everybody, whether good or evil, worthy or unworthy, but only to those who truly merit help (Sir 12:1-6).

Love of self is advised in the counsel to prudent enjoyment of the goods of this world (Eccl 9:7-9; 11:7-10; Sir 30:21-25). "Wine drunk in season and temperately is rejoicing of heart and gladness of soul. Wine drunk to excess is bitterness of soul, with provocation and stumbling" (Sir 31:28f). Man is warned not to

---

[1] Cf. V. Warnach, art. "Love" in: Encyclopedia of Biblical Theology, 1969, vol. II, 525.

be stingy and grudging to himself (Sir 14:4-7), though also not to indulge in gluttony and luxury (Sir 37:27-31). Love of self and love of neighbour are united in the admonition to share the enjoyments of life with one's friends (Sir 14:11-16).

Furthermore man is taught to love wisdom as the source of a happy life (Sir 4:12f; Prov 9:12), to avoid sin as the cause of unhappiness (Tob 12:10; Ps 34:13-15; Prov 8:36; 16:17; Sir 7:1-3), and to have care for his good reputation. "Have regard for your name, since it will remain for you longer than a thousand great stores of gold" (Sir 41:12; also 10:28f).

Love of nature finds strong expression in the frequent praise of the wonders and beauty of creation. Israel's attitude to nature is profoundly religious (Ps 8; 19; 104; 148; Job 37-40). The OT regards everything that is good and useful in creation as the work of God's wisdom (Prov 8:22-31; Sir 42:15-43:33) and love (Deut 7:13f). Hence the praise of the beauty of nature is ultimately always a praise of God. Love of nature manifests itself also in goodness to animals and care for them. "A righteous man has regard for the life of his beast, but the mercy of the wicked is cruel" (Prov 12:10; cf. Ex 20:10; Deut 25:4). The messianic reign, finally, which Israel is hoping for, will not only be a universal kingdom of justice and love for men, but it will also comprehend the abundance of blessing for the whole of creation, for earth and animals (Is 11:6-9; 65:25).

2. *The New Testament*

"The early Church, and with it Christianity throughout the centuries, was profoundly convinced that the greatest of Jesus' achievements in the moral sphere was the promulgation of the chief commandment of love of God and one's neighbour. The message of Christian agape, the model and highest expression of which is the mission of the Son of God to redeem the sinful human race, brought something new into the world, an idea and a reality so vast and incomprehensible as to be the highest revelation of God."[1] The repercussions of Jesus' chief commandment can be traced throughout the New Testament writings.

Love of neighbour is motivated, in the NT not less than in the OT, in an essentially religious way, above all by the example of God's love for every man without exception and by Christ's self-sacrificing love. Since God makes his sun rise

---

[1] R. Schnackenburg: The Moral Teaching of the New Testament. — London: Burns and Oates, 1967, 90.

on the good and on the evil, the love of Christians ought to be of the same, universal nature (Mt 5:44-48; Lk 6:32-36; 1 Jn 4:9-11). And since Christ has washed his disciples' feet and sacrificed his life for them and for the redemption of all mankind, the disciples should imitate this example and do the same (Jn 13:12-16.34; 1 Jn 3:16). "To this you have been called, because Christ also suffered for you, leaving you an example, that you should follow in his steps" (1 Pet 2:21). Besides, love of neighbour is also the express commandment of the Lord, and that—together with the love of God—the greatest one (Mk 12:28-31 par; cf. Rom 13:8-10). According to John the commandment of love of brethren is the great legacy of Christ. All the other commandments ultimately amount to this one (Jn 13:34; 15:12; 1 Jn 2:7-11; 4:21). It is the will of God that we should love the brethren, so much so that fraternal love constitutes the proof for the sincerity of our love for God (1 Jn 4:7f.12.20).[1] Luke 6:35 still adds to the motives of fraternal love the promise of heavenly reward. "Your reward will be great, and you will be sons of the Most High; for he is kind to the ungrateful and the selfish."

Because God's love and the love of Christ extend to every man, just and unjust, friend and enemy, Jew and pagan, also the disciple is to love everyone (Mt 5:43-48; Lk 6:32-36; Gal 3:28). This is beautifully exemplified by the parable of the good Samaritan (Lk 10:30-37). The neighbour to be loved is not merely the fellow member of one's nation or religion and eventually still the alien in the country, as it had in the OT. Christ extends the commandment of fraternal love to every man, no matter to which race or religion he belongs, no matter whether he is a friend or enemy. In concrete, the neighbour to be loved is everyone who by God's providential disposition is brought near to the Christian in order that he should serve and help him. The universality of Christ's commandment of love is also made plain by the mission of the disciples to all the nations for the preaching of the gospel and for the salvation of the world (Mt 28:18-20; Mk 16:15; Acts 1:8).

A particular love however is due to the brethren in Christ. Especially John points first to the community of brethren in the faith as the sphere in which the Christian should express his love. Other NT writings likewise stress the love of brethren (Gal 6:10; 1 Thess 3:12; 4:9-12; 1 Pet 1:22). Paul distinguishes between

---

[1] Cf. Schnackenburg, 1. c. pp. 323-329: Active love for the brethren in St. John.

the brothers in the strict sense, who have been justified in Christ, and those "outside". His norms for conduct towards the latter are sometimes of a restrictive caution (1 Cor 5:12f; 2 Cor 6:14-17; Eph 5:6f; Col 4:5). But the demarcation of the Christian brotherhood is by no means aimed at producing an esoteric exclusiveness. It puts a special emphasis on love for the brethren insofar as the Christian owes especially much to the community of the brethren. But it does not mark a frontier. Since Jesus loved and died for all of us, love of neighbour must embrace all men in their spiritual as well as in their material needs.

As the measure of love the NT repeatedly points to love of self. "You shall love your neighbour as yourself" (Mk 12:31 par). This measure is again expressed by the golden rule, which however, in contradistinction to the OT, is presented in its positive form by Christ: "Whatever you wish that men would do to you, do so to them" (Mt 7:12; Lk 6:31). Yet love of self is for the NT not the ultimate and most complete measure of fraternal love. The perfect measure is the boundless love of the Father in heaven for all his creatures (Mt 5:43-48) and above all the self-sacrificing love of Christ. Christ's commandment of fraternal love is called a "new" commandment precisely because Christians should love each other according to the measure of the love of Christ. "A new commandment I give to you, that you love one another; even as I have loved you, that you also love one another" (Jn 13:34; cf. 15:12).

Furthermore fraternal love has not only its measure in God's love, but its very ontological reality is rooted in God. "The agape of God and of Christ is the sphere of life 'in' which believers are firmly 'rooted and grounded' (Eph 3:17; see also Col 2:2; Rom 8:35-9; 1 Tim 2:15; 2 Tim 1:13; Jn 15:1-10), and in which they must therefore 'walk' (Eph 5:1f; see also 1 Cor 16:14; Phil 2:1f)."[1] Love comes from God, engendered by the divine Spirit in the human heart. "God's love has been poured into our hearts through the Holy Spirit which has been given to us" (Rom 5:5). Agape is a new form of being from God, a sphere of existence in which man finds himself placed as a result of the salvific deed of Christ, in which he must remain and according to which he must act (Eph 3:17; Jn 17:26; 1 Jn 3:14; 4:7.16; etc.).

Fraternal love verifies itself in the faithful fulfillment of every commandment of the second table of the decalogue, since

---

[1] V. Warnach, art. "Love" in: Encyclopedia of Biblical Theology, 1969, vol. II, p. 538.

the whole law is summed up in the commandment of love (Mt 7:12). Nevertheless there are some manifestations of fraternal love which the NT considers as particularly distinctive. Unbounded and genuine, heart-felt forgiveness of the brethren is a primary duty of Christian love. This duty is included in the "Our Father". If our petition for forgiveness shall be granted, we too must be ready to forgive each other (Mt 6:12-15 par). The parable of the merciless servant demonstrates that God's infinite mercy is given us in the expectation that we deal mercifully with our fellowmen (Mt 18:23-35; cf. 7:1-5 par; 18:21f par). "As the Lord has forgiven you, so you also must forgive," warns the Apostle (Col 3:13; also Eph 4:32). Love of enemy is the most lofty proof of the spirit of forgiveness.

Together with this spiritual work of mercy Jesus lays equal weight on practical help in bodily needs, as illustrated above all by the judgment scene (Mt 25:31-46; cf. also the parables of the good Samaritan Lk 10:30-37 and of the rich glutton and the poor Lazarus Lk 16:19-31). If we have received benefits from God, we likewise must give to those who ask or who are in need (Lk 6:30-36 par; 14:12-14; Jas 2:14-17). "The measure you give will be the measure you get, and still more will be given you" (Mk 4:24 par). Another outstanding feature of Christian love is the disinterested service of the brethren. Jesus himself provided the best example of this, even to the extent of giving his life "for many" (Mk 10:45 par). "I am among you as one who serves" (Lk 22:27). According to this great pattern of Jesus the disciples are required to serve each other, if necessary even by the sacrifice of their lives for the brethren (Mt 20:26-28; Jn 13:13-17; 15:12f; Phil 2:4-8; 1 Jn 3:16).

Love of self is nowhere expressly enjoined or advised in the NT. But it is presupposed as a fact in the norm to love the neighbour as oneself. *Love of nature* equally does not find the same attention in the NT as in the OT. It finds expression in Christ's parables (e.g. Mt 6:26-30, which calls attention to the beauty of the lilies of the field) and in the hope of redemption and perfection pledged to all creation (Rom 8:19-23; Rev 21).

II. Nature of fraternal love

1. *Notion of fraternal love*

In a very concise way fraternal love or fraternal charity has been defined as "willing the good of another". The good to be willed is that good which another possesses as natural gifts or as acquired faculties and also the good which he ought to possess and to develop or perhaps also to regain. The others to be loved are finite persons, not God, who is the object of divine love.

A more detailed description of fraternal love says that "Christian love of neighbour consists in wanting for our neighbour that natural and supernatural development to which he is destined by God and also in working for this."[1] It is not enough only to wish good to another, but one must also work for the realization of what is lacking in goodness according to one's possibilities. The good to be promoted is material and spiritual, bodily and intellectual, natural and supernatural values. This promotion must take place within the frame of a man's divinely appointed task as destined by God.

Not sufficiently specified by the wording of the latter definition is perhaps the fact that love not only desires the perfect development of the neighbour, but besides and prior to it accepts and appreciates the good endowments he possesses, independently of any development which is to come about in the future. Integrating this aspect, fraternal love could be defined as the sincere esteem for one's neighbour's natural and supernatural gifts and their protection and furtherance in accordance with his calling by God.

The object of fraternal love are all the saints and angels in heaven, all the souls in purgatory, and all men on earth. The damned in hell are excluded from this love insofar as by their own decision they definitively reject every bond of love with God and the community of saints.

The aim or objective of fraternal love consists, first, in the sincere esteem of all the good a person has received and realized; second, in the active protection, restoration and furtherance of a person's natural and supernatural gifts in accordance with the task of life set to him by God.

The saints in heaven can be loved only by the esteem for their saintly life and their holiness, since they have consummated their earthly pilgrimage. Nevertheless this love is "supremely fitting", as is pointed out by Vatican II. For it draws a man to God and inspires him to his praise (LG 50). It leads the faithful to the imitation of the saints, since love for the saints grants them "example in their way of life, fellowship in their communion,

---

[1] Karl Hörmann: An Introduction to Moral Theology. — London: Burns and Oates, 1961, 239.

and aid by their intercession" (LG 51). Finally the communion with them and with one another in mutual charity and in one praise of the blessed Trinity makes believers partake "in a foretaste of the liturgy of consummate glory" (LG 51).

The active furtherance of our neighbour's welfare and development must be guided by some criterion. This criterion could not simply be a person's contentment and satisfaction. It is not befitting to give a child ample opportunity for travels and entertainments, while he should better prepare for life by serious studies. Or it is not appropriate to procure a government position for a person who is not able to handle the job competently and responsibly, even though he desires it. The criterion and measure of fraternal love is often given in the form of the "golden rule". "Whatever you want that men do to you, do you to them." Even Jesus and Holy Scripture use it. It is certainly a rule of practical wisdom. But it is a preliminary and not an ultimate norm. For it may well be that one wants to receive benefits which contradict love towards oneself and which would equally contradict love towards the other one, if he received them. They are unjust if given and unjust if received.[1]

Hence the New Testament transcends this norm in giving the example of Christ's love for us men as a new, more perfect measure of fraternal love. And the example of Christ lastly leads men to the needs of the kingdom of God as the ultimate criterion. Love of neighbour is all the more perfect, the better it prepares and enables him to cooperate in the realization of the Creator's plan with this world and to serve God's reign. And since God has assigned to each one his particular task in the unfolding and completion of the work of creation and salvation, each person's special calling within this universal scope ought to be the ultimate guiding principle of fraternal love.

Because of this close link between love of neighbour and completion of God's work, Vatican II can rightly say that the new commandment of love is "the basic law of human perfection and hence of the world's transformation." It frees all men so that by "bringing all earthly resources into the service of human life they can devote themselves to that future when humanity itself will become an offering accepted by God" (GS 38).

The motive of fraternal love is God's love for every person, by which he makes man share in his goodness and beauty and wants him to participate more fully in it. This participation in

---

[1] Cf. Paul Tillich: Love, Power, and Justice. — London: Oxford University Press, 1954, 79.

God's goodness is described by Holy Scripture also as man's likeness to God, or in metaphors such as child of God, brother of Christ, temple of the Holy Spirit. Of course Christian love of neighbour receives its motive also from the repeated, emphatic command to fraternal love in Holy Scripture, which is even qualified as the greatest commandment, and from the example of Christ. Yet this command by no means imposes upon man something that is extraneous to his nature. It profoundly agrees with his own joy over the goodness he discovers in another person and with his hope and longing that God's likeness and beauty may be perfected more and more in all fellowmen and in all creation.

From this follows that fraternal love is not only and not even primarily motivated by a person's virtues and merits, although they certainly contribute to love of him. Love is still more motivated by the desire to perfect God's likeness where it is yet deficient. Agape loves the neighbour even when he, of himself, does not inspire love or has actually shown himself unworthy of it (love of sinners and enemies). "It loves the other person, therefore, not because he is good, pleasant or suitable to be helped, but in order that he may become good."[1]

Love of self, rightly understood, calls for the realization of the same objectives as fraternal love and is motivated by the same motives. "The motive of love for ourselves and for others is absolutely the same. It is unique and indivisible. The most eloquent and most pressing command and invitation to this twofold and unique love comes to us from the example of Christ, from His divine-human love for us and for all the brethren."[2] God wills his likeness in us as much as he wills it in our neighbour. Love of self has to realize the same objectives as those pointed out for fraternal love: acceptance of oneself and promotion of one's divinely willed growth in accordance with one's calling within the all comprising scope of God's eternal design.

Love of nature is equally grounded in God's goodness and amiability which every creature reflects. Since nature is the work of God's hands, it ought to be loved as well. "Man is able to love the things themselves created by God, and ought to do so. He can receive them from God, and respect and reverence them

---

[1] V. Warnach, art. "Love" in: Encyclopedia of Biblical Theology, 1969, vol. II, 534.

[2] B. Häring II, 1963, 357.

as flowing constantly from the hand of God" (GS 37). This love will realize itself in appreciation for the goodness and beauty of nature and in respect for the purpose it has been destined for by God.

2.   *Qualities of fraternal love*

In the canticle of love in first Corinthians, Paul enumerates a number of qualities that distinguish love. "Love is patient and kind; love is not jealous or boastful; it is not arrogant or rude. Love does not insist on its own way; it is not irritable or resentful; it does not rejoice at wrong, but rejoices in the right. Love bears all things, believes all things, hopes all things, endures all things" (1 Cor 13:4-7). These qualities mark a perfect love. Yet especially two qualities are usually pointed out as belonging to the very essence of genuine charity: love must be interior and active.

Love must be interior, i.e. sincerely affirm and accept another person's value and good endowments without envy and curtailment; furthermore, the interest it shows for the neighbour must be true and genuine. A charity which practises external works without inner concern for the neighbour's welfare does not merit the name. Thus it may happen that people perform works of charity for the sake of their reputation, but internally do not really care for the fate of their neighbour. This kind of "charitable works" lacks the true spirit of love and is not love at all. Sentiments and emotions of love however do not belong to the essence of love, although their presence will contribute to its vital force.

Love must be active by an effective concern for the welfare of the other. Although external works of charity may largely be absent because of a person's poverty and his own misery, to the extent that practical aid is possible, it ought to be offered. "If a brother or sister is ill-clad and in lack of daily food, and one of you says to them, 'Go in peace, be warmed and filled,' without giving them the things needed for the body, what does it profit?" (Jas 2:15f). "Little children, let us not love in word or speech but in deed and in truth" (1 Jn 3:18). Hence love not only wills that things go well with the neighbour in need, but it endeavours to do good to the other in a concrete way and to do all the good for him that is possible. It does so not only on extraordinary occasions of particularly great misfortune, but proves itself "chiefly in the ordinary circumstances of life" (GS 38). The intimate bond of unity in the one Body of Christ makes of our natural sentiment a real and effective sympathy for our neighbour in his suffering and in his joy. "If one member suffers, all suffer together; if one member is honoured, all rejoice together" (1 Cor 12:26). Active, solicitous love creates a sense of responsibility for others in a spirit of solidarity. It extends to the neighbour's temporal needs as much as to the spiritual good of his salvation.

Another, most indispensable quality of love appears to be humble, reverent respect for the person who is loved and helped. Whether it is the love of friendship, or the most intimate union of conjugal love, or the love towards those in distress, humble reverence for the unique value and dignity of every person is a precondition for the development and permanence of any true love-relationship.

On the other hand a caution is in place not to confound love with yielding weakness. Love and the use of force have often been contrasted in such a way that love is identified with a resignation of force and the use of force, especially by political power, with a denial of love. Powerless love and loveless power are contrasted. But such an opposition is error and confusion. One can readily say that constructive social ethics is impossible as long as power is looked at with distrust and love is reduced to kindness or to an emotional quality. Such a division will either result in fear of engaging in the political realm or, if an involvement is nevertheless sought, in the rejection of the norms of Christian ethics for politics. "It leads to the separation of the political from the religious and the ethical and to the politics of mere compulsion on the political side. Constructive social ethics presuppose that one is aware of the element of love in structures of power and of the element of power without which love becomes chaotic surrender."[1]

Love must destroy what is against love. Although it will try to save the one who is the bearer of injustice, because as a creature of God he remains a creation of love, it will resist him in his assaults against love. Remorse of conscience and the hell of despair are the "strange work" that divine love itself does within us in order to dispose us for the work of justification and salvation. "The Cross of Christ is the symbol of the divine

---

[1] P. Tillich: Love, Power, and Justice. — London: Oxford University Press, 1954, 12.

love, participating in the destruction into which it throws him who acts against love: This is the meaning of atonement."[1]

III. Universality and order of fraternal love

The universality of charity is the special characteristic of Christian love in contrast to natural love of relatives and friends and to Jewish and ancient love of fellowmen. "There is neither Jew nor Greek, there is neither slave nor free, there is neither male nor female; for you are all one in Christ Jesus" (Gal 3:28). The Church faithfully preserved the great legacy of Christ and preaches it anew in today's world. "Christian charity truly extends to all, without distinction of race, social condition, or religion. It looks for neither gain nor gratitude. For as God has loved us with a spontaneous love, so also the faithful should in their charity care for the human person himself by loving him with the same affection with which God sought out man.... The Church, through her children, is one with men of every condition, but especially with the poor and the afflicted" (AG 12). For the same reason Vatican II turns against any distinction between men or peoples in the matter of human dignity and human rights and against any discrimination. "As a consequence, the Church rejects, as foreign to the mind of Christ, any discrimination against men or harassment of them because of their race, colour, condition of life, or religion" (NA 5; cf. GS 29).

The practical realization of the commandment of universal love poses however some problems, since man has only limited means and possibilities to help his brothers in need. Nobody is able to help all his needy fellowmen. Whom then is he to help first? For whom has he the greatest responsibilities? To what extent has he ordinarily to sacrifice his means and goods for the poor and destitute? Special problems and difficulties, finally, are encountered in the case of love of enemies and malefactors.

1. *Order of love with regard to persons*

a) Well-ordered love of self

A saying of wisdom runs: Qui sibi nequam, cui bonus (Sir 14:5). If a man is mean to himself; to whom will he be good? That is to say, if a man does not know how to love himself rightly, he will also not be able to love others well. The same view is expressed by St. Augustine in one of his sermons: "First learn to love yourself.... For if you do not know how to love yourself, how will you be able to love your neighbour truly?"[1] The findings of recent psychology coincide with these experiences of old. But on the other hand the fear is not unfounded that from such principles the step to an egotist attitude is not far. They might lend countenance to a preferential treatment of self, which always thinks first of its own well-being and reserves for itself the bigger share. Hence some clarifications and distinctions are in order.

As to appreciative esteem and benevolence, one must love the neighbour in the same full measure as one loves oneself. Since the appreciative esteem ought to be greater according to a person's greater holiness and closeness to God, this may even imply that one is bound to love a person more as oneself because of his greater holiness. The same is true if a person is of considerably greater importance for the common good than we ourselves. We ought to prefer his life to our life. Therefore it does not seldom happen that in times of war simple soldiers sacrifice their lives for the life of their general or other leaders. On the other hand a person important for the common good may, for the same reason, have the obligation not to expose his life to dangers, which he must nevertheless request others to undergo. Likewise one cannot claim for works of the same quality greater reward for oneself than one would concede to others, and one ought to allow greater recompense for a neighbour's service of better quality than one's own, though the reverse is equally true.

Equality of love of self and of neighbour as to intensity of affection is not required. Such an emotional equivalence is not even possible for man, because he is necessarily much more present to himself than others can ever be. Furthermore greater emotional involvement usually corresponds to greater responsibilities whose fulfillment nature wants to secure. And a man has greater responsibilities towards himself than towards any other person.

Love of self requires that a man prepares and enables himself to serve efficiently God and his kingdom, and that he

---

[1] "Primum dilige Deum, deinde te ipsum, post haec dilige proximum sicut te ipsum. Prius tamen disce amare teipsum . . . Nam si teipsum non nosti amare, quomodo proximum poteris in veritate diligere." *Sermo* 368, n. 5; cf. St. Thomas, II-II, q. 26, a. 4 and 5.

works for his salvation. In other words he has responsibilities towards himself which love of self requires him to fulfill. This responsibility for one's self in many ways takes precedence over responsibility for one's neighbour. Our own development, sanctification and salvation depend more on our own responsible acts than does the salvation of our fellowmen. The reason is that we have received from God an immediate dominion only over our own self with its spiritual and bodily goods. From this it follows that our personal development and salvation is more immediately our obligation than that of our neighbour.

Of course the same responsibility that obliges us to be concerned with our sanctification and salvation will at a certain stage include increasing duties in the service of others. For we cannot attain to full maturity without placing ourselves at the service of others, and the way to salvation will lead the adult Christian to growing solicitude for his neighbour's salvation too.

b)   Well-ordered love of neighbours

As to inner appreciation, those persons merit a greater love who are closer to God. The more dedicated a person is in his service of God and the more perfect the likeness of God and Christ in him, the more he ought to be loved by inner esteem. This love consists above all in the joy over a person's goodness, which joy naturally includes the wish and will that this goodness may not suffer harm but be preserved.

As to active assistance, those persons ought to receive greater love who are in greater need and misery (spiritual or temporal). In instances of equal need, one ought usually to help first those who are more intimately related to oneself by bonds of kinship and friendship or who are entrusted to one's care. As a rule the order to be followed among one's relatives is: a person's spouse, children, parents, brothers and sisters, other relatives and friends. Those entrusted to one's care, like orphans to a foster-mother or foster-father, will ordinarily have the same claim to one's help as one's more distant relatives and friends, if not even precede them in the order of love. Under ordinary circumstances it would be sinful and may even be gravely sinful to overturn the order in essential matters, e.g. to give preference to one's more distant relatives to the neglect of one's spouse, children or parents. St. Thomas holds that in extreme need our parents must be preferred to all others, since we owe them our being. Yet B. Häring justly remarks that it is not easy to determine who among spouse, children and parents has the prior claim to help in instances of equal necessity.[1]

If however a spouse has abandoned the family and does hardly or not at all care for it any more, the abandoned spouse may well be justified in giving prior assistance to his children, parents, and even brothers and friends. The same is true if a brother or sister has alienated himself from the family, while other relatives or friendly neighbours have shown much attention to the remaining parents and children. The charitable benefactors rather than the alienated sibling will merit priority of assistance in cases of need.

Exception from the usual order of love can moreover be demanded for persons who are especially important for Church and society, or for the sake of the common weal in general. As a man must be ready to sacrifice his own life in defence of his nation and people, so must he be ready to sacrifice his wife or children for the same reason too, in spite of the close bonds of affection which unite him with them.

2.   *Order of love in relation to the gravity of needs*

Not all indigencies and calamities of our neighbours are equally great, but they differ in degree. Accordingly also the assistance to be given and the sacrifices demanded by fraternal love will vary. The needs may be spiritual or temporal, and both may be extreme, grave or ordinary. A person is constituted in extreme need if he is almost or completely unable to escape imminent danger of spiritual or temporal ruin, as there is danger of death (also spiritual death by loss of grace), heavy mutilation, long imprisonment. The need is grave if a person is not able to escape or free himself from great spiritual or temporal distress and harm without help, e.g. dire poverty, painful sickness. The need is ordinary if the difficulty to escape an evil is not great or the evil itself is slight.

a)   If a person is constituted in a need of the same order and gravity as his neighbour, Christian love does not command him to sacrifice his own goods for the neighbour's sake, thus placing himself in a condition worse than that of his neighbour. Never is it allowed to endanger one's own salvation seriously in order to help a neighbour in any kind of need. One can never further the true good of another by inflicting hurt on one's own

---

[1] B. Häring II, 1963, 363.

soul. Whoever harms his own salvation will, in a last analysis, cause detriment to the neighbour's true welfare too. Therefore if concern for the salvation of others involves a person in grave and imminent danger of sin, he must first concern himself with his own weakness. In such instances he himself is the neighbour most in distress and need. Obviously this does not apply to every little risk of spiritual graces in the service of others, for only in confrontation with such risks does a person mature and grow strong.

b) In extreme need of the religious and civic community one must be ready to defend and save it even at the sacrifice of fortune and life. The sacrifice of Christ was of this nature. He gave up his life in order to save mankind from spiritual death. The public witness for the faith and the martyrdom of Christians in times of persecution is in a similar way a defence of the spiritual values of the Christian community. Likewise soldiers must be prepared to sacrifice their lives in defence of their country.

c) In extreme necessity of one's neighbour one must assist him even at great personal inconveniences and material sacrifices. One is however not obliged to the sacrifice of one's life, unless the common welfare demands such a sacrifice for a person of particular importance. Moreover one is obliged to utmost sacrifices in property, health or other means only if there is an obligation of justice (for priests, physicians) or piety (obligations towards close relatives and benefactors). Priests and physicians will be obliged to greater risks of health and life in the service of the sick than ordinary persons. Nevertheless they must always view the welfare of the entire community and are not permitted to consume themselves for the one or for a few to the neglect of the many.

If handbooks traditionally demand that fraternal love ought to assist a neighbour in extreme *spiritual* need even at the risk of life and fortune, then this ruling seems of a rather theoretical nature. The manuals always further specify that there must be a well-founded hope of success and that the common weal does not forbid such sacrifice. These exceptions seem to apply to all instances in which the salvation of one or the other individual only is at stake. A priest is not obliged to baptize a child (e.g. in a burning house) or to assist a sick person (e.g. in times of persecution) if this would mean a more or less certain death. To the above reason that the common weal forbids such a sacrifice, one can furthermore add that the sick person has still the possibility to care for his salvation by means of perfect contrition, and that God will provide for the salvation of the unbaptized child as he does for so many others. The number of children who die without baptism and of people who die without the last sacraments is so great that one must earnestly assume that God has his own means to safeguard the universality of his salvific will by still other possibilities of salvation. This does not exclude that it may be easier for a person to obtain salvation with the aid of the sacraments and under assistance of a priest.

Under certain circumstances a very generous spirit of love may prompt a person to go much beyond what is laid down as obligatory. Parents are not seldom ready to sacrifice their lives in order to help their children in extreme need. Handbooks do not consider such a sacrifice as an obligation of love. In fact objectively it may often be better if parents preserve their life for those children who, in case of the parents' death, would remain without sufficient care. But such self-sacrificing love is doubtless worthy of great admiration.

d) In grave need one is obliged to assist one's neighbour as far as this is possible at ordinary sacrifice. Piety and office however may here again demand considerably greater sacrifices to avert or relieve great need of close relatives or of those entrusted to one's care. Thus, painful sickness of one's spouse, children or parents can demand the sale of one's car or of other property not necessary for one's life, if the sick relative can by this means be helped. Yet since love of self does not oblige to extraordinary treatments in cases of personal illness, one is not obliged to procure such means for another person's sickness either.

e) In ordinary need one is obliged to the ordinary works of charity, but not in every individual case. The extent of this charity will depend on a person's wealth. The wealthier a person, the more he is obliged to frequent and generous help for the needy.

3. *Love of enemies*

The Old Testament already enjoins love of enemy on repeated occasions, as has been pointed out earlier (Ex 23:4f; Lev 19:17f; Prov 24:17f; 25:21f; Sir 28:1-9). Outstanding examples of love of enemy are Joseph's love towards his brothers, who had sold him as a slave to Egypt, and David's high-minded forbearance towards king Saul's ill-will. In fact the OT nowhere says: "You shall hate your enemy" (Mt 5:43). But rabbis interpreted the texts of Scripture that refer to love of enemies as mere counsels and finally came to the construction: "You shall love your neighbour, but you may hate your enemy." Besides, the OT restricted love of enemy, just as love of neighbour in general, to fellow Israelites only, at best still extending it to the aliens in the country. The surrounding heathen nations were not included in this love. Moreover the lex talionis and many prayers still betray a revengeful attitude.

By contrast Jesus broadened the concept of love of enemies by extending it to every adversary without distinction of race and nation. Against the softening interpretation of the rabbis of his time he emphasized the truly obligatory character of the command. "But I say to you, Love your enemies and pray for those who persecute you" (Mt 5:44; cf. Lk 6:27f.32-36; Rom 12:14-21).

Faithful to the command of the Lord, Vatican II exhorts the believers to reverence and love for enemies. "The teaching of Christ even requires that we forgive injuries, and extends the law of love to include every enemy" (GS 28). Yet the same article calls attention to the necessary distinction between error, which always merits repudiation, and the person in error, who never loses the dignity of a person and hence remains entitled to respect and love. With this the traditional distinction between hatred of repudiation and hatred of enmity agrees (odium abominationis et odium inimicitiae). Hatred of repudiation is directed towards a person's errors, bad qualities, evil doings. It desires and aims at the elimination of these grievances and depravities. If it is a question of veritable evils, such hatred and the endeavour to remove them are justified. Hatred of enmity, on the other hand, is rejection of the enemy's person himself and the wish to inflict harm upon him and to destroy him. This hatred is the direct contrast to love of benevolence. If love effects unity, this hatred effects separation. In its perfected form it is gravely sinful. To it St. John's words apply: "Any one who hates his brother is a murderer" (1 Jn 3:15). The elemental tendency of hatred appears imperfectly in wishes to inflict minor evils upon an enemy.

The objective of love of enemy in general is the same as that of every fraternal love: sincere esteem of the good a person has received and possibly realized, even as an enemy; and furtherance in the task he is called to accomplish in the service of

God. This latter aspect of fraternal love, furtherance of a person in his divine calling, will assume a particular mode in the case of enemies. The particular objective of love of enemies is removal and destruction of the evil roots and causes of enmity. But lastly this negative goal takes aim at a positive one: restoration of the goodness and wholeness which has been damaged or lost by the enmity. God's love for sinners, which is in a very true sense love for enemies, most clearly reveals this characteristic of love of enemies: destruction of the roots of sin and restoration of man's lost integrity by the renewed gift of divine grace.

The decision on the means and ways by which a man is to confront an enmity must be guided by this objective of love of enemy. Christ's admonition to turn the other cheek to one who strikes us (Lk 6:29f), for example, calls the disciple to a most loving patience. "However, we must be ready for the external, literal fulfillment of such a lofty ideal only when it is necessary or at least useful for the conversion of our enemy. But such restraint is not required or even permitted when our forbearance would merely confirm insolence and intransigence. Our Lord's own example in His conduct toward the servant of the High Priest is the best illustration of the passage about 'turning of the other cheek'."[1] Hence those means ought to be adopted that secure best the aim of a conversion of the enemy and reconciliation with him, yet also his necessary restraint: be it by most generous forbearance, or be it by energetic resistance and, if need be, by invocation of the law.

Love of enemy must verify and manifest itself above all in the following ways:

a) *Spirit of forgiveness.* Love of enemy always excludes malevolent hatred and revengefulness. Positively it demands readiness to reconciliation with the offender if he sincerely tries to make up for the offence. Of course as long as the offending or hostile party does not even acknowledge the faultiness and guilt of his behaviour, no pardon is possible. Only sins and offences can be pardoned. If the offender does not truly admit of any fault from his side — which includes the determination to continue in his way of acting — no matter for pardon is at hand. An oppressor can hardly be forgiven as long as he continues to victimize and to exploit his subjects without any scruples. Even God can only forgive those sins for which we repent. But

[1] Häring II, 1963, 364.

just as God is always ready to forgive the sinner as soon as he converts, so a man must always be ready to reconcile with his enemy as soon as he repents.

Therefore the offended party is bound in charity to respond favourably to a sincere offer of reconciliation and to accept a reasonable restitution for the injury inflicted. In principle the offender or the one with greater guilt is obliged to take the first step towards reconciliation. Yet the spirit of forgiveness may not seldom demand that the offended side, especially if in the course of the conflict he has also incurred some guilt, prepares the way to reconciliation by a positive step. In instances of deeply rooted enmity of long standing, as may happen between neighbours or even close relatives and even religious, it is best to demand that both parties make a decisive step towards reconciliation. Opportune occasions for this are parish missions or retreats. Apologies need not always be explicitly made. In many cases an apology can be made implicitly, e.g. by a special mark of attention or by a courteous greeting.

Spirit of forgiveness does not require a general renunciation of the right to restitution and compensation. The offender has the obligation to restore the damage caused, and the offended party has the right to demand it. Even though an offender has asked for forgiveness, judicial action may still be brought against him, e.g. if this is the only safe way to secure restitution, or if it is necessary to protect the community against similar offences. But the motive for legal action ought not to be hatred and thirst for revenge. The warning of St. Alphonsus is certainly in place: "Love of justice is only too readily made a cloak hypocritically masking the spirit of revenge."[1] If the damage inflicted were insignificant, charity will often oblige to renounce one's right to restitution. Such an obligation exists above all if the other's loss through restitution would be unduly great.[2]

b) *Ordinary signs of respect and regard.* Such signs are especially response to greetings and prayers, although the signs will differ according to person, places and times. If an enmity exists between close relatives (brothers, sisters, children and parents), visits at special celebrations (weddings, baptisms) and other occasional visits or casual greetings by mail will easily pertain to the ordinary signs of respect. These signs are required

---

[1] Homo apostolicus, tr. 4, n. 17; cf. Theologia moralis, lib. II, n. 29, footnote.

[2] Cf. Jone, 1963, nr. 137.

in order to counteract a still further deepening of hatred, to give proof of one's readiness for reconciliation and not seldom also to avoid scandal. Thus open enmity between two priests would be the cause of a rather great scandal among the faithful.

For serious reasons however the customary signs of respect may be temporarily refused, e.g. in order to bring a misdoing home to a person and to call forth a change of his heart. Married people might well show their deep displeasure and grief in this way towards one who has seduced the other spouse and is endangering the unity and harmony of the family. Parents may act in a similar way towards their children, if this seems the appropriate means to correct their misbehaviour. Yet these reasons do not equally hold for a refusal of prayers for the offender and enemy. At least in a general way he should be included in prayers for conversion and correction of those who do wrong. For this is the will of Christ, that we ought to pray for those who hate us and do good to them (Mt 5:44; Lk 6:27f).

c) *Assistance in case of necessity.* In instances of extreme need, one is bound to help one's enemy just as one is bound to help everybody else as far as one can do so, e.g. by alms, food, clothing, first aid in accidents, etc. " 'If your enemy is hungry, feed him; if he is thirsty, give him drink; for by so doing you will heap burning coals upon his head.' Do not be overcome by evil, but overcome evil with good" (Rom 12:20f). Assistance in other needs is usually not commanded, but may often be advised. If further help should prove a means of bringing about conversion of the enemy and reconciliation with him, one would be obliged to it. Likewise one would be obliged not only to the ordinary but also to the particular signs of respect and love in such circumstances.

The practical realization of the above principles and demands will in concrete often encounter great difficulties. Spiritual guides and directors need great prudence in dealing with instances of enmity, hatred and resentment at offences. They "should not make excessive demands from one who has been very deeply hurt. One should not demand complete and utter forgiveness in one brief moment."[1] Rather they ought to allow for the psychological fact that tempers cool slowly. In the meantime they will at least endeavour to lead those who have turned to them for assistance, to pray for the grace of pardoning love and for the conversion of their enemies. Note that the forgiveness of injuries and the

---

[1] Häring, II, 1963, 369.

patient suffering of injustice belong to the spiritual works of mercy (fifth and sixth works).

B. Primary manifestations of fraternal love

Fraternal love manifests itself most directly in the bodily works of charity, such as relief for the poor, the sick, the crippled, those stricken by catastrophies, and in the spiritual works of charity, like education of the neglected, encouragement of the afflicted, promotion of a healthy public atmosphere, propagation of the Christian message. According to the "Decree on the Apostolate of the Laity" (AA) by Vatican II, all these works belong to the tasks of the Christian apostolate and constitute the apostolic activity of the People of God. In many instances this apostolate is carried out in private by individuals or by private institutions, but it is also pursued by official organizations of the Church, like the Catholic Action and similar groups.

The duties of the apostolate concern all members of the Church and in many instances particularly the laity. It is simply a consequence of Christ's commandment of love that no individual member of his mystical body, the Church, is dispensed from the duty of making each other's welfare their common care (cf. 1 Cor 12:25).

The goal of the apostolate is of a very comprehensive nature. It comprises the salvation of men as well as the renewal of the whole temporal order, i.e. all the spiritual and corporal needs. "The mission of the Church is not only to bring to men the message and grace of Christ, but also to penetrate and perfect the temporal sphere with the spirit of the gospel," and thus "to appropriate the whole universe into a new creation, initially here on earth, fully on the last day" (AA 5).

Christians have received a special equipment for this task by baptism, through which they obtain the graces necessary for a Christian life, and still more by confirmation, which is intended to strengthen them for their work in the world. These graces must be activated by a life of intimate union with Christ in the Church. For the Lord has said, "He who abides in me, and I in him, he it is that bears much fruit, for apart from me you can do nothing" (Jn 15:5).

Insofar as particularly the official apostolate of the Church is concerned, "union with those whom the Holy Spirit has assigned to rule God's Church (cf. Acts 20:28) is an essential element of the Christian apostolate" (AA 23). Though the priests are not the leaders but only spiritual counselors in the apostolate of the lay people, there must be obedience to the directives of the hierarchy to guarantee the effective cooperation of all the forces.

Finally "the common heritage of the gospel and the common duty of Christian witness resulting from it recommend and frequently require the cooperation of Catholics with other Christians, a cooperation exercised on the part of individuals and communities within the Church." Moreover the promotion of common human values frequently calls for cooperation with non-Christians as well (AA 27).

I. Corporal works of charity

Holy Scriptures of the Old and New Testament regard practical help in bodily needs as a foremost expression of fraternal love, as already mentioned earlier. Christ himself wanted such works to be signs of his messianic mission (cf. Mt 11:2-5). In a like manner Vatican II regards assistance in bodily needs as an especially vivid expression of Christian charity. While the Church "rejoices in the undertakings of others, she claims works of charity as her own inalienable duty and right. For this reason, pity for the needy and the sick, and works of charity and mutual aid intended to relieve human needs of every kind are held in special honour by the Church." Charitable works "can and should reach out to absolutely every person and every need. Wherever there are people in need of food and drink, clothing, housing, medicine, employment, education; wherever men lack the facilities necessary for living a truly human life or are tormented by hardships or poor health, or suffer exile or imprisonment, there Christian charity should seek them out and find them, console them with eager care and relieve them with the gift of help. This obligation is imposed above all upon every prosperous person and nation" (AA 8).

1. *The corporal works of charity in general*

Tradition lists seven corporal works of charity or mercy: to feed the hungry, to give drink to the thirsty, to befriend the homeless, to clothe the naked, to visit the sick, to console the captive, to bury the dead. Lactantius first compiled this number, following the judgment discourse of Mt 25:35ff, from where the first six corporal works are taken, and Tobit 1:17, from where the last one is added. In evaluating this list, one must keep in mind that it corresponds to the needs of the ancient world, and besides is also influenced by the pleasure in symbolic numbers. Love must sense the particular needs of each time anew and find out where assistance of fraternal charity is called for.

Concern for the poor and the needy has been an outstanding characteristic of the Church throughout the centuries. History gives evidence of the Church's solicitous care for the needy at all times. The first Christian community held almsgiving in high esteem (Acts 2:44f; 4:34-37) and soon chose deacons and widows to dedicate themselves in a special way to the needy members of the community (Acts 6:1-6; 1 Tim 5:9f). At the suggestion of Paul, the better-off communities collected alms for the poor community of Jerusalem (2 Cor 8-9). Almshouses and hospices were founded in the time of the earliest Fathers of the Church. For many centuries the organized care for the poor and the orphans, for the crippled and the sick, and for other groups in need was almost exclusively in the hands of the Church. In particular, religious orders and other pious communities of men and women dedicated themselves to this task. And although the modern state has created many public social services for different kinds of calamities, there is still much room left for the charitable work of the Church.

As fields of charitable love in the society of today the following can be listed: The sick and especially the incurably and chronically ill need nursing. The handicapped and mental defectives need assistance and care. Families with special marital or educational problems should be helped to overcome their difficulties. Youths in precarious conditions need sympathetic direction and centres or clubs open for recreation and entertainment during free time. Orphans should be given homes, preferably by families who adopt them. Workers far from home and emigrants are in want of friendly interest and contacts. Addicts and those in danger of addiction must be helped out of danger. Former prisoners are to be rehabilitated. Those who are victims of loneliness and abandonment, especially old people, should be reintegrated in the community. And institutes for the training of the many types of social welfare workers are to be established and maintained.[1] Yet besides these more specialized works of charity, also the ordinary ones still largely retain their relevance,

---

[1] Cf. art. "Charity, III. Charitable Organizations" by Erich Reisch, in: Sacramentum Mundi, vol. I, 1968, 295f.

such as to give alms to the needy (if not at home, then abroad) or to visit the lonely and the sick.

A new and immense field of Christian love has been opened by the great wants and problems of the developing nations, which need financial help, socio-economic cooperation by voluntary workers, training of experts in all fields, etc.

Whether assistance is given to individuals or to groups and nations, it must always be governed by certain fundamental virtues. The very documents of Vatican II call attention to this. The Council Fathers warn that "the purity of one's charitable intentions should not be stained by a quest for personal advantage or by any thirst for domination" (AA 8). All help ought to be motivated by a sincere concern for the true welfare of those in need and by reverent solicitude for their peculiar calling in the design of God.

Furthermore not only the motive of the giver must be correct, also the mode of giving must reflect the spirit of charity. Gentleness, tact and delicacy in the offer of help ought to accompany the gift of fraternal love. A condescending or sour and impatient attitude towards the poor mars the most generous aid. "God loves a cheerful giver" (2 Cor 9:7; cf. Rom 12:8; Sir 35:9). Those who are truly needy ought to be treated with sincere regard and sympathetic kindness. "The dignity of the person being helped should be respected with the utmost delicacy" (AA 8).

Finally the exercise of charity must also be governed by prudence. The warning of Scriptures not to give indiscriminately but only to those who merit help, is certainly in place (Sir 12:1-7). Those who are too lazy to work do not deserve the same assistance as those who cannot work and are helpless, or who are willing to work but destitute. "If any one will not work, let him not eat" (2 Thess 3:10). Besides, prudent charity will endeavour to help, if possible, in such a way that the recipient may gradually be able to help himself and become self-sufficient.

Fraternal love has quite appropriately been characterised as the "sacrament of love".[1] It is not only apt to open the heart of the recipient to divine love and possibly also to the Christian message. Fraternal charity is still much more a sacrament of divine love for those who practise it in word and deed. If Vatican II says that even those can attain to salvation who through no fault of their own have not arrived at an explicit

---

[1] Häring II, 1963. 390.

knowledge of God but "who strive to live a good life, thanks to his grace" (LG 16), then their good life becomes the sacrament that saves them. A good life will most naturally manifest itself in works of fraternal charity. They are a means and sacrament of salvation for those who do them.

2.   *Principles concerning material assistance*

In the past the obligation to material assistance in instances of calamity and need was usually looked upon as an obligation concerning the individual person. But recent documents of the Church justly stress that such an obligation also applies to entire political communities, if they enjoy abundance of material goods, while other countries exist in extreme poverty. This obligation is plainly stated by Vatican II: "As for the advanced nations, they have a very heavy obligation to help the developing peoples" (GS 86). The duty of solidarity that rests on individuals exists also for nations. "We must repeat once more that the superfluous wealth of rich countries should be placed at the service of poor nations. The rule which up to now held good for the benefit of those nearest to us, must today be applied to all the needy of this world" (Pope Paul VI).[1] Nations are often not yet sufficiently aware of this obligation. It must be admitted that the application of the principle of fraternal responsibility and solidarity to the level of political communities was not so much stressed until now and is of a recent nature. Yet it is thoroughly justified. Hence it is necessary to educate the conscience of nations, especially of those who are more blessed with the goods of this world, to recognize this obligation and to act accordingly.

a)   Prior to works of charity are the demands of justice. With good reason Vatican II insists that "the demands of justice should first be satisfied, lest the giving of what is due in justice be represented as the offering of a charitable gift" (AA 8). Therefore a man is strictly obliged first to pay just wages and to give the just compensation for any work, materials and products he has ordered and asked for. Landlords who do not pay the full wage to their employees but provide housing, schooling for the children, assistance in sickness, etc., cannot consider these benefits for the workers as charitable works, but they constitute obligations in justice, at least to that part which is compensation for the

---

[1] Paul VI: Populorum Progressio, nr. 49; cf. John XXIII: Mater et Magistra, nr. 157-165.

reduction of the wage. This does not preclude that such a system may be warrantable in certain circumstances and of advantage for the workers too.

No employer or customer can make up for defrauded remunerations by means of alms or other gratuities. He must restore the defrauded amount in justice. It belongs to this context when Pope Paul VI calls attention to the fact that "the rectification of inequitable trade relations between powerful nations and weak nations" is a "duty of social justice".[1] Where economic conditions differ too widely from country to country, the rule of free trade can produce unfair results. In particular the prices of raw materials, the predominant export of less industrialized countries, can prove to be unjustly low. Hence the developing countries gain "the impression that what was being given them with one hand was being taken away with the other."[2] It is an urgent duty that such inequality and overreaching be eliminated by international agreements among all the parties and nations concerned.

Justice equally requires that prior to charitable donations citizens first pay the taxes which the state imposes for the general welfare. The duty to pay taxes is an obligation of legal justice. "Only in instances of great need in which the state cannot or will not render necessary assistance is one permitted, under certain circumstances, to substitute for the tax imposed a form of direct contribution under the guise of alms."[3]

b) All superfluous goods must be used in a socially responsible way, and that in particular for the needy. It is not demanded that all the superfluities be spent in alms. A socially fruitful use of material goods in other ways may often prove even more advantageous for the welfare of one's fellowmen. But the social character of all property requires that one's excess in possessions be used with a sense of social responsibility for the good of the needy and of society.[4] That is the truth behind the sharp statements of the Fathers of the Church that all superfluous goods belong to the poor. "You return to the poor

---

[1] Paul VI: Populorum Progressio, nr. 44.

[2] Ib. nr. 56.

[3] Häring II, 1963, 399f.

[4] Cf. Leo XIII: Rerum Novarum, nr. 36: "Whoever has received from the bounty of God a greater share of goods, whether corporeal and external, or of the soul, has received them for this, namely that he employ them for his own perfection and, likewise, as a servant of Divine Providence, for the benefit of others."

something of his own", writes St. Ambrose of the surplus in wealth which a rich man ought to distribute to the poor.[1] And St. Augustine declares in one of his homilies: "The superfluities which you possess should be the necessities of life for the poor."[2] It contradicts the right order if a man does not use his superfluities in one or the other way for the good of his needy fellowmen.

A most effective and praiseworthy way of placing one's wealth at the service of one's fellowmen is the creation of opportunities for work. In fact the establishment of industries and commercial enterprises makes the aggregation of greater funds desirable, since such enterprises give work to numerous people and essentially contribute to the progress of a nation. Other ways to use one's wealth for the good of the community are provision of opportunities for education, support of social services, furtherance of other community concerns like scientific investigation or cultural programs. Naturally there is also the obligation to alms in the strict sense if there is need.

c) Assistance in form of alms or material donations is a strict obligation where this is the only way to help the needy and where one's wealth permits it. Not everybody is well-to-do. Some have just enough to support their own life; others have the means necessary for the maintenance of their social status but not beyond; and again others have superfluities in the strict sense. The obligation to alms is of course different for the different groups.

(1) One is not obliged to give alms from the goods necessary for one's own life. Such a man is poor himself. And every man has the obligation and right to care above all for his own life and that of his dependents.

(2) One is obliged to give alms from the goods necessary for one's social status in extreme necessity of one's neighbour. But if a person has not more than what is necessary for his state of life, he is not strictly obliged to do more than to alleviate the extreme need. Furthermore this obligation does not equally urge in case of calamities in far away regions. The obligation to such drastic sacrifices concerns first those who live in the very region of calamity and in the corresponding country. The duty to emergency aid from *strict* superfluities however is incumbent

---

[1] St. Ambrose, De Nabuthe 12,53 (PL 14, 747).
[2] St. Augustine, Sermo 61 (PL 38, 413).

on all wealthy people, even if they live in far away places, provided they can reach the needy with their aid.

(3) One is gravely obliged to give alms from one's super-fluous possessions, especially in grave necessity of one's neighbour. There is also a serious obligation to help the poor in ordinary need, though not in every instance. If a loan suffices, one need not make a donation. This holds in instances of extreme necessity too.

Those who have only enough for a life according to their social status are not obliged to the same generosity towards the poor as those who possess superfluities. Nevertheless they sin venially if they never do anything for the poor.

It is to be noted that the obligation to assist a person in extreme necessity from one's superfluities is considered by St. Thomas[1] and by Leo XIII[2] as an obligation not of mere charity but of justice, just as there is a right to food-theft in such a condition. In extreme need the social character of possessions prevails against the right to private property, i.e. of that private property which is not necessary for one's life. John XXIII also applies this principle to emergency aid between nations. "There are countries which produce consumer goods and especially farm products in excess, while in other countries large segments of the population suffer from misery and hunger. Justice and humanity demand that the former come to the aid of the latter. To destroy or to squander goods that other people need in order to live, is to offend against justice and humanity."[3]

II. Spiritual works of charity

Just as the great commandment of love obliges one to have concern for the material needs and welfare of one's fellowman, so it likewise obliges to have concern for his spiritual needs. The life of grace and man's eternal salvation certainly constitute a most essential good of the spiritual order, more important than any other. Nevertheless it would be one-sided and wrong to limit the spiritual works of charity more or less to the protection and promotion of the life of virtue and grace. There are other spiritual values as well whose furtherance is a true work of

---

[1] St. Thomas, II-II, q. 118, a. 4, ad 2, citing St. Basil.

[2] Leo XIII: Rerum Novarum, nr. 36.

[3] John XXIII: Mater et Magistra, nr. 161.

fraternal charity, such as the goods of education, of capability to efficient work, of social integration, of successful confrontation with the problems of life. In fact instruction of the ignorant and consolation of the afflicted have always been considered works of spiritual mercy.

1. *The spiritual works of charity in general*

Tradition again lists seven spiritual works of mercy: to instruct the ignorant, to counsel the perplexed, to console the sorrowing, to correct the erring, to forgive injuries, to bear wrongs patiently, to pray for the living and the dead. All these works still retain their validity today, although their scope has to be broadened and completed. Fraternal love includes the following fields of spiritual assistance and mercy:

(1) *Prayer.* Christians ought to be apostolic in their prayers, i.e. not merely centre their prayers around their own needs, but also include the needs of their fellowmen. St. Paul therefore urges "that supplications, prayers, intercessions, and thanksgivings be made for all men, . . . This is good, and it is acceptable in the sight of God our Saviour, who desires all men to be saved and to come to the knowledge of the truth" (1 Tim 2:1-3). The prayers of the Church and especially the prayers of the liturgy have always been exemplary of this (cf. the Prayers of the Faithful in the Mass and other liturgical services). It is natural that a person's special attention will often be directed to those close to him and to their particular needs. But Christian charity cannot limit itself to a man's relatives and friends. It will extend prayers to the needy neighbour too. And the wants of the civic community and the great concerns of Christ's reign should no less be close to his heart, such as the equitable distribution of goods, a just and prudent government, the restoration of Christian unity, the universal establishment of Christ's kingdom of justice and peace.

(2) *Vicarious suffering.* In the Mystical Body of Christ all suffering must be borne together with Christ for love of our fellowmen and for the redemption of the world. This apostolate is to be exercised especially by patient acceptance of the trials and sufferings of life, yet also by voluntary, expiatory renunciations. The whole order of the Mystical Body of Christ is the salvific order of vicarious atonement of the Head for the members

and of the members for one another. "I rejoice in my sufferings for your sake, and in my flesh I complete what is lacking in Christ's afflictions for the sake of his body, that is, the church" (Col 1:24). "Therefore I endure everything for the sake of the elect, that they also may obtain the salvation which in Christ Jesus goes with eternal glory" (2 Tim 2:10). The Christian can truly be convinced that all his sufferings, willingly accepted for love of God and love of fellowmen, serve the growth of God's kingdom and have redemptive value, even though human insight cannot fully understand how.

(3) *Good example.* Holy Scripture is aware of the great power and influence of a concrete, good example. In the Gospels Christ set his own person and life as an example for his disciples (Mk 10:44f par; Jn 8:12; 12:26; 13:15.34; 15:12), and so do the other writings of the New Testament (1 Cor 11:1; 1 Thess 1:6; 1 Pet 2:12; 1 Jn 2:6). The fast spread of Christianity in the early period was largely due to the personal conviction and example of the first Christians. In a similar manner the great saints have been examples and guides on the way to God for their contemporaries and beyond for later ages. This is one of the reasons why the Church appreciates and promotes the veneration of the saints. It does not come as a surprise that the findings of present-day psychology have confirmed the old conviction of the significance of exemplary persons.[1]

In the Decree on the Apostolate of the Laity, Vatican II regards the witness of a Christian life as one of the first forms of the apostolate. "The very testimony of their Christian life, and good works done in a supernatural spirit, have the power to draw men to belief and to God; for the Lord says, 'Even so let your light shine before men, in order that they may see your good works and give glory to your Father in heaven' (Mt 5:16)" (AA 6; also AG 11; 21; 36).

Consequently charity obliges one to the example of a good life. No individual, regardless of his state of life, is exempt from this obligation, though certain groups of people have a particularly grave obligation because of their office, like priests, religious, parents, educators or public officials, whose conduct may easily influence others. The good example is not primarily constituted by individual acts of exemplary character, but by a person's entire

---

[1] "The religious flame is enkindled much more by men than by books" (Eduard Spranger: *Psychologie des Jugendalters.* — Heidelberg: Quelle und Meyer, 1963, 262).

way of life which flows from the conviction of the values it professes. There are however occasions where consideration of the effect which an objectively lawful action or omission may have on others demands a person to omit or to perform the act, in order not to be taken for a bad example and for an excuse to sin.

(4) *Encouragement in hardships and sympathy in suffering.* Words of encouragement and recognition are of greatest importance for children and youths, who have no sufficient standards yet to evaluate their work themselves. But also for adults encouragement and approval do not seldom constitute a great benefit, especially in times of depression and loneliness. Besides, with the reassurance of others every good and useful work will easier be accomplished. Therefore Scripture exhorts: "Let us consider how to stir up one another to love and good works, not neglecting to meet together, as is the habit of some, but encouraging one another" (Heb 10:24f; also 1 Thess 5:11.14). Likewise sympathy in sickness, at the loss of a close relative or good friend, and in other sufferings very often signifies for the afflicted a great work of mercy and consolation, which is most gratefully felt.

(It is to be noted that the visiting of the sick as the fifth corporal work of mercy and the consolation of captives as the sixth lastly amount to the consolation of the sorrowing as the third spiritual work of mercy. Hence these two corporal works of mercy could more correctly be placed under the spiritual works of mercy.)

(5) *Apostolate of instruction.* Ignorance can rightly be considered as a kind of spiritual poverty, which gives a man less opportunity to unfold his abilities and resources. It puts him at a disadvantage with regard to those who are well instructed and deprives him of the possibility to compete with them efficiently. Hence instruction of those who lack knowledge certainly belongs to the works of charity. This applies to general human, to professional and to religious knowledge. Vatican II is fully aware that developing nations need not only financial assistance, but also opportunities for both basic and more advanced training. "Through education and professional formation, the citizens of each nation should be prepared to shoulder the various offices of economic and social life. Such preparation needs the help of foreign experts" (GS 85; cf. AG 41).

Religious instruction often goes hand in hand with scientific and professional training, though at other times it is an independent task of its own. Even in so-called "developed" countries the message of Christ is often not sufficiently known and appreciated. Hence, "the law of love, which is the Lord's greatest commandment, impels all the faithful to promote God's glory through the spread of His kingdom and to obtain for all men that eternal life which consists in knowing the only true God and Him whom He sent, Jesus Christ (cf. Jn 17:3). On all Christians therefore is laid the splendid burden of working to make the divine message of salvation known and accepted by all men throughout the world" (AA 3; also 6).

(6) *Apostolate of the social milieu and public life.* The nature and need of this apostolate have been aptly formulated by Vatican II. "The apostolate of the social milieu, that is, the effort to infuse a Christian spirit into the mentality, customs, laws, and structures of the community in which a person lives, is so much the duty and responsibility of the laity that it can never be properly performed by others . . . ; it is here in the arena of their labour, profession, studies, residence, leisure, and companionship that laymen have a special opportunity to help their brothers" (AA 13). Naturally priests and religious are not exempt from this task. They too have opportunities to penetrate the social milieu with the Spirit of the gospel. But it remains true that laymen have more and better chances to work in this way for the spiritual weal of fellowmen and of the community.

An important part of this apostolate is the responsible engagement in the public life of the community. "Catholics should feel themselves obliged to promote the true common good. Thus, they should make the weight of their opinion felt, so that civil authority may act with justice, and laws may conform to moral precepts and the common good. Catholics skilled in public affairs and adequately enlightened in faith and Christian doctrine should not refuse to administer public affairs, since by performing this office in a worthy manner they can simultaneously advance the common good and prepare the way for the gospel" (AA 14). In these latter instances, works and obligations of charity already turn into civic duties. Nevertheless they also have a place here, since one will hardly be able to draw a clear-cut distinction between the two types of duties.

Correction of the erring is a further work of spiritual mercy. Since the conditions and the order of correction demand a more extensive treatment, this work shall be dealt with in a separate section.

2.   *Fraternal correction*

Fraternal correction is the instruction of a neighbour on a fault of his in order to turn him away from this evil. Today the same reality is often expressed by the term criticism, which criticism of course ought to be constructive. The term is especially applied to correction of those in authority by their subjects.

Fraternal correction is of a private nature, not of judicial force nor seconded by any legal sanctions. Also correction by an authority in its quality as father and helper can still be considered as fraternal correction, though it is usually called paternal correction. Judicial correction, which includes canonical correction, on the other hand is the official correction of a member of a community by an authority, performed under certain formalities (written or before witnesses) in order that its execution can be attested and that it can serve, if there be need, as basis for legal actions.

Holy Scripture repeatedly comments on the subject, of fraternal correction. Wisdom literature of the OT already exhorts: "Question a friend, perhaps he did not do it; but if he did anything, so that he may do it no more. Question a neighbour, perhaps he did not say it; but if he said it, so that he may not say it again" (Sir 19:13f). Christ himself gives the question express attention and instructs his disciples not only on the obligation but also on the right order of correction. "If your brother sins against you, go and tell him his fault, between you and him alone. If he listens to you, you have gained your brother. But if he does not listen, take one or two others along with you, . . . If he refuses to listen to them, tell it to the church; and if he refuses to listen even to the church, let him be to you as a Gentile and tax collector" (Mt 18:15-17). The words "against you" in verse 18:15, that seem to limit corrections to instances in which one's own rights are at stake, are omitted by the best Greek manuscripts and by the parallel passage in Luke 17:3. The text in Luke simply reads: "If your brother sins, rebuke him." St. James strongly emphasizes the charitable, meritorious character of brotherly correction. "Whoever brings back a sinner from the error of his way will save his soul from death and will cover a multitude of sins" (Jas 5:20). The general duty to correction is expressed by Paul in 1 Thess 5:14 and the duty to paternal correction in 1 Tim 5:20: "As for those who persist in sin, rebuke them in the presence of all, so that the rest may stand in fear."

The inner reason for the duty to fraternal correction is the same as for all works of mercy: the duty to avert evils from a neighbour if one can morally do so, and to enable him to serve the welfare of the community and to promote God's glory efficiently. Yet at times fraternal correction is also required by the right and duty to defend one's own rights or the rights of others and the community.

Object of fraternal correction are all faults of our neighbour that cause detriment to him or to others, most especially grave sins, but also lesser sins and even imperfections and defects in good manners. It can be a great benefit for a brother to inform him, for example, on correct table manners and proper dress, since deficiencies of this kind can easily handicap social contacts and relations.

a) *Conditions of fraternal correction.* In order that a fraternal correction be obligatory or often even merely opportune, the following conditions must be fulfilled:

(1) The neighbour must be in real need of one's help. That is to say, he must be unable to improve himself sufficiently without fraternal aid. And besides, nobody else more capable or at least equally capable is willing to help him.

(2) There must be a well-founded hope that the correction will prove fruitful. For this reason there is usually no obligation to correct strangers.

Especially persons in authority will nevertheless sometimes be bound to correction, even though there is no hope of success, in order not to give the impression of silent approval from their side. A bishop, for example, will easily have the obligation to object against disregard of at least more important liturgical prescriptions by one or the other of his priests, even if his chance to change the attitude of his subject is slim.

Persons who are obliged to correct others, but know from experience that they are not likely to succeed, may at times be advised to find somebody else who is willing to undertake the task and who will more easily be successful.

(3) The correction must be possible without dispropor-tionate personal sacrifices. A certain amount of courage and effort is involved in almost every correction and hence to be

assumed as part of the obligation. This is due to the fact that correction of others frequently exposes one to the risk of non-acceptance or indignant reaction from the side of the one corrected, even if performed in a proper way. Yet if one must fear great disadvantages in case one's correction is badly accepted, one is not obliged to it, except the fault in question constitutes a serious threat for the common good. Even in the latter case at least some reasonable hope of success must exist (cf. condition 2); if not, other means ought to be adopted to protect the common good. Bishops, pastors, parents, etc. are in virtue of their office and state obliged to correct those entrusted to their care even at the cost of great personal sacrifices.

The degree of the obligation to fraternal correction depends on the gravity of the harm to be feared. The greater the harm to be feared from a neighbour's fault for him or for others, the greater the obligation to correct him.

b) *The right manner of correction.* Fraternal correction must have its motive in sincere concern for the neighbour's welfare and in zeal for God's glory and reign. Also justified defence of one's own rights or the rights of a third person can warrant the correction of a neighbour. On the other hand corrections may not proceed from personal dislikings, resentments and revengefulness, since criticisms from such sources are not of a truly constructive nature and therefore not sufficiently justified. Besides, they tend to enlarge shortcomings unduly or to find apparent but not real mistakes, which causes the correction to be unjust and therefore condemned to almost certain failure.

The manner of correction ought to be marked by modesty, prudence and benevolence. As far as possible the correction or admonition should be produced in a kind and gentle way. "If a man is overtaken by any trespass, you who are spiritual should restore him in a spirit of gentleness. Look to yourself, lest you too be tempted" (Gal 6:1; cf. Mt 7:4). Only when a person proves insensitive to friendly words and does not take them serious, would an energic and harsh demeanour be permitted, or when an arrogant and ruthless behaviour calls for a severe response. Yet even then the correction ought to be tempered by modest awareness of one's own insufficiencies.

Prudence will further know how to choose the right moment and wait for an opportune time, even though new faults may meanwhile be added. To nag one's subjects or fellowmen for every petty failure is a gross violation not only of prudence but also of charity, since by force of natural limitations man is not capable of absolute perfection. It also includes a disregard of the first condition of fraternal correction, inasmuch as a good deal of defects tend to correct themselves in the course of time, which process can be given play especially in the case of minor faults.

Finally, in order to save the feelings and not seldom also the reputation of the one to be corrected, corrections should preferably be performed in private, in particular if the fault is not public. This leads us to the order of correction.

c) *The right order of correction.* As to the question of who among a person's fellowmen has the prior obligation to correct, first in this duty are those who are closest to a man in the order of love.

The order as to the different kinds of private and public correction is normally the following: A neighbour who commits a fault or errs should first be corrected alone in private. If this is of no effect, one or the other person should be called in to confirm the fact of the fault and the need of a redress. If even then he will not listen, he should be reported to those in authority, that in virtue of their office they correct him, though at first by a paternal correction only. If also this correction does not meet with success and remedy of the situation is necessary, the case must be handed over to the judicial authority, whose judicial correction is usually enforced by sanctions in case the person in fault should refuse to amend (cf. Mt 18:15-17).

There are however exceptions to this order. Immediate report to the authority is justified or even required if the fault will become public at any rate; if authoritative correction promises to be much more efficient; and especially if the common good or the good of another person is at stake. Although especially in families and institutions of training for youth petty denouncing should be avoided, serious dangers for members of the community must be reported to the respective authority as soon as the case requires. "Subjects should be instructed in this duty, particularly since so many entertain the erroneous notion that every kind of reporting is dastardly, even though it may be essential to prevent great evils."[1] Of course the superior must carefully weigh the information and the character of those who report to him. Besides, he must also grant the accused

---

[1] Häring II, 1963, 429.

opportunity to defend himself ("audiatur et altera pars"), a rule which he should not easily ignore.

Anonymous denunciations are on principle to be declined, from the side of the subjects as well as of the superiors, since such procedure opens the door to vicious, untrue charges for motives of rivalry, resentment or revenge, against which there is no defence. On the other hand the person who reports a fault has naturally also the right that he be protected against retaliation and therefore his name be kept secret by the superior. This holds above all for instances of more serious nature, where revengeful reactions are more easily to be feared. If there is a real need to reveal the name of the one who reports, he should first be asked for his permission.

C.   The virtue of justice[1]

Justice is a much invoked claim and virtue. All men appeal to justice and demand justice. But at the same time justice is a much controverted concept. It is the subject of many disputes and arguments. Justice is one of those fundamental notions of moral and juridical life which cannot easily be defined, though they are very essential to them.

I.   Virtue of justice in Holy Scripture

Justice or righteousness is one of the centrally important biblical concepts. But being rather many-sided, it is difficult to define. In the context of Holy Scripture the usage of words pertaining to justice is much wider than the usage of these words in the present profane and even religious language.

In one of the biblical usages, justice is the familiar moral virtue, sometimes in the sense of a social norm, more often with its scope so enlarged as to extend to the total observance of all God's commandments. Correlatively God demonstrates his justice in that he is a model of integrity; first of all in the guidance of his people and of each individual person; and then as the God of retribution, rewarding or punishing according to one's works.

---

[1] References: Giorgio del Vecchio: Justice. An Historical and Philosophical Essay. — Edinburgh: University Press, 1956. Otto A. Bird: The Idea of Justice. — New York/London: Frederick A. Praeger, 1967. Josef Pieper: The Four Cardinal Virtues: Prudence, Justice, Fortitude, Temperance. — University of Notre Dame Press, 1967. John Rawls: A Theory of Justice. — Cambridge, Mass.: Belknap Press, 1971.

Another biblical theme gives justice a more immediately religious value. Justice in this second meaning is God's mercy and the gift of salvation. "The justice of God, which man attains through faith, ultimately coincides with His mercy; and, like the divine mercy, designates at times a divine attribute, at other times the concrete gifts of salvation which this mercy dispenses."[1] The Old Testament already has this notion of justice. In the New Testament St. Paul in particular speaks of justice in this sense ("justice of God", "justification").

Since only justice as a moral virtue interests us in this context, the exposition shall limit itself to the first usage alone.

1. *The Old Testament.* Justice in the sense of a moral virtue can sometimes have the more restricted meaning of civil justice and at other times the wider meaning of uprightness and integral goodness.

Civil justice is demanded by the ancient legislation of Israel from the judges, who are required to show integrity in the performance of their duties (Lev 19:15.35f; Deut 1:16; 16:18-20). Justice as respect of other people's rights is also demanded from every member of the Jewish community (Ex 23:6-8; Deut 25: 13-15). Likewise justice is expected from the king (Jer 22:1-3; Ps 72:1-4), who is praised for it (2 Sam 8:15; 1 Kings 10:9; Prov 16:13). The prophets repeatedly and forcefully denounce the injustice perpetrated by judges and kings in their oppression of the poor (Amos 5:7.11-15; 16:12; Is 5:7.22f; Jer 22:13-18; Ezek 45:9). They foretell divine vengeance for such iniquity; for the Old Testament never views injustice as a mere violation of human rules or customs, but always in the religious dimension of a breach of God's covenant and an insult to God's holiness. Knowing the weakness of human justice, the prophets look above all to the future Messiah as the righteous prince who will administer a faultless justice (Is 9:7; 11:4f; 16:5; 32:1; Jer 23:5).

In the wider sense justice signifies fidelity to the law and perfect observance of the divine precepts (Gen 18:19; Deut 6:25; Prov 11:3-10; 12:28; Is 56:1f; Ezek 18:5-24). The just man is the upright. blameless man, the irreproachable servant (Gen 6:9; 7:1; 18:23-32; Prov 12:10.26; etc.; Wis 1:1).

2. *The New Testament.* The exhortation to a juridical type of justice is not central to Jesus' message nor to that of the apostolic Church. "The gospel does not lay down regulations

---

[1] Art. "Justice" in: Dictionary of Biblical Theology, ed. by Léon-Dufour, 1967. 244.

regarding the duties of justice, it makes no insistent appeal to an oppressed group, nor does it present the Messiah as the righteous judge."[1] The most serious fault of Jesus' contemporaries is not so much social injustice as the more specifically religious vice of formalism and hypocrisy. Therefore the prophets' denunciations of injustice find their correspondence in Jesus' denunciation of pharisaism.

"In Jesus' manner of speaking, justice preserves its biblical meaning of fidelity to the Law. Although this is not the central point of His message, Jesus does not hesitate to define the moral life as true justice, as spiritual obedience to God's commandments."[2] In the sermon on the Mount Jesus defines the true justice of his disciples (Mt 5:17-6:18). Their justice ought to be greater than that of the Pharisees, who content themselves with an external, legalistic fulfillment of the rulings of the law, but disregard the spirit of justice, which consists in true concern for the neighbour's welfare (Mt 5:20; 23:23).

Inasmuch as justice signifies the moral virtue, it is usually used in the wide sense of a perfect life and of holiness, by the Gospels as well as by the apostolic Church. The expression "the way of justice" (Mt 21:32; 2 Pet 2:21) means life lived according to the commandments of God. In this sense the just man is he who fulfills the commandments of God. Thus the adjective just or righteous is used of various persons in the Old and New Testament and also of Christ in the sense of upright and holy (Mt 1:19; 13:17; Lk 1:6; 2:25; 2 Pet 2:7). And when Jesus says at his baptism that he came "to fulfill all justice", then he proclaims the glad event that in him the ancient justice is brought to culmination and perfection (Mt 3:15).

At times justice also appears as a virtue besides and distinct from others, that is, probably in the sense of civil justice and the social virtue (Eph 6:14; 1 Tim 6:11; 2 Tim 2:22).

II. Nature of justice

1. *Concept of justice*

Authors are not of one mind as to the concept of justice and sometimes differ widely. Nevertheless they are in agreement on three characteristics of justice. "Three such common notes can be distinguished. The first is that justice is a social norm,

---

[1] Dictionary of Biblical Theology, l. c. 245.
[2] Ib.

that is, a directive for guiding men in their actions toward one another. The second note is that justice is approbative in the sense that judging an action to be just manifests approval of that action. Third, justice is obligatory in that judging a certain course of action to be just entails that a person in the like situation ought to do the same thing."[1] Alongside of justice still other rules exist which also provide guidelines for men in their association with one another, such as norms of manners, decency or grammar. But they are not approbative in the sense that their observance qualifies a man as good or bad, nor are they obligatory, and that distinguishes them from justice. Justice is more closely associated with the norms of law or of morality, although it is a matter of controversy whether and how justice is related to both.

There are basically three theories as to the essence of justice: the positive law theory, the social good theory, and the natural right theory.[2] The first one defines justice as conformity to the law, and therewith reduces the just to the legal. The concept of justice could as well be replaced by legality. Against such a definition stands the argument that justice is also appealed to in matters where there is no positive law, and moreover that justice supplies a criterion of law and judges its justification. Therefore justice cannot be identical with legality, since it transcends it and is its critical measure.

The social good theory defines justice as doing what is useful for the social good. Hence justice is a wider concept than legality. Justice obliges a man to do what promotes the social good already prior to the demands of positive law, beyond positive law, and even against it, if the law should contradict the demands of the social good. The definition has the merit that it provides an objective criterion of law by which its justification can be judged, which criterion is the important value of the social good. Nevertheless the definition does not prove fully satisfactory. It presents itself as at the same time too wide and too narrow. Not every contribution to the social good

---

[1] Otto A. Bird: The Idea of Justice (Concepts in Western Thought Series). — New York/London: Frederick A. Praeger, 1967, 10f.

[2] Otto Bird. 1. c., lists 23 authors for the positive law theory, among them Hobbes, Holmes, Kelsen, Spinoza (p. 45). For the social good theory he lists 19 authors, among them Bentham, Hume, Mill, Radbruch, Sidgwick (p. 81). For the natural law theory he lists 42 authors, among them Aquinas, Aristotle, Augustine, E. Brunner, Grotius, Leibniz, Locke, Maritain, Messner, Pufendorf, Suarez, Del Vecchio, Vitoria, Wolff (p. 121).

is an obligation in justice, works of benevolence for example. Obligations in charity are not obligations in justice. Yet according to the definition there are no different obligations in charity. They all belong to the virtue of justice. On the other hand the duties of justice do not exclusively derive from the needs of the social good, but also from the individual's right to maintain and to promote his bodily and mental life and to improve the conditions of his existence, even when the social good should have no profit therefrom. This is no denial that the social good constitutes a very important criterion for the demands of justice; but it stands in need of completion.

The natural right theory holds that natural right is the ultimate basis of justice. Man has rights not primarily because he has received them by society, but because his nature as a human being confers rights upon him. The rights that are to be respected by justice primarily derive from the laws inherent in nature itself. Men and human communities have a natural right to well-ordered existence, self-realization and progress. On a secondary level man's rights also derive from the further determination of natural rights by the positive law of a community. For the demands of natural right can usually be complied with in different ways (e.g. property and inheritance rights), and it is left up to the community to determine in which concrete forms these demands shall be met with and realized. But positive law must agree with the demands of natural right as much as possible and may never contradict it, if it wants to be legitimate and binding. (For further clarification confer the treatise on natural law.)

Following Plato and Aristotle, Thomas Aquinas, as one of the outstanding representatives of the natural right theory, defines justice as "the firm and constant will to give to each one his due."[1] This definition has been adopted by many scholars of philosophy and theology. Nevertheless, confronted with the common notion of justice, it is a rather wide definition. Thomas himself extends the concept of justice beyond the duties of strict right to the obligations of gratitude, obedience, respect of persons, even friendliness and worship of God.

Therefore other authors try to narrow the definition down. Justice is then more aptly defined as "the fulfillment of that to

---

[1] II-II, q. 58, a. 1.

which our neighbour has a strict right",[1] or as "rendering to each what is his own or due by right".[2] Since the duties of worship are usually not considered as obligations of justice, although they constitute strict duties of man and a divine right, the last definition might be further explicated as: rendering to each *man* or human community what is their own or due by right. The mention of the human community in the definition makes plain that not only individuals but also communities are subjects of rights. Attention is also to be called to the distinction between a person's *own* and *due* by right. Justice for one leaves to every man what is rightfully his own, and for another gives a man what he does not yet own but what is rightfully his due, usually according to the principle of equality in exchange, distribution and contribution. Since obligations of gratitude, common respect, friendliness are not due by right, they are not included in this definition.

2. *Properties of justice*

Justice is characterized by certain properties which it owes to the fact that its demands constitute basic and essential requirements for the existence and development of man and society.

(a) The demands of justice on principle are enforceable. Every community takes provisions and creates authorities to enforce the rights of its members against those who disregard and violate them. Of course the violation must be sufficiently grave in order to have recourse to enforcement by authorities. Occasional small frauds and thefts or small inequalities in distributive justice do not constitute matter for legal intervention. Justice "on principle" is enforceable means to say therefore that it is enforceable if the matter is sufficiently grave.

(b) The demands of justice are of definite and determinable nature, at least as a rule. Insofar as justice excludes certain actions as strictly unlawful, it states in a definite way what must be omitted. And insofar as the services due to others in justice are usually ruled by the principle of equality in exchange, distribution and contribution, a rather precise determination of what justice exacts can be provided.

---

[1] Karl Hörmann: An Introduction to Moral Theology. — London: Burns and Oates, 1961, 244.

[2] Thus summarized by Otto Bird: The Idea of Justice. — New York/London: Frederick A. Praeger, 1967, 164.

(c) Violated claims of justice on principle demand restitution, or at least compensation if the damage inflicted cannot be repaired, e.g. in a case of mutilation. Where the demands of justice are less definite and precise, as not seldom in distributive and particularly in social justice, the demands of restitution are accordingly also less definite and cannot easily be urged. Of course justice as a virtue will never limit itself to what is enforceable by law. Motivated by sincere concern for the rightful claims of others, it will strive to give them what is indispensable for their existence and self-realization and for serving God and his divine plan efficiently.

III.   Classifications of justice

Justice has been defined as rendering to each man or human community their own and due by right. Two basic forms of justice are distinguished in this definition. Firstly, justice leaves to every man what is his own by right and attributes to him what he really is. This form of justice has been termed *attributive* justice.[1] It includes the right to one's person, to the property which one has acquired, to one's honour and merited reputation, to one's discoveries, to impartial acknowledgement of one's qualifications. Secondly, justice renders to every man what is his due by right, i.e. what he does not yet own but what he is entitled to receive as a remuneration, compensation or benefit, or what he is also obliged to accept as a burden in the service of the community. Since the proportion of goods or burdens due to a person is usually rendered according to the principles of equality in exchange, distribution and contribution, this second form of justice can be termed *proportional* justice. It could also be called tributive justice inasmuch as it *gives* to every man what he is entitled to receive. Proportional justice is subdivided in the subspecies of commutative, distributive, contributive (legal) and social justice. Thirdly, since the demands of justice are basic requirements for social coexistence and human development, their violation cannot be tolerated but calls for reparation of the injury inflicted. This leads to a last form of justice, retributive or *vindicative* justice. It demands indemnification of the injured person and active punishment of the culpable offender.

The four forms of commutative, distributive, contributive

---

[1] Cf. Paul Tillich: Love, Power, and Justice. — London: Oxford University Press, 1954, 63f.

and social justice still require some further explanation. They are characterized and distinguished in the following ways:

(a)   Commutative justice commands that exchange of goods and services takes place according to strict equality of values (unless one party voluntarily resigns full compensation). Since rights and claims of commutative justice are mainly based on contracts, it is also called contractual justice. It operates above all in commercial exchange and just regulation of prices, in just remuneration of work, and in recent times on an ever larger scale also in insurance contracts. (That means to say, the frequently practised cheating of insurance agencies is an offence against commutative justice too.)

(b)   Distributive justice regulates the relations of a community with its members. It demands that benefits and burdens be distributed in the community according to proportionate equality. Distributive justice has to guide those in authority, be it in the state, in the Church, in smaller communities like religious orders, or even in the family. Insofar as individuals and groups are not all equal in their qualifications, resources and dedication to the common welfare, aids, burdens and honours must be distributed in proportion to needs, capabilities, merits, i.e. according to proportionate equality. An example of this is the gradation of direct taxes according to income. Disproportion in the distribution of burdens and partiality in the award of favours are contrary to distributive justice.

(c)   Contributive or legal justice obliges the members of a community to comply with the demands of the common good. Whereas distributive justice is concerned with the individual members of a community, contributive justice is concerned with the general good of the community (therefore this form of justice is sometimes also called general justice). Within the state contributive justice obliges the citizens above all to comply with the just demands of laws, e.g. tax laws, social legislations, military service; and it obliges authorities to contribute to the common good by appropriate laws. Because of this close relation of contributive justice to the law within the state community, it has been named legal justice. However it would be wrong if this term misled one to the assumption that contributive justice is almost exclusively operative in the realm of law. Even independently of positive law and prior to it, man has the strict duty to contribute his share to the common good of those communities which essentially help him in securing his existence and self-realization or assist him in the fulfillment of strict obligations. Hence this duty is also effective in the Church, in intermediate communities like local communities or religious congregations, and even in the family.

States themselves as members of the community of nations are bound by legal justice to comply with the laws enacted by a legislative authority of this community.

(d)   Social justice is a rather recent concept and has been accepted in Catholic moral teaching since Pius XI, whose great social encyclical "Quadragesimo Anno" is characterized by this term.   Authors are of different opinions concerning the meaning of this concept.   Some regard it as merely another expression for legal justice and equate the two.   For others the term comprises legal and distributive justice in one.   And others again consider social justice as a different kind of proportionate justice, distinct from the other forms.

Social justice refers to the economic welfare of social groups. As such it demands a proportionate share of the social partners in the fruits of their economic cooperation.   Pure profits of excessive nature on the part of the management as well as overdrawn wages on the part of the workers, which endanger productivity and further expansion of an enterprise, offend against the demands of social justice.

Social justice further demands a proportionate and equitable distribution of the wealth of a nation among the different classes in society.   Hence the concentration of a nation's wealth and landownership in the hands of a few extremely rich families, while the majority of citizens live in poverty and even misery, offends against social justice.

Finally social justice also imposes obligations upon nations in their mutual relations.   It binds the economically advanced countries to assist nations in poverty and misery, so that they can live in a manner worthy of human beings.

All the different applications of social justice have in common that they order the proportionate share of social groups in the economic wealth according to the demands of an equitable distribution of wealth in enterprises, in a nation, and in the entire family of nations.   They have further in common that they do not order relations between states or communities and their members, as in distributive justice, but of social groups which are equals. They also do not regulate the contributions of subjects to their respective, superior communities, as in contributive justice. Of course in an indirect way social justice contributes to the welfare of the whole community, but that is true of every form of justice. Hence the conclusion seems to be justified that social justice is a fourth form of proportionate justice. Social justice demands the equitable distribution of wealth among social groups and among nations according to their share in the economic process, to their contribution to the general welfare, and to their right to a worthy human life.

IV. Justice and love

No solid social order and no lasting peace are possible without respect for the demands of justice. Charitable offerings and works can never substitute for denied justice; at best they can sometimes constitute an atonement for violations of justice in instances where restitution is not possible. On the other hand justice must be animated by love even in the social order. Although justice is the indispensable precondition for peace among men, respect for the dignity of other people and nations "as well as the studied practice of brotherhood, are absolutely necessary for the establishment of peace. Hence peace is likewise the fruit of love, which goes beyond what justice can provide" (GS 78).

Duties of justice and duties of love are not identical. The demands of love exceed the demands of justice. Yet there is no antithesis between justice and love, at least if these virtues are rightly conceived. On the contrary, there is a close relation between the two. Whatever is demanded by justice, is also demanded by love, although not vice versa. That means to say, love is the more comprehensive virtue, and the demands of justice constitute its minimum requirements. The fundamental relation between justice and love consists in this that every duty of justice is a duty of love, though not every duty of love is a duty of justice, since love transcends justice. From this it follows that justice may never contradict love. Any requirement which conflicts with love cannot be a requirement of justice.

Although love then comprises justice, this should not lead to the conclusion that justice could be dispensed with and simply be replaced by the universal virtue of charity. The various virtues like truthfulness, temperance, gratitude, respect, justice translate charity into particular fields of human activity. They develop more clearly what love demands in man's different relations and conditions of life. Justice unequivocally sets down where love has to begin, before undertaking any further initiatives of good will. It secures the most basic, indispensable requirements for human existence, self-realization and life in community.

But it remains equally true that justice is substantially in need of the spirit of love. The ultimate reason is that only love is able to know the neighbour truly and, accordingly, to know fully what is his proper due. For this reason love has been characterized as the condition enabling justice to see rightly.[1] Based on the concrete knowledge and understanding of a person, love must temper the rigid demands of justice whenever this is more in agreement with the true welfare of a neighbour and the community. Justice may not be used as an instrument in the service of merciless enforcement of rights. "Summum jus, summa injuria." Under the influence of love, "nobler justice" will not only pardon the neighbour if he repents, but also remit material debts when this is demanded by his condition, especially when insolvency is caused by misfortune arising through no fault of his. The requirements of social justice in particular are clearly discernible only in the brotherly view of love.

Inasmuch as the duties of justice are the minimum requirements of love, they are always graver and more urgent than duties solely imposed by love. Moral teaching must therefore demand that obligations of justice be fulfilled prior to any works of charity. But on the other hand Christians may never lose sight of the higher ideals and most exalted objectives of Christian love, which have been pointed out by Christ in the Sermon on the Mount and in his commandment to love each other as he has loved us.

---

[1] Cf. Nikolaus Monzel: Die Sehbedingung der Gerechtigkeit; in: Solidarität und Selbstverantwortung. Beiträge zur Christlichen Soziallehre. —München, 1959.

Chapter II

MORAL RESPONSIBILITY IN COMMUNITY LIFE

Man is by nature a social being. This is a truth which is beyond doubt for a mind open to reality. In order to exist and to develop himself, man needs the support of the community in many regards. In particular the spiritual development of the individual is almost ˙entirely dependent upon the education. instruction and help of others, which education is above all taken care of by the family, tribe, state and Church. This fact has forcefully been confirmed by recent ethnology and cultural anthropology, which show "how very farreaching an influence on man's spiritual formation is exercised by social tradition, the world of experience and knowledge handed down, modes of thought and imagination, beliefs regarding values and rights, customs and attitudes."[1] With this corresponds man's instinct for social fellowship, which is one of the strongest impulses in human nature. Only through social completion can man fully develop his being as his nature demands. "How little are we, or do we possess, what we in the strictest sense call our property. We must all receive and learn not only from our predecessors but also from our contemporaries. Even the greatest genius would not get very far if he had to rely solely on what he had in himself" (Goethe).[2]

Given the great importance of community and society for man's life, he has on the one hand the right to be helped by society, but on the other hand he has also the obligation to give to society his support. Concern for society is concern for one's own welfare, concern for one's neighbour, and ultimately concern for that final goal which every man, every community, and all mankind is called to serve and to bring about: God's kingdom and glory.

---

[1] Joh. Messner: Social Ethics. Natural Law in the Western World. — St. Louis/London: Herder Book Co., 1965, 96f.

[2] Quoted by J. Höffner: Fundamentals of Christian Sociology. — Westminster, Md.: The Newman Press, 1962, 21.

A. Nature and order of society in general

I. Nature of society

1. *Notion of society*

Society in the wide sense is a lasting association of men for the attainment of a common goal, necessitated by nature or freely willed. Family, tribe or nation are necessitated by nature. Although men usually accept their belonging to these societies and by free consent agree to it, they necessarily pertain to them, even if they should dislike their being a member of them. Other societies are freely willed, like religious societies, educational societies, joint stock companies, clubs for sports and entertainment, etc. The common mark of all these associations is their determination by an immanent end or inner principle. As such they are distinguished from associations whose unity rests on an external will or external compulsion. Thus the term society does not apply to a military formation, which is organized from without for an external purpose.

In a more restricted sense society is defined as a lasting association of men for mutual help in the attainment of their existential ends.[1] This definition applies to communities necessitated by nature, to religious communities, to educational societies, but not to a joint stock company or a bridge club. Only societies in the restricted sense impose more serious societal obligations (e.g. the strict duty to obedience) and hence are of particular interest for moral theology.

The terms society and community are often used interchangeably, which indicates that there is no definite distinction between them. Nevertheless the two terms imply a difference in emphasis. The expression 'community' is preferably used for associations of men primarily concerned with the inner development of the group, i.e. with the building of values important for the personal growth of their members and of mutual ties of solidarity. Characteristic example of a community is the family. The term 'society' on the other hand rather designates associations of men which are characterised by systematic organization and external institutions (laws, administrative bodies, governing officials) for the achievement of their goals. The state exemplifies this form of association in a typical way. But the terms are never

---

[1] J. Messner, 1. c. 99.

totally exclusive of each other. No community is possible without a minimum of external organization and no society is possible without a minimum of solidarity and personal interest of the members for one another.

Societies are divided in necessary and voluntary societies, as already indicated by the first definition. Necessary societies, also called natural or primary societies, are necessitated by nature. Voluntary or secondary societies result from freely chosen purposes.

2.   *The common good: aim and function of society*

The common good consists in those goods and values by means of which a society is to help its members in the realization of tasks which they alone cannot sufficiently achieve. The functions of the common good are basically two. Firstly it promotes and makes possible an integral human existence for its members. In this regard the common good comprises such values as a sound state of physical and mental health in society as a whole, a sufficient degree of education and schooling of its members, opportunities of work for all, favourable conditions for religious and cultural life, social and economic progress, the good of social justice. In the realization of these values and goals man is helped by different societies, which all have their own common good in order to assist him in the attainment of full humanity.

The second function of the common good is to preclude antisocial impulses in human nature from interfering with the rights of others and with the social order. This aspect of the common good is realized by the establishment and securing of peace and order. The most efficient means to it is the law of the state, which has the power of coercion behind it.

In view of the explanations given, the common good could also be described as the sum of those conditions of social living whereby men are enabled more fully to achieve their perfection and appointed ends (cf. GS 74; DH 6). But note that the common good ultimately consists in goods and values actualized in the members of society. This must be stressed against inclinations to view progress too much in terms of institutions, organizations and technique. Genuine progress consists in greater material security, in a better state of health, and above all in the spiritual, intellectual and moral development of the human person. The helps of the common good are meant to assist man in the realization of his tasks and existential ends. Its function is therefore subsidiary and complementary. From this it follows that the common good is not an end in itself. It stands in the service of the human personality and of God's creative and salvific design. This signifies that the human person can never become a mere means towards the common good and the purposes of society. Man is always more than merely a part and cell of society. He is directly responsible to God.

Spontaneously men usually associate the reality of the common good with the state and its institutions. Yet not only the state but also all other societies have their own social ends, their own functions and competences, and therefore their own common good. The family, religious communities, charitable organizations, trade unions, sport clubs, they all possess their own common good. Naturally this pluralism of the common good does not mean a mere coexistence of different communities. The different societies and their common good are hierarchically structured. Although each society is autonomous within the sphere of its own ends, the smaller society is subordinated to the greater one insofar as the wider end of the latter is concerned.

The common good of a society is promoted by the members who belong to it. Theirs is the responsibility and obligation to respect and to advance it. But the different societies and their different ends are not all of equal importance. The gravity of the obligation to respect and to serve the common good of a specific society depends on the importance a society possesses for the realization of man's existential ends and ultimate goal. That means to say: the more closely the good of a community is related to the basic tasks and existential ends of man, the graver is the obligation to respect and to promote it. This obligation is incumbent upon those in authority as well as upon the subjects. The binding force of the common good is graver in the family than in a sporting club, in the state than in a joint stock company.

3.   *The complementary function of society (principle of subsidiarity)*

The principle of subsidiarity states that social institutions have an auxiliary and complementary function concerning the tasks and needs of the smaller groupings and individuals. That means to say that on the one hand societies must leave to the smaller groupings or individuals what they can do by their own power; and that on the other hand they must assist the smaller groupings or individuals where they are unable to accomplish a necessary or at least useful task.

The term "principle of subsidiarity" is rather recent, although the truth it names has been known for a long time past. Coined at the beginning of the twentieth century,[1] it has found entrance in the encyclical "Quadragesimo Anno" of Pius XI.[2] The pertinent text defines the principle chiefly in its negative role, i.e. as a restrictive law by which limits are set to the intervention of society. "Just as it is wrong to withdraw from the individual and commit to a group what private enterprise and industry can accomplish, so too it is an injustice, a grave evil and a disturbance of right order, for a larger and higher association to arrogate to itself functions which can be performed efficiently by smaller and lesser societies. This is a fundamental principle of social philosophy" (nr. 79). It is noteworthy that Pius XII declared that the principle is also valid in the life of the Church.[3]

The principle of subsidiarity protects the particular rights and competencies of individuals against excessive domination by societies as well as the competencies of minor associations against oppressive and totalitarian claims of a larger society. It stands opposed to the omnipotence of organizations just as it is opposed to the omnipotence of the state.[4]

Besides the restraint imposed upon the power of societies by the principle of subsidiarity, the very term also indicates the obligation and competence of societies to "subsidize" and to aid the minor groupings and individuals. This intervention by society

---

[1] Coined by Gustav Gundlach, born 1892.

[2] The essential passage is repeated verbally by John XXIII in "Mater et Magistra" (nr. 53), who in two other places still refers to the principle (nr. 117 and 152).

[3] Allocution of February 20, 1946; AAS 38 (1946), 144f.

[4] Where the spheres of responsibility and of competence belonging to the individual or corporate members of society are unfairly diminished, the common good itself will be impaired and diminished. "Great harm is done to the reality of the common good if society arrogates to itself in the fields of science, of art, and of literature, the function of regulating or directing creative activity instead of confining itself to its auxiliary function. Anyone who is not dazzled by collectivistic ideology will admit this. In regard to economic life, on the other hand, today there is a widespread inclination to look to state planning, organization, direction and control for everything essential. Little reflection, however, is needed to see that even in economic life the common good cannot be fully realized if its function is expected to be more than subsidiary" (J. Messner, 1. c. 144).

is called for in all those many instances in which necessary or important tasks cannot be accomplished without its help. Secondarily it is also called for in cases in which individuals or minor organizations fall short in their appropriate duties, whether by incapability or by negligence and disregard.

The need of help by societies will widen or contract according to the abilities of their members and according to the will and energy by which they take up their responsibilities. To the extent that the members of a society lack competence or fail in the will to responsibility, to that extent the common good function and the need for intervention by society expands. The burden of proof that any extension of powers in society is justified however lies with the social authority claiming such extension. It has to be shown that those primarily responsible and competent are either not able or not willing to carry out their responsibility. Furthermore the principle of subsidiarity requires that intervention and assistance by social authority be made superfluous as soon and as far as this is possible, and subjects be helped to fulfill the tasks falling within their competence by their own responsibility.

The principle primarily binds those in authority, but secondarily also confers obligations upon the member societies and individuals. For in protecting the personal rights and responsibilities of subjects, it also demands that they use their rights and meet their responsibilities. In fact the principle of subsidiarity can also be formulated in the following way: As much individual responsibility as possible, as much intervention by society as necessary. On the one side authority is bound to respect the limits set to it by the order of subsidiary function. On the other side the members of society have the right but also the obligation to use their competence with vigour and to comply with their responsibilities (cf. GS 75).

A final caution is in place. In actual life the order of subsidiarity, like the order of justice in general, will never take shape in perfect form. The reason is not only human limitation and imperfection, but also the dynamics in society which bring about constant changes and always again outpace any order in society. Hence subjects must not approach society with exaggerated demands and expectations, but take into account the necessary limitations of human institutions and authorities. Besides, there also exists a legitimate free play for societies, which allows them within certain limits to place greater emphasis either on personality values or on social values. "In all this lie the origins of the rich diversity in the life of nations and in their political and social systems of which history tells us."[1]

II. Responsible use of authority[2]

No community can exist without an ordering and coordinating authority. If a community "is not to be torn into pieces as each man follows his own viewpoint, authority is needed" (GS 74). Yet although this is most true and incontestable, there is a widespread distrust of authority among people of today. They know the abuses of authority and feel threatened by its frequent totalitarian trends. An antidote is sought in a general democratization of society, which would grant subjects a greater influence on the appointment of officials and the government of society. Nevertheless the growing complexity of civilization and social life inevitably implies a continual extension of authority. All the more it is imperative that the power of authority be used in a responsible way.

The term authority derives from the Latin word "auctoritas", which has its root in the verb "augere", i.e. to increase or to enrich. Hence authority is an institution meant for the enrichment and promotion of those over whom it is exercised. This is indeed the true and proper mission of authority.

Authority can be defined as the superiority of a person by which he is entitled to make demands on others for the sake of their individual good or that of society. It is distinguished in personal and official authority. Personal authority is based on a person's intellectual, professional, spiritual or moral superiority. It can result from a profounder knowledge, richer experience, greater technical and professional skill, maturer character, or also from a special charism of leadership. Official or social authority is that authority which a person has by reason of a governing or ruling function conferred on him by society. Although it exists independently of the personal qualities of its bearer, it is desirable that he also possesses personal authority. Nevertheless official authority can impose obligations even when its wielder

---

[1] J. Messner, 1. c. 216.

[2] References: Yves R. Simon: A General Theory of Authority. — University of Notre Dame Press, 1962. Problems of Authority; ed. by John M. Todd. — London: Darton Longman and Todd, 1962. Freedom and Authority in the West; ed. by George N. Shuster. — Notre Dame/ London: University of Notre Dame Press, 1967. Paul Verghese: The Freedom of Man. An Inquiry Into Some Roots of the Tension Between Freedom and Authority in Our Society. — Philadelphia: Westminster Press, 1972.

is inadequate or unworthy, naturally within the limits of the office.

1.   *Authority in Holy Scripture*

In the Old as well as in the New Testament authority essentially and primarily belongs to God himself and signifies his absolute sovereignty. It is one of his most important attributes. All other authority has its origin in God and is appointed to serve him. In the creation that God has made, all power of men over nature proceeds from him (Gen 1:28; Sir 17:2). This is in particular true of the authority of kings and rulers over their subjects and the nations (Sir 10:4; Is 45:1-5; Jer 27:6). "There is no authority except from God, and those that exist have been instituted by God" (Rom 13:1; cf. Jn 19:11). Authorities are the servants and ministers of God for the good of their subjects (Rom 13:1-7).

Since those in authority are appointed as God's ministers and as servants of the common good, they are taught to exercise their authority in a spirit of service. "Whoever would be great among you must be your servant, and whoever would be first among you must be slave of all. For the Son of man also came not to be served but to serve" (Mk 10:43-45; cf. Lk 22:25-27). Christ illustrates this truth concretely by washing his disciples' feet at the last supper. The disciples call him Teacher and Lord, and rightly so. If then, he the Lord and Teacher, has washed their feet, they should follow his example and do the same (Jn 13:1-17).

The apostolic writings exhort to considerate and benevolent exercise of authority, just as they exhort subjects to willing obedience and to respect of authority. Husbands should love their wives and not be harsh with them (Eph 5:25-30; Col 3:19; 1 Pet 3:7). Fathers should not provoke their children but treat them judiciously (Eph 6:4; Col 3:21). Masters should be well disposed towards their servants and treat them justly and fairly (Eph 6:9; Col 4:1). And the elders in the community should take care for those in their charge with true concern for their welfare (1 Pet 5:1-4). Motive and model of such love and concern is Christ's self-sacrificing love for all men and in particular for the Church. For they are his flock, entrusted to him as the envoy of the Father in order to save them and to make them members of his kingdom.

2.   *Reason and function of authority*

a)   Reason of authority

Men are by nature differently gifted. Some have better endowments and qualities than others. These they have received not primarily for their own contentment and fulfillment, as little as anybody exists and lives only for his individual pleasure and happiness. They are called to place their abilities in the service of the common welfare and lastly of the great goals of God, his glory and his kingdom. They render this service by communicating their greater knowledge and better skills to others and by giving them guidance, which naturally vests them with authority over those who are guided and trained by them.

Yet apart from the differences in talents, authority is an essential constituent of society, which cannot exist and operate without it. If men need the help of society for the realization of their tasks and ends, they inevitably also stand in want of a coordinating and leading authority. For many different people go to make up a community, and they are inclined towards diverse ways of doing things. An ordering power is needed to coordinate the multiple activities and to dispose them towards the common good. "A social life cannot exist among a number of people unless under the presidency of one to look after the common good; for many, as such, seek many things, whereas one attends only to one. Wherefore the Philosopher says, in the beginning of the 'Politics', that wherever many things are directed to one, we shall always find one at the head directing them."[1] Since then man by his nature is dependent on society for the realization of his goals, authority as an essential constituent of society is equally based on human nature. And since God is the creator of human nature, authority ultimately has its foundation and origin in God himself (cf. GS 74).

Wherever a common good is to be realized, there must be a social authority to guide and harmonize the activities of the many. The needs of the common good require a governing authority and are the immediate source of its rights and duties. But inasmuch as social authority is established for the purpose of the common good, it is also limited by this purpose and may not demand what is not required by it.

---

[1] Thomas Aquinas, S. Th. I, q. 96, a. 4.

b)   Function of authority

Authority is appointed to assist man on the way to maturity and full manhood, to mediate perfection, to further personal and social values. It has to serve the common good by securing order in the community and by creating favourable conditions for development and progress in all realms of human life. Thus parental authority assists the child to reach human maturity and to stand on his own feet. Teachers and masters communicate knowledge and skills and stimulate personal insight and discovery. Political authority again furthers and increases the common good.

The means by which authority is to fulfill its tasks is primarily persuasion of subjects concerning the necessity of its demands and appeal to their free consent. Authority must direct subjects to their welfare and to the common good "not mechanically or despotically, but primarily as a moral force which depends on freedom and the conscientious discharge of the burdens of any office which has been undertaken" (GS 74). Only secondarily may authority have recourse to coercion, namely when subjects refuse to submit to just and necessary demands and thereby impair and injure the common weal or even their own welfare. Although coercion would not be needed in a community of perfect human beings and therefore does not constitute an essential feature of authority, it is indispensable in the concrete, sinful condition of men.

Two basic functions of authority can be distinguished: the educational and the coordinating function.

(1)   Educational authority assists man in the attainment of personal maturity. It intervenes and leads where subjects lack the autonomy to take their fate fully in their own hands. It aims at the self-reliant person who is able to meet his duties independently and responsibly and to serve the community in a dependable way. As long as children cannot be responsible for their own destiny, their parents must guide them in order to prevent disaster. Also state authority must sometimes intervene by educational measures where subjects lack the necessary insight or will-power to provide for their good, e.g. by compulsory schooling or by measures in prevention of addiction. However the continuous effort of educational authority must be to make itself superfluous, for only thus can it attain its real goal. Therefore parents, educators and all other authorities must grant as much freedom as the maturity of their subordinates permits. But since the goal of perfect maturity is only seldom reached, some

kind of educational authority is most of the time needed. "In one respect or another we all need care of a paternal or maternal kind, and hence of an authoritative nature."[1]

(2) Functional authority on the other hand has by its nature a permanent task. It consists in the preservation of order in society, which may be considered as its primordial charge, and in the coordination of forces in the pursuit of common goals. A unity of action must be realized if the values of civilization and culture are to be promoted and progress is to be achieved. The need for authoritative order grows with the growing complexity of human life. The greater the evolution of a society, the more necessary authority becomes. Hence the essential task of social authority is not conditioned by the inadequacies of its members, but by the nature of the tasks and goals which man is called to serve and which transcend the forces of the individual.

3. *Exercise of authority in a spirit of service*

Superiors must look at their authority not as dominion, but as service after the example of Christ (Mk 10:42-45; Jn 13:1-17). They must be convinced that their subjects are not just instruments in the achievement of goals, but fellow-workers who also have a direct responsibility to God and who are called to their personal contribution in the promotion of God's creative and salvific design.

Those in authority are invested with power over others not for their own benefit, but for the benefit of the individuals and communities they rule. Their office is one of service to them. Accordingly they are bound to use their authority for the good of their subordinates. Against this duty superiors may fail not only by over-protective and despotic use of authority, but also by neglect of its necessary exercise. Ease and indolence or incompetence and the feeling of inadequacy may be the reason for such neglect. "Not to give due authoritative directives would be to hinder or waste the potentialities of the subjects. Since authority is equally responsible to the values it represents and to the men it seeks to persuade, the golden rule is 'fortiter in re et suaviter in modo'."[2]

Since authority exists in order to promote the common good and to coordinate the forces for the achievement of the common

---

[1] W. Molinski, art. "Authority" in: Sacramentum Mundi I, 1968, 131.

[2] W. Molinski, 1. c. 132f.

tasks, men can command only within the sphere delimited by the purpose of the community concerned. They must keep within the limits of the laws, constitutions and ends of the community. Besides, those in authority are equally bound by the laws of the community. For the laws are established for the sake of the common good, whose promotion precisely is the task proper to authority. This does not preclude that superiors may more frequently have reasons for exceptions or dispensations than simple subjects, but they too need a sufficient cause for it. The superior's example is of great importance for the willing obedience of subjects. They expect that the personal attitude of the bearer of authority agrees with the values he represents.

Finally superiors must be able to avail themselves as much as possible of the contributions their subjects can make to the common welfare. They must be heedful not to stifle personal initiative, but on the contrary promote it as a source of enrichment and fruitfulness. The admonition given by Vatican II to religious superiors in this regard holds equally good for everybody in authority. Superiors are requested to give the kind of leadership which will encourage subjects "to bring an active and responsible obedience to the offices they shoulder and the activities they undertake. Therefore a superior should listen willingly to his subjects and encourage them to make a personal contribution to the welfare of the community" (PC 14). The text continues that this however should not weaken the superior's authority to decide what must be done and to require the doing of it.

Inasmuch as superiors have received their authority for the welfare of their subjects and of the society they govern, all their just commands stand in the service of this welfare. Obedience therefore in a last analysis does not really submit subjects to the superior's will, but rather orientates them to their own good and to the good and goal of the community.

III. The virtue of obedience[1]

The word obedience has its origin in the Latin and is derived from the verb *audire,* to hear. Also the Hebrew and the Greek words meaning "to obey" are connected with the

---

[1] References: The same as for authority. See also Bernard Häring: The Liberty of the Children of God. — Staten Island, N.Y.: Alba House, 1966.

words for "to hear".[1] The literal sense of obedience then denotes a readiness to listen to the expression of another's will and to do it. As virtue it is the promptness of the will to carry out a command given by somebody in authority.

In the past the virtue of obedience has always been held in high esteem. Hellenistic philosophy and specially neo-Platonism was of the conviction "that man attains perfection only by giving up his own will and submitting to God's heteronomy and to divinely-established authority, because only in this way is man's dispersion overcome by recollection."[2] Scholasticism, the teachers of Christian ethics and ascetics, and also philosophers like Kant valued obedience highly. The emphasis was occasionally so strong that self-determination in general appeared as a lesser good and the abandonment of self-will as the higher value. Blind obedience, which carries out the command for its own sake, was then regarded as the ideal form of obedience. This overstatement however cannot be pictured as the common doctrine of classical theology.

Modern men on the other hand often show great reservation towards obedience and submission to another person's will. Obedience is suspected as an obstacle on the way to self-reliant, creative independence. It is felt to impair a person's coming to maturity. "Obedience largely appears to be merely a necessary evil, not a virtue. In other words, people realize that without some obedience education and social life are impossible, but they would like to see it reduced to a minimum, on the ground that man's goal should be maximum possible self-determination. This ideal can on this view only be attained if obedience is rendered superfluous."[3] The order in a community would be preserved by personal responsibility and by common decisions. Hence the inclination exists to replace obedience by co-determination.

1. *Obedience in Holy Scripture*

In the Old and New Testament, as well as in higher religions in general, obedience to God represents itself as a basic religious attitude. It appears as the response to the claim

---

[1] This is also the case in the other Semitic and Indo-European languages.

[2] W. Molinski, art. "Obedience" in: Sacramentum Mundi IV, 1969, 37.

[3] Ib. 237.

of the "holy" and as due submission to the will of God, whose creatures, subjects and children men are. This obedience permits man to make of his life a service of God and to attain salvation and joyful communion with him. The readiness to obey God is of course not the same as obedience to men. The first must be unconditional, whereas the second can only be conditional; i.e. obedience to men is justified and can be demanded only as long as the human command is in agreement with the will of God.

Old Testament religion is essentially "a religion of obedience to the revelation of God in the word of the law and the prophets."[1] The covenant which God has made with Israel demands obedience to the covenant statutes (Gen 17:9; Ex 19:5f; 24:7f; Deut 4:1-6). The essential demand of Israel's religion is expressed in the sentence: "Hear, o heavens, and give ear, o earth; for the Lord has spoken" (Is 1:2; cf. 1:10; Jer 2:4; 7:21-28). Disobedience to God's command is the very essence of sin, as exemplified in the narrative on the fall of the first parents in the paradise. Through the mouth of his prophets God reproaches his people for their disregard of his word and ordinances. "When I spoke to you persistently you did not listen, and when I called you, you did not answer" (Jer 7:13; Hos 9:17). True love of God proves itself by love of his law, and true worship essentially consists in obedience. "Has the Lord as great delight in burnt offerings and sacrifices, as in obeying the voice of the Lord? Behold, to obey is better than sacrifice, and to hearken than the fat of rams" (1 Sam 15:22; cf. Ps 40:6-8). God's command is most purposeful and therefore also the obedience he demands. God wants men to obey his command because he has a plan to fulfill and wants men to be saved.

Obedience to the commandments of God is however by no means limited to the merely internal law of man's conscience or to that inscribed by God in man's nature. The precepts of the Lord comprise the entire law of the Torah. This also includes Israel's civil and ceremonial laws. Obedience to them is therefore likewise the will of God.

Particular attention is given to the duty of obedience towards parents. The obligation is incorporated in the decalogue as one of the commandments. "Honour your father and your mother, that your days may be prolonged and that it may go well with

---

[1] A. Stöger, art. "Obedience" in: Encyclopedia of Biblical Theology II, 1969, 616.

you" (Ex 20:12; Deut 5:16). Father and mother are mentioned side by side. Both have equal claim to being honoured by their children. The duty of honouring parents is likewise an important point of instruction in the Wisdom literature (Sir 7:27; 23:14; Tob 4:3-5). The synagogue elaborates a set of exact rules concerning the duties of reverence and obedience towards parents. But it also debates the limits of the commandment. In a conflict between the honouring of God and of parents, the duty to obey God naturally prevails.

The New Testament equally grants obedience a basic place in its morality, though faith and love still more frequently describe man's relation to God. Obedient fulfillment of the Father's will is a most characteristic feature of Christ's mission and passion. He has not come down from heaven to do his own will, but the will of him who sent him (Jn 6:38; cf. 4:34; Mt 26:39). From his entrance into the world until the death on the cross, his life was obedience (Heb 10:5-7; Rom 5:19; Phil 2:8). In turn, obedience to God and to Christ is also the proof of man's love for God and Christ (Mt 7:21; Jn 14:15.23f) and the first condition for attaining salvation (Mk 10:17-19; Rom 6:16-19; Heb 3:6-11).

Obedience to men and human laws flows from obedience to God's will, for authorities are willed by God. They command as his representatives. Christ himself obeys his parents as a matter of course (Lk 2:51) and fulfills the law (Mt 5:17), although he is conscious of being sent to modify it where deficient (Mt 5:27-48). The apostolic letters regard obedience as the foundation of Christian community life. Wives must be subject to their husbands (Eph 5:22; Col 3:18; 1 Pet 3:1-6), children to their parents (Eph 6:1-3; Col 3:20), servants to their masters (Eph 6:5-8; Col 3:22-24; 1 Pet 2:18), the younger members of the community to the elders (1 Pet 5:5), citizens to civil authority (Rom 13:1-7; 1 Pet 2:13f). According to Paul "there is no authority except from God, and those that exist have been instituted by God. Therefore he who resists the authorities resists what God has appointed, and those who resist will incur judgment" (Rom 13:1f). Yet not only because of God's wrath but also for the sake of conscience Christians must be subject to authority, for it is the minister of God (Rom 13:5f). Complementing this thought, the letter to the Hebrews motivates obedience by the fact that authority stands in the service of the subjects themselves and accordingly also obedience to authority. "Obey your leaders and submit to them, for they are keeping watch over your souls, as men who will have to give account. Let them do this joyfully, and not sadly, for that would be of no advantage to you" (Heb 13:17).

The NT view of the limits of obedience is summarized in the phrase of Acts 5:29: "We must obey God rather than men" (cf. Mk 12:17; Acts 4:19f).

2.   *Need and value of obedience*

Obedience in its theological sense primarily consists in the determination to accomplish the will of God in all things, as this is the constant teaching of Holy Scripture. Man is essentially ordained to serve God by fulfillment of his will. In this sense obedience can be regarded as the foundation of all other moral virtues and it is always morally good to obey. The problem of this theological obedience however consists in the question, how a man can recognize the will of God. God reveals his will through the demands and laws of nature and through his word in revelation. The ethical and theological sciences try to discover and to formulate the divine command more precisely. But God also reveals his will through human authority. "Man as a communicative being only fulfills himself through personal relations with his fellowmen. Being one of them, he is dependent on them and must obey them in proportion as he recognizes that their orders are directed to the welfare of the community and the individual, for that is the extent to which human orders express the will of God."[1] The obedience to men is the proper subject of this paragraph.

a)   Obedience in the service of personality growth (educational obedience)

A human being, left to himself, is not capable of unfolding his personality and of developing his abilities to the full. He needs the help and guidance of others in order to reach that moral, intellectual and spiritual maturity which enables him to meet the demands of the community, to serve it usefully and to be a member of full value. From this dependence on the assistance of others arises the obligation to be obedient. For guidance is not possible without obedience.

The younger the human being, the more he is in need of

---

[1] W. Molinski, art. "Obedience" in: Sacramentum Mundi IV, 1969, 239.

guidance and instruction. Most of all the child must allow himself to be led and advised by his parents, for their knowledge of life surpasses the knowledge he possesses. The young human being must also reach out to grasp the means which are offered to him by the community in order to unfold his own capabilities and thus ripen to a useful occupation in life. He owes obedience to his teachers and masters within the educational role assigned to them. For unless the pupil relies on the teacher, he cannot achieve his full capacity. Most of the time the child renders obedience spontaneously and without questioning, since his dependence and need of help is too apparent.

Yet also the adolescent has still much to learn from others and therefore is largely in need of obedience for the sake of his education. With the growing age of the young person, though, an always greater stress must be laid on an obedience which is conscientious and aware of its reasons. The Decree on Priestly Formation of Vatican II offers the following indications for the training of seminarians, which can equally be applied to the training of young men in general. The discipline of the seminary life is "a necessary part of the whole training program designed to provide self-mastery, to foster solid maturity of personality, and to develop other traits of character which are extremely serviceable for the ordered and productive activity of the Church. Let discipline be exercised, then, in a way which will develop in the students an internal attitude by which the authority of superiors will be accepted through an act of personal conviction" (OT 11). But at the same time, so the Decree continues, the rules of discipline ought to be applied in accord with the age of the students, so that they can gradually learn to govern themselves, to make wise use of their freedom, and to act on their own initiative and energetically.

Educational obedience ought to become superfluous once a person has reached perfect maturity. This is the ideal. But inasmuch as personality growth is hardly ever a fully terminated process and only saints reach the stage of perfect maturity, educational obedience may seldom be totally superfluous in a human life.

Educational obedience stands in the service of a person's development and growth, as has been pointed out. Consequently it is not an impediment but a condition of self-realization. It "offers man favourable opportunities, the neglect of which would inevitably lead to his impoverishment. Proper obedience is therefore not a necessary evil but a virtue."[1] But it would become an impediment to a person's maturity if he preferred dependence on educational figures out of reluctance or fear to take upon himself his own responsibility within that scope where he has reached competence. The same is true if parents or other educators tried to keep their subjects in a state of dependence which is no longer required and justified by their age and maturity. A certain tension between the duty to obedience and the need for growing personal responsibility will often be inevitable. There are limits on both sides, limits on the right of educators and authorities to regulate activities, and limits on the right of those trained and of subjects to demand freedom for independent decisions. But an incompatibility of these needs and rights cannot and does not exist.

   b)   Obedience in the service of the community
         (functional obedience)

In every community obedience to the laws of the social body and to its authority is absolutely necessary to ensure the common welfare of its members and efficiency in the accomplishment of its tasks. Obedience of this kind has a lasting function, since it is not conditioned by transitory, educational needs, but by the permanent needs of a well-ordered functioning of society. It is by obedience to the social rulings and laws and to the governing authorities that the efforts of the members of a society are unified, coordinated and focused on the common goal. In a last analysis obedience is necessary in order that a society can contribute to the greater glory of God, to the unfolding of his creative design, and to the establishment of his kingdom. Therefore it is willed by God himself, just the same as authority has its origin in his will.

No community can exist and work if there is no order in it. This can be illustrated by the operation of an orchestra in which many musicians must work together to achieve a good, pleasing performance of a musical composition. The skills of everyone are needed. Yet there must be one to coordinate the activities of all. He has to select the soloists; he has to beat time; he has to inspire the whole performance by his interpretation of the composition. This one is the conductor. Perhaps there are some among his musicians who would prefer other soloists; or who would give another interpretation to the composition or to

---

[1] W. Molinski, 1. c. 239.

some parts of it. But they have to subordinate themselves, even if their opinion is really a better one. If they did not want to submit and went their own ways, they would endanger and ruin the whole performance, in spite of their good ideas, since they are not the conductor. And to safeguard his undertaking, the conductor would have to replace them. Of course the conductor should be open to the suggestions of his musicians. But they must know that the last word is left to him as long as he is the leader and qualifies as the leader. He is expected to make the final decisions, and his subjects must be ready to submit to them.

A community needs laws and authoritative leadership, for the individual is not instinctively aware of the duties that fall to his share in the common work and life. This is still much more true in the always more complicated organisms of society of today. He is not in the position to possess sufficient expertise in all the spheres of common life. And even where he possesses expertise in a certain field, there are most often several approaches possible to the accomplishment of a task, and the unity of action must be ensured. Consequently every community is in need of authority and subordination, for they alone can guarantee efficiency and unified action.

Such obedience is by no means in conflict with the dignity, maturity and liberty of the human person. Genuine liberty means freedom from inordinate self-love; it means unhampered dedication to the welfare of the community; it means service to the common goals, unimpaired by interests conflicting with them. Vatican II justly dissociates itself from those "who seem inclined to use the name of freedom as the pretext for refusing to submit to authority and for making light of the duty of obedience" (DH 8). It rather requires Christians to "give conspicuous example of devotion to the sense of duty and of service to the advancement of the common good. Thus they can also show in practice how authority is to be harmonized with freedom, personal initiative with consideration for the bonds uniting the whole social body, and necessary unity with beneficial diversity" (GS 75).

3. *Practice of obedience in a spirit of co-responsibility*

Obedience is not simply abandonment of one's own will, nor mere mechanical fulfillment of an assignment given by a superior. Superiors are supposed to help subjects in their personal development and to promote the common weal and common tasks of the community. The subjects' obedience stands in the service of the same tasks and goals. Consequently it should be rendered with a sense of responsibility. Subjects cannot submit to orders that contradict the goals authority is appointed to serve. On the other hand they ought to set about the tasks superiors justly request them to perform with personal concern and engagement.

a) Responsible obedience. In the Christian view all men are of equal dignity and no human being has an absolute claim to the obedience of another. Man can never subject himself to other human beings unconditionally and without reservations. He can only submit to them to the extent that they stand in the service of divinely willed goals. Purely blind obedience and mere mechanic submission to an order is unworthy of the human person and irresponsible. Obedience is only virtuous to the extent that it is internally recognized as rightful and good. This insight must not always be explicit and direct. The well-founded conviction of the honesty of a person can also be sufficient guarantee for the legitimacy of a command. Children for example cannot judge the implications of an order, but only need to know that their parents want the best for them. Also adults often lack the competence to judge the appropriateness of an order. If they have sufficient grounds for assuming moral probity and adequate competence in the commanding authority, their obedience is warranted. In this sense obedience for obedience's sake as an educational and ascetical training is possible and can be meaningful.

Nevertheless where explicit insight in the meaning of a command can be given and acquired without undue difficulties it should be aimed at. Ideally "obedience is not this kind of formal and implicit obedience for obedience's sake; it springs from fully explicit awareness that what is commanded does in fact stand in the service of man",[1] and beyond in the service of God and his kingdom. For in this way the order given can be complied with more meaningfully and perfectly. Superiors on their side should readily help their subordinates to gain this insight into the meaning and value of a command.

b) Cooperative obedience. Subjects should understand that authority is appointed to aid them in their personal growth and

---

[1] W. Molinski, art. "Obedience" in: *Sacramentum Mundi* IV, 1969 239.

to take care of the successful performance of the common tasks. Correspondingly they must look at their obedience as willed by God for their own welfare, the welfare of the community, and the growth of God's kingdom.

For this reason subjects should take pains to cooperate with superiors by willing and cooperative obedience. They will not limit themselves to the mere literal fulfillment of an order, but strive to execute it in such a way that a true service is rendered to the common task. The request addressed by Vatican II to subjects of religious orders can equally be applied to other subject relationships. Since subjects ultimately serve by their obedience a common task and the realization of God's design, they are asked to "bring to the execution of commands and to the discharge of assignments entrusted to them the resources of their minds and wills, and their gifts of nature and grace" (PC 14). The common good must be their true concern as well. They are expected to contribute their share to it. This also includes participation in common deliberations and the responsible use of one's right to vote.

Furthermore subjects must be reasonable in their expectations and not demand a degree of perfection in a superior which usually cannot be presupposed. Not every human frailty disqualifies a superior and is reason to be upset with him. Such petty expectations only create an atmosphere of dissatisfaction and hamper the superior in fulfilling his duties efficiently.

Obedience will sometimes impose upon subjects the sacrifice of their own will. Opinions often differ with regard to the means and policies which ought to be adopted in the pursuit of a certain goal. Subjects have the right to voice their dissenting opinions, and their sense of responsibility may even oblige them to do so, although with due respect. But only one can make the final decision, and this is the right and duty of the superior. If his decision does not agree with the choice of one or some of his subjects, they are not already for this reason justified to refuse their cooperation. Submission will often be required for the sake of unity and efficient operation. Even an occasional incorrect decision on the part of a superior causes less harm than the subjects' disobedience would cause, were they to disobey in all those instances in which they believe a superior's decision ill-founded.

Nevertheless there are instances where a subject feels convinced in conscience that he may not obey, because the superior's decision seems to him not only less good but harmful and perhaps even immoral. If even after an exchange of views with the authorities the subject believes that he cannot in conscience comply with the order given, then he must "disobey" for the sake of the obedience he owes to God, following the example of Jesus as Paul did (Gal 2:11-21).[1]

c) Spheres of obedience. Human authorities share in the authority of God in different ways, and therefore obedience to them takes different forms. The extent to which obedience is due to an authority is fundamentally defined and delimited by the purpose and common good proper to a community. The child owes obedience to his parents within the framework of their task to assist him in the physical and spiritual development of his personality. Their authority also extends to the external order required for a consonant, peaceable family life. The pupil owes the teacher obedience within the range of his work of promoting the pupil's education to social life and his intellectual and professional training. The employee has to obey as far as obedience is necessary to the correct performance of his work. The member of a religious order is bound to submit to his superiors as far as this is demanded by the religious and apostolic goals of his order and defined by the respective constitutions. The citizen owes obedience to the state within the framework of the constitutional laws and the requirements of the common good. The Church can demand obedience to the extent that this is necessary for her pastoral and sanctifying care in the service of salvation. Rights and duties of superiors and subjects in family, state and Church still demand some more extensive treatment in the following pages.

B.   The family

The family is the primordial community. As the font of new human life, it is the normal, if not the only centre in which the human person can develop bodily and spiritually in a healthy fashion. The moral and religious life of man and his capability to love are first awakened by parental love. Through the family as its cell, society maintains and renews itself. Vatican II justly observes that "the well-being of the individual person

---

[1] Concerning the questions of civil disobedience and dissent in the Church see the sections "The right of resistance against unjust state authority" in this chapter and "Duty of submission to the teaching authority of the Church" in the chapter on faith.

and of human and Christian society is intimately linked with the healthy condition of that community produced by marriage and family" (GS 47). Therefore the restoration of human society as a whole constantly begins with the renewal of the family.[1] Its protection, formation and furtherance must be of foremost concern to state and Church (GS 52).

I. Nature and functions of the family

Family is the community of parents and children. The needs and inclinations of the child, the affections and innate tendencies of the parents, and the ties of blood with all the implied bodily and spiritual affinities leave no doubt of its natural constitution.

The purpose and tasks of the family consist in the upbringing of children and in the care for the daily needs of its members. Three basic functions of the family can be distinguished. It is the primary economic community, the primary educational unit, and the primary spiritual community for man.

As *economic unit,* the family provides for man's everyday wants in food, shelter and clothing. This is very largely a task of housekeeping, and hardly any of its other tasks is entirely independent of this. All who belong to the family and are able to contribute their work or their earning to the upkeep of the household, are obliged to do so, at least to the extent that the family community is in need of this contribution.

Since at present the economic condition of a family is to a considerable extent a question of family income, it is an important task of the state to secure a just family wage to wage-earners who have to support a family. But the economic condition is equally half a question of household management and responsible use of money. Girls therefore who intend to marry ought to prepare themselves for proper housekeeping. Equally husbands have the serious responsibility not to waste their money through gambling, drinking, exorbitant smoking, etc. Economic misery and penury caused by incompetent or irresponsible spending of wife or husband are known as "secondary poverty".

---

[1] The biological and moral strength of society essentially depends on the state of its families. "History provides sufficient evidence that the decay of family life is the deepest cause of the decline of nations. The consequence of the position of the family as the cell in society is that all true social reform must begin with the family. All so-called social reform which overlooks this law or acts against it is ultimately doomed to failure" (J. Messner: Social Ethics. — St. Louis/London: Herder Book Co., 1965, 420).

The intellectual and moral development of the human person decisively depends on the *education within the family*. In its circle the young person receives his first knowledge and understanding of the world around him. Here he is first taught the unselfishness of mutual love. "The two most important social virtues, charity and justice, are basically taught in family life. Next to these come the two social virtues of due obedience and just rule. . . . Until he has learned both how to obey and how to command in the family, a man is not in a position to give authority in society a form compatible with the dignity and rights of a human being."[1] The life in the family also lays the foundation for many other virtues, such as readiness to help, consideration, fairness, sincerity, diligence.

Man's decisive formation takes place in the earliest years of life, long before his intellect is capable of critical discernment, as is confirmed by modern psychology. The reason is that the child is most impressionable at this stage and that knowledge and attitudes are conveyed to him by the most winning force of his parents' dedicated love.

Yet family education is by no means limited to the educational role of the parents. Every member of the family has both an active and a passive share in it. The education which the children give one another can hardly be overrated. Such education is lacking where there is only one child, and it attains its greatest effect in a large family. Children who have brothers and sisters learn from the very beginning by the experiences of daily life to control themselves, to claim no more rights than the others, to help the other, to be obliging, to be self-sacrificing. "The fact that greater sacrifices and greater self-denial are demanded of the children in larger families, is the very reason why these families give their children more inward strength to carry them through life."[2]

Last but not least the family brings an educative influence to bear on the parents, who are challenged to put forth their best self in order to achieve fully the great and noble aim of a happy family. Responsibilities complied with are one of the most efficacious means of education. Parental responsibilities are an educative stimulus for the parents themselves. Thus "children contribute in their own way to making their parents holy" (GS 48).

---

[1] J. Messner, 1. c. 419.
[2] J. Messner, 1. c. 409.

The family finally provides the most important *spiritual home* for its members. "In daily living, based on love, trust, esteem and respect, there is also an exchange of ideas, convictions, values and attitudes, a sharing of the experience of joys and sorrows, successes and trials, such as we find in no other group."[1] The family is the "domestic sanctuary", called to pass on the faith of the ancestors, to cultivate the religious traditions, to offer common prayers to God, and to translate into daily life its religious convictions (cf. AA 11). Man's longings for communication, friendship, beauty, play and recreation find their primordial source of fulfillment in the circle of his parents, brothers, sisters and relatives (even though the circle of playmates and friends must gradually reach beyond the family as the child grows older). Many of the finest values of culture and civilization received the first seed and development in its midst.

II. Mutual obligations of spouses

The union of husband and wife calls for a most intimate partnership of mutual love and assistance. A common house, table and bed are as desirable for the sake of union, as are common planning, finances and action. The marriage bond means a most comprehensive solidarity in all needs of body and soul, in all sorrows and joys. Husband and wife are united in closest intimacy, which expresses itself particularly in conjugal love. Spouses have a mutual right and duty to the marital act, but also the obligation to live their sexuality with due respect for the dignity of the other. "Sexuality should be used in this encounter between partners to the extent that it will foster union, and subordinated to the extent that it would hinder it. That is the law of marital chastity."[2] The intimate, mutual belonging and dependence of the spouses account for the demand of their absolute fidelity to each other, apart from the children's need of a stable and harmonious family.

Both spouses have the duty to see to the material and spiritual welfare of the family, though partly in different roles. The husband is usually the primary bread-winner of the family and provides the material means for its sustenance. The wife's duties comprise in a particular way the management of the house-

---

[1] Jakob David, art. "Marriage, III. Family" in: Sacramentum Mundi III, 1969, 413.

[2] W. Molinski, art. "Marriage, I. Institution and Sacrament" in: Sacramentum Mundi III, 1969, 401.

hold, i.e. the preparation of the food, the care for clothing and for an orderly home; although today she very frequently also contributes to the income of the family by an employment of her own.

Spouses will hardly ever be totally of one mind and heart from the very beginning of their marriage. Differences in up-bringing, differences in interests, differences in behavioural attitudes cause frictions. Such difficulties have to be realistically evaluated and approached as part of every marriage. Spouses must take pains to adjust themselves and to overcome the tensions by educating each other, particularly themselves, by gradual growth in understanding and love. It is to be noted that the obligations towards the future family begin even before marriage is contracted. The future husband and wife must exercise the essential family virtues already in the bosom of their own families, such as industriousness, thrift, consideration, respect for others, readiness to sacrifice, concern for the home. The girl must prepare herself by acquiring the necessary knowledge of housekeeping. And both must know how to handle money responsibly. The man in particular may not waste it in drinking, gambling or immoderate smoking, but must save it for the good of his family, future or present.

Spouses can of course sin against each other by all the different sins against charity. More particular for their status as married people are the following offences: petty jealousy, which fosters groundless suspicion regarding the partner's faith-fulness and suppresses friendships beyond the family circle, squandering of community goods or their use for personal, partial interests to the neglect of the rights of the other; despotic government of the family by one or the other partner; long lasting absence from the family without justified reason; offences against conjugal faithfulness.

III. Parental duties and rights

The responsibility of parents for their child arises from the fact that they have given life to him and that the young human being comes helpless into the world, entirely dependent on their loving care. He needs parents to feed him and to help him in his spiritual and mental development in all regards.

The authority of parents is first of all personal, but it is also official. Parents have a personal authority over the child because of their overall physical and spiritual superiority. Since they are closest to the child emotionally, in natural tendencies and gifts, and by responsibility, their authority is primary and fundamental, while that of Church and state is secondary and subsidiary. The duties and rights of parents extend as far as is necessary to ensure the development of the child into responsible adulthood (educational authority). Besides, parents can also claim authority over the children with regard to the requirements of the domestic order (functional authority). The state as well as the Church universally confirm the rights and duties of parents by customs and laws, which grant parents also an official authority over their children. If any parental functions are being exercised by foster-parents, the corresponding rights and duties will pass to them to the same extent.

Since children are born of both parents, both have equal duties and equal rights. But as the two parents play different roles in the begetting, rearing and education of their children, a certain division of labour naturally occurs and therefore a certain division of duties and rights. This division of tasks partly arises from the nature of fatherhood and motherhood (e.g. feeding of the baby), and partly it results from the customs of society. Hence it cannot easily be determined a priori and in a universal way.

Decisions of common concern should generally be made by the parents jointly. But when the parents cannot agree and decisions are necessary, the ultimate power of decision usually rests with the father. This is also the mind of the apostolic writings, which regard the husband as the head of the family (Eph 5:22-24; Col 3:18; 1 Pet 3:1-6).

Parents may lose their rights over their children if they neglect them or prove unable to provide a suitable education. However forfeiture of parental rights does not automatically absolve from parental duties. This can be important, e.g., in the case of illegitimate children or divorce.

1. *Parental duties*

The primary duty of parents, which precedes all the others, is responsible assumption of parenthood. Parents "may only bring a child into the world if they have reasonable hopes that they will be able to rear and educate him in a way worthy of a human being."[1] They may not give more children life than they can hope to feed and to provide for sufficiently. For the

---

[1] Waldemar Molinski, art. "Marriage, II. Parents" in *Sacramentum Mundi* III, 1969, 408.

same reason procreation outside marriage must be regarded as impermissible.

If nevertheless an illegitimate child is born, the duties of the unmarried parents are in principle the same as those of married parents, but the educational rights as a rule rest with the mother alone. For a good reason parents are justified to place their illegitimate child in an orphanage or to give him to a family that is willing to accept or even to adopt him, if they know that he is well cared for by them. Adoption of illegitimate children, who cannot be well taken care of by their parents, is certainly a very praiseworthy work of Christian charity. Besides, such adoptions may signify a blessing and rewarding joy especially for childless families, to whom these children can give enrichment and new meaning.

a) *Well-ordered love.* Love is the fundamental obligation of parents. As a natural feeling, it motivates almost always the hearts of the parents in a stronger and more forceful way than the hearts of the children. Inner alienation and hatred on the part of parents are therefore rarely to be found. But parental love can prove deficient in different degrees and ways, be it by defect or by excess. By defect, parents can offend against love through neglect of parental duties, partiality, harshness and fits of anger, unjust or rude punishment. A most grievous fault in this line is the obstruction and prevention of a child's marriage for reasons of profit, personal compensation, self-centred love or other unjust motives. By excess, they can offend against love through pampering, too great leniency, undue preference. Exaggerated love is no less detrimental for the child than too little love. The coddled child at times does not gain sufficient independence and self-reliance and in consequence does not grow strong enough to master difficulties in life on his own; or at other times he does not learn how to subordinate himself and to integrate socially with others, which will easily lead him into opposition to the community and leave him in isolation.

b) *Provision for life, health and material well-being.* Parents must care for the child's well-being already before his birth. During the time of pregnancy they must avoid everything injurious to the unborn child. The mother must shun every type of violent exertion and emotional upheaval. The father must show still greater consideration for his wife than usual. He would be guilty of grave irresponsibility if he frequently treated her in a harsh and rude way.

Parents have the serious duty to look after their children in a manner worthy of human beings. They have to provide for food, clothing, health, lodging and home. Furthermore they must also procure some degree of material security for their children's future and help them to found their own homes when the time comes. It is most important that the children are aided to learn a useful profession. College and university training or a similar education can substitute for an inheritance.

These duties also hold good for illegitimate children. Both, father and mother, are equally obliged to support them. The father is bound to aid the unmarried mother with material means in the upbringing of his child, in accordance with his own financial condition and the need of the mother and child. Even though he may be able to escape the legal impositions obliging him to contribute to the sustenance of the child, he still has the natural duty to provide a livelihood and professional training for him.

c) *Education.*   Parents are absolutely bound to educate their children to the best of their abilities and to look after their spiritual welfare. The development of the children's personality is the most excellent task of the parents. Vatican II considers the work of Christian education as of so great importance that it dedicates an entire declaration to it (Gravissimum Educationis = GE). With regard to the role of parents in the children's education the Council writes: "Since parents have conferred life on their children, they have a most solemn obligation to educate their offspring. Hence, parents must be acknowledged as the first and foremost educators of their children. Their role as educators is so decisive that scarcely anything can compensate for their failure in it. For it devolves on parents to create a family atmosphere so animated with love and reverence for God and men that a well-rounded personal and social development will be fostered among the children" (GE 3). The children, especially the younger ones, need the care of their mother at home. Therefore her domestic role must be safely preserved, at least to the extent that this is demanded by her educational task. Although there is no need of an equally intensive care from the father's side, his active presence is likewise most beneficial for the children's formation (cf. GS 52).

The educational task requires that parents look after the moral and personal development of their children. The human person must be formed in view of his ultimate goal and of his future responsibility in society. This includes the training in the social, religious and all those other virtues which are necessary for a well-ordered, happy life. As long as children cannot be expected to cope with moral dangers by their own forces, parents are obliged to protect them against such evil. This also demands a certain supervision of the children's activities outside the family. On the other hand, to the extent that the children grow older, their ability for independent, responsible decision must be fostered, and they must be helped to stand on their own feet. Children "should be helped to acquire gradually a more mature sense of responsibility toward ennobling their own lives through constant effort, and toward pursuing authentic freedom. As they advance in years, they should be given positive and prudent sexual education. Moreover, they should be trained to take their part in social life, so that . . . . they can become actively involved in various community organizations, be ready for dialogue with others, and be willing to act energetically on behalf of the common good" (GE 1).

Intellectual training and schooling is another aspect of great importance in the child's education. Parents have the duty to provide for schooling and formation, making the best of their children's capabilities. They would seriously fail in this duty if they did not care for that basic schooling of their children which states usually offer to all youths and even demand from them. A special duty in this connection is that of providing for religious education and instruction. "The family is, so to speak, the domestic Church. In it parents should, by their word and example, be the first preachers of the faith to their children" (LG 11; cf. GE 3). They are to teach the young child the knowledge and worship of God. During the years of schooling they are obliged to see to it that the child receives religious instruction as offered by the school or by the Church, in accordance with their own faith and convictions.

As the child grows up, he must be accustomed to work, even if the parents are well-to-do. For only thus will he be able to make a decent living, be a useful member of the community and not a burden to it. The child's education must finally be completed by enabling him to learn a useful profession, by which he can sustain himself and a possible future family.

Parents are also the advisers of their children regarding the choice of state and vocation; although they may not interfere with the children's right to a free decision. "Parents or guardians should by prudent advice provide guidance to their young with respect to founding a family, and the young ought to listen gladly. At the same time no pressure, direct or indirect, should be put on the young to make them enter marriage or choose a specific partner" (GS 52).

d) *Prevention of defective, injurious education.* There can be no doubt that parents can also seriously endanger the educational purpose by their deficiencies, and they ought to make every effort to avoid and to eliminate such perils. "Nothing so readily undermines the confidence of children and frustrates the purposes of guidance as confusion and inconsistency in direction."[1] If a child cannot be certain whether the parents will approve or disapprove of his actions because they often change their mind, he is exposed to truly desperate feelings of frustration, which almost necessarily must result in some kind of neurosis. His condition is not much better in instances of constant contradiction of the parents' advice, which will vitiate every good effort. Although discipline and the will to efficient work are justified goals of education, exaggerated demands, lack of acknowledgement, continuous discontentment and criticism will finally result in quite adverse results. Too harsh or even unjust punishment will not yield the betterment of the child, but only provoke opposition, bitter resentment and a spirit of resistance against all authority. Over-possessiveness, which is above all a danger from the mother's side, isolation in the family circle and lack of social contacts deprive the child of precious and necessary means of spiritual and emotional development. Psychology has shown how deeply and negatively such defects can affect the personality growth of the child.

If parents seriously neglect or disregard their educational duties or if they prove unable to comply with them, the state would have the right to intervene. It can, for example, force parents to carry out their educational duties and to send their children to school. In extreme cases it even has the right to take children from their parents, temporarily or permanently, and to place them under guardians in an institution or in another family.

2. *Parental rights*

Just as parents have the duty to take care of their children's needs and education, so they also have the right to it. Above

[1] B. Häring III, 1966, 96.

all parents are entitled to decide on the form and content of the education of their children according to the opportunities available. This right is frequently endangered by an over-powering state intervention in matters of education, which unduly narrows down the rights of parents. Such unwarranted interference is an offence against a fundamental human right and must be resolutely put in its proper place.

Nature clearly speaks in favour of the parental function of education by the strength of the parents' love for their child, which love predisposes them as his most concerned and best educators. For love is an unsurpassable and essential power in education. Besides, nobody else can usually understand a child as well as parents can, because nobody else is so close and akin to the child in character, temperament and dispositions as the parents from whom he is descended. The educational right of parents is further corroborated by their striving to leave an image of themselves in their offspring. Education is the only means that can develop this image in the child. Since parents dedicate more care and effort to the upbringing of the child than anybody else does or can, it is also their right and privilege to educate him according to their own principles and convictions. Vatican II firmly upholds and defends this right, declaring that parents "have the first and the inalienable duty and right to educate their children" (GE 6).

In detail the parents' educational right embraces (1) the exclusive right to determine the child's basic religious and moral education (cf. DH 5); (2) their primary right to educate in every respect, i.e. to instruct the child as far as they are able and willing; (3) the right to select and provide schools where the child's training is in accordance with their religious and moral outlook (cf. GE 6; DH 5); (4) the right of parents who maintain their own schools to a proportionate contribution from the state, namely to that amount which is equivalent to the expense saved to the state through such private schools.[1]

Vatican II justly demands that the use of the right to free choice of schools and other means of education "is not to be made a reason for imposing unjust burdens on parents, whether directly or indirectly" (DH 5). The state certainly has the right to require that private schools fulfill the standards of instruction set by it. Yet if this condition is complied with, such schools have a right to subsidies just as other schools have. The parents'

---

[1] Cf. J. Messner: *Social Ethics*, 1965, 411.

freedom of choice in regard to educational institutions is greatly impaired if they have to carry all the expenses of private schools, while public schools offer instruction at very much reduced fees or without any fees. Such inequality in support is against distributive justice. Parents who send their children to private schools pay their taxes as much as other citizens. It is a violation of justice if their money is not used in their interest, but only for schools they cannot fully agree with. Public authorities therefore have the duty "to see to it, out of concern for distributive justice, that public subsidies are allocated in such a way that, when selecting schools for their children, parents are genuinely free to follow their consciences" (GE 6).

A further right of parents is their right to an income sufficient to maintain a family, as long as they show industriousness and are willing to work. "The way this family wage is to be achieved will vary with different economic and social systems, but there can be no doubt that there is a parental right to an income sufficient to maintain a family. It is not only a question of personal dignity, but also of the service parents render to society by bringing up and educating their children. It is against distributive justice if responsible parents are expected to accept a lower standard of living than childless people of the same social group . . . . , especially if those without children are not making any particularly outstanding social contribution."[1]

The educational role of state and Church. Although the educational rights of parents are primary, the tasks of education surpass the abilities of parents to a continuously increasing extent. Therefore the subsidiary help of state and Church is required. The need of such help also vests state and Church with certain educational duties and rights.

Under present-day conditions the state is undoubtedly entitled to require of everyone a certain general knowledge and schooling. For the common good demands that citizens be sufficiently trained and instructed to cope with the claims made upon them in the political and economic life of present-day society (cf. GS 60). The state has therefore the right and duty to prescribe standards of education and to watch over their implementation. It is commissioned to oversee the duties and rights of parents and of others who have a role in education and to provide them with assistance (GE 3).

---

[1] W. Molinski, art. "Marriage, II. Parents" in: *Sacramentum Mundi* III, 1969, 410.

In order to secure the attainment of the educational standards for everybody, it is entitled to maintain its own schools and institutes, as the common good may demand. "It is incumbent upon the state to provide all citizens with the opportunity to acquire an appropriate degree of cultural enrichment, and with the proper preparation for exercising their civic duties and rights. Therefore, the state itself ought to protect the right of children to receive an adequate schooling. It should be vigilant about the ability of teachers and the excellence of their training. . . . But it must keep in mind the principle of subsidiarity, so that no kind of school monopoly arises" (GE 6; cf. 3). There is no jural basis for a state school monopoly, i.e. the elimination and prohibition of private schools. Parents as the primary educators have a natural right to private schools, as long as the standard of instruction is maintained. However undue insistence on the right to denominational schools, which would interfere with other educational necessities, could equally constitute an injustice and offend against the common good.

The right of the state to demand a certain standard of education includes the right to enjoin compulsory schooling in order to secure the attainment of its educational goals. Yet this compulsion may not go farther than is absolutely necessary for the carrying out of the state's own task.

The Church as the community whose mission concerns man's religious vocation, eternal salvation and ultimate end is equally invested with educational rights, since such rights are essential for the fulfillment of her task. This is also true of other religious bodies, as is made plain by the Declaration on Religious Freedom of Vatican II (cf. DH 4). But it also holds for all of them, just as for the state, that their educational role is only a subsidiary one. They are called to assist parents in the task of education and to supplement what parents cannot or do not carry out.

In detail the Church has the right to impart religious instruction as well as to watch over education in general insofar as religion and morality are concerned. The Church is bound and entitled to give the "children of hers the kind of education through which their entire lives can be penetrated with the spirit of Christ, while at the same time she offers her services to all peoples by way of promoting the full development of the human person, for the welfare of earthly society and the building of a world fashioned more humanly" (GE 3). In order to achieve this mission, the Catholic school retains its immense importance still in the present times. Vatican II insists on this right very forcibly, and gravely sets forth: "This sacred Synod proclaims anew a right already made clear in numerous documents of the Church's teaching authority, namely, the Church's right freely to establish and to run schools of every kind and at every level. At the same time, the Council recalls that the exercise of this right makes a supreme contribution to freedom of conscience, the protection of parental rights, and the progress of culture itself" (GE 8).

3. *Limits of parental duties and rights*

Parents do not possess an unrestrained authority over their children, but their rights and duties are limited by the rights and duties of others, directly by those of their children, indirectly by those of state and Church and by those of other educators, e.g. relatives and teachers.

a) Parental authority is limited by the rights of the children. For children are not their parents' property, but in principle equal partners with equal and inalienable human rights. "Thus they owe obedience to their parents to the extent to which they are not yet capable of making their own decisions and taking full responsibility for their own actions, but parents may only expect obedience to that extent and no more. Parents must not attempt to limit or influence their children's wills except as far as is necessary in the children's interest, properly understood. This applies particularly to important things, such as choice of occupation and marriage, but also to unimportant matters such as fashion."[1] Also in religious education the child's freedom must be respected. Religious education should primarily aim at the guidance and shaping of conscience and may never simply force a person into a certain faith. Genuine religious development is only possible on the basis of personal conviction. Naturally parents as their children's tutors and advisers must object if a child offends against God's law. Not every punishment and physical force is against the rights of the human person. Physical punishment however should be resorted to only if urgently necessary for the good of the child, and in the case of adolescents only most exceptionally.

b) Parents are obliged to grant the state and Church the exercise of their subsidiary rights, especially in educational matters, since they themselves are not in a position to provide everything their children need and the common good may demand.

---

[1] W. Molinski, 1. c. 411.

Therefore the state has the right to enforce an educational standard appropriate to the needs of the community and its culture. If parents neglect their duties and do not care for a proper schooling of their children, the state can force them to carry out these duties. The Church too can insist that parents allow her the opportunity for religious instruction, although it can only use moral means and sanctions to enforce her rights.

c) Teachers, guardians, relatives or other persons with educational functions equally have rights with regard to the guidance and instructions of the children, which must be respected by parents. Parents cannot advise or order a child what is in contradiction to the justified commands of the other educators. On the contrary, they must support their educational efforts and constructively cooperate with them.

IV. Duties of children towards parents

According to St. Thomas the children's obligation of love and reverence is based on the fact that the parents are, after God, "the second source of life, growth and education." Doubtless, in a normal family the children owe their parents many benefits. Consequently the child has the obligation to love, reverence and gratitude. The parents' responsibility for a good education moreover demands obedience on the part of the child. All these obligations are already spontaneously experienced by the child in his emotional life. Difficulties arise if the parents do not fulfill their obligations, if they do not love their child justly, or even do not want it. That may modify the obligations of the child, though the obligation of general Christian love never ceases.

1. *Reverence and honour*

The fourth commandment of the decalogue directly stresses the child's duty to revere and honour his parents. "Honour your father and your mother, that your days may be long in the land which the Lord your God gives you" (Ex 20:12; Deut 5:16). Christ quotes this commandment twice and confirms it (Mt 15:4; 19:19). Reverence for parents flows from the mystery of life, in which they are cooperators with God. It is likewise founded in the great responsibilities which parents have for the child before God. Naturally if parents fail or prove incapable of grounding their life and authority on the veneration and adoration of God, and still more so if they are found to be irresponsible, they will greatly hinder the development of true reverence in the child's heart.

The inner spirit of reverence must manifest itself in external signs of honour. Children sin against the honour due to parents if they are ashamed of them and disown them because of their humble state or poverty; or if they use offensive speech, treat them contemptuously, or raise their hand against them. It is not against reverence to restrain one's parents in a case of necessity even by force if they are insane, intoxicated, or for some other reason out of control.

2. *Obedience*

For St. Paul the relation of children to parents is characterized by the duty of obedience. He requires children to obey their parents in all things (Eph 6:1; Col 3:20) and includes disobedience in the list of vices (Rom 1:30; 2 Tim 3:2). Obedience is the acceptance of the hierarchical order of creation, and ultimately the acceptance of God's rights, for he has so constructed and ordered human existence that men depend on and are subordinate to each other. The child's entire development requires the help and guidance of parents and educators and therefore enjoins obedience to them (educational obedience). As long as children need parental guidance and are not yet fully able and competent to make their own decisions, they must obey parents in all good and lawful matters related to their education and training. The domestic order too claims submission to the authority of parents (functional obedience), and this also from adult children as long as they stay at home. All children must obey in things necessary for the domestic order. Besides, parents retain a very extensive right and duty to admonish their children in what is good for them.

As men are fallible, confidence in the commands of men has also its limits. It must be the concern of parents or educators themselves to awaken in the child the capacity for discrimination and to teach the right attitude towards mistaken commands. As long as the critical spirit of the child rests on reverence for divinely ordained authority, this spirit of discernment is morally wholesome for the child's development.

Children sin if they disobey their parents' just commands, more or less seriously according to the importance of the matter; or if they obey, but only grudgingly and with harsh retorts;

if they leave home prematurely without good reason in order to escape parental authority; if they scorn their good counsel.

The child is however not obliged to obey his parents in matters that are immoral. It is not even allowed to do so, except where a positive divine or ecclesiastical law is concerned (e.g. the obligation to Sunday Mass) and the child must fear severe reprisals. He has also the right to free himself from exaggerated dependence and is not bound to obey against his own justified interests, at least in concerns of great moment. For this reason children are not obliged to follow their parents' will in matters involving choice of vocation or marriage partner, though they must at least consult them and listen to their advice.

3.   *Love and gratitude*

Filial love must above all be a grateful love (cf. GS 48), since children owe to their parents their life, livelihood, education, and many other benefits. Usually and in a normal family children are indebted to their parents more than to anybody else. Naturally love and gratitude increase with the magnitude of the benefits received. Egotist interests and aims of parents can also be sources of harm for the child. Hence the child's love will to a certain extent be relative to the parent's love.

Love and gratitude must express themselves in words and signs. Children should show interest in family concerns and be ready for active help. Grown-up sons and daughters will assist their old parents if they are indigent and gladden them by their visits and similar tokens. Children sin against this love if they foster sentiments of hatred; refuse to speak, to write or to see them; curse or speak ill of them; refuse to support them when they are old and indigent; fail to call the priest in a critical illness; show no concern for a decent burial; fail to pray for them.

From the love for parents love for the entire family must grow, above all for sisters and brothers, then for grandparents and the others who are more closely related. According to the degree of kinship they have a claim to special love and, in case of need, to help and support. Every family member should cooperate for the family welfare and be concerned with safeguarding the family name and honour.

V.   The wider family

Domestic servants and maids belong to the family in the wider sense, and the employer should see in them more than just workers and wage earners. Apprentices have a similar standing and also form part of the wider family circle.

In modern times the relationship between domestic servants and the family has often been treated as a mere labour contract. The masters come to expect certain definite services, and the domestics are paid for these services with a fixed sum of money. This often implies a depressing burden of degradation, loneliness and frustration for the servants. Against such misconceptions the Christian ideal of a household is still valid. "It is true that service in a family does depend on a free contract, but from its very nature a contract of this kind includes much more than exactly calculated work and payment. The relationship between the family and its domestic servants is, on both sides, one of loyalty. The family, in the performance of various tasks, needs help whose value cannot be precisely measured in terms of money, as can the labour of a worker in a factory, but depends upon a sympathetic interest on the part of the domestic servants in the welfare of the family. In the interest of the domestic staff the contract of service, by its nature, includes more than mere payment of money for service rendered; the family is responsible for the welfare of its domestics in body and mind."[1]

a) *Duties of justice.* Employers and servants have both to follow the terms of the contract. Employers are in justice obliged to pay just wages, not to overburden the servants with work, to grant them a reasonable measure of free time, not to dismiss them without sufficient reason before the contract expires. Violation of these duties carries with it the obligation to restitution.

Servants are in justice bound to measure up their work to the wage and benefits they receive, to obey with regard to work and domestic order, and to follow any further agreements of the contract.

b) *Duties of loyalty and personal care.* Employers have parental duties regarding the younger servants. This obliges them to look after their corporal and especially spiritual welfare. It is their duty to prevent blasphemy, cursing and impure language. They have to be watchful regarding the danger of sin. A twofold mortal sin it would be for the master or other members of the family to exploit their position by leading their employees into sin. On the other hand the master must take precautions against servants who might endanger his children or other employees.

---

[1] J. Messner: Social Ethics. — St. Louis/London: Herder Book Co., 1965, 421f.

Regarding servants of long service, employers have special duties of loyalty and respect. "For when these give their services for a long time and link their lives with the burdens and joys of a growing family, they are indeed part of the family community. Since they devote their lives to it, the family must provide for their essential needs, especially for their need of respect, of affection, of recreation, of security in sickness and in old age, and of suitable lodging, time off, holidays and whatever else concerns their external good."[1]

Servants have the duty of sympathetic interest in the family. They are held to discreet silence about family matters. And they are obliged to respectful and proper deportment.

C.   The state[2]

The state is the society vested with the highest sovereignty among earthly communities. It enjoys pre-eminence over all the other natural societies for the reason that it has to take care of the universal common good of the civic community. This means that it is not subject to any other earthly power, whereas all the other natural groups are in some way subordinate to the state.

I.   Nature and origin of the state

The moral rights and duties of the state as well as the limits of its power on the one hand and the moral duties and rights of the citizens regarding this state on the other essentially depend on the conception of its nature.

If the state is the goal of human development and if the state is the "moral universe" with the highest, even divine rights,

---

[1] J. Messner, 1. c. 422.

[2] References: Jacque Maritain: Man and the State. — University of Chicago Press, 1952. Oscar Cullmann: The State in the New Testament. — New York: Charles Scribner's Sons, 1956. Jacque Maritain: The Person and the Common Good. — University of Notre Dame Press, 1966. J. N. D. Anderson: Into the World — the need and limits of Christian involvement. — London: Falcon Books, 1968. James A. Gould and Vincent V. Thursby: Contemporary Political Thought. — New York: Holt, Rinehart and Winston, 1969. Alan Richardson: The Political Christ. — London: SCM Press, 1973. Karl H. Hertz: Politics Is a Way of Helping People. — Minneapolis: Augsburg Publishing House, 1974. Jürgen Moltmann a. o.: Religion and Political Society. — New York: Harper and Row, 1974.

as Hegel teaches[1] and as it was adopted by Marx, then the power of the state is almighty and every resistance against it immoral. Or if the state is nothing else than an instrument in the service of individual claims and interests and of the personal well-being of its citizens, it cannot reach out to supra-individual and supra-national goals, e.g. the advancement of less developed nations, but will be narrowed down to individualist and nationalist functions.

Quite contrary to these and similar concepts of the state, Christian philosophy looks upon the state as a servant in the attainment of the common good (cf. Rom 13:4: "for he is God's servant for your good"), which in turn is only a means to the final end of man (cf. Rom 13:6: "for the authorities are ministers of God"). The state is not the highest purpose of human existence, so that men were accorded rights only to the extent that they harmonize with the aims of the state entity. Man has his own existential and natural rights, which the state power has to respect. Essentially they are summarized in the "rights of man".[2] The state is likewise not merely the servant of the individual's welfare and interests. Man has an eternal destiny, which transcends all earthly realities. Neither the individual's perfection nor the state's progress are ends in themselves. The individual citizen as well as the entire state community are ultimately called to serve God's kingdom and his salvific plan with history.

1. *Concept of the state.* The state can briefly be described as the independent (or sovereign) political community. As independent community it is distinguished from the many smaller communities which depend on the protection and assistance of the state. As political community it is distinguished from the independent religious community, which is the Church.

In a more complete way the state is defined as a geographically delimited society endowed with supreme authority for the establishment of the universal common good. The following characteristics are commonly singled out as the constitutive elements of the state: (a) a plurality of people, usually belonging together by common culture or at least common interests; (b) a

---

[1] According to Hegel, "the state is divine will, as present spirit unfolding itself to actual form and organization." And he comes to the conclusion that the state "has the supreme right against the individual, whose supreme duty it is to be a member of the state" (quoted by J. Messner: Social Ethics. — St. Louis/London: Herder Book Co., 1965, 571).

[2] J. Messner, 1. c. 326-330 lists 14 human rights or rights of man.

distinct territory permanently settled by this people; (c) a public
authority with power of ultimate decision, which has the primacy
over all the other temporal societies within the territory; (d) a
positive legal and constitutional order for the attainment of the
common good, which also determines and legalizes the political
authority.

The state (as also the Church) is traditionally termed a
"perfect society", because it possesses all the means necessary
for the attainment of its needs and ends and thus is independent
of other societies. The qualification "perfect" is of course not
to be taken in the moral sense, but rather in the existential
sense of a society which is independent from other societies and
in principle self-sufficient. Because of its independence and
sovereignty the state tends more than any other temporal community towards perpetuity and survival into an indefinite future,
as the name already implies.[1]

2. *Origin of the state.*   In this context only the question
of the ontic and juridical origin of the state shall be posed,
not of the historical origin.

Every philosophy of state agrees that the state is not a free
invention of the human will, but a necessity founded in human
nature. Since no society "can hold together unless someone be
over all, directing all to strive earnestly for the common good,
every civilized community must have a ruling authority and this
authority, no less than society itself, has its source in nature,
and has, consequently, God for its author" (Leo XIII[2]; cf. GS
74). The necessity of the state and of state authority has
ultimately its source in God himself, who has created man as
a social and political being. St. Paul can therefore say that
"there exists no authority except from God, and those who exist
have been appointed by God" (Rom 13:1). This does not mean
that every individual ruler has been appointed by God; but rather
that political authority as such is willed by God.

In larger human groups many important and necessary tasks
cannot be achieved without the help of the state, as experience
compellingly proves. Even with regard to his own perfection
man can only realize his existential ends fully under the protection
and with the help of the state. Much less can men achieve the

[1] Cf. H. A. Rommen, art. "State" in: New Catholic Encyclopedia,
vol. 13. 1967, 645.

[2] Quoted by John XXIII in: Pacem in Terris, nr. 46.

universal goals of mankind, which are the unfolding of the Creator's work and the realization of the divine plan with history, without the coordinating and organizing power of the state.

Since man "finds political fellowship predesigned in his nature and morally commanded",[1] the state cannot be considered the result of a plain, free contract among its members in the individualist sense. The institution of the state as such is founded on human nature and in its substance is a demand of man's natural constitution. The concrete form of a state, however, and the concrete political order depend on the free agreement of the citizens. "The state and its structure pertain at least as much to men's free will and pleasure as does the style in which they build their houses."[2] The form of government (monarchic, aristocratic, democratic, etc.), the constitutional structure of the state, the leaders and parties in power derive their authority from the people, either by direct consent or at least by tacit approval. To assume that individual persons are directly chosen by God and placed in power (divine right of kings) contradicts human experience and God's way of working through secondary causes. The role of the people in the choice of the bearer of state authority is the fundamental reason why an incompetent or corrupt authority can be removed by the citizens.

According to the Church's teaching different forms of government are possible and acceptable as such (GS 74).[3] Obviously one must exclude the totalitarian state, because it does not recognize any limits to its arbitrary power. However not every absolute and dictatorial government may immediately be considered as totalitarian. Danger from corrupt or demagogic groups could justify such rulers. The decisive factor in every form of government, by which its basic right to authority is judged, is its willingness and ability to serve the common good and its disposition to respect man's fundamental rights. Yet it also holds as a general principle that in the choice of a concrete form of government the maturity of the citizens must be taken into account. The greater the political maturity of the people, the greater is their right of cooperating in the government.

For certain Christian thinkers the state has its origin in sin. For them the state is indeed willed by God, but only after the fall of man. The state is founded on human nature, but

---

[1] J. Messner, 1. c. 557.

[2] J. Messner, 1. c. 562.

[3] Cf. also John XXIII: Pacem in Terris, nr. 67f.

only on man's present sinful nature. Man's sinful aspiration must be restrained and curbed, and this makes the state with its coercive power necessary.[1] But such a view does not fully do justice to the nature of the state. Even independently of the threat of sin, man would stand in need of the coordinating and guiding function of the state in the pursuit of the common goal. The state is not merely a necessary evil, but truly a minister of God in his creative as well as salvific design.

3. *Purpose of the state.* The purpose of the state is the promotion of the general, political common good, which consists in the establishment of justice and order, the securing of domestic tranquility, the provision of common defence, the promotion of general welfare, and the ensuring of the blessings of liberty for all. It is especially important that the common good of all be promoted without preference for any single citizen or civic group. This will not seldom demand that more attention be given to the less fortunate members of the community, since they are less able to defend their rights and to assert their claims.

Two main functions of the state can be distinguished. The first one is the ordering function. It consists in the establishment and protection of the legal order, which is the prerequisite for all other characteristic activities of the state. Unless this function is fulfilled, not only is men's social coexistence impossible, but also their cooperation in the realization of common goals and tasks. This function also includes the task of common defence, since only thus the preservation of the legal order can be guaranteed. The second basic function is the welfare function. It consists in the promotion of the general economic and cultural welfare of the citizens. This function has been disregarded by

---

[1] Especially for orthodox Protestant theology the nature of the state consists in power and force to make possible a social life among sinful men. The Holy Spirit and the gospel do not rule in it, but only a kind of natural law. Therefore the state (worldly realm or kingdom) is completely independent of the Church (spiritual realm or kingdom). This spiritual realm only is ruled by the Holy Spirit, by the gospel, by charity. Outside of the Church another law is in force, which often contradicts the law of Christ.

This doctrine leads to the following dangers: 1. Either the good Christians withdraw to the spiritual realm, leaving the state on its own; 2. or the Christians live in a double morality: one for the private, religious life and another for the public, political life.

The most important concern of Luther in this doctrine was to free the state from the regimentation of the (medieval) Church and to confine the Church to its proper task: the preaching of the gospel (cf. Soe: Christliche Ethik, 1957, 323-330).

individualist liberalism, which restricted the competence of the state to the legal order alone. Today however the true idea of the state is endangered from the opposite direction through over-emphasis of this function by forms of socialism. The principle of subsidiarity must be safeguarded in order to allow for the full development of the human personality and for the optimum development of the civic community itself. The functions and the subsidiary nature of the state shall still find more detailed consideration in the following.

From the purpose of the state flows as a necessary consequence its endowment with political power; because the state cannot execute its functions unless entitled to combat arbitrary, illegal powers that endanger the common good. In two respects power belongs to the state: as an association for the establishment of internal justice and order; and as an association for self-defence.

4. *Moral character of the state.* Since the state has its foundation in human nature and lastly in God's will, it is part of the moral order. Regard for the common good is a very important part of the moral responsibility of the human person. Inasmuch as the functions of the state "are fundamental for the performance of all man's tasks in the material and cultural spheres, its value is the most comprehensive in comparison with the individual values in these spheres; hence, it is a distinct moral value of very high rank."[1]

This means that the state as a realization of the moral idea can appeal to each one's duty in conscience to collaborate readily for the common good of all. A particular indication of the moral nature of the state is its securing of a minimum of morality among men. This moral character of the state is also what gives moral justification to the use of force in the service of its order.

Citizens from their side are expected to feel responsible for the state. They are obliged to support it by their cooperation in the realization of the common tasks. Above all they are conscience-bound to obey lawful political authority.

II. Tasks and moral duties of state authority

"Political authority, whether in the community as such or in institutions representing the state, must always be exercised within the limits of morality and on behalf of the dynamically

---

[1] J. Messner, 1. c. 571.

conceived common good, according to a juridical order enjoying legal status" (GS 74). All the officials concerned, also the absolute monarch, are obliged to be faithful servants of the state. They must exercise their authority with discretion and with full knowledge of the law. They have to administer and distribute public goods impartially. The equitable order of society also demands that the private rights of individual citizens as well as intermediate organizations be carefully respected.

A good and efficient administration can only be achieved if only worthy and able candidates are appointed for public office and if the unqualified are removed from it. Distribution of offices according to patronage or to membership in favoured groups (of a religious, political, social nature, etc.) is unjust and inadmissible. Likewise acceptance of an office is forbidden to anyone incapable of filling it. On the other hand it is thoroughly respectable and praiseworthy if those who are suited for civic offices, or can become so, prepare themselves for "the difficult but most honourable art of politics" (GS 75). He who possesses the abilities may even be obliged to accept a public office if no other capable person is available and if there is no valid excuse.

Governing authorities and officials are bound to just, impartial and reliable administration of their office. Vatican II very appropriately requires them to exercise their charge "without thought of personal convenience and without benefit of bribery" (GS 75). Those who accept bribes must be threatened with proper penalties, most especially if they violate their duties by accepting them. The same holds for those who abuse their office for private advantages or who reveal official secrets, particularly state secrets, but also official secrets concerning individual citizens.

Since social life in the modern world is so complex and so much in a state of flux, even a juridical structure which has been prudently and thoughtfully established is always to a certain extent inadequate for the needs of society. This requires from civil authorities clear ideas about the nature and true meaning of laws and great flexibility in their application. "They must be men of great equilibrium and integrity, competent and courageous enough to see at once what the situation requires and to take the necessary action quickly and effectively" (John XXIII).[1]

---

[1] Pacem in Terris, nr. 72.

1. *Tasks of state authority in general*

The tasks of the state authority result from the purpose of the state, which is the protection and promotion of the general common good.

In relation to other nations, the governing authority has the duty to defend the rights of the state against foreign encroachments, if necessary even by war. (Because of the many questions connected with the national right to defence by war, a separate section shall be dedicated to this subject.) It has to safeguard the state's interests in international politics with moderation and respect for foreign rights. It has to cooperate in the community of nations and, if this is necessary for the best of this community, to renounce a part of its sovereign rights in favour of an international authority. The same holds good for confederations of states of which a nation is a member.

In relation to its own nation, the tasks of state authority can be divided into three major groups: legislation and administration of justice, promotion of the socio-economic welfare, and care for cultural concerns. The first task belongs, together with the provision for common defence, to the ordering function of the state; the two others pertain to the welfare function.

a) Legislation and administration of justice

Through the enactment of laws and through the application of sanctions when necessary, the state must uphold and defend the rights of all citizens, maintain public order and tranquility, and promote the common welfare. The conditions of a just legislation are dealt with in the treatise on the moral law (cf. the general principles of moral theology). The basic criteria for every law are the common good, the law of nature, and man's divinely appointed end. On this basis state authorities have to determine, enunciate and apply positive law. Consequently the legislative authority is clearly limited: nothing that conflicts with the common good, with natural right and divine revelation can become law through any enactment of the state. Besides, civil authority has also to respect acquired legal titles. On the other hand there is no natural law foundation for unalterability of a constitution or a civil code. None can be considered so final as to be unalterable. Hence every constitution must provide for tranquil evolution and ordered change.

Parliamentary representatives and congressmen must contribute their share to the promotion of good laws and must make the full force of their influence felt in the prevention of evil legislation. Participation in the deliberations and in the passing of resolutions is obligatory; the duty urges more strongly, the more important the matter in discussion is. Cooperation in evil legislation is sinful, except when a greater evil is to be avoided. In such cases representatives must make their position clear.

Legislative authorities must beware of delegating too easily legislative rights to inferior, executive authorities when charging them with the working out of the details of general laws. Experience shows that the use of skeleton laws cannot easily be checked and that they leave great latitude as to the concrete application. The duty of the legislator does not permit a shifting of one half of his responsibility. "When it is a question of more than merely technical matters, parliament has no real right to delegate. For no one can give up a right rooted in a duty unless the attainment of the object of the right is assured; this is not left to his discretion, but he remains responsible for it. Such responsibility lies upon the legislator, whether monarch or elected body."[1]

The administration of justice has the purpose to enforce laws and to defend against injustice, but also to impart to the citizens proper insight into their rights and duties. Lawyers and judges are required to possess a particularly solid knowledge of the law. They must also be well acquainted with the concrete conditions of modern life, to which the laws are to be applied. This acquaintance can often only be gained by practice. Lawyers are liable for damage done to others resulting from their culpable ignorance.

One of the foremost obligations of judges and lawyers is the incorruptible and impartial application of the law according to the principle of equality. Although modern states usually profess equality of all before the law, much remains to be done to realize it fully in practice. The high costs of litigation, e.g., often place poorer people at a disadvantage. Arrangements ought to be made to provide poorer people with legal facilities at moderate fees, perhaps by cooperation between the state, the local authorities and the lawyers associations.

---

[1] J. Messner: Social Ethics. — St. Louis/London: Herder Book Co., 1965, 640.

ction for legal security is finally the
independence of judges from state influence, so that they are
fully free to follow their conscience. Modern constitutional states
usually guarantee this independence by the separation of the
judiciary from the executive.

b) Promotion of socio-economic welfare and public health

This task includes the care for economic growth, social
progress and hygienic conditions of the nation.

With regard to economic planning, liberalism advocates a
minimum of state intervention, while socialism favours a
maximum of state regimentation. Yet both systems have dangers
which must be avoided. On the one hand "individual initiative
alone and the mere free play of competition could never assure
successful development. One must avoid the risk of increasing
still more the wealth of the rich and the dominion of the strong,
whilst leaving the poor in their misery and adding to the servitude
of the oppressed" (Paul VI).[1] On the other hand the unlimited
right to state intervention in economic matters tends to stifle
private initiative. State authority must therefore take care to
associate private initiative and intermediary bodies with its own
economic planning.

The state is appointed to coordinate, stimulate and integrate
the economic activity of the nation; but at the same time it must
leave as much economic self-responsibility to individuals and
intermediary associations as compatible with the common good.
Individuals and associations themselves are required not to seek
excessive and inappropriate conveniences from the state. Rather
they ought to be on guard against granting governments too much
authority with a consequent weakening of the sense of responsibility on the citizen's part (cf. GS 75).

Labour conditions and income security are two of the most
important concerns of social policy.[2] As regards labour conditions,
social legislation comprises the protection of the worker's person,
life and health by regulations concerning the workshop plant.
Compliance with these regulations is a moral duty for the
employer. Workshop inspectorate through representatives of the

---

[1] Populorum Progressio, nr. 33.

[2] "Social policy consists in measures and institutions of the state to
protect social groups against a disadvantageous position in regard to
sharing in the common weal as a result of the social system" (Joh.
Messner, l. c. 647).

state and of the workers ought to assure their implementation. Income security is primarily served by general and compulsory social insurance. It must provide for instances of misfortune, such as sickness, accident, disability and unemployment, but also for increased family responsibilities, so that "no person will be without the necessary means to maintain a decent standard of living." Furthermore "the government should make similarly effective efforts to see that those who are able to work can find employment in keeping with the laws of justice and equity" (John XIII).[1]

c) Care for cultural and moral values

The cultural function of the state includes the general instruction and schooling, the cultivation of sciences and arts, and fostering of good morals.

The right of the state to require a basic, general schooling of its citizens, to prescribe standards of education and to maintain schools for their attainment has already been discussed in the section on parental rights and duties. It pertains to the tasks of the state to provide the citizens with the benefits of the basic culture. Civic and political education ought to constitute part of it, since this is today supremely necessary in order that all citizens can make their contribution to the political community (cf. GS 75). Moreover "efforts must be made to see that men who are capable of higher studies can pursue them," so that they be able to serve the community to the best of their natural aptitudes (GS 60).

The duty of the state to respect the parents' right to private schools, as long as these schools fulfill the prescribed standards, has equally been mentioned before. Also in its own schools the state has to respect the parents' wishes, particularly with regard to religious and moral education of the children. For the state acts in these matters as the representative of the parents, who have delegated part of their educational rights to it.

The state's function in the sphere of culture consists in the protection of the cultural values against any threats of misuse and oppression, as well as in their promotion to the end that all citizens be enabled to share in them. Likewise the state has the duty to defend the citizens' right to worship and to religious freedom (cf. DH 7).

---

[1] Pacem in Terris, nr. 64.

With regard to public morality, Christian ethics has always upheld, against liberalist indifferentism, that it belongs to the highest goods of the common weal. The state as defender of the common good has to avert destructive forces in this sphere. Vatican II mentions the duty of the state to protect and promote the authentic nature of marriage and the family and to shield public morality in this regard (GS 52). Likewise government is "to help create conditions favourable to the fostering of religious life." Society itself will profit by the religious and moral virtues which originate in men's faithfulness to God's will (DH 6).

In the modern state the discussion on public morality centres in a special way on radio, motion pictures, television, literature and amusements that are accessible to the young. It is true that very strict and rigid measures may do more harm than good at times. But there can also be no doubt that particularly the young and adolescents need protection against influences that are destructive for morality. For this reason it is most praiseworthy and necessary that states enact laws in protection of the young, as has indeed already been done in many countries.

2. Criminal jurisdiction of the state[1]

a) Punitive right of the state in general

The right of the state to punish evil-doers and criminals is indispensable for the maintenance and restoration of order and justice in society, which constitute highly important aspects of the common good. Holy Scripture says: "If you do wrong, be afraid, for he (the person in authority) does not bear the sword in vain; he is the servant of God to execute his wrath on the wrongdoer" (Rom 13:4). God himself can be regarded as the author of this right, since it is an essential requisite for the carrying out of those tasks which the state is appointed to serve in God's creative design.

The authorization of the state to impose punishments is supported by the following reasons: (1) The common weal requires that the community of citizens be protected against the dangers of delinquency and crime. This is only possible if the state has the right to punish evil-doers. (2) Subjects inclined to evil are

---

[1] References: Rudolph J. Gerber and Patrick D. McAnany: Contemporary Punishment. Views, Explanations, and Justifications. — Notre Dame/London: University of Notre Dame Press, 1972. A. Regan: The Problem of Capital Punishment. — Studia Moralia 14 (1976), 209-237.

to be deterred from crime through the fear of punishment. (3) Violations of the legal order and of justice call for reparation and atonement (retaliation-theory). Damage inflicted on the rights of others must be repaired and compensated, and atonement rendered for the offence. (4) Criminals ought to be educated to mend their ways and to become better men. This requires limitations of their misused freedom and corrective measures. Amendment of the criminal can however not be regarded as the only or even main reason for the punitive right of the state. The fundamental good of the common weal calls for this right even where such amendment cannot be obtained for some reason.

b) Right of the state to death penalty

Granted that the state has the right to punish in general, it is today controverted whether it also has the right of death penalty. The latter right is recently often questioned on humanitarian grounds, and in several states capital punishment has lately been abolished. Thus it must be discussed whether the state has the right and maybe also the obligation to inflict the death penalty for major crimes.

Holy Scriptures in the OT expressly attribute to the state both the right and the obligation of death penalty for more serious crimes. "For blood pollutes the land, and no expiation can be made for the land, for the blood that is shed in it, except by the blood of him who shed it" (Num 35:33; also Gen 9:6; Ex 21:12-25; Num 35:16-34). Besides murder also other serious crimes are punished with death, e.g. blasphemy, grave sexual offences, idolatry, etc.

Since however the NT is the perfection of the OT, the regulations of the old law cannot, without further examination, be applied to the present order of grace. The NT is less explicit than the OT. Nevertheless it nowhere denies the state the right to capital punishment. And the text of Rom 13:4, which was already quoted, doubtless presumes the authority of the state to penalize with the sword. From this teaching of the Bible as well as from the entire Christian tradition we must conclude that the state in principle has the right to inflict capital punishment for serious crimes.

The four reasons listed for the right of the state to impose punishments in general do not all equally prove the right to inflict the death penalty as well. The transgressor is not able to be reformed by this penalty. And criminologists question whether the deterrent effect of death penalty is any greater than that of other grave penalties (e.g. of lifelong imprisonment). The validity of this objection however still needs further careful examination. A comparison is often made between states which have abolished death penalty and others which theoretically still retain, but hardly ever inflict it. On this condition it cannot be surprising that the deterrent effect in the latter states is no greater than in the states which have abolished the penalty. But in states where death penalty is still more resolutely inflicted and therefore a real threat to the criminal, such as for example Taiwan, the crime rate seems to be reduced effectively. The strong and very common conviction of people of all times that death penalty has a deterrent effect may after all be more than a plain deception.

The retaliation theory cannot prove why the atonement for grave crimes has necessarily to be death and cannot equally be some other severe kind of expiation. Nevertheless people of all times judged that the most commensurate atonement for very serious crimes should be the death of the criminal. It is up to the prudent judgment of each nation to decide which kind of atonement is to be required.

Of special importance in this question is the argument taken from the protection of the common weal.[1] Criminals who seriously endanger the welfare of other citizens and of the community have to be hindered from their pernicious activity. Whether this necessity to protect the public requires the death of the criminal or not depends on the question whether his death is the only efficient and morally possible means to safeguard the life and well-being of the community of citizens. That means in its consequences: Different penalties can be justified for the same crime at different times and in different circumstances (e.g. peace and war). The death penalty can be both justified and necessary in certain circumstances; in other circumstances it may not be necessary. That largely depends on whether or not a state is morally in the condition to keep the criminals under safe detention.

Under the presupposition that a state is able to protect the common weal against crime just as well by other penalties as by capital punishment, the latter can in principle be substituted

---

[1] Cf. the important text with St. Thomas Aquinas in S. Th. II. II., q. 64, a. 2.

by these other penalties. For it cannot be proved that the
state must unconditionally avail itself of the right to inflict the
death penalty; although it is not equally evident that the state
is even obliged to abolish the death penalty in this case
altogether.

At any rate wherever the death penalty is in force, sufficient
precautions must be taken that an error of law and a judicial
murder are precluded. Moreover some authority in the state
must have the right of pardon to commute the death sentence
into other penalties.

3. *Requirements of a just fiscal policy*

Fiscal and budgetary policy are of great importance for the
common good in general and for the economic development of
a country in particular. In order to accomplish its tasks and
functions, the state is in absolute need of the financial income
by taxes. The very necessities of the common good found the
state's right to levy taxes. But the requirements of the common
weal also limit this right.

Taxes may be either direct taxes, which include income
and profit taxes, personal taxes, trade taxes, real estate and
property taxes, or indirect taxes, which include customs and
purchase taxes, e.g. revenues levied on luxury goods, alcoholic
drinks, tobacco, tickets for motion pictures, gasoline. It is a
fundamental principle of just fiscal policy that tax burdens be
distributed equitably and in accordance with capacity. This
implies the obligation to impose taxes in such a way that the
poorer classes be not disproportionately burdened in comparison
with the wealthier classes. Accordingly tax laws ought to provide
for an increasing taxation of higher incomes and the progressively
lower taxation of goods generally needed in contradistinction to
luxury goods.

Besides procuring the necessary financial means for the
expenses of the state in the service of the common good, taxation
also serves as an instrument of economic policy. Taxation can
influence economic development chiefly in three directions. "It
can influence the order of magnitudes by differential taxation of
medium and small businesses in comparison with large businesses
and combines; it can further the desired expansion of branches
of the economy or restrain that which is not desired; it can be
used for a policy of industry location by means of differential
treatment of desirably or less desirably situated undertakings and

businesses."[1] Taxation is equally a means to adjust the social order by taking influence on income and property distribution.

The limits of taxation are determined by the principle of economic productivity. Too high taxes have a retarding effect on economic progress. It is asserted that taxes substantially exceeding the twenty-five per cent limit of national income have results that ultimately run contrary to the common good.[2] Taxes must be considered as harmful if they stagnate the will to economic venture, impair capital formation, cause inflationary pressure and cripple economic productivity. It must also be noted that, on the whole, public institutions cost more in administration and deal with goods less economically than private concerns. High tax levies therefore mean that considerable portions of the economic output do not find optimal use.

Taxes are unjust if they distribute burdens unfairly, if they hit the small income relatively much harder, or if they place families with many children at a disadvantage. Taxes may also not disregard the right to private property, which lastly would result in the mentioned, negative consequences of too high taxation. In this line the sharply progressive rates of death duties in some countries give rise to misgivings. An independent class of property owners has an importance of its own for the common good. "As the entire history of nations shows, greater possessions carry with them the means for nurturing values surpassing the material values, which are essential for the life and the growth of culture."[3]

III. The national right to self-defence by war[4]

War is an armed conflict between states or large organized groups similar to states. The definition includes large organized

---

[1] J. Messner: Social Ethics, 1965, 685.

[2] Messner, 1. c. 683.

[3] Ib. 688.

[4] References: Paul Ramsey: War and the Christian Conscience. — Durham, N. C.: Duke University Press, 1961. Justus George Lawler: Nuclear War. A Catholic Assessment. — Westminster, Md.: Newman Press, 1966. William V. O'Brien: Nuclear War, Deterrence and Morality. — Westminster: Newman Press, 1967. Paul Ramsey: The Limits of Nuclear War. — New York: The Council on Religion and International Affairs, 1968. Robert F. Drinan: Vietnam and Armageddon. Peace, War and the Christian Conscience. — New York: Sheed and Ward, 1970. Ralph B. Potter: War and Moral Discourse. — Richmond, Virg.: John Knox, 1973.

groups similar to states in order to account for instances such as the Spanish Civil War (1936-39), where the country was split into the two opposing forces of facists and communists, and in which war also other nations participated. Sometimes the concept of war is also used in a wider sense for conflicts carried out by means other than military weapons, especially by economic pressures and propaganda campaigns. For such instances the term "cold war" has been coined. The following considerations however primarily view war in the strict sense of an armed conflict.

The horror of recent wars and still more so the dreadfulness of modern atomic weapons have raised a sharp discussion on the moral admissibility of war. There are many voices today which condemn any war for our times, but especially atomic war. Although war may have once been justified as a means of defence, they say, it can no longer be regarded as justified in the present conditions, since the evils it causes always outweigh the harm that might otherwise befall a state. And yet the unconditional rejection of force in the protection of rights shows itself not less destructive in its consequences. It would be nothing but license for might to prevail with impunity over right. And this means that humanity will be abandoned to the disorder of moral ravishment by brutal violence and to the dereliction of moral and religious freedom, losses of still greater value than physical destruction.

1. *Moral admissibility of war*

Holy Scripture in the OT regards war as a justified means to protect the chosen people and to defend its faith. Yahweh himself orders war against his enemies. The fate of the Jews in the time of the Maccabees, who refused to obey the blasphemous laws of the foreign oppressor Antiochus, but who at the same time declined to fight on the Sabbath day, served their compatriots as a warning against inappropriate practice of religion. For they all who decided not to fight were massacred together with their wives and children by the enemy. Therefore their fellow Jews drew the conclusion: "If we all do as our brethren have done and refuse to fight with the Gentiles for our lives and our ordinances, they will quickly destroy us from the earth." And they decided to fight for their lives and faith (1 Mac 2:29-41).

The NT nowhere condemns the soldiers' class or war. John the Baptist, in his exhortation to the soldiers, does not reproach their state of life (Lk 3:14). And Jesus simply takes military service for granted, without objecting in any way against it (cf. the centurion of Capernaum Mt 8:5-13).

Theological tradition always maintained that the state has the right to defend its existence and the fundamental welfare of its citizens by war as a last means. This right has recently again been confirmed by Vatican II. "As long as the danger of war remains and there is no competent and sufficiently powerful authority at the international level, governments cannot be denied the right to legitimate defence once every means of peaceful settlement has been exhausted. Therefore, government authorities and others who share public responsibility have the duty to protect the welfare of the people entrusted to their care and to conduct such grave matters soberly" (GS 79).

Reason proves the right of the state to self-defence by war from the insight that the authority which is responsible for the common good of a nation cannot lack the means necessary for this purpose. Now war is sometimes the only means to defend the weal of a nation efficiently against unjust aggression. The higher a good that is in peril, the higher the sacrifices that are justified and demanded in its defence. Where an unjust aggressor endangers the highest goods of a nation, namely its existence and especially its moral and religious freedom, any state has the right and even the duty to defend these values against the assault. "Even nuclear weapons cannot provide a valid argument against such a proposition, precisely since the totalitarian state is, because of this weapon, given a real chance of world domination, and is, according to all recent experience, not likely to be reluctant to use any weapon for such a purpose. Thus, the old principle of the traditional natural law doctrine holds good in theory: War becomes a right and even a duty when the highest goods of the state community or of a community of states are in danger from an aggressor."[1]

2. *Conditions of a just war*

Because war is bound up with most fearful evils, it is never justified as an ordinary means of politics, but only permissible for the gravest reasons and under verification of the various conditions for a just war.

---

[1] J. Messner: Social Ethics, 1965. 666.

a)   War is lawful only for a just cause, i.e. in defence of vital goods of the state community. Just cause for a war is the unjust military aggression by another nation (but not military actions taken by the other nation in order to enforce justified claims), the withholding of state territories and sovereign rights, the violation of essential commercial or other vital interests of a nation. The existence of a justified cause must be morally certain. Offensive war waged to expiate the honour of a nation must be judged immoral in our times. Equally insufficient reasons are the aspiration to territorial rounding off, the principle of nationality, the increasing power of the neighbour state.

b)   All other means of non-belligerent nature must have been exhausted. One of these means is the attempt to a peaceful settlement of the conflict by mediation and arbitration of a neutral or superior authority, like the UNO. All the measures of a cold war are doubtless to be preferred to an armed conflict.

c)   The war must not jeopardize still higher goods than those to be defended. "When the damages caused by war are not comparable to those of 'tolerated injustice', one may have a duty to 'suffer the injustice'."[1]

d)   The military action may not extend beyond the needs of just defence and the restoration of the violated rights. Continuation of a war becomes unjust after the essential goals of it have been achieved. To continue a war only with the intention to punish the adversary is immoral. Furthermore the combatants must at all times be prepared for a peaceful settlement of differences if there is a chance of it.

Writers on international law not seldom incline to the view that a just war can only be a defensive war against an actual armed aggression, and that the guilty party is he who first takes up arms. But this must be regarded as too great a simplification. A preventive war against an unquestionably threatening, deadly aggression must equally be regarded as justified. Naturally this war of defence against an imminent, extreme threat must be clearly distinguished from a preventive war against a feared, but not certain and imminent aggression or even against a merely possible aggression. Such a preventive war is always an unjust war of aggression. Again, the right to defence of the common weal also includes the right to force claims of great importance for a state community which are withheld by a hostile nation.

---

[1] Pius XII: Address to the International Office of Documentation for Military Medicine, AAS 45 (1953), 748f.

The armed enforcement of such claims cannot simply be condemned as an unjust war of aggression. However the very horror of modern war restricts this latter right much more today than in former times.

3. *Means and methods of warfare*

Also a just war does not justify all the means. The means and methods employed must not be unlawful in themselves, and they must be proportionate to the just cause and objectives of the war. All acts of force (destruction of life, devastation of property, etc.) which do not essentially contribute to the attainment of the just ends of the war are evil. "Any act of war aimed indiscriminately at the destruction of entire cities or extensive areas along with their population is a crime against God and man himself" (GS 80).

Immoral are all means and actions which are forbidden by natural or by international law. Actions which deliberately conflict with the universal natural law, "as well as orders commanding such actions, are criminal. Blind obedience cannot excuse those who yield to them. Among such must first be counted those actions designed for the methodical extermination of an entire people, nation, or ethnic minority" (GS 79). Other examples of means forbidden by natural law are perjury and falsehood; wholesale killing of innocents as reprisal; killing of innocents as hostages; rape, cruelties and torture; deportation of enemy workers and their forced employment in war industry. Forbidden by international law as well are the following means and methods (cf. the international conventions of The Hague 1907 and of Geneva 1949): deliberate killing of non-combatants; destruction or expropriation of enemy property for other than military purposes; killing of wounded enemies or of captured enemies merely because they are enemies; foul assassination of combatants or enemy population; military actions by persons not clearly recognizable as militaries; use of poisonous weapons (e.g. poisonous gas); use of weapons designed to cause unnecessary suffering (e.g. dumdum bullets); abuse of the flag of truce, of the enemy flag and military emblems, of the red cross or white flag; killing of persons declared immune: envoys, army chaplains and hospital orderlies.

Guerilla warfare of partisan groups in areas unjustly occupied by enemy troops cannot entirely be condemned as immoral. Nevertheless the utility of guerilla warfare must be weighed most carefully, for as a rule it merely aggravates the bitterness of the struggle and the suffering of the occupied country. Partisans too must be recognizable as militaries.

4.   *Problem of atomic warfare*

The most urgent objective with regard to atomic war is to prevent it. The reason is that it "can inflict massive and indiscriminate destruction exceeding the bounds of legitimate defence" (GS 80). Therefore the second condition of a just war cannot easily be verified, i.e. that the war does not jeopardize still higher goods than those to be defended. This is why nuclear war constitutes a special problem for ethics.

J. Messner distinguishes between nuclear weapons uncontrollable and controllable in their effects. "Nuclear weapons which are uncontrollable in their effect owing to radioactive fall-out, or for other reasons, are inadmissible, since not only large masses of the noncombatant population of warring states but also, on account of the drifting fall-out, large numbers of non-participating states would suffer severe injury . . . . The objections mentioned are not applicable when atomic weapons have no, or hardly any, fall-out, and are used for the purpose of rendering unserviceable military objects and formation".[1] But even in the case of controllable nuclear weapons the proximate danger exists that once nuclear warfare has begun, it will almost inevitably lead to the unlimited use of these weapons. B. Häring therefore views the unleashing of any atomic attack as a grave crime.[2] This judgement has also been adopted by the American bishops in their pastoral letter on war and peace of 1983 (nn. 150-153). Indeed, any offensive use of atomic weapons in a war seems to be as reprehensible as the offensive use of gas.

Granted however that a hostile power threatens an aggressive war with atomic weapons of any kind, must the nations thus threatened even then be ready to renounce the use of similar weapons? The most urgent aim will be to avert such a war. This gives the right to the nations so endangered to arm with similar and more effective weapons. The use of inadmissible weapons, such as gas and bacteria, has been prevented above all because of the fear of retaliation with like weapons. "A one-sided renunciation of such weapons in a defensive war against such an aggressor would mean a renunciation of self-defence; in

---

[1] J. Messner, 1. c. 513f.   [2] B. Häring III, 1966, 131.

this situation, the threatened state is not justified by natural law principles in such a renunciation, since the highest goods of mankind, freedom of mind and of conscience, including the values of religion, are gravely threatened."[1]

Yet also in the case of a defence by nuclear weapons every effort has to be made to avoid the devastation of open towns or of regions which are of no greater significance for the waging of the war. Therefore only controllable nuclear weapons may be used in defence against an atomic aggression, if available, even though the enemy uses uncontrollable nuclear weapons. Only if no other nuclear weapons are at disposal, those uncontrollable in their effect may be employed against the aggressor.

Since the consequences of any atomic war — whatever its justifications — cannot be but most dreadful, it must be a most urgent aim of international politics to ban nuclear weapons, just as other atrocious types of weapons have already been banned by international agreements.[2] And beyond it, the ultimate aim would be the ending of the very production of nuclear weapons and the destruction of existing stocks of them, both under international control.

5. *Participation in war*

In case of a just war the citizens have to obey the call to arms. They have no objective moral right to refuse military service, because the state authority can justly demand their contribution in defence of the common weal. If citizens doubt the justice of their country's cause, they may not volunteer for service, but they may follow the call to arms. Probably they are even obliged to obey also in this case, because it is to be assumed that the better insight in these difficult decisions is with the state authority. Citizens are not allowed to take part in an evidently unjust war, though it is almost always impossible for the individual to reach certainty concerning the justice or injustice of a war. Whoever is forced to take part in an unjust war may neither wound nor kill the enemy, unless the enemy attempts to kill him, notwithstanding his surrender.

No military or civilian subordinate is allowed to obey immoral orders. Yet as long as the lawfulness of the order is doubtful, the presumption is in favour of the authority. Moreover

---

[1] J. Messner, 1. c. 514f.

[2] Cf. John XXIII: Pacem in Terris, nr. 112.

if the consequences of the refusal of obedience were an even greater evil for the subordinate, he would be entitled to obey the unjust order (e.g. to destroy a church in order to save his life).

With regard to conscientious objectors of war, the Church never favoured such refusal in principle. But Vatican II declares: "It seems right that laws make humane provisions for the case of those who for reasons of conscience refuse to bear arms, provided however, that they accept some other form of service to the human community" (GS 79). The genuine conviction of conscience can more easily be tested in instances of objection based on religious convictions of a sect or denomination (Quakers, Mennonites) than in cases of individual moral convictions. At any rate conscientious objectors can justly be required to contribute to the defence of the state in some other and equally dangerous way, e.g. in ambulance units at the front. Since clergy and monks have dedicated their entire lives to the service of religion, they are in a particular and unique way representatives of the idea of universal brotherhood and peace. For this reason their exemption from combatant service must be regarded as most appropriate.

Promotion of the cause of peace.   Peace and war are not only the concern of the leaders of nations. All citizens and especially the powers which form the public opinion have their influence in this regard, and a very important one. "A firm determination to respect other men and peoples and their dignity, as well as the studied practice of brotherhood are absolutely necessary for the establishment of peace" (GS 78). It is a sin against fraternal love and against the duty to promote peace among men if citizens foster hatred for other nations or for groups of different race or conviction within their own nation. And it is a particularly grave sin if this is done by those who influence the mass media. For government officials "depend on public opinion and feeling to the greatest possible extent. It does them no good to work at building peace so long as feelings of hostility, contempt, and distrust, as well as racial hatred and unbending ideologies, continue to divide men and place them in opposing camps" (GS 82). Hence arises the duty of those who mold public opinion, of educators and of all citizens to promote the cause of peace. It must be born of mutual trust between nations and grow as the fruit of the will to ever greater

justice and brotherly love. The building of peace is indeed a
work of supreme love for mankind.

IV. Duties of citizens

The basic duty of the citizens is love for their country.
This duty rests in the law of nature, because the fatherland is
the community of people to which the citizens are bound by
common mores and culture; and because they are indebted to
their country for protection and promotion of the common weal.
The love of one's country should manifest itself in interest and
concern for the country's welfare. The acid test of genuine
patriotism is the readiness to defend the just cause of one's
country in a war and to pay heavy taxes in critical times.

Love of one's country should however not be confounded
with narrow nationalism, which in an egotist way is only concerned with the benefit of one's own nation, or overvalues it
and disregards the rights of others or thinks little of them. "It
is only natural that communities which have recently reached
their political independence should be jealous of a national unity
which is still fragile, and that they should strive to protect it.
Likewise, it is to be expected that nations endowed with an
ancient culture should be proud of the patrimony which their
history has bequeathed to them. But these legitimate feelings
should be ennobled by that universal charity which embraces the
entire human family. Nationalism isolates people from their
true good. It would be especially harmful where the weakness
of national economies demands rather the pooling of efforts, of
knowledge and of funds" (Paul VI;[1] cf. GS 75). True patriotism
is at the same time characterized by the spirit of love and
justice towards other nations, even towards the enemy nations
of yesterday.

1. *Civil obedience and respect*

Obedience to civil authority is a basic duty of citizens
which binds them in conscience, and which they owe not merely
to an authority that satisfies all reasonable requests, but also
to uncomfortable and hard rulers. This is the teaching of Scripture. "Be subject for the Lord's sake to every human institution,
whether it be to the emperor as supreme, or to governors as
sent by him to punish those who do wrong and to praise those

---

[1] Paul VI: Populorum Progressio, nr. 62.

who do right" (1 Pet 2:13f). "Therefore he who resists the authorities resists what God has appointed, and those who resist will incur judgment. . . . One must be subject, not only to avoid God's wrath but also for the sake of conscience" (Rom 13:2-5). Paul also admonishes the Christians to pray "for kings and all who are in high positions" (1 Tim 2:2).[1]

The nature of obedience in general has already been explained in an earlier context. With regard to state authority in particular it holds that the same social needs of human nature which demand the institution of the state also demand civil obedience. For without the citizens' obedience and cooperation the state could not exist, but would end up in anarchy and chaos. "When, in fact, men obey their rulers, it is not at all as men that they obey them. Through their obedience it is God, the provident Creator of all things, whom they reverence, since he has decreed that men's dealings with one another should be regulated by an order which he himself has established."[2] Civil obedience is by no means a particular homage paid to the person of the ruler, but it is subordination of one's personal interests to the needs of the common good. One of the chief consequences of this is that citizens "must bring their own interests into harmony with the needs of the community, and must dispose of their goods and services as civil authorities have prescribed, in accord with the norms of justice, in due form, and with the limits of their competence."[3]

The fact that civil authority is instituted and willed by God and that it renders a most important and often difficult service to the community obliges citizens furthermore to show due respect to their bearers. Contumelious treatment of one in authority must be regarded as a serious sin, especially when it occurs in public or may easily become public.

2.   *Obligation to pay taxes*

The duty to pay taxes is pronounced by Christ himself. When asked by the Pharisees and some of the Herodians, whether it is lawful to pay taxes to Caesar or not, his answer is: "Render to Caesar the things that are Caesar's, and to God the things that are God's," thus acknowledging the emperor's right to levy

---

[1] Cf. R. Schnackenburg: The Moral Teaching of the New Testament, §25: The Attitude to Public Authorities, 235 ff.

[2] John XXIII: Pacem in Terris, nr. 50.

[3] Ib. nr. 53.

taxes (Mk 12:13-17). St. Paul likewise requires the Christians to pay their taxes conscientiously. "Pay all of them their dues, taxes to whom taxes are due, revenue to whom revenue is due, respect to whom respect is due, honour to whom honour is due" (Rom 13:7).

The duty to pay taxes derives from the citizens' obligation to contribute their share to the necessities of the state, whose help they need, by which they profit, and which also assumes certain obligations in the citizens' place and stead. For the purpose of taxes is the maintenance of the machinery of the government and its institutions, e.g. police and army; provision for the common needs of the community, e.g. roads, ports, schooling, social welfare work; and redistribution of wealth according to social justice, whether on national or international level. Each citizen is in justice and charity required to contribute to these goals and is consequently conscience bound to pay just taxes. The assumption of many traditional manuals that taxation laws are in principle only penal laws does not seem to do justice to the real importance of taxes and is more and more abandoned in recent times.

It is however a fact that tax evasion is widely practised and commonly taken lightly. "One of the most serious aspects of our present-day problem is not so much that taxpayers are dishonest as that dishonesty in tax matters is condoned. This is a grave symptom of the lack of public spirit."[1] The following reasons are usually brought forward in justification of tax evasions.

(1) Everyone cheats over taxes. Hence one is allowed to do the same, and one may even be compelled to do so in order to compete with the others in business life. Yet this assertion is true only for a rather limited group of citizens, as statistic studies have shown. The very large group of wage and salary earners evade taxation only to a slight extent and contribute by far the biggest portion to the national income (60-70%). Since their payrolls are declared by the employer, there is indeed little opportunity for cheating. The second group is constituted by firms, which evade taxes to a moderate extent. Independent businessmen and the liberal professions are the group which evades taxation to a considerable extent. Of course a businessman who is unscrupulous in defraudation of taxes makes more

---

[1] Saint-Séverin Catechism for Adults, vol. IV: The Christian Social Conscience, by a Group of Laymen. — London/Dublin: G. Chapman, 1965, 57.

money than his honest competitor. But such financial advantages are gained by other kinds of fraud, injustice and dishonesty as well; nevertheless they do not constitute any justification for competitors to use the same unlawful means.

(2) Taxes are too heavy. If one pays them all, one will never get ahead in the world. But this argument is not convincing either. Just liabilities cannot be refused simply because they are heavy. Naturally if taxes are so high that they result in being unjust, citizens would be allowed to defend themselves against them. But as long as this injustice is doubtful, presumption stands for the lawfulness of tax legislation.

(3) The government takes tax evasions into account and bases tax-rates on the assumption of such evasions. Yet this is an unhealthy situation. The government imposes as many taxes as are necessary or feasible to meet the expenditures of the state. It imposes them there where it can expect sufficient income, but hardly by preference there where more taxes seem to be evaded. Could it really be asserted that the state imposes higher taxes on businessmen or liberal professions because they defraud more? This does not seem to be so. Yet even if this were the case, it must be considered as regrettable. "Taxation is becoming a battle which must gradually demoralize or immoralize both sides."[1] Tax evasion is an evil and proof of lack of public spirit. It is an important task of the civil authorities to insist on a reasonable fulfillment of the tax obligations. Special care should be taken to prevent tax collectors from accepting bribes for non-fulfillment of tax duties. Taxpayers from their side ought to be led by a sense of solidarity with the community to which they belong and by which they profit.

Vatican II resolutely turns against an individualist morality which makes little of certain social obligations, among them tax duties. It declares that the obligations of justice and love are fulfilled only if each person contributes to the common good according to his abilities and the needs of others. Those are reproached who "make light of social laws and precepts, and do not hesitate to resort to various frauds and deceptions in avoiding just taxes or other debts due to society" (GS 30).

Citizens need to be educated to a better understanding of their civic duties as taxpayers. The payment of taxes is an essential part of one's public responsibility. Only the taxpayer is a good citizen. Tax paying is a sign of communal spirit and good

---

[1] Saint-Séverin Catechism, 1. c. 55.

citizenship. Fiscal policy and economic policy are means by which society is being built. They are also instruments of the brotherhood of men, for nowadays brother helps brother frequently not by almsgiving, but through public institutions and organizations. These institutions are supported by the money of the citizens which they contribute in the form of taxes.

From the obligation to pay taxes arises the duty to make a corresponding declaration for assessment. A person need not be scrupulous in the appraisal of his possessions. Scholars discuss whether there exists a proper duty of restitution in cases of tax defraudation. It is certainly difficult to fix the exact amount to be paid in restitution according to natural law. One also claims that society does not need such a restitution, because it is able to enforce the necessary funds by public measures. And since the individual is contained in the totality of the citizens, the realms of law are not as clearly separated in instances of legal justice as in those of commutative justice. But on the other hand citizens have a right to demand the contribution of their fellow citizens to the common weal, just as they themselves render their contribution. Restitution of a certain amount of defrauded taxes in form of contributions to charitable works is at least very recommendable, if not an obligation in instances where the defrauder is able to do so.

3. *Civic responsibility and participation*

The concerns and needs of society ought to be at the heart of every citizen, for they are lastly always his own concerns and needs. The weal and woe of the civic community sooner or later affects all its members. Everyone is called to contribute his share to the furtherance of the common good. "Let everyone consider it his sacred obligation to count social necessities among the primary duties of modern man, and to pay heed to them" (GS 30). This obligation includes, besides the duty to pay just taxes, also the duty to respect the other norms of social life, e.g. those designed for the protection of health or traffic laws. Citizens are likewise called to make the weight of their opinion felt, so that civil authorities may act with justice and laws may conform to moral precepts and the common good (AA 14).

A particularly important right and duty of citizens in the modern democratic state is their right to vote. Nobody may say that his vote is of no importance and that it does therefore not matter whether he uses this right or not. The final result of the voting only comes about through the contributions of the many individual citizens. Voting is a civic duty and moral obligation (cf. GS 75) which binds in conscience, at least whenever a good candidate has an unworthy opponent. Refusal to vote for no valid reason would be a serious sin if the election is to decide whether a regime hostile or sympathetic to religion and to freedom of conscience will take over the government. To be sure, Christians are not bound to support only Christian candidates. But they must consider whether their vote is likely to affect the freedom of the Church and of conscience. One may vote for an unworthy candidate only when this is necessary to prevent a still less worthy candidate from obtaining office. Bishops and priests have the right and duty to instruct the conscience of the believers how to vote in a responsible way. However in doing so they ought to avoid entering into party politics and only explain the basic, general principles.

Finally those suited for public office ought to be ready to accept such charges in the service of the common good, whether in the national or local government, in parents' associations, in professional groups, etc. Only strenuous activity within society can make it a fellowship of responsible citizens rather than a flock of discontented or indifferent sheep. "Catholics skilled in public affairs and adequately enlighted in faith and Christian doctrine should not refuse to administer public affairs, since by performing this office in a worthy manner they can simultaneously advance the common good and prepare the way for the gospel" (AA 14; cf. GS 75).

V. The right of resistance against unjust state authority

Political authority "must always be exercised within the limits of morality and on behalf of the dynamically conceived common good, according to a juridical order enjoying legal status. When such is the case citizens are conscience-bound to obey . . . . Where public authority oversteps its competence and oppresses the people, these people should nevertheless obey to the extent that the objective common good demands. Still it is lawful for them to defend their own rights and those of their fellow citizens against any abuse of this authority, provided that in so doing they observe the limits imposed by natural law and the gospel" (GS 74). Although the Church is very cautious and slow in granting the right to civil disobedience and to resistance against state authority, nevertheless in principle she admits of such a right. State authority can be unjust on two different grounds: The state authority has been usurped in a violent and illegitimate way; or a lawfully acquired state authority turns to be abusive and tyrannical. The two instances have to be treated separately.

1. *Resistance against illegitimate rulers*

An illegitimate ruler or usurper is one who gets hold of the government without a just title. Usurpers may come to power as rebels against their own, lawful government, or in the sway of an invasion by enemies who have gained actual control of the state or a part of it and who install their own government.

In principle citizens do not owe any obedience to usurpers. Rather they are obliged to assist their own lawful government in the resistance against the illegitimate ruler. For the legitimacy of state authority is not based on the forcible seizure of power in a territory, but on legal titles approved by the consent of the people, i.e. in modern states usually the constitutional transfer of power.

There is a limited obligation of obedience to the orders of the usurper once he has gained assured control and as long as he is in power. "The legal basis for this lies not in the fact of assured control but in the necessity of insuring public order in the political community, which would otherwise fall a victim to anarchy and chaos."[1] The duty is confined to the requirements of the common good, i.e. of ordered legal and political adminis-tration. It may not involve recognition of the illegitimate authority, e.g. by participation in a government formed by the usurper or in a "constituent assembly" convoked by him in order to "legalize" his government. This qualified obedience to the usurper does not prejudice the right of the legitimate rulers to call the citizens to active resistance against the usurping government in due time. Yet once the usurper has obtained firm control over the state, the legitimate authority is allowed to resort to violent measures in order to regain power only if there is a well-founded hope of success.

After the illegitimate ruler has attained the peaceful posses-sion of power, his authority can become legitimate in the course of time. The reason is not the fact that success creates right,

---

[1] J. Messner: Social Ethics. — St. Louis/London: Herder Book Co., 1965, 594.

but the necessity to save the civic community from further disastrous struggles. Yet such legitimation only takes place under the condition that right and justice are in principle respected by the new ruler and the common weal is maintained and promoted. A tyranny can never obtain legitimacy, even if it succeeds in holding power over a long period of time. The recognition of a former usurper as the legitimate authority of a country cannot come about without the explicit or tacit consent of the citizens, by which they acknowledge that the common good is assured under the new government and that its authority has itself become a constitutive element of the actual common good. In this case every legal claim of a former legitimate ruler becomes obsolete. "The validity of this legal principle, that the de facto government becomes legitimate in time, finds confirmation in the legal consciousness of peoples; this has often been manifested in the course of history after revolutionary changes."[1]

2. *Resistance against legitimate rulers*[2]

Obedience to legitimate authority is not an unconditional duty. It has its limits in natural and divine law. Where state authority becomes unjust and contradicts the law of God, the citizens are no longer bound to obey. To such situations apply the words of Peter and John before the Sanhedrin, when they were forbidden to preach further Jesus Christ: "We must obey God rather than men" (Acts 5:29; cf. 4:19f).

However not every dissatisfaction with the social and economic conditions of a country and not every (culpable or inculpable) inability of its leaders to cope with them sufficiently justifies the violent overthrow of the government. The word revolution is often used today, especially in nations which are in the process of industrial and social development and which frequently suffer from many problems. There are groups of people who, in the unsatisfactory and disappointing conditions

[1] J. Messner, l. c. 595.

[2] References: William R. Miller: Nonviolence. A Christian Interpretation.—New York: Shocken Books, 1966. Howard Zinn: Disobedience and Democracy. — New York: Random House, 1968. Abe Fortas: Concerning Dissent and Civil Disobedience. — New York: World Publishing Co., 1969. New Theology No. 6: On Revolution; ed. by M. M. Marty and D. G. Peerman. — London: The Macmillan Co., 1969. Oscar Cullmann: Jesus and the Revolutionaries. — New York: Harper and Row, 1970. Robert T. Hall: The Morality of Civil Disobedience. — New York: Harper and Row, 1971. Thomas A. Shannon: Render Unto God. A Theology of Selective Obedience. — New York: Paulist Press, 1974.

of their nation, would like to resort to something like a revolution
as a means to bring about greater justice and faster progress.
Pope John XXIII, while being aware of the justified concerns
of these "souls, particularly endowed with generosity", still at the
same time cautions them that progress is not to be sought in the
line of revolution but evolution. "It must be borne in mind
that to proceed gradually is the law of life in all its expressions.
Therefore, in human institutions, too, it is not possible to renovate
for the better except by working from within them, gradually.
Pius XII proclaimed: 'Salvation and justice are not to be found
in revolution, but in evolution through concord. Violence has
always achieved only destruction, not construction; the kindling
of passions, not their pacification; the accumulation of hate and
ruin, not the reconciliation of the contending parties. And it
has reduced men and parties to the difficult task of rebuilding,
after sad experience, on the ruins of discord.' "[1]

The sometimes unjustified use of authority, which is to a
greater or lesser degree always bound up with its exercise because
of the limitations of human nature, does not yet divest a government of its legitimacy. Governments do not become illegitimate
because of occasional cases of unjust laws or slow solution of
national problems. But they become illegitimate through continuous misuse of their power contrary to the common welfare.
In such instances citizens are entitled to resist the tyranny of
their government with the purpose to remove and to replace it.
The following are the means against unjust oppression by state
authority and its abusive exercise:

a) *Utilization of the legally afforded means.* In a well-
ordered state citizens must have the opportunity to safeguard
their rights through legal means against oppression by political
authority and to remove an abusive government. The presence
of such means distinguishes an equitable, sound state system
from the dictatorial state. As long as the right of the citizens
to judicial protection against oppression by civil authorities is
respected, there is little possibility of the emergence of state
totalitarianism.

b) *Passive resistance.* It consists in the non-violent refusal to obey the law. Citizens are not bound to obey unjust
laws and orders of their government. They have the right and
not seldom even the obligation to defend themselves by public
opposition in word and writing and by refusal of obedience.

---

[1] John XXIII: Pacem In Terris, nr. 162.

Laws and commands are unjust if they conflict with man's human rights and existential ends; e.g. if the ruler imposes oppressive laws that are not required by the common good, but spring from his avarice or pride; if he exceeds the authority granted him by the constitution; if burdens are inequitably apportioned. Infringement of rights by modern states especially affect the spheres of education, marriage legislation, right to private property, taxation, freedom of religion and conscience. The injustice of the laws in question must be certain. In instances of doubt presumption stands for the lawful authority.

If laws or orders are unjust but do not command immoral actions (e.g. if they prohibit free expression of opinion, peaceful public association, public processions), obedience may be refused, although there is generally no strict obligation to do so. Submission to such laws is permissible in order to escape the severe penalties attached to their disregard. Thus under totalitarian systems fathers of families may be justified in showing an external loyalty in order to keep their jobs and to be able to support their families. Exceptionally observance of unjust laws of the kind mentioned can be obligatory for the sake of the common good to avoid still greater harm to peace and order. Obedience must however be refused if the law commands immoral actions (e.g. mercy killing or denial of faith).

c)   *Active resistance.* It is the organized defence of citizens against the abuse of state authority. This defence may be carried out with or without the use of force. Non-violent, active resistance may take the form of mobilizing the public opinion, of appealing to a higher judicial tribunal (the Pope was such a tribunal in former times), of mass-demonstrations, or of a general strike. Traditional Christian ethics has always held that, apart from very special circumstances, non-violent resistance is the only permissible means to defend the citizens' rights against unjust, despotic state authority. Civil war is mostly a greater misfortune for the common good than the abuse of power by state authority.

Violent resistance is the armed insurrection against lawless tyranny. After the experiences with recent tyrannies of nazist and communist nature, theologians of the present are more inclined to grant an oppressed people the right to violent resistance, not excluding the killing of the tyrant himself,[1] than were the

---

[1] Pribilla, Laros, Th. Meyer, E. Welty, Mausbach-Ermecke, Messner, Häring.

theologians of the past.[1] The following are the reasons for a
nation's right to violent resistance against the dictatorship of
tyrants and their reign of terror:

(1)   Natural law may not leave the people without just
and efficient means of defence against unjust power. But if
every species of violent resistance were forbidden, the people
would indeed be left without the efficient means of defence
against the oppression by unscrupulous tyrants.

(2)   Moral theology grants individuals the right to self-
defence against violent aggression without hesitation. If this right
is accorded to individuals, it cannot logically be denied to the
people in its entirety.

(3)   State authority has its power only for the common
good. If the ruler himself turns against the common good by
extreme abuse of his power, undermining justice, morality and
religion, then he surrenders the title upon which his right to
authority is based. The power of civic authority returns to the
people, on whose consent its rightful and legitimate use depends.
The citizens can take over the care for order, offer armed
resistance and even decide the tyrant's death.[2]

In order that active, violent resistance against tyrannical
abuse of state authority be justified, the following conditions
must be fulfilled:

(1)   The government must be guilty of gross abuse of
civic authority, i.e. of such abuse that it no longer fulfills its
function of serving the common good. This is the case if, e.g.,
the essential freedoms of the citizens are suppressed or if the
foreign policy of the ruler only serves his own ambitions and
glory to the detriment of the country's true good and to the
right of other nations.

(2)   All peaceful and non-violent means of resistance have
been exhausted without success.

(3)   There must be a well-founded hope that the violent
resistance will prove successful and that the evil conditions will

---

[1] Protestant ethics was even more resistant to grant the citizens
the right to disobedience against the tyranny of legitimate rulers. E.
Brunner accuses Catholic moral theology (in its traditional form before
World War II) that its teaching on resistance against unjust laws signifies
"an unbearable endangering of the positive-legal order" (Gerechtigkeit.
— Zürich: Zwingli, 1943, 110).

[2] Already Bellarmine and Suarez justified with this argument active
resistance against despotic state authority. Yet it ought to be inves-
tigated whether they included in this right also the permission to tyrannicide.

not worsen rather than improve because of it. Theologians therefore require that the resistance be sufficiently organized, and this for two reasons: first, in order to bring about a quick decision against the existing tyranny and to avoid a long civil war; second, in order to prevent the rise of a new tyranny by small, radical groups, which often attain to power as the result of political disturbances.

(4) The use of force must not exceed the measure necessary and sufficient for the removal of the oppressive power. But for the sake of an assured success it is better to exert some greater force than necessary rather than too little.

(5) The decision regarding the justice and actual exercise of the violent resistance must be taken in the name of the community, and may not be the private affair of only some discontented individuals. Therefore only men of great competence and high sense of responsibility, acknowledged by the people as its exponents, are qualified to decide on this matter. These men however are in case of extreme necessity of the country not only permitted but also obliged to make this decision, even at a very great personal sacrifice.

In setting forth the principles of Christian ethics on the right of active resistance, social ethics can admittedly only indicate some general norms and conditions. In political reality the concrete facts and presuppositions are, as a rule, of great complexity and obscurity. Ethics must show the gravity of the moral responsibility. Yet the practical decision must be made in conscientious judgment by those people who live in the concrete situation and on whom the care for the nation falls.

D. The Church

"By her relationship with Christ, the Church is a kind of sacrament or sign of intimate union with God, and of the unity of all mankind. She is also an instrument for the achievement of such union and unity" (LG 1). As the state is the society instituted for the universal establishment of the secular common weal, thus the Church is instituted by Christ himself for the universal promotion of the spiritual and religious weal of mankind. According to the above mentioned text, this spiritual weal essentially consists in the achievement of an intimate union with God and of the unity of all mankind.

I. The Church authority

Church authority is represented by the pope, the bishops and the priests. They govern the Church as the mediators between God and men and are the teachers of the divine truths.

1. *Mediator between God and men*

"Pursuing the saving purpose which is proper to her, the Church not only communicates divine life to men, but in some way casts the reflected light of that life over the entire earth" (GS 40). The Church's function is to serve men in their religious and spiritual needs and to promote the values of faith and religion. She is called to imbue the everyday activity of men with a deeper meaning and to serve as a leaven and as a kind of soul for human society, with the goal to renew it in Christ and to transform it into God's family (cf. GS 40).

The Church performs her tasks and functions through her priests and ministers. Vatican II has dedicated to the state and office of the priesthood the "Decree on the Ministry and Life of Priests" (Presbyterum Ordinis = PO). Priests are men appointed for the things which pertain to God. "By their vocation and ordination, priests of the New Testament are indeed set apart in a certain sense within the midst of God's people. But this is so, not that they may be separated from this people or from any man, but that they may be totally dedicated to the work for which the Lord has raised them up" (PO 3).

One of the foremost duties of priests is the preaching of the word of God. They "have as their primary duty the proclamation of the gospel of God to all . . . For through the saving Word the spark of faith is struck in the hearts of unbelievers, and fed in the hearts of the faithful. By this faith the community of the faithful begins and grows" (PO 4). Another basic task of the mediating function of priests is the celebration of the liturgy and the worthy administration of the sacraments, among which the holy Eucharist excells as the source and apex of them all.

The universal spiritual welfare of the believers must be at their heart. "They must lead the faithful along to an ever-improved spirit of prayer offered throughout the whole of life according to the graces and needs of each. They must persuade everyone to the discharge of the duties of his proper state in life, and bring the saintlier ones to an appropriate exercise of the evangelical counsels" (PO 5). The office of the pastor is also to be extended to the formation of a genuine Christian community; and with missionary zeal priests ought to embrace the concerns of the universal Church.

As leaders of the Christian people on the way to God, clerics must be unceasingly concerned to foster their personal union with God and life with Christ. To secure the necessary devotion to God and to the service of souls, the Church has prescribed for the clergy of the Latin rite from the diaconate onwards the obligation to the Divine Office and the commitment to celibacy.

Priests and deacons "are bound to pray the entire Office every day, either in common or individually" (SC 96). The reason for this provision is not only the concern of the Church for the personal sanctification of her ministers. Priests and clerics are also to pray in the name of the entire Christian community and indeed for the whole world (PO 5). This is their special vocation. The lasting failure to recite the Divine Office must therefore be reckoned as a grave neglect of a serious, vocational duty. The clergy is deputized by the community of believers to this office of prayer, so that at least through them the commission of the community to divine worship be continuously fulfilled and the prayer of Christ unceasingly continued. The General Instruction on the Liturgy of the Hours enjoins that particular importance be attached to Lauds and Vespers, which should not be omitted except for a grave reason (nr. 29).

Through celibacy the Church seeks to keep her ministers as free as possible for the service of God and men. For through evangelical virginity, observed for the sake of the kingdom of heaven, priests more easily hold fast to Christ with undivided heart. "They more freely devote themselves in Him and through Him to the service of God and men. They more readily minister to His kingdom and to the work of heavenly regeneration, and thus become more apt to exercise paternity in Christ" (PO 16).

The external behaviour of the clergy must befit their office. They will keep away from everything that would be unbecoming for their state, e.g. vanity in their affairs, a luxurious way of life, engrossment in totally profane business, and the like. More than the other followers of Christ they will avoid the things which can offend the poor in any way (cf. PO 17).

The universal call to perfection, at length, is extended to priests with particular urgency. For by their ordination, by their daily sacred actions, by the entire ministry which they exercise, they are being directed towards perfection of life and "bound by a special claim" to it (PO 12).

In order to perform their pastoral work efficiently and as fruitfully as possible, priests ought to exercise their ministry in close cooperation and unity with their bishop and confreres. "No priest can in isolation or singlehandedly accomplish his mission in a satisfactory way. He can do so only by joining forces with other priests under the direction of Church authorities" (PO 7).

2. *Teacher of the divine truth and the moral law*

Christ is "the way, and the truth, and the life" (Jn 14:6). He communicates his life and his truth to the believers through the Church. Even Holy Scriptures are not a source of doctrine divorced from the Church. Rather Scriptures are given to the believers by God through and in the Church.

It is the Church which teaches the law of Christ, giving to men his gospel and helping them to understand its significance. The meaning of the written mystery can only belong to that community which carries within itself the revelation of that mystery. The individual, left on its own, would not be able to give an adequate interpretation of Holy Scriptures. Thus when the believers are instructed to consult tradition and to listen to the magisterium, it is not that they should prefer the Church to Scriptures, but rather the explanation of the Scriptures given by the whole Church to their personal explanation. The unavoidable differences arising from diversity of opinion on certain positions in theological teaching are possible only within the bounds of the doctrinal magisterium.[1]

Priests and pastors themselves are required "not to teach their own wisdom but God's word" (PO 4). The word must be preached impartially, without regard for persons or human factions; not influenced by the wish to win men's favour, but only led by the will to transmit faithfully Christ's message and command (cf. PO 6). Intrepidly and staunchly priests should teach and admonish men according to the words of the Apostle: "Be urgent in season and out of season, convince, rebuke, and exhort, be unfailing in patience and in teaching" (2 Tim 4:2).

In order to be well prepared for their teaching office, priests

---

[1] The question of assent and dissent in the Church is dealt with in detail in the section "Duty of submission to the teaching authority of the Church" in the treatise on the divine virtue of faith.

must constantly perfect their knowledge. They must be well acquainted with the documents of the Church and keep abreast of developments in the theological science.

Being teachers of the moral law, they "should help men see what is God's will in the great and small events of life. Christians should also be taught that they do not live for themselves alone, but, according to the demands of the new law of charity, every man must administer to others the grace he has received" (PO 6). All men should find in the bishops and priests defenders of their rights, of justice, love and truth. For through her ministers the Church is to prove herself as the conscience of the nations.

3.   *The Church as servant in her ministry*

The Church is meant to be a sign of the redemptive obedience of Christ to the Father, which has as its aim the salvation of all men. Thus the Church is not called to exercise dominion over men in a spirit of self-aggrandizement or to seek glory before the world. Most characteristic of her is her mission to serve men in their spiritual needs and to carry out the work of redemption in humility and self-sacrifice (cf. LG 8). She is conscious of her duty to hearken to the will and example of Christ and to live in imitation of Mary, the humble handmaid of the Lord, who is the primordial type of the Church. All aspiration for power and earthly prestige and all arbitrary exercise of ecclesiastical authority by Church officials obscure the role of the Church as servant of the spiritual, religious kingdom of God.

"Priests therefore should preside in such a way that they seek the things of Jesus Christ, not the things which are their own. They must work together with the lay faithful and conduct themselves in their midst after the example of their Master, who among men 'has not come to be served but to serve, and to give his life as a ransom for many'" (PO 9). Priests must sincerely acknowledge and promote the role which is proper to the laity in the mission of the Church and confidently entrust to it duties in the service of the people of God, allowing them freedom and room for action.

The mission of the Church as a manifestation of the king-dom of God also suffers from any dishonourable self-defence and untruthful apologetic. Anyone who seeks to justify what is in reality a deplorable conformity with the spirit of this world diminishes the effectiveness of the Church and the respect for her. False justifications have however to be distinguished from a mere silence on these faults. All members of the Church must be conscious of their duty to protect the honour of their Church as far as possible, even when criticism appears necessary and wholesome.

Since the Church is a social organism, it cannot be governed without certain rules and laws. The Church is entitled to issue such directives. Yet everyone who participates in the pastoral office of the Church must endeavour to look upon her laws and directives in the light of the rule governing the kingdom of God, which is Christ's love for the Church and the Church's love for Christ. All the laws of the Church, e.g. the liturgical prescriptions, and even the ecclesiastical law on censures, all must flow from zeal for the glory of the Lord and for the salvation of men, and must be interpreted in this spirit.

II. Duties of believers

The nature of Christ's redemptive work is such that his followers can share in his vivifying life and death, in his grace and glory, only insofar as they turn to the Church and accept her mission as a mediator of the divine mysteries. It follows that only in the Church and in union with her can believers please God by their praise and join in the prayer by which Christ glorifies the Father. In fact if Christian piety is to be pleasing to God, it must be ecclesial.

God can certainly disclose himself to men in a direct way through interior enlightenment and immediate religious experiences. Yet such privileges cannot dispense from the constancy and regularity of participation in the worship of the Church, which keeps her believers in balance and preserves them from one-sidedness and eccentricity.

More in detail, the following obligations of believers can be outlined:

1) Love and reverence for the Church and her ministers. Love for the Church is love for Christ who lives in her as in his mystical body. It is a love of gratitude for the immeasurable gift of supernatural life which she bestows on her members. It is also gratitude for her care by which she gives growth to her believers' religious life, helps the indigent, sick and poor, and defends right and justice in public life. This love becomes active in inward thinking and feeling with the Church (*sentire cum Ecclesia*) and in outward cooperation in her apostolate.

Reverence for the Church and for those who hold office in her is based on the fact that she is founded by Christ, that her most important offices go back to Christ, and that her ministers are — by their priestly ordination — representatives of Christ and mediators of his grace. They follow him in closer imitation, especially by celibacy. Furthermore they are servants of the believers' religious and spiritual weal.

2) Obedience to the Church. The duty of obedience arises from the fact that the Church has her authority from Christ and is the appointed and competent guide in matters of faith and morals. "He who hears you hears me, and he who rejects you rejects me" (Lk 10:16). "Whatever you bind on earth shall be bound in heaven, and whatever you loose on earth shall be loosed in heaven" (Mt 18:18). This imposes duties of responsibility for the faithful upon the ministers of the Church. And "the Christian faithful, for their part, should realize their obligations toward their priests and with filial love they should follow them as their shepherds and fathers" (PO 9). Knowing that the Church wants to provide them with supernatural life, Christians will indeed be glad to share in her sacramental life and to follow her directions which aim at fostering this.[1]

3) Material sustenance for priests and their work. Dedicated to the religious and spiritual welfare of the believers, priests are worthy of receiving a just recompense. For "the labourer deserves his wages" (Lk 10:7), and "the Lord commanded that those who proclaim the gospel should get their living by the gospel" (1 Cor 9:14). "Hence, where a fitting recompense of priests is not otherwise provided for, the faithful themselves are bound by a genuine obligation to see that the needed means can be procured for them to lead a respectable and worthy life. For it is in behalf of the welfare of the faithful that priests labour" (PO 20).

Besides being adjusted to the situation of the pastors and priests, their sustenance should also allow them to give a suitable recompense to those who assist them and dedicate themselves to their service. "It should also enable them to give some kind of personal assistance to the needy. From her earliest beginnings the Church has always held this ministry toward the poor

---

[1] The question of disobedience in the Church is examined in a sober way by Robert J. Banks: Ecclesial Disobedience.— The Jurist 30 (1970), 91-102.

in high regard. Moreover, this recompense should be such as to allow priests a requisite and sufficient vacation each year" (PO 20).

4) Apostolic cooperation. Not only ordained priests but all members of the Church have the task of taking part in her redemptive work. They are bound to do so through love of God and of fellowmen. "Indeed, the law of love, which is the Lord's greatest commandment, impels all the faithful to promote God's glory through the spread of His kingdom and to obtain for all men that eternal life which consists in knowing the only true God and Him whom He sent, Jesus Christ" (AA 3). All Christians have been equipped for this task by baptism and particularly by confirmation, which is intended to strengthen them for the apostolate in the world. Hence lay people should assist their priests by prayer and work to the extent possible and "assume their duty of carrying on the apostolate, each according to his state in life and his ability" (CD 17; cf. PO 9). (For a more detailed treatment on the different forms of the lay apostolate confer "Primary manifestations of fraternal charity.")

All the faithful are equally obliged to cooperate in the propagation of the faith (cf. LG 17; AG 23) and in the promotion of Church unity (UR 5). The particular duties in this regard are dealt with in the chapter on the divine virtue of faith ("Duty of spreading the faith" and "Promotion of unity of faith").

III. Church and state[1]

1. *Guidelines for the relation between Church and state*

God has given over the charge of the human communities to two powers, the ecclesiastical and the civil, the one being set over religious and divine things, the other over temporal needs. Each in its kind is supreme, each has fixed limits within which it is contained, limits which are defined by the nature and special

---

[1] References: Sidney Z. Ehler: Twenty Centuries of Church and State. — Westminster, Md.: Newman Press, 1957. Luigi Sturzo: Church and State. — Notre Dame, Ind.: University of Notre Dame Press, 1962. E. Y. Goerner: Peter and Caesar. The Catholic Church and Political Authority. — New York: Herder and Herder, 1965. J. M. Cameron: Images of Authority. A Consideration of the Concepts of Regnum and Sacerdotium (Compass Books 11). — London: Burns and Oates, 1966. Church-State Relations in Ecumenical Perspective, ed. by Elwyn A. Smith. — Duquesne University Press, 1966. Donald Eugene Smith: Religion and Political Development. — Boston: Little, Brown and Co., 1970.

objects of each community. "In their proper spheres, the political community and the Church are mutually independent and self-governing" (GS 76). Yet both communities are also related to each other as public institutions which have to a large extent the same subjects who belong to both spheres. Furthermore the Church also has temporal and material needs, and the state has to serve God's goals and therefore does by no means stand outside the religious sphere. If we look at the state in its full reality, "it becomes evident that the state itself has a religious existence, that religion is also a public affair, and that the state community, no less than the individual himself, has obligations to God, the Creator of his nature, which is ordered toward the state. A dogmatic political secularism finds as little basis in social reality as does a dogmatic anarchism." [1]

Following are some basic guidelines which indicate the way to a harmonious and equitable relation between Church and state.

(I) The Church has the right to work and to govern herself in full freedom from state intervention. According to the Declaration on Religious Freedom (Dignitatis Humanae = DH), "the freedom of the Church is the fundamental principle in what concerns the relations between the Church and governments and the whole civil order" (DH 13).

Provided the just requirements of public order are observed, the Church and religious bodies in general rightfully claim freedom in order that they may govern themselves according to their own norms. They "have the right not to be hindered, either by legal measures or by administrative action on the part of government, in the selection, training, appointment, and transferral of their own ministers, in communicating with religious authorities and communities abroad, in erecting buildings for religious purposes, and in the acquisition and use of suitable funds or properties. Religious bodies also have the right not to be hindered in their public teaching and witness to their faith" (DH 4). Likewise they are not to be prohibited from freely undertaking to show the special value of their doctrine in what concerns the organization of society and the inspiration of the whole of human activity. Finally they are entitled to establish educational, cultural, charitable, and social organizations (ib.).

---

[1] J. Messner: Social Ethics. — St. Louis/London: Herder Book Co., 1965, 661.

(II)   The Church does not possess any political power over the temporal order.   This means that she has no jurisdiction over the political realm, even though she possesses the plenitude of teaching authority.   Outside the sphere of religion and morals the Church possesses no competence.   Refraining from direct involvement in politics, the Church will be able to proclaim the royal dominion of God over the entire world all the more efficiently and unerringly.

(III)   The state does not possess any authority over the spiritual, religious order.   The state is never entitled to subject the work of the Church to a control founded on state interests (Gallicanism).   If the state should assume any position of power in the Church, attempt to dominate her or even to enlist her service in its political programs, it would infringe the divinely ordained separation of powers and violate the rights of the Church.

It is true, the government ought "to take account of the religious life of the people and show it favour, since the function of government is to make provision for the common welfare. However, it would clearly transgress the limits set to its power were it to presume to direct or inhibit acts that are religious" (DH 3).   Vice versa of course the Church may never place herself at the unqualified service of a particular political system or state, which would mean a betrayal of her mission (cf. GS 76).

(IV)   The Church possesses a plenary teaching office, which also extends over the moral laws governing the political life.   Though Christian regents and political leaders may rightly protest when individual ecclesiastics go beyond their proper bounds, they should at the same time be aware that God is the Lord of the political domain and of civic life as well.   The Church "has the right to pass moral judgments, even on matters touching the political order, whenever basic personal rights or the salvation of souls make such judgments necessary" (GS 76). She has the right and duty to manifest her grave concern over evils in the social order, and she may not be accused of meddling in politics if she denounces any attempt to expel God from public life or censures patent violations of the moral law on the political scene.   Recognition of this function of the Church by the state is in no way subjection to the Church, but a recognition of the subordination of both, Church and state, to God.

(V)   The state has the right and duty to protect religious freedom and to promote conditions favourable to religious life. For the state itself has a religious existence and must be subordinate to God's eternal goals.   It has to contribute to God's glory and to the unfolding of his creative design.   Furthermore society highly profits from the values of love of God and neighbour, of justice and peace, promoted by the Church.   "Therefore, government is to assume the safeguard of the religious freedom of all its citizens, in an effective manner, by just laws and by other appropriate means.   Government is also to help create conditions favourable to the fostering of religious life, in order that the people may be truly enabled to exercise their religious rights and to fulfill their religious duties, and also in order that society itself may profit by the moral qualities of justice and peace which have their origin in men's faithfulness to God and to His holy will" (DH 6).

Since Church and state serve the same human being, it is unavoidable that their interests intersect in certain areas.   Examples of such so-called mixed areas are: education and school, marriage, establishment of Church institutions such as hospitals, orphanages or asylums, holy days, the filling of ecclesiastical positions endowed by the state (e.g. army chaplains).   Conflicting interests in these areas are most expediently settled by agreement. They form the main object of treaties between the Church and the state, known as concordats.   The more that both societies foster cooperation between themselves in such instances, the more effectively will their service be exercised for the good of all.

Modern states frequently profess a separation of Church and state.   In fact in nations with mixed religion the state cannot give preference to the religion of one group without causing conflicts with the other groups.   In such instances the best solution for the state seems to be the avoidance of any official identification with one of the religious groups.   A separation of Church and state in this sense is to be accepted.   Catholics or Protestants cannot expect that the state gives preference treatment to their religion before that of the other religious groups. But since on the other hand the state too has a religious existence, a complete separation of state and religion in general is unnatural and not acceptable.   The state has to grant religion a place in education and society, not only practically but also officially, and has to protect and to promote its cause.

2. *Religious tolerance*[1]

Since within the same state there are frequently various religious groups represented, the question arises which attitude the state should adopt towards them, and especially in which way rulers and government officials, who have their own religious convictions, ought to practise tolerance towards the other religious groups. The teaching of the Catholic Church on this question found an explicit reformulation in the "Declaration on Religious Freedom" (DH) by Vatican II.

Though the Second Vatican Council expresses its belief that the "one true religion subsists in the Catholic and apostolic Church, to which the Lord Jesus committed the duty of spreading it abroad among all men", it likewise expresses its conviction that it is upon the human conscience that the obligation falls to seek the truth, especially in what concerns God and his Church, and to embrace the truth it comes to know (DH 1). "It is one of the major tenets of Catholic doctrine that man's response to God in faith must be free. Therefore no one is to be forced to embrace the Christian faith against his own will. This doctrine is contained in the Word of God and it was constantly proclaimed by the Fathers of the Church" (DH 10).

Therefore "all men are to be immune from coercion on the part of individuals or of social groups and of any human power, in such wise that in matters religious no one is to be forced to act in a manner contrary to his own beliefs. Nor is anyone to be restrained from acting in accordance with his own beliefs, whether privately or publicly . . . This right of the human person to religious freedom is to be recognized in the constitutional law whereby society is governed. Thus it is to become a civil right" (DH 2).

Religious freedom does not only include the right for all religious bodies to worship God privately or publicly, but also the right to public teaching and witness to the respective faith. According to the Declaration on Religious Freedom, the same freedom which the Church claims for herself is to be granted to religious bodies of every kind (DH 4).

[1] References: A. F. Carillo de Albornoz: Religious Liberty. — New York: Sheed and Ward, 1967. Louis Janssens: Freedom of Conscience and Religious Freedom. — Staten Island, N.Y.: Alba House, 1967. Enda McDonagh: Freedom or Tolerance? The Declaration on Religious Freedom of Vatican Council II; Text and Commentary. — New York: Magi Books, 1967. Richard J. Regan: Conflict and Consensus: Religious Freedom and the Second Vatican Council. — New York: Macmillan, 1967.

Only in the case where a religious group commits abuses on pretext of freedom of religion has the state the right and duty to intervene. "It is the special duty of government to provide this protection. However, government is not to act in arbitrary fashion or in an unfair spirit of partisanship. Its action is to be controlled by juridical norms which are in conformity with the objective moral order" (DH 7).

Thus, by way of a conclusion, the religious tolerance taught by Vatican II is not an indifferentism which regards all the different religions and denominations as equally true or false. It is the firm belief of the Council that the true religion subsists in the Catholic Church. But in the public, civil life the subjective convictions of every citizen and of the different religious groups have to be respected as long as they do not imperil the common weal, and the same rights of religious freedom have to be granted to everybody.

Chapter III

BODILY LIFE AND HEALTH

Respect for a person's life, his bodily and mental integrity and health belongs to the fundamental rights of man. To this right corresponds the duty of respecting the health and life of others as well as of one's own person. Vatican II made it a point to stress reverence for men as a particularly urgent demand and to denounce the manifold violations against human life: "Whatever is opposed to life itself, such as any type of murder, genocide, abortion, euthanasia, or willful self-destruction, whatever violates the integrity of the human person, such as mutilation, torments inflicted on body and mind, attempts to coerce the will itself; whatever insults human dignity, such as subhuman living conditions, arbitrary imprisonment, deportation, slavery, prostitution, the selling of women and children; as well as disgraceful working conditions, where men are treated as mere tools for profit, rather than as free and responsible persons; all these things and others of their like are infamies indeed" (GS 27). The various responsibilities for health and life together with the offences against them are to be stated and explained in the following chapter.

A. Christian view of the body and of bodily life

The Christian attitude towards the body occupies a central position between spiritualistic-dualistic hostility to the body and its materialistic idolization. Body and soul as a whole were created in the image of God (cf. Gen 1:27). And through the fall of man into sin not only the body was affected, but both body and soul were wounded and are inclined to evil.

The Pauline *sarx* (flesh) is not to be conceived in such a way as if it were the corrupted principle, hostile to God, the soul itself remaining intact. Even sins which we consider sins of the spirit, such as envy, jealousy and anger, are works of the *sarx* (Gal 5:20f). In St. Paul's as well as in the Hebrew and Semitic anthropology man is always a whole, but can be viewed

307

from various aspects.   *Sarx* signifies the entire man in his frailty, liability to temptation and slavery to sin.

The *pneuma* on the other hand, the participation in the life of the divine Spirit, is the principle of a holy life, which must renew both soul and body. Thus R. Schnackenburg judges: The theory is untenable "that St. Paul thought of the realm of the body and the senses as corrupt in itself and so depreciated what belongs to the body and matter, in a Platonic or Gnostic manner, and held there is a dualism within man himself. His more Jewish presuppositions make it certain that this was not the case." [1]

In his incarnation the Lord assumed a truly human body endowed with a human soul and sanctified both. St. Paul concludes: "Do you not know that your body is a temple of the Holy Spirit within you?" (1 Cor 6:19; cf. 6:13f). "I appeal to you therefore, brethren, by the mercies of God, to present your bodies as a living sacrifice, holy and acceptable to God" (Rom 12:1). The sanctification of the body embraces a well-ordered care for bodily health, hygiene and bodily culture; conformity with God's will in pain, illness and death itself; devotion of our bodily energies to all good works for the glory of God.

Bodily life is a gift of God, and a long life is considered as a blessing by Holy Scripture. "With long life I will satisfy him" (Ps 91:16; cf. Ex 20:12; Prov 10:27; Eph 6:2f). Yet life is given to men not at will but in stewardship. "None of us lives to himself . . . If we live, we live to the Lord" (Rom 14:7f). Thus life must not be considered as the highest value, but rather is to be placed in the service of God and neighbour. If attachment to our earthly life becomes an obstacle to the imitation of Christ, we must "hate life" (Lk 14:26; Jn 12:25), which really means that we must place it in its true perspective. In a last instance the Christian must even be ready to sacrifice his earthly existence for Christ and the brethren in a supreme act of love. "Greater love has no man than this, that a man lay down his life for his friends" (Jn 15:13).

B. Responsibility for health

Bodily life and health are goods entrusted to man by God. Accordingly there is an obligation to take care of one's health. Normally man's instinct for self-preservation already makes him

---

[1] R. Schnackenburg: The Moral Teaching of the New Testament. — London: Burns and Oates, 1967, 267; cf. 264f.

attentive to this duty. St. Paul finds it self-evident. "For no man ever hates his own flesh, but nourishes and cherishes it" (Eph 5:29).

Everyone is bound to maintain life, health and integrity of his members and to provide what is necessary for this end: food, clothing, housing, recreation. Everyone has to drive off from himself or from others what might injure life and health. With suitable means one has to restore impaired health. Civil legislation in matters of hygiene and health binds in conscience to the degree in which it is concerned with an important service for public health (cf. GS 30). Examples of such services are: vaccination against various diseases, pure food and drug regulations, hygienic measures for the prevention of contagious disease, etc.

The concept of health is however not only to be taken in the sense of bodily health. Health of mind and soul is of even greater importance. A relatively feeble body, compliant to the spirit and subservient to the needs of love of God and neighbour, comes closer to the ideal of human health than an exuberant vitality which oppresses the freedom of the spirit. The overall criterion for human health is not sheer physical vitality. It rather is a person's best possible aptness for his total vocation.[1]

Modern psychology and psychiatry have shown to what extent disturbances of mind and soul influence the health of the body. The ancient Roman saying "a sound mind in a sound body" can as well be interpreted in the sense that a sound body presupposes a sound mind. A person is therefore also responsible for his psychological health and for the health of those entrusted to him. Right and morally sound living is a most important precaution against the disorders of the soul.

Man has always seen a relation between sickness and sin. But the relation between psychoneurotic sickness and human failure is particularly evident. The burden of serious sins bears heavily upon one's soul. And thence it affects the body-soul relation, above all if speedy healing of the spirit through sorrow is neglected. It must however be noted that the proper psychoneuroses (in contrast to neurotic reactions) are caused not so much by the failures of the sick person himself, than by the failures and shortcomings of his surrounding, especially by lack

---

[1] Cf. B. Häring: Medical Ethics. — Slough, England: St. Paul Publications, 1973, 152-155.

of true love.   Thus man bears in these as well as in many other sicknesses often also the guilt of his ancestors.

1. *Nourishment*

In contrast to the Old Testament, there are no longer "unclean" foods in the New Testament. According to Mk 7:14-19 nothing defiles man what enters into his stomach from the outside. "For everything created by God is good, and nothing is to be rejected if it is received with thanksgiving" (1 Tim 4:4; cf. Rom 14:14). The decision as to what one should or may eat is based solely on the demands of temperance, the concrete requirements of health and hygiene, and the demands of love (cf. 1 Cor 8:8.13).

Eating and drinking have to be morally ordered. Self-preservation requires sufficient nourishment. In order to secure the taking of sufficient food and the fulfillment of this moral duty, God has associated it with pleasure — as he did with other instincts. To take this pleasure is not wrong as long as it remains subordinated to the purpose of nourishment. But there is a danger of man's overstepping the limits of right order in taking food, doing this for the only sake of pleasure and in contradiction to the demands of health.

The right order is clear from the aim. That amount and form of food is right which serves the preservation and development of bodily life; that which is opposed to this end is wrong.

A person who is willing to keep to the right order in taking food practises in this respect the virtue of temperance, which as a whole consists in the moderation of the sense appetites. A person sins against this virtue by the quantity of food or drink if he takes more than is permissible or less than is required for his health. He sins in regard to quality if he seeks pleasure in things which injure his health; or if he indulges in wasteful luxury, especially if the other family members have to suffer from it, if his economic security is endangered by it, or if other people in the surroundings are starving at the same time (cf. the parable of the rich man and the poor Lazarus, Lk 16:19-31).

Fasting is a help to control the disorderly desire for eating and drinking and for pleasure in general. Our Lord himself practised fasting (Mt 4:2) and recommended it (Mt 6:16-18; Mk 9:28f), though he also states that not all seasons are compatible with it (Mt 9:15). The Church always appreciated fasting and leads her believers there by her commendation and her fasting laws. The motivation for this is expressed in the Preface of Lent: Through the observance of Lent (which includes fasting as one of the important practices) "you correct our faults and raise our minds to you, you help us grow in holiness, and offer us the reward of everlasting life."

2. *Clothing and housing*

Clothing as well as housing have an influence on bodily and mental health of man. Both have the purpose to provide physical protection against the weather and must be adapted to this task. Yet they also serve other ends.

Thus clothing serves as adornment, as protection of modesty, and as distinction between sexes and classes or professions. With regard to health, clothing may endanger it and thus become a moral problem, be it because of fashion and vanity, or be it because of negligence and uncleanliness. In fact fashion exercises a tyranny over women which is often harmful to health, as physicians assure. Though a healthy fashion should also be a concern of the society, the individual himself ought to retain so much independence in this matter as to refuse a fashion harmful to health.

Dirt and uncleanliness in clothing as well as in housing are an opposite danger to health, as under such conditions vermin and germs of illnesses develop more easily. At least under this aspect a reasonable hygiene in clothing and housing is also a moral demand.

Housing should provide a wholesome setting for living in an environment of positive formative influence. An insufficient housing harbours perils for physical and mental health. All endeavours to remedy housing shortage merit therefore the support of state and Church, of employers and communities.

3. *Recreation and sports*

Recreation and sufficient sleep are necessary to restore exhausted working energy. They are a demand and command of nature.

An important element of recreation is joy, which may be found in sociability, in occupation with arts, or in contemplation of nature (e.g. on walking-tours). Games are also suitable in order to provide recreation and enjoyment, not excluding gambling, if not practised passionately or, what would be worse, to the detriment of one's economical condition.

The attitude of Christian moral teaching towards sports is altogether positive. Many natural and Christian virtues are exercised by its performance. But here also the proper balance is in place. Sports may not be practised without due regard for other obligations and without sufficient protection against possible injuries (e.g. in boxing or rugby). The use of strong stimulants to achieve higher performances is against the true spirit of sports. Moreover they may damage the organism and are judged by experts as a means of cheating. Training and strengthening of the body ought to remain the proper function of sports.

4.   *Stimulants and drugs*[1]

Stimulants (intoxicating drinks, tobacco, coffee, tea, cola, betel) used in smaller quantities can serve health, relaxation and sociability. "Use a little wine for the sake of your stomach and your frequent ailments" (1 Tim 5:23), writes St. Paul to Timothy. "Wine is like life to men, if you drink it in moderation" (Sir 31:27; cf. Ps 104:15).

Temperance in stimulants is however still a stronger obligation than temperance in eating, as they damage health more easily and can lead to addiction. This holds especially for tobacco and still more for intoxicating drinks. Abuse of alcoholic drinks has too often already destroyed the happiness of individuals and families. From this point of view the abstinence organizations merit great praise as a warning against the grave abuses and as an encouraging example to weaker brethren.

A particularly great danger for physical and psychological health in our times is drug abuse. All drugs however are not equally dangerous, and one should not fall into the rather common error of treating them all as more or less alike. Four groups of drugs, qualitatively different from each other, can be dis-

---

[1] References: Hagmaier/Gleason: Counselling the Catholic. — New York: Sheed and Ward, 1964, 113ff. Problems in Addiction: Alcohol and Drug Addiction; ed. by W. C. Bier. — New York: Fordham University Press, 1968. James Cassens: Drugs and Drug Abuse. — London/ St. Louis: Concordia, 1970. Henlee H. Barnette: The Drug Crisis and the Church. — Philadelphia: Westminster Press, 1971. Paul M. Goldhill: A Parent's Guide to the Prevention and Control of Drug Abuse. — Chicago: Henry Regnery Co., 1971. Roger E. Meyer: Guide to Drug Rehabilitation. A Public Health Approach. — Boston: Beacon Press, 1972.

tinguished: namely, marijuana, LSD, barbiturates, and the opium derivates.

One of the most widely used drugs today is marijuana and hashish, both produced from the Indian hemp plant. In spite of its bad reputation, this drug seems to be of a rather harmless nature. "It is not addictive, having none of the physiological effects or withdrawal symptoms of heroin, opium, or other narcotics... It is not as habit-forming as tobacco, resulting in no such agonies as many tobacco smokers go through to quit the habit. It leaves no hangover or sluggish feeling as does alcohol, no damage to internal organs such as results from extensive use of alcohol and tobacco. It does not heighten sexual desire or prowess, nor does it lead to crime or violence."[1] If this judgment is correct, one cannot, from the moral point of view, object to the use of marijuana and hashish more strongly than one can to the use of tobacco.

A caution is however in place. The widespread use of marijuana is of a rather recent nature, and so are the studies about it. "For the moment, there remain serious gaps in our knowledge with regard to the mental and public health implications of chronic marijuana use."[2] Some studies assert that habitual use of hashish causes inactivity and apathy and has a sluggish pattern of life in its train.[3] Here as much as in the case of alcohol, moderation may lend itself as the most prudent advice.

Not quite as common, but still rather widespread, is the psychedelic drug LSD (d-lysergic acid diethylamide), which causes a kind of ecstasy and can lead to deep psychological and even mystical experiences. LSD too is not physiologically addictive. "No matter how often one takes it, the body does not build up a need for it."[4] There are however dangers from the

---

[1] James Cassens: Drugs and Drug Abuse. — London/St. Louis: Concordia, 1970, 59f.

[2] Roger E. Meyer; Guide to Drug Rehabilitation. — Boston: Beacon Press, 1972, 120. As to the known effects of Marijuana, Meyer essentially comes to the same conclusions as J. Cassens.

[3] Cf. B. Häring: Medical Ethics. — Slough, England: St. Paul Publications, 1973, 190. A pamphlet of the Ambassador College on Marijuana claims that it has the following negative effects: "Investigations from all over the world — especially in North Africa and the Orient — have demonstrated that the long-term users of the cannabis drugs all fall into the same sluggish pattern of life: typically passive, lethargic, lazy, non-productive, slothful, sedentary and completely lacking in drive and ambition" (1970).

[4] J. Cassens, 1. c. 41.

psychological side, since a user may also have negative psychic experiences and may not be able to cope with them. Cases of homicide, suicide, psychotic break have been known. Though such reactions are most rare, they nevertheless occur. All experts therefore demand that LSD be only taken in carefully controlled, supervised conditions, i.e., an LSD user must be accompanied by an experienced, trustworthy guide.

Barbiturates (Membutal, Seconal, Luminal, Amytal) are usually given as sleeping pills, though they also have many other medical uses (e.g. treatment of high blood pressure or epilepsy). They are freely prescribed by doctors, and many people depend on them. But they are not as innocuous as they appear. Taken without medical advice or in an accidental overdose (the users of these drugs experience different reactions at different times to the same dosage), they are often lethal. Besides, "barbiturates are physically addicting. In order to achieve the effect of the drug consistently, increasing dosages are needed. Withdrawal symptoms accompany sudden stoppage of the drug. The symptoms are so severe (cramps, nausea, delirium, convulsions) that most doctors recommend that withdrawal should take place over a long period of time in the safety of a hospital. Withdrawing from barbiturates is considered harder to deal with than withdrawing from narcotics."[1] Hence it is imperative that these drugs be not used without medical advice, and that physicians be more careful in prescribing them. One may add that quite in general there is a need for more restraint in the use of the different energizers and tranquilizers ("up and down pills"), which many people get accustomed to without real lasting profit.

The most dangerous of drugs are the opium derivates such as morphine, codeine, paregoric, and worst of them all heroin; others are of synthetic nature such as Demerol and Dolophine. They are the genuine narcotics. Addiction comes fast for those who trifle with them. The body continually craves for them, and if deprived of them, punishes the addict with terrible spasms of pain and nausea that seem unbearable. Moreover narcotics addiction is very expensive and often (especially in the case of heroin) swallows more money than any job can make. So most addicts steal constantly, and their families get ruined. Finally narcotics constitute a direct threat to a person's health and life. Death because of heroin abuse is a frequent occurrence. If one

---

[1] J. Cassens, 1. c. 84.

therefore excepts the medical use of narcotics, their pleasure can for all the indicated reasons not be allowed.

Nevertheless, in spite of the known dangers of alcoholism and the detrimental character of the hard drugs, addiction is a widespread phenomenon. The reasons are multiple. They may consist in lack of self-discipline and permissive pleasure-seeking, feelings of insecurity and anxiety, a troubled social background, familial or marital conflicts, despair under dehumanizing life conditions such as poor housing, joblessness, social contempt, and the like. There are also certain character traits which are common among addicts and seem to predispose for dependency. "Chronic alcoholics and confirmed narcotic addicts are generally described as immature and excessively dependent individuals, often sexually inadequate and having a history of poor inter-personal relationships. Drugs or alcohol enable them to deal with their personal deficiencies by escape into a make-believe world."[1]

One of the root causes of the problem of addiction in our present society is a materialistic, pleasure-seeking philosophy and outlook on life which lacks true ideals and is unable to give deeper meaning to man's existence. The whole society is sick. It is affected by a "neurosis pervading the whole environment and finding expression in aimlessness and meaninglessness in the midst of economic success and comfortable life."[2]

The successful control of addiction therefore often demands a thorough re-orientation of a person's entire life. It must be given new and deeper meaning by the commitment to true ideals. Yet also the family of the addict will at times have to examine the basic attitudes which govern their conduct and relations with each other. Finally the problem of addiction is a challenge for society at large to fight the dehumanizing social conditions and to reform its outlook on life. Poverty and destitution, which are gravest in the developing nations, call upon the whole society of mankind for a concerted effort to alleviate and overcome them. The mass phenomenon of addiction in the wealthier groups and nations however may well be a lesson from God for men. Prosperity, comfort and pleasure are not the values which can fill the human heart. Man needs worthier ideals to live and work for.

---

[1] B. Häring: Medical Ethics. — Slough, England: St. Paul Publications, 1973, 194.

[2] Ib.

C. Medical Treatments and operations[1]

Bodily life is a gift of God entrusted to man not in ownership — the Lord and owner of our life is God who created it — but in stewardship and in right of usufruct. Therefore man is not allowed to use and to damage this life and the integrity of his body arbitrarily. On the other hand he is obliged to restore injured health in a responsible way.

Integrity of members is not an absolute value, as every Catholic theologian admits. It may and often even must be sacrificed (by amputation or mutilation) for the well-being of the whole body. The preservation of the whole organism is more important than the conservation of a part, which in most instances of such necessities anyway became useless because of illness. Nevertheless this principle of the part-for-the-whole (principle of totality) is not only applicable to sick organs, but also to perfectly healthy ones if by their sacrifice the life as a whole can be saved. Thus it would be allowed to cut off a foot caught in a railroad track if this is the only means to save one's life.

The use of the principle of totality has traditionally been limited to the preservation of the physical health of the sick or endangered person himself. Sterilization of a woman would not be allowed in order to cure a psychotic disturbance resulting from the fear of a further pregnancy. It would also not be allowed in order to prevent sick off-spring. On the other hand the sacrifice of a kidney for the salvation of another person's life is allowed according to a solidly probable opinion. The justification for this sacrifice is no longer the principle of totality in its traditional understanding. The justification is rather the critical need of the sick fellowman and the dispensability of the organ for the donor's life. This sacrifice transcends the principle of totality as interpreted and applied by tradition.

B. Häring judges in this regard that "medical ethics for the future must rest on an all-embracing concept of 'totality': the dignity and well-being of man as a person in all his essential

---

[1] Apart from the standard works on medical ethics by P. Finney/O'Brien, E. Healy, G. Kelly, J. Kenny, C. McFadden and T. O'Donnell, the following, more recent literature can be mentioned: Harmon L. Smith: Ethics and the New Medicine. — Nashville and New York: Abingdon Press, 1970. James B. Nelson: Human Medicine. Ethical Perspectives on New Medical Issues. — Minneapolis, Minn.: Augsburg Publishing House, 1973. George V. Lobo: Current Problems in Medical Ethics. A Comprehensive Guide to Ethical Problems in Medical Practice. — Allahabad: St. Paul Publications, 1974. Charles J. McFadden: The Dignity of Life. — Noll Plaza, Huntington, Ind.: Our Sunday Visitor, 1976.

relationships to God, to his fellowmen and to the world around him. In view of the breadth and depth of the human vocation, man can and must use his knowledge and art to manipulate the chaotic forces of the physis for the creation of a more humane order not only in the physical world but also in his psychosomatic nature. If it is more humane, it is also more pleasing to God."[1]

I. Medical and surgical treatments in general

1. *Moral rights and duties of the physician*

The ethos of the physician has at all times been characterized by the understanding of his vocation as service to his sick neighbour. In all circumstances it is his commission to alleviate the sufferings of his patient and to heal him, to the best of his knowledge and ability. He may never use his skill in order to incapacitate or destroy a person, e.g. for political motives or utilitarian reasons of any kind.

In view of the constant progress and improvements in medical care, the effort to keep abreast of the developments and to increase the professional competence by continuous education is, today more than ever before, an important duty of the physician. Besides, modern medicine with its ever increasing possibilities and demands necessitates an ever growing specialization of physicians. Doctors are not equally competent in all realms of medicine. Hence they must be aware of their limitations. They will seek the services of other physicians whenever the conditions of the patients require it. An ethos of teamwork and mutual recognition is therefore of mounting importance.

The physician cannot ignore the norms for morally good action established by the ethical sciences. As a Christian, he will be committed to the spirit of the gospel and respect the approved principles of moral theology. He will be ready to listen to the pronouncements and moral judgments of those whose special duty it is to proclaim the word of God and to speak up against any violations of love and justice.

On the other hand ethics, moral theology and Church authority are not in a condition to offer ready answers for every moral problem a physician may encounter. There are many situations where the laymen alone are sufficiently knowledgeable of all the data pertinent for the moral evaluation of an action.

---

[1] B. Häring: Medical Ethics. — Slough, England: St. Paul Publications, 1973, 62.

The right and duty of the decision is then with them. "Laymen should also know that it is generally the function of their well-formed Christian conscience to see that the divine law is inscribed in the life of the earthly city. From priests they may look for spiritual light and nourishment. Let the layman not imagine that his pastors are always such experts, that to every problem which arises, however complicated, they can readily give him a concrete solution, or even that such is their mission. Rather, enlightened by Christian wisdom and giving close attention to the teaching authority of the Church, let the layman take on his own distinctive role" (GS 43; cf. 33).

State authority is obliged to honour the conscientious convictions of the physician. No just law can constrain him to give medical treatment and practice surgeries which are against his conscience, nor may it deprive him of any rights because he feels in conscience bound to decline certain medical interventions as immoral, e.g. direct abortion.

The patient too has the obligation to respect the physician's conscience — just as the physician has the same obligation towards the patient. No human considerations can allow a physician to perform medical treatments which contradict his moral convictions. "The argument that the patient will, regardless, obtain what he wants from a less competent physician can never justify an action which is against the physician's conscience."[1]

2. *Ordinary and extraordinary treatments*

Medicaments are allowed if their direct purpose is to heal or alleviate an illness or to ease pain. This is true even if they incidentally shorten life. This presupposed, the question arises to what extent a person is obliged fo use medicines or to undergo medical treatments. Catholic moral theology answers the question by distinguishing between ordinary and extraordinary treatments.

Ordinary treatments (in the context of ethical considerations[2]) "are all medicines, treatments, and operations, which offer a reasonable hope of benefit for the patient and which can be obtained and used without excessive expense, pain, or

---

[1] B. Häring, 1. c. 41.

[2] From the physician's standpoint, a medicament or procedure is extraordinary if it is fanciful, bizarre, experimental, incompletely established, unorthodox or not recognized.

other inconvenience."[1] Such other, grave inconvenience would be had, e.g., if a patient had to move to another climate or country to be helped and cured. The medicine, treatment, etc., must be obtainable with relative convenience *and* offer reasonable hope of benefit. If either of these conditions is lacking, the means is extraordinary.

Extraordinary means, accordingly, are "all medicines, treatments, and operations, which cannot be obtained or used without excessive expense, pain, or other inconvenience, or which, if used, would not offer a reasonable hope of benefit."[2] For example a young woman has a rare cardiac ailment. There is a chance of curing her with an extremely delicate operation; but it is only a chance. Without the operation she can hardly live a year. With the operation she may die on the table or shortly afterwards. But she also has a slight chance of surviving and of being at least comparatively cured. This is an extraordinary treatment because of the expenses and especially because of the great uncertainty that it involves.

Ordinary medical and surgical treatments, necessary to cure a serious illness or also to protect against it, are obligatory. "Natural reason and Christian morals say that man has the right and the duty in case of serious illness to take the necessary treatment for the preservation of life and health. This duty that he has towards himself, towards God, towards the human community, and in most cases towards certain determined persons, derives from well-ordered charity, from a submission to the Creator, from social justice and even from strict justice as well as from devotion towards his family. But normally, one is held to use only ordinary means — according to circumstances of persons, places, times, and culture — that is to say, means that do not involve any grave burden for oneself or another. A more strict obligation would be too burdensome for most men and would render the attainment of the higher, more important good too difficult. Life, death, all temporal activities are in fact subordinated to spiritual ends" (Pius XII).[3]

On the other hand one is not forbidden to take more than strictly necessary steps to preserve life and health, as long as one does not fail in some more serious duty. Exceptionally the use

[1] G. Kelly: Medico-Moral Problems. — Dublin: Clonmore and Reynolds, 1960, 129.

[2] G. Kelly, 1. c.

[3] AAS 49 (1957), 1030.

of extraordinary means may be obligatory, e.g. if the prolongation of a person's life were necessary for the common good, as might happen in the case of a great soldier or stateman; or if an at least limited prolongation of some days enabled a person to regulate important family or business matters; or if it were necessary to prepare for a good death.

These considerations primarily mark the duty of the patient. The doctor's problem is more complicated. He has not only to do what the patient would be obliged to do. He also must do what the patient reasonably wants him to do. Therefore he has above all to ascertain the wishes of the patient or of his representatives. If this is not possible, he should do what he thinks the patient would want or what he sincerely judges to be in the patient's best interest. In such instances the golden rule should be helpful: What would the doctor himself want if he were in the patient's condition?

It is important to note that means which were extraordinary in past times may become ordinary later on for different reasons. Major operations used to be considered extraordinary treatments, first because the pain was practically unbearable for most people; and secondly because the outcome was often very uncertain, e.g. because of the danger of infection. Today medicine is in a condition to control both the pain and the danger of infection. Likewise, formerly expensive treatments may become less expensive as medicine and production techniques progress. Hence many operations and treatments that would have been extraordinary in former times, have now become ordinary.

These explanations make it obvious that the distinction between ordinary and extraordinary means is not sharp and clear-cut but flowing. "In concrete cases it is not always easy to determine when a given procedure is an extraordinary means. It is not computed according to a mathematical formula, but according to the reasonable judgment of prudent and conscientious men."[1]

Unnecessary procedures, whether diagnostic or therapeutic, are morally objectionable. A procedure is unnecessary when no proportionate reason requires it for the welfare of the patient. Most often branded as unjustifiable are removal of the appendix or of the gall bladder, cesarean section, removal of the ovaries or the uterus. A fortiori unnecessary is any procedure that is opposed to sound medical standards.

---

[1] G. Kelly, 1. c. 135.

The removal of an apparently healthy appendix while the abdomen is open for some other reason may be allowed at the discretion of the physician. The reason is that the appendix itself, as far as we know, serves no useful purpose, and its removal under the mentioned circumstance precludes the probability of future surgery without undue present risk or expenses of the patient.[1]

3. *The duty to preserve life*

The question of ordinary and extraordinary treatments is especially acute in the situations of terminal sickness. A rather widely accepted principle in medical circles holds that the duty of doctors and nurses is not only to heal and to relieve suffering, but also to prolong life as much as possible. Death is considered the enemy which is to be kept away by all means and as long as this can be one.

But it not seldom happens that relieving pain and preserving life do not neatly coincide. Instead they may present themselves as alternatives which are in conflict with each other and occasionally mutually exclusive. Prolongation of life at times means prolongation of hopeless suffering.

At other times only a biological life is maintained with all kinds of pharmacologic and surgical means and mechanical devices. The patient lies in a permanent coma, if not even his brain is already destroyed. The question must seriously be asked whether the prolongation of a merely vegetative life can still qualify as a medical assistance in the service of human life. Human life is more than mere biologic vitality.

Again, the tendency to regard death as a wholly negative reality must be questioned. In fact it is false. In the perspective of Christian faith, death is reunion with Christ, the entrance into eternal life, the final unification with God (cf. Phil 1:21-23). If death is the enemy, then physicians are waging a losing fight. Sooner or later they are always defeated. However the ultimate purpose of the medical profession is not to defeat death. Rather it is to assist men to serve God and his divine plan as efficiently as possible and to work their eternal salvation. Therefore when a person's task on earth is terminated by God's will, the physician's task is terminated as well.

Medical conscience must learn to be willing not only to

---

[1] G. Kelly remarks that this is fairly routine practice in good (at least American) hospitals (Medico-Moral Problems, 1960, 253).

begin treatment but also to stop it. If someone's life has already been despaired of, then there is no need to prolong it indefinitely by means of medicines and equipments, especially if the life in question is purely vegetal, without signs of human reaction. In this case all extraordinary means may be omitted and the natural process allowed to take its course. The conviction is expressed that after brain death the omission of these means is even obligatory. "After brain death, the surgeon has the moral obligation to stop all artificial methods of sustaining life by respirators."[1]

This also holds true for cases of incurable, painful illness. Though the physician must devote the normal measure of medical care to the incurable patient, he is not obliged to prolong such a life by special efforts and extraordinary means. On the contrary, more and more voices assert "that it is immoral to prolong life artificially when, in particular situations, this means only prolonging suffering, the agony or the act of death."[2]

It is a thoroughly sound Christian attitude if sisters in a home for incurable cancer patients do not use such things as intravenous feeding.[3] In these circumstances the most appropriate assistance is indeed if all patients are given devoted nursing care (including the food and drink they want); if their pain is alleviated as much as possible; and if they are helped to make a good preparation for death. There is no obligation to use any other medical treatments of prolonging life, whether they are defined as extraordinary or ordinary.

These norms apply to those incurable cases where there is no hope that the patient may regain consciousness or where the prolongation of life only means a prolongation of suffering. But as long as there is hope of curing a patient or of prolonging life in such a way that a reasonably happy and significant existence can be anticipated for a short or longer period of time, the doctor should use every probable remedy at his command. The common good demands this rule of conduct from the doctor.

The patient however is entitled to refuse any treatment that would be extraordinary. His desire is to be respected even if one of his chief motives is to avoid added burdens and harmful debts for his family. This motivation is not merely one of

---

[1] L. A. Brewer: De Humanitate. — The American Journal of Surgery, 118 (1969), 136; quoted by B. Häring: Medical Ethics, 1973, 133.

[2] B. Häring: Medical Ethics.— Slough, England: St. Paul Publications, 1973, 140.

[3] Cf. G. Kelly: Medico-Moral Problems, 1960, 139.

utility, but of responsible concern for his dependants. Much more is his wish to be respected if the situation is beyond hope. Almost absurd cases are reported where in hopeless situations even the written wish of the patient has been grossly disregarded to discontinue further medical steps to prolong his life.[1] One may wonder whether in such instances the physicians responsible should not be obliged to carry the additional expenses.

It is not contrary to the common good for a doctor to admit that a patient is incurable and to cease trying to effect a cure. Naturally the reasonable wishes of the patient as to further life-sustaining treatments should likewise be respected and complied with. The same holds for the wishes of his representatives if the patient is under age or unable to make a decision. Nevertheless "the doctor must not allow the family to seduce him to the point of using the most expensive procedures for the sole purpose of appeasing them when there is practically no hope that it would be of any avail to the patient. An expensive treatment for a life already doomed may constitute a grave injustice towards the members of the patient's family. Often the heavy financial burden is incurred by the family solely through fear for their reputation. The attending physician would be acting irresponsibly were he to yield to family pressures in such a case."[2]

Physicians may offend against the true well-being of the patient, of his family and other patients, and ultimately against the common good if they needlessly prolong a life in suffering or sustain the merely vegetative life of a person whose brain has ceased to function. It deserves asking whether we can say "that doctors who refuse to allow an accident victim to die (for example, one whose brain is destroyed) are not aggressors against the well-being of the patient's family and all their resources so long as the patient's death is artificially postponed? Or that the hundreds of hours and millions of dollars expended in the care of mechanically metabolized human organisms, for whom there is no real medical hope of recovery, do not constitute in some sense an assault upon the common good?"[3]

[1] The example of an absurd prolongation of life against the patient's written wish is reported by W. St. C. Symmers, Sr., in his article "Not Allowed to Die" (British Medical Journal, 1968, 442); reprinted in Harmon L. Smith: Ethics and the New Medicine. — Nashville and New York: Abingdon Press, 1970, 133f.

[2] B. Häring, 1. c. 141.

[3] Harmon L. Smith: Ethics and the New Medicine. — Nashville and New York: Abingdon Press, 1970, 156.

In order to spare patients who are beyond hope extension of their distress, their families needless anxiety and expense, hospital personal and facilities needless consumption of skill and resources, and waiting patients needless delay in receiving attention — for these and other worthy reasons doctors must be ready to terminate a treatment which does not serve the health and well-being of the patient any more.

4. *Cooperation in illicit operations*

It does not rarely happen that nurses are called to assist operations which they cannot approve of in their conscience by preparing the patient, handing instruments to doctors and so forth. May they take part in these operations? Or must they refuse such cooperation and rather resign than assist?

The actions by which the nurses render assistance are in themselves not evil. They are morally neutral. If the nurses disapprove of the doctor's evil action and evil purpose, they are rendering a material cooperation only. Such cooperation is permissible under certain conditions.

Of course if it is possible for the nurses to refuse the assistance in an illicit operation, they should do so. If they judge that their request to be excused would be futile, but that it would not be held against them, they ought to make the request as a definite way of showing their disapproval. Yet if they foresee, or know from past experience, that the request would not only be futile but would also be a source of serious inconvenience to them, they could omit the request and show their disapproval in some other way. However nurses should not be too ready to judge that their conscientious request will not be honoured. Very often they are respected for asserting their principles.

Suppose the refusal of cooperation in the objectionable operation is not possible, then such unwilling assistance is allowed when it cannot be avoided without incurring some proportionately serious inconvenience. The danger of losing one's position without the hope of getting another would be a sufficient reason to justify the material cooperation. Another reason would be the fact that a nurse can do at lot of spiritual good in a hospital, e.g. by summoning the priest or minister for the patients, in helping the dying to make their peace with God, in baptizing dying babies, etc.

But if these conditions are not verified, or if the demands

for such cooperation are very frequent, or most especially if the operations performed are not only condemned by the Church but also by the state (e.g. abortions prohibited by state law, mercy killing of defective babies, unlawful experiments), the nurse will be obliged to withdraw from such a hospital and to get employed in another one. Nevertheless G. Kelly judges that a nurse seldom finds herself in a situation in which resignation is her only legitimate choice.[1]

II. Particular surgeries

1. *Cosmetic surgery*

Cosmetic surgery is an operation performed in order to improve a person's appearance. In general there is no moral objection to such surgery. The removal of repulsive bodily blemishes may even be morally obligatory. Moral psychology explains how such a defect can be profoundly prejudicial to the entire spiritual development of character. Moreover certain physical defects may prove a serious obstacle to professional advancement or to chances of marriage. For this reason under certain circumstances parents may have a grave obligation to care for the removal of a mole or birthmark or a similar cosmetic defect of their children by means of a surgical operation, as long as it does not involve serious and disproportionate risk for the patient. It must be performed at such an early age that perfect success is to be expected. Physicians have the obligation to inform a child's parents that the defect ought to be corrected in due time.

On the other hand a physician will not readily resort to surgery in order to satisfy motives of pure vanity or worse. He would not be allowed to do a face-lifting operation in order to help a dangerous criminal escape detection.

2. *Transplantation of organs*

Transplantation of organs is a rather recent surgical procedure. The first experiments with skin grafts were made in 1923-24. The first successful human renal homograft was carried out between adult identical twins in 1954. The recipient died 8 years later of coronary artery disease and glomerulone-

---

[1] G. Kelly: Medico-Moral Problems, 1960, 335.

phritis in the transplanted kidney. The first human heart transplant took place in 1967. The recipient died 18 days later. By June 1970, 160 heart transplants had been performed, but only 10 of the recipients were still alive.[1]

Transplants may be autografts, heterografts or homografts. Autografts are transfers of tissue, e.g. skin or bone, from one part of the patient's own body to another part. They are justified for any reason of health. Heterografts are transplantations of animal tissue to a human body. They are permissible as long as they do not effect changes of personality. Since the transfer of animal sex glands to a human recipient involves such serious changes, it must be rejected as immoral. Homografts consist in the transfer of tissue from one human being to another. The tissue may originate from the body of a deceased person or from a living donor. Some of the questions connected with homografts have to be discussed more in detail.

There is no moral objection to the making of grafts from cadavers (skin, cornea from the eye) and from legitimately amputated organs (bones).[2] Transplantation from cadavers would usually not be permissible — apart from exceptional cases — without the consent of the family or the responsible relatives, or contrary to the explicit refusal of the deceased.

Heart transplants naturally have as their exclusive source the bodies of deceased persons. This raises the question as to when precisely the moment of death occurs and a person can be considered dead. This question is of special urgency today, since the vegetative life of a person can be sustained by various machines long after the brain has ceased to function. It is here not the place to enter in the discussions physicians have had and have concerning the moment of death. According to B. Häring a general consensus has by now been reached that brain death is the end of the earthly history of a human person. "The arguments for the equation of the total death of the person with brain death are fully valid."[3]

Evidently for any instances of heart transplant the death of the donor must be fully assured. In order that this be the

---

[1] Cf. Harmon L. Smith: Ethics and the New Medicine. — Nashville and New York: Abingdon Press, 1970, 102.

[2] "Bone banks" are usually made up of bone removed at operations; "skin banks" have as their main, if not only source the cadaver.

[3] Medical Ethics, 1973, 136.

case, the World Medical Association and many national groups of physicians have agreed to the principle that "if transplantation of an organ is involved, the decision that death exists should be made by two or more physicians and the physicians determining the time of death should in no way be immediately concerned with the performance of the transplantation."[1] The norms concerning the physician's duty to preserve life have been given above. They are not altered by the fact that the dying person is the possible donor of a heart. But there is reason to apply them with still greater caution.

Granted that the conditions are fulfilled which protect the donor's life against any violations, heart transplants are in principle permissible. Nevertheless in view of the very limited success with them, the question must still be asked in all seriousness whether these operations do really provide reasonable therapeutic benefit to the patient. One must wonder whether there is sufficient benefit to justify the sufferings the transplant generally entails for the patient, the many precautions which have to be taken, and the tremendous medical efforts necessary for the performance of the operation.

Another discussion concerns the transplants of tissues or organs from one living person to another (homografts inter vivos). It is universally admitted that such things as blood transfusions and skin grafts are lawful. (Medicine considers blood and skin as organs too.) Some theologians reason that these are permitted because the blood and skin restore themselves; or because it is not the organ as a whole that is transplanted, but only a small part of it. This would mean that man is allowed to dispose of parts of his body to the benefit of his neighbour as long as the parts sacrificed are of minor importance to the donor. Transplantation of more important organs is according to these authors (Ermecke[2], Zalba[3]) an unallowed disposal of one's body. Thus transplantation of a kidney (probably the only case coming into consideration at present) would not be permitted. (Yet also in this case not the entire organ is transplanted but only one half, since the entire organ consists of two kidneys.)

---

[1] British Medical Association News (October, 1968); quoted by Harmon L. Smith, 1. c. 132.

[2] Mausbach-Ermecke: Katholische Moraltheologie III, 1961, 253.

[3] M. Zalba: Theologiae Moralis Compendium I (B.A.C. 175), 1958, nr. 1576.

Other authors (G. Kelly,[1] T. O'Donnell,[2] J. Kenny,[3] C. McFadden,[4] B. Häring,[5] G. Lobo[6]) argue that love of one's neighbour would justify the minor as well as the major transplants. In a last analysis there is no difference in principle between the different kinds of transplantations. The justifying reason is the same for all. Love of one's neighbour warrants such procedures as long as the donor's organism does not suffer serious harm. There is only a difference in the degree of the sacrifice. Of course the graver the sacrifice is, the graver the reason must be for which the transplant is performed. This opinion is sufficiently well represented among moral theologians so as to form a solid basis for lawful action. Provided the transplants are not contrary to good medicine, they can be performed.

Note however that there is no general duty in charity to make such a sacrifice like the offer of a kidney for the sake of a suffering fellowman. This is to be considered a heroic and therefore completely free act of Christian love. For this reason the consent of the donor must be given with full freedom and knowledge. Serious questions arise as to whether anybody, adult or child, can give consent for a minor to become an organ donor. It seems that the answer should be negative. But in this case kidney transplants between twins under age, for example, would not be lawful. Perhaps the age of consent should be extended downward to the age of conscription or universal suffrage, as has been suggested.[7]

At any rate, since the medical trend is to replace kidney transplants from living donors more and more by transplants from deceased donors, the problem loses somewhat of its urgency. The progress in medicine made it possible to achieve almost the same results with kidneys from dead donors. Homo-

[1] Gerald Kelly: Medico-Moral Problems. — Dublin: Clonmore and Reynolds, 1960, 246.

[2] Thomas J. O'Donnell: Morals in Medicine. — Westminster, Md.: Newman Press, 1960, 126-130.

[3] John P. Kenny: Principles of Medical Ethics. — Westminster, Md.: Newman Press, 1962, 163.

[4] Charles J. McFadden: Medical Ethics. — London: Burns and Oates, 1962, 266-268.

[5] Bernard Häring: Medical Ethics. — Slough, England: St. Paul Publications, 1973, 137.

[6] George V. Lobo: Current Problems in Medical Ethics. — Allahabad: St. Paul Publications, 1974, 83f.

[7] Cf. Harmon L. Smith, 1. c. 107.

grafts of such important organs from deceased persons are naturally to be preferred in every regard, if they are possible.

Finally also consent of the recipient must be sufficiently assured for any transplants which must be considered extraordinary treatments. If the patient is unconscious or under age, the consent of his representatives (husband, wife, parents) is required. Physicians may not treat or operate against the will of the recipient or his representatives, certainly not if extraordinary treatments are concerned.

3. *Sterilization and castration*

The term sterilization is often used in the wide sense of any mutilating procedure which deprives man or woman of the power of generation. In this sense it also includes the procedures of castration. More precisely however sterilization only comprises those medical interventions which merely suppress the generative functions by certain surgical operations (e.g. ligation or section of the tubes, vasectomy) or by medications, while leaving the reproductive glands intact. Castration on the other hand consists in the removal or destruction of the reproductive glands (testicles in the male and ovaries in the female). Removal of the entire uterus of the woman is called hysterectomy.

Sterilization and castration are forms of mutilation. They deprive the body of functions and organs which it possesses for the purpose of procreation and which also influence and determine the distinctive physiological and psychological traits of man and woman. These functions and organs cannot be suppressed and destroyed arbitrarily, but only for a sufficiently weighty reason. Such reason is, according to traditional moral theology, the bodily health of the person who is to suffer the mutilation. Since castration is a more drastic mutilation than sterilization, a graver reason is required to justify the former than the latter.

The ultimate criterion for good and evil, lawful and unlawful however is not exclusively a person's bodily health. The ultimate criterion is man's final goal, as has been explained in general moral theology. For this goal man has been created. And for this goal he has received his body from God in usufruct. Man's ultimate goal is also the ultimate destination of his body. By means of his body man is to cooperate in the realization of the divine plan to work his salvation. Any mutilation and consequently also any sterilization and castration, must receive its justification from this goal. A person's health evidently is of great importance for the efficient realization of God's divine plan. But one cannot a priori exclude the possibility of other reasons which likewise may justify a mutilation and sterilization for the sake of the superior goals of God. Naturally such interference with the integrity of the body has always the burden of proof.

Sterilization and castration are permitted, according to traditional moral theology, when they are immediately directed to the cure, diminution or prevention of a serious pathological condition and a simpler treatment is not reasonably available. The sexual organs themselves ought to be sick, or they must be the physiological cause of a sickness in some other part of the body. Thus removal or irradiation of the ovaries is allowed in treating carcinoma of the breast or ulcer resulting from them. But sterilization or castration would not be allowed in order to remedy psychological disturbances in a woman which result from fear of further pregnancies. In this case the procedures are immediately directed to the suppression of the procreative function and only mediately to the cure of a disease. This would be unlawful, direct sterilization.

If a uterus is the serious cause of a pathological condition, there is no need to subject a woman to almost appalling hardships — financial, physical and psychological — in order to preserve it. Though unnecessary removals of the uterus are frequent, there are nevertheless cases where this operation is in order. Such an instance would be had, e.g., if a woman's menstrual period regularly lasted from ten to fifteen days, during which time she suffers great pain and the bleeding is so excessive that she is prevented from doing her work. If all other, less drastic treatments fail, the uterus can be removed in order to help the woman to lead a normal life again.

Object of a controversy among Catholic moral theologians has been the question whether a uterus which has severely been damaged by previous cesareans could be removed, although it does not create danger here and now as long as the woman is not pregnant. Yet because of the weakness of the wall or scar, it is very likely that it will cause serious danger in another pregnancy. Some theologians (e.g. Healy,[1] O'Brien[2]) think that,

[1] Edwin Healy: Medical Ethics. — Chicago: Loyola University Press, 1956, 174f.

[2] P. Finney/P. O'Brien: Moral Problems in Hospital Practice. — St. Louis: Herder Book Co., 1956, 224.

since the actual danger would arise only from a further pregnancy, the removal of the uterus would be a contraceptive measure. The means to prevent the danger should rather be avoidance of the further pregnancy. Others more justly think (and it seems that they are in the majority, e.g. G. Kelly[1], Paquin[2], O'Donnell[3], Häring[4]) that, since the condition which would cause the danger is already present, the uterus may be removed now, because it is already seriously pathological and a useless organ. Organs are essentially functional rather than static. A damaged uterus which is not capable of any further pregnancy is without purpose. Therefore, if reasons of health recommend its removal, there is no obligation to preserve it. Since this opinion is sufficiently well represented among theologians, the damaged uterus may in good conscience be removed, naturally with the consent of the patient. Would the same reason also justify a permanent — although in this case direct — sterilization, since it is less drastic?[5] One could hardly blame a physician who gave preference to this simpler treatment, since it involves lesser risks for a woman's health.

There are still other instances of sickness which may be fatal for a woman if she becomes pregnant again, and where therefore sterilization seems to be recommended as the safest means of prevention. If for example a woman has a very weak heart, she may not be able to survive another delivery. Yet in contradistinction to the cases discussed until now, the generative organs are in this instance in no way pathologically affected nor do they condition a sickness. The heart disease is not conditioned by the generative organs and can therefore also not be cured by their suppression or removal. Consequently a sterilization of a woman under this condition would have to be considered a direct sterilization; and this is according to the traditional principles of Catholic moral theology not admissible.

For people not trained in the distinctions of Catholic moral theology, it is extremely hard to follow these differences in conclusions. The lives of two women are equally endangered by

---

[1] Gerald . Kelly: Medico-Moral Problems, 1960, 215-217. He includes a bibliography of authors who deal with the problem and indicates their respective positions.

[2] Jules Paquin: Morale e Medicina. — Roma: Catholic Book Agency, 1958, 248.

[3] O'Donnell, 1. c. 149.

[4] B. Häring: The Law of Christ III, 1966, 246f.

[5] This conclusion is drawn by E. Tessen: Discussion morale. — Cahiers Laennec 24, June 1964, 69f.

a further pregnancy. In the one case the danger results from a uterus badly damaged by repeated cesareans, in the other case it results from a weak heart. The one woman may be sterilized or castrated in order to prevent the danger of another pregnancy, the other not. It is in view of such and similar cases that B. Häring remarks that the vocabulary of direct and indirect sterilization "is hardly intelligible to medical thought today".[1] Protestant theologians find the distinctions between direct and indirect procedures "circumlocuitous". They feel that precisely this kind of moral posture has given casuistry "a bad name as a synonym for legalism".[2]

The customary distinction between directly and indirectly willed effects in Catholic ethics is certainly not an arbitrary invention or mere hair-splitting. It has a real basis in the nature of human actions. The distinction is often of help in the formulation of moral guidelines. But there are time and again instances, generally borderline cases, where the distinction leads to queer results. The moral conclusions drawn seem unreasonable and opposed to common sense. The root of the difficulty lies in the affirmation that directly willed evil effects are never and under no condition admissible, while indirectly willed evil effects sometimes and for a sufficiently grave reason are. This principle is established by general moral theology and subsequently taken for granted in the different sections of special moral theology. But the question must be asked whether this supposition is really sufficiently substantiated and truly absolutely valid.

The proposition has been explicitly discussed in the first volume of this moral theology under the heading "problems and controversies" in the section on the imputability of indirectly willed effects (chap. IV). The root issue is the argument in justification of indirectly willed evil effects under certain conditions. The argument says that life would be unbearable if it were never allowed to admit of indirectly willed evil effects, that much good could not be done, and that it would be unreasonable to act contrarily. The question now is whether this argument would not also hold true for some instances of directly willed evil effects. True, there are many more instances where the argument will justify indirectly willed than directly willed evil effects. As a rule of thumb therefore it can indeed be said that

---

[1] B. Häring: Medical Ethics, 1973, 90.

[2] Harmon L. Smith: Ethics and the New Medicine. — Nashville and New York: Abingdon Press, 1970, 33.

directly willed evil effects are generally not permissible. But this is not an absolute principle without any exception. The mentioned argument is also able to justify at times a directly willed evil effect, even though only rarely.

Another serious difficulty against the absolute inadmissibility of directly willed evil effects results from the argument that moral theology cannot be under the sway of several absolute values and claims. Inevitably such a position must at times lead to frictions and conflicts. Also Catholic moral theology knows only one supreme value absolute in its own right. This is the absolute value of God's glory, the promotion of his kingdom and the unfolding of his creative designs. If other absolute values exist, then only because the preservation of these other values is always an unconditional demand of the supreme value of God's glory, and because their violation would always and with no exception cause detriment to it.

Applied to the present issue, the question then would be: Is the integrity of the generative organs such a value and is direct sterilization always and with no exception an offence against God's glory and his creative designs? Or is in the case of the woman whose heart is too weak to allow any further pregnancy not perhaps the opposite the case? Is her own good, the good of the family and the creative purpose of God not perhaps best served by a direct sterilization?[1]

A positive answer to the latter question however is controverted by a Responsum of the Congr. for the Doctrine of Faith of 1975, which rejects, with reference to the declarations of the magisterium and especially Pius XII, every direct sterilization as absolutely forbidden. Inasmuch as this sterilization has the direct purpose and immediate effect of rendering the generative organs unfit for procreation, it must be considered intrinsically evil.[2]

---

[1] The question receives a positive answer by Charles E. Curran: New Perspectives in Moral Theology (Notre Dame, Ind.: Fides Publishers, 1974), 206f, and George V. Lobo: Current Problems in Medical Ethics (Allahabad: St. Paul Society, 1974), 143. Both authors also consider sterilization as a possible "ultima ratio" in situations which demand of a couple birth control (Curran p. 211 and Lobo p. 144f). Their view is shared by B. Häring: Medical Ethics, 1973, 90f, Franz Böckle: Ethische Aspekte der freiwilligen operativen Sterilisation; in: Stimmen der Zeit, 1974 (192. Band), 755–760, Vitaliano R. Gorospe (ed.): Freedom and Philippine Population Control (Quezon City: New Day Publishers, 1976), 30f, and Johannes Gründel, in: Handbuch der christlichen Ethik II, ed. by Anselm Hertz et alii (Freiburg: Herder, 1978), 157.

[2] See AAS 68 (1976), 738–740. It is however to be noted that the Responsum was formulated at a time when the above arguments in favour of exceptions were rather new and still in the process of development.

4. *Operations in cases of difficult pregnancy*

The treatments to be studied here are operations on the child before it is born, or operations on the mother which entail the probable or certain death of the fetus or unborn child, but only in an indirect way. The problem of direct therapeutic abortion shall be dealt with later in the section on abortion.

Fortunately the evolution of medical science reduced to a very large extent the cases in which a therapeutic abortion or the direct killing of the fetus by craniotomy could seem indicated.[1] In many cases help is offered by means of cesarean section, which is now a relatively safe procedure.[2]

As a general principle, medical interventions bearing with them a probable or even certain danger for the life of the child as an undesired and indirect consequence are allowed in cases of a hazardous, morbid condition of the expectant mother which endangers her life. Thus the surgical removal of a cancerous womb of an expectant mother can be permitted, although this operation includes the death of the fetus. But it should be made sure that there is no other way to save both, the mother and unborn child. This is an obvious prerequisite for the licitness of such operations. Some of these surgical interventions have to be studied in particular in the following.

a) Treatment of hemorrhage during pregnancy and before the fetus is viable: Hemorrhage in this case is generally treated by emptying the uterus of the fetus or by administering ergot preparations, which staunch the bleeding by contraction of the uterus.

These treatments only apply to excessive hemorrhage, where the mother's life is in imminent danger and that of the fetus cannot be saved. The basic treatment for a moderate bleeding is bed rest and sedatives.

In cases of excessive hemorrhage the physician may empty the uterus if he has good reason to believe that the fetus is

---

[1] The article "Abtreibung" in "Lexikon für Theologie und Kirche" however warns against too naive a judgment in this matter: "Wenn aber behauptet worden ist, daß es überhaupt keine 'Fälle' gäbe, bei denen die Schwangerschaftsunterbrechung das einzige Mittel wäre, um das Leben der Mutter zu retten, so entsprechen solche Behauptungen nicht den Tatsachen" (LKTh I, 1957, 97).

[2] Nevertheless also this intervention should not be performed except in cases of real necessity. Primary section creates at least a high probability that future deliveries must be by cesarean as well.

already dead or that the placenta is already completely detached. But if the fetus is still alive and still attached to the uterus, Catholic moral theologians commonly judge that no procedure is permitted which has as its sole, immediate purpose the emptying of the uterus, because it would constitute a direct abortion. However physicians also judge that with every strong and protracted hemorrhage the death of the fetus is to be definitely presumed.

If an ergot preparation is used to staunch excessive bleeding, the resultant contraction of the uterus will not only seal off the blood vessels, but it may also sheer off the placenta. May such a medicament nevertheless be used? Ergot does not stop hemorrhage by means of the expulsion of the fetus but — independently of the presence or absence of a fetus — by means of contraction of the uterus. If therefore an abortion is connected with this treatment, it is only indirect and on this account permitted. It is also to be noted that ergot would not disturb a firmly attached pregnancy unless given in large doses.

b) Operations on the infant in utero: The two questions to be discussed are the surgical operation of cleidotomy and the delivery of the hydrocephalic infant.

Sometimes when the infant has died in the uterus, it is necessary to cut or break the collar bone (clavicle) in order to effect a vaginal delivery. These procedures are known as cleidotomy and osteoclasis respectively. The question arises whether the same procedures may be used on a living baby in cases in which the head is already born, but the size of the shoulders is an obstacle to complete delivery. Physicians assure that cleidotomy (cutting of the clavicles) is not necessarily a fatal type of surgery nor mutilation beyond recovery. As to the fracture of the collar bone, it can be performed without doing any permanent harm to the fetus. The break readily heals after birth.

The second treatment concerns a hydrocephalic fetus, whose head contains too much fluid and is therefore too big for a vaginal delivery. In such cases physicians have recourse to drainage of the hydrocephalic head by means of a small cannula introduced through the anterior fontanelle. Thus one withdraws so much of the excess fluid as is necessary to reduce the fetal head to a relatively normal size and to permit a normal delivery. This withdrawal can usually be effected without injury to the brain. Though death might occur, this is not the necessary consequence. Therefore it is not a direct attack on the life of the fetus. After all it is the very same operation that would be performed in favour of the child if the hydrocephalic were already born and gave hope of survival.

c) Ectopic operations: These operations concern pregnancies developing in a fallopian tube or ovary. In such a condition the fetus is unable to reach viability.

According to the principle that directly willed evil effects are never permissible, Catholic moral theologians commonly consider the shelling out of a living fetus, the killing of the fetus by means of an electric current, and so forth, as illicit. All would also agree that the ligation of the maternal arteries and removal of the tube is morally justifiable in order to check hemorrhage resulting from rupture of the tube. In this case the loss of fetal life — if indeed the fetus is not already dead — would be merely the indirect effect of a procedure designed to take away a dangerously ill part of the body and to stop hemorrhage.

The opinions of theologians differ regarding the proper treatment of a tubal pregnancy before rupture occurs. According to some theologians, the ligation of the arteries and removal of the tube and fetus before rupture actually occurs constitute a direct attack on the life of the fetus and are therefore morally unjustifiable. This opinion is based on the view that the only source of danger in this case is the fetus itself and not a sick organ. But progress in medical research has shown that the tube itself is pathologically affected already before the definitive rupture occurs, namely by a constant disintegration of blood vessels with consequent hemorrhage. The rupture of the tube simply adds more hemorrhage. For this reason other theologians judge that the operation in discussion can already be performed before the actual rupture of the tube takes place. The direct object of the surgery in this case is not the removal of the fetus, but the prevention of the danger inherent in the disintegration of the blood vessels of the tube. This second opinion is by far the more common today and can safely be followed.

d) Abdominal pregnancy: Sometimes it happens that an ectopic fetus enters into the abdominal cavity and attaches itself to the mother's intestine. Is it allowed to terminate such a pregnancy whenever it is discovered?

For a serious reason the fetus may be removed as soon

as it has attained minimum viability, though medical authorities judge that it would generally be much safer to wait till almost full term.[1] It would not be allowed to remove an inviable fetus simply because it is found in the abdominal cavity. This would be unlawful, direct abortion. On the other hand if the mother's intestine is already damaged and in urgent need of treatment in order to save her life, the damage may be repaired, even though the fetus perishes in the process. Also if the mother were bleeding, the ligation of maternal blood vessels required for stopping the hemorrhage would be permissible, even though this procedure would also cut off the blood supply for the fetus. In these two last instances the termination of the pregnancy is to be considered indirect.

III. Psychotherapeutic treatments

Psychotherapy deals with neurotic and psychosomatic illnesses which result from unresolved psychic conflicts. The illnesses may arise from the unsuccessful attempt to meet the difficulties of life or from the lack of courage to do so. The pure neuroses are disturbances of purely psychic nature, e.g. phobias, obsessions, scrupulosity, etc. The psychosomatic illnesses on the other hand affect the body, e.g. by paralytic phenomena, rash, ulcers, etc.; yet the cause of the sickness is ultimately not organic but psychic. An efficient cure can therefore only be effected if the psychic cause is discovered and resolved.

Psychotherapy aims at relieving the patient of his psychopathical symptoms. The ultimate goal is to dissolve the psychic conflict that led to the sickness. Thus the patient should be brought into emotional equilibrium with his environment again.

Physicians must possess some basic knowledge concerning psychologically conditioned sicknesses. They must be able to recognize the psychogenic nature of an ailment or at least know when to take this possibility into consideration. In such cases they will have to refer their patient to a competent psychotherapist. Here as much as in other fields of therapy, medical practitioners must beware of trespassing their competence by attempting psychoanalytic treatments without sufficient expertise. They must know the limits of their abilities, just as psychotherapists from their side must remain conscious of their confines.

---

[1] Cf. G. Kelly: Medico-Moral Problems, 1960, 111.

1.   *Methods of psychotherapeutic treatment.* The special methods to elicit the hidden psychic conflicts and the unconscious material which are at the root of the psychic illnesses are free association, hypnoanalysis, narcoanalysis and psychoanalysis.

a)   The method of free association is a time consuming, but frequently successful method of bringing to light experiences which have been suppressed or forgotten. It is based on the laws of psychological association. The patient is made as comfortable as possible and told to verbalize the thoughts which may run through his mind in this state. No effort should be made to select them. Any interrupting thought should be mentioned.

The aim of the method (also called cathartic method) is, with or without hypnosis, "abreaction". The reproduction into full consciousness of memories, representations and emotional experiences makes the patient face them as they are. He is made to reactivate and actually relive the psychotraumatic events of his past life that were forgotten, suppressed and not completely digested. Lived through again, the original experiences become "abreacted" together with the emotional component that caused the neurotic state. The experiences which had previously been repressed through fear are recalled and then rationally and consciously rejected. Thus they "die a natural death". Most of these emotions were experienced in early life.

b)   Hypnoanalysis is a psychoanalytic technique in which the patient is hypnotized and then asked to recall his past experiences. Through the use of this method the period of treatment for most, if not all, psychopathological conditions can be shortened effectively without loss to the patient.

c)   Narcoanalysis is effected by means of drugs such as sodium amytal and sodium pentothal. These drugs have been referred to as "truth serum". This designation is however far from accurate. They are useful in lowering the patient's inhibitory level, if he finds it difficult to talk about some painful conflict. If however the individual deliberately intends to conceal certain facts, he is quite unlikely to reveal them under the influence of the drug, at least when direct questions are asked. Nevertheless the drug is not without dangers, since it heightens suggestibility by the therapist considerably. Great professional and moral competence is demanded of the therapist who uses it.

d)   Psychoanalysis again aims at eliciting unconscious conflicts and interpreting these to the patient. This method includes besides the use of free association also dream interpretation and the manipulation of the transference phenomenon. (Transference means the patient's reaction to the analyst as though he were not himself but some other person in the patient's past.)

2. *Moral considerations*. The goal of the different methods of psychotherapeutic treatment for the patient should be the rational and spiritual approach to his conflicts and true self-education. He should be helped to develop a true philosophy of life. This includes discussions of maturity and immaturity, of the hedonistic principles of conduct, and the necessity of establishing purposes and goals in life.[1] Under such circumstances it must be hazardous to place oneself under the care of a psychotherapist who does not accept the Christian faith. The analyst can hardly avoid applying his own standards of morality and religiosity to the case. Persons of Christian and Catholic conviction therefore must be careful in selecting a psychotherapist for treatment.

Psychotherapists are bound to observe the cautions dictated by sound morality, such as: avoiding the error of pansexualism (which has been propagated especially by the psychoanalytic school of Freud); respecting secrets which the patient is not permitted to reveal; avoiding the disproportionate risk of moral dangers, e.g. by deliberate reactivation of sexually stimulating situations; never counselling even material sin. The latter demand must not be interpreted in the sense that a therapist is forbidden to allow the patient to act according to his conscience if it is erroneous. Already Pius XII pointed out that psychotherapy "can tolerate what, for the moment, remains inevitable."[2] But the therapist will not positively counsel actions of objectionable nature which the client himself does not intend to do. The use of

---

[1] "According to the logotherapeutic school of Viktor Frankl, about twenty per cent of all psychoneuroses today develop in an 'existential vacuum,' that is, the existential predicament of the person who finds no meaning or significance in his life. It seems that there is a mounting incidence of 'nöogenic' neuroses in a materialistic welfare society. The 'existential vacuum' is often nothing less than the collective neurosis of the whole entourage, of a social environment devoid of sense and ideals" (B. Häring: Medical Ethics, 1973, 169f). The goal of logotherapy is therefore to guide the patient to a deeper spirituality, personal responsibility, openness and responsiveness to the needs of fellowmen, and the discovery of the meaning and purpose of life.

[2] Allocution of April 13, 1953; AAS 45, 1953, 286.

narcosis or hypnosis for the cure of mental illness moreover demands the consent at least reasonably presumed of the patient.

There should also be a sufficiently grave reason for undergoing a psychotherapeutic and psychoanalytic treatment. A Monitum of the Holy Office rejects the opinion that everybody who wants to enter priesthood or the religious life should first be subjected to a psychoanalytic examination.[1] Such an examination in fact is not necessary at all, except in cases of pathological conditions which make a person unable to live a normal, social life.

IV.   Experimentation on human beings[2]

Medical experimentation means either the use of treatments not sufficiently established for the benefit of the patient, or the use of procedures which have for their purpose the advancement of medical science and thus the benefit of others. Ordinarily experimentation in hospitals should be limited to procedures that are primarily for the good of the patient. In exceptional cases however experimentation which is primarily or even exclusively for the good of others may be admitted.

All clinical research should be conducted only by scientifically qualified persons and under the supervision of a qualified medical man. Before applying the treatment to human persons, the experimenters must be in possession of thorough information from laboratory and animal experiments or other scientific research. Moreover the expected benefit for the patient or the importance of the objective for medical science must be in proportion to the inherent risk to the experimental subject. Special caution is required in experiments with drugs or other research procedures which may alter the personality of the subject. All reasonable precautions must be taken to avoid physical or psychic harm to him. The experimenting physician must show true concern for the person who submits to his experiment. "It is considered a valuable criterion not to invite others to cooperate when the investigator himself would not like to be an experimental subject or would not dare invite members of his own family or personal friends to volunteer for the project."[3] The use of a

---

[1] July 15, 1961; AAS 53, 1961, 571.

[2] Cf. the *Declaration of Helsinki*: Recommendations Guiding Doctors in Clinical Research, a resolution adopted in June 1964 by the World Medical Association. The full text is reprinted in B. Häring: Medical Ethics. — Slough, England: St. Paul Publications, 1973, 209-212.

[3] B. Häring: Medical Ethics, 1973, 214.

fellowman as a means in the service of the physician's scientific ambitions is a serious violation of the reverence and love due to the person of the other.

Experimental procedures for the benefit of the sick patient may be used if in the judgment of the physician they offer hope of saving life, re-establishing health or alleviating suffering. This is the case if none of the standard procedures affords any founded hope of improvement in the patient's condition, or if the standard remedy for a disease is a long, difficult and very expensive treatment, while the experimental treatment is less inconvenient, though also by supposition less certain. If the condition of the patient permits, his free consent must be obtained after a full explanation of the nature of the experiment. Otherwise consent of his legitimate guardian is to be procured.

When experimentation is primarily for the good of others, the experimental person must understand and voluntarily consent to the procedure. He must receive full and objective information on the nature, methods, duration and purpose of the experiment, and on all inconveniences and risks reasonably to be expected. The fully free consent of the subject is absolutely essential. The forced experimentations made on prisoners of war or other prisoners are reckoned among the crimes against humanity. The subject of clinical research must be in such a mental, physical and legal state that he is able to exercise his free choice without the intervention of any element of coercion or constraint. If the subject is legally incompetent, experiments are generally considered lawful with the consent of the legal guardian. Paul Ramsey however forcefully vetoes any kind of non-therapeutic experimentation with children.[1] Psychopaths and neurotics should generally likewise be excluded, since in most cases they are unable to consent freely.

At any time during the course of the experiment the subject or his guardian should be free to withdraw permission for research to be continued. Physicians from their side are obliged to discontinue the experiment if in their judgment its continuation would be harmful to the subject.

D. Endangering of health and life

Since health and life are great and important goods, it is not allowed to place either one's own life or that of others

---

[1] Cf. Paul Ramsey: The Patient as Person. — New Haven: Yale University Press, 1975, 19f.

carelessly in danger. Each individual and society as a whole must respect this rightful claim of the human body and life to protective love. But since health and life are not the highest values, they may be exposed to danger for the sake of values more important than they themselves. Yet the greater the danger is, the weightier the reasons must be which permit such an endangering.

I. Permissible endangering of health and life

Works of penance are lawful as long as their practice is reasonable and does not endanger one's health seriously. Unhealthy work done in smelting plants or brass foundries, in mines, glass factories and chemical plants is permitted, and the owner of the enterprise may employ under such working conditions, if and insofar as a protection against the dangers is not possible and if the work done is of concern for society. In like manner the individual or the state may undertake tasks which are necessary or very profitable for the common welfare, even though they involve a degree of danger to the life of individual workers. But in no way may the state undertake economic or similar projects involving the life of thousands of people.

Equally permitted and sometimes even obligatory is the care of the plague-stricken, though it exposes one's life to danger. Steeplejacks, test pilots, etc., may likewise expose themselves to the dangers necessarily involved in their occupation.

Difficult is the question whether stage exhibitions (tight rope stunts, acrobatics, trapeze) and certain types of racings warrant the taking of serious risks of life and limb. The judgment of moralists on these performances is hesitant, but generally they do not forbid them outright. The reason is that in most cases of circus performers, funambulists, high-divers, bullfighters, etc., it is possible for the performers by their skill to avoid any real danger to their lives. The danger is more apparent than real. If the spectator were up on the high wire, it really would be dangerous, but for the trained artist it is not. Yet justly John C. Ford judges: If the trapeze artist removes the net which protects him in case of a fall in order to increase the attractiveness of his performance, such a way of acting is immoral, because he greatly and unnecessarily increases the danger to his life.[1]

---

[1] J. C. Ford: Current Theology. — Theological Studies 6 (1945), 534.

The unjustly imprisoned may attempt escape at the risk of his life to avoid execution or a life sentence. Equally one may leap from a dangerous height to escape burning to death. And there are many other instances in which one may for good reasons undertake a dangerous course of action, however directly aiming at some important good, e.g. the rescue of a drowning person with a certain risk for one's own life.

II. Sinful endangering of health and life

The sinful endangering of health and life may have its reason in simple carelessness. The evil effect of an action is not really foreseen but only, because of culpable negligence, overlooked. According to the degree of subjective guilt and of the possible damage which could be caused, this carelessness is gravely sinful. Yet greater is the guilt if the endangering has its reason in indifference and ruthlessness. Here the risk connected with an action is foreseen and the action set nevertheless without a sufficiently weighty motive. In cases of serious endangering this is always a grave sin against love. More frequent forms of sinful endangering are the following:

1. Endangering in traffic. The enormous development of vehicular traffic has extremely increased the possibility of injuries and fatalities of all kinds. The driver in particular, but also the pedestrian, must seek to prevent accidents through avoidance of all recklessness and the observance of the traffic regulations. Besides, drivers must sufficiently master the technique of driving, e.g. the approaching of a turn. They ought to possess some knowledge of the behaviour of their fellowmen and be able to estimate their reactions. They have the serious duty to be in sufficient command of their senses and reactions, so as not to become causes for accidents through their own fault.

Drunkenness ranks first among the causes of traffic accidents. Even a little alcohol may already diminish the ability to safe reaction and clear judgment. Overtiring at the wheel is another cause. Too many drivers do not sufficiently reckon with their fatigue. It is self-deception to believe that driving brings relaxation after exhausting work. Overspeeding likewise constitutes a frequent danger in the traffic. Especially younger men are tempted to handle driving as a kind of competitive sports. On the other hand drivers may also be too slow and thus bring about accidents. Nobody should ever drive without adequate knowledge of the traffic regulations or sufficient mastery of the car. If drivers realize that because of old age, sickness or similar reasons they are no longer able to drive safely, they must be realistic and humble enough to acknowledge their insufficiency and discontinue driving. Drivers as well as cars ought to undergo regular tests on their safety in traffic.

Who offends against these duties because of gross carelessness sins gravely, even if he is fortunate and nothing happens. Sin in this case is the attitude which ruthlessly conjures up great dangers for oneself and for others. Though the traffic rules do not oblige without exception, they oblige at least normally in conscience. The more important rules also bind the pedestrian.

2. Negligent practice of one's profession. This concerns above all officials responsible for the safety in traffic (gate-men, switchmen, supervisors of airports, etc.), physicians and related professions (pharmacists, hospital nurses, midwives), but also housewives and maids who have to look after little children. Quackery, which holds sick persons back from regular medical treatment, is a most serious form of such incompetence and irresponsibility.

3. Deficient labour conditions. Careless damaging of health or manslaughter may be caused by insufficient safety measures for workers, inadequate hygienic conditions, ruthless exploitation. That holds true especially for mining and industry.

4. Lack of caution in pregnancy. Expectant mothers may be guilty of careless damaging and even killing of the unborn child by gross lack of caution, for example by carrying too heavy loads, driving on motorcycles, etc. Husbands may be guilty of the same by rough treatment of their wives, especially by beating them.

E. Destruction of human life

For the moral judgment on actions destructive of human life the distinction between direct and indirect killing is important in Catholic moral theology.

One speaks of direct killing when the death of a person is intended as the aim of an action or as a means to achieve this aim. Thus the poisoning of an enemy out of hatred or the taking of an overdose of sleeping pills in order to shorten an excruciating illness are direct killing.

One speaks of indirect killing when the killing of a person is not intended as a means for the achievement of an end, but is merely permitted as a concomitant effect. Thus the destruction of a military object which includes the death of some civilians is indirect killing.[1]

I. Suicide and indirect killing of oneself

1. *Suicide*

Suicide is the direct taking of one's life done on one's own authority. It is gravely sinful. It is not suicide in the strict sense if a man who is ordered by the civil authority to carry out a legitimate death sentence upon himself would do so (cf. Socrates). Moral theologians dispute if the execution of such a sentence is allowed. Several important authors judge that it is permitted.[2]

Psychologists assert that there is a suicidal tendency in life, the longing for rest without conflict. Especially in moments of intolerable, insuperable and meaningless pain there is the desire to escape the pain by getting rid of one's self. Thus despair is the most common motive for suicide. Yet there are also other motives of a more altruistic nature. A father kills himself because he endangers the existence of his family (e.g. by a long-lasting, costly illness). Prisoners (especially spies) kill themselves in order to prevent the danger of betraying secrets and other persons.

Statisticians tell us that more men kill themselves than women, more Protestants than Catholics, more city-dwellers than country-folks, more elderly people than youngsters.[3] Public opinion in general considers suicide as dishonourable and morally reprehensible. Members of a suicide's family and his friends will always attempt to hush up the manner of the death. Catholic moral theology rejects every kind of suicide. The reasons are the following:

    a) Man has not the right of ownership over his body

---

[1] This is the explanation of Zalba (I, 1958, nr. 1568 and 1586). Somewhat different is the definition of Mausbach: Direct killing is the destruction of human life either with the intention to kill or the use of means which cause death by their nature. It does not matter whether death is the purpose intended by the acting person or not, if only the means used for the achievement of the purpose aim by their very nature at the destruction of human life. Indirect killing, then, is the destruction of life which excludes the intention to kill as well as the use of means fatal by their nature (III, 1961, 243). With such a definition it is harder to permit the destruction of a military object which includes the certain death of some civilians.

[2] Cf. St. Alfonsus (III, 369), Marc (I, 753), Merkelbach (II, 350), Prümmer (II, 112), Genicot-Salsmans (I, 361), Häring (III, 1966, 200f).

[3] Cf. Claus Menzel: The right to kill oneself must be discouraged. — The German Tribune, 10 July 1975, no. 691, 14.

and his life. He has only the right of responsible administration and usufruct. The owner and master of his life is God. He gave it to man in order to use it in the service of the divine plan with man and the world. And this plan is that through the cooperation of man the work of creation be unfolded and brought to perfection. Suicide is therefore a violation of God's sovereign rights. Of course God himself could theoretically give a person the order to sacrifice his life by directly killing himself, if in a very exceptional case this should prove to serve his creative and salvific designs best. Yet a certain example of such an order cannot be pointed out.[1]

b)   Suicide is very often, though not always, a crime against a person's dependents and human society. This is the case if somebody takes his life without consideration for his responsibilities and obligations towards others. But there are also instances where precisely the concern for the common good might move a person to sacrifice his life. A case in point is the suicide of a captured spy who kills himself in order not to betray his fellow spies and to endanger the security of his country. The argumentative force of the second argument is therefore conditioned and not absolute. It permits of exceptions.

c)   Suicide is a violation of one's duty to love oneself and to strive after perfection. The person who kills himself deprives himself of the possibility to any further personal growth. He refuses to bring himself to that full perfection to which he has been called by God. Yet here again one could object that, though this assertion is normally very true, there might be exceptions. Since a very important means of perfection is sacrifice, why not also in certain instances the sacrifice of one's life, especially since the indirect sacrifice of one's life for a higher good is allowed and sometimes even demanded? This argument is therefore valid for most cases of suicide, but — like the second argument — not for all.

The general law of the Church formerly laid down that suicides are deprived of ecclesiastical burial. This is no longer

---

[1] The question may however be asked whether God does not reveal his will in this matter, just as in so many other matters, also indirectly through natural causes and conditions. In confrontation with a concrete situation it might become evident that the preservation of one's life is the lesser value, and the defence of other, still higher values more urgent, e.g. the values of freedom, justice or the welfare of the entire community. If this can be shown with certainty, must one not conclude that in such a condition the sacrifice of one's life is willed by God, even the direct sacrifice? This question still needs further discussion among theologians.

the case. The new code of canon law only provides that manifest sinners, whose Christian burial would cause public scandal, should be denied this honour (CIC 1184). Physicians judge that about 20% of the suicides have their reason in psychiatric disorders (psychoses) and another 60% of the people committing suicide are psychopathic personalities.[1] Though psychopathies (the latter group) do not cancel the freedom of will, they may diminish it. Therefore it is very difficult to judge the subjective guilt of anyone who takes his life. On the other hand it is also statistically proven that a living faith and religious convictions are the best protection against suicide. Religion is of decisive importance for the prevention of suicide.[2] In critical situations man needs restraints from authority and tradition, when his own ability to decide fails.

2. *Indirect killing of oneself*

Indirect killing of oneself may be permitted and in certain cases even be obligatory for a proportionately grave reason. The greater the danger for one's life, the graver the reason must be. Proportionate reasons for the sure sacrifice of one's life are values higher or at least as high as one's bodily life,· especially one's faith and the common welfare. If Christ demands that whoever wants to be his disciple must hate his life (Lk 14:26; Jn 12:25), then this means that he must be ready to sacrifice it for Christ's sake and for his kingdom. Yet also the love of brethren must dispose a man to the same sacrifice. "Greater love has no man than this, that a man lay down his life for his friends" (Jn 15:13).

A striking example of the indirect sacrifice of one's life in the spirit of Christ is the Polish priest Maximilian Kolbe. A prisoner in the concentration camp Auschwitz, he voluntarily took the place of a family father condemned to death from starvation in retaliation for the escape of another prisoner (1941).

If in case of shipwreck a life-boat is overcrowded, passengers may voluntarily jump into the sea, even if there is no possibility of being saved. It is equally allowed in this case to force a passenger destined by lot to leave the boat. One may in wartime blow up a fortification or sink a ship which can no longer be held against the enemy, although one forsees that one's life will

---

[1] Georg Siegmund: Sein oder Nichtsein. Die Frage des Selbstmordes. —Trier: Paulinus, 1961, 119f.

[2] Ib. 111f.

be lost in doing so. It is allowed to navigate a weapon against an enemy ship under the same condition (so Zalba I, 1958, nr. 1573). It is also permitted to jump from a burning building with certainty of one's death to avoid thus the more cruel death in the fire.[1]

II.   Murder and indirect killing of fellowman

Immoral and gravely sinful is every direct and illegal killing of a fellowman. It is called murder. "Illegal" means in Catholic understanding (a) every killing of an innocent, included his killing by authorization or order of the state authority, and (b) the killing of a criminal outside the legal order by lynch law. — The indirect killing of a fellowman can be justified by serious reasons. If however it is not justified, it is murder as well.

The criminal law distinguishes murder as a premeditated killing from unpremeditated forms of homicide, due to a sudden fit of passion. Though in the second case the crime would be less grave, it is a great sin against love as well. The moral concept of murder comprises both forms of killing.

Murder may be motivated by hatred or lust for revenge, by sexual passions, by greed for power or money. It may be political murder, mob law, deadly dueling for the sake of honour or similar motives, mercy killing, infanticide and abortion for different reasons. Mercy killing or euthanasia and abortion need to be dealt with in separate sections because of the special problems connected with them.

1.   *Murder and indirect killing in general*

a)   The crime of murder

Already on the first pages of Holy Scripture the murder of Abel by his brother Cain is condemned. "The voice of your brother's blood is crying to me from the ground" (Gen 4:10). The basic judgment on murder is given by the fifth commandment Ex 20:13 and Deut 5:17: "You shall not kill." The verb used

---

[1] Moralists commonly judge that also a spiritual good, in particular that of virtue, is a sufficient reason to kill oneself indirectly. Thus a virgin or woman may leap from a tower to avoid being violated by a libertine, and even more so if there is danger of consent. — Yet one may question if corporal integrity is really so high a good to justify the sacrifice of life. The danger of consent, besides, is very much reduced in such cases.

in the Hebrew language is *rasach*, a rather rare verb, signifying an unallowed, unlawful killing. Beer-Galling states that in Ex 20:13 four things are not comprised: war, suicide, execution of a criminal by force of a judicial sentence, and killing of animals.[1] Ex 23:7 condemns the killing of an innocent in particular: "Do not slay the innocent and righteous, for I will not acquit the wicked." The reason for the condemnation of murder is that it interferes with the rights of God and man. "Whoever sheds the blood of man, by man shall his blood be shed; for God made man in his own image" (Gen 9:6). Jesus underlines the validity of the fifth commandment (Mt 19:18; Mk 10:19) and already condemns the roots of murder: anger and hatred (Mt 5:21f).

The intrinsic reasons for the criminality of murder are the following: (1) The owner and master of human life is God alone, as already explained in the discussion on suicide. As man is not allowed to dispose of his own life, so much less is he allowed to dispose of other people's life, except the case that a higher good whose safeguarding is willed by God even more urgently justifies and demands such a sacrifice.

(2) Life is the highest temporal good of man, indispensable for his earthly existence. This good gives origin to a correspondingly high right of man. According to the principle of justice, such a right cannot be robbed of a person by any worldly power except in defence of a still higher right. Such a higher right is in question if a criminal endangers basic rights of others and the community. In this case the still higher right of justice and of protection of the common weal could command the death of the criminal.

According to the common teaching of Catholic moral theology there is no earthly right in the case of an innocent which would be higher than man's right to be protected from any direct assault against his life. Not even the demands of the common weal create a higher right in this instance. The reason is that man does not exist on behalf of the state (like a member exists on behalf of the whole body), but rather the state on behalf of man.

Ultimately however man and state alike exist for God and his glory. Both are called to serve his plan. And this

---

[1] Exodus, Tübingen 1939, 102.

plan not only aims at a transcendent, heavenly kingdom. It also includes the unfolding of God's creation here in this world (cf. GS 34;57;67). The rights of this divine plan must be considered still higher than the rights of any individual or state.

Note that in the case of a guilty person the right to decide whether or not the person is guilty of death does not belong to private individuals, but to the representatives of the community, because the judgement in such a grave matter cannot be left to the unreliable insight of a single person.

(3)   The welfare of society demands the protection of human life. If people were allowed to kill each other on private authority, the safety of society would be done for. The commonweal would cease to exist. — This argument however cannot prove that the sacrifice of an innocent (by direct killing) for the sake of the commonweal is unlawful under all circumstances.

b)   Indirect killing of a fellowman

The indirect killing of an innocent person is not always murder, but is sometimes allowed for the safeguarding of a proportionately higher good. The reason is that otherwise important values, especially of the common welfare, could not be defended or preserved. Naturally the more certainly an action will result in the indirect death of the innocent, the graver the reasons must be which justify the action.

It is allowed to bomb military objects or industries important for the waging of a just war, though one foresees that also some civilians will be killed. Innocent persons may be handed over to a tyrant who wants to kill them if thus a whole town can be saved. One may return the fire of unjust aggressors or rebels, even though they seek shelter behind women and children and innocent lives are thereby lost, presupposing that there is no other way to defend oneself. If the brakes of a car fail and it begins dashing downhill, the driver is not obliged to steer over an embankment or the railing of a bridge, even though thereby he endangers another car or a pedestrian's life. Naturally he would be obliged to steer in a field at a moderate risk, if in this way greater disaster can be prevented. In principle the indirect sacrifice of innocent life for the rescue of other lives or values is only then justified when the lives or values to be saved are of greater or at least equal importance than those to be sacrificed.

2. *Euthanasia*[1]

Euthanasia or mercy killing is the direct killing of the incurably sick, be it at their own request, or be it at the request of the legal representative in the case of incurables who are incapable of deciding for themselves, e.g. infants and mental defectives. Euthanasia comes to its extreme when it means the officially planned and directed destruction of the mentally sick and of the incurably crippled, i.e. of all who are considered a burden on society. Yet this extreme is the exception, and it would be unjust to attribute this kind of outrage to the usual defenders of mercy killing. Nevertheless there is a danger inherent in the support of any kind of mercy killing. The arguments may not only serve to justify the more limited forms, but also mercy killing on a larger scale.

Euthanasia as the active killing by lethal agents or means must be distinguished from the passive withholding of artificial means of prolongation of life, e.g. of a respirator. This distinction is very fundamental and important. The questions connected with the duty to preserve life have been discussed earlier in detail.

From the moral point of view all forms of mercy killing are unlawful and murder, with or without the consent of the sick person. They involve suicide and cooperation to suicide or simply murder of the innocent. Not only the Church magisterium absolutely condemns euthanasia (Pius XII,[2] GS 27). A great number of competent men in the fields of ethics and law reject it, and not least the very people who would have to perform the act, the physicians.

---

[1] References: John F. Dedek: Euthanasia; in: Human Life. — New York: Sheed and Ward, 1972, 119–141. Daniel C. Maguire: Death by Choice. — Garden City, N.Y.: Doubelday, 1974. Arthur J. Dyck: The Good Samaritan Ideal and Beneficent Euthanasia: Conflicting Views of Mercy. — Linacre Quarterly 42 (1975), 176–188. John A. Behnke and Sissela Bok (ed.): The Dilemmas of Euthanasia. — Garden City, N.Y.: Anchor Books, 1975.

[2] "To our profound grief we see at times the deformed, the insane, and those suffering from hereditary disease deprived of their lives, as though they were a useless burden to society; and this procedure is hailed by some as a manifestation of human progress, and as something that is entirely in accordance with the common good. Yet who that is possessed of sound judgement does not recognize that this not only violates the natural and divine law written in the heart of every man, but that it outrages the noblest instincts of humanity?" (Mystici Corporis, AAS 35, 1943, 239). Note also the *Declaration on Euthanasia* by the S. Congr. for the Doctrine of Faith of May 5, 1980; AAS 72 (1980), 542–552.

The essential and generally only reason for euthanasia among those who defend it in the more cautious form of mercy killing of the incurably suffering is the viewpoint that destruction of life is preferable to pain and senseless misery. This argument is however already somewhat weakened by the medical fact that, so far as pain is concerned, medicine can relieve it to a large extent and can take care of it neurosurgically.[1]

One must also get down to the evil consequences that would follow if euthanasia were permitted. Trust in physicians and hospitals would vanish, particularly if mercy killing were allowed without the consent of the sick person. Yet even when only permitted with the consent of the sick patient, the danger of surreptitiously obtained or falsified consent would create feelings of unsafety and mistrust. To exclude abuse, society would be compelled to establish sufficient cautions. This might involve considerable financial expenses, thus reducing at the same time the weight of possible arguments taken from the financial commonweal, obviously a rather insufficient argument.

In the last analysis the philosophy behind the euthanasia movement is largely of a utilitarian, immanent, secularistic nature. If the meaning of human life exhausts itself in temporal happiness, progress and self-fulfillment, if it has no dimension which reaches beyond this world, then misery and suffering which cannot be cured or improved are without sense and value. Yet this is not the Christian understanding of human life. Christian theology interprets man's existence from the life of Christ, from his suffering, death and resurrection. In this light even the poorest cretin has his special role in the divine plan of salvation. His helplessness is apt to awaken the capacity of love in fellowmen. Just as Christ's suffering had a salvific value, so has the suffering of his brothers. Often enough men may have to atone for their own sins. And at all times they are called to participate by their suffering in the redemptive work of their Lord and thus to complete what is lacking in his suffering (cf. Col 1:24).

Obviously this does not mean that the fight against suffering could be regarded as less urgent at any time. In the fellowship of the Good Shepherd men have to exert themselves to heal what is wounded and to cure what is sick. They are requested to combat misery and pain in all its forms as much as they can. To the extent that this is possible, they must strive to diminish and to relieve it. Furthermore when a life has already been

---

[1] Cf. G. Kelly, 1. c. 123.

despaired of, there is no obligation and often enough no justification to prolong it further by special medical efforts and any extraordinary means, as has been explained earlier.

3.   Abortion[1]

a) Concept

Abortion is the removal of the non-viable human being from the mother's womb by human intervention, whether by killing him before removal from the womb, or whether by exposing him to a certain death outside the womb.

Abortion is direct when the ejection of the non-viable fruit or the destruction of the offspring in the womb is intended as the aim of an action or as a means to achieve this aim, e.g. abortion in order to save the reputation of an unwed mother. It is indirect if the death of the fetus is merely permitted as a concomitant effect of a directly willed end, e.g. the death of a fetus caused by the removal of the cancerous uterus of a pregnant mother.

The offspring is viable approximately after 28 weeks. In a properly equipped hospital it may be considered viable after 26 weeks. If pregnancy has been interrupted before the twentieth week by causes which are beyond the control of free will, one speaks of miscarriage; if after the twentieth week, one speaks of premature birth. Some degree of guilt would be present if these acts were resulting from carelessness.

A special problem is raised by the question as to when the precise beginning of human life is to be set. When does the animation of the fertilized ovum by a spiritual soul take place? And consequently from which time on is the embryo to be considered a human being in the strict sense? From of old two theories were held among philosophers and theologians. Aristotle and following him St. Thomas Aquinas, for instance, were of the opinion that the rational soul is infused into the

---

[1] References: Enda McDonagh: Ethical Problems of Abortion. — The Irish Theol. Quarterly 35 (1968), 268-297. Daniel Callahan: Abortion: Law, Choice and Morality. — New York: Macmillan, 1970. Germain Grisez: Abortion. The Myths, the Realities, and the Arguments. — New York and Cleveland: Corpus Books, 1970. Theological Studies, March issue 1970. David Granfield: The Abortion Decision. — Garden City, N.Y.: Doubleday 1971. Peter A. Facione: Callahan on Abortion. — Am. Eccl. Review 167 (1973), 291-301. Richard A. McCormick: The Abortion Dossier. — Theol. Studies 35 (1974), 312-357. National Conference of Catholic Bishops: Documentation on the Right to Life and Abortion. — Washington: United States Catholic Conference, 1974.

body only after the fertilized ovum has reached a certain state of development. Until then the embryo is solely animated by a life of vegetative and animal nature. The time of animation by the spiritual soul was often set at approximately six weeks after conception. For a long time this theory was very commonly held; then it was more or less abandoned. More recent scholars usually inclined to the opinion that from the very moment of conception the fertilized ovum is animated by a human soul. Today however the idea that there must be some development of the material before the infusion of the spiritual soul takes place is again proposed by many scholars as the more acceptable explanation of the beginning of human life.

There is no official pronouncement of the Church which approves or condemns either theory. However since both opinions are probable and since we deal with the great good of human life, theologians commonly hold that in the practical order one must follow the safer course of action and always treat a living fertilized ovum as a human person, whatever its stage of development, with all the rights of a human being. This rule of prudence is to be observed as long at least as there is no certain proof for the opinion of St. Thomas and those who take sides with him.

Until now it seemed that such a proof could never be established. Yet there are present findings of medical science which are able to contribute to a further clarification of the issue. After conception the fertilized ovum still remains in a mobile state in the fallopian tubes and in the uterus for 7 to 8 days[1] (others state about 12 days[2]). Then nidation takes place, i.e. the implantation of the fertilized ovum in the uterus wall, which is completed at about 12 days after conception. Physicians assume that in the period before nidation 40-50% of the fertilized ovums get lost and are naturally expelled. The new finding consists in the discovery that in the period until the termination of nidation and even two to three days beyond it cell division of the tiny cell cluster into identical twins remains possible. That means to say that until that moment one cannot speak of the cell cluster as a human individuum, and hence not of a human person.[3] There is likewise some evidence that in the early stage

---

[1] J. Gründel: Unterbrochene Schwangerschaft. Ein moraltheologisches Tabu? — Theologie der Gegenwart 13 (1970), 204.

[2] Harmon L. Smith: Ethics and the New Medicine. — Nashville/New York: Abingdon Press, 1970, 18.

[3] Andre E. Hellegers: Fetal Development. — Theological Studies 31 (1970), 4f.

the twins may recombine again, or even that one human being be formed from the fusion of two fertilized ovums. One must conclude that the animation or hominization of the fertilized ovum only takes place at a time after the individualization of the embryo is definite, i.e. not before 14 days after conception. This view has been adopted by P. Schoonenberg,[1] J. Donceel,[2] J. Gründel,[3] C. Curran,[4] B. Häring,[5] G. Lobo,[6] G. Pastrana.[7]

The proposition has indeed much in its favour. A cell or cell cluster which is still subject to segmentation resulting in two or more human beings cannot yet be considered a human individuum and therefore a human being itself. The assumption finds a strong confirmation in the factor that nature itself permits the loss of 40-50% of the fertilized ovums in this early stage. Such unconcern of nature could not sufficiently be explained if we were already dealing with the great value of human life. Furthermore the presupposition that there are different levels of life in the human being is proven by the fact that cells of the human body, e.g. skin or blood cells, can continue to live separated from the body and independent from the animation by the soul.

In view of these insights one could not speak of abortion in the strict sense before the elapse of a period of about 14 days. Consequently one could also not simply classify the IUD or those medicaments and pills that possibly or certainly hinder the fertilized ovum from nidation as "abortive" means, as J.

---

[1] Piet Schoonenberg: God's World in the Making. — Pittsburg: Duquesne University Press, 1964, 49f.

[2] Joseph F. Donceel: Immediate Animation and Delayed Hominization — Theol. Studies 31 (1970), 96-101.

[3] J. Gründel, 1. c. 206.

[4] Charles Curran: New Perspectives in Moral Theology. — Notre Dame, Ind.: Fides Publishers, 1974, 188.

[5] Bernard Häring: Medical Ethics. — Slough, England: St. Paul Publications, 1973, 84. Häring and Donceel even consider the possibility of a still later term for the beginning of human life. They think of that stage where the cerebrum of the fetus and the functions of the brain are sufficiently developed, which falls in the second or third month after conception. But since at times deformed children without a cerebrum are born, who still must be considered human beings, this term for the animation by the human soul does not seem acceptable. The assumption that the fetus is a human being must be favoured until the contrary is demonstrated with sufficient certainty. This proof has not been established convincingly.

[6] George V. Lobo: Current Problems in Medical Ethics. — Allahabad: St. Paul Society, 1974, 104-106.

[7] Gabriel Pastrana: Personhood and the Beginning of Human Life. — The Thomist 41 (1977), 282.

Gründel rightly observers.[1] In fact the British Council of Churches already in 1962 expressed its opinion that a fertilized ovum not yet settled in the uterus is not yet human life. The Council of Churches therefore does not regard the prevention of a fertilized ovum from nidation as abortion.[2] Nevertheless the fertilized ovum is already a living organism, which will develop into a human being, if the circumstances are favourable. Therefore there is a duty to respect and to protect it. For this reason contraceptives which prevent a fertilized ovum from nidation cannot simply be put on par with the other contraceptives. There is greater reason to avoid them.

Lobo draws a further conclusion for instances of rape. He considers it a clear case where the view could be followed that the fertilized ovum is not yet a human person during the first two weeks after conception and where the use of the "morning after pill" would be permissible to prevent nidation.[3] This opinion is also supported by J. Dedek,[4] J. Gründel[5] and R. McCormick.[6]

A recent declaration of the Congr. for the Doctrine of Faith makes reference to the opinion that animation of the fetus by the soul takes place only some weeks after conception. Without intending to make a final decision in this matter, it however advances that interruption of pregnancy even during the first days after fertilization was nevertheless always considered a grave offence by Catholic moral theology. But the declaration admits of the possibility that the state may refrain from legal sanctions in certain instances of interruption of pregnancy.[7]

---

[1] J. Gründel, 1. c. 206.

[2] Cf. Human Reproduction: A Study of Some Emergent Problems and Questions in the Light of the Christian Faith. The British Council of Churches, London, 1962.

[3] G. Lobo, 1. c. 105.

[4] J. Dedek judges that the theory of delayed hominization has a great probability in its favour, although a full certainty cannot be reached. Nevertheless a lethal action against what is only doubtfully a human person — so he argues — does not constitute a conditional will to homicide, as traditional manuals commonly reason, but rather the risk of homicide. Therefore in instances of rape he considers the removal of the fertilized ovum justified before the beginning of the third week (Human Life. Some Moral Issues. — New York: Sheed and Ward, 1972, 87-89).

[5] J. Gründel, 1. c. 206.

[6] Richard A. McCormick: Notes on Moral Theology. — Theological Studies 39 (1978). 128

b) The morality of abortion

Abortion is advocated as a way out of different kinds of complications and dilemmas. The circumstances which are alleged as justifying reasons for abortions are called "indications". — Four indications are distinguished:

(1) The eugenic indication calls for abortion in instances where the expected offspring with great probability will be affected with serious defects. The defects may be caused by genetic disorders or by acquired sicknesses, e.g. German measles of the mother during pregnancy.[1] But it is rarely possible to predict a defective child with certainty. Chromosomal defects such as mongolism may occur in one out of three live births if one of the parents is a carrier. There is danger that more healthy than defective babies may be aborted for eugenic reasons. Besides, in the case of some genetic disorders it is possible, and it may become more possible in the future, to minimize the danger through appropriate therapies. The same holds for acquired sicknesses, such as the mentioned German measles.[2]

(2) The ethical indication is had when a pregnancy is due to rape. Abortion is considered justified in this case since the child is an undue burden forced upon the mother against her will, who therefore will find great difficulty to love the child. His existence moreover exposes the mother to great moral strains and social shame. Some authors also include incest and adultery in this indication.

(3) The social indication would be present if the (additional) child were too great a social or, more specifically, too great an economic burden for the family or for the mother. The ultimate basis for the social abortion is however often enough not serious financial pressure. It has been proven that abortion is in fact more common among those who enjoy greater economic security than among the poor, although dire poverty does actually contribute to the dangerous situation.

(4) According to the medical or therapeutic indication abortion is indicated if the life of the mother is in serious danger

---

[1] "In the 1964 rubella epidemic almost 90 percent of the women who caught the disease in the first three months of pregnancy produced babies that were damaged, although some only slightly. When the disease was contracted later in the pregnancy, the incidence of damage fell to 25 percent" (The Terrible Choice: The Abortion Dilemma; ed. by R. Cooke a. o. — New York: Bantam Books 1968, 76).

[2] "Medical experts expect that the German measles problem will be eliminated in the next few years" (Ib.).

because of pregnancy. Non-Catholics generally agree that in this circumstance even directly procured abortion is justified. — Closely related to the medical indication in the traditional sense is the indication for reasons of mental health, which could be called the psychiatric indication. While the number of therapeutic abortions has steadily declined, the number of those granted for psychiatric reasons is on the increase. Yet psychiatrists themselves are greatly divided in their judgment on the need and justification of psychiatric abortions. Their reactions range from rejection of any abortion for psychiatric reasons to great permissiveness.

Catholic ethics absolutely rejects any kind of abortion for eugenic, ethical and social reasons and considers it simply as murder of the innocent. More difficult is the question of therapeutic abortion. Catholic moral theology at least always admitted of the lawfulness of indirect abortion in cases of serious danger for the mother's life. The problem has to be studied more in detail below.

Holy Scripture does not contain express references to abortion and its reprehensibleness. But it repeatedly condemns the crime of murder (Ex 20:13; Mk 10:19), the shedding of innocent blood (Ex 23:7; Deut 21:9; Prov 6:16f; Jer 22:3) and the murder of children and defenceless beings by their parents (Wis 12:3-7). It emphasizes the sacredness of life by teaching that God is the author of life and man is created in his image. Man is the steward of life and not its master. The basic commandment of fraternal love extends to all human beings and bids respect and reverence for every human life.

On the background of these biblical doctrines and also influenced by the inheritance from Judaism, the young Christian Church formulated its judgment on abortion. From the earliest times it was one of decided rejection.[1] The condemnation developed in sharp opposition to the attitude of the Greco-Roman world, in which abortion and infanticide were not viewed as serious moral offences. Throughout the centuries Christianity continued to consider abortion as a crime.[2] Grave sanctions were issued by the Church against Christians who would dare to commit this sin already in the first centuries. Present canon law

---

[1] The first explicit condemnations of abortion occur in the earliest postscriptural documents, the Didache (2:2) and the Epistle of Barnabas (19:5).

[2] Cf. John T. Noonan, Jr.: An Almost Absolute Value in History; in: The Morality of Abortion. — Cambridge, Mass.: Harvard Press, 1970, 1-59.

inflicts an excommunication reserved to the Ordinary upon those who procure abortion (CIC 1398). Vatican II once more takes a severe stand against it. It writes: "From the moment of its conception life must be guarded with the greatest care, while abortion and infanticide are unspeakable crimes" (GS 51) — The intrinsic reasons for the abjectness of abortion are the same as those which militate against the crime of murder and the killing of an innocent in general.

c) The problem of direct therapeutic abortion

While abortion in general has universally been rejected in the Church, therapeutic abortion as a means to save the mother's life is a more controversial issue. Among the Fathers the problem is mentioned by Tertullian (died about 220), who seems to approve of therapeutic abortion as a "cruel necessity". Although he rejects abortion in general as murder, he writes concerning the special case of therapeutic abortion: "But sometimes by cruel necessity, while yet in the womb, an infant is put to death, when lying awry in the orifice of the womb he impedes parturition, and kills his mother if he is not to die himself."[1] Noonan argues that here Tertullian is merely describing what sometimes occurs as a matter of fact, but is not expressing any moral judgment about it.[2] Yet others maintain that Tertullian made an exception to the general rule.[3]

The theologians of the Middle Ages universally considered direct abortion as unlawful and only admitted of indirect therapeutic abortion. From the 15th to 17th century several theologians held the opinion that the direct abortion of a nonanimated fetus is permissible in order to save the mother's life.[4] But since animation was believed to take place about 40 days after conception, this doctrine was hardly able to offer much help for cases of difficult childbirth. For the critical condition usually develops at a much later state, and after animation only

[1] De anima 25:4.

[2] John Noonan, 1. c. 13.

[3] Cf. J. Dedek: Human Life. Some Moral Issues. — New York: Sheed and Ward, 1972, 35f.

[4] Authors quoted for this opinion are St. Antoninus of Florence, Sylvester da Prieras, Martinus Azpilcueta (better known as Doctor Navarrus), Franciscus Torreblanca, Leo Zambellus, Joannes Baptista de Lezana (cf. Charles E. Curran: New Perspectives in Moral Theology. — Notre Dame, Ind.: Fides Publishers, 1974, 175-177).

indirect abortion was considered lawful even by these theologians.[1]

At the turn of the 19th century the question of therapeutic abortion underwent another reexamination. This was probably conditioned by the development of new medical aids and technics. Several theologians taught that craniotomy and other forms of direct abortion are allowed for therapeutic reasons in order to save the mother's life. Among the authors mentioned are Ballerini, Avanzini, Constantini, Apicella,[2] Linsenmann[3] and Lehmkuhl.[4]

It was then that the magisterium of the Church for the first time officially commented on the issue. In several answers to questions concerning the permissibility of direct abortion and of craniotomy in particular in order to save the mother's life (between 1884 and 1902)[5] the Holy Office stated that the lawfulness of such operations cannot be taught safely. The contrary opinion is not declared as certainly false, but it is qualified as not sufficiently assured.

The first express and absolute disapproval of therapeutic abortion occurs in the encyclical "Casti Connubii" of Pius XI. He plainly rejects the "medical and therapeutic indication" as "a sufficient reason for excusing in any way the direct murder of the innocent."[6] This position was likewise adopted by Pius XII[7] and Paul VI.[8] A recent declaration of the Congregation for the Doctrine of the Faith once more reconfirms this rejection.[9]

---

[1] The conclusion drawn by J. Dedek that "from the fourteenth century many theologians allowed both embryotomy and abortion to save the mother's life" can in this general form not be considered precise and correct. The same holds for his conclusion that the lenient opinion permitting therapeutic abortion was tolerated by Rome during all these centuries, so that the stricter decisions of the Holy Office at the end of the 19th century appear as innovations contradicting the tradition (J. Dedek, 1. c. 54-56).

[2] Quoted by M. Zalba: Theologiae Moralis Compendium I, 1958, 880, footnote 50.

[3] Lehrbuch der Moraltheologie, Freiburg 1878, 491ff.

[4] Lehmkuhl retracted this doctrine after the decree of the Holy Office of July 24, 1895; cf. Theol. mor. I, nr. 841.

[5] DS 3258; 3298; 3337.

[6] DS 3720.

[7] AAS 43 (1951), 838.

[8] In the encyclical "Humanae Vitae" Paul VI declares that direct abortion, even though procured for therapeutic reasons, is absolutely to be rejected (AAS 60, 1968, 490).

[9] AAS 66 (1974), 739.

The refutation of direct therapeutic abortion by the magisterium of the Church and by Catholic moral theologians is based on the same principle as the refutation of any other kind of direct abortion: The direct killing of the innocent is always immoral and forbidden under any circumstances whatsoever. Non-Catholics on the other hand generally do not agree with this strict attitude and regard therapeutic abortion as justified in certain instances. Also among Catholic theologians the dispute revived again after the Second Vatican Council.

Four arguments have been advanced by the older theologians in defence of direct therapeutic abortion. First, it is lawful to accelerate the anyhow imminent death of the fetus somewhat in order to save at least the life of the mother. Second, one can justly assume that in a crisis where the mother's life is at stake the fetus would be ready to sacrifice his life, if in this way the mother can be saved. Third, placed between two evils one may and even must choose the lesser one, which in this case is the killing of the fetus. Fourth, the fetus is an unjust aggressor and may be killed as such in order to save the mother's life.

However it is objected against the first three arguments that they are not able to show that the abortion of the fetus is not a direct killing of an innocent, which is by presupposition always immoral. Direct acceleration of the death of the fetus is unlawful direct killing. The "sacrificial" death of the child is brought about by the intervention of a physician who again directly kills the unborn child. And one can never choose an immoral action as the lesser evil, namely the direct killing of the fetus, against another evil which is only a physical one, namely the natural death of the mother or of mother and child together.

The fourth argument tries to show that the therapeutic abortion is not merely the killing of an innocent, but rather the killing of a materially unjust aggressor, which is lawful. Yet the objection is that the fetus is not carrying out an "aggression" in any reasonable interpretation of the word, not even a material one. He does not overstep his rights and rob by any unjust means the mother of her rights. Rather one could call the mother a materially unjust aggressor of the infant, because it is her pathological condition which hinders the infant to leave her womb alive.

Nevertheless the arguments point out some truths which merit attention. The spontaneous judgment of common sense is that the death of the fetus alone is certainly preferable to the death of mother and fetus together, even though the death of the fetus has to be anticipated by direct human intervention. Doubts and hesitations concerning the absolute inadmissibility of direct therapeutic abortion never totally ceased to persist among Catholic moral theologians. The distinction between lawful, indirect and unlawful, direct therapeutic abortion does not seem to do full justice to the claims of reality. C. Curran judges: "In general, I do not believe that the theory of direct and indirect.... adequately comes to grips with all the problems of conflict situations involving the fetus."[1] If applied with rigorous consistency, it may lead to rather absurd consequences. It is not merely lack of good will if laymen and Protestant theologians generally stand uncomprehending before it.

B. Häring reports the case of a pregnant woman who suffered from a tumor in the uterus which caused profuse bleeding. In order to prevent the woman from bleeding to death, the attending physician decided to open the womb and to empty the uterus. Thereupon the uterus contracted and the bleeding ceased. Yet according to the principle of directly and indirectly willed evil effects, this procedure must be considered illicit. The emptying of the fetus from the uterus constitutes a direct abortion, which is unlawful. The circumstance that in this way the uterus could be saved for the woman who was still childless is not a reason which could justify the procedure. But it would be licit to take out the whole uterus as a sick organ, together with the child, because this is indirect abortion. Häring justly doubts whether this is sound morality.[2]

Here as much as in the case of sterilization the question must be asked why a directly willed evil effect is never admissible, while an indirectly willed evil effect often is. The reflections had in the context of sterilization also hold good for the present issue. Fundamentally the problem has been dealt with in general moral theology (chap. IV, D). The crucial point is the argument in justification of indirectly willed evil effects under certain conditions. Reasoned out with consistency, it would hold true for some instances of directly willed evil effects as well, and also for some instances of direct therapeutic abortion. For much good which could be done is left undone or made impossible, and

---

[1] Charles E. Curran: A New Look at Christian Morality. — Notre Dame, Ind.: Fides Publishers, 1968, 240.

[2] B. Häring III, 1966, 212.

it is unreasonable and morally unbearable for those concerned if the uterus is removed together with the fetus, instead of only removing the child; or if the mother has to die together with the child, instead of saving at least the mother through therapeutic abortion of the fetus.

Yet it is argued that, confronted with the choice between a moral and a physical evil, one must opt for the latter, even if it seems to be greater. And the direct killing of an innocent, also of a fetus by direct abortion, is a moral evil. But this precisely is the object of the controversy, whether directly willed abortion is always a moral evil. The indirect admission of the evil effect of abortion is considered lawful. Yet it has been shown that the arguments by which this is proven at times also hold for direct therapeutic abortion. Consequently direct therapeutic abortion seems to be admissible the same as indirect therapeutic abortion is, as long as it constitutes the lesser evil in terms of physical damage to health and life. It is not opposed to the realization of the divine goals; rather the admission of the greater evil is.

In the discussion of the crime of murder it is argued that God alone is the owner of human life and man only its steward. Therefore man is not allowed to dispose of other people's life, *unless* a higher good is at stake, whose safeguarding is willed by God even more urgently. As far as human insight reaches, the preservation of the uterus through direct abortion of the fetus is a higher good than the destruction of uterus and child together; the preservation of the mother's life through direct abortion is a greater good than the death of mother and child together.

It is also argued that life as the highest good of man establishes the highest temporal right of man. Nevertheless the earthly life of a person is not the highest good altogether and therefore also not the highest of rights. The highest good, besides a person's eternal salvation, is the realization of God's plan with mankind and the world. This plan also includes the unfolding of his creation. Viewed in this perspective, the anticipated death of a fetus constitutes a lesser evil and offends against a lesser right than the death of mother and child together. Because the mother can still contribute, and perhaps much contribute, to the realization of God's plan with the world. This is especially evident if she is the mother of several children; but it can also be shown in other regards. The fetus, on the other hand, who is unable to survive the mother's death, is therewith also unable to contribute to God's creative plan. Hence his right to be

kept alive for some days more must yield to the higher claims of the divine plan, which demand that the mother's life be saved, if necessary by the direct removal of the unviable fetus.

In view of such considerations, J. Dedek judges that a sufficient reason for a therapeutic abortion "would be to save the physical life of the mother or, what I would think equivalent, her mental sanity."[1] A similar opinion is held by C. Curran.[2] However, insofar as the mother's mental sanity is concerned, one may wonder whether abortion will be ever the right and necessary means to save it. This is too doubtful a reason in such a serious matter.

Other recent, Catholic authors who consider therapeutic abortion permissible in order to save the mother's life are R. Springer,[3] J. Noonan,[4] B. Häring,[5] the Belgian bishops,[6] W. May,[7] J. Stimpfle,[8] H. Rotter,[9] L. Janssens,[10] F. Böckle,[11] J. Gründel,[12] and L. Cornerotte.[13] The latter permits abortion only if otherwise mother and child together had to die. If either one of them can be saved, one rather has to wait and leave the outcome to providence. It seems that this is a correct restriction, inasmuch as in this last case we have no means to establish which of the two lives is of the greater value.

---

[1] J. Dedek, 1. c. 87f.

[2] C. Curran, 1. c. 243.

[3] Robert H. Springer: Notes on Moral Theology.—Theol. Studies 31 (1970), 493.

[4] J. Noonan, Jr.: An Almost Absolute Value in History, in: The Morality of Abortion, ed. by the same. — Cambridge, Mass.: Harvard Univ. Press, 1970, 58.

[5] B. Häring: Medical Ethics. — Slough, England: St. Paul Publications, 1973, 108f.

[6] Déclaration des évêques belges sur l'avortement. — Documentation Catholique 70 (1973), 433.

[7] William E. May judges that the killing of a fetus in order to save the mother's life is justified as the indirect killing of a materially unjust aggressor (The Morality of Abortion. — Linacre Quarterly 41, 1974, 74f).

[8] J. Stimpfle, bishop of Augsburg, in a declaration of April 27, 1974; quoted by Franz Scholz: Durch ethische Grenzsituationen aufgeworfene Normenprobleme. Theol. prakt. Quartalschrift 123, 1975, 342.

[9] Hans Rotter: Konflikte um das Leben. — Innsbruck: Tyrolia Verlag, 1976, 45.

[10] Louis Janssens: Norms and Priorities in a Love Ethics. — Louvain Studies 6 (1976/7), 214.

[11] Franz Böckle, in Handbuch der christlichen Ethik, vol. II, ed. by Anselm Hertz et alii. — Freiburg: Herder, 1978, 55 and 58.

[12] Johannes Gründel: Normen im Wandel. — München: Don Bosco Verlag, 1980, 184.

[13] L. Cornerotte: Loi morale, valeur humaines et situations de conflit. — Nouvelle Revue Théologique 100 (1978), 528f.

III. Self-defence

1. *Concept and conditions of self-defence*

Self-defence is the violent resistance against an actual and unjust threat to oneself or to a third person. The defence may even include the killing of the unjust aggressor if he threatens vital goods of a person.

Conditions for self-defence:

a) The aggression must be unjust, i.e. not justified from the side of the aggressor. (It would be justified, e.g., in the case of distress emergency, which would warrant theft of food.) It is sufficient if the assault is at least materially unwarranted, and it does not matter whether the aggressor is subjectively (formally) guiltless. Therefore one may also resist an insane or intoxicated person in self-defence.

b) The aggression must be actual, i.e. imminent or present or still lasting. One may strike in preventive defence as soon as it is evident that an unjust attack against oneself or one's own is both certain and inescapable. After the aggression has taken place, killing is no longer self-defence but revenge. Consequently a woman may not kill the man who has ravished her. Yet self-defence is still permissible against a thief making off with his loot.

c) The defence must limit itself to means which are proportionate to the greatness of the danger. Hurting severely or killing the aggressor is only allowed in defence of great values such as life, integrity of one's members, bodily integrity in attempts of rape, temporal goods of great value. One may defend the life and possessions of others in the same way as one may defend one's own.

d) The resistance must be confined to that minimum of violence which is necessary and sufficient to obtain the justified purpose of defence. Among various possible means the least harmful for the aggressor must always be chosen. Therefore if one can save one's life by flight, one must flee (unless flight would be very disgraceful, e.g. in the case of an officer). Killing is unlawful if the assailant can be rendered harmless by wounding him. However because of his excitement the person attacked is often excused if he exceeds the bounds of a blameless defence.

2.   *Arguments in justification of self-defence*

a)   Holy Scripture and tradition

Holy Scripture does not offer any kind of a developed doctrine on self-defence. The only text referring directly to the question is Ex 22:2. It permits the killing of a thief breaking in during the night. If he were robbing during day-time, it was not allowed to kill him, probably because the one concerned could call for help or recognize the robber more easily and then accuse him before the judge.

Some teachings of the NT seem to speak against the right to self-defence. Thus Jesus teaches to turn to the striking also the other cheek (Mt 5:39) and St. Paul preaches to overcome evil with good (Rom 12:21; 1 Cor 6:7). However it would be wrong to press these texts too much and to see in them a denial of the right to self-defence. When Jesus, standing before the high priest, was struck by one of the officers, he did not offer the other cheek, but asked of the officer what was justifying such a punishment (Jn 18:22f). The very mission of Jesus demanded this defence against the unjust treatment, to avoid wrong suspicion.

Some of the Church Fathers show scruples regarding the right of self-defence (Tertullian, Cyprian, Ambrosius, Basilius). St. Augustin however approves of this right.[1] In the scholastic and in the later theology the right to self-defence is generally accepted.[2]

From ancient times the right to self-defence is rooted in the judicial convictions of the nations, at least in cases of aggression against one's life. In modern times this right became fully acknowledged by nearly all the criminal laws.

b)   The arguments of reason

(1)   There exists a natural order of law which assures every individual and every community the rights necessary for their existence and their connatural development. At the same time this order obliges one to respect the identical rights of other

---

[1] Epist. 153, 17.

[2] Some decisions of the Popes (Alexander VII, DS 2037f and Innocence XI, DS 2130f), though directly limiting the right to self-defence, approve of it implicitly and in principle by setting these limits.

people and communities. The existence and inviolability of such a natural order of law follows from the fact that without it well-ordered human life and successful development would be impossible.

Because of its strict necessity this natural order must permit and demand its safeguarding and defence even by means of force, to the extent requisite for its preservation. An order of law protecting the absolute inviolability in the private sphere of those who destroy the order would protect its own violation and destruction. This contradicts its necessity.

In the case of self-defence the natural order of law must grant the attacked person the possibility to defend his rights by force as far as this is necessary for their safeguarding. Only by this means the rights of the individual as well as of the community can be protected effectively.

Note that the citizen defending his or other people's rights only tries to safeguard a natural order still intact. He does not inflict punishment. Punishment is inflicted after the violation of the law has been completed. The right to punishment is reserved to the public authority, because this is a sufficient and even safer means to restore the broken order.

(2) Regard for the people entrusted to one's care (the family, the relatives, the welfare of a community or organization) and regard for a committed work very often not only justify but demand defence against an unjust aggressor. The same commandment of love which commands one to spare an evil-doer as far as possible, also commands to protect the welfare of our unjustly endangered neighbours.

(3) A last argument for self-defence is taken from the evil consequences which would result if those attempting robbery or murder were inviolable for a private person. This inviolability would encourage brutal individuals to even more crimes and thus multiply them.

An objection against direct killing as means of self-defence is raised by some authors[1] on the grounds that direct killing in self-defence would violate the order of being, according to which all people are of equal value and equal rights. It contradicts this equality if in the case of self-defence the killing of a person is made a means to save another person's life. These authors

---

[1] Cf. W. Rauch: Abhandlungen aus Ethik und Moraltheologie, Freiburg, 1956, 202-205.

therefore allow only indirect killing as a means of self-defence. This opinion is also backed by St. Thomas.[1] (Of course the objection would concern every kind of direct killing, also killing in war or execution of a criminal. Regarding war, this theory in fact only permits indirect killing. In the case of death penalty it thinks direct killing justified because it is ordered to the restitution of the *gloria Dei*.)

In answering this objection one must consider the following: Bodily life naturally cannot be subordinated to lower or equal values, but it can justly be subordinated to higher values. In the case of self-defence there is a value superior to individual life justifying the direct killing of the aggressor. This value is not just the possessions or the life of the unjustly attacked. This value is the inviolable natural order of divine law, whose contempt cannot be tolerated. — In instances of an unjust assault against another person's life one might also wonder whether the life of the criminal in action is really entirely of the same value as the life of the innocent whom he attacks; or whether the life of the innocent is not after all a higher value.

c)   The obligation to self-defence

There is generally no obligation to defend one's rights by means of killing the aggressor. Christian love may refrain from taking the life of an unjust aggressor and choose to suffer injustice.

But one would be obliged to kill an aggressor in self-defence if one's life were necessary for the support and protection of one's family or of a community. A duty of charity can oblige to defend others (wife, children, parents, or those specially committed to one's care). Officers of the law, policemen, watchmen are often obliged by reason of their office to defend others against unjust aggressions.

F.   Acceptance of suffering and death

The afflictions of sickness and old age cause men to experience more deeply the agonizing problem of suffering and death. The answer to this problem depends on the idea men have of the world and especially on their religion. Christian faith sees in suffering a means to unite a person to Christ, who went through suffering and death to the glory of his Father. We bear "in the body the death of Jesus, so that the life of Jesus

---

[1] Summa II-II, q. 64, a. 7.

also may be manifested in our bodies" (2 Cor 4:10). By accepting infirmities generously and even heroically, man grows unto the full measure of maturity in Christ. Moreover the Christian's suffering is also seen as a source of grace for the entire people of God. Through his infirmities he makes up in his own flesh "what is lacking in Christ's afflictions for the sake of his body, that is, the church" (Col 1:24). As the sick man is the image and sign of Christ, serving the sick is to serve Jesus himself. "I was sick and you visited me," he will say on judgment day (Mt 25:36).

The sacrament of the sick strengthens the Christian in the affliction of suffering and death. It would be wrong to consider this sacrament exclusively as a preparation for death. In the letter of St. James the sacred anointing is much more considered as a help to heal the sick body (Jas 5:14ff). A hospital chaplain therefore would fail in his vocation were he to consider himself merely as the appointed comforter of the dying and neglect to bless and to strengthen in the name of Christ the patient's will to live.

We cannot speak of a grave obligation of the person who is seriously ill to receive the anointing of the sick. He can provide for the needs of his soul through the sacraments of penance and the holy Eucharist. But the Church ardently desires that a Christian who is sick should not neglect the graces offered him by the sacrament of anointing and that those around him should help him in this regard, particularly by summoning the priest.[1]

Death ends earthly existence. The Christian dies united with Christ in a union begun in baptism, renewed and strengthened in the sacraments of penance and the Eucharist, and now brought to final perfection. In dying he offers God his final act of self-surrender. The Christian dies for the Lord just as he lives for him (Rom 14:7f; cf. Phil 1:20).

Though in death bodily life comes to an end, it does not on that account vanish into insignificance. For the story of man's earthly life is the story of God as well, and much more so if a life was lived in union with Christ. As the man who walks

---

[1] The lawful reception of the anointing of the sick requires the state of grace. If it is impossible to recover the state of grace by confession or perfect contrition, the sick person should at least elicit an act of imperfect contrition. The sacrament of the sick with imperfect contrition will remit mortal sins. But if a person in mortal sin is able to confess, then he is obliged to do so.

towards death reviews his life from the childhood and youth to his full maturity and to his decline, he reviews the ways of God, the things of God. For in a backward glance he discovers across the story written by himself the story written by God. The priest can help the dying to discover in the life, which is now past, the paths of divine love and the tracks of God's work.

The death of man is filled with bitterness because of the sin of Adam. However as a fruit of Christ's bitter suffering and death, the death of the Christian is also filled with heavenly hope, the hope of immortality and resurrection and of final union with Christ. "He who raised Christ Jesus from the dead will also give life to your mortal bodies" (Rom 8:11). Since dying means the perfect union with Christ, death for the Christian is in the last analysis a gain (Phil 1:21-23). The present, earthly condition is an exile from the Lord, and therefore dying is going home to him. This accounts for the Christian's desire to leave in order to be with him (2 Cor 5:8; Phil 1:23).

Under this aspect death is no longer an evil to be feared, but the desired release from the earthly exile. Of course the desire of death can also have its origin in less perfect motives, such as impatience resulting from temporal misfortune, or even in sinful motives, such as tiredness with the ordinary hardships of life. But it is perfectly lawful when the desire to leave this world is inspired by the wish of union with Christ in heaven and of eternal rest in God.

Chapter IV

SEXUALITY AND MARRIAGE

Sexual morality attempts to explain the meaning and purpose of human sexuality and the moral significance of those human acts and relations which are of an erotic and sexual nature. The elaboration of a sexual ethics encounters particular difficulties today. Profound changes are taking place in man's attitudes towards sexuality. Traditional Christian sexual ethics is largely found unsatisfactory and rated as no longer convincing. Its view of sexuality is regarded as too narrowly centred round the procreative function of the sexual act. Besides, dualistic theories deriving from Gnosticism and Manichaeism are accused of having gained influence in Christian ethics. All sexual desire and pleasure was suspected or even outrightly disparaged as ignoble and degrading. The gratification of the flesh was supposed to stand in opposition to the spirit. Sexual pleasure was relegated to the dark realm of the irrational. The tendency was to ban it as something evil. Readily the moral qualifications of sin and mortal sin have been used against it.[1] The result was a sexual ethics full of warnings and prohibitions with hardly any appreciation for the good values of sexual love and with little constructive guidance.

Against this sexual negativism a strong counter-reaction has risen. Traditional norms are simply being abandoned and taboos brushed aside. One may justly speak of a "sexual revolution". A positive approach to sexuality is advocated. Against all false repressions the demand for a genuine personalization of sexual relations is made. Sexual love is discovered and exalted as a human value, willed by the Creator and therefore wholly good.

Without doubt a re-evaluation and re-appreciation of sexuality is in place. Nevertheless a naive optimism concerning an easy, unpreoccupied enjoyment of sexual love and its spontaneous regulation by the instincts of human nature is not adequate

---

[1] Cf. the very enlightening study of Michael Müller: Die Lehre des hl. Augustinus von der Paradiesesehe und ihre Auswirkung in der Sexualethik des 12. und 13. Jahrhunderts bis Thomas von Aquin. — Regensburg: Pustet, 1954.

either. The fallen state of man cannot be ignored. The mastering of sexuality poses problems which are not of an easy nature. Not without reason the sexual drives have been termed "passions". The tensions caused by them not seldom expose man to suffering. And even though one cannot agree with the degradation of sexuality by ancient pagan philosophies such as Stoicism, Gnosticism and Manichaeism, their negative attitude points to the dark forces at work in it. Time and again the sexual passions threaten man's spiritual self, peace and true happiness. Great pagan religions like Hinduism and Buddhism share this apprehension and teach their adherents to show restraint in the use of the sexual powers. A sound sexual ethics will have to do justice to the entire reality of human sexuality: to its creative powers of enriching love, as well as to its eroding forces of dehumanizing abuse.

A.   Nature and meaning of human sexuality[1]

To be human is to be born of other men. There was a man and a woman and a family behind every man. Two currents of humanity come together in a marriage, and at a given moment there is a human being. At one time there was I.

It is a "given" moment when a life comes into existence, a moment given by God. Neither father nor mother could say with certainty that a new life would come to be. In the fecundation there are forces at work which human ingenuity cannot imitate and which are always unpredictable to some extent. "Lo, sons are a heritage from the Lord" (Ps 127:3). It may still be affirmed that, though new human life comes about according to laws that we have not made, we can study these laws and to some degree gain control over them. But there is one thing which remains an inviolable wonder outside of all human control: that it was precisely this human being who was born, that it was precisely "I".

---

[1] References: Dietrich von Hildebrand: Man and Woman. — Chicago: Franciscan Herald Press, 1965. August Adam: The Sixth Commandment. — Cork: The Mercier Press, 1966. Frederick Von Gagern: Marriage Partnership. — Westminster, Md.: Newman Press, 1966. Leonhard M. Weber: On Marriage, Sex and Virginity (Quaestiones Disputatae 16). — New York: Herder and Herder, 1966. Alphonsus Jansen: The Meaning of Love and Marriage. — Techny, Ill.: Divine Word Publications, 1968. Sexual Ethics and Christian Responsibility; ed. John C. Wynn. — New York: Association Press, 1970. Sex: Thoughts for Contemporary Christians; ed. Michael J. Taylor. — Garden City, N. Y.: Doubleday, 1972. Felix M. Podimattam: A New Look at Chastity. — Bangalore: Asian Trading Corp., 1974.

The beginning of a new human life is a sacred moment in which God's continuing creative power is especially evident. After all parents cannot want this particular child. At best they wanted "a boy" or "a girl". Only God wanted "me". Hence a child is born in cooperation between man and God. The power to cooperate with God is bestowed on parents as they give new life to a child. This cooperation begins with conception and birth and is completed in the education of the child. God nourishes, loves and guides the new human life through its parents. They have a serious and joyful responsibility.[1]

At the beginning of a new human life stands the affection and utter love of two people, father and mother. This love and its fruitfulness is based on the differences of sexes. The differences of sexes are however not only of significance in the creation of new life. "Sexuality must be numbered among the essential determining factors in man. It characterizes the entire structure of the human being, whether as man or woman, and affects the behaviour of the individual even in his mental attitudes and processes."[2] Man's sexual differentiation permeates his whole person always and for ever; it stamps all his actions and is creative also under other aspects than procreation.

1. *Biblical view of sexuality*

a) The statements of the *Old Testament* and in particular of the book of Genesis have preserved mankind's primal understanding of man's sexual differentiation. Human heterosexuality is the work of the Creator. "God created man in his own image, in the image of God he created him; male and female he created them" (Gen 1:27). The text speaks in the same breath of man as God's image and as differentiated in two sexes. And the sacred author adds to this that this is very good (Gen 1:31). "The entire man is created good. Therefore sexuality too, as a gift of God, is wholly acceptable. Although any projection of a sexual difference on God and the Trinity is inadmissible, the relationship of man and woman united in love reflects something of God's love, in its free giving of itself, and of the unity within the Divine Trinity."[3] Since man has been created in the image of God, his nature must primarily be understood from the nature

---

[1] Cf. the "Dutch Catechism" for adults: A New Catechism. Catholic Faith for Adults. — Herder and Herder/Burns and Oates, 1967, 381f.

[2] J. Gründel, art. "Sex" in: Sacramentum Mundi, vol. VI, 1970, 73.

[3] Ib. 73.

of God if it is to be grasped rightly, and not from the nature of the animal.

The purpose of sexuality according to the first chapter of Genesis is the bearing of offspring. "Be fruitful and multiply, and fill the earth and subdue it" (Gen 1:28). Just as the purpose of all heterosexuality is generation, so it also applies to men. God charges men to multiply, for by this means the plan of the Creator is to be continued and the work of creation unfolded. In view of his wife's motherly function Adam called her Eve, "because she was the mother of all living" (Gen 3:20).

The second chapter of Genesis adds another purpose to the first, why God created the first couple as man and woman. After Adam had been called into existence, God said: "It is not good that the man should be alone; I will make him a helper fit for him" (Gen 2:18). Man has been created as a being in need of companionship. God therefore made the woman in order to give Adam a partner and to free him from loneliness. The narration relates very graphically how God took one of Adam's ribs and made this into a woman (Gen 2:21f). God took part of the man away and formed it into his female partner. Therefore man and woman go together and complete each other.[1] This completion is not only a biological but also a spiritual one. Sexuality reaches deep into the human soul. The total man, not only his body, is sexually man or woman. For the sake of this completion and mutual companionship, man and woman leave their parental family. They establish their own community, which culminates in that mutual self-giving by which they form so intimate a union that they can be called "one flesh" (Gen 2:24).

The original relations between the sexes were, according to the biblical account, guileless and free from all feeling of shame (Gen 2:25). But the primordial state of integrity was lost when man fell into sin. This caused a disturbance in the entire order of creation and also in the relationship between the sexes. "The eyes of both were opened, and they knew that they were naked" (Gen 3:7). The carefree naturalness of the sexes in their mutual relationships is lost. Sexuality is experienced as

---

[1] Plato tells in the Symposion how, according to a Greek myth, Zeus originally created man as a bisexual being. Only later he cut him asunder. From there comes the love of the sexes, because each half now searches for the other (Symp. 190f). This tale agrees with the Bible in the two fundamental truths: 1. it is God who created man and woman; 2. both belong together like the two halves of a whole which cannot do without each other (cf. M. Müller: Grundlagen der katholischen Sexualethik. — Regensburg: Pustet, 1968, 30f).

a vulnerable possession which man must protect against abuse by others and also by himself.

Apart from the first two chapters of Genesis, the Old Testament views sexuality primarily from the aspect of procreation. "Having children was considered as the first and foremost value, to which all else was subordinated."[1] The blessing of children is a gift of God and a reason for joy (Ps 127:3-5; 128:3-6). Conversely childlessness is a misfortune and a penalty from God"(Lev 20:20f; 1 Sam 1:1-20; Is 47:9; etc.). Thereby the needs of the community take precedence over the wishes and interests of the individual. Nevertheless the spontaneity of love is not missing altogether. The free, ardent love between man and woman finds a most poetic portrayal in the Song of Songs. Even though the book allegorically speaks of the love between the soul and God, it does so with words and attitudes which were at that time those of human love.

b) The *New Testament* displays a natural attitude towards sexuality. It offers no encouragement to a dualistic, Manichaeistic contempt of sex. Jesus treated women with equal regard and concern as men. Women were among his disciples and friends. He did not permit Jewish traditions to constrict him in his dealings with them and to interfere with his mission as their saviour. There is no trace in his teaching or conduct which would suggest a depreciation of women or the marriage state.

One can however not overlook that the early Church was much concerned with self-control and discipline in sexual life. In the time of the emperors the old Roman strictness had given way to frightful libertinism and lewdness, which led to an increasing decline in social life. "The warnings to flee from licentiousness, to follow the Lord and not prostitutes, and to regard the body as the temple of the Holy Spirit, were urgently necessary. It is, therefore, no accident that in the lists of vices, idolatry (which was often combined with debauchery), unchastity and avarice are given a prominent place."[2] In 1 Thess 4:4-8 St. Paul sees the sanctification required by God first of all as purity in married life. In the list of vices in 1 Cor 6:9f he warns that "neither fornicators, nor idolaters, nor adulterers, nor the effeminate, nor liers with mankind . . . will inherit the kingdom

---

[1] Art. "Marriage" in: Dictionary of Biblical Theology, ed. by X. Léon-Dufour, London 1967, 294.

[2] Rudolf Schnackenburg: The Moral Teaching of the New Testament. — London: Burns and Oates, 1967, 248.

of God." All these things should belong to the past pre-Christian life of his readers. Christians must sanctify their bodies and sexuality because they are the temples of the Holy Spirit (1 Cor 6:13-20).

Married people are exhorted to maintain mutual love for each other (Col 3:18f; 1 Pet 3:1-7). This love is immeasurably ennobled by the parallel which is drawn in the letter to the Ephesians between the bond that unites Christ with the Church and the bond of the marriage covenant (Eph 5:21-33). Husbands should love their wives as Christ has loved the Church and given himself for her. And wives should adhere to their husbands as the Church does to Christ. From this parallel marriage derives a unique dignity and particular stability.

A peculiar trait of New Testament sexual ethics is the recommendation of virginity. The fulfillment of sexuality in marriage no longer appears as the only way for man in this world; the way of virginity appears beside it as a second form of life (Mt 19:11f). "Between the time of the OT, when bearing offspring was a primary duty to perpetuate the people of God, and the parousia, when marriage will be abolished (Mt 22:30 par), two forms of life coexist in the Church: marriage, transfigured by the mystery of Christ and the Church, and consecrated celibacy, which Paul considered better (1 Cor 7:8.25-28)."[1] It is not a question of undervaluing marriage. For Paul marriage is a divinely willed and divinely instituted bond. "Each has his own special gift from God, one of one kind and one of another" (1 Cor 7:7). But by becoming attached undividedly to the Lord to please him alone (1 Cor 7:32-35), one bears witness that the structure of the present world, to which the institution of marriage is correlated, is transitory and that man finds his ultimate fulfillment in the love and service of God.

2.   *Man's sexual constitution in general*[2]

The sexual difference between man and woman is a constitutive part of human nature. The two sexes are not only distinguished by their sexual organs and systems of glands. Their whole anatomic structure differs. Thus the man has more robust bones and a stronger build, while the woman's constitution is softer, her pelvis broader, her breast more developed. Also their

---

[1] Art. "Marriage" in: Dictionary of Biblical Theology, 1967, 296.

[2] Cf. Michael Müller: Grundlagen der katholischen Sexualethik. — Regensburg: Pustet, 1968, 78-123. August Adam: The Sixth Commandment. — Cork: The Mercier Press, 1966.

psychological qualities and spiritual dispositions differ. The male is more active and outgoing; he possesses greater courage to assail. The female is more receptive and protective; she shows greater fortitude to endure. The man is ordered towards things and more concerned with goals of objective nature. The woman is interested in persons and consecrates herself to those whom she loves with her soul and entire being. The logic of facts and keen penetration are characteristic of the man; the woman is more led by emotion, sensitivity and intuition. He is ruled by principles, she by love. Popular wisdom expresses the difference in the saying: In man the head reigns and in woman the heart. As the symbol of charity artists time and again chose the image of the woman, not of the man.

Each sex has its own strength and weakness. Man and woman complement each other. Any contempt of the other sex is therefore unfounded conceit and ultimately an offence against the Creator. Man and woman must rather show mutual respect and cooperate with each other.

The complementary constitution of man and woman results in erotic tensions which have important repercussions on the life of the individual and the community. They are the source of many achievements, especially in cultural life. The erotic is a marvellous and creative power in man. But it is likewise terrifying on account of its force. When sexual desires and genital satisfaction are detached from the totality of eros and human love, unsuspected depths of evil can be revealed. Only when integrated in the totality of man's being is sexuality good, amiable and constructive.

The insights into the diversity of the sexes take to some conclusions. The very nature of the masculine and feminine demands that the characteristics of each be maintained and given favourable opportunities to unfold. A blurring or disregard of the two would be unnatural and do injustice to man's sexual nature. Accordingly the two sexes ought to be educated separately to a great extent. For their biological and spiritual maturing process proceeds at different speed, and the properties of each must first be developed before the corresponding qualities can become fecund in a mutual encounter. Even though financial considerations may recommend common schools, pedagogic deliberations rather favour separate education for boys and girls during puberty.

There should be no alien and unnatural imitation of the other sex, no tasks and commitments totally foreign to a person's sexual individuality. Against a simplistic egalitarianism, a sober realism is called for. The principle "suum cuique" must not be falsified into the maxim "idem cuique", which can only result in the detriment of mankind and especially of the woman. The complete equalizing of the sexes, which is sometimes advocated today, will again ultimately result in a predominance of the male standards at the expense of the proper feminine values. Justice does not demand the same duties and tasks for everybody, but a division of obligations and works in accordance with the proper abilities and gifts of each.

3. *Nature and purpose of sexual love*

The attraction and love of the sexes finds its most intimate, most bodily, and at the same time most ecstatic expression in the act of sexual love. By its nature sexual love aims at a partner of the other sex. Every other form of sexual actuation is incomplete, if not immature or in certain instances perverse.[1] Man "can never meaningfully actuate his sexuality if he sees in it only a purely egocentric value; he must see it in terms of partnership."[2]

The sex instinct incites man to maintain the human race in the same way as the instinct of self-preservation impels him to maintain his life as individual by taking food. The Creator has attached pleasure to the satisfying of these instincts in order to bring them into play and to reach the goal. But pleasure is not the purpose and aim of their functioning.[3] It is rather the divinely instituted allurement of human beings to use these powers and thereby to maintain and to propagate life. The enjoyment of the pleasure is justified and good. However it must always remain subordinated to those aims whose realization it is destined to serve. "Therefore sexuality cannot and may not become purely the means to private satisfaction of instinct nor a sort of easily available drug. It gives man a goal beyond himself."[4]

---

[1] Sexual maturity, according to Viktor E. Frankl, has two elements: to be able to direct one's sexual desire towards the opposite sex, and to be able to love him/her with his/her whole being. The first one he calls sexual love and the second he calls erotic love. To be sexually mature means to be able to have sexual desire or fulfillment with another sex and to be able to love the opposite sex with one's whole being.

[2] J. Gründel, 1. c. 81.

[3] "To hold that the principal purpose of this faculty is the gratification of the individual is absurd, at least to anyone who admits the wise designs of God in the formation of human nature" (John R. Cavanagh: Fundamental Marriage Counselling. — Cork: Mercier Press, 1966, 519).

[4] J. Gründel, 1. c. 81.

What then is the goal or purpose of sexual love? This question has been lively discussed in the past decades. Traditional moral theology most strongly emphasized the procreative function of the sexual act. Any other purpose, at which men might aim in the actualization of marital love, had to be totally subordinated to this basic function. Recent theologians find this view of sexuality incomplete and not satisfactory. Independent of the procreative function the sexual act still serves another end which is good and worthy in itself; namely it is a means to express mutual love. The Pastoral Constitution on the Church in the Modern World of Vatican II takes up this question. It completes and further unfolds the teaching of Catholic theology on the purpose of sexual love (GS 47-52).

a) **Sexual love** has as its purpose the propagation of mankind through procreation of children. Any unprejudiced evaluation of sexuality will have to agree with traditional sexual ethics in this affirmation. Procreation of children is the innate, ultimate purpose of man's sexual faculties. The whole sexual structure and inclination indicates the child as its aim. The Creator's ultimate intention in providing man with the sexual faculties is the propagation of mankind. The urge for sexual union and the sexual organs themselves would not exist without the necessity of procreation. This is the presupposition of Christ's retort to the Sadducees that men in heaven are like the angels. When people "rise from the dead, they neither marry nor are given in marriage, but are like angels in heaven" (Mk 12:25).

Procreation of children is also for Vatican II the nature-ordained end of sexuality. "By their very nature, the institution of matrimony itself and conjugal love are ordained for the procreation and education of children, and find in them their ultimate crown" (GS 48; cf. 50). Insofar as the text not only speaks of the purpose of conjugal love (for the Council there is no other sexual love than conjugal love) but also of matrimony, it adds to the end of procreation the education of children. Education is the purpose of the marriage institution as a whole. It can however not be considered the purpose of the marital act in itself. The purpose of this act is the procreation of children, in which the Council sees the innate end and ultimate crown of conjugal love.

It follows however as a consequence that sexual activity should take place in such a way that the new life which may result from it will be responsibly taken care of. Hence, even though education of children cannot be considered the purpose of the sexual act, the readiness to their education is certainly the precondition for the lawful actualization of sexual love. And since the upbringing and education of children is a lengthy process, mother and father must be permanently united for it.

In keeping with the necessity of a permanent union between a child's parents, human love already by its natural aspiration aims at more than temporary companionship. Man and woman wish to belong to each other wholly. Moreover the desire for the total expression of the mutual love in the conjugal act is not limited to the moment of conception, but longs for fulfillment always anew and thus demands permanent companionship too. This already leads over to the second purpose of sexual love.

b)　Conjugal union is also suited to give expression to the mutual love and esteem of husband and wife and to deepen their intimate unity. "The actions within marriage by which the couple are united intimately and chastely are noble and worthy ones. Expressed in a manner which is truly human, these actions signify and promote that mutual self-giving by which spouses enrich each other with a joyful and thankful will" (GS 49).

The marital act is apt to express mutual appreciation and love. For if a person accepts this act in its whole significance and value as suited and intended for the procreation of children, he will be ready for such intimate love only with a partner whom he would like to be the mother of his possible child, and vice versa. Rightly therefore can Vatican II regard the bodily expressions of conjugal love "as special ingredients and signs of the friendship distinctive of marriage" (GS 49).

Sexual love is able to create community. It binds people together, and this all the more, the more body and soul participate in it. It brings about an atmosphere of love which calls forth a mood of gratitude, generosity and joy. These dispositions will not fail to have their effect on the entire family and build community even in the wider environment.

The expression of marital love and friendship is sufficient reason for the conjugal act. Therefore the Church has always permitted marriage between people who for reasons of age or health are unable to have children. But where the conditions are adequate, the child as the ultimate end should never be excluded from the union of love. That would mean the deliberate frustration of the Creator's aim, who ultimately wished sexual love as a means to propagate mankind.

The aim of mutual love is again all the more perfectly gained, the more man and woman are bound together by a permanent union of common life. It provides the best conditions for man to seek in a true spirit of love his partner as a person, not desiring his own sexual satisfaction in a purely selfish spirit, but offering safety and shelter to the companion. A permanent union alone answers the deeper psychological structure of sexual love. "Inasmuch as the sexual act is the expression of the unity of both partners and their total mutual love and acceptance and is capable of bestowing a knowledge which has a most fundamental formative effect, the indispensable prerequisite for its legitimacy is the mutual and publicly proclaimed will to a binding acceptance which is total and permanent. Thus only in validly contracted monogamy is the full meaning of such a self-giving secured."[1]

4. *Social dependence of sexual actuation*

Since sexuality orders a man towards other human beings and since its complete actualization involves a partner, it necessarily affects the social life of a community. Nobody can arbitrarily use another for the satisfaction of his sexual desires. He has to respect the rights of the partner to his body, to the free disposition of himself, to a treatment worthy of a person, to responsible care. And the community has to protect these rights.

Furthermore sexual relations are of greatest concern for every society because they give life to children who are the future of the community. The survival, well-being and growth of a society depend on a strong, rising generation which is bodily and spiritually healthy. This demands that sexual relations be ordered in such a way that a healthy youth is guaranteed. A sound family life will be an essential condition for that.

There is general agreement on the need of giving form and direction to man's sexual instincts, though not an equal agreement on the criteria for these norms. The need is confirmed by behavioural research. Human sexuality possesses specific qualities which demand a control of its energies for social living. Thus human sexuality — in contradistinction to that of the animal — continues to be active also outside the mating seasons. Man's sexual desire can be isolated from conception. His instincts are of a generalized and uncertain nature, which entails the possibility of sexual excess. All these factors point to the need for institutionally supported direction and order in sexual relationships.

---

[1] J. Gründel, art. "Sex" in: Sacramentum Mundi VI, 1970, 75.

Accordingly in no society has sexuality been left to the arbitrary will of the private individual. It has been subjected to social norms. The social implications of sexuality demand that the concerns and needs of the community be taken in account. This remains true even though ethnology has shown that the normative systems are not everywhere the same, but are historically and culturally conditioned in their content.

The observation of a certain relativity of sexual norms made modern man critical towards the norms presented to him by his own community. No longer does he consider arguments based on tradition and authority alone as sufficient. He wants to know the intrinsic grounds for the validity and necessity of these norms. This is certainly a justified concern. Nevertheless sexual norms as such continue to be of importance in contemporary society too. The experiences and moral guidelines of past generations should not simply be thrown over board. Rather they should dispassionately be scrutinized for whatever they can offer in valid contributions to the difficult task of the elaboration of a sexual ethic.

"Sociological and anthropological studies of culture continue to emphasize the basic need for human behavioral norms for guiding the natural instinctual powers and relieving them of burdens, and for ensuring human freedom."[1] Even though the norms of sexual conduct constitute a certain limitation of man's sexual freedom, this is primarily the limitation of an arbitrary license. They relieve man much of the burden to find a meaningful and safe way through the tangle of sexual inclinations, desires and passions. Through this he is helped to devote his energies in greater freedom to other tasks, energies which might otherwise unnecessarily be absorbed by the struggle with the demands of an unguided, straying sexuality.

5. *Christian reverence for the dignity of woman*[2]

The encounter of the sexes in genuine love and a happy, holy family life strongly depend on the reverence for the dignity

[1] J. Gründel, 1. c. 82.

[2] Cf. the very instructive expositions by Michael Müller: Grundlagen der katholischen Sexualethik. — Regensburg: Pustet, 1968, 49-77. For further reference: Thierry Maertens: The Advancing Dignity of Woman in the Bible. — De Pere, Wisc.: St. Norbert Abbey Press, 1969. Religion and Sexism. Images of Woman in the Jewish and Christian Traditions; ed. by Rosemary R. Ruether. — New York: Simon and Schuster, 1974.

of woman. The history of cultures shows that the equitable esteem for woman often left much to be desired. All the more is it imperative for Christians to recall the attitude of Christ towards women, which is characterized by sincere esteem, and the authentic teachings of the faith.

The disdain of women is not merely an occasional phenomenon in the history of cultures and religions, but rather widespread. According to the Indian theories of reincarnation and karma, a woman cannot enter the nirvana or paradise. She must first be reborn in a man; while vice versa a man who leads a wicked life will reincarnate as a woman in his next life. It is however not correct to say that according to the Koran women have no soul; they have. Persian dualism, which exercised a great influence in the mediterranean world, posits a good principle, which created the world of spirits, and an evil principle, which created matter. Man is seen as related to the good principle and woman to the evil one. The theory was adopted by the gnostics. From there it gained entry into Judaism and also into some Christian circles (e.g. in Manichaeism and later in Catharism).

There are numerous misogynic utterances in the Greek classics. Because of the great appreciation these writers enjoyed in the Christian Middle Ages and in later humanism, they inevitably also influenced Christian thinkers. Of particular great import was the adoption of the Aristotelian biology by high scholasticism of the 13th century. According to Aristotle the man is the active, life- and form-giving principle in procreation. The woman is merely passive and only offers the matter. Consequently, since man alone is supposed to be the form-giving principle, only men ought to be born. If nevertheless women are in fact born, then it is by some failure and defect. Aristotle therefore regarded the woman as a "maimed man", which term was rendered in Latin by "mas occasionatus". Unfortunately the misguided doctrine found entrance in the writings of Albert the Great and Thomas Aquinas, who made it their own. The doctrine cannot claim support from Holy Scripture. It is evidently of non-Christian provenance.

In spite of such deviations the consciousness of the equal dignity of man and woman was never lost in Christianity. St. Ambrose writes: "Everybody, man as woman, must know that he bears God's image and likeness."[1] St. Basil declares: "The woman

---

[1] Exhortatio virginitatis 10 n. 68, PL 16, 356.

no less than the man possesses the privilege of being created after God's image. Both sexes have the same dignity, both the same virtues."[1] And St. Francis of Sales adds: "The woman is equal to the man, especially in the claim to grace and glory, which glory is the fruit . . . of the image and likeness of her Creator."[2]

The quotations all refer to the narrative of creation, which offers the basis for the Christian evaluation of woman. "God created man in his own image, in the image of God he created him; male and female he created them" (Gen 1:27). The woman is created by God in the same way and with the same dignity as man. Adam expresses this truth when he calls Eve bone of his bones and flesh of his flesh (Gen 2:23).

Christ treated women with equal respect as men. He did not differentiate in his preaching between men and women. Although he did not undertake to make changes in the legal status of women, which in Judaism was far from being one of equality, in practice he recognized them as persons of equal rights and dignity. He demands absolute faithfulness from husband and wife and rejects the Jewish right to divorce, which the woman never possessed, for the man as well (Mt 19:3-9 par). His actual behaviour bears witness to high esteem and delicate tact, rarely encountered in later Judaism. He allowed women among his followers and accepted the help they gave him (Lk 8:2f), visited the friendly family at Bethany and wished the sisters Mary and Martha to listen to what he had to say (Lk 10:38-42; cf. Jn 11:20-36). When it seemed necessary to him for his messianic mission, he even overstepped the bounds of Jewish customs in his dealings with women. Thus he spoke to the Samaritan woman in public at Jacob's well, to the astonishment of his disciples (Jn 4:27). He allowed himself to be touched by the woman with an issue of blood, though that made him ritually unclean (Mk 5:25-34 par). He showed sympathetic love and mercy for women known as sinners and prostitutes, which was totally incomprehensible from the point of view of the Pharisees (Mt 21:31f; Lk 7:36-50; Jn 8:2-11).

The factual recognition of the woman as a person of equal dignity by Jesus was bound to exercise a profound transforming influence on her social status in the Christian world and beyond. In the long run the concrete attitude of Jesus raised the dignity

---

[1] Hom. 10 in Gen.. PG 30, 54.
[2] Opuscules. Oeuvres 25, 291-293.

of the woman more effectively than any particular legal reform. Jesus saved women from being thought of as merely sexual beings by honouring them as human persons and children of God.[1]

The new condition of equality for women and men before God finds apt expression in St. Paul's letter to the Galatians: "In Christ Jesus you are all sons of God, through faith . . . . There is neither Jew nor Greek, there is neither slave nor free, there is neither male nor female; for you are all one in Christ Jesus" (Gal 3:26-28). He gives Timothy the well adapted advice, as a practical guideline for his behaviour towards women, to honour the elder women like mothers and the younger women like sisters (1 Tim 5:2; cf. Mt 12:50). And St. Peter exhorts husbands to honour their wives for the reason that they both are joint heirs of the divine life of grace (1 Pet 3:7).

In one text however statements do occur which appear to disparage the female sex. This is 1 Timothy 2:9-15. As a reason why women should be silent in church it argues that Eve was created after Adam, and that she, not Adam, allowed herself to be deceived by the serpent. The task of the wife is maternity, through which she will be saved. "But for this text it should be remembered that Jewish views are being taken over here and that a definite abuse was being fought, namely the appearance of 'prophetesses' at the service, accompanied by an unhealthy aspiring to extraordinary gifts and activity which were diverting women from their proper tasks in home and family."[2] Also on other occasions Paul had to fight turmoils in the community services, resulting from a disorderly use of charismatic gifts, like the speaking in tongues and the gift of prophecy. Therefore he laid down rules as to who should speak in the church and when and in what order (1 Cor 14). "Let all things be done for edification" (ib. 14:26).

Christian respect and esteem for women is especially evident in the mariology of the Catholic Church and the devotion to Mary, the virgin mother of Christ. From early times Christian writers contrasted the image of Eve, which incriminated the woman so gravely, by the radiant figure of Mary. The woman is for the man not only a seducer, but also a guide to lift him up. In the person of Mary Christians are shown the real vocation

---

[1] Cf. R. Schnackenburg: The Moral Teaching of the New Testament. — London: Burns and Oates, 1967, 132-135.

[2] R. Schnackenburg, l. c. 254.

of the woman: to be mother, and not to be just an object of sex. Through her lofty ideal the Church teaches the believers reverence for the dignity of woman in the concrete language of an example.

B. Mastery of sexuality and failures in it

Christian morality sees in the body and in sexuality the Creator's work. Against all contempt of matter and sexuality it must defend the genuine biblical view of these realities. For Holy Scripture the body and its sexual constitution do not stem from an evil principle but from God. Therefore it values them as good and accepts them as worthy. Not contempt but respect and reverence must characterize the attitude of the Christian towards them.

Sexuality is a creative power. But as any other powerful, natural force, it must be rightly channeled. It must be curbed to serve man and not to oppress him. Otherwise it may turn to be a source of servitude, frustration, disgust, egotism and destruction. "The special nature of human sexuality and the dynamism it contains make it imperative for man that he should not drift in this matter but should provide for a formation and discipline of these powers."[1] Where no such formation takes place, the road to personal maturity remains blocked. As a result of it, immature fixations, compensative attitudes and perversions are to be feared.

I. Virtues of modesty and chastity

1. *The virtue of modesty and its offences*

Modesty respects the demands of shame in the realm of sexuality. In order to understand this virtue well, some reflections on the sense of shame are called for.[2]

Antiquity and the Middle Ages regarded shame essentially as a sentiment of inferiority. The feeling of shame arises at everything that is either really evil or that is considered as dishonourable by general opinion. Thereby it can be observed that one is less ashamed of defects which result from no personal

---

[1] J. Gründel, art. "Sex" in: Sacramentum Mundi VI, 1970, 76.

[2] Cf. Michael Müller: Grundlagen der katholischen Sexualethik. — Regensburg: Pustet, 1968, 159-185 (ch. VII: "Die Umfriedung der Sexualität durch das Schamgefühl").

failure than of those which spring from one's own guilt.[1] Nevertheless one is also ashamed of things which imply no sin at all, such as poverty, patched clothing, lowly work. The reason for shame here lies in the disregard by the public.

However this does not cover the entire realm of shame. If for example a student is praying in his room and suddenly a companion of his enters, he will usually try to hide his act of devotion by turning to another occupation. In this instance the feeling of shame arises at an action which is not at all inferior, so that it could be blamed. On the contrary, the student wants to conceal something which is most worthy, but of a very personal, intimate, sacred nature. The deeper an action reaches in the depth of the soul and the more delicate a sentiment is, the more it wants to be guarded as a secret. The sense of shame spontaneously reacts as a protective instinct against interference by others. The soul divines that certain values can only ripen in secret and only unfold their deepest beauty in seclusion.

A principal realm of shame is sexuality. The sense of shame not only strives to hide the act of sexual intercourse, but also all the expressions of the libido, such as looks, touches and kisses. This shame is felt in the most lawful manifestations of conjugal love. Married people withdraw them from the looks of outsiders. The reason primarily lies in the need to protect these intimacies against all importunate curiosity and unwarranted intrusion by others. Only in this sense of a personal protection does the shame at nakedness become fully understandable, which veils the body before others. This is so not because the body is something inferior, which a man must be abashed of, but because it needs to be guarded.

The feeling of shame is inborn in man, even though it shows considerable differences in its expressions. It is kindred to conscience. In a certain sense it is an intimate part of conscience which protects man's self in the field of sex. Its existence even among races which go naked is shown by the fact that also these keep sexual activities out of sight of others. And as soon as foreigners direct their attention to the sexual organs, they cover themselves.[2]

The reactions of shame show differences according to age, sex and customs. What demands protective cautions for one person and in a particular situation, does not always demand

---

[1] Thomas Aquinas, S. Th. II-II, q. 144, a. 2.
[2] Cf. M. Müller, 1. c. 175f.

them for others. Feelings of sexual shame cannot be detected in children under five years. The awakening sense of shame first extends to the anal zone. Sexual shame in the proper sense makes itself only felt when the corresponding maturity of body and mind has been reached. In older age the sense of shame retrogresses again. The reason is that because of the reduced production of hormons the responsiveness to sexual incentives is lowered. Usually also the self-confidence of the spirit to dominate the passions has grown.

Differences likewise exist between the sexes. The sexual act of intercourse has a fundamentally different momentousness for the man and the woman. The man works outwards in the sexual act and is able to experience it as an incidental happening which is terminated with the act. The woman however experiences the act as an inroad into her self. The defloration signifies for her the end of a period of life and the beginning of a new one. She becomes a different being, not only bodily but also psychologically. The shrinking back from this inroad constitutes an important factor in the female sense of shame. Furthermore the woman feels a particular sexual stimulation in being passively looked at. The sense of shame therefore induces her to withdraw from intrusive looks and to cover her body before the man. On the other hand women among themselves shy from denudation less than men.

A very important role is played by customs and the social environment in the specific articulation of the innate sense of shame. Among some races denudation of the breast or even total nudity before the other sex do not cause feelings of shame. The reason is that nudity or a certain fashion which are customary in a region will ordinarily not provoke the sexual desire. On the other hand uncustomary denudation of the body or parts of it attracts attention and arouses the sexual passions. It is even true that the dressing of the body where it is not customary will stirr up the sexuality, while nudity does not. Hence the rules of modesty must always carefully take into consideration the particular conditions of time and place. But this relativity does not question the basic importance of such rules.

The significance of the sense of shame is fundamentally that of a protective instinct, built in by nature between a person and his fellowmen. It functions as a kind of brake when a person is sexually incited. The barriers of shame restrain the bodily desires. This prevents a too rapid diffusion of the libidinous agitation, which impairs the activity of the intellect. The sense of shame secures a person the possibility of deliberation and free decision, whether he must resist the sexual urge or whether he can or maybe should yield to it. Often it spontaneously blocks a rash, imprudent proceeding. Hence the sense of shame works as a guardian of the personal, intimate, sacred sphere.

The moral virtue which disposes a man to meet the demands of shame in the realm of sexuality is modesty. It is a readiness to keep away from all dangers rising against a person's sexual integrity from fancies, words and exterior demeanour. It provides an important protection for chastity and is its custodian.

Disregard of the sense of shame offends against the virtue of modesty. The offences may be mere imperfections, they may be venial sins, they can also at times constitute grave sins. This depends on the danger of impermissible sexual excitement and misguided actions which are to be feared for oneself, and on the provocation and scandal which is to be feared for others.

In the following some particular fields of modesty shall be mentioned. The guidelines laid down constitute prudential norms. They give orientation but cannot free from the obligation to personal examination of one's motives and to responsible investigation of the possible implications of one's action. Each one must also be responsive to the demands of his individual sense of modesty.

a) Conversation. Vulgar and off-colour talk on sexual matters is in conflict with the attitude of modesty and reverence for the source of life. "Immorality and all impurity or covetousness must not even be named among you, as is fitting among saints. Let there be no filthiness, nor silly talk, nor levity, which are not fitting" (Eph 5:3f). Nor may one speak of these matters in any and every group, particularly in mixed company. Conversations are unchaste and seriously sinful if they openly manifest the clear-cut consent to grave sins of impurity or, still worse, if they serve the purpose of seduction.

It is however not against modesty if married people give their total love for each other verbal expression. They are even advised not to silence their feelings of love, but to give them utterance in words. On the other hand exhibitionism of one's sexual and erotic experiences before third persons must be rejected as unbecoming. Men usually feel it as a betrayal of the marital secret if their wives talk with each other about their erotic life.

It causes damage to the marital love and makes the woman trivial, empty and banal.

b) Reading. Reading of pornographic literature is generally sinful, except when it is an object of study, which will not be a very frequent case. The right attitude of modesty will leave off reading as soon as one notices that the sense of decency is violated and that the brochure is a temptation to impurity. It must also be kept in mind that literature suitable and lawful for one group of people, e.g. married people, may be unsuitable for another one, e.g. those in the state of virginal chastity or unmarried people in general.

c) Theatre, radio, motion pictures and television. The indiscriminate use of these means of entertainment constitutes one of the principal hazards to modesty today. Anyone who goes to a movie theatre where immoral films are frequently shown sins against modesty, unless he first checks on the moral character of the film he is to see. Precautions must also be observed regarding radio and television programs, particularly where children share in this form of entertainment. The moral judgment must distinguish between the different ages and states of life. Performances which may have to be rejected for young or unmarried people, may be permissible for adult or married persons.

Christians must be concerned with the christianization of these tremendous sources of influence in the community. They will give voice to their convictions, be it by letters to those concerned or by signatures under protests and ·petitions or by membership in organizations destined to promote noble standards of morality (e.g. the American "Legion of Decency" established to advance good motion-picture entertainment).[1] Not least they will cast their votes only for those who have Christian principles at heart.

d) Looks. The woman in particular feels sexually stimulated by looks turned on her as a sexual being. It is therefore immodest to gaze in curiosity or much more so in erotic pleasure at the naked or indecently clad body of another person for a considerable time. This holds true especially of a person of the other sex to which one is not united by the bond

---

[1] Cf. Alfred P. Klausler: Censorship, Obscenity, and Sex. — St. Louis: Concordia Publishing House, 1967.

of marriage. If however the motive is reasonable and proper, there is no question of indecency or sin. Medical examination, for example, would constitute such a reasonable motive.

The portrayal or the contemplation of the naked in the art — insofar as it is really art and not pornography — is in principle not immodest. By means of the external presentation the artist wants to express a deeper reality, for example the marvel of creation or the beauty of the soul. The naked is not presented for the sake of sexual excitement, but for the sake of a spiritual value.

e) Touches. The normal person should be entirely unaffected in dealing with his own body in bathing, dressing, etc. Immodest would be the unnecessary trifling with one's sexual organs.

As regards the body of others, particularly those of the opposite sex, reverence and modesty demand great caution and tact. But when charity occasions and demands bodily contact (e.g. in the care of the sick), experience shows that normal people have nothing to fear. Obviously the signs of respect and affection customary in a region and in use towards members of the family are permitted and good. The question of touches and caresses shall still be studied more in detail farther below in the section on necking and petting.

Dances are in principle a lawful and also welcome means for the encounter of the sexes. They constitute an entertainment of a social and also aesthetic nature. Dances are suited to facilitate acquaintances among young people and to help them in the choice of a future marriage partner. Yet not all dances are equally acceptable. Some are calculated, in their entire nature, to excite the passions by the movements and the contact of the sexes as well as by the musical accompaniment. They must naturally be declined as immodest. It is to be remembered that such dances among primitive peoples are often the deliberate prelude to copulation.

However what holds for other areas of modesty also applies to dances, that originally provocative innovations can lose their offensive character once they become customary. The waltz is a known example for this. Initially not only Christian but also liberal critics opposed it as indecent and immoral, while now it is commonly accepted.

f)   Dressing and fashions. There is no objection to moderate beauty culture for women. God wanted them to have the wholesome desire of attractive cultivation of appearance. In accordance with reasonable customs they have the right to please by their dressing and fashion. They are also allowed to make use of such aids like powder, lipstick, rouge, dyed hair, etc., though in many cases the natural, unaffected beauty may be more refreshing.

In the moral judgment on the decency of dress and fashion one should bear in mind that no mathematical rules are possible concerning the slight or serious immodesty of a fashion. Too-short, low-necked and diaphanous clothing or scant bathing attire easily give scandal and lead to sins against chastity. In forming a judgment on fashions, the following rule is of special importance: "The latest modes, by the very fact that they are unusual, readily have an improper and exciting effect, whereas those of long standing appear less enticing even though they may offend the tender sense of modesty."[1]

Priests must insist that women at divine services or at Catholic gatherings appear in becoming garb. Yet the sacraments should be denied only if the scandal is really shocking. The preacher cannot fail to say a word occasionally against indecent dress. But he should be most cautious in his statements and avoid crude forms of criticism. Exhortations to feminine modesty must not fall prey to any dualism and appeal to an alleged inferiority of the body as against the spirit. Rather they must be motivated by the sense of reverence and protective care for the sphere of intimacy and the sacredness of one's person and body.

2.   *The virtue of chastity*

a)   Nature of the virtue

Chastity is the moral force which keeps order in the sphere of human sexuality. This order is deduced from the purpose and nature of sexual activity. "Man is duty bound either to use his sexual capacity in accordance with its character, or else to renounce it. If he acknowledges this duty without limitation, and if he seriously endeavours to reach the appropriate attitude in his thinking, speaking and actions, he lives in chastity."[2]

---

[1] B. Häring II, 1963, 490.

[2] Josef M. Reuss: Modern Catholic Sex Instruction. — Baltimore/Dublin: Helicon, 1964, 35.

In the past the virtue of chastity was often rather narrowly identified with continence and abstinence from unlawful sexual desires and pleasures. The essence of the virtue was seen in renunciations and denials. Presented in this negative light, chastity is not able to exert much attraction or to awaken much enthusiasm. It rather conjures the danger of being regarded as a cheerless, irksome burden.

Chastity is more than continence. It must be viewed in the light of the value which it is called upon to assert and to protect. It is an attitude of reverence for the mystery of life and for the personal dignity of the partner, who may not be abused in a selfish way, but who has a claim to protective love. Chastity shapes and orders the sexual powers in such a way that they are truly able to serve the human relation of conjugal partnership and the social need of the propagation of the community. "It neither disdains the sexual nor makes an absolute of it. To the very essence of the virtue belongs a reverence which penetrates to the very depth of the mystery of sex and which is nonetheless fortified against making it the ultimate and absolute."[1]

Unchastity naturally has to be defined in negative terms. But is must be kept in mind that chastity is more than avoidance of unchastity, just as fraternal love is more than avoidance of loveless actions. Unchaste is the unlawful use of one's sexual powers and the unlawful desire for it. But also a purely functional, biological approach to sexuality must be regarded as unchaste, because it isolates sexuality from the total context of human love. Sexual satisfaction may not be sought in a way which disregards man's character as a person and degrades him to the animal level. Even if performed within a legitimate marriage bond, such actuation of sexuality contradicts the ideal of chastity.

The early Church was much concerned about self-control in sexual life and valued the virtue of chastity highly. Our Lord requires chastity not only in deed but also in thought (Mt 5:28). He counsels the most perfect form of chastity: virginity for the sake of the kingdom of God (Mt 19:10-12). St. Paul repeatedly warns his Christians against the vices of unchastity, from which they should abstain themselves as those who belong to Christ (1 Cor 6:9-20; Gal 5:19-21; Eph 5:5; 1 Thess 4:3-8). He urges them to lead a chaste and pure life (Gal 5:23; 1 Tim 4:12; 5:2; Tit 2:5). Something more is required from the Christian than the civic morality of the Gentiles. "Each one of you should

---

[1] B. Häring III, 1966, 286.

know how to control his own body in holiness and honour, not in the passion of lust like heathen who do not know God" (1 Thess 4:4f).

Admittedly chastity is not the first of the virtues, as some presentations of piety and morality seemed to suggest. Our Lord as well as the apostles clearly and repeatedly singled out charity as the most important of all virtues. Unambiguously the law of love has been set up as the chief commandment under the new covenant. But it also remains true that after charity it was chastity that most distinguished the early Christians from their heathen neighbours.

The ideal of Christian chastity is a high one. Often enough it will not be a quiet possession for man, but an aim towards which he has to orientate himself again and again and to strive in patient endurance. A sincere aspiration and earnest moderation will keep the soul open to the values of chastity. If "the proper basic attitude is present and if it is constantly striven after, even with individual lapses, one can rightly speak of chastity; for the virtue is entirely lost only by an abandonment of the purpose or basic attitude."[1]

b) Questions of imputability

Sins against chastity are only possible after the sexual powers develop and the sexual urges awake, i.e. with the age of puberty. Children cannot commit sins of unchastity. There is the quite common phenomenon of infant manipulation of the genitals. It is often called infant masturbation, although of course no orgasm is possible. The term "masturbation" merely indicates a handling of the genitals for reasons of curiosity or perhaps for some sensual feelings. Especially in the years from three to six the young child shows curiosity about his sexual organs. His manipulations in no way involve guilt or sin. "It is generally unwise to call attention to the phenomenon by 'no—no's,' hand slapping, or threatening admonitions. Such concentration upon the genitals can only suggest to the child that this part of his body is less desirable, fearsome, or 'bad'. In other words, parents should be encouraged to ignore the masturbatory practices of their young children."[2]

After the sixth year the pronounced curiosity about the

---

[1] J. Gründel, art. "Sex" in: Sacramentum Mundi VI, 1970, 84.

[2] G. Hagmaier/R. Gleason: Counselling the Catholic. — New York: Sheed and Ward, 1964, 74f.

sexual organs usually recedes. Fears and worries about matters quite unrelated to sex may cause a child to trifle with his sexual organs (to "masturbate") between the years of six and puberty. "As in the case of the infant masturbator, it is useless and often harmful for a parent or counsellor to concentrate, by admonition and disapproval, on the habit itself. They should seek, rather, to determine the deeper causes and anxieties underlying the symptom."[1] If a child is excessively preoccupied with masturbation and becomes withdrawn and tense, psychiatric help may be necessary.

Reproaching children for unchaste conduct misses its mark, since they are ignorant of sexual excitements and pleasures. They likewise do not know sexual fantasies in the proper sense. Nevertheless the growing child slowly develops a sense of shame and can offend against it, although never gravely. In due time he should be trained to shun what offends against modesty. Not infrequent among children is playing the doctor, in which they mutually examine their sexual organs, or the playing of father and mother, in which they attempt and imitate sexual intercourse. This cannot simply be dismissed as a harmless joy in discoveries. If this happens repeatedly, a predisposition to relapses develops, which easily has fateful consequences in puberty. Children who are corrupt in this regard are a danger of seduction to others, especially to those who lack education. It is quite in place to warn children against this kind of indecency and to teach them the beauty of modesty.

From the age of puberty onwards a person is able to sin against chastity, and also to sin gravely. But especially in this realm offences against the right order not seldom stem from a considerable diminution of insight and free will. The reason is that the conditions of sexual tension inhibit the activity of the brain cortex, the seat of mental processes. Reflection is lessened and the usual caution is abandoned. Only after the sexual release from tension does the "fogging" of thought come to an end.

"Seen from this point of view, it becomes clear that an isolated judgment of individual acts is necessarily insufficient, that instead it is essentially a question of the person's total basic attitude and approach. He who seeks the right order of the sexual and is aware of the dynamism of these powers will not incautiously expose himself to the 'proximate occasion'. Where, however, in spite of earnest endeavour — in some cases because

---

[1] Ib. 75.

of previous failure — he is simply once again 'overcome', one should also be cautious with the assertion that the individual failure is a grave sin and in case of doubt decide 'pro reo'."[1]

Not every consent of the will is a fully free consent. Especially in the case of young people during puberty, that degree of maturity is often absent which is necessary for a fully imputable action. Most important is the question whether a person is letting himself be carried along by his sexual impulses without any real effort to control them, or whether he is seriously striving after the right ordering and integration of his sexual powers. A person who in full freedom takes to arbitrary gratification of his sensual and sexual desires without consideration for the consequences for his spiritual self and for others, who enjoys sexuality in a hedonistic way, and who is not ready to accept responsibility for his actions, adopts a fundamentally wrong attitude. If he does so knowingly and willingly, he sins gravely. But if in spite of his good will a person is not yet able to integrate his sexuality successfully, his shortcomings merit a milder judgment. In such instances encouragement is required rather than harsh reproaches.

II.   Sexual fantasies and impure thoughts[2]

Sexual fantasies are all images, mental pictures and day-dreams of an erotic nature, whether their contents are merely erotic sights, ways of dressing, touches, etc., or whether they are imaginations of complete sexual actuations. Psychologists assure that no one can avoid sexual fantasies altogether. They equally hold that a man must learn to control them.

Fantasy and imagery are a very important part of a person's psychic life and are crucial to smooth, successful conduct. Among others, fantasies are used to plan future behaviour, to decide on the reactions to prospective challenges and to anticipate responses to probable situations. They have a positive function in the psychological adjustment of a person and in the mastery of his sexual drives. This does not mean that one may plunge into elaborate daydreams. But a total suppression of all sexual fantasies does not lend itself as a sound solution either.

Traditional morality assumes that for a normal person there

---

[1] J. Gründel, art. "Sex" in: Sacramentum Mundi VI, 1970, 86.

[2] Cf. Robert P. O'Neil and Michael A. Donovan: Sexuality and Moral Responsibility. — Washington/Cleveland: Corpus Books, 1968, 81-97.

is a rather proximate danger of progression from flitting images to welcome fantasy to elaborated daydreams to sexual arousal to masturbation or sexual intercourse. Control of sexual behaviour therefore ought to begin with and concentrate on the first faint stirrings of fantasy. Otherwise the ability to resist temptation will be strongly weakened.

This view is however not shared by scholars of presentday psychology. What is known about wholesome adjustment of sexuality does not favour automatic rejection of fantasy as in the best interest of the person. Each fantasy must be considered on its merits. Indiscriminate repression is too simplistic a policy of conduct. A person must learn to accept normal erotic fantasies, i.e. to appreciate the sensual attraction and values which they entail, and to evaluate correctly when a fantasy must be declined as inadmissible.

For the moral evaluation of sexual fantasies two basic criteria have to be taken into account. Sexual fantasies may be objectionable either because of the intrinsic immorality of their contents or because of their intensity by which they result in sexual arousal. Furthermore different standards must be applied to the different states of life. The traditional distinction between two states of life only, the married and the single state, is not sufficient. More discerning differentiations are called for, namely between the dating youth, the engaged person, the married adult, and the celibate religious.

a) Sexual fantasies may be sinful because of a content which in principle is inadmissible. The deliberate enjoyment of actions in the imagination which are immoral because they are never admissible (e.g. adultery, incest, fornication, homosexuality), the approval of offences against chastity committed in the past or the regret at not having exploited the occasion, and most of all the desire to commit unchaste deeds are interior sins against chastity. Especially the serious desire to commit gravely sinful actions is gravely sinful itself and condemned by our Lord in express words: "Every one who looks at a woman lustfully (ad concupiscendam eam) has already committed adultery with her in his heart" (Mt 5:28).

If one excepts the "efficacious desire", i.e. the serious wish and intention to commit gravely unchaste actions, Catholics normally do not accuse their impure thoughts as grave sins or make further distinctions. The confessor need not insist on stricter norms. "We should not overlook the fact that mere sins of thought usually have less determination and intensity of will than external sins, and accordingly less malice."[1] The consent to the unchaste actions in these impure thoughts is still imperfect; otherwise it would develop into an efficacious desire. And even what sometimes seems to be an efficacious desire, often proves to be an imperfect consent in the concrete situation which would offer the possibility to translate the desire into action.

Nevertheless, even though unchaste thoughts are in most instances not grave sins, they are inordinate and sinful and must be shunned. What is plainly immoral should also not find acceptance in a person's imagination. Every sin first occurs in the mind before it is externalized. "For out of the heart come evil thoughts, murder, adultery, fornication, theft, false witness, slander. These are what defile a man" (Mt 15:19f).

b) Sexual fantasies may also be objectionable if they turn to be so intense that they cause sexual arousal. The reflections on the psychological significance of fantasies have shown that not every erotic imagination can automatically be considered as reprehensible and evil. Sexual fantasies are part of the psychic life and have a positive function. But a person must be able to control them.

Sexual fantasies must generally be dismissed before they reach the level of strong bodily excitation. Because in the state of sexual arousal the freedom of will becomes progressively impaired and the ability to control the sexual desires is increasingly diminished. Excitations however which result from sexual fantasies related to lawful conjugal love may be legitimate as long as they do not aim at solitary satisfaction.

"Obviously the person cannot make a responsible moral decision once passions are aroused, and this fact is what led to the traditional ban on the admitting of erotic thoughts and images at their very outset. However, the person can develop a habit of suppressing these fantasies before they reach a critical level of intensity and still allow the normal pleasurable fantasies to be enjoyed. The development of this type of conscious, habitual decision, based on the uniqueness of the person's arousal level and normal fantasy life, prevents the damming up of sexual tension that occurs when fantasies are suppressed or rejected the moment they appear."[2]

---

[1] B. Häring III, 1966, 298.

[2] O'Neil/Donovan, 1. c. 91.

As a rule it is an elaborated fantasy or daydream that produces sexual arousal, not a relatively short-lived image. The possibility of moral evil arises when a person, knowing his general level of response to fantasy through experience, continues to allow fantasies to cause sexual arousal that leads to complete sexual gratification. Sinful is the deliberate disregard of the limits which a person ought to set himself in his life of fantasy. The occasional lapse however by a person whose orientation is towards responsible sexual adjustment must be judged differently and milder. It is through experience and trial that a person must come to know his individual threshold of arousal and the point at which he ought to suppress a fantasy as inadmissible because it begins to escape the control of the mind.

c) Some distinctions are furthermore to be made for the different states of life. The unmarried person may lawfully reflect on erotic relations with a possible partner for life, coupled with a sense of appreciation for the divinely willed values inherent in sexuality. These thoughts are neither unchaste nor immodest. This holds true especially for the young dating person. Dating activities will give rise to sexual fantasies, and that is normal. The person who is at a dating age must include the sexual aspect in his evaluation of the other and in the mutual relationship, since this belongs to the essence of the community for life which is to be tested and ultimately intended. Still wider must be the moral boundary line for sexual fantasies of the engaged. From the beginning the person who is going to marry must be aware that sexual fantasies are a normal aspect of conjugal life, although — as in everything else — overindulgence in them can lead to problems.

For the married person sexual fantasies constitute an integral part of conjugal love. "Generally, sexual fantasies are able to stimulate a sexual relationship and can keep it from becoming dull or mechanical. If sexuality in a marriage is limited to intercourse, it loses its integral character; and it is only a short step to misunderstandings, sexual rejections, or merely physical coupling. It is unfortunate that so many married persons still apply moral standards of the single life to their sexual fantasies."[1] Fantasies concerning the conjugal relations of married people enrich the expression of their mutual love and enhance enjoyment. They should be encouraged.

---

[1] Ib. 93.

There also exist misconceptions among many married people concerning the kind of fantasies which are normal and permissible. Changes of position in intercourse or certain intimacies by touches are considered as deviations by them, but wrongly so. "In reality, sexual deviation is limited to activities in which the object is inappropriate, that is, activities which take the place of sexual intercourse. Generally, if any sexual activity is in the nature of foreplay, serving to arouse desire and ending in sexual intercourse, it is not deviant but normal. Common examples include variations in position and kissing parts of the body other than the mouth. Fantasies of these activities, therefore, are also normal, not evidence of a warped mind."[1] Naturally married people must show consideration for each other's feelings and not demand from the other what is repulsive to him.

As to those finally who have definitively decided to dedicate their life in celibacy to God, they must apply stricter norms for their fantasy life. They will have to abstain from reflections on relations which cannot find fulfillment in this state of life. In order to achieve this, the religious person will have to develop a strong habit of sublimation. This presupposes a high level of psychosexual development, great vigilance and self-denying effort on his part.

On the other hand many religious come in constant contact with the opposite sex, due to their pastoral and charitable work. They must be able to encounter the other sex not in stiff rigour or impersonal neutrality, but in natural ease and sincere sympathy. This supposes that they come to terms with their sexuality and do not have to fear it. Ideally the religious or priest should have been able to confront and to value the challenges of erotic and sexual love before the final commitment to his vocation. This is not possible without some experience of the sexual attraction at least in fantasy. Many troubles of religious celibates in the realm of sexuality seem to result from a lack of frank confrontation with it, which again has been impeded by an unhealthy fear of all sexual imaginations and their rigorous suppression. Those who make the final commitment to the celibate life of a religious vocation must at least possess so much emotional knowledge of the values of sexual love that they are enabled to make a basic choice and judicious option for a state of life which implies a total renunciation of sexual love.

---

[1] Ib. 91f.

III. Moral perspectives of masturbation

Masturbation or pollution is complete sexual satisfaction (orgasm) either obtained by some form of self-stimulation or procured by immodest actions with the other sex, exclusive of sexual intercourse. Mostly however the term masturbation designates sexual gratification by self-stimulation, which is also the more frequent form. It is also called self-abuse, the solitary sin, ipsation. Orgasm is usually brought about by manipulation or friction of the genitals (therefore the term "masturbation"); but it can also be procured by sexual fantasies, desires and touches of another person. The term onanism, which is likewise sometimes used, refers rather to unlawful avoidance of conception in the sexual union of married people.

1. *Occurrence, causes and effects*

According to the general estimate of studies on the subject, about ninety percent of boys and fifty percent of girls masturbate once or more than once during adolescence. The average fifteen-year-old boy may masturbate two or three times a week, and the habit may continue from a few months to four or five years. Nevertheless between fifteen and twenty percent of boys and more than fifty percent of girls pass through their adolescent years without falling into the habit. They never or seldom masturbate. This fact is often too readily ignored at present. "Contrary to what some psychologists would have us believe, those boys who never or seldom masturbate do attain to a healthy maturity,"[1] which of course also holds good for girls.

Although the age of onset varies, masturbatory practices are frequent already during the years from ten to twelve. It might be wise therefore to instruct the youths of this age group on the moral dangers and responsibilities in this regard. Above all they should be given sufficient knowledge about the reality of sex and its true meaning.

Puberty by its very nature presents an imperious invitation to masturbate. The awakening of the sexual drive tempts the adolescent to try the feelings of pleasure and to experiment with them. He is still ignorant of the mechanism of sexual fantasies, sexual arousal and orgasm, and has to wrestle to control his

---

[1] Eugene J. Weitzel: Masturbation: Some Practical Considerations; in: Contemporary Pastoral Counseling, ed. by the author. — New York: The Bruce Publishing Co., 1969, 83.

sexual wishes and impulses. Incitements by fellow teen-agers and by modern civilization with its load of sex symbols in the mass media do their share to add to the provocations. Adolescent masturbation is therefore a rather universal phase of psychosexual development. It ought not to be an object of grave preoccupation or fear.

About twenty percent of those who practise masturbation during adolescence continue with it in adulthood. Although this is a more serious matter than adolescent masturbation, it is wrong to conclude that adult masturbation is, for the large majority of cases, a sign of a pathologic personality. "There is good reason to contend that the vast number of unmarried adults who masturbate do so primarily because they are presently deprived of sexual intercourse with persons of the opposite sex."[1] The same holds for those married people who practise masturbation because it is difficult or impossible for them to have normal marital relations, e.g. on account of advanced pregnancy, serious illness of the partner, the use of the rhythm method, military service or other employment that takes the husband away from the home for extended periods of time, separation through imprisonment, etc. They find themselves in the same situation as the unmarried adult.

There are doubtless also instances of habitual masturbation which are indicative of pathology. This is certainly the case when masturbation is preferred by adults to normal heterosexual intercourse. Ipsation may also be a means to relieve sexual tension denied any other outlet because of neurotic inhibitions or latent homosexuality. These types of habitual and compulsive masturbation are however rather the symptom of a neurotic conflict than its cause. They require treatment by a psychotherapist.

In the past, popular belief and medical studies have attributed many physical and mental disorders to masturbation. But such contentions are unfounded. Masturbation is not physiologically harmful. No sickness can be traced back to it. There are some effects of minor importance which are brought in relation to masturbation, such as symptoms of bodily exhaustion, pains in the region of the loins, loss of appetite, loss of sleep, lessening of attentiveness and of memory. But they do not assume dangerous proportions.[2]

[1] Ib. 81.
[2] Cf. Eugene Weitzel, l. c. 80.

The emotional and psychological effects are not too serious either, although such effects are not totally absent. The unreal character of the sexual situation in ipsation calls forth a feeling of inadequacy of such satisfaction. The sensual and erotic aspects of sexual love cannot unfold. The gratification of the libido is restricted to the imagination and to the genital actuation. Frequently feelings of depression and guilt follow upon the act itself. They tend to be the stronger the more ipsation stands in discrepancy to the developmental stage of the growing or adult person.

Masturbation which becomes habitual leans to emphasize the sexus at the expense of the eros. This in turn is easily linked with a growing introversion and preoccupation with oneself, instead of an increasing opening to the outside world and a concern for others. "Definitely, therefore, one can regard the flight from responsibility and an increasing inability to aspire to the realization of the highest values in life as a danger. This aspect leads us back to the problem of narcism."[1]

People who enter marriage with such a frame of mind see themselves handicapped in the development of a personal, dedicated love. This has negative repercussions on the harmony and happiness of the married couple and their family. Even though these effects are usually not of a very serious nature, they can nevertheless not be ignored.

2. *Moral evaluation*

Psychology considers masturbation as a passing phase of life on the way from childhood to the adult age. Under this aspect masturbation is the expression of a still immature personality. If not overcome in due time and if continued in a habitual way, psychologists are inclined to suspect emotional conflicts, inability to give sex and love their proper place in healthy emotional living, or some similar disturbance.

The inner reason for the defectiveness and disorder of masturbation lies in this that the sexual power is used in a way not intended by the Creator. The basic purpose of sexual activity is the procreation of offspring and the expression as well as fostering of mutual love between husband and wife in the service of their family life. This double end of sexual activity is

---

[1] André Alsteens: Tabu im Reifungsprozess. Masturbation — Symptom oder Vergehen? — Luzern/München: Rex-Verlag 1969, 92; cf. pp. 88-92.

frustrated in the solitary practice of masturbation. The true, proper meaning of sexual activity is not realized. With this conclusion from the nature of sexuality agree the emotional and psychological effects of masturbation outlined above: the experience of the inadequacy of this satisfaction, the feelings of depression, and the impairment of an outgoing, personal love.

Holy Scriptures do not contain any express condemnation of masturbation. The word *malakoì* in 1 Cor 6:9 has sometimes been translated with masturbators. The text has then been quoted as a condemnation of masturbation, since the *malakoì* are listed among the sinners who are excluded from the kingdom of heaven. However this translation is no longer upheld. *Malakoì* literally means the soft or effeminate, and in this context it most likely signifies the passive party in homosexual relations.

Yet there is a very strong and common theological tradition of old which considers masturbation objectively as gravely sinful. This tradition is naturally also reflected in some utterances of the magisterium of the Church. Its documents refer to masturbation as an abomination and qualify it as an intrinsic violation of the moral order.[1] The recent Declaration on Sexual Ethics by the S. Congregation for the Doctrine of Faith expressly states that this act is a grave disorder.[2]

The reason given by the Declaration why masturbation must be considered a grave disorder is the following: "Whatever the motive for acting in this way, the deliberate use of the sexual faculty outside normal conjugal relations essentially contradicts the finality of the faculty. For it lacks the sexual relationship which realizes 'the full sense of mutual self-giving and human

---

[1] The ruling of Leo IX on the admission to the sacred orders includes masturbation in a group of sexual offences which he calls abominations (DS 688). But neither this declaration nor the condemnations of Alexander VII (DS 2044) and Innocent XI (DS 2149) contain clear statements that masturbation is always objectively gravely sinful.

July 24, 1929, the Holy Office declared that it is not permitted to obtain semen for the scientific detection of the contagious disease gonorrhea by means of direct masturbation (DS 3684). The negative decision certainly presupposes that direct masturbation is always sinful, but it does not say that it is always *gravely* sinful. Likewise Pius XII declares that it is illicit to procure semen for any kind of examination by means of masturbation (AAS 45, 1953, 678). In a later allocution, which discusses the issue of masturbation in more general terms, he states that direct masturbation for whatever reasons is always an intrinsic violation of the moral order (AAS 48, 1956, 472f). But in all these declarations the qualification "gravely sinful" is not used.

[2] Declaration of Dec. 29, 1975, nr. 9.

procreation in the context of true love' (GS 51). All deliberate exercise of sexuality must be reserved to this regular relationship."[1]

The qualification of masturbation as objectively a grave sin was the common doctrine of moral theologians up to the present time. Nevertheless theologians of the last decades with ever increasing emphasis pointed out that, particularly in the case of this sin, freedom is very often and for various reasons considerably diminished. Masturbation was regarded as gravely sinful only if one deliberately sought out the temptation or the occasion for self-abuse; or if there were no resistance against a temptation which comes unsought for, in spite of clear insight and full freedom of the will. Insight and will may be impaired, e.g., by pre-sleep or half-sleep conditions, by initial inadvertence due to some deflecting, critical situation, by strong emotional stress, or by a deep-rooted habit. The judgment more and more prevailed that at least subjectively masturbation is more often a venial than a mortal sin.

On the basis of these considerations the counsellor and confessor was helped by the following, practical guideline to judge the gravity of an act of masturbation: "If a penitent is making serious efforts to lead a life pleasing to God; if he is sincerely trying to overcome this habit and avoid the individual acts; if he avoids the occasions that are avoidable, frequents the sacraments and is constant in prayer; and especially if on the individual occasion when temptation comes he does not yield except after a long struggle or a hard one — the confessor should be lenient in judging the case."[2]

The recent Declaration of the S. Congr. for the Doctrine of Faith in principle agrees with this more differentiated approach. But it cautions that "the absence of serious responsibility must not be presumed; this would be to misunderstand people's moral capacity."[3]

In the course of the general re-examination and critical revision of theology after Vatican Council II, however, more and more voices made themselves heard who feel that masturbation is also objectively not so grave a matter that the qualification "grave sin" could be regarded as adequate. They judge that

---

[1] L. c. nr. 9.

[2] John C. Ford: Autosexuality. Moral Aspects; in: Personality and Sexual Problems, ed. by W. Bier. — New York: Fordham University Press, 1965, 224f.

[3] L. c. nr. 9.

masturbation is also objectively not more than a venial sin, at least in principle. This point of view has been expressed by Robert P. O'Neil and Michael A. Donovan[1], Eugene J. Weitzel[2], Charles E. Curran[3], John F. Dedek[4], Felix M. Podimattam[5], and François Reckinger.[6] Doubts about the grave sinfulness of the act are raised by L. Rossi.[7]

According to these theologians the arguments raised against masturbation prove indeed that it is a moral disorder. But they do not equally prove that the disorder is of a gravely sinful nature. Masturbation, it has been said, contradicts the finality of the sexual faculty. This is true. But lying contradicts the finality of the faculty of speech too. And yet it is not considered gravely sinful for that reason. It has always been rated as a venial sin only, unless aggravating circumstances occur. Guilt is to be proven, not to be presumed. Reason can pinpoint certain negative effects of masturbation. But they are not of such a serious nature that they could justify the qualification "gravely sinful".[8]

---

[1] O'Neil/Donovan: Sexuality and Moral Responsibility. — Washington/Cleveland: Corpus Books, 1968, 107f; 110.

[2] E. Weitzel: Masturbation: Some Practical Considerations; in: Contemporary Pastoral Counseling. — New York: The Bruce Publishing Co., 1969, 91; but confer also 99 and 102.

[3] C. Curran: Contemporary Problems in Moral Theology. — Notre Dame, Ind.: Fides Publishers, 1970, 175f.

[4] J. Dedek: Contemporary Sexual Morality. — New York: Sheed and Ward, 1971, 60f. The author explains: "I think that it is fair to say that it is very unlikely that anyone changes his fundamental option two or three times a week. One can presume that the average adolescent who has a fairly deep-rooted habit of masturbation is not guilty of mortal sin in every act. Each case, of course, must be judged in its own circumstances, but I think that this presumption is valid and can be acted upon in almost all cases. This does not mean that there is no culpability and no sin, only that it is not mortal" (ib. 64).

[5] F. Podimattam: A Difficult Problem in Chastity: Masturbation. — Bangalore: Asian Trading Corp., 1973, 2nd ed., 153-180. The author offers a very clear and most comprehensive study on the question from the moral and pastoral point of view. His book was very favourably accepted in the Indian Church.

[6] F. Reckinger: Wird man morgen wieder beichten? — Kevelaer: Butzon und Bercker, 1974, 113-120.

[7] L. Rossi, art. "Masturbazione", in: Dizionario enciclopedico di teologia morale (Roma: Ed. Paoline, 1981), 619f.

[8] "An adolescent should feel remorse for acts of masturbation, just as he or she should for indulging in any potentially bad-habit forming activity, such as cheating or reckless driving" (O'Neil/Donovan, 1. c. 110).

It is also advanced that an act which is so frequent, and statistically and psychologically the norm during the adolescent years, establishes a presumption against mortal sin.[1]

The possibility of a grave sin is however not excluded altogether by these theologians. If a person does in no way care to resist his urges to masturbation, he exposes himself to grave sin. That is, if a habit of masturbation causes an attitude of severe self-centredness, or if it seriously impairs a person's ability to self-giving and conjugal love, one would have to consider it as gravely sinful.

However the Congr. for the Doctrine of Faith disagrees with such a conclusion, certainly in conformity with a long-standing tradition of the Church. It judges that every directly willed act of masturbation is objectively a grave sin. The same judgement is once again expressed in the document on sexual education, issued 1983 by the Congr. for Catholic Education. But it likewise advises educators that "it is necessary to be cautious in evaluating the subjective responsibility of the person. In order that the adolescent be helped to feel accepted in a communion of charity and freed from self-enclosure, the teacher 'should undramatise masturbation and not reduce his or her esteem and benevolence for the pupil'. The teacher will help the pupil towards social integration, to be open and interested in others, to be able to be free from this form of autoeroticism, advancing towards self-giving love, proper to mature affectivity; at the same time, the teacher will encourage the pupil to have recourse to the recommended means of christian asceticism, such as prayer and the sacraments, and to be involved in works of justice and charity".[1]

A special thought must still be given to the need of confession at the reception of the Eucharist. The fact that masturbation is at least subjectively often only venially sinful, raises the question whether it is still necessary to go to confession before receiving Holy Communion in each case. To be logical one would have to admit that there is no such strict obligation, if it is reasonably certain that no mortal sin has been committed. Presuppose a penitent displays good will, sincerely strives to live a good Christian life and regularly avails himself of the sacraments,

---

[1] Congr. for Catholic Education: Educational guidance in human love. Outline for sex education. Rome, 1983, no. 99f.

the confessor has reason to assume that not every act of masturbation is a mortal sin for him. He can allow him to receive Holy Communion without confessing after every individual lapse. The penitent should however also be advised that his problem with masturbation is a serious challenge to his growth and demands in response a serious effort on his part to rid himself of these acts.[1]

Nevertheless the frequent and regular approach to the sacrament of penance is strongly to be recommended. Every person addicted to masturbation must maintain and build up the sincere will to be chaste. That is why reception of the sacraments is usually all important, including the regular reception of the sacrament of penance.[2]

Note: Spontaneous, nocturnal emissions are not sinful at all. The adolescent should be taught in due time to look upon them without any anxiety or scruple as something quite natural. It is difficult to see that in such cases it should be venial sin if some "pleasure is experienced while half awake", as moral theologians sometimes teach,[3] since this pleasure is simply a spontaneous result of natural proceedings.

It is lawful to perform actions which not by their nature but only due to one's particular excitability easily provoke pollution, such as bathing, riding, or other kinds of sport (indirectly voluntary pollution).

IV.   Encounter of the sexes

1.   *Genuine growth in human love*

Integration of sexual love within the love of agape

There is no doubt that man and woman instinctively gravitate towards each other on account of the sexual drive. But sexual union entirely based on this instinctive drive is not a complete human love. Besides and even prior to the expressions of sexual love the relationship of the sexes must be a personal encounter

---

[1] Cf. J. Dedek: Contemporary Sexual Morality. — New York: Sheed and Ward, 1971, 65; and B. Häring: Shalom: Peace. The Sacrament of Reconciliation. — Garden City, N.Y.: Doubleday (Image Books), 1969, 232.

[2] A very helpful orientation for the pastoral guidance of persons who suffer from the problem of masturbation is given in the book of George Hagmaier/Robert Gleason: Counselling the Catholic.—New York: Sheed and Ward, 1964, 73-93.

[3] E. g. H. Jone, 1963, nr. 229.

of mutual reverence and charitable concern. The great commandment of love also applies to the domain of sexuality. Sexual affection needs illumination and guidance by the self-forgetful love of Christian agape.

"Sex and eros find in agape their personal and religious integration and meaning. The testimonies of revelation proclaim that human love must be essentially characterized by altruism. Hence an egocentric, narcissistic love is radically condemned by Christianity. Every erotic and sexual love which does not have the backing of the total person, which is therefore not prepared to take on responsibility and obligations, cannot be regarded as genuine love."[1] The egocentrism which regards the partner simply as an object of one's own satisfaction or which does not see sexuality in its social aspect is clearly wrong.

Sexual love and Christian agape are however not entirely separate realities. Human sexuality possesses an immanent bent towards the loving devotion to the other, which wants to care, to serve, to protect. This loving care must be gradually developed in the boys and girls who are growing up, and continuously increased as the mutual companionship grows closer.

Maturing in love during the years of adolescence

Boys and girls must first mature in their own characteristic manner in order to become real men and women. This recommends a separate education and schooling in the years of puberty and early adolescence, as has been mentioned earlier. But they must also little by little learn to encounter each other in an amicable, courteous way and in mutual regard. Such encounters take place in the wider circle of the family and its friends, leisure time, youth organizations, the places of employment and advanced education.

"The young person must learn to meet people of the other sex in a fair way, without sexual provocation. It is necessary that he gets to know the individuality of the other sex in order that he gradually comes to a deliberate choice of the partner for his future marriage or can consciously decide himself for the renunciation of marriage. Though the danger exists that these encounters get into sexual intimacy and a premature commitment, it is not correct to reject or to leap over this necessary stage of

---

[1] J. Gründel, art. "Sex" in: Sacramentum Mundi, vol. VI, 1970, 83.

maturing in the human ability to love."[1]

Parents, priests and teachers should not be overwhelmed by their knowledge of bad experiences here and there. They should rather create good opportunities for proper encounters between boys and girls. It is a great help for the healthy development of the young people if boys and girls can meet within their families in fellowship with their parents. Well-organized dances are another means to foster proper relationship between boys and girls. Here they can learn to meet without losing themselves. However young people should be somewhat more developed for this form of encounter, i.e. girls should be beyond the age of sixteen and boys beyond the age of seventeen.

"During the time when boys and girls become infatuated with one another, they must be helped to be happy in this affection from the bottom of their hearts. Such an encounter should neither be considered nor described as a necessary evil, or as an opportunity to sin. Young people should be told how beautiful such encounters can be, and what they can do to allow them to remain beautiful. This occurs when the affection of being infatuated grows into the affection of love. But boys and girls must learn to be good to each other for the sake of the 'you' they love. This means that a young man and a young woman must learn to protect one another."[2]

Since the maturing process in the love of the sexes is slow, it needs time. As much as the young people "may feel urged to express their affection for each other in a more sensitive manner, caresses do not belong to their form of companionship. Caresses are only for those young people who are testing themselves seriously, in order to determine whether they want to remain together and grow together in the exclusive companionship of marriage."[3] Too early a solid bond places an adverse effect on the maturity of the young person, and its later dissolution may have tragic consequences for the girl.

There exist many pressures today which invite early and unrestrained enjoyment of sexual pleasure. They make little of self-control, maturing in love and pre-marital chastity. The representatives of sexual freedom boost their playboy mentality, even though they cannot show the fruits of maturer personalities

1 Hirtenbrief der deutschen Bischöfe zu Fragen der menschlichen Geschlechtlichkeit. — Herder Korrespondenz 27 (1973), 339.

2 Josef M. Reuss: Modern Catholic Sex Instruction. — Baltimore/Dublin: Helicon, 1964, 64f.

3 Ib. 65.

and of more stable or happier families. The youth who does not want to be infected by the sexualized public atmosphere urgently needs the courage to be different. Anyone who will go along with all possible programs and presentations of sexual nature and who indiscriminately takes to every reading matter cannot succeed in the mastering of sexuality and in the growing up in a mature love. Association with others who are likewise striving for a clean and decent attitude, especially in Christian youth organizations, is an important aid to achieve this goal. And it is also to be observed that there are more boys and girls who earnestly strive to live their youth in a pure and responsible way than the loud voices of sexual licentiousness make believe.

When a young man and a young woman have learned to love each other so that they think of matrimony, they have the right to express their love in more affectionate ways. The embrace and the kiss are for the engaged couple justified expressions of their love. But they should not forget that their deepest happiness lies in the protection rather than in the possession of each other.

Agape as sustaining force in conjugal love

Devoted love finally must be the sustaining force where married people encounter each other because they desire to have a child, or because they want to give themselves to each other in mutual affection. Certainly husband and wife are fully entitled to be unreservedly happy in their bodily affection and sexual love for each other. No reservations and misgivings should be allowed to affect the deep gladness and blissful rapture of their mutual self-giving in conjugal love. But this happiness is not contradicted, it is rather supported by the demand that sexual love ought to be embedded in the more comprehensive, more lasting love of self-forgetful agape.

"For the personal meeting of bodies to be an encounter in love, a man and woman must respond to each other selflessly. The more they do this, the more and deeper happiness will sexual pleasure bring them. Purely drive-conditioned mating, on the other hand, permits indulgence in sexual pleasure, but does not result in genuine happiness."[1] Husband and wife will generally not be able to realize their mutual love in its perfect form from the very beginning. They have to mature towards the consummation of their love in patient endeavour. Yet the goal of the perfection of love should never be lost sight of.

---

[1] J. Reuss, 1. c. 43.

Christian agape as the soul of virginity

From the first beginnings of Christianity there have been many men and women who in the fellowship of Christ remained unmarried "for the sake of the kingdom of heaven" (Mt 19:12). This exclusive dedication to the direct service and love of God is meant when Catholic theology speaks of virginity. Virginity also has its great importance for the service of one's fellowman. The virginal person becomes free to serve his neighbour, whether this be in the priestly service for the salvation of the world, or the charitable service for the welfare of the ill and weak. Beyond this, in a time that lives so much only for temporal comfort and happiness, the virginal person provides an immensely valuable testimony to the truth that man does not find the ultimate fulfillment of his life in this world, but that he is called to a greater life in communion with God.

Also in the state of virginity man does not become a-sexual, as little as in any other form of celibacy, whether voluntary or involuntary. "He remains developed in his personality as a male or female person who, quite naturally, keeps an innate desire for fully human companionship with a partner of the opposite sex. If the unmarried person is not to become an egotistic bachelor or an embittered spinster, he must go a step beyond himself in his acceptance of God and in service to his fellow man. This enables him to carry abstention from the desired loving companionship between man and woman without distortion or damage (celibacy hurts, regardless of whether it is voluntary or involuntary)."[1] Only in the selfless, devoted love of agape can celibacy be mastered and become fruitful.[2]

2. Necking and petting

The question arises which expressions of affection or erotic and sexual love are meaningful and therefore justified before, outside of and on the way to marriage. Different rules ought to

---

[1] Ib. 44f.

[2] A virginal life, properly lived, has no detrimental effects on the full maturity of the person. It may be true that man and woman can reach human maturity in marriage more readily. Anyone who follows the call to virginity has·a harder time of it. But ultimately it is not the question of marriage or virginity that is decisive in the maturing of a personality. Fundamentally it is the question of a person's calling to which he must respond, and of his faithful, devoted service to the task which has been appointed to him in the service of the greater intents of God.

be applied to the single and as yet uncommitted person, to engaged couples, and to the celibate religious.

From the very beginning however an important caution is in place. Cultural customs and usages play a weighty role in the forms the encounter of the sexes take. What may be admissible and inoffensive in one culture, may be scandalous and an occasion to sin in another. The standards of the Western World cannot simply be transferred to the cultural conditions of Africa or Asia. Especially priests and educators have to be careful not to cause confusion and havoc among their people by the naive transference of behavioural norms from one culture to another. They must be sensitive to the differences in cultural patterns. What is admissible in the abstract and in principle, may be objectionable in the concrete and particular.

The manifestations of mutual affection are often covered by the terms necking and petting. They designate caresses and fondlings which range from hand-holding and kissing to genital contacts short of intercourse. The terms are often used interchangeably. But already the etymologic origin of the words indicates differences which are meaningful and worthwhile to note.

The term necking is derived from 'neck' and designates caresses of a lighter nature (above the 'neckline'), such as stroking of the hair, the usual forms of kissing, patting of the shoulder and the like. Complete bodily contact and strong sexual excitement are avoided. Petting on the other hand is derived from 'pet' (pet animal, lapdog, darling) and designates more intimate forms of caresses, such as hugging, embraces, or bodily contacts of a kind which ordinarily produce sexual arousal, especially in the man. It is obvious that the forms of necking can be admitted more readily as expressions of mutual affection than the caresses of petting.

The single person who is of dating age will have to tackle the problem of his relationship to the other sex in one way or another. He must learn to encounter it in a natural, appropriate manner. If he is not yet committed to any particular state of life or to any particular person through engagement, he will have to test himself and the partner in relationships of friendship. Because the sensual, erotic attraction is an essential component of marriage, some physical contacts such as hand-holding, dancing, kissing (though not in its passionate forms) and limited necking have a legitimate place in the dating acquaintance.

At this stage the manifestations of mutual liking should in

principle be confined to the level of mere affectionate expressions. There is no place yet for caresses of a sexual nature and erotic petting. "The limits of affectionate and sexual expression should be defined primarily in terms of the young man, since sexual arousal in women is more diffuse and emotional. A pattern of actions which regularly evokes an erection in the man is morally questionable."[1]

This does not mean that if a couple inadvertently go beyond this, they have already sinned, or if they yield with some negligence to the sexual inclinations, they have already sinned gravely. But it does mean that they have to make allowance for the danger and be more heedful in their love. "If on occasion a young man is sexually aroused, he need not feel that this is seriously sinful. His responsibility lies in changing the situation so that he does not fall into a pattern of overt sexual gratification. Human nature is such that an individual or couple cannot for long control sexual arousal at a level of partial gratification. Sexual arousal creates increasing tension that pushes toward complete gratification."[2]

Premature petting and sexual caresses prejudice the more mature and more difficult development of an integral love, which does not only feel in terms of eros and sexuality, but also of selfless concern and devoted friendship. There is moreover too much emotional preoccupation in a sexual relationship than to allow a sober, realistic evaluation of the partner as a possible companion for life. The actual dating practices have in fact often little to do with a preparation for marriage. Frequently they rather constitute a competition for greater popularity and prestige. The results of teenager petting and dating are by no means better marriages. Girls who have played the game of petting over several years, at times over a period of ten years before marriage, and who had always to withhold the total self-giving after the emotions had been aroused more or less to their peak, often suffer in their later marriage from frigidity. They are not capable of a complete sexual surrender. There is also the danger of a premature, total commitment at an age when young people are not yet able to enter a lasting bond of love with sufficient responsibility. It is therefore not surprising that the frequency of unsuccessful marriages and of divorce has not

---

[1] Robert O'Neil/Michael Donovan: Sexuality and Moral Responsibility. — Washington/Cleveland: Corpus Books, 1968, 139.

[2] O'Neil/Donovan, 1. c. 140.

decreased by means of the dating practice but rather increased.[1]

The period of free dating must have restraints, and the responsibility lies with both the man and the woman. "It has been a common mistake to place the greater part of the burden of premarital prudence upon the woman. The attitude often has been that the woman must set the limits of physical intimacy."[2] But this unduly reduces the responsibility of the man. Besides, the woman is generally much slower in sexual arousal and therefore not sufficiently in a position to draw the line of permissibility for the man as well. Without restraints it is too easy to confuse passion with lasting love, infatuation with commitment.

Different norms however apply once a couple has become engaged and decided to commit themselves to each other permanently. They have entered the period of immediate preparation for marriage, which entitles them to greater intimacies, as has always also been recognized by traditional moral theology. O'Neil/Donovan indicate three goals which ought to be achieved during this period. These goals also state the reasons why more intimate expressions of the mutual love are justified.

The first goal to be achieved "is the gradual unlearning of defenses and inhibitions built up over several years in the area of sexual attitudes and behavior. It is critical at this time that the couple abandon a 'do not touch' attitude that may have served to control impulses in the past." The formerly necessary controls can turn into an obstacle if they are carried over into the new condition of the married state. "Physical intimacies must be seen not as a tolerated weakness, but as a psychologically and morally necessary preparation for marriage."[3]

A second goal of the engagement time is the integration of the sexual aspect of love with its spiritual, personal dimension. Young men and women tend to separate their sexual inclinations from the more spiritual affections of esteem and admiration for the idealized person of their love. They place the beloved one on a pedestal and suppress sexual impulses towards this person. If the individual happens to have many good qualities, it often adds to the dichotomy. This attitude, which is characteristic of adolescence, must be replaced by the conviction that sexuality is an integral part of a love relationship. "This neces-

---

[1] Cf. Heinz Loduchowski: Teenager und Koedukation? Jugend der freien Welt in Gefahr. — Freiburg: Herder, 1964, 47-50.

[2] O'Neil/Donovan, 1. c. 140.

[3] Ib. 141.

sary integration cannot be achieved in a context of modesty appropriate for the celibate life. It needs reinforcement through demonstration that the idealized love object is indeed capable of expressing sexual feelings and that these feelings flow from love for the other person. Maturity of psychosexual development is achieved when this integration of the person-affectionate and the sexual aspects of love occurs."[1]

The third major goal is that of free communication in sexual matters. A couple needs to discuss all aspects of their current and future sexual relationship with each other. They must learn to understand their mutual emotions, reactions, anxieties, reserves and inclinations. The open discussion of these questions, which are of great concern for both partners and which are nevertheless so often silenced, is generally felt as liberating, removes wrong ideas about the other and false inhibitions, and contributes much to a mutual consonance.

3.   *The problem of premarital intercourse*

Premarital intercourse has always been regarded as sinful and gravely sinful by Christian ethics. On the other hand it is a rather frequent phenomenon. Even though statistics on sexual behaviour vary considerably on this issue and must be carefully read, one will have to admit that premarital intercourse does not occur only as an exception.[2] It cannot surprise that the

---

[1] Ib. 142.

[2] Surveys in the United States reveal that between 60 and 85 percent of the unmarried men experience premarital intercourse. (The average is higher for those who only attended grade school and lower for those with higher education.) For unmarried women the figures rate between 20 and 50 percent. (In their case, it is the other way round: the average is considerably lower for those who only attended grade school, while it is higher for women with advanced education.)

But it must be noted that these figures include all those who even only once experienced intercourse before marriage as well as those who are already engaged. Of the 50 percent of the women who had premarital intercourse according to Kinsey's interviews, one half experienced it only with the man they eventually married. Furthermore the statistics include both fervent and indifferent Christians, believers and unbelievers alike. Yet there is good reason to assume that the sexual attitudes of those who have strong Christian convictions are different from the attitudes of those who are lacking in faith.

Noteworthy is also a recent study which reveals that while 75 percent of college girls think that their classmates are sleeping around, only about 20 percent have themselves had intercourse (cf. John F. Dedek: Contemporary Sexual Morality.—New York: Sheed and Ward, 1971, 25f).

present critical re-examination of traditional sexual ethics concerns itself precisely also with this problem. Is premarital intercourse really always or even generally wrong and therefore faulty and sinful? Are not rather good reasons advanced in its favour? Which are the arguments that really speak against it?

The teaching of Holy Scripture

The Christian attitude towards premarital intercourse has been strongly determined by the decided rejection of all fornication on the part of the New Testament. Already the Old Testament strenuously combats sacral as well as secular prostitution (Lev 19:29; Deut 23:17f; Jer 5:7; Amos 2:7; Sir 9:6). It even orders that a young woman shall be stoned to death if the man who marries her finds that she is not a virgin anymore, "because she has wrought folly in Israel by playing the harlot in her father's house" (Deut 22:21). There is however especially for the man no general proscription of all premarital intercourse. Nevertheless later Jewish tradition tends to be more strict and extends the prohibition of *zenut* (sexual immorality of a heterosexual nature) to all fornication. "In later Rabbinic usage *zenut* applies not merely to all extra-marital intercourse but also to intercourse in marriages which run contrary to Rabbinic decisions."[1]

The New Testament categorically rejects all fornication (*porneía*) as opposed to the justice of the kingdom of God. "The NT is characterized by an unconditional repudiation of all extra-marital and unnatural intercourse."[2] Christ lists fornication together with adultery among the evil things which come from within a man's heart and defile him (Mt 15:19f; Mk 7:21-23). Repeated reprobations of sexual immorality and fornication occur in the letters of St. Paul. "It is noteworthy that he speaks much more often of unchastity or fornication (*porneía*) than of adultery (*moicheía*); probably because Christian demands went so much further than Stoic ethics. Frequenting of prostitutes and any kind of illegitimate satisfaction of desire is bound gravely to endanger the exclusive and close mystical relation of the Christian with the Lord (cf. 1 Cor. 6:17; 7:32ff.)."[3]

---

[1] Hauck/Schulz, art. porneía in: Theological Dictionary of the New Testament, ed. by G. Kittel and G. Friedrichs, vol. VI. — Grand Rapids, Mich.: Erdmans Publ. Co., 1968, 589.

[2] Ib. 590.

[3] Rudolf Schnackenburg: The Moral Teaching of the New Testament. — London: Burns and Oates, 1967, 298f.

The question must be asked whether Paul uses the concept fornication (*porneía*) in the same sense as it is used today, or whether it has a different, more limited meaning for him. In 1 Corinthians 5:1 he qualifies as *porneía* the incestuous union of a member of the community with his step-mother. And in 6:13-20 he speaks of association with a prostitute and thus seems to understand the term in the sense of prostitution.

In 1 Cor 7:2 on the other hand *porneía* has a wider meaning. Paul judges that it is well for a man not to touch a woman. But because of the temptation to *porneíai* each man should have his wife and each woman her husband. "In this context, the plural *porneíai* must be understood in a very general sense. It refers to all extra-marital activities."[1]

1 Thessalonians 4:3-8 equates fornication with the selfish lust of the pagans. "For this is the will of God, your sanctification, that you abstain from immorality (*porneía*); that each one of you know how to control his own body in holiness and honour, not in the passion of lust like heathen who do not know God." Paul condemns the sexual promiscuity and license so widely practised among the pagans. "As in 1 Cor 7:2, the word here takes a very general sense and refers to any possible kind of sexual license outside of the legitimate marriage."[2]

In the list of vices *porneía* regularly appears among the denounced sins (2 Cor 12:21; Gal 5:19; Eph 5:3-5; Col 3:5; Rev 9:21). But the simple enumerations do not permit any further conclusions as to the precise nature of the sin.[3]

Taking into consideration the totality of the texts, one will have to conclude that the New Testament probably condemns all extra-marital, sexual relations.[4] This agrees with the Jewish background of the New Testament writers, where all extra-marital

---

[1] A. Humbert: Les péchés de sexualité dans le Nouveau Testament; in: Studia Moralia VIII. — Roma: Academia Alfonsiana, 1970, 160.

[2] Ib. 162.

[3] In Acts 15:20 and 29 the term *porneía* has probably a special and more restricted meaning. The council of the apostles and elders decreed not to burden the pagan Christians with any demands of the Mosaic law except that they should abstain from what has been sacrificed to idols, from blood, from what is strangled and from unchastity. Exegetes observe that the things here forbidden seem to be four of the things proscribed by Lev 17-18: meat offered to idols (17:8f), the eating of blood (17:10-12), the eating of strangled animals (17:15) and intercourse with close kin (18:6-18). Against this background, *porneía* would refer to sexual union with certain degrees of kinship.

[4] Humbert, 1. c. 182.

intercourse was rejected. In this sense the New Testament was also understood by the early Church.

The doctrine of the magisterium

The magisterium of the Church has repeatedly expressed its conviction that premarital intercourse is a grave sin, although not by any infallible definition.

The thirteenth ecumenical council at Lyon under Innocent IV in 1245 decreed: "But concerning fornication, which an un-married person commits with another unmarried person, there is no doubt that it is a mortal sin, since the Apostle asserts that fornicators as well as adulterers are excluded from the kingdom of God (cf. 1 Cor 6:9f)."[1] Several condemnations of theological and moral errors by the magisterium state or at least clearly presuppose that extra-marital intercourse is sinful[2] and gravely sinful.[3] The recent Declaration on Sexual Ethics by the S. Congregation for the Doctrine of Faith once more reconfirms this position of the Church. "Sexual union is only legitimate if a definite community of life has been established between the man and the woman."[4]

The decisions reflect the universal doctrine of the Church, which has been taught by her at all times, and which up until now constitutes the practically unanimous opinion of Catholic theologians.[5] J. Gründel is right when he judges: "A change in the attitude of the Church so as to favour pre-marital intercourse is not to be expected; this would essentially mar the concept of marriage. The step to promiscuity would then be a minor one."[6]

---

1 DS 835.

2 DS 1367; 2148; Pius XI in Casti Connubii, AAS 22 (1930) 558f.

3 DS 897; 2045.

4 Declaration of Dec. 29, 1975, nr. 7.

5 The same attitude towards extra-marital intercourse was also adopted by the British Council of Churches. In 1966 it passed the fol-lowing resolution: "That the Council, while convinced that Christians must always show compassion to those who fall below the highest standards, and neither condemn nor condone, affirms as Christian the rule that sexual intercourse should be confined within the married state. It believes that the maintenance of this rule is in accordance with the will and purpose of God and that God's grace and strength are available to help all who seek to reach that demanding and rewarding standard" (Sex and Morality. A Report to the British Council of Churches October 1966. — London: SCM Press, 1966, p. 4).

6 J. Gründel, art. "Sex" in: Sacramentum Mundi, vol. VI, 1970, 77.

Arguments in support of premarital continence

Two of the arguments in defence of premarital continence are derived from the nature and purpose of sexual love. Premarital intercourse contradicts the very purpose of sexuality. Therefore it cannot be accepted as meaningful and proper. A third argument argues a posteriori. It shows that only a lasting marriage bond provides the conditions for a sexual relationship which is truly happy.

Sexual love has as one of its most fundamental purposes the propagation of mankind through procreation of children. This purpose is in principle undesirable and excluded in premarital and extra-marital intercourse. Intercourse and procreation are radically dissociated, which involves a distortion of human sexuality. Not that procreation and sexual union must always go together. But the absolute exclusion of one of the natural ends of intercourse breaks up the balance, meaning and unity of human sexuality.[1]

The close relation between the sexual act and procreation is shown by the fact that in spite of the effort to avoid pregnancy, nature often asserts itself nevertheless and a child is conceived all the same. This is a serious hazard especially for the child, but also for the couple themselves. For the child will not find the protection and security of a family, which he needs for a well-ordered up-bringing and a healthy education.

Even contraceptives are not an absolutely safe means to preclude the conception of a child. Their regular use and absolute efficiency is not always assured. "There are other related factors such as carelessness, suddenness of emotion and spontaneity, as well as some girls' conscious or unconscious desire to become pregnant. Therefore it is not too much of a surprise that Vance Packard's recent survey of college students reveals that while the fear of pregnancy has declined among young people the incidence of it has not."[2]

The traditional argument for premarital continence has therefore also today not lost its validity. Sexual intercourse is responsible only if it is performed by a couple who are able to

---

[1] Cf. R. F. Hettlinger: Living With Sex, SCM Press, 1967; quoted by Francis Manning: The Human Meaning of Sexual Pleasure and the Morality of Premarital Intercourse, Part III. — AmEcclRev 166 (1972) 311.

[2] John F. Dedek: Contemporary Sexual Morality. — New York: Sheed and Ward, 1971, 39.

secure the healthy education of a child, since the natural end of intercourse is the generation and education of children. And the proper education of a child can be guaranteed only within the permanent state of marriage (or its equivalent).[1]

This argument is completed by a second, which is derived from the other purpose of the sexual act, namely to give expression to the mutual love of the partners and to deepen it. Current theological literature generally gives preference to this second argument of a more personalistic nature. Sexual intercourse is a natural sign of a total gift of oneself, the culmination of a mutual relationship of love. Such a meaning is naturally inherent in this act, as explained earlier. Sexual intercourse which is not the sign and expression of true love, but mere tension reduction or even only exploitation of the other for the sake of bodily pleasure, falls short of its authentic meaning. It is a delusion and lie.[2]

The character of the sexual act as a unique, exclusive expression of love is confirmed by the manner how men spontaneously experience such relationships. Once a boy begins to feel a special, erotic affection for a girl, she "becomes singled out for a certain exclusive and possessive relationship. Other female acquaintances he may have are no longer on the same level. Consider the love songs of our culture, the poems, the popular music — in every man's heart there is a desire for the endurance, even the 'eternity', of this love. We cannot do much about the way we are made. There are strong reasons for believing that when a given sexual relationship contains the elements of exclusivity, possessiveness (without jealousy), and permanence it will bring happiness. Where one of these elements is missing or uncertain, it will engender destructive tension and unhappiness."[3] It can therefore not surprise that uncommitted extra-marital intercourse is not accompanied by a feeling of deep gratification and self-realization, but leaves a sense of incompleteness and malaise.

A limitation of sexual intercourse to marriage alone is finally also demanded by the preconditions which are necessary in order that man and woman can be unreservedly happy with

[1] Cf. J. Fuchs: De Castitate et Ordine Sexuali. — Roma: Università Gregoriana, 1960, 35.

[2] If sexual intercourse is less than the expression of a love that is total self-donation, "it is a lie, a betrayal of the genuine meaning of the sign and trivialization of the genuine meaning of human sexuality. But if it is not less, then it is what we mean when we say 'marriage'" (John Dedek, 1. c. 40).

[3] O'Neil/Donovan: Sexuality and Moral Responsibility. — Washington/Cleveland: Corpus Books, 1968, 131.

each other in their bodily love and union. Although the conditions taken individually do not constitute absolutely conclusive proofs for the inadmissibility of premarital intercourse, since a couple might also content itself with less ideal conditions and a lesser degree of common happiness, they nevertheless are indications of the inadequacy and deficiency of intercourse before or outside marriage.

In order to be entirely happy with each other a couple needs time. Under time pressure sexual love cannot sufficiently unfold. Every time limit disturbs. They equally need a room, a room for themselves where they will certainly not be disturbed. And the room must be comfortable for them. The narrowness of a car does not offer the necessary ease. Even a room in a hotel cannot be compared with a person's own dwelling. There must also be the possibility of a repetition of their togetherness. How can they be fully happy if they must fear that this might be the only or the last time for them to meet? They must be sure of each other and of their meeting again. Besides, true love desires more than only the togetherness of sexual intercourse. True love wants to share with the other his interests and ideas, his sorrows and joys. Even that the two can eat together is expression of their feelings of tenderness for each other. The conversation belongs to it, the movie, theatre, concert, dance, and similar things. Already before they actually meet, they have tender thoughts for the other. If two people are in love, they would like to share as much as possible with each other. In other words, the union of love and sexual self-giving wants to be a union of life. And in this total union of love also the wish for a child must find a legitimate place. Finally, even though the love of the sexes is a most personal matter, every couple ultimately wishes that people recognize their belonging together. Constant stealthiness and exclusiveness is not pleasant nor possible. Hence the couple which belongs together in love wants to be accepted in public. All these conditions make up the pre-requisites for a fully happy realization of sexual love. They are only fulfilled in the lasting, public bond of marriage.[1]

Objections

The demand of premarital continence is frequently attacked today as the product of a taboo-morality which is unreasonable

---

[1] Cf. Martin Goldstein: Anders als bei Schmetterlingen. Er und sie und ihre Liebe. — Jugenddienst-Verlag Wuppertal, 1967, 116-124.

and unwarranted. Several arguments are advanced against it. They require an examination.

A first argument asserts that the sexual drive needs its satisfaction as any other drive. Continence imposes an unnatural strain. And since in our present civilization the interval between sexual maturation and marriage is rather long, the natural and normal way to gratify the drive in this meantime is premarital intercourse. Evidence from psychopathology and psychotherapy is supposed to confirm that repression of sexual impulses is psychologically harmful.

The facts however do not support this contention. A great number of young people remain continent without damage to their psychological health. And is this not even a substantial majority? Because an occasional act of intercourse, e.g. during engagement time, cannot be counted as a shift to bridge the gap between maturation and marriage. One must indeed ask for evidence that those who do not engage in premarital intercourse experience more problems in interpersonal relations and in their future marriage than those who do; or whether not even the contrary is true.

A second argument contends that the partners must know whether they will truly match, also under the sexual aspect. This experience is to be gathered before the final marriage pledge and not afterwards, when a withdrawal from the bond is no longer possible.

But do people need to experiment by means of intercourse whether they really match? Such a necessity is certainly not given under the physiological aspect. The two always fit together, unless some malformation of the genitals has taken place. Of this the person thus affected would naturally have to inform the other. As to the psychological compatibility, it can sufficiently be tried by expressions of love and affection other than premarital intercourse. They have been mentioned earlier. Besides, for a gladsome, bodily experience of love it is necessary that the couple have played up to each other. This cannot be reached the first time or after a few times. To try out a few times does not permit a definite judgement re compatibility. Furthermore intercourse before marriage can never anticipate the conditions of conjugal love and therefore also not be a meaningful test of it. Being married cannot be tried out.

A third argument finally claims that the repression of sexual pleasure for the sake of an allegedly necessary premarital continence lacks justification. Man must be liberated from the oppression of moral taboos which deprive him of his legitimate fulfillment and happiness. What difference does it ultimately make whether a couple practises petting short of or even up to orgasm or whether they go all the way through to premarital intercourse? The real criterion for the immorality of any sexual act is whether "it hurts or exploits others". As long as this is not the case, it is lawful.[1]

This contention, that the ban on premarital intercourse is the unjustified oppression by an unenlightened taboo morality, is answered by the arguments which vindicate the traditional position. They have already been explained. Some remarks however shall still be added here. The promise of greater happiness from a liberated premarital sexuality is not verified by the facts. The longing for true happiness, loving companionship and personal reassurance is not fulfilled in premarital intercourse. The tragedy is that it is not a way out of frustration and loneliness, but rather a way into greater desolation. "For to use sex in this way, without lasting commitment, is to empty it of meaning and depth of affection, thereby surrendering even sexual love to the meaningless void, and becoming even more alone and alienated than ever."[2] In simply setting up "honesty" and "true love" alone as the norm for the lawful use of sexuality, young people are overtaxed. For it is perhaps nowhere more difficult to be honest with oneself and to know what true love demands than in the realm of sexual love. True love must not only take into consideration the immediate consequences, but also the more remote ones. And this is not even sufficiently done by the philosophers of the sexual liberation.

As to the equation of heavy petting with sexual intercourse, such a view appears too simplistic. Intercourse is the expression of the definite gift of oneself, but petting is not. A couple may engage in various types of passionate kissing and petting, but this does not reach the symbolic meaning of that most intimate bodily union which is intercourse. Moreover petting up to orgasm has never been considered by Christian morality as a rightful expression of affection among the sexes.

---

[1] Cf. J. Fletcher: Moral Responsibility. — London: SCM Press, 1967, 131; 134; 137f.

[2] Francis Manning: The Human Meaning of Sexual Pleasure and the Morality of Premarital Intercourse, Part III. — AmEcclRev 166 (1972), 316.

Some further considerations and clarifications

A distinction has been made between premarital and pre-ceremonial intercourse. The distinction means that if for a couple intercourse is really the expression of the fact that their lives are united and if they are now willing to accept all that is entailed in the sexual act, then they are in the moral sense already married, even though their union is not legalized by any official ceremony. The sexual act of intercourse is in this case preceremonial but not premarital.[1]

But the question must be asked whether preceremonial inter-course will really do good to the couple and whether it will really contribute to strengthen their union. If they deceive them-selves, the opposite may become true: Premature intercourse may weaken and even destroy the bond that unites them. Sexual acts are expression of a relationship of love, not its cause. Hence the love they express must have grown and matured prior to the sexual actuation. Premature sexual acts can cripple and cut short the full development of love. On the other hand a love that can wait with its genital expression until the moment of marriage is the surest proof for a couple that they do not merely desire sexual gratification from each other, but that their sexual need for one another is really subordinate to their love.

For the sake of the greater strength of their love and of a convincing proof of their sincerity, a couple ought to avoid pre-marital intercourse. "Before marriage a couple must grow in their love for each other in a physical as well as psychological way, but they must not have intercourse. This will result in considerable tension. This tension, far from being harmful, is the most important element in the development of sexual love. It must not be avoided — it should be anticipated and even encouraged. Tension, contrary to some popular misconceptions, is not a bad thing. Some tensions are creative. To eliminate all tension is to eliminate all human striving, growth, and accomplish-ment. We want to say that the tension resulting from the denial of complete sexual gratification before marriage is the only effective means of establishing the foundation of mutual trust essential to the future of the marriage and also of forcing the love relationship to expand itself into all the other dimensions."[2]

---

[1] Cf. Paul Ramsey: A Christian Approach to the Question of Sexual Relations Outside of Marriage. — The Journal of Religion 45 (1965), 100-118.

[2] O'Neil/Donovan: Sexuality and Moral Responsibility. — Washing-ton/Cleveland: Corpus Books, 1968, 135.

The other dimensions, which profit from this tension, are tenderness, affection, intellectual communality, sensitivity and sacrifice.

One may also question whether the distinction between premarital and preceremonial intercourse in the sense described is truly legitimate. Marriage is not only a personal bond, but also a social and ecclesial reality. Hence one cannot speak of a marriage on the basis of a personal consent of two partners alone without its social and ecclesial acceptance and sanction.

Nevertheless Catholic moralists and canonists have always admitted of certain exceptions in difficult cases. For instance there may be conditions where it is very hard for Catholics to approach a priest. They may live in a remote region where a priest only rarely comes for a visit. Or a time of persecution can make it impossible for a priest to attend to the needs of his parishioners with sufficient regularity. In such cases the couple would be allowed to marry without the official ceremonies and make good for the omission whenever the opportunity lends itself (cf. CJC 1116).

If sexual intercourse is carried out in a marriage-like liaison between two partners of different sex, yet without the intention or possibility to marry, it is called concubinage. However marriages which are invalid because contracted by a Catholic partner in an external form which is not recognized by the Catholic Church, i.e. not in the canonical form and without proper dispensations, may not be called concubinage if there is the will to a permanent marital union. Although these marriages are invalid before the Church, they possess all the other elements of a legitimate marriage.

4.   *Other sins of heterosexual nature*

a)   Prostitution

If sexual intercourse is offered for hire, it is called prostitution. The term "fornication" in Holy Scripture and particularly in the Old Testament often applies to this form of sexual immorality, be this profane or sacred prostitution.

All the arguments which argue against premarital intercourse also and even more so militate against prostitution. Sex is right only for two people who are in love. But prostitution involves less personal love than any other form of extra-marital sexual union. Therefore it is the source of still deeper malaise and depression than other extra-marital, sexual relationships. Prostitution is carried out without any proper love between man and woman. Besides, the women which the man meets in the brothel are generally passive and do not cooperate much with him. Consequently he does not find the desired gratification. The result is that the young man who frequently visits the brothel quickly acquires a profound contempt for women, if not even also for himself.

b) Adultery

Adultery is sexual intercourse between two partners of different sex, of whom at least one is married. Besides the sin against chastity, adultery is also an offence against justice and fidelity.

Holy Scriptures of the Old and New Testament condemn the sin of adultery in rather severe terms. In the decalogue God commands his people: "You shall not commit adultery" (Ex 20:14), and: "You shall not covet your neighbour's wife" (Ex 20:17). Severe punishments are ordered for those who trespass this command (Lev 20:10; Deut 22:22; Sir 23:18-27). Christ confirms the prohibition given by the decalogue and emphasizes it again (Mt 5:27-32). For St. Paul it is one of the sins which exclude from the kingdom of God (1 Cor 6:9; Heb 13:4).

The inner reasons for the sinfulness of adultery are first those that contend against extra-marital unions in general. Above all they tend to bring children into the world who will not be properly cared for because their parents are not permanently united. This is especially true if the woman in the adulterous relation is not married. If she is married, true, the child is born into a family, but injustice is done to the husband and to the legitimate children, insofar as the husband will be obliged to rear another man's child and the legitimate children be forced to share their inheritance with a stranger. Moreover if some suspicion as to the real father of the adulterous child arises, the child may not be fully accepted by the family he is born into.

Besides, adultery involves destructive consequences for the love, harmony and stability in the family of the married partners. The love of the partners who commit adultery will usually be divided. They will be drawn away from their first partners and families, which inevitably will weaken the stability of the original bonds. Further damage to love and harmony will be done if the innocent partners discover the unfaithfulness of their marriage mates.

Finally adultery violates the fidelity promised by the marriage partners to each other, and among Catholics it further-

more offends against the sacramental consecration of the matrimonial union. Should the husband or wife who are not involved
consent to their partner's adultery, the adulterer would not
offend against justice; but chastity and the sacramental consecration of the marriage are violated nevertheless.

Many a time adultery could be prevented if the husband
and wife did not neglect the mutual love and concern for each
other. Adultery is unlikely to happen where the partners are
truly united in sincere love. David R. Reuben judges that
"although perhaps one in four wives commits adultery at least
once in her life, it is usually only with the greatest reluctance
that a woman abandons the sexual security of her husband for a
new and relatively unknown partner." The reason for unfaithfulness is more often than not the neglect by the husband who
takes his wife sexually and emotionally for granted. "Every
human being needs attention — but a wife particularly needs that
special kind of attention that involves tenderness, understanding
and reassurance. The moment a woman decides her husband
doesn't 'care' about her anymore, she becomes vulnerable to the
temptation of infidelity. An ounce of prevention on the part of
the husband is worth years of constant worry."[1]

Substantially the same holds for the husband. "Many
husbands are deliberately, although unconsciously, pushed into
the arms of other women by careless or indifferent wives." Men
who find a nagging, self-assertive, indifferent wife at home and
who are in vain looking for a companion with whom they could
share their fears and hopes, may finally look for somebody else.
Naturally husbands also seek sexual fulfillment from their wives
(as women likewise do from their husbands). Also a married
woman must care for her appeal and avail herself of the charms
of novelty. Nevertheless the dissatisfaction of husbands is more
often of an emotional nature. "Erotic sexual techniques are
not nearly as important to a man as the knowledge that his wife
loves him and wants him sexually."[2]

The foundation for sexual happiness or misery is laid not
in the bedroom but at the dining-table. A marriage which is solely
founded on sexual gratification cannot be lasting. Sexuality grants
happiness and fulfillment only where it is the expression of a
sincere, personal love. Husband and wife must be true com-

[1] David R. Reuben: Why Wives Cheat on Their Husbands. —
Reader's Digest, vol. 21, Sept. 1973, 73-76.
[2] David R. Reuben: Why Husbands Cheat on Their Wives. —
Reader's Digest, vol. 20, Febr. 1973, 65-68.

panions of life for each other, allies, helpers and friends. "If both partners are willing to sacrifice their individual egos and give up the luxury of self-justification, they should not only be immune to infidelity, they should find true happiness in marriage."[1]

c) Sins of violence

Rape is illicit sexual intercourse with a woman against her consent. Besides the grave sin against chastity, it is a grave sin against justice, because the woman's right over her body is violated. In addition the violation may bring social (though unjustified) dishonour to her and obstruct a future marriage.

Rape can be committed by the use of physical or moral force (grave fear, including reverential fear, fraud and deceit); likewise by a sin committed with a woman who has not the use of reason (because insane or intoxicated). The exploitation of one's position as superior in order to make a subject compliant to acts of lust is considered by nearly all civilized countries as an offence against morality and punished severely. The same is true of the seduction of a girl under sixteen years of age (statutory rape).

The victim of an immoral attack is allowed to resort to the most suitable means of defence, which in some instances may even include the killing of the unjust aggressor. But as in other cases of unjust aggression, there is generally no obligation to defend one's rights by means of killing the aggressor. Some form of active resistance however is normally expected of a ravished woman, though she may abstain from external resistance or cries for help when this cannot be done without danger to her life or reputation. Yet she must always offer the external and particularly internal resistance necessary to avoid sinning.

Similar to rape is the sin of abduction (violent seizure) or violent detention of a person of either sex for impure purposes, which is likewise a grave sin against justice and chastity. The force employed may be physical or moral, and used either upon the person ravished or upon those under whose authority the person is constituted.

d) Incest

Incest is sexual intercourse between persons who are closely related by blood or affinity.

---

[1] Ib. 68.

Most experts agree that in no known society is it conventional or even permissible for father and daughter, mother and son, or brother and sister to have intercourse or to marry.[1]   Society justly rejects marriage between close relatives, because inbreeding proves prejudicial to healthy offspring, biologically as well as psychologically and socially.[2]   Some exceptions to this universal prohibition have been noted especially among royal families of the ancient Egyptians, the Incas and the Hawaiians. Sick offspring was usually killed in these instances.

The Old Testament forbids incestuous unions in a somewhat wider range than the few cases mentioned above — as it is also the norm in most societies. Prohibited are incestuous unions between mother and son or step-son (Lev 18:8; 20:11; Deut 27:20), father and daughter or step-daughter (Lev 18:17), grandfather and granddaughter or step-granddaughter (Lev 18:10.17), brother and sister or half-sister (Lev 18:9.11; 20:17; Deut 27:22), nephew and aunt (Lev 18:12-14; 20:19f), mother and son-in-law (Lev 20:14; Deut 27:23), father and daughter-in-law (Lev 18:15; 20:12), and brother and sister-in-law (Lev 18:16; 20:21). The New Testament seems to adopt these norms inasmuch as it does not make any changes in this regard. John the Baptist reproaches Herod's marriage with his sister-in-law during his brother's lifetime as a particularly grave depravity (Mk 6:17f); and St. Paul excommunicates a man sexually linked to his step-mother (1 Cor 5:1-13).

Incest according to canon law is a still broader concept. It includes the following relations between persons related by blood or by affinity: marriage between all ascendants and descendants in the direct line; in the collateral line between brothers and sisters and between first cousins (CIC 1091; cf. 108); between

---

[1] Cf. art. "Incest" in: New Catholic Encyclopedia, vol. 7, 1967, 420.

[2] A study on children of incest was performed by the Czechoslovakian researcher Dr. Eva Seemanova. She examined and kept records of 161 children born to women who had had sexual relations with their fathers, brothers or sons. The same group of women also produced 95 children by men to whom they were not related. The children of incestuous unions were often doomed from the start. Fifteen were stillborn or died within the first year of life; in the control group, only five children died during a comparable period. More than 40% of the incest group suffered from a variety of physical and mental defects, including severe mental retardation, dwarfism, heart and brain deformities, deaf-mutism, enlargement of the colon and urinary-tract abnormalities. By contrast none of the children of the control group showed any serious mental deficiency, and only 4.5% had physical abnormalities (Newsweek, Oct. 9, 1972, p. 32).

those who are related by affinity in any degree of the direct line, i.e. between a man and his mother- or daughter-in-law and between a woman and her father- or son-in-law (CIC 1092). However the prohibition of marriages between first cousins is an impediment from which the Church dispenses, although reluctantly. Rarer is dispensation from affinity in the direct line.

The incest prohibitions result from the concern for a healthy offspring, for a sound family and the stability of social life. They eliminate sexual competition and therefrom ensuing tensions within the nuclear family and restrain sexual abuse of the close family relations. By forcing the children to leave their next of kin in seeking mates, the prohibitions foster the integration of the young in the society as a whole and prevent concentration of undesirable familial peculiarities and oddities.

Because of its special perversion incest adds to the sin of unchastity a sin against familial piety, which is greatest when committed between grandparents, parents and children, brothers and sisters.[1]

V. Sexual deviations and the problem of homosexuality

Sexual deviations are abnormities of sexual behaviour. The object of the sexual desire is abnormal, e.g. an animal, or the kind of act by which sexual arousal is caused, e.g. sadism.

1. *Homosexuality*[2]

Homosexual problems are much more common than is generally supposed. One must not be induced to think that homosexuality is relatively rare because one does not often come across it in the confessional or the parlour. Owing to the stigma which society has placed upon the homosexual, the latter shuns away from revealing his tendencies to people of normal sexual constitution. Though for this reason accurate statistics are difficult to obtain, five percent of the total population is an

---

[1] Justly B. Häring distinguishes between the canonic concept of incest and that of moral theology. The latter is less broad and in the main the one of Holy Scripture (The Law of Christ, vol. III, 1966, 300f).

[2] References: John J. McNeil: The Christian Male Homosexual. — Homiletic and Pastoral Review 70 (1970), 667-677; 748-758; 828-836. Martin S. Weinberg and Alan P. Bell, eds.: Homosexuality: An Annoted Bibliography. — New York: Harpers, 1972. John F. Harvey: The Controversy Concerning the Psychology and Morality of Homosexuality. — American Eccl. Review 167 (1973), 602-629. C. E. Curran: Catholic Moral Theology in Dialogue. — Univ. of Notre Dame Press, 1976, 184-219.

estimate which appears in a number of reliable studies.[1] But it should be understood that not all people with a homosexual constitution also engage in active homosexual practices.[2]

Concept and nature of homosexual relations

Homosexual relations are sexual activities between persons of the same sex. Often they consist in mutual masturbation. The unnatural imitation of a carnal copulation (mostly rectal coition) by persons of the same sex is called sodomy.[3] Introduction of the penis of one man into the mouth of the other is called fellatio.[4] Homosexual activity between women is often named lesbian or sapphic love. If committed between an adult and a youth, it is called pederasty.

An important distinction is to be made between homosexuality as a psychic, constitutional deviation on the one side and a more or less occasional homosexual activity on the other. Many boys engage towards the end of the prepuberty period and on into the early years of adolescence in at least occasional sex plays of a homosexual nature. These plays very often represent no more than an extension of masturbatory techniques. Absence of heterosexual outlets (e.g. among soldiers, in prison camps, etc.) can be the reason for temporary, homosexual activities also among adults. Such activities are not yet signs of constitutional homosexuality (though — of course — they do not exclude it). In true homosexuality the normal heterosexual attraction is substituted by an abnormal attraction towards persons

---

[1] Cf. G. Hagmaier/R. Gleason: Counselling the Catholic. — New York: Sheed and Ward, 1964, 94f. Norman Pittenger: Time for Consent. — London: SCM Press, 1970, 30.

[2] According to studies of H. Ellis in England and M. Hirschfeld in Germany, 2.2 and 2.3 percent of the population have regularly and exclusively sexual relations with members of their sex (Paul G. Ecker: Homosexuality. Genetic and Dynamic Factors; in: Personality and Sexual Problems, ed. by W. Bier. — New York: Fordham University Press, 1965, 154f). A. C. Kinsey arrives at 4 percent of the male population in the U.S.A. who are exclusively homosexuals all their lives. But this seems to include also those constitutional homosexuals who have only occasionally had homosexual relations. The percentage for women is considerably lower (D. J. West: Homosexuality. — Penguin Books, 1968, 36-43).

[3] Rectal intercourse practised by persons of different sex is called 'imperfect sodomy'.

[4] The term fellatio is also used for mouth contact of the genitals by partners of different sex. As long as this is only a prelude to the normal act of intercourse, it is not a sexual deviation. If performed among married partners, it is not necessarily objectionable.

of the same sex. In most cases the heterosexual attraction is simply missing. But there are also bisexual types capable of both homosexual and heterosexual stimulation.

Often it is assumed that the typical homosexual or invert, as he is also called, is an effeminate man and a masculine type of woman. But this is not the case. A small proportion of homosexuals do have bodily characteristics of the opposite sex and some occasionally affect the mannerisms or clothes of the opposite sex. But the great majority have no outer physical characteristics that identify them in their sexual predilections. Indeed many feminine-appearing men are exclusively heterosexual. Yet it may be true that many homosexuals are people of a sensitive and gentle character.

Even among experts the opinions as to the cause and nature of constitutional homosexuality are intricate and diverse. The theory that homosexuality is an innate propensity is not supported by biological evidence. No physiological differences between the homosexual and heterosexual individual have been discovered so far. Hence its causes must rather be searched in psychological factors. Homosexuality is probably the result of an interaction between a person's early life experience and his particular constitutional make-up. There is a good chance that the mother of a homosexual will be a dominant, inclusive and aggresive female, and that the father is submissive by temperament. As a child the homosexual may have been induced to seek affection and emotional warmth from the father rather than from the mother. The result is an abnormal inhibition vis-a-vis women and an equally abnormal attraction towards men, or vice versa in the case of lesbians. "The flight from heterosexual relations is a neurotic symptom, produced in much the same way as other irrational fears and inhibitions."[1]

Moral evaluation

A distinction must be made between the homosexual constitution, which is contracted very often without any personal guilt and therefore not more culpable than any other sickness, and overt homosexual activity. Only the latter, the activation of

---

[1] D. J. West: Homosexuality. — Penguin Books, 1968, 17. Others regard homosexuality as an arrested state of sexual development. According to their theory the individual is drawn first to the same sex, because he relates to the known more easily than to the unknown. Only at a later stage he turns to heterosexual relationships. The homosexual is not able to take this second step.

homosexual tendencies, must be judged upon as an imputable disorder, and as such it cannot simply be tolerated. Under this aspect the homosexual is expected to practise self-control and continence in the same way and with the same spiritual helps as the heterosexually oriented, unmarried person.

Holy Scripture definitely regards homosexual actions as sinful.[1] The Old Testament bids: "You shall not lie with a male as with a woman; it is an abomination" (Lev 18:22). Those who do such actions shall even be put to death (Lev 20:13; cf. the account on Sodom and Gomorrah, Gen 19:4-14). To St. Paul homosexual activity between men as well as between women is one of the most shameful pagan vices. "God gave them up to dishonourable passions. Their women exchanged natural relations for unnatural, and the men likewise gave up natural relations with women and were consumed with passion for one another, men committing shameless acts with men" (Rom 1:26f). He lists homosexuality among the sins which exclude from the kingdom of God (1 Cor 6:9f; 1 Tim 1:9f).[2]

With this agrees the constant teaching of the Church and of moral theologians. The recent Declaration on Sexual Ethics by the S. Congregation of Faith wishes that especially confirmed homosexuals who are definitively such should be treated with understanding. "Their culpability will be judged with prudence. But no pastoral method can be employed which would give moral justification to these acts on the grounds that they would be consonant with the condition of such people. For according to the objective moral order, homosexual relations are acts which lack an essential and indispensable finality. . . . Homosexual acts are intrinsically disordered and can in no case be approved of."[3]

---

[1] Also the Koran condemns homosexual acts in explicit terms (ch. IV, v. 20). On the other hand a number of primitive societies are quoted where some form of homosexual activity was considered normal and acceptable. The practice of homosexuality in ancient Greece and Rome is known from Holy Scripture. Other societies in turn are rigidly condemnatory (cf. D. J. West, 1. c. 19-30).

[2] The judgment of St. Paul is so unequivocal that N. Pittenger, in his attempt to justify homosexual partnerships, sees no other way out to plead his cause than to contest the correctness of Paul's statements. They are, he writes, doubtless "an expression of the horror which he felt when confronted by the open licentiousness of many of the great cities of the Graeco-Roman world of his time. But St. Paul's precise comments on the subject are not infallible" (Time for Consent. A Christian's Approach to Homosexuality. — London: SCM Press, 1970, 105). This indeed is a very drastic solution. But is it acceptable and in harmony with the Christian faith?

[3] Declaration of Dec. 29, 1975, nr. 8.

The intrinsic reason for the disorder of homosexual acts lies in this that they frustrate the purpose of sexuality. Evidently homosexual acts exclude all possibility of transmission of life, which is the most basic purpose of the sexual power. The other purpose of the sexual act, the expression and fostering of mutual love between husband and wife, is equally not obtained. Advocates of homosexual liaisons often claim that the sexual act can also serve as an expression of love between two persons of the same sex. But a closer inspection reveals that this is not so. The sexual act is apt to be an expression of love and appreciation in the last analysis because it is able to generate new human life. Every man and every woman would like to have a child only with a partner whom they sincerely esteem. The readiness of a man and a woman to unite together in the sexual act is therefore a sign of their mutual esteem, at least if they do not superficially plunge into the sexual encounter, but do so in a responsible decision. Sexual acts between two persons of the same sex however are never apt to procreate offspring. Therefore they can also not be the expression of a love and esteem which is based on the possibility to give life to a child. The precondition is missing which imparts to the sexual act the quality of a sign of love.

Furthermore homosexual acts never constitute a real sexual union, but basically remain on the level of mutual masturbation. Homosexuality is not able to fulfill the deepest sexual longings of the other, nor the longings for a home, a family and emotional security, as conjugal love does. It is only a surrogate which is not able to come up to the veritable needs of the other, and which is therefore also for this reason not in a condition to be an authentic sign of love.

These insights from the nature of sexuality are confirmed by the psychological implications which homosexual activity entails. Homosexual gratification is experienced as ultimately inadequate. Feelings of frustration and depression often go with it. "Few homosexuals, if any, are actually at peace with their perversion, the pathway of gratification being unstable and incomplete, and the degree of gratification in the perversion always limited. The factor of unconscious guilt looms large in many of these individuals."[1]

---

[1] Paul G. Ecker: Homosexuality: Genetic and Dynamic Factors; in: Personality and Sexual Problems, ed. by W. Bier. — New York: Fordham University Press, 1965, 165.

Homosexual relationships not seldom prove to be ambivalent. The partners are at the same time attracted to each other by emotions of love and repelled by feelings of hostility. After all, this kind of sexual relationship is only a poor surrogate for the authentic love between the sexes.

In old age many homosexuals eventually find that they are left without family, roots or purpose. They are no longer attractive as partners of sexual satisfaction. And friendships based on the deeper, more lasting foundation of a spiritual love have not matured. The dread of growing old is a noticeable feature especially of male homosexuals. "The normal man, restricted as he may be by family routine, has little cause to envy the so-called 'gay' life."[1] Homosexuals themselves concur in this judgment. Inquiries conducted among male inverts reveal their overwhelming desire, were they to be fathers, to see their sons free of this problem.[2]

In view of these insights homosexuality cannot simply be treated as a neutral phenomenon. It cannot be approved. Also the promotion of marriage-like liaisons between homosexuals does not lend itself as a veritable solution to the problem. Ultimately it does not render a real service to the invert. Both nature and social circumstances work against this solution. Experience shows that homosexual "marriages" are most of the time not lasting, particularly among men.[3] The truth is that they do not offer the love the partners are really looking for. They have no lasting foundation.

Against the qualification of overt homosexuality as inadmissible and sinful the objection is made that this deprives the homosexual person of any possibility of sexual fulfillment, at least if he is an absolute invert. And yet the power of the sexual drive is in him no less strong than in his heterosexual peers. In answer to this it is to be observed that the sexual drive is in the homosexual also not stronger than in other persons. There are always a number of heterosexual persons who do not marry. Christian ethics does not approve of extra-marital relationships for the satisfaction of their sexual inclinations either. Hence the condition of homosexuals is not worse than that of unmarried

[1] D. J. West: Homosexuality. — Penguin Books, 1968, 57.

[2] Cf. Eugene C. Kennedy: The New Sexuality. — Garden City, N.Y.: Doubleday (Image Books), 1973, 137.

[3] It is however asserted that homosexual unions of a certain stability, even though not of a permanence until death, occur more often than is generally assumed.

people with a heterosexual constitution. Naturally, those who feel that premarital or extra-marital sex must be granted as a means to appease the sexual urge, will consequently also have to approve of homosexual outlets. But this is not the mind of Holy Scripture and Christian tradition, nor does it constitute the general conviction of theologians.

On the other hand there is no need to give homosexual acts a severer judgment than fornication and adultery, among which it is listed in the letters of St. Paul. This also holds for civil legislation.[1] On the contrary, there are certain mitigating circumstances in the case of homosexuality insofar as the invert has often a more difficult time avoiding stimulatory situations. He has also no hope for a possible fulfillment of his sexual inclinations.

The element of possible compulsion must also be taken into consideration. Since homosexual behaviour is to a considerable extent a neurotic disorder, it is not surprising to find compulsive elements in the invert. Psychic compulsion diminishes liberty and imputability. Yet this should not be understood in a sense as if the homosexual who suffers from compulsive urges is absolved from all responsibility for his homosexual acts. "If the homosexual temporizes with this interior disorder by fostering habits of indiscreet reading or by cultivating dangerous friendships, he is guilty of placing himself unnecessarily in the proximate occasion of sin." It is necessary for the homosexual to be rigorously honest with himself. "In many instances of the *almost* irresistible urge the individual could have stopped the whole process of mounting passions at an early stage, but he did not do so."[2] To the extent that he is able to control his urges, he is also responsible for his actions.

---

[1] The punishment of homosexual actions with imprisonment, appointed by the civil law of several nations, is contaminating rather than rehabilitative. A revision of the laws in this regard is to be advocated. The Report of the Roman Catholic Advisory Committee on Prostitution and Homosexual Offences, published in the Dublin Review of Summer 1956, recommends "that the criminal law should be amended in order to restrict penal sanctions for homosexual offenses as follows, namely, to prevent: a) the corruption of youth, b) offenses against public decency, c) the exploitation of vice for the purpose of gain. It should be clearly stated that penal sanctions are not justified for the purpose of attempting to restrain sins against sexual morality committed in private by responsible adults" (quoted by G. Hagmaier/R. Gleason: Counselling the Catholic. — New York: Sheed and Ward, 1964, 104).

[2] John Harvey: Some Pastoral Reflections on Homosexuality; in. Contemporary Pastoral Counseling, ed. by E. Weitzel. — New York: Bruce, 1969, 113f.

Homosexual plays among adolescents should essentially be judged as an infantile, though nevertheless inadmissible phenomenon.

Practical considerations[1]

To the extent that homosexuality is a psychic disorder, its cure would be desirable if possible. Yet this illness constitutes a rather difficult psychiatric problem. It necessitates the change of a person's essential identification with his psychic role. This may be possible where the motivation is very great. But it requires exceptional effort on the part of both analyst and patient. Many homosexuals are not able to afford the treatment or to exert the effort. They are like men born crippled. They have to live with their alien tendencies to the end of their lives.

Healthy people, who are happy enough not to suffer from this distortion, must learn to accept the homosexual for what he is: not an abomination but rather an afflicted person in need of understanding, encouragement and sympathy. The confirmed homosexual has usually a kind of hopeless air about him. He cannot solve his problems. He feels himself rejected and abandoned by his fellowmen. He not seldom even dislikes himself. Because of this he is tempted to bitterness towards God and society. And bitterness leads to isolation and loneliness.

The homosexual must therefore be helped to regain a conviction of his own worth. Though he has to face the fact that something is wrong with him, there is no need to feel guilty and vile because of his abnormal constitution. He cannot be blamed for it. He is a human being worthy of acceptance as much as any other person. Disgust and rejection only reinforce the bondage of unconscious complexes. Love and sympathy offer him the help he needs to integrate healthily in society and to believe in the possibility of a holy life also for him.

If it is certain that the male homosexual is a true invert, he should not attempt marriage. Petting and dating practices of the bisexual must sometimes be viewed as attempts to test a genuine heterosexual relationship. Female inverts are able to perform the marital act and to raise children without as many difficulties. In any case, the opinion of a qualified psychologist or psychiatrist should be obtained if possible.

---

[1] Cf. the very good pastoral considerations in G. Hagmaier/R. Gleason: Counselling the Catholic. — New York: Sheed and Ward, 1964, 94-111.

The homosexual should feel encouraged to participate in all social and sport activities which bring him satisfaction. In many cases such involvements help to drain off a more basic urge of physical contact. A limited risk of possible sexual stimulation must be run, and abstention from a given activity only required if it proves a proximate source of seduction. Teachers, social workers, athletic directors, scout leaders, etc., who have been involved in actual homosexual activity with their students and subordinates should of course be dissuaded from continuing in such positions. On the other hand such occupations can be desirable and healthy outlets for those who have no problems with overt seductive behaviour.[1]

Finally the invert must seek an outlet for his energies in works of love and service. His efforts must be accompanied by earnest prayer for God's grace. The person who declines all commitment to some overarching and dominant purpose is indeed living without love. But the person who is able to forget himself in the service of his brethren possesses love in its truest sense. The Christian believer finds the way of love in Jesus Christ. He discloses to every man that true love which is the way to reconciliation and salvation.

2. *Other sexual deviations*

a) *Bestiality.* So is called the coition of a human being with an animal. It is severely condemned by Holy Scripture (Ex 22:19; Lev 20:15f). The evil consists in the perverted affect to an animal, in which the human sexual act can never achieve its proper meaning. It cannot give life to a child, nor is it in any way an expression of love. It is only a means for the release of sexual tensions. The total divorce of the sexual satisfaction from the erotic and spiritual aspiration is necessarily degrading and a cause of frustration.

b) *Forms of sexual paresthesia.* Sexual paresthesia is had when sexual excitement is aroused exclusively or at least primarily through things which are altogether alien to sex life: in sadism through active exercise of cruelty on others; in masochism through endurance of cruelty and humiliation; in fetishism through such objects as clothing, shoes, hair, without reference to a

---

[1] It is possible for an invert to be constituted in such a way that he has difficulties only in his private, off-the-job hours, while he remains unaffected in his vocational contacts, tempting as they might appear.

person. In sadism these anomalies can lead to most terrible crimes (sadist cruelties and rapist killing).

The moral evil of such behaviour is obvious. True, at its root a psychological disturbance may often be found which was contracted without personal guilt. But everyone must control the manifestations of his inclinations and passions and renounce unlawful satisfactions, also the sexually abnormal; and much more so if these passions do harm to other people.

C. Moral responsibility in the marriage state[1]

I. The time of engagement

The ordinary preparation for marriage is, after a period of acquaintanceship, a time of engagement. The motive which in many instances brings two people together is the love they experience for each other. A young man and a young woman discover something in each other that no outsider can fully see, and that makes them feel they should belong together. In other instances the motives which determine the choice of the partner are more of a pragmatic, rational nature, e.g. common professional or economical interests. Though people today are rather antipathetic to these latter motives, experience shows that marriages with such reasons in view often develop surprisingly well, supposing the motives are not purely egoistic. Yet also in the cases of a great, spontaneous love reason and conscience cannot be left out. The partners must examine responsibly if they really harmonize together, and this is the purpose of the engagement period.

1. *Meaning of the engagement time*

The engagement allows the young people to see whether their first love is based on a solid foundation. They confront each other in conversations, on walks or entertainments, alone or together with other young people. In their families or at

[1] References: Pierre Grelot: Man and Wife in Scripture. — New York: Herder and Herder, 1964. Daniel Planque: The Theology of Sex in Marriage. — Notre Dame, Ind.: Fides Publishers, 1965. Wilfrid J. Harrington: The Promise to Love. A Scriptural View of Marriage. — London: G. Chapman, 1968. Marc Oraison: Man and Wife. The Physical and Spiritual Foundations of Marriage. — New York: Macmillan, 1969. Bernard Häring: Love is The Answer. — Denville, N. J.: Dimension Books, 1970. Paul F. Palmer: Christian Marriage: Contract or Covenant? — Theol. Studies 33 (1972), 617-665. Mark C. Taylor: In Defense of Marriage. — American Eccl. Review 167 (1973), 164-177.

work they can witness each other's behaviour and moods, and gradually become acquainted with their mutual background and interests. This is necessary if they are to choose each other with the sufficient insight which such a vital decision deserves. Though the parents stand more aside than they formerly did in most cases, the engaged will not despise their advice, but weigh it carefully.

The nature of the engagement as a time of examination requires that it must have a certain length to become effective, i.e. at least the length of several months. On the other hand it ought not last too long. An engagement time of two years or more involves the risk of repression of vital affections with the danger of mutual alienation or the risk of a compromise: marriage de facto but not de jure. Both can lead to tensions, constraints and great encumbrances for the future marriage.[1] Engagements therefore without the hope of a speedy marriage should be avoided.

2. *Rights, duties and chastity of the engaged*

Since the engagement is a first decision of two people to bind each other for life, it is still provisional; and since it is meant as a time in which they are supposed to examine whether they are fitted for each other, they owe each other love, fidelity and frankness. Sexuality, in the broadest sense of the term, plays an essential part in the engagement, both spiritually and physically. As the fully human eroticism develops, it is concerned with the You alone, and any third person is automatically excluded. Gradually the young people recognize (and should be guided to do so) that they are responsible for each other's future. Genuine love will prevent their courtship from becoming egoistic.

Timidity and anxiety as well as unbridled passion are both out of place. The engaged are permitted manifestations of love which would be deemed improper for other unmarried couples. The exchange of caresses forms a positive and essential element of the time of engagement.[2] The primary question must be whether through the caresses the common love is enriched and the partner made happy. The man should also know that place

---

[1] Cf. Böckle/Köhne: Geschlechtliche Beziehungen vor der Ehe. — Mainz: Matthias-Grünewald-Vlg. 1967, 58f.

[2] Böckle/Köhne, l. c. 57. The authors mention that the mutual demonstrations of love can sometimes cause pollution, but this should not be sought after primarily or intended directly.

and circumstances of intimate caresses are not rarely more irksome and disappointing than enchanting for the bride. It is quite convenient and should be quite natural that the young people speak honestly and conscientiously about the caresses they may indulge in at the various stages of courtship.

The greater freedom of intimacy should however not induce the engaged to adopt too quickly the attitude of the future husband and wife. "As long as the bond has not been confirmed by Church and State, it is not definitive. Hence, though the young people may have become very intimate, sexual intercourse in such a situation is irresponsible. The reason is that it has by its very nature a definitive character. It implies that it is 'for good'. If they surrender themselves to it, there is an inner change in the young man and the young woman. From then on they experience each other as husband and wife, and each act of union conjures up one to follow. This brings with it on the one hand the sense of being married, and on the other, the conflict of knowing that they are not married. And a step backwards — at any rate if a long period is involved — is only possible at the cost of profound inner tensions" (Dutch "New Catechism").[1]

Failures need not cause inhibitions, but may be occasions for new courage, once the will of God is acknowledged. The fact that sexual intercourse took place and even that a child is on the way does however not create the obligation for the man to marry the girl. The father remains of course responsible for the child and its mother, especially under economic aspects. But it is better for the child to grow up in an incomplete family than in a bad marriage. The question to be asked is whether one would marry this partner even if there were no child on the way.

From the pastoral point of view talks and courses in preparation for marriage are very much to be recommended and usually greatly welcomed by the young people.

The majority of mankind is called by God to enter the state of matrimony. The biblical text: "It is not good that the man should be alone" (Gen 2:18) expressly refers to marriage. Normally a man does not attain to his full stature in relation to life until he is married and starts a family. This fulness is reached through responsibility towards those who look to him

---

[1] A New Catechism. Catholic Faith for Adults. — London: Burns and Oates, 1967, 387; cf. also Böckle/Köhne, l. c. 32; 56f.

for support and through escape from the dangerous limitation of an existence based on purely personal convenience.

II. Nature of marriage

1. *The ends of marriage*

The ends of marriage are closely related to the ends of sexual love, as discussed in the section "Nature and purpose of sexual love". But they are not completely identical. Marriage has as its purpose not merely the procreation but also the education of children. And the other purpose of marriage is mutual assistance in a very comprehensive sense, in which the expression of mutual love by means of the conjugal act only forms one aspect among others.

a) Procreation and education of children

The procreative aim of sexual love is also a fundamental end of marriage. "Marriage and conjugal love are by their nature ordained toward the begetting and educating of children. Children are really the supreme gift of marriage and contribute very substantially to the welfare of their parents. . . . Hence, while not making the other purposes of matrimony of less account, the true practice of conjugal love, and the whole meaning of the family life which results from it, have this aim: that the couple be ready with stout hearts to cooperate with the love of the Creator and the Saviour, who through them will enlarge and enrich His own family day by day. Parents should regard as their proper mission the task of transmitting human life and educating those to whom it has been transmitted" (GS 50; cf. 48).

Only the institutions of marriage and family create the truly proper conditions for the procreation and upbringing of children. They prepare the necessary scope for conjugal love and its fruit and goal: the child. Therefore sexual relations are lawful only within a marriage. For sufficient reasons however married people would be allowed to avoid offspring by mutual consent. Thus a marriage would be valid if both parties agree to have intercourse only in the infertile periods because they are congenitally afflicted and want to avoid sick offspring. Yet this must always be done by mutual consent, notwithstanding the basic and full right to a fertile marital union. (Canon law regards a marriage invalid which excludes the right to a fertile marital union.[1]).

---

[1] This at least is the interpretation of the marriage rights given in CIC 1096 §1 and 1101 §2.

Instances in which children are completely avoided must remain rare exceptions and justified by weighty reasons. Interpreting the Creator's intention, the Scriptures rightly regard the propagation of mankind an essential purpose of marriage. The blessing of God on the first human couple in the Six-Day account "Be fruitful and multiply" (Gen 1:28) granted fertility to marriage for all ages. This marriage blessing of God is an expression of Israel's belief that children are a gift of God and that in God's plan marriage serves the spread and expansion of mankind.[1]

There are certain tendencies today which emphasize the aspect of mutual love and assistance in marriage at the expense of its function for the propagation of mankind. Yet such tendencies are not consistent with the mind of Holy Scripture and the distinctive, nature-ordained purpose of marriage. "In opposition to the neo-pagan rejection and neglect of the child in relation to marriage we are doubly warranted to focus special attention on its creative aspect, constituting its distinctive or specifying end and purpose: in this sense we speak of children as the purpose of marriage. Marital love attains the lofty heights of reverential chastity only after it is committed in joyful service to life."[2]

b)   Mutual assistance and completion in love

Still another important end is obtained through the marriage covenant: mutual assistance and completion in love of the two spouses. In marriage man and woman "render mutual help and service to each other through an intimate union of their persons and of their actions" (GS 48). Man and woman with their different gifts and abilities complete each other in this covenant in the most perfect way.

This end of marriage is confirmed by the Garden-of-Eden account in the book of Genesis. The reason why God gave a wife to man is for mutual help and company. "It is not good that the man should be alone; I will make him a helper fit for him" (Gen 2:18). So God created the woman. When seeing her, Adam called out: "This at least is bone of my bones and flesh of my flesh." And Scripture concludes: "Therefore a man leaves his father and his mother and cleaves to his wife, and they become one flesh" (Gen 2:23f). The wording "flesh of my

---

[1] Cf. G. N. Vollebregt: The Bible on Marriage. — London: Sheed and Ward, 1965, 71.

[2] B. Häring III, 1966, 330.

flesh and bone of my bone" implies that marriage is not merely a bond, but moreover constitutes a new being, a being-together, an actuality which we can never undo.[1] Thus the expression "one flesh" asserts in a very concrete and vivid way the mutual completion of man and wife effected by marriage.

The ideal of marriage as a very close union of undivided love is also pointed out by the prophets' use of the marriage image as a means of portraying the relationship between Yahweh and Israel (Jer 2-4; 31; Is 54; Ezek 16; 23). The same comparison is later used by Paul, only that it is now reversed and thereby given a still deeper meaning. It is not that Jesus' love for the Church is like married love. It is that marriage is like Jesus' unity with the Church. "Husbands, love your wives, as Christ loved the Church and gave himself up for her, that he might sanctify her. . . . Even so husbands should love their wives as their own bodies" (Eph 5:25ff). Marriage manifests on its own level something of the unfathomable depths of giving and loving, of mutual absorption and beatitude within God himself.

The mutual assistance which man and woman give each other in the marriage bond must however not only be understood as a companionship in joys and blissful togetherness, but also as a solicitous solidarity in sorrows and distress. "The comparison between human marriage and the union between Christ and the Church is only verified in so far as our family shows the sort of love which Christ taught and inspired. It must be love of the other as of oneself. It is the love. . . . in which the cross has its place. Thus it is a love which is proof against disappointment, a loyalty which is proof against failure — failure to come up to each other's expectations, to make joy full, to find love satisfying. It is love and loyalty which persist even where humanly speaking there seems to be no reason for it — just as the cross of Jesus was humanly speaking hopeless, but brought salvation and goodness."[2]

This alone is wholly "marriage in the Lord". Of course the truth that the cross has a place in Christian marriage does not mean surrender to unhappiness and failure. Christians will always make every effort to build up and preserve a happy family life. But it means that even the misfortunes which befall a family can become a school of love and a source of fruitfulness of a higher order for the kingdom of God.

---

[1] Cf. Vollebregt, 1. c. 58.
[2] A New Catechism. — London: Burns and Oates, 1967, 391.

As a third end of marriage is usually listed the remedy and restraint of concupiscence (*remedium concupiscentiae*), though this end could also be considered as part of the second end. In this regard marriage is looked upon as a help to allay concupiscence, to prevent sexuality from straying wildly and to place it under the firm control of married love. This purpose of marriage is pointed out by Paul in 1 Cor 7. His recommendation for the unmarried and the widows is to remain single; yet he adds: "But if they cannot exercise self-control, they should marry. For it is better to marry than to be aflame with passion" (v. 9). In a later letter he even drops the recommendation not to marry in the case of younger widows. On the contrary, he would have them marry because some had already strayed away (1 Tim 5: 11-15). The reason why they should marry is again the appeasement of the passions.

Still the appeasement of the passions ought not to be aimed at in an isolated way with the determination simply to satisfy the sex instinct as such. The spouses should show concern for the possible sexual need and temptation of the other partner, in this way going beyond mere satisfaction to mutual love and solicitude. Meaningful realization of the sex instinct finally must place it in the reverential service of the other marriage ends, as intended by the Creator. Only true conjugal love has healing power.

2. *Unity of marriage (monogamy)*

Historically some evolutionists assumed that the origins of marriage could be traced to a condition of primitive promiscuity. But there is no evidence that a completely promiscuous society has ever existed. Polygamy however was rather far spread in the ancient world. Exceptions were the Greeks and the Romans, who did not sanction it, but who practised concubinage. Nevertheless normally only the rich have been able to avail themselves of the privilege of polygamy. In practice monogamy has been the most prevalent form of marriage even where polygamy was permitted. Of old there have also been societies, not excluding primitive societies, which rejected polygamy completely and only permitted monogamy.[1] The number of these societies has been steadily increasing. This has gone hand in hand with the fact that the mutual dedication of husband and wife has become more

---

[1] Cf. New Catholic Encyclopedia, vol. 9, 1966, art. "Marriage", 258f.

profoundly human and that both partners came to stand more and more on the same footing.

In the Old Testament the marriages of the patriarchs followed the usual pattern that we find in the ancient East in the second millenium, namely polygamy. In the time of the Judges and the Kings the possession of many wives was a sign of wealth and power. But we find scarcely any polygamous marriages of ordinary men after the settlement of Israel in Canaan. The reasons may have been partly of economic nature and partly the limited number of women. Yet there is also a constant growth of a monogamous ideal of marriage in Israel itself, as reflected in the preaching of the prophets and in the Wisdom literature. Later on the monogamy of the Greco-Roman world would also have its influence. And even while polygamy was admitted, Israelite love showed a tendency towards exclusiveness. The love praised is the jealous love that chooses one among dozens, as depicted by the Song of Solomon in its ardent manner. Lastly this song is a passionate plea for monogamous marriage and for the faithfulness of which this is the foundation.

Although the prophets accepted polygamy as an existing state of affairs, their ideal of marriage is monogamous, as for example shown by the use of the marriage covenant for portraying the relationship between Yahweh and Israel. In the Wisdom literature there are no further references to having several wives. It is assumed that the reader observes monogamous marriage.

The description of the first marriage in the Garden-of-Eden account — the prototype of every subsequent marriage — is close to the ideal of the prophetic and Wisdom literature in being monogamous (and permanent). The expression "a help fit for him" and the usage of the formula of relationship "my bone and flesh" in this account testify to a lasting communal life for the two, and for the two only. That the Yahwist as well as the priestly tradition regard monogamous marriage as normal is furthermore corroborated by the remark in the list of Cain's descendants that Lamech was the first to take two wives (Gen 4:19), and that the patriarchs of the family of Seth are represented as monogamous (Gen 5 and 7).

Jesus and the New Testament do not discuss the question of monogamy explicitly — monogamy was looked upon as self-evident. In Christ's words: "From the beginning of creation, God made them male and female. For this reason a man shall leave his father and mother and be joined to his wife, and the two shall become one" (Mk 10:6-8 par), monogamy is implied rather than stated. Yet it clearly lies behind the expression: "these two shall become one flesh". Equally for St. Paul monogamy is so self-evident that it is not even prescribed (1 Cor 7:2.10f). Since in the Greco-Roman world marriage was, legally at least, generally monogamous, on this point Christians were not faced with any particular problem or unusual restriction.

Throughout the centuries Christians adhered to monogamous marriage as prescribed by the Lord. The prohibition of polygamy for Christians is a dogma of the Tridentinum.[1] Vatican II briefly summarizes the arguments of reason when it states: "As a mutual gift of two persons, this intimate union, as well as the good of the children, imposes total fidelity on the spouses and argues for an unbreakable oneness between them" (GS 48). "Firmly established by the Lord, the unity of marriage will radiate from the equal personal dignity of wife and husband, a dignity acknowledged by mutual and total love" (GS 49).

Polyandry (several husbands and one wife) and polygamy or polygyny (several wives and one husband) are contrary to the ends of marriage because they dusturb the union of love between man and wife and render their necessary cooperation in the education of the child difficult or even impossible. This contradiction is most obvious in polyandry, which is more of a hindrance than a help, not only to the education of children but even to their propagation. Polygamy is less opposed to the propagation of children than it is to their education and to the mutual love and devotion of man and wife. It also lowers the dignity of woman. If the social conditions of more primitive times did not absolutely exclude polygamy (so that scholastic theology judged that it was allowed in these ancient times on the basis of secondary natural law), they surely exclude it at least today.

3. *Indissolubility of marriage*[2]

Most societies provide the possibility of divorce in cases of incompatibility of the marriage partners. Among the innumer-

---

[1] DS 1798; 1802.

[2] References: The Bond of Marriage. An Ecumenical and Interdisciplinary Study; ed. William W. Basset. — Notre Dame/London: University of Notre Dame Press, 1968. William W. Basset: Divorce and Remarriage. — Am. Eccl. Review 162 (1970), 20-36; 92-105. Richard A. McCormick: Notes on Moral Theology. — Theol. Studies 32 (1971), 107-122; 33 (1972), 91-100; 36 (1975), 100-117. Divorce and Remarriage in the Catholic Church; ed. Lawrence G. Wrenn. — New York: Newman Press, 1973. Val J. Peter: Divorce and Remarriage. — Communio. Int. Cath. Review 1 (1974), 261-274.

able grounds for divorce that may be recognized, adultery, particularly on the part of the wife, is perhaps most widely included. But it is also observed that in the majority of societies divorce is never considered to be an ideal solution, so that, although it may be easy to obtain among primitives in general, it is not at all uniformly prevalent.[1]

The Old Testament

The attitude of the Old Testament to divorce agrees with the general findings of social anthropology. In the period of the patriarchs only one case of divorce is mentioned: Abraham sent away his concubine Hagar at the request of Sarah (Gen 21:9-14). The fact that at the repudiation of a wife the bride-price was not returned to the man certainly worked as a protection for the woman against arbitrary divorce. To dismiss a woman was to abandon property. But in principle divorce was possible, and the later Jewish law recognized it as existing and legal. If a man marries a wife and "if then she finds no favour in his eyes because he has found some indecency in her," he may send her out of his house by writing her a bill of divorce (Deut 24:1). (The significance of the bill is that the wife should be free to enter a new marriage without committing adultery.)

The manner in which the grounds for divorce are specified in the mentioned text is rather casual and not very enlightening. It became the occasion for many discussions and widely different opinions among the later Jewish scribes. At the time of Jesus the two most important interpretations of this text were given by the school of Shammai, the stricter one, which regarded only adultery by the wife as a sufficient cause for divorce; and the school of Hillel, which concluded from Deut 24:1 that any reason was good enough. Among possible reasons are mentioned the wife's burning the food, or even the husband's finding someone better looking.

The prophets show an acceptance of the factual situation on the one hand. On the other hand they look upon the indissolubility of marriage as an ideal. "What is certainly clear from the whole of their preaching on the subject of marriage and marital fidelity is that divorce was something which ought not to happen."[2]

---

[1] Cf. New Catholic Encyclopedia, vol. 9, 1966, art. "Marriage", 261.
[2] G. N. Vollebregt, l. c. 43.

Like the ideal of monogamy, so is also the ideal of indissolubility comprised in the prophets' comparison of the relationship between Yahweh and Israel with the marriage covenant. The climax of the Old Testament ideal of marriage is perhaps Malachi 2:14-16. "The Lord was witness to the covenant between you and the wife of your youth, to whom you have been faithless, though she is your companion and your wife by covenant. Has not the one God made and sustained for us the spirit of life? And what does he desire? Godly offspring. So take heed to yourselves, and let none be faithless to the wife of his youth. For I hate divorce, says the Lord the God of Israel." This ideal is equally reflected in the passage about the creation of woman in the Garden-of-Eden account, in which the first marriage is described not only as monogamous but also as permanent.

The New Testament

The Jewish controversies on the question of divorce gave rise for Jesus to deal with this subject explicitly, and to oppose strongly the indulgence and also laxity of the Jewish scribes on this point. Jesus decreed that according to the will of God marriage was originally indissoluble and was now obligatorily so again. Already in the Sermon on the Mount there are sharp words pronounced against divorce (Mt 5:31f; cf. Lk 16:18). But he also took up a definite position on this question in a discussion recorded by Mark 10:2-12 and Matthew 19:3-9. The way the discussion between Jesus and the Pharisees went left Jesus annulling the right to divorce granted by Moses, which right was established only because of the "hardness of heart" of the Jews. Jesus brought two earlier scriptural passages into the field against the Mosaic dispensation allowing a bill of divorce. By the book of Genesis woman is assigned equality of dignity with man. "Male and female he created them" (Gen 1:27). "And they shall become one flesh" (Gen 2:24). The husband forms with his wife a new community and becomes so completely one with her that they can never again be separated.

One cannot escape the conclusion that Jesus' words signify the unequivocal and absolute prohibition of any kind of real divorce. Yet many have claimed to find a basis for making an exception in the text of the New Testament itself, in the much-quoted "fornication clause" at Matthew 5:32 and 19:9. "I say to you that every man who divorces his wife, except on the ground of unchastity (*porneía*), makes her an adulteress; and whoever marries a divorced woman commits adultery." In the parallel texts of Mark and Luke the clause is missing.

How is the clause to be interpreted? The problem is rather difficult, and all the explanations hitherto suggested encounter objections. However it is not possible to nullify or relax Jesus' fundamental and universal prohibition of divorce by the addition of Matthew, as pointed out by R. Schnackenburg, for the following reasons: (1) This is clear from the meaning of the context of the two quotations. In the Sermon on the Mount (5:31f), Jesus' purpose was to go beyond the law as it had been, and to replace it with a new commandment from God. If Jesus had actually accepted unchastity (adultery) as an exception, he would have been going scarcely any further than Shammai. Furthermore in the discussion 19:3ff we find the sentence "What therefore God has joined together, let no man put asunder", in its absolute form. (2) Mark and Luke know nothing of this exception. It is hardly conceivable that they would have omitted so important a pronouncement. (3) 1 Corinthians 7:10f, the earliest interpretation of our Lord's words, bears witness to the absolute prohibition of divorce, although v. 11 does acknowledge the possibility of separation without divorce. "The conclusion drawn by Protestants and Orthodox from the clause, that in Jesus' mind adultery was a true exception is therefore untenable. (Modern Protestant theologians are coming to concur in this judgment.)"[1]

Scholars have made many different attempts at an explanation of the "fornication clause". The various theories can be learned from the exegetical commentaries and studies of biblical theology.[2] The following explanation possesses great probability: The term *porneía* in the clause refers to marriages which were forbidden by the Old Testament and therefore considered illegal by the Jews as well as by the early Church, while they were often regarded lawful among the gentiles. This concerns in particular certain marriages between blood relations (cf. Lev 18: 6ff; Acts 15:20.29). Such marriages, which could sometimes be found among applicants for baptism, had to be dissolved. This gave the impression of a divorce to the gentiles, and the Matthean redaction is an attempt to meet this problem. Hence, although

---

[1] Rudolf Schnackenburg: The Moral Teaching of the New Testament. — London: Burns and Oates, 1967, 138.

[2] Cf. Schnackenburg, 1. c. 138-141.

on assumption of this explanation the clause seems to say something that is self-evident, this is only true for the Jewish Christians but not for the Christians converted from paganism. For them the dissolution of such marriages had the appearance of an exception from Christ's prohibition of divorce.[1]

Granted the absolute rejection of divorce and remarriage by Christ, there is still another interpretation of Jesus' teaching which recently received attention. According to this understanding Jesus' absolute rejection of divorce expresses an ideal, not an absolute law. This opinion finds support in the fact that Mt 5:31f falls within the Sermon on the Mount, where Christ in radical formulations calls to an ever surpassing perfection, but does not mean to put down laws for literal observation. There are many apodictic statements in the Sermon which the Church has taken as ideals and not as precepts (e.g. the teachings on oaths and on violence). Hence Christ's insistence on the indissolubility of marriage possibly likewise constitutes an ideal to be seriously pursued rather than a law to be literally enforced. On the other hand Lk 16:18 and especially Mt 19:3-9 and Mk 10:2-12 place the prohibition in a context where it has very much the character of a real precept.

In summary one will have to admit that the NT teaching on divorce poses some difficulties which cannot easily be solved. Nonetheless the mind of Christ is plain: He opposes any kind of real divorce.

The teaching of the magisterium

The great majority of the Fathers of the Church uphold the absolute indissolubility of marriage. Yet there are also some who advocate exceptions in difficult cases. They usually quote the fornication clause of Matthew in support of their opinion.[2]

The attitude of the supreme magisterium is characterized by the abiding conviction that the marriage bond is indissoluble. The teaching of the Roman Pontiffs and general councils is consistent and practically unanimous: no remarriage is possible

---

[1] Cf. A. Humbert: Les péchés de sexualité dans le Nouveau Testament; in: Studia Moralia VIII. — Roma: Academia Alfonsiana, 1970, 158f.   William J. O'Shea: Marriage and divorce: the biblical evidence. — Theology Digest 19 (1971), 6.

[2] Cf. G. Pelland: De controversia recenti, relativa ad testimonium traditionis de divortio. — Periodica 62 (1973), 413-421.

after divorce.[1]

Two instances are quoted where popes seem to have deviated from the principle of absolute indissolubility: Gregory II (died 731) and Stephan II (died 757). But it is not clear whether they admitted of a remarriage of divorced partners in the true sense or whether they rather tolerated second marriages in controverted cases in order to avoid greater evil. A third instance is an undue extension of the Privilegium Paulinum to a divorce case by Coelestin III (died 1198).[2]

The Catholic Church has defended the absolute indissolubility of marriage even at the price of great sacrifices and sufferings. A particularly prominent example is the firm attitude of the Roman authorities to king Henry VIII of England, who caused the Anglican schism because the pope would not comply with his request of dissolution of his first marriage.

The Catholic doctrine of indissolubility is unambiguously stated by the Council of Trent.[3] But it is important to note that the Council Fathers consciously avoided to condemn the practice of the Eastern Churches in matters of divorce. According to these Churches there is likewise no valid sacramental marriage in the lifetime of the first partner. But the second marriage is tolerated and reception of the sacraments permitted. The Tridentine decision therefore simply says that the Church has not erred in not allowing remarriage after divorce.[4]

Vatican II again proclaims the indissolubility of marriage — in spite of some suggestions favouring divorce in difficult cases. "By that human act whereby spouses mutually bestow and accept each other, a relationship arises which by divine will and in the eyes of society too is a lasting one. For the good of the spouses

---

[1] The Code of Canon Law further specifies that a sacramental marriage of Christians which has been consummated by the conjugal act cannot be dissolved by any human power, nor by any cause save death (CIC 1141). However a non-consummated sacramental marriage can be dissolved for a just cause (CIC 1142). Moreover a legitimate marriage between non-baptized persons, even though it has been consummated, can be dissolved in favour of the faith by virtue of the Pauline privilege (CIC 1143). This privilege is based on 1 Cor 7:15, where Paul declares that if the unbelieving marriage partner of a convert to the Christian faith "desires to separate, let it be so; in such a case the brother or sister is not bound."

[2] Cf. Bruno Primetshofer: Zerbrochene Ehe und Ehescheidung. — Theol. prakt. Quartalschrift 119 (1971), 122-124.

[3] DS 1797; 1805; 1807.

[4] Cf. Piet Fransen: Divorce on the Ground of Adultery — The Council of Trent. — Concilium, May 1970, 80-100.

and their offspring as well as of society, the existence of this
sacred bond no longer depends on human decision alone." The
goods of matrimony argue for an "unbreakable oneness" of the
spouses (GS 48).

The intrinsic reasons

In pronouncing the absolute prohibition of divorce against
the more permissive law of Moses, Jesus himself appeals to the
original order of creation as the reason for the precept. The
union of man and woman in the marriage bond is a work of
God. He willed this unity to be stronger than the closest ties of
blood. Indeed the law of the Creator is such that the two become
"one flesh" (Gen 2:24; Mt 19:4-6; Mk 10:6-8). Separation of
this oneness therefore is an offence against the intrinsic laws of
marriage, implanted in this union by the Creator himself.

The text of Vatican II enumerates three reasons which
militate against divorce: the good of the spouses, of their offspring
and of society. A fourth reason is of theological nature and
taken from the sacramental status of the Christian marriage.

(1) Divorce is opposed to the good of the spouses. It
frustrates the end of mutual assistance and completion in love.
A husband and wife cannot surrender themselves fully to one
another when there lurks in the mind of either one even the
possibility that their union might be broken. Already by its
psychological structure human love aspires after permanent
companionship. The aim of mutual help and protection, precisely
when it is most necessary, namely in the more difficult situations
of life, is fully granted only in a permanent union of husband
and wife. Thus a true spirit of love appears incompatible with a
matrimony limited as to time.

The certainty that the marriage bond is indissoluble is in
addition a powerful incentive to safeguard the good of conjugal
fidelity and love. It provides a strong motive for the spouses to
bear each others limitations in patient forbearance and to preserve
unity and harmony among each other.

(2) A dissoluble marriage is prejudicial to the child. Whenever the bond is severed, the children are deprived of either parent
or both, and this inevitably affects their confidence, security and
education. The loss to the child is irreparable. The offices of
divorce courts, marriage counselors, psychiatrists, doctors and
pastors are filled with evidence of the havoc wrought on the
child of the divorced couple.

(3)   The good of society requires stable families. For only in this way can the healthy education of the young generation be assured and sure dependence and solidarity within the community protected and aided.

(4)   A last argument is of theological nature. It is founded in the sacramental status of Christian marriages and therefore only holds for Christians. According to Eph 5:21-33 the marriage between baptized Christians is entered after the model of the union of Christ with his Church. With the same faithful love with which Christ loves the Church, husbands must love their wives. And with the same unbreakable bond of devotion and love with which the Church is linked to Christ, wives must be linked to their husbands. "This is a great mystery, and I mean in reference to Christ and the church" (Eph 5:32).

The sacramental nature of the Christian marriage explains why it can never and for no reason whatsoever be dissolved, suppose it is a valid marriage. While marriages of partners who are not baptized can at times be dissolved for the greater good of the faith (cf. 1 Cor 7:12-16).

Separation from bed and board

For a very serious reason the most that is possible is separation from bed and board (judicial separation), i.e. the discontinuation of the common life, while the bond of matrimony remains. Holy Scripture mentions this possibility and permits it (1 Cor 7:10f). An immoral or criminal way of life and danger to soul and body of the other family members give the innocent party the right to a separation as long as the grievances persist. The education of the children is in this case a matter for the innocent party. Judicial separation may also come about without any fault of the partners, e.g. if no children are to be supported and one of the spouses wishes to enter the religious life. But such instances require the consent of the other party.

At first glance all the arguments of reason brought forward against complete divorce seem to militate likewise against judicial separation. Yet this is not fully true. The fidelity of the partners to their marriage promise even in such an onerous situation cannot fail to command the children's respect. The hope and possibility of at least a minimum of mutual help and of an eventual reunification is considerably greater in the case of judicial separation. And most of all the temptation to this kind of separation is much less in degree. Spouses will have recourse to a separation from bed and board only as a last resort — as it should be — , which is far less certain if remarriage is permitted.

Pastoral considerations concerning instances of conflict

Civil laws commonly admit the possibility of divorce with remarriage. There are also quite a number of Catholics who live in marriages where one or both partners are divorced. These marriages are not valid before the Church. That means to say, the Catholic partners of such marriages live at odds with the ecclesial community and its beliefs about marriage. That is why they cannot receive the sacraments, which are signs of unity in faith and Christian living.

Nevertheless the Catholic partners of such marriages often display much good will, they educate their children in the practice of the faith, they go to Mass and would very much like to receive the sacraments. They are distressed because of their exclusion from the sacred rites. But they also feel that they cannot break up their present homes and families and live separately. Can anything be done for them? Especially are there any possible means for pastors to help them?

A solution can hardly be expected from doctrinal changes, at least not for the near future. It is not likely that the Church will suddenly reverse her teaching on divorce and remarriage. What one might more realistically look for is a better understanding of the impediments which render a marriage invalid because of lack of full consent or of psychic or moral impotence (e.g. in instances of homosexuality) or of similar reasons, and a corresponding adaptation of canon law. A greater decentralization in matrimonial jurisdiction could help to accelerate the decisions of the marriage courts. A less rigorous interpretation of the juridical presumption in favour of the marriage bond may at times likewise suggest itself.

There are many instances where an invalid marriage can be revalidated on the basis of present ecclesiastical legislation, suppose the legislation is sufficiently known. Moreover canonical jurisprudence began to recognize various, additional grounds for nullity, especially on account of defective consent (cf. CIC 1095), which were formerly not so clearly distinguished, such as sociopathy (chronically antisocial behaviour), incurable and especially fixed homosexuality, hyperaesthesia (i.e. nymphomania and satyriasis) and psychasthenia (a habitual state of basic indecision).[1] The cases are not rare where something could be done but was not done because of a priest's indifference, or more often because of his simple ignorance of canon law.

But apart from this there will always remain quite a number of agonizing cases where no legal solution is possible. Do the Catholic partners of invalid marriages have any possibility to be admitted to the sacraments, even though they are unable to separate? Traditional moral and pastoral theology sees a way out in the brother-sister arrangement. If the invalidly married couple promises to live together as brother and sister, i.e. to abstain from marital intercourse, they can be allowed to receive the sacraments again. "It is obvious that this is not the solution to all difficult cases, but it would be a mistake to think a priori that it is a viable solution only for old people who have lost interest in sex."[2] In some situations it will provide the best help for the troubled couple. Even though the partners will at times fall short of their promise, because of the condition of proximate occasion in which they live, it can still be an honest attempt to cope with a faulty situation which is otherwise unsolvable.

A more recent approach to the problem starts from the possibility that a Christian may come to the conviction that the former marriage does not bind him in conscience and that he is justified to enter a second marriage. For the law, and also canon law, is never perfect. On this earthly pilgrimage there will never be a total identification between law and conscience, canons and love, regulations and faith.

Such instances may occur where a marriage is truly invalid in the internal forum, but no sufficient proof can be produced for it in the external forum. This is the situation of the so-called "unprovable case". The partners of such marriages may feel justified in conscience to enter a second marriage.

Could they be admitted to the sacraments? Several theologians, if not many, are confident that they can. The priest "has a right to advise the penitent to follow his well-informed conscience even if it is in conflict with external legislation."[3] Naturally the spouses themselves have to attain the final certainty that their

---

[1] Cf. Lawrence G. Wrenn: Annulments. — Canon Law Society of America, 1972, revised edition.

[2] John F. Dedek: Contemporary Sexual Morality. — New York: Sheed and Ward, 1971, 159.

[3] Ladislas Örsy and others: Relief in difficult marriage cases. — Theology Digest 19 (1971), 21.

former marriage is invalid. The priest can help to form their conscience. But he cannot make the decision of conscience for them. If however after sincere consideration and prayer the Christian spouses come to the conclusion that they are not really living in sin, they would in principle be allowed to receive the sacraments. (Of course in doing so they ought to avoid public scandal and harm to the Church; i.e. as a rule they ought to receive Holy Communion in places where they are not known, just as spouses of invalid marriages who promise to live together as brother and sister have always been expected to observe this precaution.)

A situation which can be equated with that of the unprovable case is the condition of a couple that is confronted with an impediment which is not officially recognized, but nevertheless precludes a real marriage. The history of canon law shows a development in the understanding and interpretation of marriage impediments. Some defects which were formerly unknown as marriage impediments are now admitted as sufficient reasons for the annulment of marriages. This is illustrated by the above mentioned examples of psychic and moral impotence. One may justly ask the question whether such marriages have not always been invalid, even before the impediment was officially recognized. A person who happened to contract such a marriage may have come to the sincere conviction that this marriage is not valid in the sight of God. There may still exist other impediments which objectively invalidate a marriage because of impotence or lack of genuine consent or similar basic defects, but which are not recognized by the law. Also in these instances people may feel justified in their conscience to enter a new marriage after the first one failed and had to fail. And one would have to conclude that they too can be allowed to receive the sacraments, the same as the remarried partners of the unprovable cases.

There are finally the "insoluble cases", which create the greatest problem. These are the cases where the first marriage was certainly valid. It fell apart because of the fault of the partners, of one or of both. Having married a second time, they live in invalid marriages. Could it at times be justified to readmit also them to the sacraments? Certainly as long as reconciliation between the parties of the first marriage has not become really impossible, admission to the sacraments is not warranted. Sincere repentance of the wrong committed must prove itself in the will to repair the damage and to restore the first marriage.

But how should those instances be dealt with where the first marriage is irreparably broken and the second firmly established? Maintenance of the union may have become a new moral obligation towards the partner and the children of the second marriage. If the spouses sincerely repent of their former fault, may they be admitted to the sacraments? The "New Catechism" for adults of the Netherlands judges that "in this world of failures, the sacraments are given to men to nourish and strengthen them."[1] If their conscience does not condemn them, the spouses of the second marriage may receive the sacraments. Other theologians express the same conviction, while further specifying the conditions for a re-admission.[2]

The Commission of Cardinals appointed to examine the "New Catechism" however raised strong objections against such a practice. The Commission demands that the solution is to be sought within the framework of the moral theology of the Church. "In some cases the partners of the invalid marriage will agree to live together simply in mutual friendship. (If they are seriously prepared to do this, and if the danger of scandal is completely excluded, they may receive the sacraments.) In other cases (if they do not make this resolution) they can take part, in humility before God in the Church's life of prayer, practising justice and love towards their fellow-men. This is no slight matter in the economy of salvation which the Lord Jesus announced."[3] The Commission justly points out that the sacraments are not the only means of grace. If spouses accept their exclusion from them in the spirit of true repentance, this also can be a powerful source of grace for them.

---

[1] A New Catechism. Catholic Faith for Adults. — London: Burns and Oates, 1967, 397.

[2] Cf. Karl Lehmann: Indissolubility of Marriage and Pastoral Care of the Divorced who Remarry. — Int. Cath. Review 1 (1972), 249. Most radical in his solution is Charles E. Curran: Divorce; in: New Perspectives in Moral Theology. — Notre Dame, Ind.: Fides Publishers, 1974, 212-276. He definitely judges that the Church must change her attitude towards divorce. He not only expresses the conviction that also the sacramental marriage of Christians can be dissolved and a remarriage of the divorced partners permitted. He also feels that the opinion possesses sufficient certainty, so that in practice he sanctions such second marriages by "a small Eucharistic celebration and an exchange of vows", whether the partners regard their first marriage as invalid or not (246f). But he also cautions the couples that these marriages do not enjoy official recognition in the Church, and justly so.

[3] Eduoard Dhanis and Jan Visser: The Supplement to A New Catechism. On behalf of the Commission of Cardinals appointed to examine A New Catechism. — London: Burns and Oates, 1969, 57.

Perhaps the practice of the Eastern Churches might still merit some further discussion and study in this context. They grant the possibility of a second marriage to separated partners, as has been mentioned earlier. This is tolerated for grave reasons, such as abandonment, insanity, plot against one's life by the spouse. The Eastern Churches did not develop a consistent and systematic doctrine on this matter. They unfold their teaching more often in liturgical rites than in canonical texts. They provide guiding principles rather than explicit legislation. The sacramental marriage is indissoluble according to orthodox theology, and the Church never divorces it. However she acknowledges that in certain situations the first marriage has ceased to exist as an external reality. And in these circumstances she gives permission to the innocent party to marry again. But the second marriage is not put on par with the first. This finds expression in the marriage rite, which is more of a penitential service than of the joyful betrothal and coronation of the first.[1]

Could certain elements of this practice prove acceptable to the Roman Church? Perhaps it will need a long time of reflection and re-evaluation before an answer can be given.

4.   *Marriage as a public act*

Since the marriage of two people is an important act of public interest, it must be entered into publicly and made known to the community. Marriage has also need of protection by society. Therefore it is a concern of society itself and of those responsible for the common welfare, who are required to ratify and to protect the marriage covenant by their laws. A good law is not contrary to love, but signifies the recognition and protection of the bond of love in the public sphere.

The public nature of marriage varied at different times and in different regions. After the Council of Trent in the sixteenth century precise legal forms were instituted for Catholic marriages in canon law. (This is possible because marriage is also a sacrament, and the Church is guardian of the sacraments.) It was laid down that marriage must be contracted before the parish priest and two witnesses. This juridical form is still today a condition for the validity of a Catholic marriage, save a few exceptions in

---

[1] References: Olivier O. Rousseau: Divorce and Remarriage: East and West. — Concilium, vol. 4, nr. 3, April 1967, 57-69. Alexander Schmemann: The Indissolubility of Marriage: The Theological Tradition of the East; in: The Bond of Marriage. — University of Notre Dame Press, 1968, 97-116.

danger of death or when it is foreseen that a priest will not be available for some time, in which case the presence of two witnesses suffices, or when dispensation from the canonical form has been granted by the local Ordinary in the case of a mixed marriage.

It is understandable and even desirable that the state too feels responsible for the protection of the marriage contract and provides the required legal security for it. This led to the introduction of civil marriage. Some countries avoided a double ceremony by admitting the religious ceremony as legally valid. In others they remain distinct.

From the necessity and obligation to protect the values of marriage for the best of society, marriage laws and impediments result. The impediments usually stem from the very nature of marriage: a marriage bond already in existence; one or other of the pair being too young; compulsion or fear; too close a degree of blood relationship; physical or psychic impotence. They set out in detail what is contrary to the nature and dignity of marriage.

5. *Marriage as a sacrament*

a) Sacramental sign and grace

In Ephesians chapter 5 St. Paul uses the Christ-Church relationship as a model for marriage. The customary admonition to the woman takes on a mystical basis: Man is the leader of his wife, as Christ is the leader of the Church; as the Church is subject to Christ, so are wives to their husbands (vv. 22-24). The man on the other hand is not given lordly authority, but is admonished to love. "Husbands, love your wives, as Christ loved the church" (v. 25).

Thus God himself has located a mystery with a deep meaning in marriage. It has a bearing on the unity of Christ and the Church (v. 32). The total, surrendering love of Christ for his Church, and of the Church for her Lord, is model and measure for the mutual love of man and wife in marriage.

On these mystical reflections of St. Paul the Catholic as well as the Orthodox Church base their doctrine of the sacramental character of marriage. For what Paul does in this passage is more than merely to motivate a moral warning with the relationship between Christ and the Church, as for example he urges slaves to serve their masters as in Christ (Eph 6:5-8). He describes the relationship as a mysterious reality, of which marriage is a sacramental sign. The permanent bond of marriage is a symbol of the eternal unity of Christ and the Church. This is the deepest reason for the absolutely unitary and unbreakable nature of the sacramental marriage.

Also the Second Vatican Council expresses the sacramental reality of marriage in the context of Christ's union with the Church: "Authentic married love is caught up into divine love and is governed and enriched by Christ's redeeming power and the saving activity of the Church. Thus this love can lead the spouses to God with powerful effect and can aid and strengthen them in the sublime office of being a father and a mother. For this reason, Christian spouses have a special sacrament by which they are fortified and receive a kind of consecration in the duties and dignity of their state" (GS 48).

The Christian spouses themselves administer the sacrament by their mutual consent and promise. By means of this sacrament all the love, tenderness, help and counsel that married people offer each other is a source of grace and of Christ's presence. The fact that the spouses themselves administer the sacrament also symbolizes the relationship of spiritual care which they enter towards each other. The sacrament likewise equips them for a priestly service towards the children whom God may give to them.

b)   The Church's responsibility for the marriage covenant

The character of marriage as a sacrament implies that the Church has a responsibility for the God-willed order and holiness of this covenant. Therefore marriages of Catholics are subject to the law of the Church. And Catholic spouses must, in all matters concerned with marriage, adhere to the doctrine and directives of the Church. It follows that for Catholics a purely civil marriage without observance of the canonical form is not a valid marriage, unless dispensation has been granted by the competent ecclesiastical authorities. However if the couple actually has the firm will to enter a matrimonial union, we should not term it a concubinage but rather an "invalid marriage".

Equally civil divorce does not dissolve a valid marriage bond between Catholics. Nevertheless for serious reasons it could be permitted that Catholics sue for civil divorce in spite of a valid, sacramental marriage. This would be the case if civil divorce is the only safeguard of rights after a "separation from bed and board" has lawfully been obtained from the Church authority, e.g. to prevent the loss of property or support for mother and children, or to avoid the danger of legal sanctions, or to guarantee the custody of the children and their Christian education.

c) Mixed marriages

Ecclesiastical legislation makes a distinction between the mixed marriage of a Catholic with a non-Catholic Christian (the prohibitive impediment of mixed religion) and the mixed marriage of a Catholic with a non-baptized person (the diriment impediment of disparity of cult). Mixed marriages always constitute a problem, but most of all in cases where the non-Catholic partner has strong religious convictions. Not less unfortunate are marriages of a Catholic with an avowed Marxist, even though he has not broken with the Church externally. In the open society of today mixed marriages cannot be totally avoided. Yet Catholic as well as Protestant ministers agree that these marriages often cause detriment first of all to the faith, but also to the harmony in the family in general.

If husband and wife do not agree on their faith and religious convictions, their longing for unity will remain unfulfilled in important regards, and tensions are caused. After all a couple would wish to be together in their experience of the great values of life. But in a mixed marriage it often happens that the partners are at variance with each other in the most essential things. And even where two people are able to accept each other's convictions with reverence, love and tolerance, the question of the baptism and religious education of the child is not yet solved. Neither Catholics nor Protestants are able to do justice to the religious convictions of both partners at the same time, suppose both are really convinced of their faith.[1] In which religion shall the child be brought up? There is also a serious danger of growing indifferent to the things of faith. "For these reasons the Church, conscious of her duty, discourages the contracting of mixed marriages, for she is most desirous that Catholics be able in matrimony to attain to perfect union of mind and full communion of life."[2]

The present, modified norms for marriages of Catholics with non-Catholic partners are laid down in the Motu Proprio of Pope

---

[1] A very instructive study of the provisions of the Protestant Churches of Germany for mixed marriages is given by Georg May: Bestimmung über die Eingehung und Behandlung von Mischehen in den Ordnungen des deutschen Protestantismus. — Trierer theologische Zeitschrift 73 (1964), 22-44.

[2] Motu Proprio of Pope Paul VI *Matrimonia mixta* of March 31, 1970; AAS 62 (1970), 258.

Paul VI *Matrimonia mixta* and in CIC 1124–9. The faculty to dispense from the impediments of mixed religion and disparity of cult is with the local Ordinary. In some countries however the power to dispense from the prohibitive impediment of mixed religion has been delegated by the bishops' conferences to all the priests who possess general permission to assist marriages.

In order to obtain this dispensation, the Catholic party must declare that he is ready to remove dangers of falling away from the faith. He is also gravely bound to make a sincere promise to do all in his power to have all the children baptized and brought up in the Catholic Church. At an opportune time the non-Catholic party must be informed of these promises which the Catholic party has to make, so that it is clear that he is cognizant of them. It is for the bishops' conferences to determine the way in which these declarations and promises shall be made: whether by word of mouth alone, in writing, or before witnesses.

Attention is to be called to the fact that the promise of the Catholic party is to be made with the restriction that he will do *all in his power* to have the children brought up in the Catholic faith. The content of the promise is only the sincere intention, not the actual realization of a Catholic education of the children. If therefore the circumstances should make it impossible for one or the other party to educate the children in his faith, this would not deprive him of the possibility of salvation.

The canonical form is to be used for contracting mixed marriages, just as for all other Catholic marriages, i.e. the marriage consent is to be given before an authorized priest (the parish priest or the local Ordinary or a priest delegated by either of them) and before two witnesses. This form is required for the liceity of a mixed marriage of a Catholic with a member of the separated Eastern Churches, as long as it is celebrated in the presence of a sacred minister and the other requirements of the law are honoured,[1] and for the validity of all other mixed marriages.[2] However if serious difficulties stand in the way of observing the canonical form, local Ordinaries have the right to dispense from the canonical form in any mixed marriage. The marriage can then be contracted validly before the Protestant minister or even before the civil authorities. But the bishops should see to it that there is always some public form of ceremony. — It is to be noted that the Catholic Church regards purely

---

[1] Cf. the Decree *Crescens matrimoniorum* of Febr. 22, 1967; AAS 59 (1967), 166.

[2] Motu Proprio *Matrimonia mixta;* AAS 62 (1970), 261 (nr. 8).

Protestant or non-Christian marriages as valid, i.e. their validity does not depend on the canonical form in any way.

Ecumenical marriages are possible in the sense that at a mixed marriage, which is performed in the Catholic or Protestant rite, also the minister of the other Church or religious community participates in the liturgical celebration. Simultaneous weddings are however forbidden, i.e. the celebration of marriage before a Catholic priest or deacon and a non-Catholic minister, performing their respective rites together. Nor is it permitted to have another religious marriage ceremony before or after the Catholic ceremony, for the purpose of giving or renewing matrimonial consent.

III. Responsible parenthood and regulation of birth[1]

God blessed the first human couple with the words: "Be fruitful and multiply" (Gen 1:28). This blessing expresses the conviction that sexuality and marriage serve the propagation of mankind. A wealth of children is considered by Holy Scripture a favour from God and a reason for joy. Conversely childlessness is a misfortune and a divine punishment (Lev 20:20f; Is 47:9; Jer 18:21). "Sons are a heritage from the Lord, the fruit of the womb a reward", prays the psalmist (Ps 127:3). And before Rebecca departed from Mesopotamia to marry Isaac, her mother and brother had given her this blessing: "Sister, be the mother of thousands of ten thousands" (Gen 24:60). Such blessings were customary at Jewish marriages (cf. Ruth 4:11f).

Today as much as in the past, children are rightly to be considered a gift and a blessing from God. "A babe in a house is a well-spring of pleasure", writes a poet. The baby is the fulfillment of human matrimony and the pride of his parents.

Because this is so, many parents took it for granted in former times that they should accept the children as they come. This is not a compelling conclusion. But it created no problem

---

[1] References: Germain G. Grisez: Contraception and the Natural Law. — Milwaukee: Bruce Publishing Co., 1964. John T. Noonan, Jr.: Contraception. A History of Its Treatment by the Catholic Theologians and Canonists. — Cambridge, Mass.: Harvard University Press, 1965. G. Egner: Contraception Vs. Tradition. A Catholic Critique. — New York: Herder and Herder. 1967. Ambrodgio Valsecchi: Controversy. The birth control debate 1958-1968. — London: G. Chapman, 1968. A. M. J. Kloostermann: Family Planning and Christian Marriage. — Fontana Books, 1970. J. Horgan, ed.: "Humanae Vitae" and the Bishops. — Dublin: Irish University, 1972. John and Sheila Kippley: The Art of Natural Family Planning. — Cincinnati, Ohio: The Couple to Couple League, 1975.

up until recently. Today however we are suddenly confronted with the fact that population in many parts of the world is growing too fast and that especially the young developing nations have great difficulties to absorb the rapidly increasing numbers of their people. Many parents also encounter individual difficulties of economic, pedagogic or other nature, which cause obstacles to a greater number of children. This raises the question of the justification or even need of birth control, of its limits and the means to achieve it.

1. *Justification and limits of birth control*

Religious quarters are sometimes inclined (or at least were in the past) to minimize the importance of the problem of birth control. It is pointed out that the roots of the problem are much more to be sought in the inequality of the distribution of wealth and in the lack of efficient utilization of the inexhaustible resources of nature. God who has charged men to multiply and who calls them into being has also provided the means to satisfy their needs and the demands of life. Hence the real means to cope with the situation is an increased scientific and technical effort on the part of man to extend his dominion over nature, to amend and improve deficient economic and social conditions, and to enhance a greater solidarity of the affluent nations with the poorer ones.

One will certainly have to agree that all these means must be used to the full, much more today than in the past. The world can still feed many more people, if only all the available land is well cultivated, if technology is everywhere applied and further improved, if also the immense oceans are utilized in their capacity as food resources. But nevertheless there is a limit to these possibilities. If the population increase is too rapid, as this is the case in many young nations, then the economic development of the country can simply not keep pace with it. The result is malnutrition, lack of housing, unemployment, deficient school facilities, want of medical care and hygienic conditions.[1] Besides, some countries have already reached a point of density of population where they cannot absorb great increases in population anymore.

---

[1] A particularly striking example of population explosion is Bangladesh. In 1961, it had a population of 50.8 million. By 1971, the population had grown to 75 million. The annual growth rate is 3.15%. The Philippines had 27.1 million inhabitants in 1960 and 38 million 10 years later in 1970. The annual growth rate is 3.01%.

At times it is argued that more people means a more powerful nation. But this is true only if these people are well nourished, well educated, well equipped and able to work.

The need and obligation to responsible parenthood has ever more clearly been recognized by theologians during the past decades and always more clearly stated in the official documents of the Catholic Church. Parents are obliged to give birth to their children in a responsible way. This duty also finds expression in the documents of Vatican II. Parents "will thoughtfully take into account both their own welfare and that of their children, those already born and those which may be foreseen. For this accounting they will reckon with both the material and the spiritual conditions of the times as well as of their state in life. Finally, they will consult the interests of the family group, of temporal society, and of the Church herself" (GS 50).[1]

The Council also recognizes the fact that population control is not merely the concern of individual couples who have particular difficulties, but that also public authorities have the right and duty to contribute to the solution of the population problems in their nations. "Within the limits of their own competence, government officials have rights and duties with regard to the population problems of their own nation, for instance, in the matter of social legislation as it affects families, of migration to cities, or information relative to the condition and needs of the nation" (GS 87). The Council however adds that the question of how many children should be born ultimately must be left to the conscientious dicision of the parents. "The question can in no way be committed to the decision of government" (ib.).

Taking into account the health of the parents, the spiritual and material welfare of the family, and the interests of society, the following reasons would justify a limitation of the number of children:

1. danger for the mother's health and life;
2. eugenic considerations in cases of hereditary defects;
3. economic difficulties, e.g. a low income of the family, continued danger of unemployment, lack of housing space;
4. pedagogical difficulties, such as caused by the higher educational demands of the industrial societies;

---

[1] Cf. likewise the encyclical *Populorum Progressio* by Paul VI, nr. 37 (1967).

5.   national needs conditioned by limited resources. Especially less developed nations may find it impossible to support too great a number of needy citizens with sufficient aids and social benefits.

On the other hand there also exists a trend at present in precisely those nations which are economically better developed, to have only one or two children. Nor is this by any means regarded as the ideal answer to the problems of world population by the Catholic Church. A healthy and economically safe couple which is able to educate their children well can account for more than only one or two children. It is particularly in view of the present aversion against more children in the developed nations that the Council praises those couples "who with wise and common deliberation, and with a gallant heart, undertake to bring up suitably even a relatively large family" (GS 50).

In fact although pedagogical considerations may sometimes advise a certain limitation of the number of children, they advise at the same time to have more than only one or two. Even the interest of the temporal society requires more than an average of only two children per family. For at such an average a society will not only not increase, but even decrease, since two children are already required to replace their parents, and no further child is available to replace those who do not marry, who remain childless, who die early.

Hence the interest and welfare of the society demand a number of children which is neither too large nor too small. The desirable number of children in a family seems to be a number of three to five, although there are certainly well-founded exceptions to this rule.

Responsible parenthood includes the policy of prudent spacing of the birth of children. However the pedagogical insight that the age differences between the children in a family ought not to be too great would advise a spacing of not much more than two and a half years.

The need of responsible parenthood and the justification of a sober population control are universally recognized and not a matter of controversy in the Catholic Church. Controverted are the means by which the goal is to be achieved. The Council did not resolve the question concerning the methods of birth control that can harmonize the needs of conjugal love with the responsible transmission of life. It limited itself to a general ruling, which however contains some basic principles. "The moral aspect of any procedure does not depend solely on sincere intentions or on an evaluation of motives. It must be determined by objective standards. These, based on the nature öf the human person and his acts, preserve the full sense of mutual self-giving and human procreation in the context of true love. . . . Relying on these principles, sons of the Church may not undertake methods of regulating procreation which are found blameworthy by the teaching authority of the Church in its unfolding of the divine law" (GS 51). Hence some further considerations must be dedicated to the admissible and inadmissible means of birth control in the light of Catholic teaching.

2. *Natural family planning*

If one leaves out of account sexual abstinence and the somewhat controversial practice of the "amplexus reservatus",[1] which both are of a very limited value, the Catholic Church has so far officially only recognized the so-called rhythm method or natural family planning as a lawful means of birth control. This position has recently been reconfirmed by the encyclical of Pope Paul VI *Humanae Vitae* of 1968.

The rhythm method is based on the findings of the physicians Ogino from Japan (1930) and Knaus from Austria (1929). They discovered that the woman is not equally fertile at all times, but has fertile and infertile periods. The reason for this is that only once during the menstrual cycle of the woman an ovum matures, namely twelve to sixteen days before the beginning of the next menstrual period. Since the ovum has a life duration of only 12 hours to two days at most, the woman is infertile for the rest of the period. A couple who wants to avoid further pregnancies, temporarily or for good, is advised to have intercourse

---

[1] "Amplexus reservatus", also called "copula sicca", is a full marital union with deliberate avoidance of the perfect sexual satisfaction by orgasm. One must appreciate the mastery of self required by this method and the determination of a couple to use this form of union of love in order not to offend against life. Nevertheless according to a warning of the Holy Office in 1952 a priest may not speak of the matter in his spiritual guidance as though there were no misgivings about it from the standpoint of the Christian moral law (DS 3907). The reason for this warning is probably to be found in the fear that people might frequently not be able to have this degree of restraint and therefore expose themselves to the danger of onanism. The caution is however not a condemnation of the method. In principle couples are allowed to use it.

only during the infertile days when no mature ovum is to be expected.

An additional help in the use of this method is the record on the daily body temperature of the woman (biphasic record). It is based on the discovery that at the time of ovulation the basal temperature of the woman rises to a higher level and maintains that level until the onset of the next menstrual period. Then it falls to the original level again.

Lately still another aid for the determination of the moment of ovulation has been developed in the so-called mucus method. Basis of the method is the circumstance that the body of the woman discharges a cervical mucus as fertility approaches. The method consists in the observation of this mucus. Absence of the mucus indicates infertility.

From the time when the rhythm method has been discovered first, it has been accepted as lawful by Catholic moral theology and by the papal teachings. The reason is that in this method man avails himself of natural laws and rhythms of fecundity which God himself has implanted in human nature. Man does not interfere with the openness of the marriage act to the transmission of life. If no conception takes place during the infertile days, then this is so because nature itself suspends fecundity during these times. In contradistinction to this, all the other methods positively impede the development of natural processes, either by interruption, mechanical devices or chemical intervention.[1]

At times the use of the rhythm method is rendered difficult or even impossible if the menstrual cycles are too irregular, at least if the method is employed without the daily measurement of temperature or the observation of the cervical mucus. The menstrual cycle may, for example, at one time last 20 days, at another time 30, and still at another time 28. But the same progestin compounds which are used as the "pill" for temporal sterilization, can also serve to normalize too irregular menstrual cycles. The lawfulness of such medical use of the compounds is agreed upon in Catholic moral theology. It is up to the physician to decide how long the compounds have to be tried for the purpose of normalizing the cycle and whether after an unsuccessful attempt another trial should be made at a later date.

It is to be admitted that the rhythm method is not absolutely safe. But if carefully observed, it is safer than most of the other

---

[1] Cf. *Humanae Vitae,* nr. 11-16.

methods, such as withdrawal, condom, diaphragm and jelly.[1] Only the IUD[2] and the sterilizing medicaments are still safer.

It is also true that the careful observation and calculation of the infertile and fertile days is somewhat irksome, especially if combined with the temperature and mucus method. In addition the method requires the sacrifice of periodic continence.[3]

But all the methods have their pros and cons, and the disadvantages of the rhythm method are not among the greatest. It allows the couple an integral marital union. In contradistinction to the "pills" it precludes harm to health and is by far more inexpensive. It also uses no artificial means foreign to the body, a circumstance which makes IUDs to many women less desirable.

3.   *Unlawful means of birth control according to "Humanae Vitae"*

Pope Paul VI only restates the traditional Catholic teaching when he writes in article 14 of the encyclical *Humanae Vitae:* "We must once again declare that the direct interruption of the generative process already begun, and, above all, directly willed and procured abortion, even if for therapeutic reasons, are to be absolutely excluded as licit means of regulating birth. Equally to be excluded, as the teaching authority of the Church has frequently declared, is direct sterilization, whether perpetual or temporary, whether of the man or of the woman. Similarly excluded is every action which.. . . . proposes, whether as an end or as a means, to render procreation impossible. . . . It is an error to think that a conjugal act which is deliberately made infecund and so is intrinsically dishonest could be made honest and right

---

[1] Dr. med. J. Rötzer gives the following statistics of failures for the different contraceptive methods (Empfängnisregelung — nur eine Frage der Technik? — Theol. prakt. Quartalschrift 115, 1967, 169; cf. 174). The percentages indicate the number of undesired pregnancies within one year for 100 couples who have regular intercourse:

coitus interruptus (withdrawal): 12 to 38
lavage of vagina after intercourse: 36
diaphragm plus jelly: 6 to 29
jelly alone: 9 to 39
condom: 6 to 19.

[2] But also the IUD is not absolutely safe. Its rate of failure is estimated at 1-3%.

[3] At times the rhythm method is accused of requiring continence precisely during the time when the sexual inclination is strongest, i.e. during ovulation. This opinion is however not uncontested. Experts assert that an increased libido during the time of ovulation is not provable (cf. J. Rötzer: Die natürliche Empfängnisregelung als vorgezeichneter Weg. — Theologie und Glaube 11, 1968, 232).

by the ensemble of a fecund conjugal life''. The doctrine is reiterated once again by Pope John Pauls II in his apostolic exhortation *Familiaris Consortio* of 1981. In its main assertions it repeats the very words of *Humanae Vitae.*[1]

Noteworthy is that the encyclical avoids qualifying all or some of the listed offences explicitly or implicitly as "gravely sinful". The two moral qualifications given, namely "absolutely excluded" and "intrinsically dishonest", emphasize that the actions thus qualified are never allowed, but it is not determined by the expressions whether these actions are venially or gravely sinful. In the following some further explanations must be given to the different kinds of rejected means.

a)   *Abortion.* Abortion is the kind of birth regulation which finds the strongest rejection in the papal encyclical. Christian moral teaching always considered abortion as gravely sinful (cf. GS 51), and canon law inflicts an excommunication reserved to the Ordinary upon those who successfully procure an abortion.

A particular problem is at hand with regard to those means of birth control which hinder a fertilized ovum from nestling in the uterus. The British Council of Churches is of the opinion that a fertilized ovum not yet settled in the uterus is not yet human life. Procedures to hinder the ovum from nestling therefore would not be abortion.[1] In view of recent medical findings also some Catholic moral theologians are inclined to the opinion that before the nestling of the fertilized ovum in the uterus wall one cannot speak of a human individuum yet. Hence one could not simply classify the IUD or those medicaments which possibly hinder the fertilized ovum from nidation as "abortive" means. For a more detailed discussion of the question see "Abortion" in chapter III: "Bodily life and health".[2]

b)   *Permanent sterilization.* It is gravely immoral to destroy human fertility arbitrarily by means of permanent sterilization not effected for reasons of health. This is the common judgment of traditional Catholic moral theology.

For the confessor a somewhat difficult question arises here. What measures has he to take if a penitent accuses himself of this sin? Must the confessor require a reversion of the surgical

---

[1] Cf. Familiaris Consortio, no. 32 (1981).
[2] Human Reproduction: A Study of Some Emergent Problems and Questions in the Light of the Christian Faith. The British Council of Churches. London 1962.

act of sterilization? Suppose a new pregnancy now and later on would be against the principle of responsible parenthood, there is no such moral obligation.[1] But also in other cases the reversion of the sterilization could hardly ever be insisted upon, since the difficulties and expenses involved in such attempts are generally of serious or grave proportions.[2] But true repentance would require an adequate satisfaction. In case the motive for the sterilization was an unjustified refusal to have further children, an adequate satisfaction might for example be a regular aid for an orphanage.

c) *Interrupted intercourse.* There is of old a very common tradition in the Catholic Church which regards interrupted intercourse as gravely sinful. Interrupted intercourse is also called onanism because of Onan, who was supposed to give offspring to this brother who had died childless. But Onan did not want to fulfill this his duty and to create offspring with his brother's wife Tamar. Therefore he spilled the semen on the ground. For this reason he was slain by the Lord (Gen 38:9f).

Yet B. Häring justly remarks: "Only a couple who act out of egoism in refusing the service of life without any reasonable motive can be compared with Onan whose sin God punished with death (Gen 38:9f). A great injustice would be done to married people who follow the fundamental principle of responsible parenthood with the greatest generosity, if in their case an interrupted intercourse were to be called 'onanism'. It does not follow, however, from this distinction that in their case a deliberate or systematic use of the method of interrupted intercourse can be considered as morally indifferent."[3]

d) *Artificial means of birth control.* Until recently the use of all artificial means of birth control was — supported by the magisterium of the popes — judged as gravely sinful. But since these means are of rather recent origin, this moral doctrine does not look back on a long tradition. The encyclical *Humanae Vitae* simply states that they are illicit. The number of theologians and bishops rejecting the traditional qualification — namely that the use of all these means without further distinctions is gravely sinful — is at any rate very considerable today.

Some of the artificial means, as e.g. the condom, obstruct the natural integrity of the conjugal act in its expression as an act of union; they are therefore more opposed to the natural

[1] Cf. B. Häring III, 1966, 346.
[2] Cf. the translator's note in B. Häring III, 1966, 346.
[3] Häring III. 1966, 354f.

performance of the marital act. Others obstruct this integrity less or not at all, as e.g. certain antiseptics, which kill the spermatozoa, or spermicidal jellies and diaphragms, both introduced into the vagina to occlude the mouth of the uterus and thus prevent entrance of the spermatozoa, or sterilizing drugs (usually progesterone compounds), or intrauterine devices (IUD). But some of these means might also constitute dangers to health, at least in the long run. Many physicians judge that the drugs should not be taken longer than one year, after which an interruption of several months should follow. As reason for this is mentioned changes in the ovaries. In principle the sterilizing drugs should not be taken without previous consultation of a physician.[1] All these factors have to be considered in a moral, psychological and medical evelution of the various artificial means.

The therapeutic use of the sterilizing drugs (progesterone compounds) is always lawful, as indicated by the encyclical itself (nr. 15). It was already mentioned that they are used to normalize a woman's period. This is permissible even if a temporal impediment to procreation should result therefrom. Whether the use of the progesterone compounds during the time of lactation is medically indicated and from the moral standpoint justified is still under discussion by physicians and moralists. It is argued that during the time of lactation the organism of a healthy woman would produce hormons similar to the progesterone compounds which hinder ovulation, and this usually for a period of six to nine months. Thus a time of rest is granted to the woman by nature itself. In case the maternal organism does not produce those hormons preventing ovulation during the time of lactation — as this happens rather frequently today —, medicine would be allowed to remedy this defect of nature by providing the woman with artificial progesterone during lactation. The use of such drugs in this case is favoured by L. Janssens, O'Callaghan, Ford, Kelly, and others more.[2]

---

[1] It is reported that users of oral contraceptives run twice the risk of acquiring gallbladder disease as women who do not take them, and two to five times the risk — and even more, depending on the number of years the pill is taken — of developing benign liver tumor (The International Family Planning Digest, June 2, 1976, published by the Alan Guttmacher Institute for Planned Parenthood, U.S.A.). The danger of a thrombus is said to be seven to ten times higher for those who take the pill.

[2] Other supporters of the opinion are De Guchteneere, Healy, Fuchs, Weber, Salazar, Perico, Vimercati, Böckle, Demmer, Aldunati and Navarro; cf. Ambrogio Valsecchi: Controversy. The birth control debate 1958-1968. — London: G. Chapman, 1968, 21.

Note that a husband or wife who does not agree to his partner's using unlawful means of birth control and who cannot change his partner's mind, is nevertheless allowed to render the marriage debt. He may even ask for it, except for the days during the fertile period in case he also agreed to have no more children. The cooperation of the innocent spouse would only be material. It would be allowed for a moderately grave reason, such as domestic peace or the avoidance of the dangers of abstinence. According to B. Häring the simple fact of the mutual marriage rights constitutes a sufficient reason for the material cooperation.[1]

4. Echo on *Humanae Vitae* and interpretations

The encyclical *Humanae Vitae* received a very divided echo and is probably the most controverted encyclical ever written. This must be understood against the background of the discussions preceeding the encyclical in the Church; of the hopes of a revision and the petitions for a change of the traditional doctrine; of the Pope's decision to withdraw the matter from discussion in the Council and to reserve it to his own competence; and, last not least, of the vote of the papal commission for birth control, whose theologians and lay experts voted with a strong majority for the admission also of other means of birth control than only the rhythm method.[2]

The controversy does not concern abortion. It is rejected with great unanimity among Catholics as a means of population control. The principal issue of the dispute is the artificial means of birth control. Many theologians and lay people are convinced that at least under certain circumstances their use is not contrary to moral law. They find themselves in conflict with the teaching of the encyclical. How is this conflict to be solved?

Many bishops' conferences issued pastoral letters on the question.[3] All acknowledge the pronouncement of the supreme teaching authority with reverence, honour it as the expression of

---

[1] B. Häring III, 1966, 358.

[2] Only four theologians of the commission, which at the end counted over 60 theologians and lay experts, signed the minority report, while the others favoured a more liberal attitude of the Church towards the artificial contraceptives. (Cf. Pope and Pill. More documentation on the birth regulation debate; ed. Leo Pyle. — London: Darton, Longman and Todd, 1968, 84).

[3] The comments of 33 bishops' conferences, issued between July 1968 and February 1969, have been gathered and published in their essentials by Eduardus Hamel: Conferentiae Episcopales et Encyclica "Humanae Vitae". — Periodica 58 (1969), 243-349.

the Pope's sincere conviction, and respect his duty to speak up in matters which concern faith and Christian living. But several are at the same time keenly aware of the moral difficulties which the papal statement is attended with for many married couples. They give therefore further interpretations of the encyclical and try to reconcile its teaching as far as possible with the dilemma of married people. Since also the bishops speak in the name of Christ (LG 25) and are "vicars and ambassadors of Christ" (LG 27), the comments of the bishops possess a special authority. These documents "possess greater weight than the studies of private theologians. They are truly acts of the ordinary teaching office of the Church."[1] Several of the comments are very valuable contributions.

Spouses in difficulty not separated from the love of God. Various bishops' conferences, such as Austria,[2] England,[3] Brasil,[4] Japan[5] and Italy,[6] point out that the encyclical contains no threat of condemnation. Far from being excluded from the sacraments, those in difficulties are invited to receive them frequently. If spouses, in spite of good will, are unable to follow the directives of the encyclical because of inevitable circumstances, they should never think that they are separated from the love and grace of God. "If somebody, notwithstanding his good will to fulfill the directives of the encyclical, is unable to observe it in some matters because of objective and necessary circumstances, he should never think himself separated from the love of God".[7] Confessors on their part ought not to keep away from the holy Eucharist those who did not yet arrive at the conviction of the truth of the official doctrine or who find themselves in difficulties because of a sickness or other grave reasons.[8]

[1] E. Hamel, l. c. 331.   [2] Ib. 273.
[3] Ib. 276f.   [4] Ib. 303.
[5] Ib. 318.   [6] Ib. 270f.
[7] The Japanese bishops, Hamel 318.
[8] Francois Reckinger remarks that the encyclical would permit the interpretation, according to German, French and Italian experts who take a favourable stand to it, that the use of the controverted means of birth control is only venially sinful. (Wird man morgen wieder beichten? — Kevelaer: Butzon und Bercker, 1974, 122f.).

Choosing the lesser evil in conflicts of duties. The Canadian and French bishops foresee that spouses who are confronted with the problems of birth control, will not seldom find themselves in a conflict of duties. They do not know how to reconcile the demands of conjugal love with the needs of responsible parenthood. The Canadian bishops explain that spouses who sincerely try to conform to the norms of the encyclical, but are not able to attain this goal, can nevertheless "be certain that they are not separated from the divine love, if they honestly choose that alternative which appears to them the better one."[2]

The French bishops develop this thought still further. They advance the following considerations: "Contraception can never be a good. It is always a disorder, but this disorder is not always culpable." The reason is that spouses are often confronted with two evils of which they can avoid but one. If circumstances force them to some kind of birth control, and if they are not able to take refuge in the lawful rhythm method, they see themselves placed before the alternative either to use unlawful, artificial means of birth control, or to abstain from the physical expression of marital love and to endanger thereby the stability of their family life. "With regard to this", the bishops write, "we simply recall the constant teaching of moral theology: if someone is in an alternative of duties where, whatever decision he makes, he cannot avoid some evil, the traditional wisdom foresees that one must seek before God which of the duties in question is greater. The spouses will make their decision after a common deliberation, guided by that care which the greatness of their conjugal vocation requires."[2]

Against the solution of the Canadian and French bishops it is at times advanced that the dilemma of a perplexed conscience can only be due to a subjective lack of insight into a person's veritable moral obligation, which obligation objectively is always only one. This is correct. But it is not precise to assume that only individuals can be subject to such dilemmas. Also social bodies as a whole can at times, even if only temporarily, find themselves in a state of perplexity vis-a-vis certain moral problems of a complex nature. In the present issue it is most especially the dilemma of those couples who cannot avail themselves of the method of natural family planning, because the woman's rhythm is too irregular. This seems to resist an answer which could do justice to all the claims the spouses have to answer.

A similar conclusion as the one drawn by the Canadian and French bishops is reached by the bishops of Switzerland.[1]

Right to follow one's conscience if it dissents for weighty reasons. Several episcopal conferences indicate the possibility of a conscientious dissent from the encyclical, among them the bishops of Belgium,[2] Germany,[3] Austria,[4] England,[5] Canada[6] and Scandinavia.[7] All point out that everybody has the serious obligation to form his conscience. This includes the duty to attend carefully to the doctrine of the Church and to listen to it with reverence and docility (cf. DH 14). But an encyclical is not infallible. This leaves the possibility open that a Catholic, after careful study of the matter, may at times also come to different conclusions. (And of course, while the individual Catholic may not feel sufficiently sure of his divergent opinion if he stands alone — and justly so — , he will be more easily convinced of it if many others come to the same conclusion. This precisely is the situation of many Catholics in the present issue.)

Thus the German bishops explain that the magisterium of the Church can issue doctrinal directives of the kind given by the encyclical, even at the risk of error in detail. Otherwise the Church could not proclaim its faith as the decisive reality of life at all, or expound and apply it to each new human situation. A Catholic who is rightly disposed will accept also these doctrines with a positive frame of mind and make them his own. On the other hand "anyone who thinks that he must deviate in his private theory and practice from a non-infallible doctrine of the Church's magisterium — and such a case is conceivable in principle — must ask himself soberly and self-critically whether he can take responsibility for this before God."[8] Yet even if it should be that spouses come to a decision which differs from the teaching of the encyclical, "the actual way of achieving responsible parenthood must not be injurious to the dignity of the human person nor endanger marriage as a creative community of love."[9] Pastors are admonished to respect the conscientious

---

[1] Hamel 322f.	[2] Ib. 259f.	[7] Ib. 293f.
[3] Ib. 264f.	[4] Ib. 272f.	[8] Ib. 262.
[5] Ib. 276f.	[6] Ib. 279f.	[9] Ib. 265.

decision of the faithful, especially in the administration of the holy sacraments. They must make allowance for the case, as the Scandinavian bishops further note, that a spouse may feel justified in his deviant judgment. "In such an instance perhaps no sin is committed which must be confessed or which excludes from Holy Communion."[1]

5. *Artificial insemination*

Artificial insemination is impregnation not by means of natural intercourse, but by means of mechanical, artificial aids, e.g. a syringe, used for the transfer of the sperm. If the sperm is obtained from a donor (generally unknown) other than the husband, one speaks of heterologous insemination. If the sperm derives from the wife's husband, it is called homologous insemination.

Heterologous insemination, whether outside of marriage or whether in marriage, effected by the sperm of a third party, is to be rejected plainly as immoral. Catholic moral theologians agree on this.[2] A child conceived under such conditions is illegitimate and, if born by a married person, adulterous. All the reasons that militate against illegitimate and adulterous childbirth also militate against heterologous insemination. Marriage alone safeguards the dignity of the woman who is to become a mother. And it alone sufficiently provides for the well-being and education of the child. The donor-child born within a marriage has, it is true, an apparent family. But to the supposed father he is in reality a stepson and worse. He is to him a constant, humiliating reminder of his sterility. To the mother the developing child will bring none of the joy that comes to women as they see the characteristics of a beloved husband bud forth in the child. In a most unnatural way the child's father is totally unknown to her. By nature's plan children should be a bond of union between their parents and bring them joy and a sense of mutual fulfillment. But the donor-child is much more likely to be a source of humiliation, jealousy and anxiety. — If childless parents intensively desire children, a much better solution is for them the adoption of a child.

---

[1] Eduardus Hamel: Conferentiae Episcopales et Encyclica "Humanae Vitae". — Periodica 58 (1969), 295.

[2] In an address on medical ethics of 1949, Pius XII decidedly condemns heterologous insemination as absolutely inadmissible (AAS 41, 1949, 557ff).

As far as artificial insemination with the husband's sperm is concerned, the moral question is essentially different. "One does not necessarily proscribe the use of certain artificial methods intended simply either to facilitate or to enable the natural act effected in a normal manner to attain its end" (Pius XII).[1] A technical means to facilitate insemination is the cervical spoon, used to aid sperm migration through the cervical os. One might rather call it "assisted insemination" than "artificial insemination". Another form of assisted insemination avails itself of a syringe, in which the semen is collected after a normal coitus between husband and wife and then placed further into the wife's genital tract. These methods are permissible.

Controverted are procedures which obtain the semen for insemination from husband to wife by condomistic intercourse. coitus interruptus or masturbation. From a practical standpoint masturbation presents itself as the easiest and safest way to collect the necessary semen. However Pius XII rejects any homologous insemination where the semen is procured "by acts that are contrary to nature".[2] He undoubtedly refers to such methods. as the three mentioned ones.

Nevertheless one will have to admit that, where the sperm comes from the husband, the child is conceived as the fruit of a legitimate marriage and is therefore a legitimate child. The procreative meaning of the sexual act is by no means frustrated in this kind of artificial insemination, but on the contrary supported. The direct purpose of the insemination is the conception of a child. And inasmuch as husband and wife desire a child together because of the mutual love for each other, the sexual act also retains its meaning as an expression of love. In this sense the spouses will doubtless evaluate it.

Hence the double end of sexuality is secured in homologous insemination. At a first sight the procuration of the sperm has the appearance of an act of masturbation or onanism. But it is of a different nature. This explains the misunderstanding in its evaluation.

On the basis of such considerations B. Häring comes to the conclusion: "There are no convincing arguments to prove either the immorality of ejaculation by the husband in view of fatherhood nor the immorality of introducing that sperm into the wife's uterus".[3] This is also the opinion of Rodger Van

[1] L. c. 561. [2] L. c. 561.
[3] Medical Ethics. — Slough, England: St. Paul Publications, 1973, 93.

Allen,[1] F. Podimattam,[2] G. Lobo,[3] A. Regan[4] and others.[5]

It has been objected that homologous insemination is not able to retain the "unitive aspect" of the sexual act. This is true if this aspect is understood in a merely physical sense. But in such a sense it is commonly not listed among the primary ends of the marital act. If it is however understood in the more comprehensive sense of a union of love, then it seems still verified in homologous insemination, since the child is precisely the fruit of this love.

Note that the possibility of resorting to artificial insemination does not, according to the explanation of Pius XII, make valid a marriage between persons who are unfit to contract a marriage by reason of the impediment of impotence. By impotence is understood the inability to have coitus. If this condition certainly exists before the marriage and if it is also certain that the condition is perpetual and not merely temporary, the person so afflicted is incapable of contracting marriage (cf. CIC 1084 § 1).

IV. Marital love and conjugal intimacies

Marriage is more than a physical relationship. It is a spiritual union as well. "The right to each other's body" must not be understood in a materialistic way. If in the exercise of the conjugal rights sexuality is aimed at apart from love for the other person, this can hardly be called chastity. Sexuality does not exist apart from the other as fully a person; it cannot be isolated from the whole of married life and from the countless attentions which married people pay each other.

1. *The right to the conjugal act*

The right to the marriage act constitutes an essential element of the marriage covenant. For this reason the rendering of the conjugal debt is a serious concern. The refusal of the marital

---

[1] Rodger Van Allen: Artifical Insemination (AIH): A Contemporary Re-analysis. — Homiletic and Pastoral Review 70 (1969/70), 363-372.

[2] F. Podimattam: A Difficult Problem in Chastity: Masturbation. — Bangalore: Asian Trading Corp., 1973, 2. ed., 185-187.

[3] George V. Lobo: Current Problems in Medical Ethics. — Allahabad: St. Paul Society, 1974, 152.

[4] A. Regan: The Accidental Effect in Moral Discourse. — Studia Moralia 16 (1978), 118f.

[5] Other authors are — according to Lorenzo Leuzzi — E. Chiavacci, A. Delepierre, M. Di Janni, L. Rossi, A. Valsecchi and M. Vidal (Il dibattito sull'inseminazione artificiale. — Medicina e morale 22, 1982, 357-361).

submission for a considerable time, perhaps even under certain circumstances for one single instance, without just motive is a grave sin. This is especially true if the fulfillment of the marital debt appears necessary to guarantee marital love and fidelity and to safeguard the other spouse from incontinence or even adultery. But also the need to strengthen conjugal love brings about an obligation in conscience to render the marriage act. It is an infringement upon mutual rights and a violation of the love spouses owe each other if they deny each other without sufficient reason this expression of marital affection.

By mutual agreement, of course, spouses have the right to renounce intercourse for a certain time, but never to the point of dangerous temptation to the virtue of chastity and fidelity. In this regard married people should lend an ear to the advice of St. Paul: "The husband should give to his wife her conjugal rights, and likewise the wife to her husband. For the wife does not rule over her own body, but the husband does; likewise the husband does not rule over his own body, but the wife does. Do not refuse one another except perhaps by agreement for a season, that you may devote yourselves to prayer; but then come together again, lest Satan tempt you through lack of self-control" (1 Cor 7:3-5).

Spouses may not simply await the formal demand of the other as though unconcerned. Rather they must prepare for the approach the other may make with sympathetic concern. The husband in particular must know how to understand an implicit demand, e.g. by the wife's showing signs of affection; though, on the other hand, he should also beware of interpreting indiscriminately every sign of affection as a demand. Mutual love must teach the spouses ever more to meet each other in sympathetic understanding.

The right and duty to the marriage debt is also given in instances of sterility of one or the other spouse. Sterility does not interfere with the normal consummation of the sexual act.

2. *Causes excusing from the marriage debt*

a) Reasons of bodily indisposition and health. Love in marriage that is considerate excludes the request for marital union in the following circumstances: (1) during the time of the menstrual indisposition of the woman; (2) during the final (four to six) weeks of pregnancy and the first (four to six) weeks after confinement of the woman; (3) during an illness which would render the marital union physically or psychically painful and distasteful. However in instances of protracted illness carrying out the marital debt can indeed be justified, even though the sick spouse finds the act distasteful and suffers some slight pain; (4) during the fertile period if a new conception would constitute a serious danger for the woman's life, or in cases of gravely contagious diseases (e.g. gonorrhea, syphilis, etc.). Urging the marital debt in the cases mentioned under (4) must be regarded as gravely sinful.

b)   Unreasonable demand. This is principally the case when one party desires intercourse too frequently. There is no obligation to warrant a request for marital union more than once in a day. Hence more frequent demands need not be granted. Consultation of a physician would be advisable in such cases. — The marriage debt may, but need not be rendered to the insane nor to the completely intoxicated person.

c)   Sinful demand. Though in certain cases material cooperation with a spouse using unlawful means of birth control is allowed and perhaps sometimes even a debt, there is no obligation to render the marriage debt if requested in the presence of a third person or in a sodomistic way (rectal intercourse) or in other similar circumstances.

d)   Adultery. The right to demand the marital act is lost by the partner guilty of adultery. Nevertheless the injured party, even though not guilty, may have obligations arising from Christian love and from concern for the good of the whole family. Yet the adulterer, even though he has repented of his sin, does not have the right to demand the restoration of marital relations, but merely to plead for it.

e)   Failure to support wife and children. If the husband squanders the income and compels his wife to provide for the livelihood, she need not render the marriage debt. But if the family must live in poverty through no fault of the husband, there is no reason for refusing the debt.

3.   Care for affectionate love

Intimacy and tenderness belong to the entire married life, not merely to the marital union. Conjugal fellowship must be penetrated by the expressions of a tender, affectionate love. The intimacies between married people nourish their love and keep it alive. Therefore caresses and acts of affection expressing marital attraction are not only lawful, but often enough even required. Nor do they simply become illicit if orgasm should at times result from it, contrary to the couple's will and intention.

If marital attachment is to be permanent, it must be fostered. This includes that spouses must make themselves attractive, desirable and lovable to each other under every aspect. They will understand that marital love is not simply a given fact, but that it is an "art" which must be cultivated.

Acts of tenderness are also necessary prelude to the harmony of a marital union. Especially the husband must exercise his love with moderation and tender consideration for his spouse. "He must bear in mind that as a rule the experience of sexual emotion is more gradual in reaching its climax and completion in woman than in man. An abrupt demand for sexual union without the preparatory prelude of affectionate acts and brusque termination of the act without consideration of the differences in the emotional pattern of the woman must wreak havoc on the wife in many instances. She often will be frustrated because she is bereft of the lawful sexual gratification. In consequence she may gradually look upon sexual union as burdensome and crude or brutal, and feel incapable of responding in deep and tender love to the demands of her husband, which seem merely lustful and offensive to her."[1]

Dominion over passion is for the spouses a task of common effort. Both must work together in a spirit of solidarity rather than practise an individualistic form of asceticism. Spouses with tender consciences may at times be excessive in restraining the manifestations of conjugal affection. A rigorous effort to control desire can readily deprive them of the joy in mutual love and leave their longing for a total devotion unfulfilled. Acts of endearment serve to foster and confirm conjugal love, to console a married partner in depression or sorrow, to give him the feeling of acceptance, belonging and appreciation.

According to St. Paul husbands and wives must love each other with the same permanence and devotion as Christ loves the Church and the Church is dedicated to Christ (Eph 5:21-33). The selfless solicitude of this love ought to guide and to inspire the relations between the spouses. And their love too must remain consecrated to the service of God and to his plan of creation and salvation.

---

[1] B. Häring III, 1966, 363.

Chapter V

WORK AND PROPERTY[1]

Social life in society, economy and state is essentially determined by the conditions of work and property. The order of work and property determines the distribution of the total product of economy. It is therefore no surprise that social and political revolutions are most of the time inflamed by conditions of work and property which are considered exploitative and unjust. The moral order of work and property are the two problems which are at the root of the modern "social question".

Two fundamentally opposed social theories have greatly influenced society and economy in the technical age: individualist liberalism and marxist socialism. The theory of liberalism centres in the demand of the greatest possible economic freedom of the individual. Free enterprise, free competition, free trade are its slogans. The law of supply and demand ought to regulate the entire economic process and also the employment and compensation of workers. The freedom for economic enterprise combined with sound self-interest are held to be the best conditions for progress and prosperity. The result is liberalist capitalism with the concentration of wealth in the hands of a few and extensive

---

[1] Jean-Yves Calvez and Jacques Perrin: The Church and Social Justice. The Social Teaching of the Popes from Leo XIII to Pius XII (1878-1958). — Chicago: Henry Regnery, 1961. Jean-Yves Calvez: The Social Thought of John XXIII. Mater et Magistra. — Chicago: Henry Regnery, 1964. John C. Bennett, ed.: Christian Social Ethics in a Changing World. — New York: Association Press, 1966. Richard L. Camp: The Papal Ideology of Social Reform. A Study in Historical Development 1878-1967. — Leiden: Brill, 1969. Charles Rodger: The Christian Social Conscience. — Cork: Mercier, 1970. Ronald Preston, ed.: Technology and Social Justice. — Valley Forge: Judson Press, 1971. Denis O'Callaghan: A Just Society for Mankind: Recent Writing. — Irish Theological Quarterly 39 (1972), 79-87. Norbert Brockmann and Nicholas Piediscalzi, eds.: Contemporary Religion and Social Responsibility. — Staten Island, N.Y.: Alba, 1973. Gary North: An Introduction to Christian Economics. — Nutley, N.J.: Craig Press, 1973.

poverty among the masses.

The theory of marxist socialism, on the other hand, can be summed up in the demand that private property must be abolished. All property is to be transferred into the hands of the state. This will create the classless, socialist society with equal prosperity for all. Combined with this theory is the doctrine of the struggle of the classes. The two classes of the capitalist owners and the propertyless masses are irreconcilably opposed. The struggle, by an intrinsic necessity, leads to the elimination of the few capitalists and the nationalization of all property. The philosophical frame of the theory is, at least *de facto,* an atheistic determinism. The practical result of the ideology is marxist collectivism with the concentration of power in the hands of a totalitarian state and masses deprived not only of the right to property, but of other basic human rights as well.

The social doctrine of the Catholic Church is opposed to both systems. They build upon concepts of man which are deficient and wrong. Consequently their theories of the social order are deficient and wrong as well. The fundamental fallacy of individualist liberalism is its evaluation of human work as merely an impersonal commodity and the disregard for the social character of the economic life. The principal error of marxist socialism is its global rejection of private property and the inability to understand the positive function of personal ownership for society and the economic process.

The Church, in her answer to the social question, seeks "help neither from liberalism nor socialism; the former had already shown its utter impotence to find a right solution of the social questions, while the latter would have exposed human society to still graver dangers by offering a remedy much more disastrous than the evil it designed to cure" (QA 10). This judgment of Pius XI is the judgment of the Church also today (cf. MM 57f; PP 26; 33).

The Catholic social doctrine has found its official formulation especially in the five great social encyclicals and in the documents of Vatican II (above all in GS 63-72; 83-90). The five encyclicals are: *Rerum Novarum* (RN) by Leo XIII, *Quadragesimo Anno* (QA) by Pius XI, *Mater et Magistra* (MM) and *Pacem in Terris* (PT) by John XXIII, and *Populorum Progressio* (PP) by Paul VI. To them has recently been added as a sixth one *Laborem exercens* by John Paul II.

A. The moral order of work[1]

Man is called to serve God by his work. This is one of his basic duties. Work is also the primary title by which he takes possession of things and acquires the right to own them. Work, whether manual or intellectual, is furthermore the most decisive factor in the economic process; every economic process takes its origin in man's work (cf. GS 67). For this reason the moral order of work shall be dealt with first, followed by the moral order of property and of social economy.

I. Christian evaluation of work

1. *Work in Holy Scripture*

a) *The Old Testament.* According to the account of Genesis work pertains to the original order of creation. In spite of a current presumption, it does not come from sin. It was before the fall that "the Lord God took the man and put him in the garden of Eden to till it and keep it" (Gen 2:15). The sequence of six days of creation and a day of rest on the seventh is set before the people of God as a model and incentive for their own rhythm of week-day labour and Sabbath rest. The observance of this rhythm is Yahweh's express will. "Six days you shall labour and do all your work; but the seventh day is a sabbath to the Lord" (Ex 20:9f).

If God created man according to his image (Gen 1:26f), then this includes the obligation to imitate the Creator also by the six days of weekday work. According to God's will man should be a partner to him in the realization of the divine plan. Having once set the universe in place, God entrusted it to the hands of man. He invested him with the power, but also charged him with the duty, to command all creation and to subdue the earth. "Fill the earth and subdue it; and have dominion over the fish of the sea and over the birds of the air and over every living thing that moves upon the earth" (Gen 1:28).

In contradistinction to the surrounding pagan nations, the Old Testament does not regard work as low and degrading. The

---

[1] References: Werner Osypka: Arbeit und Eigentum. — Aschaffenburg: Pattloch, 1965. W. E. May: Animal Laborans and Homo Faber. Reflections on a Theology of Work. — Thomist 36 (1972), 626-644. John H. Redekop, ed.: Labor Problems in Christian Perspective. — Grand Rapids: Erdmans, 1972. Ronald Preston, ed.: Industrial Conflicts and Their Place in Modern Society. — London: SCM, 1974.

rabbis even made it a point of pride to know a trade by which they could support themselves. The day of rest on the other hand is a privilege not only for the free man. All men, including the slaves, are entitled to this repose. "Nowhere outside of the Bible can a similar social order be found. Elsewhere it is the freeman's privilege to be at leisure, while those in bondage are obliged to work day after day. The common weekly day of rest is a social establishment of incalculably great importance."[1]

The commandment to work is a universal obligation. It is the same for everyone. This order is simply taken for granted. "Man goes forth to his work and to his labour until the evening" (Ps 104:23; cf. Deut 5:13; Ps 90:17). Everyone who is righteous and pious performs some labour. God is described as teaching men their work (Is 28:23-29). The Wisdom books reprove the lazy sluggard and praise the industrious labourer (Prov 6:6-11; 28:19; 31:13-29; Sir 10:27). Whoever does no work, rightly starves (Prov 13:4; 19:15).

In spite of the high esteem for work, the Old Testament is also realistically aware of the painful toil and hardships which are often connected with it. Work is in a special way affected by sin. "In the sweat of your face you shall eat bread" (Gen 3:19). Laborious, often sterile work is one of the ways where sin makes its inroad. Caprice, violence, injustice, greed are others. Workers are deprived of their pay (Jer 22:13-17), peasants despoiled by taxes (Amos 5:11), whole peoples subjected to forced labour by an enemy government (Ex 1:8-14; 2 Sam 12:31) and even by their own kings (1 Sam 8:10-18; 1 Kings 12:1-14), slaves condemned to work and beatings (Sir 33:25-28). In order to protect the workers against unscrupulous oppression, the Mosaic law already introduced social legislations. The hired labourer must be paid the same day (Lev 19:13) and must not be exploited (Deut 24:14f). No interest for a loan may be exacted from the poor of the people (Ex 22:25-27). Strangers who sojourn with Israel must not be wronged (Ex 22:21; Lev 19:33f). Slaves may not be maltreated according to the whims of their owners (Ex 21:20.26f). And they too, as has been mentioned, have to be granted a day of rest on the Sabbath (Ex 20:10).

b) *The New Testament.* Christ himself was a worker. The longest part of his life he worked as a carpenter (Mk 6:3; Mt

---

[1] Karl Hermann Schelkle: Theology of the New Testament, vol. 3: Morality. — Collegeville, Min.: The Liturgical Press, 1973, 287.

13:55). Joseph, the foster-father of Jesus and his master in the workshop, is with good reason venerated as the patron of the workers by the Christian people. The immediate disciples of Jesus likewise mostly come from the labouring class (Mt 4:18-22; Lk 5:1-11).

Work is considered by Christ as a natural, integral part of human life. In his discourses and parables he often illustrates his teachings by examples taken from the world of labour: the farmer in the fields, the woman about her housework, the faithful and unfaithful shepherd, the fisherman, the hired hand in the vineyard. The parables demand industry, reliability and fidelity in work (Lk 16:1-12). The servant who buried his talent in the ground is punished as lazy and wicked. The industrious servants, who worked with their capital, are praised and rewarded as faithful and good stewards (Mt 25:14-30; Lk 19:12-27).

But there are also warnings against too great a pre-occupation and absorption by work and business. "Take heed, and beware of all covetousness; for a man's life does not consist in the abundance of his possessions" (Lk 12:15). Solicitude about the necessities of life must not prevail over the more important, spiritual concerns, which are the openness for God's word and the kingdom of God and its justice (Mt 6:25-34; Lk 10:38-42). Unaccountable is an absorption in work which leads a man to the extent of neglecting God's eternal banquet (Lk 9:25; 14:15-24).

St. Paul requires from his Christians quiet and steady work. In accord with rabbinic custom he himself practised a trade (Acts 18:3; 20:34f). Even as a preacher of the gospel, who in principle has the right to be supported by the congregations (1 Cor 9:13f; 2 Thess 3:8f; 1 Tim 5:17f), he often still worked as a tentmaker in order to provide for his living and not to burden anyone (1 Cor 9:3-15; 1 Thess 2:9; 2 Thess 3:7f).

In a pagan surrounding, which often had little appreciation for manual labour, Christians are all the more expected to earn an honest living by the work of their hands. "We exhort you", Paul writes to the Thessalonians, "to live quietly, to mind your own affairs, and to work with your hands, as we charged you: so that you may command the respect of outsiders, and be dependent on nobody" (1 Thess 4:10-12). When some Christians, as it seems, were tempted to abandon their regular work because of the expectation of the imminent return of the Lord, he energetically turns against such wrong conclusions. "If any one will not work, let him not eat. For we hear that some of you are living in idleness, mere busybodies, not doing any work. Now such persons we command and exhort in the Lord Jesus Christ to do their work in quietness and to earn their own living" (2 Thess 3:10-12).

Work is a general obligation. Idleness is disorderly living (1 Thess 5:14; 2 Thess 3:6). Through faithful work Christians are to provide for their livelihood. This is also a guarantee for their independence and personal freedom.

In addition work makes it possible to exercise charity and to serve the needy. "Let the thief no longer steal, but rather let him labour, doing honest work with his hands, so that he may be able to give to those in need" (Eph 4:28; cf. Acts 20:35).

The "rules of life" in the epistles repeatedly mention the duties of slaves, who mainly did the manual work in the society of the Roman empire, and of their masters (Eph 6:5-9; Col 3:22-4:1; 1 Pet 2:18-20). The slaves are exhorted to do their work with good will, not with eye-service, but as servants of the Lord. From him they will receive their reward. The masters on the other hand must deal with their servants in fairness; for they will find a judge in God, with whom there is no partiality. "Masters, treat your slaves justly and fairly, knowing that you also have a Master in heaven" (Col 4:1; cf. Eph 6:9; Jas 5:4).

The deepest motive of work is the service rendered to God. Work has its ultimate meaning not in this temporal order, but in the final, heavenly goal. "The form of this world is passing away" (1 Cor 7:31). But Scripture invites the hope that the fruits of man's work will persist in the new world, though in a transformed, heavenly way (Rom 8:18-24; Eph 1:10; Col 1:15-20). "Therefore, my beloved brethren, be steadfast, immovable, always abounding in the work of the Lord, knowing that in the Lord your labour is not in vain" (1 Cor 15:58).

2.   *Theology of work*

St. Thomas Aquinas gives a fourfold purpose of work. Work provides for the daily livelihood, prevents idleness which is a source of many evils, curbs the rebellious flesh, and enables a man to give alms from his material surplus.[1] Traditional ascetics add as further purposes atonement in the spirit of penance and the acquisition of graces. In this view work is related to God's glory and kingdom insofar as through its faithful execution God's

---

[1] Summa Theologica, II-II, q. 187, a. 3.

graceful presence in the hearts of men is made to grow. The intention to please God and to obey his will gives work, faithfully performed, its supernatural value.[1]

The good intention is of great importance indeed. Through it a man can impart value to all his actions. Nevertheless it is felt today that the traditional teaching on the meaning of work is not fully adequate and satisfactory. Does the purpose of work really exhaust itself in the making of one's living, in penance and the gathering of graces? Is this the total meaning of the cultivation of the earth, the exploration of the continents and the space, the creations of technics and arts? Or do the good results of one's work not possess a further significance for the kingdom of God? Does human activity not stand in a deeper relation to the mysteries of creation, incarnation and the eschatological completion of the world? Recent theology affirms such a relation. In this regard the Pastoral Constitution on the Church in the Modern World of Vatican II offers new insights of great importance. They merit special attention.

Also today the immediate purpose of work is for most people to make their living. Under this aspect the doctrine of St. Thomas did not undergo a change. Man is dependent upon material goods for the maintenance of his existence. He needs food, clothing and shelter. His work enables him to provide vital goods for himself, his family and those entrusted to him. It also puts him in a condition to practise charity towards those who lack these goods and are in need (GS 67).

In order to reach the goals of their work more effectively, men join together. This cooperation has far-reaching social consequences. It could however hardly be considered the purpose of human activity. Rather it is a means for the better realization of the objectives of work.

Having satisfied the basic needs of life, man is not able to retire. He will always aspire after new and higher aims of work. He will strive to expand his knowledge and to develop further technics and culture. In doing so, "he not only alters things and society, he develops himself as well. He learns much, he cultivates his resources, he goes outside of himself and beyond himself. Rightly understood, this kind of growth is of greater

---

[1] A very pertinent formulation of the traditional doctrine on the theological value of work is given by Theilhard de Chardin: The Divine Milieu. — New York: Harper and Row, 1965, 53f. Theilhard's concern is the presentation of a theology of work which is more comprehensive and complete. His expositions are very worthy of note.

value than any external riches which can be garnered. A man is more precious for what he is than for what he has" (GS 35). It merits attention that the Council does not primarily speak of moral virtues in this text. Rather it speaks of the perfection of a person's intellectual and cultural formation and of his professional abilities. This kind of perfection, too, makes a man grow in value.

Through his work, furthermore, man can and should "place himself at the service of his brother men" (GS 57). In sharing his insights and skills with his fellowmen, "he can do very much to elevate the human family" and "to make the conditions of life more favourable for all" (ib.).

Yet also the development of the human person is not yet the ultimate purpose of work. Why should men work for an ever greater increase of their knowledge and skills? Why should a person not rather dedicate his free energies, which are not necessary for his material sustenance, to prayer and the religious life? What makes the growth of knowledge and skills so valuable in the sight of God's plan with mankind?

The goal of personal development through work must still be seen in the wider context of man's participation in God's work of creation. After God had created the world and assigned its place to everything, he entrusted it to the hands of man to subdue the earth and to exercise dominion over it. By carrying out this order faithfully, man is to serve the plan of the Creator, so that "the name of God would be wonderful in all the earth" (GS 34).

Man complies with this commission by exploring the treasures and forces hidden in nature and by using them for always new creations of technics and culture. His striving after an ever more perfect dominion over the world ultimately results in a continuation of the divine work of creation. Human work stands in the service of the Creator. He wants to unfold and to complete his divine plan through man's cooperation. Vatican II repeatedly points to this exalted, ultimate meaning of human activity. Man's labour enables him to "be a partner in the work of bringing God's creation to perfection" (GS 67; also 34; 57).

Man is not merely the custodian of a creation which is in principle completed, as it was in accordance with the static view of the world of the Middle Ages. Rather he is the co-worker of God in a world which is in continuous evolution. God's creative activity did not end with the six-day work in the beginning of the world. It goes on through the millenia, but now with the cooperation of man as God's helper.

Even the most ordinary everyday activities of man stand in the service of this sublime goal and are indispensable for it. The services of the handy-man in a construction, the repair work on the roads, the grip at the assembly line, the work in the kitchen and in the household constitute ever so many small, but necessary contributions to the great, common task. The individual, even if he is the boldest inventor, needs the community for the realization of this task, and the community needs the services of every individual. Wherever men and women comply with their duties faithfully, they can justly consider that "they are unfolding the Creator's work, consulting the advantages of their brother men, and contributing by their personal industry to the realization in history of the divine plan" (GS 34). All the good achievements of the human race are manifestations of God's greatness and the display of his own mysterious design.

On the strength of this significance of work it becomes clear "that men are not deterred by the Christian message from building up the world." On the contrary, they are more stringently bound to do these very things (GS 34). The Christian is called to fulfill his temporal duties responsibly and to cooperate in the progress of the world, as much as he is called to adore God and to worship him. The one-sided stress of the one or the other of these poles is wrong and detrimental. Justly the Council warns against the temptation to such extremes. "Let there be no false opposition between professional and social activities on the one part, and religious life on the other" (GS 43). A sound balance and a fruitful complementation of both must be aimed at. But where a man meets his temporal duties in harmony with God's will, there he even serves the divine plan of salvation. "Indeed, we hold that by offering his labour to God a man becomes associated with the redemptive work itself of Jesus Christ, who conferred an eminent dignity on labour when at Nazareth He worked with His own hands" (GS 67).

These reflections show that human work serves God's plan in a very direct way. Even though "earthly progress must be carefully distinguished from the growth of Christ's kingdom", man's achievements are "of vital concern to the kingdom of God" (GS 39). Men are summoned "to make ready the material of the celestial realm by this ministry of theirs." In order to secure this end, Christ himself is "at work in the hearts of men through the energy of His Spirit. He arouses not only a desire for the age to come, but, by that very fact, He animates, purifies, and strengthens those noble longings too by which the human family strives to make its life more human and to render the whole earth submissive to this goal" (GS 38).

We do not know exactly how human achievements do contribute to the realization of the kingdom of God and in what form they will enter into the new earth at the end of time. As deformed by sin, the shape of this world will pass away. But the good fruits of human enterprise will be found again in the new world, "freed of stain, burnished and transfigured" (GS 39). The holy Eucharist is a sign and pledge of this hope. In this sacrament natural elements refined by man are changed into his glorified Body and Blood. In a like manner the fruits of human labour will be incorporated as building stones into the heavenly kingdom through Christ's transforming power (cf. GS 38).

Over all the acceptance of human progress, however, the Church never loses sight of the fact that the ultimate goal of her hope consists in more than earthly achievements. The goal of the New Testament hope is not merely an improved condition of this world, however progressive it may be. The goal is ultimately the Lord himself. He is "the focal point of the longings of history and of civilization, the centre of the human race, the joy of every heart, and the answer to all its yearnings" (GS 45). It is the counsel of God's love "to re-establish all things in Christ, both those in the heavens and those on the earth" (Eph 1:10). The re-establishment of all things is not their annihilation. This also holds for the fruits of man's labour. It is their completion and consummation.

II. Moral duties in work and profession

1. *The duty to work*

The purpose and meaning of work as explained above also contains the reasons for the duty to work. Work is the normal way to self-preservation. It is ordinarily by his work that a person satisfies his material needs and the needs of those entrusted to him. To the extent that a man is able to work and has no other legitimate source for his sustenance, he must acquire what is necessary for his livelihood by his labour.

Some people possess sufficient property, e.g. by inheritance, and do not have to work for their livelihood. In fact it is desirable that there are people in a community whose living does not depend on their daily work. This gives them greater freedom to dedicate themselves to concerns of common interest, e.g. to political tasks, services in the Church, arts, etc.

But also those who do not depend on their work in order to make a living are strictly obliged to work in one way or the other. Vatican II concludes, that from the Christian doctrine on work there arises "every man's duty to labour faithfully" (GS 67). For every man is called to serve his fellowmen and to cooperate with God in the unfolding of his creation, naturally to the extent that he is able to do so. Work in this context is not to be taken in the narrow sense of manual labour. It is understood in the wider sense of any serious and purposeful activity, including the adoration of the contemplative life. In this wider sense however work is a universal duty. It is an obligation towards the different communities which contribute to the welfare of a person. It is a demand of fraternal charity. It is a duty towards God, who created man to govern the world and to bring creation to perfection.

2. *The duty to conscientious preparation for one's profession*

The significance and purpose of work further demands that a person chooses his profession responsibly and prepares himself conscientiously for it.

The responsible choice of a profession requires above all the sober, realistic assessment of one's talents and capabilities. One is allowed only to choose a profession with whose demands one is able to comply sufficiently. And one should choose only that profession where one believes that one can serve God, oneself and one's fellowmen best. Of course the circumstances restrict the freedom of choice of a profession at times considerably. In these instances a person's responsibility consists in the acceptance of the concretely possible profession with the determination to dedicate himself to it to the best of his abilities.

Having made the choice of a profession, a person is morally obliged to prepare himself for it conscientiously. Negligent preparation is a sin against God, oneself and one's neighbour. Negligence in the acquisition of the necessary professional skills which results in serious harm to others, as for example in the professions of pilots, drivers, physicians, lawyers, politicians, priests, is a very grave irresponsibility.

If the practice of a profession is bound to certain certificates

of a person's proficiency and competency, he has the grave obligation to acquire them honestly and without fraudulence. Besides,
honesty and conscientiousness, diligence and perseverance in the
preparation for one's profession are rather sure signs for the
sterling quality and reliability in the future practice of the
profession.

3.   *Duties in the practice of the profession*

Every worker or professional is obliged to render the services
conscientiously which he agreed to perform and for which he is
paid. Who performs his work badly, who does not comply with
his obligations, or who conducts his job carelessly or recklessly,
sins against justice. He is obliged to restitution.

In many professions there exists an obligation to continued
education and to the up-dating of one's knowledge in order to
measure up to one's task. This holds in a special way for
lawyers, priests, teachers, and in different degrees for many other
vocations.

The service relationship not seldom establishes moral
obligations of a more personal nature, such as loyalty, respect,
discretion. This holds in a special way for domestic employees.
Personal concern and secrecy are particularly duties of priests,
physicians, psychotherapists, counselors, lawyers, and similar
professions.

III.   The right to work and to just compensation

1.   *The right to work*

Together with the duty to work, Vatican II also asserts the
right to work (GS 67). This right follows from man's right and
obligation to self-preservation, to support for his dependents, and
from his calling to cooperate with God in the plan of creation.

Every person has the right to earn a living by a meaningful
occupation, worthy of a human being. Interference with this right
through actions which thwart a person's effort to find suitable
work is an offence against social justice and love. Rather "it is
the duty of society . . . to help its citizens find opportunities for
adequate employment" (GS 67).

Naturally, if a national economy has not sufficient places of
work for all, the unemployed cannot demand jobs which are
not needed or for which no money is available. But the state is
entitled and obliged to a policy which promotes full employment.

According to J. Messner the state is empowered to enforce the social obligation of private property to create opportunities of work, if there is need for it. "A mere right to work without an obligation on the part of the state to guarantee the carrying out of the social obligations of private property is of little value to the propertyless worker; it leaves him to the benevolence of the propertied classes."[1] The state has the right and the duty to see to it that the social obligations of private property are fulfilled.

If a man who is able and willing to work and who depends on his wage for his livelihood cannot find employment, he has a claim to be assisted by the community. The right to existence also gives him the right to the necessary means for it. "For those who cannot work, there should be economic aid given in an atmosphere of dignity and compassion. Nothing less will satisfy the demands of justice and equity. Nothing less is acceptable in terms of human dignity."[2] In instances of extreme want a man can be entitled to food theft. Today states generally try to meet the problem of unemployment by unemployment insurances. Abuse of the insurance by persons who do not want to work or cannot work because otherwise occupied, for example in the household, is a sin of fraud and an offence against social justice.

The right to work however does not include the right to employment in the craft or profession a person has learned, if there is no need for it. He must be satisfied with some other kind of work. Different from the right to work is also the right to one's place of work. The latter consists in the claim not to be dismissed without valid reason. The natural law basis for this right is not a strict claim in justice, but a claim to personal concern and, where a worker has been serving his employer faithfully over a longer period of time, to a sense of obligation. Within certain limits a legal right to the place of work is often granted by the contract of work. Ultimately it amounts to a protection against unjustified notice to quit.

2. *The right to a just wage*

The wage is the contractual remuneration for labour service. It is the compensation for dependent work which is carried out on the order of an employer in accordance with a work contract.

---

[1] J. Messner: Social Ethics. — St. Louis and London: Herder Book Co., 1965, 840.

[2] John F. Cronin/Harry W. Flannery: Labour and the Church (Faith and Fact Books 50). — London: Burns and Oates, 1965, 33.

The category of wages comprises not only the remuneration for manual labour, skilled or unskilled, which is called 'wage' in the narrower sense, but also most forms of salaries.

The problem of the just wage is a main issue in the social question. It became urgent with the expansion of industry in the last century. Employers tended to deal with labour after the manner of a commodity. Its price was stipulated in a contract according to the principle of supply and demand. If many workers offer their services but the demand for labour is limited, the price for work will necessarily be low. Since the worker is free to enter the labour contract, he is not forced to accept the low wage. But if he enters the contract, he is legally bound by it. Even theologians "often held that justice demanded that a wage contract be enforced. Hence the only solution for the wretched condition of workers was to be found in works of charity."[1]

Against this economic theory Pope Leo XIII takes a decided stand in his encyclical *Rerum Novarum* (32; 61-65).[2] A worker may be forced to agree to a wage which is under subsistence minimum because there is no other means of livelihood for him. Hence he has no real freedom of choice. It is obvious that for the determination of a just wage still another factor of greatest importance is to be considered. Labour contracts are always determined by "an element of natural justice, and one greater and more ancient than the free consent of contracting parties, namely, that the wage shall not be less than enough to support a worker who is thrifty and upright" (RN 63). This also includes the means of livelihood for his wife and children (RN 65). Indeed the law ought to favour an income of a level that enables a worker to make savings and thus to acquire some property of his own (RN 65f).

The problem of wage justice is also dealt with in the eucyclicals *Quadragesimo Anno* (63-75) of Pius XI and *Mater et Magistra* (68-81) of John XXIII. They complete the doctrine of Leo XIII. They all emphasize that the just wage is to be determined not by one factor alone, but by the consideration of several factors.

The various factors to be considered are partly of commutative and partly of social justice. A systematic presentation of the criteria for a just wage can basically divide them in these two groups.

---

[1] John F. Cronin/Harry W. Flannery, 1. c. 24.
[2] Numbers and texts of the social encyclicals are quoted from the NCWC edition.

a) *Criteria of commutative justice.* Even though the norms of commutative justice alone are not sufficient for the determination of a just wage, they are nevertheless of indispensable and fundamental importance. Commutative justice demands equivalence between service and remuneration. The worker must receive a wage which corresponds to the service he renders and to the energy he spends. The employer may not seek his gain from the toils of the labourer. His gain must entirely derive from his own contribution to the production and the economic process.

It is to be noted, however, that the concrete worth of the worker's contribution to a product cannot easily be computed. Such a computation may still have been relatively easy in pre-industrial handicraft and agriculture. But in the industrialized economy of today it presents great difficulties. The total output of an economic enterprise is the result of many causes. Besides labour there are management, the service of the entrepreneur, capital (which is often invested with a certain risk) and land. Therefore workers could not simply claim the total net profit an enterprise makes. But they are entitled to that share in the profit which is the result of their labour and not of the other factors mentioned.

Commutative justice furthermore demands that equal workmanship receive equal compensation. Accordingly women could not be paid less than men merely because of their sex. The actual achievement must be the basis for the wage. On the other hand higher efficiency is entitled to higher remuneration. In the evaluation of services the following points have to be taken into account: knowledge of work and practical experience; time spent in formation; skill; responsibilities assigned; the energy employed, in which the nervous strain is not to be valued less than the use of muscular force.

Compliance with the stipulations of a justly entered wage contract is likewise a demand of strict justice. Failure to fulfill the terms agreed upon imposes the duty of restitution. This also applies to the violation of laws that establish minimum wages. Refusal to pay the minimum wage not only violates legal but also commutative justice. It obliges to restitution. The mere fact that a minimum wage is established however does not mean that it is just under all circumstances. If this wage should prove too low for any reason, for example because of a general devaluation of the currency or because of the special performance of a worker, the employer is in justice obliged to raise it.

   b)   *Criteria of social justice.*   It is clear that the worker is entitled to a wage adequate to support him and his family in decent conditions. This means an income sufficient to afford wholesome food, to rent or buy a good home, to provide for suitable education and adequate medical care. A problem arises inasmuch as not all workers have families of equal size and some have no families at all. Does the right to a family wage demand that all workers receive a pay high enough to support an average family (absolute family wage)? Or should the wage be adapted to the different sizes of the families (relative family wage)? As far as the enterprise itself is concerned, it would seem that equal services demand equal pay. This pay ought to be enough to meet the basic needs of a family. Additional support for large families should rather be taken care of by the community, for example in form of tax reductions and family-allowances.

   The wage must furthermore allow the worker to care for his spiritual and cultural needs in consonance with the entire living standard of a nation. "Payment for labour must be such as to furnish a man with the means to cultivate his own material, social, cultural, and spiritual life worthily, and that of his dependents" (GS 67).

   The social encyclicals make it a point that the wage income should be so high as to enable a thrifty worker to make some savings and acquire a moderate property. Insurances for old age, sickness, unemployment and the like are to be counted as forms of savings.

   Finally justice demands that the wage be proportionate to the development and growth requirements of the national economy as a whole. Even the needs of the entire human family should be considered. This requirement points to a twofold aspect of social wage justice: It claims a growing wage income as a nation progresses in economic regard, but at the same time it limits this claim in accordance with the present and future tasks of a nation.

   Above all a national economy must aim at providing work for everybody. Wages may therefore not be so high that they prevent the formation of the capital necessary for the further expansion of the industry. If it should happen that an individual enterprise or even the whole national economy passes through a severe crisis, social justice may at times demand a temporary reduction of wages and the renunciation of a full family wage. In such instances unreasonable insistence on a full family wage would be unjust towards the enterprise or the national economy.

Ultimately it would conflict with the worker's own true welfare.

Leads in wages of particular groups of workers easily contradict social justice. They often gain for these groups temporary advantages at the expense of the consumers, including the other groups of workers, who have to pay higher prices for the products of the highly paid enterprises. Even in the event of higher yields in certain branches of the economy, due not to services performed but to other factors, such as improved methods of production, reductions in raw material prices, a better foreign market, etc., there is not necessarily a claim in justice to higher wages. Social justice would rather demand a reduction of the prices for the goods concerned, by which all members of the economy would profit. This is also the safest and most equitable way to secure a share in the prosperity of a nation to those who have contributed in the past to the building of the economy and are now living on old-age pensions.[1]

The future development of the nation must likewise be accounted for. Increase in population demands greater production of consumer goods, more schools, more hospitals, more places of employment. A growing number of the aged in an aging society signifies higher expenses of social policy. National security and preservation of peace give rise to expenses for military defence.

Finally the requirements of the common good on the world level may demand limitations of wage claims. A nation may not profit from another nation by too low prices for raw materials or similar forms of unjust trade relations. Above all, the exigencies of development aid impose great obligations of social justice upon the wealthier nations, including their working class.

3. *The right to protection and social security*

The beginning of industrialization is not only characterized by too low, unjust wages, but also by too long working hours, want of vacations, insufficient safety measures, the overtaxing of women and, worst of all, children's labour. These were most grave abuses, and it is obvious that workers have the right to be protected against them. Today this protection is to a large extent guaranteed by social legislation.

In this regard Leo XIII demands first of all that workers are to be treated as human beings and not as slaves or mere

---

[1] Cf. J. Messner: Social Ethics. — St. Louis/London: Herder Book Co., 1965, 806f; 812.

things for gain. "It is shameful and inhuman to use men as
things for gain and to put no more value on them than what
they are worth in muscle and energy" (RN 31). He then points
out several basic rights in detail and calls upon the state to
secure them by legislation. Employers and the state are obliged
to protect the workers from religious and moral harm. They
have to be granted adequate periods of free time to attend to
their religious obligations and to renew their energy. No work
is to be imposed which is immoderate and beyond the hours
that human strength can endure. Likewise no work is to be
demanded which is incompatible with sex and age. Working
conditions for women must be in agreement with their constitution
and their duties as wives and mothers. Children are not to be
incorporated in the working process at all before they have
sufficiently matured in body, mind and soul (RN 31; 53; 56-60;
cf. PT 19). These basic rights of workers have always to be
respected. To the extent that they are threatened, the state must
intervene and secure them.

A further group of rights of workers concern their social
security. They are above all spelled out by John XXIII. "A
human being also has the right to security in cases of sickness,
inability to work, widowhood, old age, unemployment, or in any
other case in which he is deprived of the means of subsistence
through no fault of his own" (PT 11). These are rights of
every human being, just as the right to protection of labour. But
their safeguard and implementation is of special urgency in the
case of the dependent workers.

Many countries offer social security by means of different
social programs and insurance systems. Five general categories
of social insurance are common in the modern world. These are
old-age, invalid and survivors' insurance; health and maternity
insurance; family allowances; work-injuries insurance; and unemployment insurance. They contribute much to the social
security of citizens in general and of workers in particular. But
often the coverage is inadequate and incomplete. It not seldom
happens that certain groups are placed at a disadvantage, for
example the farm workers with their lower income. John XXIII
holds that this is not in harmony with social justice and equity.
"Insurance allowances made to the people should not be materially different no matter in what economic sector the individuals
work or the income on which they live." The systems of social
insurance can indeed contribute much to an equitable re-distribu-
tion of the over-all income of a nation. They can be effective

instruments in reducing imbalances between the different classes of citizens (MM 135f).

Vatican II still calls attention to other concerns in the realm of labour. The way how work is organized is too often not adjusted to the needs of the human person. Workers are made slaves of their work. This situation cannot be justified. "The entire process of productive work must be adapted to the needs of the person and to the requirements of his life, above all his domestic life" (GS 67).

In the industrialized world of today it becomes increasingly difficult for workers to identify with the work that they are doing. The production on a mass basis makes work impersonal. The worker loses his individual status and significance. The mechanized work of the assembly line leaves little or no room for creativity. Mechanization, specialization and automation, all tend to dissociate the worker from the product, leaving him without a direct link with the end product of his labour. This gives little opportunity for pride and joy in an accomplished job. The effect upon the worker is that his work is not a central life interest for him. He looks for self-fulfillment outside of his job. Vatican II for this reason demands that workers "should have the opportunity to develop on their own the resources and potentialities to which, perhaps, their professional work gives but little scope" (GS 67).

The frequent shift work still adds a further problem. Family life is disrupted. Social life is difficult. The staggering of shifts prevents a man from going to night school, from regular participation in religious services, meetings of organizations and other periodical gatherings. Certainly remedies for this situation do not lie at hand. But the industrial problems that concern men must challenge the ingenuity of technicians as much and more than the technical problems of production.[1]

John XXIII turns against impersonal and atrophying working conditions in quite energetic terms. "If the structures, the functioning, the surroundings of an economic system are such as to compromise human dignity, . . . or if they systematically blunt in them (the workers) the sense of responsibility, or constitute in any way an impediment to expressing their personal initiative. such an economic system is unjust, even if, by hypothesis, the wealth produced through it reaches a high standard and this

---

[1] Cf. the article "Some problems of the world of industry;" in: The Christian Social Conscience. Saint-Séverin Catechism for Adults. vol. IV. — London: G. Chapman. 1965. 28-43.

wealth is distributed according to the criteria of justice and equity" (MM 83; cf. PP 28; 34).

Technical, economic and financial factors have to be subordinated to man. Industrialists, managers and executives must learn to see in the worker more than an accessory to a machine or a factor in production. The worker is a human person. This creates the need for personal relationships between management and workers and between the workers themselves.

An important requirement for a more meaningful participation in the process of work is information about the significance of a worker's task in the context of the entire enterprise. He should also be given an understanding of other related work and of the meaning of his work for the community in general.

If work has lost its creative dimension for many workers, the personal dimensions of service and responsibility must more clearly be recognized and developed: responsibility for the manufacturing process, for the material used, for safety. Responsible participation of workers in the production process of their particular enterprise and in the national economy at large is carried out above all by means of the trade unions. They are the worker's natural means of expression and economic participation. They require a more detailed treatment in the following section.

IV. The right to organize and to strike

In order to enforce and protect their rights, workers have organized themselves in trade unions. They enable the workers to bargain for just labour contracts in a collective way. Collective bargaining is based on the simple principle that workers acting in concert are much stronger than the individual alone. Organized labour is normally in a position to hire lawyers and other specialists who can assist in the laying down of the labour contract. If an impasse is reached, the union can withhold labour by a strike. While the lack of wages during a strike is a hardship to workers, the employer is also under severe economic pressure to secure a settlement. The development of trade unionism doubtless brought about most far-reaching modifications in the economic and social order.

1. *The trade union*

The trade union is a voluntary organization of workers for the protection of their economic and social interests in the labour market. The unions naturally tend to organize according to the different branches of economy, since the labour market itself follows these lines of division. The basic function of the unions is the settlement of just and fair working conditions in collective bargaining with the employers and their associations. The bargaining is above all concerned with agreements about the just wage, breaks, holidays, sick leave, length of notice, etc.

The right to the formation of trade unions derives from the fundamental right of man to free association. Capitalist society tried with all its might to dispute this right of the worker, because the unions challenge and break the predominance of capital power in the economy. In many countries bitter struggles marked the rise of organized labour.

From the beginning the popes upheld in their social encyclicals that "man is permitted by a right of nature to form private societies." The state is therefore not allowed to forbid them, as long as they are not clearly at variance with good morals and the welfare of the society. On the contrary, the state "has been instituted to protect and not to destroy natural right" (RN 72; cf. 75). Among the associations for mutual aid and social assistance "associations of workers occupy first place." They are necessary to meet the present needs of the working class (RN 69). "Furthermore, if citizens have free right to associate, as in fact they do, they also must have the right freely to adopt the organization and the rules which they judge most appropriate to achieve their purpose" (RN 76; cf. MM 22).

The Second Vatican Council reconfirms this right in clear terms. "Among the basic rights of the human person must be counted the right of freely founding labour unions." A further right added by the Council is only a logical consequence of this basic right. "Another such right is that of taking part freely in the activity of these unions without risk of reprisal" (GS 68). Abuses may have led the Council Fathers to formulate it expressly.

The right to establish and organize unions is however not an absolute right. It is evidently limited by the still more basic right of a person to religious, moral and political freedom. This must be stressed against strong tendencies in trade unions to subscribe to socialist and communist ideologies as a body and to discriminate against divergent religious and political convictions. For this reason the Church encouraged Catholic workers

to form Catholic or Christian confessional unions that were free
from Marxist influence. Nevertheless it was realized that this
alternative was often not practicable. Pius XI is aware that the
necessity of uniting forces makes the formation of Catholic unions
not seldom unfeasible. Catholic workers will have to join neutral
unions. But the pope justly demands that these neutral unions
"should always respect justice and equity, and leave to their
Catholic members full freedom to follow the dictates of their
conscience" (QA 35; cf. MM 100-102). Trade unions must
honour the religious and political convictions of their members
in a fully democratic way.

The trade unions proved to be a most efficient instrument
in the defence of the rights of the workers. Their merits in this
regard are undisputed. "In the trade unions the workers themselves became a 'social power', and thus broke the economic
and social monopolistic predominance of capital power. It was
of decisive significance for the course of the social system that
now 'labour' was placed on an equal footing with capital and
for the first time was free to oppose it in the settlement of
conditions in labour contracts. Moreover, the trade union movement has proved false Marx's assertion that the proletariat would
become increasingly impoverished. With the trade union movement the workers took their social destiny into their own hands
instead of waiting for their impoverishment and the resulting
'dictatorship of the proletariat'."[1] Today organized labour is equal
in social power to finance capital, employers and the other
great social forces. The trade unions are able to enforce the
rights of the workers efficiently.

However the rise to power is also for the trade unions not
without dangers. They are not immune against the temptation
to abuse their strength in a capitalist, exploitative way. "The
trade unions act according to the profit principle of capitalism;
they seek as much advantage as their strength allows though the
wage policy of trade unionism varies in different countries.
Theoretically, everywhere it is recognized that wage demands
should not overstep the limits of the increase of economic
productivity; in practice, however, ... these limits have been
exceeded in many countries, as is shown by the progressive
inflation to which the trade union wage policy undoubtedly

---

[1] J. Messner: Social Ethics. — St. Louis/London: Herder Book Co.,
1965, 458.

contributes."[1] Pope Paul VI expresses his concern that the unions here and there profit from a position of force to impose, particularly by strikes, "conditions which are too burdensome for the overall economy and for the social body, or to desire to obtain in this way demands of a directly political nature. When it is a question of public services, required for the life of an entire nation, it is necessary to be able to assess the limit beyond which the harm caused to society becomes inadmissible."[2]

Fair labour practice is also offended against where trade unions form monopolies after the manner of cartels to the detriment of groups of workers. The "closed shop" is their instrument. A trade union compels the employer to accept labour only from the supply which the union has organized. Employers who do not comply and who give work to other workers are threatened by strikes. This practice is in conflict with the natural right of individuals to join or not to join a voluntary association. Only very special circumstances could justify the closed shop, such as defence against a grave injury to the rights of the group which can only be averted by this means.

To the social power of trade unions also correspond duties. The greater the power, the greater their responsibilities and duties. First of all unions have the duty, "when making wage claims, to consider the general economic interest and the state of their branch of industry. If they make a progressively rising income a basic principle of their wage policy, they must also share in the responsibility for a proportionate rise in productivity in the whole economy, in the separate branches of industry, and in the factories. In any case, justice demands that they consider themselves bound by a standard of output corresponding to their wage claims."[3] Wage demands which overstep increases in productivity conflict especially with social justice. They cause a creeping inflation, which harms savings and those groups of the

---

[1] Ib. 459. "In England, annual wage claims by the trade unions have become the rule, giving rise to a competition between the trade unions to raise their demands at an opportune time, before public opinion is restive and might cause them to fail. On the other hand, it is generally admitted that the 'miracle of German economy' after the Second World War and the stabilization of the West German mark would have been unlikely without the wage restraint of the trade unions" (ib.).

[2] *Octogesimo Adveniens*, Apostolic Letter of Pope Paul VI of May 14, 1971, nr. 14; AAS 63 (1971), 412.

[3] J. Messner, 1. c. 462.

population who cannot obtain corresponding increases of their income.

Another duty is that of internal democracy. The trade unions rest on free association, so that their leaders in all essential questions are dependent upon the will of their members. Certainly the leaders may try to mold the will of the members. But they have the duty to provide opportunities for them to express their will. Trade union policy may not become the affair of an oligarchy within the union.

Finally the influence unions are able to exert on social policy and in the sphere of politics in general imposes upon them the duty of responsibility and concern for the equitable development of the social order and the political community. Union members must be prepared for this task through an ongoing formation in economic, social and political matters (cf. GS 68). Above all they must learn to understand the indissoluble connection between their group interests and the general interests of the economy and political community. Their welfare is dependent on the fate and prosperity of the economy as a whole.

2.   *The strike*

The strike is the refusal to work on the part of the organized workers. The refusal of employers to admit the workers to work is called a lockout. The one or the other may occur in the course of collective bargaining, when one of the parties in the labour contract cannot otherwise obtain the conditions it desires. The same moral principles apply for both. The lockout is however comparatively rarely used today. The following considerations shall therefore only deal with the strike and the moral principles applying to it.

Leo XIII refers to the strike as an evil that should be avoided as far as possible. "Labour which is too long and too hard and the belief that pay is inadequate not infrequently give workers cause to strike and become voluntarily idle. This evil, which is frequent and serious, ought to be remedied by public authority" (RN 56). But Pius XII further clarifies that workers act in full conformity with the Church's social teaching if they vindicate their rights by all means morally permissible. From the context of the statement it is plain that these means also include the strike as a last resource.[1] The right to strike is expressly acknowledged by Vatican II. When "socio-economic

---

[1] Allocution of June 26, 1955; AAS 47 (1955), 515.

disputes arise, efforts must be made to come to a peaceful settlement. Recourse must always be had above all to sincere discussion between the parties. Even in present-day circumstances, however, the strike can still be a necessary, though ultimate, means for the defence of the workers' own rights and the fulfillment of their just demands" (GS 68).

The right to strike "is based on two natural rights: first, on the freedom of man to work or not to work according as he has agreed or not agreed about relevant conditions; and secondly, in freedom of combination for the purpose of all aims which do not conflict with the common good. The strike can be an indispensable means in the hands of the organized workers for the attainment of justified demands. However, it is always detrimental to one or more business firms or to a whole branch of industry or even to the general public; moreover, because it leads to bitterness it has detrimental effects on social peace and often on political peace. Therefore, there are limits set by natural law principles to the use of the strike weapon."[1]

The strike is permissible under certain defined conditions. They are basically the same as those applying to a just war.

(1) The objectives of the strike must be lawful, e.g. the obtainment of a just wage or important improvements in working conditions. Thus a strike is just if the employer is making good profits, but paying wages below the average. A strike is unjust if workers who are already paid wages above the industry average still strike for more. The cause for the strike must be graver the more harmful its effects are. Since strikes of civil servants are of great harm to the public order, they would only be justifiable in the case of grave injustice. The public interest demands that doctors, nurses, firemen and police should not strike. Alternate methods for a just settlement of their grievances should be available. Furthermore it must be pointed out as a general principle that, as long as a collective agreement is in force, a strike can only be justified if the agreement is not kept by the other partner.

(2) All other, peaceful means for an equitable settlement of the differences must have been earnestly tried and exhausted. There should be a reasonable period of negotiation. If this fails, it is usually proper to call in conciliators to try to mediate the dispute. In most countries today there are public and private agencies available for such a service.

---

[1] J. Messner: Social Ethics. — St. Louis/London: Herder Book Co., 1965, 463.

(3) The means employed must be morally acceptable. It certainly would be unfair for workers to leave a steel mill without first taking steps necessary for a proper cooling of the furnaces. Strikers in a food store should make provision for the orderly sale of perishable goods. No matter how bitter may be the resentment of workers against an employer, it is not legitimate to destroy his machinery or damage his property.

The political strike, which aims at objectives of a political nature, is ordinarily the misuse of an economic weapon for an alien purpose. It is not justified as long as a government does not use unconstitutional measures. Only if most important rights are in jeopardy, can a politically inspired strike be justified, for example if the general constitutional order, the basic rights of freedom or the right to free association are seriously violated by a government. The general strike is the principal means of nonviolent resistance against unlawful state authority.

No labourer or employee may participate in an unjust strike. But if he were threatened by a serious harm in case he continued to work, he would be allowed to stop working.

The misuse of the strike weapon for unjustified demands or in a manner detrimental to the common good or for political ends has raised the question of strike legislation. In principle state authority has the right to enact laws which protect the economy and society against unjust strikes. It even is obliged to do so, if this is necessary to avert grave harm to the common good. Thus a legal settlement must restrain strikes (and lockouts) which are incompatible with the duties of the state, such as self-defence, health protection or public supply undertakings. The freedom of workers must be safeguarded by law against measures of force or intimidation directed against those willing to work. Likewise the management ought to be defended against strikes intended to prevent necessary mechanization and rationalization measures or to enforce employment of unnecessary workers. On the other hand legislation must not be such that it prejudices the effective use of the strike weapon for the promotion of the just claims of the workers. The best possible protection of the interests of the common good not seldom demands the permission of a certain detriment to the common good in order to avoid greater evils.

V. Promotion of worker partnership

The need of responsible participation of workers in the social, personal and economic concerns of their enterprises and in the concerns of the national economy as a whole has already been mentioned before. It is more and more felt that workers should not be reduced to simple and silent performers in their workshop place without any say in regard to decisions that regulate their activity and without the possibility of bringing to bear their experience. This leads to the question of worker partnership and codetermination.

In the social encyclicals the question is first mentioned by Pius XI. He recommends that the wage contract should, when possible, be modified somewhat by a contract of partnership. "In this way wage-earners are made sharers in some sort in the ownership, or the management, or the profits" (QA 65).

The issue is once more taken up and further unfolded by John XXIII. He explains that men engaged in productive activity have the innate desire to employ their own responsibility and to perfect their own being through their work (MM 82). Therefore provisions must be made to permit workers some sort of codetermination in questions related to their work and to the economic development of society. Such codetermination is regarded by the pope as lawful and desirable in the workers' own workshop place and as imperative on the regional and national level.

As to the workers' own enterprise, "it is not feasible to define a priori the manner and degrees of such participation. . . . At any rate, every effort should be made that the enterprise become a community of persons in the dealings, activities and standing of all its members" (MM 91). This demands that the relations between employers and employees be marked by appreciation, understanding, a loyal and active cooperation, and devotion to an undertaking common to both. "This also means that the workers may have their say in and may make their contribution to the efficient running and development of the enterprise." The necessary unity and efficiency of direction must however be safeguarded (MM 92).

But the individual productive units are not isolated entities. They are parts of the economic and social complexity of the society as a whole and are determined by it. Therefore it is necessary that workers or those who represent them should also have a say in the economic and social decisions made on the regional, national or world-wide level. "We cannot fail to emphasize how timely and imperative is it that the workers exert their influence, and effectively so beyond the limits of the individual productive units, and at every level" (MM 97).

This distinction is also adopted by Vatican II. As the social encyclicals before, it avoids speaking of a *right* of the workers to codetermination in their enterprise, but rather formulates a recommendation. "The active participation of everyone in the running of an enterprise should be promoted." At the same time the necessary unity of operations must be provided for. Worker participation on the higher levels is not less important. "Decisions concerning economic and social conditions, on which the future of the workers and their children depends, are rather often made not within the enterprise itself but by institutions on a higher level. Hence the workers themselves should have a share also in controlling these institutions, either in person or through freely elected delegates" (GS 68).

Social ethics must sharply distinguish between two different forms of codetermination by workers in their enterprise. The one is codetermination in the social sphere and in questions of personnel, and the other codetermination in the economic sphere, i.e. in the running of the business. The first form of codetermination does not create very serious difficulties. But the second form is strongly controverted. The representatives of the Catholic workers and employers at the German Katholikentag in Bochum of 1949 declared that the codetermination of all workers in social, personal and economic questions is a natural right. Pope Pius XII however disagreed. On June 3, 1950, he explained that the right of economic joint management lies beyond the field of possible achievements. "Neither the nature of the contract of work nor the nature of the enterprise by themselves necessarily comprise such a right."[1] And once again, on Sept. 14, 1952: "The pontiffs of the social encyclicals, and also We ourself, have declined to deduct, directly or indirectly, from the labour contract the right of the employee to participate in the ownership of the operating capital, and its corollary, the right of the worker to codetermination." Economic decisions involve property ownership, and workers do not have the right to demand control over another's property.[2]

This is also the opinion of J. Messner. Natural law principles do not offer a basis for the right of codetermination of the employees in the conduct of the business. "No such basis exists. Still less is there any justification for such a right on the part of interest groups outside the plant, such as trade unions. If such a right is enforced, it means infringing the owners' right of disposal,

[1] AAS 42 (1950), 487.
[2] AAS 44 (1952), 792.

which is protected by the natural law principles of ownership."[1] Economic codetermination is in harmony with natural law principles only in the following two instances. Either codetermination is freely agreed upon by the owners of undertakings or the management representing them; this form has proved the most successful. Or codetermination is based on capital investment and thus on participation by the workers in the ownership of an undertaking.[2] However that may be, in all instances of codetermination workers must clearly realize that this right also implies an obligation. Codetermination means co-responsibility and readiness to co-entrepreneurship.[3]

B. The moral order of property[1]

The handbooks of the past centuries dealt with the right to property in a rather isolated way. Its subservient function in God's plan of creation and salvation was not sufficiently attended to. The large scope granted to civil legislation in this treatise did its share to detach it from the deeper theological foundations. Property appeared too much as an unconditional right. This gave the impression as if it were a value in itself. The patristic tradition was lost sight of, which looked upon property primarily as stewardship in the service of God and of Christian love.

Present-day theology tries to overcome the individualistic approach of the past centuries and to integrate once more the patristic concerns in the teaching on property. Material possessions are unequivocally placed under the universal dominion of God who owns all things and is the common Father of all men. The earth and all that it contains are given to all men. Property is of instrumental character, subordinated to the development of the human person, the needs of the community and the promotion of God's creative design. The social encyclicals of the popes progressively unfold the social function of property and the universal purpose of all created things. In this light property is also viewed by Vatican II.

---

[1] J. Messner: Social Ethics, 1965, 844.

[2] The problems of co-ownership find a good exposition by J. Messner, 1. c. 831-834.

[3] A more detailed presentation of the issue of codetermination is given by Werner Osypka: Arbeit und Eigentum (Der Christ in der Welt. series X, vol. 3). — Aschaffenburg: P. Pattloch, 1965. 95-104.

[4] References: Harvey Seifert: Ethical Resources for Political and Economic Decision. — Philadelphia: Westminster, 1972. Martin Hengel: Property and Riches in the Early Church — Philadelphia: Fortress, 1974.

I. Meaning and basis of private property

Ownership is the exclusive right of control over a thing. No other person except the owner is entitled to use the thing or to dispose of it. Exceptions to this right are however possible if demanded by a higher law, e.g. by the needs of the common good. Subject to ownership are not only material goods but also intellectual and spiritual creations, such as inventions, products of art, books, etc.

Ownership in the full sense or perfect ownership includes (1) the right to dispose of a thing freely, i.e. to use, consume, sell, donate or bequest it; (2) the right to the fruits of a thing, whether they are natural or industrial; (3) the right to exclude others from acting upon the thing and to restitution in the event of unlawful deprivation. Imperfect ownership is a limited and qualified right over a thing. It is direct if one owns a thing but may not use it, as for example minors or owners of rented property. It is indirect if one has only the use of the thing or the right to its fruits but not the power of disposal over its substance.

The holder of the right of ownership can be an individual person or a juridical person. The latter may be of private or of public law. Juridical persons of private law are, e.g., corporations, private organizations, religious associations, etc. Juridical persons of public law are municipalities, provincial governments, the state.

The property can consist of consumer goods like food or clothing; movables like furnishings, tools, cars, animals, jewelry; immovables like flats, land, houses, plants; intellectual property like patent rights and copyrights; claims against other parties like bank accounts, shares, securities, debts, insurance claims and money in general.

1. *Holy Scripture on the value of material goods*

The evaluation of property and wealth in the Old and in the New Testament appear rather diverse and even opposed. The Old Testament is inclined to regard riches as a divine blessing. The New Testament on the other hand rather recalls the inconsistency and danger of all earthly wealth. Still the two views can be considered complementary. If riches are perilous and if evangelical perfection consists in sacrificing them, it is not that they are evil in themselves, but they are easily hindrances for a sincere love of God. Only wealth received and administered as a gift from God is praiseworthy.

a) The *Old Testament* regards wealth as a sign of God's favour. God enriches those he loves: Abraham (Gen 24:34f), Isaac (Gen 26:12-14), Solomon (1 Kings 3:11-13), Hezekiah (2 Chron 32:27-30), or Job after his trials. The tribes counted on prosperity. Wealth is God's blessing for the righteous (Prov 10:22; 22:4). It assures a precious independence and means a full and happy life (Prov 10:15; 14:20). Its acquisition normally presupposes meritorious human qualities, like diligence (Prov 10:4; 20:13), wisdom (24:3f) and temperance (21:17).

Yet though wealth is considered a good and a blessing, it is never presented as the best of goods. Preferable to it are peace of soul (Prov 15:16f), righteousness (Tob 12:8; Prov 16:8), good reputation (Prov 22:1), health (Sir 30:14-16). Love cannot be purchased by possessions (Song 8:7). It is always necessary to prefer wisdom to wealth (1 Kings 3:11f; Job 28:15-19; Wis 7:8f). This is the treasure, the precious pearl which merits every concern (Prov 2:1-4; 3:15; 8:11).

It is furthermore not forgotten that wealth has also its dangers. It is difficult to remain faithful in prosperity, because easy living closes the heart (Deut 31:20; 32:15). Wealth is ill-acquired if it tends to exclude the majority from earthly goods and to reserve them for the privileged few. "Woe to those who join house to house, who add field to field, until there is no more room, and you are made to dwell alone in the midst of the land" (Is 5:8; cf. Jer 5:27f).

But the basic right to property is undisputed. The Old Testament takes it for granted. Property is protected by the moral order. Its violation is subject to punishments. The seventh commandment of the decalogue bids: "You shall not steal" (Ex 20:15; Deut 5:19). And the tenth commandment already condemns the evil desire of a neighbour's possessions. "You shall not desire your neighbour's house, his field, or his manservant, or his maidservant, his ox, or his ass, or anything that is your neighbour's" (Deut 5:21; Ex 20:17). Dishonesty and fraud are an abomination to the Lord. "You shall do no wrong in judgment, in measures of length or weight or quantity" (Lev 19:35; also Deut 19:14; 25:13-16; Prov 11:1). Whoever causes damage to his neighbour by his negligence, must make full restitution. And whoever is found stealing or cheating, must restore the ill-gotten goods double or more (Ex 22:1-15; Num 5:6f).

At the same time the Old Testament is also very much aware of the social obligations that are incumbent upon property. The Mosaic law provides that farmers, when harvesting their field, vineyards or olive orchards, must leave the gleanings to the widows and orphans, the sojourners and the poor (Lev 19:9f; Deut 24:19-22). In every third year all the tithe of the produce is to be given to the Levites and the needy (Deut 14:28f; 26:12-15). Every seventh year, the sabbath year, the fields, vineyards and olive orchards are to lie fallow, and whatever grows shall belong to the poor (Ex 23:10f). A fellow Jew who has been taken into slavery through purchase is to be set free after six years of service in the seventh year (Ex 21:2; Deut 15:12). In the same way a loan is to be remitted (Deut 15:1f). Again, every fiftieth year is to be hallowed as a jubilee. Any real estate that has been alienated during this period, and in special cases also the house that has been sold, is to be returned to the original owner or to his heirs (Lev 25:8-34; Num 36:4). Protection of the poor is also the purpose of the prohibition to take interest from a fellow Jew (Ex 22:25; Lev 25:36f; Deut 23:19f). Interest may however be taken from foreigners, who also charge interest (Deut 23:20).

"These laws, the like of which cannot be found elsewhere among the legal ordinances of the ancient East, act as a preventative against the amassing of enormous holdings of land and money, and against the acquiring of colossal power by any individual in the nation, while guarding the less affluent against the extremes of utter poverty and protecting the freedom and security of each and every member of the nation."[1] But it also appears that these laws, especially in the area of land tenure, were essentially idealistic projections which were rarely if ever enforced.

There is finally the general obligation to almsgiving and charity. "Therefore I command you, you shall open wide your hand to your brother, to the needy and the poor, in the land" (Deut 15:11). The obligation to deeds of beneficence was deeply implanted in the moral consciousness of the people of Israel.

b)   The *New Testament* equally accepts property as a self-evident institution. Jesus shows no intention to revise the order of property or even only to be a judge in such matters. "Who made me a judge or divider of inheritance over you?" (Lk 12:14). True, he keeps a great love for simple people who earn their living by the labour of their hands. He himself had grown up in the poor circumstances of a small artisan (cf. Mk 6:3; Lk

---

[1] Karl Hermann Schelkle: Theology of the New Testament. Vol. III: Morality. — Collegeville, Minn.: Liturgical Press, 1973, 299.

2:24). But he associates with the rich and the poor alike. The solution of economic and social problems is not his actual concern. He makes no attempt to share out the goods of this world more fairly. All that Jesus' wholly religious outlook completely excludes, by making love the supreme law, is indifference towards those in need, exploitation from above and hatred from below.

But did not Jesus direct his sharpest warnings against the rich? "Woe to you that are rich, for you have received your consolation" (Lk 6:24). And does he not call the poor blessed? "Blessed are you poor, for yours is the kingdom of God" (Lk 6:20). Yet it must be noted that this blessing is quoted by the Gospels in two different versions. The version of Luke gives the impression indeed that Jesus speaks of the economically poor. But if this were true without further qualification, it would create a problem. For not all who are materially poor are for this reason also God-fearing people. The difficulty is solved by the version of Matthew. According to him the blessing applies to "the poor in spirit" (Mt 5:3). His concept of poverty means a spiritual and religious attitude: the inner detachment from possessions; and, at a deeper level still, a person's awareness of his dependence on God and of his need for redemption.

"The different version of the Beatitude in Matthew 5:3 and Luke 6:20 must be understood as due to the fact that the two evangelists have interpreted in a special sense in the service of the paraenesis of the early Church, Jesus' originally Messianic call addressed to all men willing for redemption, Matthew more with a view to the religious and moral attitude, Luke socially in regard to the actually poor and needy, but likewise presupposing the corresponding religious disposition."[1]

Yet there are still other sayings of Jesus which seem to prove that he rejects earthly possessions. Thus he suggests that it is almost impossible for the rich to enter the kingdom of God (Mk 10:23-27). He states that one cannot serve God and mammon (Mt 6:24 par). He advises not to lay up perishable treasures on earth, but to gather imperishable ones in heaven (Mt 6:19-21). The deceitfulness of the riches chokes the good seed of the word (Mk 4:19).[2] Jesus must therefore have been closely associated with the idea of poverty. He regards it as a

---

[1] R. Schnackenburg: The Moral Teaching of the New Testament. — London: Burns and Oates, 1967, 130.

[2] Some strong warnings against riches are also found in the letter of the apostle James: 2:5-7; 5:1-6.

condition for the undivided dedication to God. Especially the preacher of the gospel is called to live the poor life of his Master (Mt 10:8-10; 19:21; Mk 6:8f).

Nevertheless Jesus makes of the demand of poverty neither a social program nor a law for all to whom his message is addressed. He permits himself to be the guest of rich men (Lk 7:36; 14:1), often accepts the hospitality of the well-to-do sisters at Bethany (Lk 10:38-42; Jn 11:1ff; 12:1-8) and the support of women of property (Lk 8:2f). He certainly did not exclude from the kingdom of God these friends of his or such people as Nicodemus and Joseph of Arimathea. Therefore one must conclude that the renunciation of earthly possessions remains a special call, which is only addressed to those who are chosen by Christ to follow him in a more immediate way.

Not the possession of property as such is evil, but wealth which becomes an idol. The scandal is not that there was a rich man and a poor Lazarus, but that Lazarus wanted to eat the crumbs which fell from the table of the rich man, and that he did not receive a particle of them (Lk 16:19-31). Property has value only to the extent that a man uses it in the service of the kingdom of God and of his fellowmen. The rich should know that wealth is precarious, and they should use it in doing good works. In this way they can store up treasures for eternal life (1 Tim 6:17-19). Whoever has possessions must not withhold them from a brother in need. How could such a one abide in God's love? (1 Jn 3:17).

The New Testament repeats the Old Testament prohibition of thievery (Mt 19:18 par; Rom 13:9). Thieves and robbers are listed together with idolaters, adulterers and the immoral. They will not inherit the kingdom (1 Cor 6:9f; 1 Pet 4:15). Now the thief must abandon his former deeds. He is to do honest work, and from his surplus he will be able to give to the needy (Eph 4:28). It is likewise the will of God that no man defraud his brother in business (1 Thess 4:6). But to the extent that a man lawfully owns property, he also has the right to dispose of it freely (cf. the parable of the labourers in the vineyard, Mt 20:1-16).

2.   *Moral basis for the right to private property*

Christian social ethics has always been of the conviction that man has the right to own private property. This right is presupposed and confirmed by Holy Scripture. It is demanded by man's needs as a person and a social being. The social encyclicals see in it a natural right and an indispensable element in the social order (RN 7-23; QA 44f; MM 104-112).[1] They firmly defend it against its contestation by socialist and communist theories from the time these theories took rise. "It is incomprehensible how the innate character of a right can be called into question that has as its main source the fruitfulness of work and is continually fomented by the same; a right that constitutes an apt means to assert one's personality and to exercise responsibility in every field; an element of solidity and of security for family life and of peaceful and orderly development of society" (MM 112). Vatican II likewise regards private ownership as a necessary institution, even though it is aware that there are limits to this right (GS 71).

Man has a natural desire for property. His innate feeling for justice tells him that he has the right to dispose of the fruits of his work. These psychological reactions show that man needs property and is entitled to it. The right to private ownership is supported by several reasons, derived from man's nature as a person and from the needs of society. Insofar as these reasons show that the nature of man and society demand this right, it can justly be called a natural right. The reasons are the following:

a) Property is an important means for exercise of personal responsibility, self-realization and creative development. "Ownership and other forms of private control over material goods contribute to the expression of personality" (GS 71). The person who does not own property cannot freely make use of the material goods necessary for his work. This will adversely affect his initiative and creativity.

b) Private property secures man a realm of independence and serves as a protection of his freedom. For the dispossessed are to a large extent dependent on the good will of those who control land and property. They are compelled to seek the favour of those in power. The fewer the people who own property, the weaker the defences against the totalitarian abuse of political power. In contrast the institution of private property tends towards a distribution of power in society and prevents its dangerous concentration in the hands of few. "Private ownership or some other kind of dominion over material goods provides everyone with a wholly necessary area of independence, and

---

[1] Texts and numbers of the social encyclicals are quoted from the N.C.W.C. Translation.

should be regarded as an extension of human freedom" (GS 71). By the same token it is also a source of security. Property makes it possible for a man to care himself for his daily needs. He depends less on the uncertain will of others.

c) Private property enables a man to provide for the sustenance and upbringing of those who are entrusted to his care. Especially for parents it is an important means to fulfill their duties towards their children. This also includes provision for their future support and security. "It is a most sacred law of nature that the father of a family see that his offspring are provided with all the necessities of life, and nature even prompts him to desire to provide and to furnish his children. . . . with the means of decently protecting themselves against harsh fortune in the uncertainties of life. He can do this surely in no other way than by owning fruitful goods to transmit by inheritance to his children" (RN 20). By means of his possessions a man is also enabled to help his friends and needy neighbours. Even where social welfare services are available, they alone never suffice to cope with all the conditions of distress. They must be complemented by private charity, which presupposes ownership of personal goods.

d) Private property serves to maintain peace in society and obviates disputes. This is true of property for consumption, but also and especially of property for production. Common property inevitably raises the question concerning who is entitled to control it. This is a precarious source of disputes and quarrels. Where a clear demarcation of mine and thine is missing, the doors are opened to dissension and social strife. These evils are avoided by the clear definition of the spheres of competency provided by the institution of private property.

e) Private property brings about a better utilization of the goods available in the interest of all. "The individual has less interest in what is common to all, he treats it with less care and is reluctant to devote work, effort, and self-sacrifice to it: this is a universal experience."[1] While the hope and possibility to acquire property fosters responsibility, diligence and thrift.

These various reasons show that private property is a necessary institution. But they also show that it is not a goal in itself. It is subservient to the needs of the person and of society. And it is a matter for the social community to give this institution

---

[1] J. Messner: Social Ethics. — St. Louis/London: Herder Book Co., 1965, 823.

the form most suited to these needs. "Thus, the system of private property in every society is, to a large extent, dependent on social and historical factors: social, including the agreement of wills in society; and historical, namely, those connected with the evolution of society and culture."[1]

For the same reason private property is not an absolute right, but a right conditioned by the needs of the individual and of the community. Material goods are given by the Creator to serve all men, and not only a selected few. Therefore, "no one is justified in keeping for his exclusive use what he does not need, when others lack necessities. In a word, 'according to the traditional doctrine as found in the Fathers of the Church and the great theologians, the right to property must never be exercised to the detriment of the common good'. If there should arise a conflict 'between acquired private rights and primary community exigencies', it is the responsibility of public authorities 'to look for a solution, with the active participation of individuals and social groups' " (PP 23). The common purpose of created things must still find some more attention in the following section.

3.   *The universal purpose of created things*

Material possessions are not values in themselves. They are meant to serve man's needs. And inasmuch as the ultimate destiny of man is the glory and praise of God, material possessions must likewise be ordained to this end. The purpose of created things is therefore not their accumulation to the greatest possible riches. That contradicts their function as instruments in the service of God and men. Since all men have material needs and all are called to serve God by means of them, it is obvious that all are entitled to have a share in the goods of this world.

"God intended the earth and all that it contains for the use of every human being and people. Thus, as all men follow justice and unite in charity, created goods should abound for them on a reasonable basis. Whatever the forms of ownership may be, as adapted to the legitimate institutions of people according to diverse and changeable circumstances, attention must always be paid to the universal purpose for which created goods are meant" (GS 69).

A first consequence from this is that all property has always a social character with corresponding social obligations. Man has not an unconditional right over his possessions. This truth has

---

[1] J. Messner, 1. c. 825.

already been pointed out by Pius XI. "It follows from the two-fold character of ownership, which we have termed individual and social, that men must take into account in this matter, not only their own advantage, but also the common good. To define in detail these duties, when the need occurs and when the natural law does not do so, is the function of the government" (QA 49; cf. MM 119; GS 69). Especially a man's excess income is not simply left to his own discretion. He has the grave obligation to use it in a socially beneficial way, e.g. by making it available for works of charity, or by creating opportunities for work, or the like (QA 50f).

If the social quality of property is overlooked, it easily becomes an occasion of social unrest and serious disturbances. Indeed, failure to use one's surplus property for a community which is in need of it is unacceptable. "Especially in under-developed areas, where all resources must be put to urgent use, those men gravely endanger the public good who allow their resources to remain unproductive or who deprive their community of the material and spiritual aid it needs" (GS 65; cf. 71). Governments are entitled to enforce a socially meaningful use of idle property.

A second consequence is that all property must be subordinated to the exigencies of the divine plan. Earthly goods provide for bodily needs and well-being, for progress and more gracious living. This makes them valuable. But this is not their ultimate purpose. "Seek first the kingdom of God and his righteousness, and all these things shall be yours as well" (Mt 6:33; cf. Lk 12:31). The true hierarchy of values must never be lost out of sight. "What will it profit a man, if he gains the whole world and forfeits his life?" (Mt 16:26; cf. Lk 12:16-21). If material possessions seduce man to forget his true calling and to turn away from God, he must rather "hate" and "despise" them (cf. Mt 10:39; Lk 14:26.33).

John XXIII expresses his great concern "that in the economically developed countries there are not a few persons in whom the consciousness of the hierarchy of values is weakened, is dead, or confused; that is, in whom the spiritual values are neglected, forgotten, denied; while progress of the sciences, of technology, the economic development, the material well-being are often fostered and proposed as the pre-eminent, and even elevated to the unique reason of life. This constitutes an insidious poison." It undermines the foundations of true civilization (MM 176f).

The fundamental purpose of production must not be profit or domination. It must not be the avaricious accumulation of goods, so often condemned by Holy Scripture. "Rather, it must be the service of man, and indeed of the whole man, viewed in terms of his material needs and the demands of his intellectual, moral, spiritual, and religious life. And when we say man, we mean every man whatsoever and every group of men, of whatever race and from whatever part of the world. Consequently, economic activity is to be carried out according to its own methods and laws but within the limits of morality, so that God's plan for mankind can be realized" (GS 64).

II. Acquisition of proprietary rights

1. *Work and accession*

The most excellent title to property is work. Most titles of acquisition derive from work. "Human labour which is expended in the production and exchange of goods or in the performance of economic services is superior to the other elements of economic life. For the latter have only the nature of tools" (GS 67).

Every person's innate feeling for justice tells him that a man has a right to the fruits of his work. "Since man expends his mental energy and his bodily strength in procuring the goods of nature, by this very act he appropriates that part of physical nature to himself which he has cultivated. On it he leaves impressed, as it were, a kind of image of his person, so that it must be altogether just that he should possess that part as his very own" (RN 15). It is against equity to defraud a man of the things his labour has produced. "Would justice permit anyone to own and enjoy that upon which another has toiled? As effects follow the cause producing them, so it is just that the fruit of labour belongs precisely to those who have performed the labour" (RN 16).

Of course to the extent that a product is the result of the work and contributions of several parties, e.g. of the workers, the management and of those who provide the machines, the profit must be divided in an equitable way among all of them. This question has been discussed in detail in the section on the just wage.

Also the intellectual and spiritual worker has a right to the fruits of his work. The scientist, artist or author of a book has the right to his product and is entitled to the material fruits accruing from it. Modern states, practically all, protect this right through patent and copyright laws. Violation of such rights is the basis for an obligation to restitution, the same as violations of other property rights.

Improvements made on a material or on land property are generally called industrial accession, e.g. carvings from wood, embroidery on cloth, house-building on land. But they all result from man's work. Hence industrial accession is the same title to property as work.

For instances in which the work and the material are supplied by different persons, the following rulings hold: If a person works on a material that belongs to another, the new object belongs to the one who does the work, provided the work is more valuable than the material used. If the material is the more valuable part, the finished product belongs to the owner of the material. But in either case the one must indemnify the other. Wherefore a statue which an artist carves from the wood belonging to another, belongs to the artist. Bread that a baker makes from flour belonging to another, belongs to the owner of the flour.

If a building is erected on a person's property with material that belongs to another, the building belongs to the owner of the property, who must indemnify the builder. The same holds good for plantations. If one sows or plants things on land belonging to another, the growth belongs to the owner of the land, who must compensate the sower or planter. But he who builds, plants or sows in bad faith on the land of another, loses according to some positive laws what is built, planted or sown without the right to indemnity.

The increment brought about through fruitful increase, e.g. fruitage of trees, pregnancy of animals, grass of land, is usually defined as natural accession. But since trees have to be planted, animals to be raised, and the land has to be cultivated, their increment can justly be considered as the fruit of man's work too.

The increase of money effected by interest seems to be a kind of accession which is indeed rather removed from work. Yet the money saved certainly is the result of man's labour. And it should in one way or another benefit and serve the owner. For this is the purpose of work. Hence a reasonable interest for money loaned is the fruit of man's work in a similar way as the fruits which grow on the trees he has planted.

2. *Occupancy*

Occupancy is the actual taking of a thing belonging to no other with the intention of making it one's own. It is a valid title to ownership, as long as it transgresses no existing rights of others and no just positive laws, because nature offers the earth and all its goods for the good of all mankind.

The act of seizure should be intentional and physical. A mere act of the will gives no title. Moreover the thing taken should be of such quantity only as can admit of immediate and proximately future use. Occupation of so large quantities of an object — such as land — as cannot be used or effectively exploited does not give a valid claim to ownership. For the seizure of soil and unexploited resources has no other purpose and moral justification than their useful development and utilization. Unrestricted accumulation of domain and other resources for the sole purpose of exercising control and gaining power is a violation of the natural right of all to share in the goods of this world provided by the Creator.

On the other hand it is likewise not correct to deny man the right to a piece of land of his own altogether. "It has been stated erroneously — and the error is apt to recur periodically — that land cannot be occupied and privately owned, because it is not the result of labour, it is not produced but exists before occupancy. If the principle were true, clothes could not be owned, nor the fruits of the earth, nor money, nor in fact anything, for the raw material of all things which we fashion existed antecedently. On the contrary, most of the valuable qualities possessed by cultivated land are due to labour, which practically changes the very nature of land."[1] To the extent that a man uses and develops a portion of land meaningfully and invests his work in it, he is also entitled to own it. (Note that a person who buys a piece of land with the money he has earned, also invests his work in land, although in an indirect way.)

In our times land can hardly be acquired by simple occupancy anymore, since most of it is already divided and owned. The things most liable to occupancy today are animals and things that are found (chattels).

Treasure-troves. A treasure long abandoned, so that it is impossible to discover the owner, may according to natural law

---

[1] Henry Davis: Moral and Pastoral Theology, vol. II. — London. Sheed and Ward, 1943, 284.

be occupied by the finder. But the civil law sometimes decides that the find must be divided with the owner of the place or with the government. At times it also establishes claims of the state to cultural and historical discoveries which are of national interest. Such laws bind in conscience, provided they are not patently unjust.

Abandoned goods. Things freely abandoned belong to him who first appropriates them, e.g. things thrown in the garbage. Fruits and crops are usually looked upon as abandoned if they are left in the field after harvest time, e.g. oranges, nuts, grain.

Lost objects. Lost property belongs to its original owner as long as there is hope of discovering him. The finder is obliged to make reasonable efforts to find the owner. The value of the object found and the circumstances involved should decide whether there is an obligation in charity to take charge of it, and which degree of care is required to search out the owner. There is no obligation to assume the burden of finding him if the article has little value and presumably also means little to the owner. The finder has a right to be recompensed for his trouble and the expense incurred. If his effort to find the owner was unsuccessful, he may use the article as his own. The prescription of civil law as to the time interval before he may begin to use the article must be observed.

According to positive law articles found in places of work or business, in offices, stores, stations, public service centres, etc., must usually be turned over to the proper authorities at a designated place, e.g. a lost property office, where the owner is expected to report his loss and recover the article.

Animals. In former times wild game had no owner and could be hunted by anyone. Today however conditions in many countries are such that, generally speaking, one can no longer look upon wild game as having no owners. Hunters must acquire the right to hunt by license fees. Unlicensed hunting or poaching must be viewed as offence against commutative justice. But the protection of one's fields and crops is not classed with poaching. The owner of fields has the right to trap or shoot animals that damage his property. Fish in the open sea belong to him who takes the pains to catch them. The same applies to wild fruits.

Tame and domestic animals may not be appropriated, however much they stray, provided they can be recovered by any reasonable means by their owners. An animal tamed or reclaimed, though it fly or run about at its will, remains in its owner's possession if it habitually returns to a place under his control. Yet wild animals that were reclaimed but have regained their complete liberty are not in this category and may be taken. The positive legislations of states often contain further provisions concerning these matters, which bind in conscience to the extent that they are reasonable.

3. *Contracts*

A contract is a mutual agreement of two or more persons founding or modifying a relationship of rights. Ordinarily the contract should involve a strict equality in what is exchanged by the parties to the agreement. Nevertheless it may also entail the free granting of a right by one party (e.g. a donation) without a corresponding service in return from the other.

A' Contracts in general

Contracts are a most important means to acquire rights of ownership. This is however not their exclusive function. Contracts are also used for the transfer or modification of other rights, such as rights of guardianship, membership in associations, titles to offices, etc. What is said in the following about the conditions and effects of contracts applies to all contracts, not only to those which transfer property rights.

In every contract the following elements can be distinguished: the object of the contract, the capacity of the contracting parties, the contractual consent and the obligations arising from the contract.

a) Object of contract

The subject matter of the contract may be things or actions subject to the free and legitimate disposal of the contractants. The object must have the following qualities:

(1) It must be *possible*. No one can oblige himself to do the physically impossible. Thus a marriage contract is invalid if one of the partners is unable to perform the marriage act because he is impotent. Nor does anyone intend to oblige himself to what is morally impossible (i.e. very difficult), unless he explicitly states this. If the impossibility is only partial, one is held to the part that is possible. In a case of bankruptcy, for example, one is bound to pay the creditors that portion of their due which

one is still able to pay. If an action becomes impossible after the contract is made, the obligation to observe it ceases. The contract to sell a particular horse ceases if the horse dies prior to the fulfillment of the contract. But whoever renders a contract impossible through his own fault, is bound to repair damage caused thereby to the other party.

(2) It must *rightfully belong* to the disposing contractants. Yet it suffices that one subsequently come into possession of the object of the contract. No one can sell or lease what is not his own. One cannot lease a flat in a house which is no longer one's property. Stolen goods cannot, in conscience, be the object of sale. One cannot contract to sell public property which is inalienable. Church law forbids and nullifies simoniacal contracts, i.e. the sale of ecclesiastical offices for money or similar considerations. State laws likewise often forbid the sale of civil offices.

(3) It must be *morally good*. No one may ever bind himself to do what is evil. Therefore if a person obliges himself by contract to pay for something which is immoral (e.g. a contract for fornication made with a prostitute), the agreement is void before its execution. If one has previously received payment for such a thing, he must return the money. However it seems to many that after an immoral contract has been executed, the party who has received the service is also obliged to fulfill his part, provided he can do so without additional sin. Likewise money given for immoral actions already performed may be kept. "The argument used here is that though an agreement to perform an immoral act is null and void, there arises in the actual performance of the act, a good contract: v.g., *facio ut des;* the act done, under the aspect, not of its immorality, but of its laborious or benefiting or pleasure-giving nature, is worth something."[1]

If in the course of an immoral contract a third party has been harmed (e.g. by robbery or assassination), the money gained must naturally be paid as restitution to the victims. Gifts offered as bribes do not effect a valid contract, and those who give or take such gifts are guilty of serious sin.

(4) It must be *estimable at a price* if one of the contractants is expected to make payment. One may not ask payment for something which costs him no effort, e.g. for showing someone the way; a gift however may be accepted.

---

[1] Henry Davis: Moral and Pastoral Theology, vol. II. — London: Sheed and Ward, 1943, 356.

If one already has a strict right to some action of another, the latter cannot exact a price for the same, e.g. a judge cannot demand payment for passing a just sentence.

In reference to contracts unenforceable in court or not recognized by law, it is to be observed that they are nevertheless sometimes binding in conscience. Thus betting contracts are often not recognized by civil law, but they are good in conscience. Therefore the bet must be paid according to the terms agreed upon.

b) Capacity of contracting parties

According to natural law every person who has the use of reason, sufficient to understand what he is doing, can enter into a contract. Incompetent are children before they attain the use of reason, those who are insane, completely intoxicated or otherwise deranged. Less competent are those who are feeble-minded, partially intoxicated, or who need a guardian in important matters.

Positive law usually still defines more in detail in which instances the contractual power is restricted. Minors, i.e. those under twenty-one years of age, have a limited capacity of contracting. With some exceptions they may annul a contract after it has been made and demand a return of the money. Hence where their inexperience has involved them in difficulties which would prove harmful to them, they are permitted to void the contract. The other party is entitled to his property. However if a minor injures another's property, he is liable for damages. Furthermore minors may not avail themselves of the benefit of the law if they have acted in bad faith, e.g. if a minor by deceit induced the other party to sell to him. The same holds for persons who have been declared legally incompetent, e.g. lunatics, habitual drunkards and spendthrifts.

c) Contractual consent

The contractual consent must have the following four qualities in order to be valid:

(1) It must be *internal*. If one has no intention to make a contract, the same is void. But civil legislation ordinarily must exclude the claim of any mental reservation and press the execution of the contract as signified externally. As to the obligation in conscience, moral theology teaches that a contracting

party who culpably withholds his consent must either carry out what he has promised in making the contract or fully compensate the other party for the damage caused. If one's intention was actually to contract but not to fulfill the implied obligation, the contract is valid.

(2) It must be *mutual*. Both parties must agree to the same thing. Mutuality requires that consent be contemporaneous, that is, that the acceptance of one be given while the offer of the other still holds good. But it does not require that the parties be in each other's presence or that they contract through direct personal communication. In order to avoid litigation, positive laws often determine a certain time within which one party must obtain knowledge of the other's consent. After the elapse of that time the offer is considered revoked.

(3) It must be *manifested externally*. That is one must manifest in some sensible way one's agreement to the proposition contained in an offered contract. Silence gives consent only when the contract is favourable to the party who is silent, or when that party should and easily could manifest his lack of consent if the proposal did not please him.

To avoid difficulties positive law often prescribes definite formulae. Contracts of this kind are called formal, in contradistinction to non-formal contracts, where no such formalities are prescribed. In instances in which the formalities prescribed are not observed, the contracts are called informal. Informal contracts can be contested in the courts and voided by a judicial decision. According to a well-founded opinion, however, such informal contracts oblige in conscience (with the exception of the matrimonial contract) until the invalidity has been declared by court. It should also be noted that even though certain contracts cannot be enforced by law, they may nevertheless bind in conscience.

(4) It must be fully *deliberate and free*. Accordingly error, fear and force impair the validity of a contract.

Every substantial error about the nature of the contract or the nature of the subject matter of the contract vitiates the agreement. Thus a contract is void if one contractant considers it a donation and the other a sale; or if one wishes to buy black textile for a particular suit, but the material one receives is blue. If the error is only accidental, that is if it concerns features of the contract that are only incidentally intended, the contract is generally valid. Thus if one gives a poor man an alms under the erroneous impression that he is a relative, one generally does not wish the gift to be invalid on account of this error. Or if one buys a pair of shoes for 50 dollars, although it is worth only 30, one usually still wants to have this pair of shoes, although that portion of the price must be restored which exceeds the just price. Nevertheless such contracts may be rescinded, especially if they were brought about by fraud. If the positive law lays down further regulations concerning these matters, as usually is the case, they must be observed in the interest of the common good, even though they do not always perfectly agree with the natural law, as long as they are not substantially unjust.

Grave fear unjustly inflicted upon a person for the purpose of forcing him to agree to a contract gives this person the right to rescind the contract, if it is not invalid from the beginning. If therefore a person agrees under threat of death to procure a certain amount of money, he need not keep this contract. But if an individual, who is being attacked by a robber, promises a passer-by money for assistance, he must keep his agreement. The reason is that the fear was not inflicted for the purpose of effecting this agreement. As to force, it renders a contract void because of lack of consent.

Positive law generally declares contracts entered into under grave and unjust fear as invalid or at least as rescindable. According to ecclesiastical law the following contracts are invalid, if made under the influence of grave and unjust fear: marriage contracts, entry into novitiate, profession of vows, ecclesiastical elections, resignation from office and benefice.

If the fear is not unjustly inflicted or if it is the effect of some necessary cause, the contract is valid and not voidable by law. He who promises another money in order that the latter may not denounce an offence committed by him, must keep the contract.

d) Obligations arising from contracts

A contract obliges in justice, either gravely or not, according to the nature of that which is contracted. The obligation to restitution for any loss caused by breach of contract is the same. An exception to this is a gratuitous promise which, according to the intention of the promisor, obliges only out of fidelity. But it may be disputed whether a simple promise of this kind is a contract in the strict sense.

The contract must be carried out as intended by the

contracting parties and as interpreted by custom and circumstances. If the object of the contract is destroyed through the moral fault of one of the parties, he is liable for the damage caused.

One who unduly delays the execution of the contract and thereby inflicts damage on the other contractant, is bound to repair the damage he has caused. If there is a clause setting a time for the fulfillment under penalty of fine, the party who does not meet the time-limit is obliged to pay the fine. But in the enforcement of the terms the partners must go beyond the mere letter of the law and the rigours of commutative justice. There must be Christian concern for unforeseen contingencies and the undeserved incapacity of a partner to comply with the stipulated terms.

An added condition makes consent and consequently the validity of the contract dependent upon the existence or fulfillment of the condition. If a contract of sale of land is made under condition that the buyer pays the amount due within three months, the contract becomes void if the amount is not paid within the stipulated time. Impossible or immoral conditions make the contract invalid.

A contract which imposes a burden makes some special action obligatory upon one of the contractants. Such a burden is for example a donation with the obligation of using it for the building of a church. If there is a burden in the strict sense, the non-fulfillment of the obligation renders the party who did not fulfill his obligation liable for restitution. But if a gift is only for the advantage of the donee, there is no burden in the strict sense. Sometimes the donor merely intends to supply another with the means to attain some goal, e.g. the priesthood, but does not require its actual attainment. In such a case there is no question of restitution.[1]

B'   Contracts of sale

Sale is a contract by which a seller transfers the ownership of a commodity to a buyer for a consideration in money, called the price. Present commercial life is largely based on the contract of sale. The basic moral principle, which ought to guide all commerce, is that the contract of sale must be a genuine service and a contribution to the common welfare. Commerce and trade are of great importance to the community.

---

[1] Cf. H. Jone, 1963, nr. 289.

An ethos of service ought to inspire those who are involved in it. — The principles which apply to contracts of sale also apply to contracts where one commodity is exchanged for another.

(1) *The just price.* The most important problem involved in the contract of sale is that of the just price. Justice demands a basic equality between what is given and what is received. The just price is however not to be regarded as an exactly determined and fixed sum, capable of mathematical determination. It is the result of the cost of production (including storage and transportation), advertising expenses, commissions for the dealers, taxation fees, and the utility of the object for the buyer. The relation of the individual price to all the other prices and hence to the entire price structure in a region or country must likewise be taken into consideration. Accordingly prices usually constitute an approximate computation, which permits of a margin. There are highest, lowest and average prices. To sell above the highest, or to force prices down below the lowest, would ordinarily be a sin against justice and would entail restitution. An exception to this are auction sales, which are justified by law and custom. Bargaining or haggling which has as its purpose a price commonly accepted is not considered unjust.

There is a theory which takes the view that the just price of a thing is what can be got for it without deceit or fraud. This may hold for normally prosperous times, where nobody will feel compelled to produce goods for sale at a price lower than the cost of production, or to pay a higher price than the service value of the good justifies. But this auto-regulation of a free market economy is not adequate in times of crisis, such as economic depression, war and post-war periods, and other situations of economic distress. In such conditions the principle will easily lead to unjust and cruel exploitation of those in need. It cannot be justified to sell an article for more than it is worth, or to buy it for less than it is worth, only because one of the contractants is in a particular distress. We may not trade with the needs of others. This applies above all to basic foods and other necessities of life.

To take advantage of the momentary market situation in order to buy or sell more profitably is within certain limits justified. A man who takes his vegetables to a neighbouring town in order to profit by the higher prices consequent upon a temporary scarcity, does not offend against commutative justice. First, because the price margin for these goods is rather large;

second, because vegetables do not pertain to the basic foods, certainly not the individual kinds, and can be replaced by other foodstuffs, though less select ones.

In order to prevent abuses the state has the right and duty to impose just legal prices. But as a rule this should remain an emergency measure, when a just price formation is, for the time being, unattainable by other means. Fixed prices tend to create black markets, which are hotbeds of usury, as experience teaches. The legal price obliges in conscience as long as it is not overtly unjust or generally abandoned. If the legal price has been fixed in the interest of the seller, it is also a sin against justice for a merchant to sell for less, if the fellow merchants thereby suffer loss.

If there is neither a common (market) price nor a legal price, the price must be determined by the free agreement of the buyer and seller, without being subject to fraud or deceit, or the estimate of an expert. This price is common for used articles or objects that are extremely rare or very precious. Works of art, curios, antiques, rare books, etc. have a species of market price among those familiar with such articles, which however allows of great latitude. Even in this area one is not allowed to exploit the ignorance of the seller or buyer.

(2) *The commodity.* An error concerning the nature or a substantial quality of the commodity voids the contract of sale. Such an error is committed if buyer and seller, for example, believe an object to be an artificial jewel, which in reality is a precious stone, or vice versa. Or if the buyer wants to buy goods of genuine and pure quality (such as genuine wine) and receives inferior or adulterated goods (e.g. wine made from orange juice), even if there is a reduction in the price.

If neither buyer nor seller knows the real value of an object and both doubt whether the price paid represents the real value of the thing, the contract is valid, since in such an instance their agreement takes on the character of an aleatory contract. If the value is unknown on account of public error reflected in the common price, the contract is both valid and just, e.g. if an art dealer buys at a low price a painting which is not valued highly by the public, but which he recognizes as a masterly piece of art.

An error about some accidental quality of a commodity does not void the contract of sale, but in some cases renders it rescindable. If the buyer does not inquire about the accidental defects, there is no obligation to reveal them, provided the price is just and no fraud has been committed. However if he inquires about them they must be disclosed to him, unless the inquiry is a general one and the object will serve the purpose of the buyer equally well. If the seller, in spite of the buyer's inquiry, does not reveal the accidental defects of the commodity, the contract is valid, but it can be rescinded if the buyer would not have bought the goods had he known of these defects; if he would have bought them in spite of such knowledge the price need only be brought within just limits.[1]

C' Last will or testament

A last will or testament is a declaration concerning the disposal of one's property after death. It can be considered as a form of gratuitous contract. The testator transfers the rights to his property to his heirs. In order that the transfer be effective, it must be accepted by the beneficiaries. As demanded for the validity of contracts in general, the testator must have the use of reason and be of age. According to the laws of some states also persons of 18 years of age and at times even below may enjoy the capacity to make a will. Testaments made under the pressure of force or grave unjust fear are invalid. Impossible, immoral and illegal conditions added to a will are void.

(1) *The right to bequeath* belongs to the institution of private property and is, together with it, in its essence based upon natural law. "Man's natural right of possessing and transmitting property by inheritance must remain intact and cannot be taken away by the state" (QA 49). There is no good reason why a person should not possess the right to decide in what way his possessions shall be used when he dies and who shall receive them. Moreover parents have a natural desire and a moral obligation to extend the care for their children beyond the time of their death, particularly if the children are not sufficiently provided for. The inheritance is an important means for them to comply with this duty. The abolition of the right to inheritance would undermine the institution of private property and soon eliminate it altogether. An important incentive to thriftiness and industry would fall away.

There are also important cultural and political points of view which support the right to inheritance. Greater possessions enable a person to dedicate himself more freely to cultural tasks

---

[1] Cf. Jone, 1963, nr. 299-303.

and to further them. An independent class of property owners is likewise vital for a strong and settled democracy. Because those who are economically independent can more readily afford to sustain their own opinions and to withstand the forces steering for a state-dependent mass society and the despotic abuse of power.

The state however has the right and the duty to supervise the right of inheritance and to determine more specifically its details. Although the freedom of the testator to dispose of his possessions must be safeguarded, his children and wife should be guaranteed their due portion. In order to forestall fraud and to secure the peace in the community, the state is entitled to set down regulations for a legally valid testament. Inheritance taxes are not unjust, as long as they remain within due limits. They must not be so high that they ultimately violate a person's right to his possessions. Such a policy is not in the interest of the common good but contradicts it, as has been pointed out.

(2) *Legal formalities* are required by civil law for the validity of a last will before the law. In general a written will is valid if it is properly signed by the testator and two witnesses with the date and place clearly stated. If the testator is unable to write, he must make his mark. At times civil law also permits a proxy to sign for the testator at the latter's express directions and in his presence. Testaments irregular in form are for that reason however not simply invalid in conscience. The wishes of the testator should be respected also in these cases and his will be carried out, provided it is reasonable and its authenticity assured. But if an informal will is contested in the courts, the judicial decision must be followed in the interest of public peace.

Can. 1299 §2 of the Code of Canon Law requests the heirs to carry our the bequests made in favour of pious causes even if the will is irregular in form.[1] However necessary heirs may always claim the portion to which they are entitled by law, even against pious causes. Statutes of civil law which void bequests made in favour of pious causes are unjust. The bequests may be retained and cannot be set aside by the other heirs without offending against justice.

---

[1] The Commentary of Bouscaren/Ellis notes that, according to an answer of the Code Commission, this canon, formerly can. 1513, is to be interpreted not merely as an exhortation but as a precept. Heirs have an obligation in conscience to carry out the provisions even of a civilly invalid testament regarding any bequest to pious causes (Canon Law. A Text and Commentary, 1966, 824).

(3) *Duties of the testator.* Natural law obliges a testator who makes a will to leave a part of his possessions to his nearest kin, especially his wife and children who need assistance. He has also a grave obligation to help his parents, brothers and sisters if they are in grave need, even in preference to pious causes. Any favouritism must be avoided, and no child should be discriminated against except for a serious reason. There is no obligation to leave everything to one's children or other near relatives if they are already sufficiently provided for. It is very praiseworthy indeed if the testator also remembers the poor and other good causes in his will.

To the extent that civil law provides for the equitable distribution of the property in case of intestacy, there is no strict obligation to make a will. Such an obligation however exists when otherwise serious quarrels may ensue; or when the merits of the children differ so that an equal distribution by the law will work an injustice; or when the poverty of one child calls for a greater share; or when debts are to be paid or restitution is to be made which will not be taken care of by the law.

(4) *Duties of the heirs.* Ordinarily there is no moral or juridical obligation to accept an inheritance. But if it is accepted, the heirs are also obliged to settle the testator's debts and other obligations, if there are, and to pay out all bequests as soon as possible. In order that heirs may not be bound to obligations beyond the amount of the inheritance, they may accept it on condition that legal inventory be made and that they have not to pay more than the value of the inheritance to liquidate the debts and obligations with which it is burdened.

"It is probable, however, that an heir is not obliged in conscience to pay out claims beyond the value of the inheritance, even though he accepted the inheritance and has been declared liable to the obligations by court sentence. Hence, one cannot be obliged thereto. The creditors can, however, make legal claim for full payment." [1]

(5) *Intestate succession* takes place when an owner of property has left no will at his death, or has property which his will does not dispose of. The will of the deceased is supplied by the provisions of the law, known as statutes of descent when referring to real property, and statutes of distribution when referring to personal property. The statutes of descent and

---

[1] Jone, 1963, nr. 321.

distribution are often similar, but not always. Debts have usually to be paid first. In exceptional cases a last will may also be revoked by operation of the law, then namely when the testator's circumstances have radically changed, such as by marriage or birth of children.

The children of the deceased, if any, usually inherit in equal shares minus the dowry. If one of them has died, his descendants take the share of the parent. Posthumous children of the intestate take as if they had been born in his lifetime. Half-brothers and half-sisters inherit alike as children of their common parent. Children born after the making of the will, or those born after the testators death, if not provided for in the will, usually take as heirs; likewise living children not provided for in the will if their omission was unintentional. Husbands and wives are made heirs of each other in most states. Next in the line of succession are parents, brothers and sisters; the order of precedence among them varies. Where there is no living descendant or ancestor, the law provides for inheritance by the next of kin, which means those most nearly related by blood. Where there is no one who under the law is entitled to take, the possessions devolve upon the state.

4. *Prescription*

Prescription is a title introduced by positive legislation by which, under certain conditions and during the period determined by the law, ownership is acquired or another's claim to a thing or action extinguished.

The acquisition of a title to property or to its use by this means is called acquisitive prescription. Suppose a farmer has for many years tilled a piece of land. He is convinced that he has rightfully inherited it from his father. His right to the land has never been contested during these years. Yet a long time after the death of his father a neighbour claims this piece of land by virtue of a title found in the archive of his family. If the farmer has been in the peaceful possession of the piece of land for the time determined by the law, usually twenty years, he then is considered the legitimate owner of it, in spite of the adverse title of his neighbour. The land has been acquired by prescription.

The liberation from the claim of another person to a service or consideration or from the obligation to tolerate an action by him is called liberative prescription. Thus claims to payment of debts, the right to legal prosecution of a misdeed, rights of way or water which are not made use of, prescribe after a certain period of time.

Prescription is justified by the needs of the common good. By means of it lawsuits are reduced and simplified. "Obviously there would be turmoil in society if possessors of property could have their claim to a rightful title contested even after long periods of tranquil possession in good faith, or if payment of debts or services of which men had long lost memory could suddenly be demanded and made the matter of endless litigation with which the state would have to concern itself." [1] The difficulty of preserving evidence for a long time complicates decisions concerning controversial facts which lie far back in the past and renders the lawsuits time consuming. It is also presumed that old claims are bad claims, since good claims are usually more readily fulfilled. The welfare of the society finally demands that uncertainties in titles and claims be obviated. In view of these reasons one may justly say that natural law itself favours and demands the title of prescription.

Valid and licit prescription presupposes the capacity of a thing or claim to be prescribed, good faith and a definite lapse of time. Acquisitive prescription in addition requires a title and actual possession or usufruct of the thing.

(1) *The thing or claim* in question must be subject to prescription. Public squares, streets, public springs are not subject to the ownership of private persons by prescription, if the people have not ceased to use them. According to canon law Mass stipends cannot prescribe, and this applies both to the person who is obliged to give a stipend (e.g. as a bequest) and to the person who is obliged to say Mass by reason of the stipend received (CIC 199 no. 5).

(2) *Good faith* consists in the conviction that the thing or right held is not unjustly held. The person who possesses jewels of which he knows that they are stolen is in bad faith. As to liberative prescription, a distinction is made between positive and negative good faith. He is in positive good faith who is convinced that he paid a debt. Negative good faith is present if one does not hinder another in the exercise of his right, for example if one does not prevent him from using his right to cross one's property.

Usually negative good faith is sufficient for liberative pre-

---

[1] Häring III, 1966, 440f.

540   *Christian Ethics*

scription. But in the case of the paying of debts and other active obligations which are not mere legal duties but moral duties, many authors require positive good faith. Some moralists however maintain that the state can extinguish an obligation in conscience also if there is only negative good faith, provided it is in the interest of the common welfare. "Practically, one may follow the milder opinion, except in cases wherein the creditor has reminded or for some reason purposely did not remind the debtor of his obligation; in such instances justice or equity forbid the debtor to appeal to liberative prescription." [1]

A law which does not require good faith for prescription has no effect in the realm of conscience. Prescription therefore does not take place if a person is convinced that the thing which he possesses belongs to another. Civil law can never establish a title in conscience where there is bad faith; it can only bar legal action. Evidently the law must limit itself to external evidence and is not in a condition to judge in the internal forum. — In case of doubt one should endeavour to attain certainty. If certainty is impossible, the possessor or person subject to a claim is considered as being in good faith.

(3)   *A definite length of time* is required, which varies according to the different rights and claims and according to the different laws. Formerly the period of possession necessary to give a title of prescription was from time immemorial, or "from the time whereof the memory of man runneth not to the contrary". Today the time is usually fixed at twenty years for immovable goods, e.g. land, and for the acquisition of rights of way, water and light. For movable goods (e.g. jewels, appliances, animals) and for most cases of liberative prescription the time required is less.

Canon law requires one hundred years in case of immovable and precious objects and rights of the Holy See; thirty years when there is question of other moral persons in the Church, e.g. a diocese or parish (CIC 1270). For ordinary movable objects which constitute ecclesiastical goods the time prescribed by the civil laws holds good (CIC 197).

(4)   *A good title* is needed, or one thought to be good, for acquisitive prescription, i.e. a reason on account of which one is convinced that a thing belongs to him. Such a title is for example a price paid (although the goods were not transferable because stolen) or the conviction that the goods are

---

[1] Jone, 1963, nr. 277.

inherited or a donation. Without any such title good faith is impossible.

(5) *Actual possession* of the thing or exercise of the right is a further condition for acquisitive prescription. The possession or exercise of the right must be certain, continuous, peaceable and open. Litigation, opposition, arrangement, apology for usage are all contrary to peaceable and open possession. Whoever possesses a thing in his own name acquires it for himself by prescription; whoever possesses it in the name of another acquires it for the latter, e.g. a guardian for his ward.

III. Moral duties concerning property

Acquisition and accumulation of property is not an end in itself, as has already been pointed out. Property has a subservient function. It is a means by which man is to be helped to fulfill the tasks assigned to him by the Creator. At all times it must be used in harmony with these tasks. Man can therefore not dispose of his property in absolute independence. He is subject to the all-embracing goals which God has set to him and the universe. He is bound to exercise his rights in accordance with the universal moral order.

Property has an individual and a social character, i.e. its function is to serve the needs of the individual as well as to promote the common good. "Whoever has received from the bounty of God a greater share of goods, whether corporeal and external, or of the soul, has received them for this purpose, namely, that he employ them for his own perfection and, likewise, as a servant of Divine Providence, for the benefit of others" (RN 36; cf. QA 45). Even though an owner does not forfeit the right to his property by the unaccountable use of his possessions, he nevertheless offends against God and his neighbour (cf. QA 47).

1. *Property as stewardship*

Christ regards men as stewards of the talents and gifts they have received. Possessions are doubtless among these gifts. Their owners have to account for them before their divine Master. They may not let them lie idle; much less may they abuse them for evildoing. The servants who have used their talents well, so that they made profit for their master, are praised and rewarded by him. "Well done, good and faithful servant; you have been faithful over a little, I will set you over much; enter into the joy of your master." But the servant who buried his talent and left it lying idle is condemned and thrown into the darkness (Mt 25:14-30 par).

Faithful and wise is that servant who administers the possessions which have been entrusted to him with concern for his household, so that each one has food to eat at the proper time. Wicked however is that servant who abuses his position as steward of the lord by maltreating his fellow servants and by not giving them their due, while he himself leads a luxurious life. He will be punished with the hypocrites (Mt 24:45-51).

No man can serve two masters. "You cannot serve God and mammon." If accumulation of money is a man's supreme goal, he will not be able to respect the dispositions of God. He will inevitably bring himself into conflict with God, and his place will be with the evildoers. On the other hand, if a man chooses God and his reign as his supreme goal, he will not hesitate to place his possessions in the service of the divine Master. And this is what Christ expects from his disciples and from every man who is a child of God. Such a man merits to be entrusted with the higher goods which are of lasting value. But if "you have not been faithful in the unrighteous mammon, who will entrust to you the true riches?" (Lk 16:10-13).

This teaching of Holy Scripture finds its echo in the social doctrine of the popes. Pius XI asks the rich to recognize "that they are nothing more than stewards of such possessions, and that they will have to render an account of them to God." [1] Authority over earthly goods is never an absolute authority. It is subordinated to the superior authority of the Creator. "If rich men are loyal and honourable, they will regard themselves as managers and dispensers of the earthly goods of God," [2] says Pius XII. Although these texts speak only of the rich, because their responsibilities are especially great, they apply to other owners too. They all are stewards of their property, accountable for its use before God.

Possessions are means by which a man provides for his livelihood, health and reasonable recreation. They enable him to attend to his education and to improve his knowledge and skills, and hence are means for his perfection. In many cases they are needed as aids for his work and profession. They

---

1 Pius XI. AAS 29 (1937), 88.
2 Pius XII, AAS 31 (1939), 642.

enable him to provide for the needs of his family and dependents. Finally property also has important social functions and serves to promote the common good. Property must be used in harmony with these needs and functions. Sinful is that use which neglects or even contradicts these needs.

2.   *Social obligations concerning property*[1]

From the universal purpose of the goods of this world it follows that "a man should regard his lawful possessions not merely as his own but also as common property in the sense that they should accrue to the benefit of not only himself but of others" (GS 69).

From of old Christian ethics has emphasized the grave obligation to share one's possessions with those in need. The chapter on fraternal love sets down the principles by which material assistance for the needy is ruled. Especially all superfluous goods must be used in a socially beneficial way. And their owners have a grave obligation to assist the poor in one way or another, and much more still those in extreme necessity. Vatican II points out that this obligation concerns both individuals and governments. Also wealthy nations and their governments are obliged to assist the many people in the world who are afflicted with hunger (GS 69).

Alms-giving is not the only way to use one's property for the benefit of others, although there will at all times be situations where this is the only way to help those in distress. The investment of one's money in securing favourable opportunities for employment is a help which is often even of greater value. It provides a lasting source of income and in addition benefits the society by the goods produced. Another form of serviceable use of one's property is improvements in the production of goods, by which their prices are reduced or their quality is raised. There are still many other ways to serve the common good by means of one's possessions, such as their employment for educational, scientific, cultural or religious purposes.

The social obligations of ownership are obviously not respected if goods are held idle and unproductive, or if they merely serve the limitless and exclusive enrichment of a small number of people. Vatican II refers to those large rural estates

---

[1] References for the duty of assistance to the developing nations: René Laurentin: Liberation, Development and Salvation. — Maryknoll: Orbis, 1972. N. B. Y. Vaughan: The Expectation of the Poor. The Church and the Third World. — London: SCM, 1972.

in many underdeveloped areas which are only moderately cultivated or lie completely idle for the sake of profit. Such situations require reforms, so that the land will be used in a way that truly benefits the community (GS 71).

Not least among the obligations of property is a duty which is of particular urgency today: the duty of the wealthy countries to help the developing nations from the abundance of their goods. Pope John XXIII speaks of a "most difficult problem of the modern world." "The solidarity which binds all men and makes them members of the same family imposes upon political communities enjoying abundance of material goods not to remain indifferent to those political communities whose citizens suffer from poverty, misery, and hunger, and who lack even the elementary rights of the human person" (MM 157). He stresses the fact that all the wealthy nations are equally responsible for the undernourished peoples and points out the urgent need to educate one's conscience in this regard (MM 158).

Vatican II states that the advanced nations "have a very heavy obligation to help the developing peoples" (GS 86). It addresses itself especially to the Christian nations who "have an abundance of this world's goods, while others are deprived of the necessities of life and are tormented with hunger, disease, and every kind of misery. This situation must not be allowed to continue, to the scandal of humanity. For the spirit of poverty and of charity are the glory and authentication of the Church of Christ" (GS 88).

Pope Paul VI once more takes up the issue and repeats "that the superfluous wealth of rich countries should be placed at the service of the poor nations. The rule which up to now held good for the benefit of those nearest to us, must today be applied to all the needy of this world" (PP 49). Each one is required to examine his conscience, whether he is truly prepared to comply with this duty of brotherly solidarity. It is his obligation to contribute his share to the relief of the destitute. Personal contributions, payment of higher taxes, or also services as development helpers abroad are various forms of realizing this aid (PP 47).

3. *Unaccountable use of property: avarice and waste*

Avarice is the inordinate desire for material goods in the form of possessions. From of old it has been reckoned among the seven capital vices. Immoderate love of riches is one of the most prolific sins which has many others in its train.

The Book of Sirach characterizes the greedy man as a person who is grudging to himself. The bread lacks at his table. Mean injustice withers his soul (Sir 14:5-10). The New Testament repeatedly warns against greed. Christ includes covetousness or greed among the evil things which come forth from the heart (Mk 7:22). To the parable of the foolish grain farmer he attaches the admonition: "Take heed, and beware of all covetousness; for a man's life does not consist in the abundance of his possessions" (Lk 12:15). Greed is several times mentioned in the catalogues of vices of St. Paul (Rom 1:29; 1 Cor 5:11; 2 Tim 3:2). It pertains to the sins which exclude from the kingdom of God (1 Cor 6:9f; Eph 5:5). Among Christian people, as is fitting among saints, immorality and covetousness must not even be mentioned (Eph 5:3). Christians ought to be content if they have the necessities of life. "There is great gain in godliness with contentment." But "love of money is the root of all evils" (1 Tim 6:6.10; cf. Heb 13:5).

The sinfulness of avarice consists in this that it does not devote the goods of this world to their proper purpose. Possessions are not employed as means to serve the utility of man and the designs of God. They are abused as an end in themselves. The feelings of security, happiness and satisfaction, which go with possessions, are set absolute. The greedy man believes that he can increase his happiness and satisfaction by ever more possessions. But he is pitifully mistaken. Man's spiritual being cannot be satisfied by material possessions. And salvation, the deepest happiness, can only be found in the communion with God and his people.

Yet greed is by no means only a matter of personal concern. Greed also affects the community, which is deprived of the social benefits which should accrue from possessions. The social obligations connected with property are neglected or completely disregarded. The greedy man is unwilling to give to the needy, even in grave and extreme need. He accumulates possessions without using them in a socially beneficial way. Often he will also succumb to the temptation of increasing his riches by immoral and unjust means. Greed therefore is the source of serious disorders, and the usual judgment of traditional handbooks that avarice, by its genus, is only a venial sin may even be too mild.

Waste offends against the responsible use of property in

the opposite way. It is an insufficient regard for material goods and their extravagant consumption. Waste, which manifests itself especially in excessive luxury, is an offence against the poorer classes. Its asocial nature must hurt and provoke them. Less offensive is prodigality, which is the extravagant bestowal of material goods on others. Nevertheless also this conduct offends against a person's responsibility for his possessions. For he is held to administer them as a steward who has to give account for them before God.

IV. Violation of proprietary rights

An offence against the proprietary rights of another is committed if one violates the strict right of another to a material possession against his reasonable will. If no strict right is violated, no sin against justice is committed, though one may sin against charity, e.g. if out of hatred one does not extinguish a fire that is destroying another's property. If the other party lawfully consents to the violation, no injustice is committed either, e.g. if a boy steals some oranges in the neighbour's garden while the owner looks at it from the window with a smile. The appropriation or violation of another's property is however unjust if the other person cannot lawfully renounce his right. Thus a guardian cannot appropriate to himself the possessions of an orphan child even with the latter's consent. Finally no sin is committed if an owner ought reasonably to consent to the appropriation of some of his property, e.g. in instances of food theft.

The gravity of the sin of injustice is measured by the actual damage done. It is obvious that not all violations against another's property are equally grave. If the damage caused is only small, the sin is only light; if the damage is serious, the sin is grave as well, suppose of course the violation proceeds from insight and free will and is not justified by a higher good.

But since men are not all equally wealthy, the same kind of violation may be light or grave according as it hurts a rich or a poor man. Cheats and thieves themselves often make this distinction and choose as their victims only people who are better off. In view of this the measure for the gravity of a violation against property will be relative. However the gravity of the injustice is also determined by the harm done to society, i.e. to its peace, security and stability. And this leads to an absolute standard concerning the question as to when a violation against the property of another is grave.

In the first case (relative standard) authors commonly regard it a grave sin if the sum involved is equivalent to the amount which is necessary to support a man and his family for one day according to their condition of living. In the second instance (absolute standard) there will be a grave sin if the amount involved is about 100 dollars or its equivalent in other currencies, measured by the purchasing power the currencies possess for basic foods and commodities.

If neither an individual nor society suffers great harm, no grave sin against justice is committed, although charity may be seriously violated, e.g. if a person is deeply grieved over the loss of a remembrance which is precious to him, although it is of little material value.

1. *Unjust damage*

Unjust damage in the narrow sense consists in violating the property of another in some unjust manner without gaining an advantage therefrom. The harm may result either from destroying or injuring a thing that belongs to another, or from hindering another in an unjust manner to receive a material benefit.

The moral judgment must distinguish between damage caused by mere accident or oversight, slight or criminal negligence, wantonness or enmity. Accidents and oversights arising from no personal fault are not morally imputable and therefore do not constitute a sin .But they can nevertheless involve obligations to restitution. If the damage is due to neglect, the sin is grave only if the negligence was serious and the damage is significant. Damage caused by wantonness or enmity is a grave or a light sin according to the gravity of the damage caused. But if the harm is an expression of sheer hatred, even a petty damage can constitute a grave sin, although not against justice but against charity.

If one inadvertently has undertaken an action which will cause detriment to another, it would be an injustice not to hinder the evil effect thereof as soon as one becomes aware of the matter. This is for example the case if one carelessly throws away a lighted match and a conflagration threatens as a consequence; or if a pharmacist by oversight gives a client a wrong and harmful medicine. One is excused from the obligation if one would suffer himself a proportionately graver harm in preventing the evil effect.

In hindering another from obtaining something, an injustice is committed either if the other has a strict right to the thing, or if one uses unjust means to prevent him from receiving a thing which he may lawfully acquire.   The first case obtains if for example someone induces parents to refuse their child an inheritance to which he is entitled; or if in a competitive contest one would not give the prize to the one who merits it according to the clear rules of the contest.   The second case obtains if one by force, fear, calumny, detraction, fraud, lies, persistent urging and similar means prevents somebody from receiving what he could lawfully acquire.   Unjust damage is therefore committed if one by calumny prevents another from receiving an alms or a position; or if one deceitfully validates an illegal testament.

No unjust damage is however done if one prevents another from receiving an alms or a bequest merely by petitioning the owner.   Neither is there such damage if one keeps someone from acquiring a thing which is unlawful for him, even if unjust means are employed.   Thus a wife is not guilty of injustice if she restrains her husband by fraud from giving to a friend inappropriate gifts.

2.   *Fraud*

Fraud is the unjust appropriation of the goods of another under the guise of right, usually in some form of contract.   It is objectively not less evil than theft.   Subjectively men are often not so keenly aware of the malice of fraud and do not ostracize it by so strong a disapproval as theft.   Furthermore fraud often involves lesser amounts than theft and is to that extent of course also a lesser offence.   Nevertheless fraud in principle obliges to restitution no less than theft.

Holy Scripture repudiates fraud in the form of false weights and measures.   "You shall not have in your bag two kinds of weights, a large and a small.   You shall not have in your house two kinds of measures, a large and a small.   A full and just weight you shall have . . . For all who do such things, all who act dishonestly, are an abomination to the Lord your God" (Deut 25:13-16; cf. Lev 19:35f; Prov 11:1).   The reprobation has also today lost nothing in its urgency.

Fraud has many forms.   It is committed if one charges more or pays less than is fair for goods and services received, under the appearance of a just compensation. It is committed if one deceives the other over the real quantity or quality of the goods which are exchanged or paid for, e.g. by secretly reducing the weight, measure or number of the goods, or by substituting inferior or adulterated goods for the quality goods which are promised. Misleading labelling and advertising or deliberate concealment of defects are equally frauds of this kind. It has already been mentioned earlier that a deception concerning the nature or a substantial quality of the commodity voids a contract of exchange or sale. Concealment of accidental defects to a buyer who expressly inquires about them makes the contract rescindable (cf. the section on contracts of sale).

Other types of fraud are unfair competition, graft, embezzlement, forgery (e.g. of money), evasion of just taxes. A frequent source of fraud today is the tapping of insurances by means of misrepresentation of the required data and facts. Bankruptcy is a special occasion for fraud. At times it is deliberately engineered to avoid payment of debts. Often, though in itself inculpable, it is accompanied by injustices, e.g. concealment of assets, transfer of property to relatives, preferential treatment of some creditors, etc. To the extent that in a bankruptcy a person unjustly retained assets which he owed to his creditors, he is obliged to restitution, even though before the civil law he may have no further obligations.

3. *Usury and profiteering*

The common opinion among the early and medieval theologians was that the taking of any interest for money or consumer goods loaned is unjust and usury. Their reason was that money and consumer goods are only good for consumption and do not produce any increment which could be the basis for demanding an additional amount of money or quantity of goods when they are returned. Interest was only considered permissible on the ground of extrinsic titles, i.e. as compensation for the expenses of a transaction or the loss of opportunity to make good bargains. This doctrine is reflected in several decisions of the supreme magisterium, which condemn any interest on capital.[1] A compensation for additional work and expenses connected with the loan is however acknowledged as justified, e.g.

---

[1] DS 764; 2062; 2141f.

the compensation for the work and expenses involved in the running of a pawnshop.[1]

This teaching is doubtless influenced by several texts of Holy Scripture which disapprove of the taking of interest. The Old Testament repeatedly forbids that an Israelite take interest from his brother (Ex 22:25; Lev 25:36f; Deut 23:19), although he is allowed to take interest from a foreigner (Deut 23:20). Christ even commends to lend without any hope of return (Lk 6:34f). On the other hand in the parable of the talents he reproaches the servant who did not trade with his talent but buried it and returned it to his master without increase. "You wicked and slothful servant... You ought to have invested my money with the bankers, and at my coming I should have received what was my own with interest" (Mt 25:26f). Hence Christ seems to approve of the practice to invest money at interest. In fact documents show that banking houses and banking operations already existed at the time of Jesus.[2] Banking is therefore not only a recent invention.

A strong money market and large capital flux, involving all the sectors of society, however only developed with the emergence of industrialization. Opportunities for investments increased, and money assumed the role of a factor of production more than ever before. The insight is now definitely prevailing also among theologians that money is productive and does fructify, and that therefore a moderate interest for money loaned is justified. "To place money, then, at the disposal of another to be employed in profitable ventures constitutes an economic service and, as such, is worth its price as any other service... So viewed, interest, or the price of money, is determined in the same way as the price of any other service; the unjust price, or usury, is an excessive price."[3] Usury accordingly consists in an interest which is higher than is justified by the worth of the loan.

If the lender does not demand more than the loan is worth but exacts it in a heartless manner, by holding the debtor to the strict letter of the agreement at a great loss to him, he does not commit usury, but he sins against charity, and may sin gravely.

---

[1] DS 1442-1444; 2548-2550; 3105-3109.

[2] Cf. the exposition by Franz Michel Willam on banking at the time of Jesus in: Das Leben Jesu im Land und Volke Israel. — Freiburg: Herder, 1960, 365-367.

[3] John A. McHugh/Charles J. Callan: Moral Theology, vol. II. — New York: Joseph F. Wagner, 1960, 279.

Loans of consumer goods are of a similar nature as loans of money, since these goods can always be converted into money. Hence if any bigger loans of consumer goods are made, e.g. grain, rice, textiles, a moderate interest for them is likewise justified, certainly if they are loaned for commercial purposes. But if the reason for borrowing such goods is the needs of daily living, Christian love demands that no interest be taken. Here the request of Christ to his disciples applies: "Do good, and lend, expecting nothing in return" (Lk 6:35). This also holds for loans of money to a needy person or family, in order that they can buy the necessary foods and goods for the daily sustenance.

The profiteer exploits the distress of others in times of great shortage by demanding exorbitant prices for wares, e.g. foods in times of famine. As means of personal enrichment through exploitation of the misery of others, profiteering and usury are especially shameless sins of injustice.

4.   *Theft*

a)   Nature and sinfulness

Theft is the secret appropriation of what belongs to another against his reasonable will. If the appropriation is done openly and forcibly, it is robbery. Robbery and burglary are aggravated thefts.

Theft is the *appropriation* of what belongs to another. Since such an appropriation also occurs if a person does not pay his debts, if patents and copyrights are violated, if lost property is unlawfully kept, these offences are considered equivalent to theft. It is however not theft in the strict sense if one takes property away with the intention of borrowing it for a time or of destroying it. Nevertheless these too are acts of unlawful possession and unlawful damage. An exception to this is the necessity to prevent a crime by taking away an object from another (e.g. a gun), in which case the seizure is even obligatory.

The goods must be taken *against the reasonable will* of the owner. Therefore it is not theft on the part of a trustworthy servant to give secretly a poor man an alms if he knows that his master would not object to this. Furthermore an owner is supposed not to be reasonably unwilling that a thing be taken if in justice or piety he is obliged to yield it. Therefore it is not stealing to take what is necessary in extreme need or as secret compensation; neither is it theft for a wife or for children to take what is necessary for their sustenance according to their social condition. But if the owner has only an obligation in charity to donate something, e.g. an alms to a poor man, he cannot be considered reasonably willing to have it secretly taken away from him, even if he disregards his obligation and refuses the alms.

Holy Scripture repeatedly states the *sinfulness of theft*. Theft is among the basic offences which are listed by the decalogue. The seventh commandment bids: "You shall not steal" (Ex 20:15; Deut 5:19). The tenth commandment even forbids the desire of the neighbour's house, his field, his ox or his ass, or anything that is his own (Ex 20:17; Deut 5:21). Christ reconfirms the prohibition (Mt 19:18; Mk 7:20f). And St. Paul enumerates theft among the sins which exclude from the kingdom of God (1 Cor 6:10).

The injustice of theft is evident from the fact that it offends against the right to private property. Above all if the goods of others could be taken without moral fault, there would be an end to social peace, stability and progress. Even countries which profess the communist ideology of common property are very sensitive against theft and punish it severely.

But it is likewise evident that not all thefts are equally grave. Petty thefts do not constitute the same threat to the common good as a bank robbery. It is therefore necessary to determine a standard by which to judge when theft is a serious injustice and when it is not. It has already been mentioned earlier that a distinction is to be made between a relative and an absolute standard. The question still requires some further study.

b)   Two standards

A relative standard for the grave matter of theft is required by the fact that not all people are equally wealthy. What might constitute a light harm for a rich man, may constitute a very grave harm for a poor person. Moral theologians choose as the relative standard for a grave matter in thefts (which will equally apply to the other violations of property) either the wages of a day of a man who has to work for his living, or the amount which would suffice for a day's sustenance for himself and his family. In the daily sustenance are included not only the expenses for food, but also the other basic commodities·such as clothing and housing. Obviously the amount will vary according to the wages and social standing of an individual and according to the different income scales in the different countries.

The second, absolute standard attempts to define that amount which is always to be considered a grave offence against justice, no matter how rich a person or an organization is. The standard implies that there is a sum of money which, if its unjust appropriation were taken lightly, would tend to make property insecure, and render men generally unwilling to work diligently and to promote their economic progress and that of the state. In the determination of this amount the judgment of common sense is also to be taken into consideration. The absolute amount has been set at 100 dollars or its equivalent in other currencies, measured by the purchasing power of the currencies for the basic commodities of life, such as food, clothing, housing, furniture and the like.[1]

However the problem with such fixed sums is that the worth of the currencies is not stable, but generally slowly·declines. Hence after a period of years the sum laid down proves to be too low again and needs revision. In order to avoid this difficulty, some theologians have attempted to give a norm which is less subject to changes. According to them that matter is absolutely grave which equals the weekly wages of a man of a moderately good income.[2] This criterion is certainly helpful and also correct in the economic conditions of most of the countries. However in prosperous nations the amount may turn out to be rather high, perhaps at 200-250 dollars. Maybe this amount indeed constitutes the absolutely grave matter in these wealthy countries. Or possibly one has to reformulate the criterion in this way that the absolutely grave matter is defined as that amount (or its equivalent) which in ordinary circumstances would suffice for the weekly sustenance of a family of a moderately good social condition, luxuries and special comforts not included.

It becomes clear from these reflections that the grave matter

---

[1] If one can buy for 100 dollars 50 kilos of basic foods, one has to ask how much money in another currency is needed to buy the same foods. This constitutes the equivalent of 100 dollars in another currency measured by the purchasing power.

[2] Cf. Noldin: Summa Theologiae Moralis, vol. II, 1959, nr. 416: "Absolute gravis censetur materia, quae aequivalet proventui hebdomadario hominum condicionis mediocris melioris." Likewise McHugh/Callan: Moral Theology, vol. II, 1960, 152.

in theft cannot be determined with mathematical exactness, but only approximately. The distinctions may seem casuistic to some. But the need to distinguish between light and grave thefts, between light and grave guilt in this matter remains. There are thefts which cause serious harm to the indiviual and which are gravely prejudicial to the security of society. They constitute a grievous moral guilt. The moral theologian cannot escape the necessity to formulate a criterion by which to judge when this objectively is the case.

c)   Special forms of theft

If dealing with *thefts in the domestic circle* (wife and children), a greater amount is required to constitute a grievous matter. For a father is presumably less unwilling to be deprived of his money by members of his family than by strangers. A serious matter would be about twice the ordinary relative amount and in the case of thefts by the wife perhaps even more. In general the obligation of restitution need not be imposed on wife or children, since the father or mother cannot usually be presumed to wish restitution to be made. But there are limits here. A son who steals the money gained by the hard work of his parents and needed for the education of the other children may indeed be obliged to restitution. — Servants seldom sin gravely by taking ordinary foodstuffs or small commodities like paper and envelops which they themselves use and consume. As to other things servants sin no less gravely than strangers.

Another problem is that of *repeated petty thefts*. No precise, clear-cut laws can be set up in this matter. Only some prudential norms can be given. Many petty thefts coalesce to a grave matter if the thief plans beforehand to steal a considerable amount in stages. Frequently repeated thefts likewise coalesce if they are made at short intervals and, though no accumulation of a larger amount was initially intended, they in fact reach such an amount. The greater the amounts taken, the greater must be the interval in order to prevent coalescence. In case the amounts are taken from different owners, more is necessary to constitute a grave matter, e.g. if a merchant commits many petty frauds in the sale of his goods.

If *several individuals conspire* to steal a bigger amount, but each one does not obtain much, a grave sin will be committed only if the whole amount taken and divided is double the ordinary amount necessary for a grave sin. But this presupposes

that the person from whom the goods are taken does not suffer
great personal harm. If the person suffers grave harm, no more
will be required to constitute a grave sin than in any other kind
of theft.

5. *Reasons which permit appropriation of another's goods*

a) Appropriation in necessity (food theft)

Extreme need justifies a person to appropriate enough of
another's goods to alleviate his need. "If a person is in extreme
necessity, he has the right to take from the riches of others what
he himself needs" (GS 69). With this right on the part of the
needy person corresponds the obligation on the part of the
wealthy owner to assist the person in extreme necessity from his
superfluities or to permit that the necessary goods be taken.
This is according to Thomas Aquinas[1] and Leo XIII[2] not only
an obligation in charity but in justice.

Necessity is extreme when a person is exposed to the certain
or very probable peril of losing life, health, liberty or goods of
similar importance, and is unable to help himself. The right
to appropriate goods of others in this situation also applies when
one alleviates the need of a third party. Since the goods which
are most of the time needed and taken in extreme necessity
are foods, this kind of appropriation is also called food theft.
But this does not mean that only foods may be taken in extreme
need. Also clothing, fuel and other basic commodities can be
appropriated for the same reason.

Food theft is lawful because in extreme need the common
ownership of things by all takes precedence over the division
of goods by private ownership which is normally necessary.
Life, health, liberty or other comparable goods are of greater
value than material possessions which are not necessary for
human life. Therefore in a case of conflict the material goods
as the lesser values must give way to the higher ones.

In order that food theft be permissible, the following conditions must be verified: (1) The need must be extreme and
not merely grave. It is sufficient if it is imminent. Suppose a
family has still to eat for three days, but they have a chance to
appropriate some foods here and now. They would be allowed
to do so if they have no hope of any other supplies. Grave

---

[1] Summa Theologica, II-II, q. 118, a. 4, ad 2.
[2] Rerum Novarum, nr. 36.

need however does not justify such action. Nevertheless Jone is of the opinion that "a poor man may take things of small value if such things can alleviate his grave need and if he could get nothing by asking."[1]   (2) There must be no other way of acquiring what is necessary, e.g. by asking for it or begging. (3) The person from whom the goods are taken must not be placed in equal need.   As far as possible the goods should be taken from owners who will not be seriously hurt by the loss, i.e. from owners who have superfluities.   (4) More may not be taken than is required to alleviate the need.   (5) If possible the goods must be taken after the manner of a loan and should be restored once the need has ceased.   But if at the time of appropriation there was no hope of giving back what was taken, there is no obligation of restoring it later, even if a person unexpectedly should get the means.

It is disputed whether a person in extreme need could take a very large sum of money, or a very expensive chattel.   Since no one is bound to save his life by extraordinary means, it seems that one is also not entitled to appropriate goods of extraordinary value.   Therefore one is not allowed to steal a large sum of money in order to undergo an expensive medical treatment to save one's life.   But if there is a reasonable hope that the goods taken can be restored, one may be allowed to appropriate them. Thus one may take a neighbour's car in order to escape from an assault against one's life, since there is good hope of restoring it.

b)   Occult compensation

Occult compensation is the secret appropriation by a creditor of what is owed to him by the debtor.   Ordinarily this is not lawful, because its frequent practice would cause grave public disturbance, menace the common good by the dangers of abuse, expose the debtor to loss by possible second payments, etc.   If a debt is not being paid, the ordinary remedy is appeal to the law.   For it is the proper function of the law to defend the citizens against injustice and crime.   Nevertheless there are situations where the individual cannot take refuge to the law because of great difficulties or prevalent injustices, e.g. the danger of serious reprisals or the liability of the courts to bribes.   If this is the case, occult compensation is justified under the following conditions:

---

[1] Jone, 1963, nr. 331.

(1) A certain and strict right to the thing concerned is required. If the claim is doubtful or if it is only a claim in charity and not in justice, occult compensation is not warrantable. A strict right is had if the stipulated wage is not paid, unjust substractions are made, extra work exacted without additional payment; or if one has been forced by necessity or fear to contract for a wage that is certainly unjust. Likewise shop-keepers who are forced to sell under the price are allowed to compensate by giving less weight. — No such right is had if a servant has merely been promised a gift out of gratitude; or if one voluntarily undertakes to do some work to which one is not obliged by agreement; or if one freely does more work than what was contracted for. It does likewise not obtain if one, without any need of help, employs another merely out of pity, or if the low wage is compensated for by tips, better food, etc.

(2) It must be impossible to obtain justice in any other way without great inconvenience. If this condition is not fulfilled, no sin against commutative justice is committed and therefore no obligation to restitution incurred. Nevertheless one would offend against legal justice.

(3) No harm thereby must be inflicted upon others. Such injury would be casting the suspicion of thievery upon another person. But since charity does not oblige under grave inconvenience, such harm may sometimes be permitted. Likewise no wrong must be done to the debtor, e.g. by taking an article which the debtor needs for earning his living. For the same reason one would not be allowed to resort to occult compensation if the debtor had been reduced to penury and cannot pay on that account. — Should the debtor later pay his debts, the occult compensator must restore the value in some way.

V. Restitution for violation of proprietary rights

The term restitution is often used in the general sense of reparation of the violated rights of another. Thus the term is not only applied to the restoration of violated rights of property, but also to reparation for physical injuries, rape, adultery, defamation and dishonour. But in most of these cases the lost goods cannot be restored anymore. Only a compensation or satisfaction is possible. Other authors reserve the term for the restoration of violated rights of property. Restitution then is the act by which the goods which a person lost through a violation of his rights to a certain possession or material benefit are restored to him.   The person can be an individual or a moral person, e.g. a corporation or the state.   Only restitution for violation of proprietary rights is the subject of the studies in this context.

Restitution for violated rights of property is manifestly a precept of natural law.   The dictate that each one should receive his due (*suum cuique*) is one of the primary principles of natural law.   Peaceful social coexistence and the progress of society depend on its observance.   The right to private property is realistic only if the owner has also the right to claim it from those who unlawfully appropriate, withhold or damage it, and if the offender has the corresponding obligation to restore it.

Holy Scripture clearly insists on the duty of restitution. The legal prescriptions of Ex 22:1-15 provide that full restitution must be made for unjust damages, and two-, four- or fivefold restitution for thefts and breaches of trust.   Stolen goods must be returned to the owner, even if one did not steal them oneself but received them as a gift or compensation for work (Tob 2:11-13).   The evildoer who wants to return to the Lord must restore the pledge and give back what he has taken by robbery. If not, "he will surely die" (Ezek 33:14f).   The penitent publican Zacchaeus promises Jesus to restore fourfold what he had gained by defrauding others (Lk 19:8).

The duty to restitution is grave or light according as the value of the goods unjustly withheld or the damage unjustly caused is grave or light.   Even if, in stealing an object, a person thought that it was of little value, he is gravely obliged to restore it if it turns out that its value is great.

If the obligation to make restitution arising from the natural law and the positive law are not precisely the same, the following rule should be observed: If the obligation arising from the natural law is more comprehensive, this more comprehensive obligation is binding in conscience.   If the demands of the positive law go beyond what is required by natural law, it is binding after the courts have so decided.   But, as B. Häring notes, one is not permitted to press such a case in court if the restitution prescribed by positive law involves an unduly great hardship for a poor man.[1]

At all times the demands of strict justice must be tempered by the spirit of Christian love.   "As in all the areas of life equity must be brought into play to balance the rigors of com-

---

[1] Häring III, 1966, 495.

mutative justice. Restitution may work great hardship on certain individuals, perhaps too great a hardship by comparison to their subjective guilt. On the other hand, the loss may be insignificant to the injured party. In such cases the guilty party must indeed show his good will, but circumstances may be such that he should not be obliged to bear the entire burden of damage."[1]

1. *Restitution on grounds of unjust possession*

The duty of restitution of stolen or unjustly withheld goods is mainly ruled by the following three principles: First, goods unlawfully taken away or withheld from their owner must be restored to him (*res clamat domino*). Second, the owner alone has the right to the natural product of his goods (*res fructificat domino*). Third, when a thing perishes, the owner is normally the loser (*res perit domino*). But as a person may hold or may have consumed the goods of another in bad or good or doubtful faith, the respective obligations to restitution will be different in these three cases and must be considered separately.

a) *Possessor in bad faith* is one who knowingly and unjustly retains another's property. This is true of the thief, of the one who acquires or accepts stolen goods knowing that they are ill-gotten, of the debtor who does not pay his debts, of the finder who does not return the found object to its owner although he could reasonably do so, and of all who defraud others of their property.

The possessor in bad faith must not only restore the ill-gotten goods together with all the fruits that they have naturally produced. He must also compensate for any depreciation in value of the goods and in principle repair all the ensuing damage which was at least indistinctly foreseen by him. The fruits of his labour he may retain. He may likewise deduct the necessary and really useful expenses he incurred.

If he still retains the object, he must return it as soon as possible. Should this betray the thief, he may restore the thing's equivalent. If he cannot even do so much, he may wait for an opportune occasion. If he has given away or sold the object and its owner cannot recover it from the recipient or buyer, or if he has consumed or destroyed it, he must restore its value to the owner.

If the object has been bought in bad faith from a thief or

---

[1] Ib. 485.

middleman, the possessor may still resell it to the latter in order to recover his money. Otherwise he has to return it to its rightful owner.

Restitution is obligatory even if the thing would have perished for certain in the possession of the owner. Wherefore everything which one has salvaged or stolen during a fire or flood must be restored. Compensation for such salvaging may be deducted.[1]

If the thing has perished in consequence of unjust retention, the possessor in bad faith must repair the owner's loss. But if it would have perished in any case, even had it remained with the owner (e.g. due to a general flood or some intrinsic defect), he is not bound to do so. This is true even if the thing would have perished in the owner's possession for a different reason. But the unjust possessor may be bound to some restitution if the owner was at a loss during the actual retention of the object.

If the rightful owner cannot be found, e.g. because the goods were stolen in a bus or train, the unjust possessor (in contradistinction to the possessor in good faith) has no right to retain the object. He must make restitution to the poor according to the principle: No one may enrich himself at the expense of another man's possession.[2] But he is permitted to postpone restitution as long as he himself is poor.

b) *Possessor in good faith* is one who unknowingly and without any fault of his holds the property of another. Thus, for example, a person may have bought or received goods from a seller or donor in the conviction that they are his property, while in reality they are stolen. He is in good faith, but not the rightful owner of the goods.

The possessor in good faith must restore tne property of another as soon as he discovers that it is not rightfully his own. Whoever for no valid reason postpones restitution must compensate the owner for the loss he suffers in the meantime.

The goods themselves and their fruits are to be returned in the condition they are in at the time when the legitimate owner becomes known. The possessor in good faith need not compensate the owner for any depreciation in the value of the goods, even if they depreciate because of his neglect. On the other hand he may also not retain a portion for himself if the

---

[1] Cf. Jone, 1963, nr. 340.

[2] "Locupletari non debet aliquis cum alterius iniuria vel iactura."

goods increased in value while in his keeping. Fruits however which derive from his own skill and diligence he may retain or, if the fruits are partly also the result of natural increment, that portion which corresponds to his labour. Likewise necessary and useful expenses made for the maintenance or the improvement of the goods may be deducted.

If the owner becomes known after the possessor in good faith has used up or destroyed the goods, he is not bound to restitution of the equivalent of the goods. If he has sold them, the owner has to reclaim them from the buyer. However if the possessor in good faith received the goods as a gift or partial donation, he is bound to restore to the owner that equivalent by which he has become enriched, either by sparing his own goods or by profiting in some manner. If in this case the goods have been sold and the owner can still recover them from the buyer, the possessor in good faith has to give the value by which he has been enriched to the latter, at least if he claims it.

The goods must always be given back to the lawful owner as soon as he claims them. If he does not claim them, for example because he does not know who has them, the possessor in good faith may return them to the thief from whom he bought them in order to recover his money, if he could not otherwise get his money back. Should he be unable to find the thief, he must give the goods to their rightful owner though he would thereby suffer loss himself.

If the rightful owner cannot be found after reasonable inquiry, the possessor in good faith may retain the goods as his own. The same holds if legal prescription has gone into effect. The ownership of movables, for example, may prescribe through uninterrupted possession of four years, the ownership of immovable property through possession of ten years in good faith. The time required of course depends on the positive law of a particular country. Stolen goods acquired in good faith at a public sale can usually, according to positive law, not be recovered by the owner unless he prosecutes the thief or reimburses the price paid therefore.

c) *Possessor in doubtful faith* is one who has good but not convincing reasons for believing that he is in wrongful possession of another's property.

A possessor in doubtful faith must make inquiry commensurate with the value of the thing as to the true owner. If his efforts are fruitless he becomes a possessor in good faith. He may retain the goods as his own.

If he neglects to make inquiry he becomes a possessor in bad faith. If, after such neglect, he again try to find the owner and fail, he has indeed been guilty of negligence, but he may keep the thing, since no one else has a clear right to it.

2.   *Restitution for tax evasions*

A particular problem is constituted by the question of restitution for tax evasions. Many traditional authors regard taxation laws as penal laws only. Accordingly citizens are not in conscience obliged to pay their taxes, but only to submit to the penalties imposed for evasions if they are caught. However, as has been explained in the treatise on human law, this theory is largely abandoned today. Payment of just taxes is considered an obligation in conscience, and violation of this duty regarded as an offence against justice. Yet if this is so, the problem of restitution for tax evasions arises.

Some authors regard the obligation to pay taxes as an obligation of legal justice. They argue that taxes have the character of a tribute from the part to the whole rather than of a payment for services rendered, as in commutative justice. Hence, though he who evades taxes offends against justice, and may offend gravely if considerable amounts are involved, he is not bound to restitution. For the taxpayer himself is part of the whole to whom taxes are due. This dispenses him from the duty of restitution. One may however wonder whether this argumentation is truly conclusive.

Others regard the obligation to pay taxes as one of commutative justice. There is an implicit contract between the government and the people. In virtue of this contract the government is bound to provide for the safety of the people and for the things necessary for the common welfare, while the citizens in return are bound to pay the expenses of the government. Consequently there is a strict obligation of restitution in instances of tax evasions.

Indeed it seems that there is a duty of restitution for tax evasions, whether taxes are an obligation of legal or commutative justice. For the citizens receive services from the government, and very important ones at that, and the state incurs expenses for these services which have to be paid. Tax fraud "is undoubtedly an injustice against the state and obliges to restitution, excepting instances in which one attempts to free himself from an obviously unjust demand." [1]

Naturally to the extent that governments abuse taxes for goals other than the common welfare, which welfare also includes justice among the nations, e.g. for their own pride or for the realization of party ideologies, to that extent taxes do not oblige in justice. In such circumstances a person is in principle allowed to withhold a portion of the taxes and rather use the amount for social and charitable purposes possibly neglected by the State. Certainly unjust taxes do not oblige in conscience and consequently do not entail any obligation of restitution if they are not paid. However in cases of doubt, as to whether taxes are just or not, presumption stands in favour of the government and the taxes would have to be paid.

The gravity of the amount of tax evasions is to be measured by the absolute standard for violations of property rights. A grave matter is the absolutely grave amount. (See the deliberations on the absolutely grave matter in the treatise on theft.)

Restitution must in principle be made to the state, if this is possible without unproportionately grave difficulty. If this should prove to be very difficult, restitution could also be made by donations for charitable purposes or for projects of social concern. Thus if a person would have to fear penalties for his tax evasions, if they become known by the fact of his restitution to the inland-revenue office, he could choose this indirect way of reparation. The reason is that such donations are a contribution to the common good as well.

In cases where a taxpayer has run into a financial distress which threatens the existence of his business, B. Häring judges that tax evasions should be condoned. If "the evasion is motivated by the desire to save his business enterprise and preserve his family from need, restitution may not at all be prescribed. Nor would it be to the interest of the state to insist on restitution in such instances." [2]

3. *Restitution for unjust damage*

Unjust damage is a loss inflicted on the goods of another without material advantage to the offender, e.g. arson or damage

---

[1] Häring III, 1966. 493f. Also Mausbach-Ermecke is of the opinion that defrauded taxes still have to be paid, unless they have come under the statute of limitations (Katholische Moraltheologie III, 1961. 555).

[2] L. c. 494.

caused by malpractice of one's profession. It is ground for the obligation to restore the loss directly caused as well as all foreseen additional losses that are strictly consequent upon the damage. In order that there should be a clear obligation of reparation, three conditions must be verified.

First, the damage must be objectively unjust. A damage is not unjust if, for example, caused by justified self-defence. But an injustice is committed if a person, by the use of unjust means, prevents another from obtaining something which he may lawfully acquire, e.g. an inheritance.

Second, the action must be subjectively sinful, i.e. deliberately and consciously unjust. The sin may consist in the evil intention to cause damage or in sinful negligence. Thus the damage done by a farmer's cattle to another's property usually has to be repaired if the farmer neglected to take the ordinary precautions. The same holds if a person neglects the care which can justly be expected from him in the performance of his profession, e.g. a physician or judge. But if unintentional harm ensues to a client, although ordinary care and skill are used, there is no obligation of restitution. Those who cause damage in a state of intoxication are responsible for the damage to the extent that they could foresee that it might possibly occur. e.g. a driver who causes an accident because drunk.

Before the law subjects are also held responsible for merely juridical faults, i.e. for damages caused by inadvertence without subjective guilt. Citizens are presumed to know the law, and it is not possible for the authorities to ascertain in every case whether the violation of the law proceeded from subjective guilt or not. One guilty of juridical fault is therefore bound to pay damages after judgment is given.

Third, the action must be the real and effectual cause of the damage, not only the occasion. Accordingly one need not repair damage caused by the wind accidentally carrying afar the sparks of a fire in one's property and starting a conflagration. However if one noticed that a change in the wind creates danger to one's neighbour, one would be obliged to extinguish the fire; otherwise one may indeed be responsible for a possible conflagration. One is likewise not obliged to make restitution if one has influenced another merely by one's bad example to injure a third person. Again no obligation of restitution exists on the part of a person who has committed a crime for which an innocent party is being punished by mistake. However if the criminal has deliberately thrown suspicion on the innocent person, he is obliged to make restitution and must, if necessary, deliver himself up to save the innocent.

The obligation to make reparation for damages deliberately caused is grave if the damage is grave, and light if the damage is light. This also holds if a person, due to a wrong judgment, believes that he only sins venially in inflicting a grave damage. The obligation to restore the grave damage is nevertheless grave. For the obligation arises much more from the fact that the harm was knowingly done and was grave, than from the theological guilt incurred.

Damages, whether light or grave, caused without sufficient advertence or deliberation do not oblige to restitution, even if the person who caused the damages was slightly at fault. This is an accepted opinion. For an imperfect human act is not the basis for a grave obligation. Nor can a certainly light obligation impose a burden which is grave. If then in this case serious damage need not strictly be repaired, it is obvious that slight damage need not be repaired either. But also in this event one must answer for a legal fault if one is sentenced to do so.

4. *Restitution for culpable cooperation in damage*

Cooperation in unjust damage may be either positive complicity, by actual help or moral support, or negative complicity, by not preventing injustice when one could and should prevent it. In order to be obliged to restitution it is required that, the same as in instances of unjust damage, the action be unjust, subjectively sinful, and the actual cause of the damage. As a general principle the following rule applies: One who positively cooperates is bound to repair the harm which is effectively and knowingly caused, even though the harm would have ensued without his help; and the one who negatively cooperates is bound to repair the harm which he could and should have prevented.

a) In cases of *positive cooperation* the most culpable is the mandator who orders an injustice to be done. He is bound in the first instance to repair all the damage inflicted in his name. Request, promise and threat entail the same obligation. If he prevailed upon the actual doer by force, fear, fraud or misuse of authority to commit the injustice, he is also liable for the damage the agent himself may suffer.

The actual doer of the harm is bound in the second instance to repair the damage done, unless reasons of force and fear absolve him from guilt. (See the norms for material cooperation in general moral theology.) Should the agent inflict damage beyond what was ordered, either out of malice or vincible ignorance, the one who commanded the deed is not obliged in rigid justice to repair the additional damage. If the command is revoked before the harm is done and the revocation has been intimated to the agent, he alone is bound to reparation if he nevertheless proceeds.

An advisor, who by counsel induces another to inflict damage or shows him how to do it, is liable for the damage to the extent that his counsel is the effective cause of the evil done. He is obliged to restitution, unless he retracts his counsel. There is however no duty of restitution if the person counselled was already determined to act unjustly independent of the counsel. Also confessors, lawyers, physicians, etc., who give wrong advice because of culpable ignorance are in justice bound to retract their counsel; or else they are obliged to restitution. The same applies to quacks and similar impostors who give wrong advice to their clients. One who inadvertently gives harmful advice is bound, if possible, to retract it with some relative inconvenience to himself. If he culpably neglects to do so, he is responsible for the harm done. If in spite of the revocation the person counselled is determined to inflict harm, the counsellor is in justice obliged to warn the one threatened, provided the person counselled is still acting under the influence of the counsel (e.g. by the use of means taught him); yet should he proceed in virtue of his own malice, the duty to forewarn is one merely of charity.

Consent, praise, flattery, ridicule may be efficacious ways of cooperating in injustice and the source of the obligation to restitution, e.g. if by these means the evil-doer is induced to refrain from obligatory restitution. Approval of parents or superiors may be the effective cause of damage inflicted by their children or subordinates, particularly if the latter be ignorant. Those who consent are bound in the second instance to repair the harm done in proportion to the efficacy of their approval.

Whoever shelters an evil-doer or receives and conceals ill-gotten goods renders himself responsible with the agent for his misdeed. He is bound to restitution in default of the main agent to the extent that he effectively cooperates in the injustice. To shield a friend for friendship's sake is not necessarily cooperation in injustice. The same holds if one gives shelter to a thief only in order to escape grave harm to oneself.

One who takes an active part in an unjust action is bound to repair the harm of which he was the efficacious and culpable cause. If he received a portion of the ill-gotten goods, he is bound to restore them. If he is a cooperator in unjust damage, he must repair the harm done. He is bound to repair the whole harm equally with the other cooperators if his cooperation was necessary for the damage. He is only bound to repair that amount of harm which he actually did if his cooperation was not necessary. Mere material cooperation for justified reasons does usually not oblige to restitution.

b) *Negative cooperation* consists in the culpable failure to prevent unjust damage to one's neighbour. Moral theologians commonly maintain that he who is bound in justice to prevent harm to another, in virtue of his position or office or by contract, and refrains from doing so, though he could have prevented it without unproportionate inconvenience, is obliged to restitution. Thus hired watchmen, guardians, caretakers, tax and custom collectors are held responsible for damage resulting from their negligence or disregard of their duties (unless it concerns an insignificant matter or the poor) and supposed to make restitution.

However in practice this seems not to be urged. A hired guard, for example, who neglects his duty in watching a jeweller's store and permits robbers to break in is hardly ever made to pay the damage, although he will be subjected to some form of penalty. The reason may be that the damage is not in any way effected by him, but by another agent. His negligence or inactivity alone and by themselves are not apt to cause any damage.

The matter is different with drunken drivers who commit actions which are damaging to others. They are truly the cause of the damage and therefore bound to restitution, as has been explained earlier. The same holds of owners of animals who neglect the necessary supervision. Since the animals are their property and subject to their dominion, they are bound to repair the damage caused by the animals to others, if they fail to control them. In purely negative cooperation on the other hand no cause is created that could produce damage. A person merely neglects, though culpably, to counteract a detrimental cause, which however proceeds from another agent. For this reason the duty to restitution is less clear and usually not urged in this case.

All authors agree that those who are only bound in charity to prevent unjust damage are not obliged in justice to repair the loss of their neighbour, although they sin by their indifference or negligence, and at times gravely. Thus a person who is not the custodian of a house is only in charity bound to turn in a fire alarm when he notices a fire. For the same reason a confessor is not bound to restitution if he fails to remind a penitent of his duty of restitution, unless his silence be equivalent to an implicit counsel.

5. Recipient of restitution, manner and excuses

a) *The recipient of restitution*. In principle the person himself who unjustly suffered material loss is to be indemnified. If he is dead, restitution must be made to his heirs. This also holds if a juridical person has been damaged, e.g. a stock corporation, an insurance company or the state. However the obligation of restitution to the state or to state-owned enterprises or to other mammoth societies can for the most part be satisfied by donations to the poor, to charitable institutions or to other socially worthy causes. In countries where the Christian schools are not supported by the state, restitution can also be made by contributions to these schools. The reason is that the support of charitable and social causes pertains to the duties of the state. Huge economic enterprises likewise are expected to patronize such purposes.

B. Häring rightly judges that "restitution may also be made to the poor if the one entitled to payment is a rich man whose social conduct toward the poor is notoriously lacking in social justice and charity."[1] Likewise one may satisfy one's obligation to restitution by equivalent payment to the creditor of the person to whom restitution is due, if the creditor could not obtain a just settlement in another way.

If it is not known to whom restitution is due or if it is morally impossible to indemnify the injured party, as for example if restitution would involve undue hardship or unproportionately great expenses, the possessor in good faith may keep the thing. But the possessor in bad faith must make restitution to the poor. If in the latter case the original creditor should appear later, the debtor is most probably free from further obligations, since he has fulfilled his obligations in the best possible way.

In all cases where restitution can or should be made to the poor, he who is obliged to make it may keep the goods if he himself is poor, as long as he is poor. A person making

---
[1] Häring III, 1966, 495.

restitution to the poor when he should do so to the injured party does not fulfill his obligation. But he may often be left in good faith.

If the person who is bound to restitution should die without complying with his obligation, it is transferred to his heirs. But they are not held to restore more than the inheritance is worth.

b) *The manner of restitution.* If possible the object belonging to another itself must be restored to its rightful owner, unless it has become worthless through its use. If this should not be possible without great inconvenience or detriment to the debtor, he is permitted to make restitution in the form of money, unless the owner is reasonably unwilling to accept the money value of the object. There is then nothing to be done but to wait.

Restitution may be made without the knowledge of the creditor. It can be made by a fictitious donation, provided the donor does not induce the reception of a favour in return. Servants and employees can restore by additional work or greater diligence.

Restitution is to be made as soon as possible. Culpable delay may, and often does, amount to additional injustice if the creditor suffers by the delay. The additional injustice carries with it additional obligations of restitution.

c) *Excuses from restitution.* Condonation excuses from restitution, whether it is express, or tacit, or reasonably presumed. But presumptions must be used cautiously, and the advice of a prudent counsellor should usually be sought.

Physical or moral impossibility postpones the obligation of restitution and even remits it when such impossibility is perpetual. Restitution is morally impossible if the debtor would thereby be constituted in really grave need, or lose the social status he has justly acquired, or suffer loss of a higher order, e.g. life, liberty, good name, etc. But this does not apply to cases where the omission of restitution would cause the rightful claimant similar or even greater hardships. For the innocent must be favoured over the guilty party.

When bankruptcy is declared, the debtor's entire possessions are subject to the regulations of positive law. They oblige in conscience as far as they do not conflict with the natural law. Opinions differ as to whether after bankruptcy the debtor still has the obligation in conscience to pay his debts in full, should he later become wealthy again. The common opinion of the older theologians and of many modern authors is that he has this obligation. But some authors are of the milder view that in the case of a bona fide bankruptcy the debtor is not obliged to any further payments after the legal settlement of the case. Although the legal extinction of all further claims does not necessarily apply to the internal forum, debts are contracted under the implied condition that they will cease in case of a bona fide bankruptcy, so the proponents of the second opinion argue. Every person involved in business knows the risks connected with it and must accept the possibility of misfortune. — Bankruptcy in bad faith does not extinguish the obligation of restitution, since the insolvency is counterfeit and not real.

VI. Socialization and land reform

Socialization is the transfer of certain properties to the ownership of the state (nationalization) or of other public law corporations, especially municipalities (communalization). Socialization is justified if it is required by the needs of the common good. But in every case in which socialization is under consideration, it must be shown that it is indeed in the interest of the general good. For socialization interferes with the sphere of private ownership and with the rights of those whose property is expropriated.

In the social teachings of the Church the right to socialization is expressly stated for the first time by Pius XI. "It is rightly contended that certain forms of property must be reserved to the state, since they carry with them an opportunity of domination too great to be left to private individuals without injury to the community at large" (QA 114).

The reason given by Pius XI is the possible abuse of economic power. Pius XII still adds further reasons. Socialization is also justified "when it is the only means to remedy an injustice or to avoid the squandering of the productive forces of the nation and to insure the coordinated use of the same forces to the benefit of the economic life of the nation."[1]

The latter text declares that socialization must be "the only means" to remedy the mentioned defects. If equally or more effective alternatives are available, they merit to be preferred. The abuse of too extensive landholdings, e.g., can more efficiently be remedied by land reform measures than by collectivization. Also in the realm of property and economics the principle of subsidiarity is of fundamental importance and must be observed

---

[1] Pius XII, AAS 37 (1945), 71.

(cf. MM 117). State control of the means of production is least desirable. Socialization should therefore be the last resort. It entails dangers for a sound social order and constitutes a hazard to democracy. The more the means of production are socialized, the more powerful the government becomes and the weaker the people.

Furthermore experience shows that state-owned economic enterprises usually work less profitably than those in private hands. "No one manages industrial concerns worse than the state."[1] The reason is that the function of the entrepreneur and the Civil Servant are quite different things. Besides, the incentives to economic venture and thrifty use of available means are wanting in public undertakings.

Keeping in mind these various considerations, J. Messner comes to the following concrete conclusions as to when socialization may be justified and when it is not. Socialization is always justified where production of the materials for nuclear energy is concerned. It may be necessary for so-called key industries upon which a large proportion of a country's industry depends, if their safe functioning cannot otherwise be guaranteed, or if the necessary private capital for its development cannot be secured. Important minerals, like coal and ores, may become an object for socialization for the same reasons, or also to prevent an exploitation which could be detrimental to the national economy. There may be grounds for socializing those consumer goods industries which supply basic needs of the community and which cannot be left to the good will of private enterprises, such as water, gas, electricity and public transportation services.

No adequate grounds exist for the socialization of the banks. "Credit possesses a fundamental importance for the whole of the social economy, which is surpassed only by that of the soil. He who controls credit controls the economy. If the state controls it, the whole of the economy is in the grip of the state. State ownership of a bank or the nationalization of the central issuing bank is a different matter, however. For obvious reasons, enterprises with cultural aims must be completely exempt from nationalization. Such enterprises are the press and book publishing. This does not preclude the state's maintaining, for example, its own printing press or publishing house or news-

---

[1] Otto Bauer, onetime head of the Austrian Social Democratic Party. Quoted by J. Messner: Social Ethics, 1965, 940.

paper, provided that these do not make use of unfair methods of competition." Finally there is no sufficient justification for the socialization of agricultural land. Political, social and economic reasons make it a rather vital task of the state to promote such a distribution of landed property that as many families as possible can obtain economic and social security by their own work on their own soil.[1]

The sound and just distribution of agricultural land is the concern of the social movement called land reform. In many countries vast landholdings have accumulated in the hands of a few landlords, who are often not able or not even interested in cultivating them well. While the tenants who have tilled the land for generations and invested their labour in it are kept in a kind of servitude, unable to acquire a farm of their own.

Vatican II regards this as a serious social evil which urgently needs to be remedied. "In many underdeveloped areas there are large or even gigantic rural estates which are only moderately cultivated or lie completely idle for the sake of profit. At the same time the majority of the people are either without land or have only very small holdings, and there is evident and urgent need to increase land productivity. It is not rare for those who are hired to work for the landowners, or who till a portion of the land as tenants, to receive a wage or income unworthy of human beings, to lack decent housing, and to be exploited by middlemen."

"Depending on circumstances, therefore, reforms must be instituted if income is to grow, working conditions improve, job security increase, and an incentive to working on one's own initiative be provided. Indeed, insufficiently cultivated estates should be distributed to those who can make these lands fruitful" (GS 71; cf. PP 24).

"Still, whenever the common good requires expropriation, compensation must be reckoned in equity after all the circumstances have been weighed" (ib.). This applies to expropriation in the train of socialization as well as for purposes of land reform. Compensation to the owner for the expropriated possessions is a question of commutative justice. Therefore it must essentially be carried out on the principle of equivalence.

There is no doubt that the ascertainment of the value of the property often meets with great difficulties. The goods to

---

[1] J. Messner: Social Ethics. — St. Louis and London: Herder Book Co., 1965, 939f.

be given in exchange are another problem. Compensation in form of money alone may not always be a sufficient equivalent, especially where the currency is steadily decreasing in value. On the other hand increases in the value of land (land rent) which result from the work of others and not of the owner or from public facilities provided by the state (like roads, water, electricity, etc.) have not necessarily to be refunded to the owner. But attention must be paid that those whose property is expropriated are not placed at a considerable disadvantage as against those of comparable property who are able to retain it. If the compensation is too low and unfair, the state would be guilty of injustice and liable to restitution. The question should be settled by an honourable agreement between the state and the owners.

Chapter VI

TRUTH, FIDELITY AND HONOUR[1]

The subject of the present chapter is values which are primarily of a spiritual and ideal nature. As all genuine values, they too claim man's respect and protection. Genuine love of neighbour must be concerned with them. It will place itself in their service in order to uphold, defend and promote them. The truth enables a man to live and act in harmony with reality. *Truthfulness* therefore is that virtue which respects the truth in whatever form it is found and assures the neighbour of it in one's communication with him. Closely related to truthfulness is *fidelity,* by which a person remains true to his conviction, word and promise. Secrecy is in many instances a demand of faithfulness, since *secrets* are often entrusted to the other under the explicit or implicit condition that they will not be betrayed. At other times however secrecy is an obligation which simply results from a person's right to privacy and protection of the intimate realm of the soul. The good of *honour* finally accords a person the esteem due to him in accordance with his true value and the dignity of his position in the community. It is a spiritual good of great social significance.

A. Truthfulness

I. Truthfulness in Holy Scripture

The biblical concept of truth is not quite the same as that of today's language. Modern parlance calls a thought or statement true if it conforms to reality or to a person's inner conviction and knowledge. This understanding of truth is close to Greek thought. The Bible on the other hand conceives of

---

[1] References: J. A. Dorszynski: Catholic Teaching about the Morality of Falsehood. — Washington: Catholic University of America Press, 1949. Gregor Müller: Die Wahrhaftigkeitspflicht und die Problematik der Lüge. — Freiburg: Herder, 1962. Karl Rahner: On Truthfulness; in: Theological Investigations. vol. VII, 1971, 229-259. Anthony Padavono: Free to Be Faithful. — New York: Paulist, 1972.

truth rather in the sense of faithfulness. Truth is faithfulness to God's law and to the message of the gospel. God's law and word are truth. Truthful therefore is the man who accepts and obeys them. Truthful is similarly also he who shows faithfulness to his neighbour. Trustworthiness of one's assertions is included in this concept of truth as one of its aspects, but it is always seen in the more comprehensive scope of the demand of faithfulness.

1. *The Old Testament.* The Hebrew word used for truth is *'emeth,* which is formed from the word *'aman.* (The liturgical word "Amen" originates from it.) The basic meaning of *'aman* is to be firm, reliable, worthy of confidence. Thus the meaning of *'emeth* is close to faithfulness.

When *'emeth* is attributed to Yahweh, it expresses that he is faithful and trustworthy. In particular God's truth is his fidelity to his covenant. "The Lord your God is God, the faithful God who keeps covenant and steadfast love with those who love him and keep his commandments" (Deut 7:9; cf. 32:4 Neh 9:33; Ps 71:22; 89; Is 49:7; Hos 2:19f). His promise is truth because it is trustworthy and sure. "The Lord swore to David a sure oath (*'emeth*) from which he will not turn back" (Ps 132:11). The truth of God is protection (Ps 91:4), light (Ps 43:3), assistance in the face of the enemy (Ps 54:5). *'Emeth* is also a characteristic of God's word and law. "Thy words are true" (2 Sam 7:28; cf. Ps 119:160). "All his precepts are trustworthy" (Ps 111:7; cf. 19:9; 119:86.142.151). Therefore the psalmist prays to be instructed in them. "Teach me thy way, O Lord, that I may walk in thy truth" (Ps 86:11; cf. 25:5).

When truth is affirmed of men, it means their loyalty to God, to his covenant, to his law. "Fear the Lord, and serve him in sincerity and in faithfulness" (Jos 24:14; cf. 2 Chron 31:20; Zech 8:3). "To walk in the truth" (1 Kings 2:4; 3:6; Tob 3:5; Ps 26:3; Is 38:3) and "to do the truth" (Tob 4:6; 13:6; Sir 27:9), both have the meaning to live in faithfulness to God's law. "I have walked before thee in faithfulness and with a whole heart" (2 Kings 20:3). In a similar sense *'emeth* can be used to indicate a relationship of faithfulness between men, as for example in the expression "to deal loyally and truly" with a person (Gen 24:49; 47:29; Josh 2:14). The righteous man is the one who is found faithful in his dealings with others. "Let not loyalty and faithfulness forsake you" (Prov 3:3; cf. 14:22; 16:6; 20:28). At times the quality of truthfulness is also attributed to judgments. A man ought "to judge in truth" and "to render true judgment" (Prov 29:14; Ezek 18:8; Zech 7:9). Here truth has the meaning of equity and justice (cf. Is 59:14).

Finally *'emeth* can also be used in the narrower sense as a quality of speech. Truth then signifies the correspondence between assertion and reality (cf. 1 Kings 10:6; 22:16). Not to speak the truth is iniquity (Jer 9:5). The Lord expects men to be truthful in their words. "Speak the truth to one another" (Zech 8:16; cf. Jer 23:28). "Truthful lips endure for ever, but a lying tongue is for the moment" (Prov 12:19).

2. *The New Testament.* The notion of truth (*alētheia*) in the New Testament is close to that of the Old Testament and resembles it in many ways. As in the Old Testament, truth can mean the fidelity of God (Rom 3:3-7) and the faithfulness to his promise (Rom 15:8). God's word is truth (2 Cor 4:2). And just as formerly the law was truth (Rom 2:20), now the gospel is truth (Gal 2:5.14; Eph 1:13; Col 1:5; Jas 1:18).

In the Pastoral and Catholic Epistles truth often signifies the sound doctrine which is in agreement with the gospel (1 Tim 1:10f; 2 Tim 4:1-3; Tit 1:9; 2 Pet 1:12). "To come to the knowledge of truth" means to accept the gospel and to live accordingly (1 Tim 2:4; 2 Tim 3:7; Tit 1:1-3). False teachers are those who are "bereft of truth" and "turn away from listening to the truth" because they falsify the faith (1 Tim 6:5; 2 Tim 2:18; 3:8; 4:4; Tit 1:14; 2 Pet 2:2). The Church of the living God however remains "the pillar and bulwark of the truth" (1 Tim 3:15).

Particularly in the Johannine writings truth is an important term. Truth is the revelation of God in Christ. "The law was given through Moses; grace and truth came through Jesus Christ" (Jn 1:17). Christ reveals the truth in that he proclaims what he has heard from the Father (Jn 8:26.40.45-47; 18:37). As the Word of the Father he himself is the truth. This is the great Christian innovation. Christ is "the way, and the truth, and the life" (Jn 14:6). As the "true light" (Jn 1:9; 1 Jn 2:8) he is the "light of life" (Jn 8:12). Truth, light and life are terms of equivalent significance if used as predicates of Christ. Since the role of the Spirit is to guide the disciples into all the truth and to bear witness to Christ, he is likewise characterized as "the Spirit of truth" (Jn 14:17; 15:26; 16:13; 1 Jn 5:7).

The divine gift of truth imposes an obligation to accept the truth and to live in accord with it. Christians must do away with "the old leaven, the leaven of malice and evil" and replace it by "the unleavened bread of sincerity and truth" (1 Cor 5:8).

They must put on the new man and achieve the holiness demanded by truth (Eph 4:20-24). Truth is opposed to wickedness (Rom 1:18; 2:8), just as the light is opposed to the darkness (Eph 5:8f). Love does not rejoice in what is evil, but in the truth (1 Cor 13:6). Therefore a Christian must not "wander from the truth" (Jas 5:19). He is sanctified by "obedience to the truth" (1 Pet 1:22).

According to John the true disciple is "of the truth" (Jn 17:17f; 18:37; 1 Jn 3:19). It frees him from sin (Jn 8:31-34). Therefore he must follow the truth (2 Jn 4; 3 Jn 3f) and do what is true (Jn 3:21; 1 Jn 1:6). This means nothing else than to fulfill the Law of Christ and to keep his commandments.

Undoubtedly the New Testament also demands truthfulness in the narrower sense. Jesus demands that in speech the "yes" and "no" of the disciples be reliable and true. Anything else is of the evil one (Mt 5:37). In the same sense Paul admonishes the Christians: "Put away falsehood, let every one speak the truth with his neighbour, for we are members one of another" (Eph 4:25; Col 3:9f). Falsehood and lying are condemned repeatedly. The problem of the lie shall still be dealt with separately below.

II. The virtue of truthfulness and its duties

Truthfulness is an attitude of the mind in which one reverences the truth as a value which can claim man's respect in every regard. It is a disposition by which one is, first, as absolutely open as possible to the truth, second, prepared to follow out in action the known truth unconditionally, and third, ready to share it with one's fellowmen as something which is, at least in principle, due to them.

Truthfulness fundamentally is receptivity, submissiveness to being, readiness not to refuse the claims of reality. Truth is not shaped by man, but rather man must suffer to be shaped by the truth and permit himself to be grasped by it. Truthfulness ultimately means that a man lets himself be grasped by the very source of truth and being, God, who is the truth himself in its most unfathomable depth.

The basis for the obligation to truthfulness is that without it the proper development of the human person, social life and religion are impossible. Man and society cannot progress if the facts and laws of reality, upon which progress must build, are concealed, misrepresented or ignored. Neither is worship compatible with the denial of the truth expressed in God's will. The knowledge and recognition of reality are the indispensable foundations of efficient and fruitful action. Untruthfulness robs a man of this foundation; truthfulness gives access to it.

1.   *Truthfulness in thought*

In order to arrive at truthfulness, a person must first of all be truthful in his thought. He must accept the truth which confronts him in many various ways and earnestly seek to find it. Of course no one is able to search for all the possible truths which can be gathered and known. The obligation to seek the truth primarily extends to a person's own self, to the tasks assigned to him in the world, and to the divine ground of his being, God, who gives ultimate meaning to his life.

The duty to seek the truth and to adhere to it is pointed out by Vatican II as a strict obligation of all men. "All men should be at once impelled by nature and also bound by a moral obligation to seek the truth, especially religious truth. They are also bound to adhere to the truth, once it is known, and to order their whole lives in accord with the demands of truth" (DH 2; cf. also 1). With this duty corresponds the right of every man "to search for the truth, voice his mind, and publicize it" (GS 59).

One of the basic demands of truthfulness is the courage to face up to the truth within oneself. A person can mask his true being and intentions, not only before others but also before himself. He can blind himself to his real motives, deceive himself as to his true obligations and escape into a world of unreal appearance. The process of self-deception can be carried to such an extreme that mendacity becomes almost a second nature and is only dimly recognized. The devil is not called the "father of lies" without reason (Jn 8:44).

In order to counter this state of deception and alienation, a person must learn to be radically honest with himself. This requires humble self-acceptance and sincere acknowledgement of one's limitations. It likewise requires the readiness to conversion wherever a person finds himself at fault. Interior truthfulness presupposes humble self-denial free from pride.

An ethics of truth must also take in account the laws of the objective order and the realities of the surrounding world. Since these are disclosed in the sciences, their findings and settled conclusions must be given due attention. This holds especially if they have a bearing on one's life and work.

A most imperative demand is finally the obligation to seek the truth in religious matters and to be open to God's saving word. Vatican II stresses this duty in a particular way. "All men are bound to seek the truth, especially in what concerns God and His Church" (DH 1; cf. 2f). Nevertheless, even though this obligation is of a special urgency, it does not justify any coercion. Truth "is to be sought after in a manner proper to the dignity of the human person and his social nature. The inquiry is to be free" (DH 3). "The truth cannot impose itself except by virtue of its own truth" (DH 1). But the person who does not live up to his obligation of seeking the truth and adhering to it in a matter of so great importance can certainly not be excused from moral fault.

Of course the knowledge of truth required in this matter is not an intellectual insight as complete as possible. Rather it is the loving acceptance of the word of God as it reveals itself in the faith of the heart. The believing Catholic will also take into account the doctrine of the Church as a source of his faith. Everyone has to be aware of the limitations to his insight and knowledge of the truth.

2. *Truthfulness in conduct*

True must also be a person's actions. They must agree with the principles he upholds and the faith he professes. Truthfulness in conduct means that a person acts and lives in conformity with his thoughts and words.

Holy Scripture speaks of truthfulness in this sense if it requires those who belong to God "to do the truth," "to walk in the truth" and to obey it. The meaning of these expressions is to live in faithfulness to God's law and in accord with the demands of faith, as has been explained. Certainly there is no truthfulness more important than this.

In a like manner Vatican II insists on the duty of all men not only to seek the truth, but also to hold fast to it and "to order their whole lives in accord with the demands of truth" (DH 2; cf. 1). As the truth is discovered, men are bound by a personal assent to adhere to it, in order that they may come to God for whom they are created (DH 3).

Untruthful accordingly are all actions which contradict the recognized truth and the convictions of a person's faith. In a special way opposed to truthfulness is hypocrisy, which dissimulates virtuous behaviour in external deeds, while the real motives are of a different nature. This is Christ's criticism against the Pharisees and scribes. He reproaches them for practising their piety and good works, such as almsgiving, praying, fasting and the meticulous observance of the law, not for the sake of God and the needy neighbour, but in order to receive praise from men (Mt 6:1-8; 23). He likewise criticizes them for another, similar form of insincerity, their insistence on rules and obligations which they themselves are not willing to fulfill. "They preach, but do not practise. They bind heavy burdens, hard to bear, and lay them on men's shoulders; but they themselves will not move them with their finger. They do all their deeds to be seen by men" (Mt 23:3-5).

On the other hand, "we must grant that the man ensnared in error is at least relatively truthful and genuine if he acts in accordance with his convictions. And if his conviction, objectively false, is subjectively sincere, he is true by will and intention."[1] Such a person is by no means guilty of falsehood, as is also noted by Vatican II. "Conscience frequently errs from invincible ignorance without losing its dignity" (GS 16).

Truthfulness equally demands that a man be able to face up to disagreeable situations without evading them. It requires him to submit to the criticism of others without yielding to sentiments of antipathy and desires of retaliation. The truthful man takes the opinions of others serious and is ready to acknowledge his own errors and mistakes.

This does not only apply to individuals but also to groups and communities and even the Church. "Care must also be taken to encourage truthfulness and courage in avowing the faith in the communal life within the Church herself, in other words among Catholic Christians. Let us allow opinions to be expressed even when we ourselves find them disquieting. Let us really allow 'public opinion' to have a place in the Church herself, where we are in a position to expand or to restrict the opportunities for expressing such opinions."[2] The apologetics for Christianity must not be allowed to measure its supporters and opponents by different standards. On the contrary, motivated by the spirit of their Master, Christians must make all efforts to remain fair in

---

[1] Häring III, 1966. 556.

[2] K. Rahner: On Truthfulness; in: Theological Investigations, vol. 7. 1971, 251.

their methods of controversy and to listen with goodwill to the opinions of others.

Loyalty to the truth of the faith which Christians have received as a privileged gift from God finally entails, as one of its essential elements, the courage to bear witness to it before others. Every Christian must be a witness to the Christian truth. Every Christian has to attest to it in the manner appropriate to his vocation and particular circumstances.

3. *Truthfulness in words*

The audible word must in some measure be an expression of the inner word of knowledge. It is true that man cannot exhaustively express his thoughts and insights in external words, and often he is not even permitted to do so. However truthfulness in words requires that whatever is stated in the external words be in harmony with a person's internal thoughts and knowledge.

Truthfulness in words is a demand of justice, reverence and love. Since the opposite, the lie, does not only deny the truth to another but in addition induces him to believe in what is not true, it leads him into error. He accepts facts and relies on securities which in reality do not exist. If he acts on this basis, he will often suffer harm himself or also cause harm to others. Sure reliance on the truthfulness of the statements and assertions of others is an essential condition for beneficial coexistence, fruitful cooperation and efficient work.

Inasmuch as fraternal love obliges to help others in their needs, it also obliges to share with them the truth. Even where a truth seems of no importance to another person, the breach of trust, which is inherent in every lie, is an offence against the other. Every lie treats the other as not worthy of the truth or not entitled to it. This offends against the dignity of the other as a person of equal value and right. Intellectual and moral fellowship can only thrive where the truth is respected.

Nevertheless, even though there is an obligation to be always truthful in one's words, one is not obliged, and often not even permitted, to impart all the truth one knows to others. Christ was absolutely truthful. But he proclaimed the mysteries of God only gradually to men, and not to all. He warns not to throw the "pearls before swine" (Mt 7:6).

"To maintain an adequate moral norm of 'true speech' we must go beyond the mere psychological concept of true speech (conformity of word to mind) and keep in mind the divine primordial pattern and the human end and purpose of the word. The goal is the building up of love in ourselves, in our neighbour, in the community." Speech must be community-forming and community-sustaining.[1]

This forbids us to use the truth and to reveal it in a manner which possibly or certainly will prove detrimental to others, unless values of a still higher order justify this. Every word of truth must be guided by discretion and prudence. The person in possession of the truth must prudently weigh whether its revelation will be truly edifying, bridge over differences, build community and contribute to the greater glory of God; or on the contrary whether it will create confusion, divide and prove destructive.

Dishonesty and hypocrisy are at times harshly counter-acted by radical frankness and blunt exposure of the truth. Brutal honesty with oneself and with others is considered the perfect, though painful realization of the virtue of truthfulness. In themselves frankness and absolute honesty are certainly praiseworthy. But they have their drawbacks if everything is voiced what a person thinks and believes to know. It is already difficult to know the truth about oneself. It is even more difficult to know it about others. Often only part of the truth is known. Disclosure of a partial truth however only gives an incomplete picture of the other and therefore tends to be unjust. Moreover charity demands that the truth, even when it really is such, be always expressed in a form which does not offend against fraternal love. As far as possible it must spare the sensitivity of others. A simple criterion for ascertaining whether one is prompted by motives of genuine truthfulness or by those of loveless arrogance is to ask oneself whether one would be willing to recommend another to criticize one's own person in the same way as one criticizes others.

Even the sincere and upright man must conceal many things because of consideration for his neighbour and the need to protect himself and others against abuse. This need often causes conflicts for the truthful man. The problem must find further attention in the following.

III. The lie and lawful concealment of the truth

The lie consists in a verbal statement which contradicts a person's internal conviction and knowledge. Catholic moral

---

[1] Häring III, 1966, 559.

theology commonly defines it as *locutio contra mentem*, a speech contrary to what a person has in mind. Following St. Augustine, some authors include in the definition the intention to deceive. The lie then is defined as a speech contrary to what a person has in mind with the intention to deceive (*cum intentione fallendi*). This would distinguish the lie from idle speeches in which, for example, a person would say to himself: "It is raining," although the sun is shining, or from the invented stories which children at times are telling as real happenings.

Many Protestant theologians and also some recent Catholic authors include in the definition the violation of the right to the truth. This of course narrows the concept of the lie down in an important regard. The lie (*mendacium*) is in this case defined as an untruthful speech which violates the right to the truth of the person addressed. An untruthful speech which does not violate the right to the truth is accordingly not a lie. It is called a false speech (*falsiloquium*) and not considered an offence against the truth by these authors.[1]

In the following expositions the traditional definition of the lie shall be taken as a basis. Lying is a speech contrary to what a person has in mind, with the intention to deceive.

1. *The lie according to Holy Scripture*[2]

The *Old Testament* formulates in the decalogue the commandment: "You shall not bear false witness against your neighbour" (Ex 20:16). The precept forbids the making of an untrue declaration before the court to the detriment of another. Hence if catechisms often render the eighth commandment in the more general form: "You shall not lie," it is not a literal translation. Nevertheless it agrees with the mind of Holy Scripture, since other texts condemn lying and the liar quite in general (cf. Lev 19:11).

---

[1] Some Catholic theologians also distinguish between formal and material speech. A speech is formal if the circumstances in which it is stated are such that one can reasonably expect the speaker to communicate his true thoughts. A speech is material if the circumstances are at least objectively such that one cannot expect the speaker to communicate his true thoughts. Only the formal speech contrary to what a person has in mind is a lie, not the material speech. Authors who hold this theory are, e.g., A. Vermeersch (Theologia Moralis II, 1928, nr. 703 and 705) and A. Tanquerey (Synopsis Theologiae Moralis et Pastoralis III, 1953, nr. 292 and 295).

[2] Cf. Karl Hermann Schelkle: Theology of the New Testament, vol. 3: Morality. — Collegeville, Minn.: Liturgical Press, 1973, 276-280.

The prophets demand truthfulness and condemn all lies, calumnies and deceptions (Jer 9:3-9; Nahum 3:1; Zeph 3:13). The Psalms bewail the prevalence of lies everywhere (Ps 59:12f; 62:4; 109:2). God abhors the deceitful man (Ps 5:6). Wisdom literature repeatedly condemns the direct lie (Prov 6:17; 12:19.22; Wis 1:11; Sir 20:24-26) as well as calumny, double-dealing and dissimulation (Prov 4:24; 26:23-28; Sir 5:14; 28:13-26).

At times the concept of lie assumes a wider meaning. It then signifies godlessness, irreligion and idolatry in contradistinction to righteousness and true religion (Ps 78:36f; Jer 13:25; 16:19f; Hos 7:13; 10:13; Hab 2:18).

The historical books relate several instances of concrete lies and frauds on the part of Abraham (Gen 12:11-13; 20:1f), Isaac (Gen 26:7-11), Jacob (Gen 27:18f), Michal, David's wife (1 Sam 19:13f.17), and David himself (1 Sam 20:6.28f; 21:1f). The exegesis is not unanimous as to whether these lies find the approval of the sacred writers or whether they are merely reported as historical facts. Certainly the texts contain no explicit or implicit disapproval of the deceptions. The lie by which the Hebrew midwives deceived Pharaoh in order to circumvent his wicked command to kill the new born boys is doubtless considered as justified. It is out of the fear of God that they so act, and therefore they are blessed (Ex 1:15-21). The same holds of the lie by which Judith deceived Holofernes and his men in order to save her people (Jud 10:12f).

In the *New Testament* Jesus repeats the prohibition of false witness as one of the commandments of the decalogue (Mk 10:19 par). Beyond it he demands absolute truthfulness from his disciples. Their "Yes" and "No" must be so reliable that no further confirmation of their words, such as an oath, is needed (Mt 5:37).

According to the letters of the Apostles lying and falsehood belong to the old, sinful man who must be put off. "Do not lie to one another!" (Col 3:9; cf. Eph 4:25). Christians must "put away all malice and all guile and insincerity and envy and all slander" (1 Pet 2:1). A very severe judgment is handed down to Ananias and his wife Sapphira who tried to lie to the community in Jerusalem and thereupon suddenly died (Acts 5:1-11).

If according to the Johannine writings truth is faithfulness to God's commandments, then its opposite, the lie, likewise assumes a wider meaning. It signifies disobedience against God, hatefulness and heretical falsehood. "He who says 'I know him' but disobeys his commandments is a liar, and the truth is not in him" (1 Jn 2:4; cf. 1 Jn 1:6; 2:22; 4:20). Ultimately the lie is the antithesis of God. The devil is the father of lies. "He has nothing to do with the truth, because there is no truth in him" (Jn 8:44). In the Apocalypse the lie is the embodiment of all vices. There is no place in the holy city for those who practise lies. The lot of the liars is "in the lake that burns with fire and brimstone, which is the second death" (Rev 21:8.27; 22:15).

2. *Historical summary*

The pagan antiquity hardly knows of an obligation to absolute truthfulness. A lie is permitted and at times even demanded for the sake of a higher good (Socrates, Plato, the Stoics). Aristotle is often quoted as an exception. He highly praises the man who is truthful in his speech even when no profit is at stake, as in matters of contracts and justice, and who avoids falsehood for its own sake because it is something base.[1] However interpreters are not of one mind as to whether by this he wanted to exclude absolutely every lie, even if the interest of the nation were at stake. A most thorough condemnation of lying and any kind of dishonesty is found in Cicero.[2] He rejects them with great determination in private as well as in public affairs. Nevertheless faith and oath must not be kept with a villain whose methods and intentions are criminal.[3]

In the Christian antiquity many Fathers of the Church condemn every kind of lie and do not want to admit of any exceptions. However this judgment is not unanimous. Other Fathers admit of exceptions in situations of emergency in order to avoid greater evil. Authors quoted for this latter opinion are usually Clement of Alexandria, Origen, Chrysostom, Hilary of Poitiers, Hieronymus (who later revised his opinion) and Cassianus.[4] A decisive influence on the Christian doctrine on

---

[1] Aristotle: Nicomachean Ethics, book 4, chap. 7.

[2] Cicero: De Officiis, book 3, 14-32.

[3] ib., book 3, 29.

[4] According to Gregor Müller: Die Wahrhaftigkeitspflicht und die Problematik der Lüge (Freiburg: Herder, 1962), also the following ancient authors and writings admit of exceptions from the obligation to truthfulness in situations of emergency: Didymus the Blind, Synesius of Cyrene, Dictinius of Astorga, Theodoret of Cyr, the Apophthegmata Patrum, Procopius of Gaza, Dorotheus of Gaza, Martin of Braga, John Climacus, Germanus of Constantinople, Theodorus of Studion, Eustratius of Nicaea, Eustathius of Thessalonica, John Apocaucus, John Contacuzenus, Antonius Melissa. The last six Greek writers belong to the 9th to 14th century.

lying was exercised by St. Augustine. He describes the lie as a false statement with the intention to deceive, and considers it as intrinsically evil. Lying is forbidden in all circumstances. No exceptions are admissible. In support of his opinion he quotes Cyprian and Ambrose. However the ultimate reason for him is the teaching of Holy Scripture.

In the Middle Ages theologians, except for a few, share the view of St. Augustine. Since also Thomas Aquinas adopted it, the weight of this opinion became very strong in Christian and particularly Catholic tradition. Thomas regards the lie as contrary to the nature of speech and on this account as evil in itself. Among the theologians of the Middle Ages who take a different view and consider a false speech permissible for sufficient reasons are William of Auxerre, Alexander of Hales and Bonaventure.

Modern times brought the division of the Church by the Reformation, and with it also a division concerning the doctrine on the morality of lying. Protestant theologians generally hold that the "officious lie" to help a neighbour and the emergency lie to defend one's own just interest are permissible. An exception to this is Calvin. A special importance was gained by the destinction made by H. Grotius († 1645) between lie and false speech. The lie is an untruth which violates the right of the other to the truth, while the false speech is not. Only the lie is morally evil.

In Catholic moral theology the beginning of the modern times is characterized by the doctrine of the mental reservation (*restrictio mentalis*). On the one hand it keeps to the absolute unlawfulness of every lie, on the other it seeks a way out for those situations where the truth has to be protected against its possible abuse. Many theologians went so far as to permit the purely mental reservation (*restrictio pure mentalis*).[1] Among them are G. de Valencia († 1603). T. Sanchez († 1610), L. Lessius († 1623) and F. Suarez († 1619). The latter regards the purely mental reservation as probably permissible. Abuses of this doctrine were countered by Innocent XI, who in 1679 condemned the proposition as scandalous that it is permissible to confirm a purely mental reservation even by oath.[2]

---

[1] According to Daniel Concina — whose statements however have to be taken with caution — as many as 50 theologians favoured the purely mental reservation in the first half of the 17th century (Theol. Christiana III. 1758, 5, dist. 3, nr. 1; quoted by G. Müller, 1. c. 191, footnote 2).

[2] DS 2126-8.

After the intervention by the Holy See against the aberrations of the morality of reservation, the theory of the purely mental reservation was no longer maintained. However the voices never grew totally silent who wanted to permit exceptions from the prohibition of lying, e.g. C. Cattaneo († 1705), C. Lacroix († 1714), G. Bolgeni († 1811), B. Stattler (†1797) and others.

The number of Catholic theologians who defend the permissibility of false speech in certain situations of emergency has increased considerably in the present century. For the first half of the 20th century Gregor Müller lists more than thirty theologians for this opinion, among them R. Brouillard, A. Dorszynski, E. Genicot, G. Kelly, M. Laros, M. Ledrus, J. Lindworsky, L. Ruland, A. Tanquerey, G. Ubach, A. Vermeersch.[1] Authors of more recent date are A. di Marino,[2] M. Huftier,[3] M. Brunec,[4] F. Connell,[5] C. Curran,[6] W. Molinski[7] and J. Metzinger.[8]

This shows that the absolute of the intrinsic sinfulness of lying is not an undisputed doctrine of Catholic moral theology. Indeed the great number of theologians who defend the possibility of exceptions justifies the conclusion that the contrary opinion is probable as well.

3. *Reasons for the sinfulness of lying*

Lying is objectionable. All theologians agree on this. Also those authors who permit exceptions do so only reluctantly and with great caution. Truthfulness is a high value which must be upheld even if at times it demands sacrifices. Various reasons are put forward in proof of it. They are basically the following:

---

[1] Gregor Müller: Die Wahrhaftigkeitspflicht und die Problematik der Lüge. — Freiburg: Herder, 1962.

[2] A. di Marino: Why is lying forbidden? — Theology Digest 4 (1956), 9-12.

[3] M. Huftier: Le Mensonge. — L'Ami du Clergé 72 (1962), 689-700; 705-716.

[4] M. Brunec: Mendacium intrinsece malum sed non absolute. — Salesianum 26 (1964), 608-685.

[5] Francis J. Connell: More Answers to Today's Moral Problems. — Washington: Catholic University of America Press, 1965, 123f.

[6] Charles E. Curran: A New Look at Christian Morality. — Notre Dame: Fides Publishers, 1968, 236f.

[7] Waldemar Molinski, art. "Truth" in: Sacramentum Mundi VI, 1970, 317.

[8] J. Metzinger: Falschaussage oder Lüge? — Zeitschrift für Kath. Theologie 94 (1972), 311-319.

a) Lying is sinful because it leads the neighbour in error and undermines mutual confidence. It does not only deny the truth to the fellowman. Worse, it gives him wrong information, which must lead him to wrong conclusions whenever it is used. This makes realistic, efficient action impossible. Very often the error misleads the deceived person to actions which are prejudicial to him or to others. The lie therefore destroys a most important fundament of individual security and fruitful work.

In consequence every man considers it as unjust if he is deliberately given wrong informations. It is for this reason that lying undermines mutual confidence, another indispensable good. Confidence is necessary for the healthy development of the person. It is equally necessary for smooth, efficient cooperation. Distrust on the other hand gives rise to aversion and ill-will. In view of these reasons it can justly be said that the lie harms the common good.

b) The lie is furthermore a breach of the promise which is contained in every assertion or statement. Whenever a person makes statements about facts or speaks of his thoughts and convictions, he implicitly gives the assurance that his statements correspond with the facts and truthfully render his thoughts. Because of this implicit promise a person is believed. And it is precisely because of this implicit promise that a person can deceive his neighbour by his lies. Since the breach of promise is a disparaging treatment of the other person, the lie has also been denounced as an offence against the human dignity.

c) A third argument is taken from the nature of speech. The natural meaning of speech, for which this faculty was given to man by God, is the representation of man's thoughts and judgments. Words are signs which by their nature are keyed to give external expression to the contents of the mind. An untruthful statement therefore contradicts the purpose which is inherent in word and speech. It offends against the order demanded by the nature of things.

For Thomas Aquinas[1] and many other Catholic theologians this is the decisive argument which conclusively proves the

---

[1] "Cum enim voces naturaliter sint signa intellectuum, innaturale est et indebitum quod aliquis voce significet id quod non habet in mente. Unde Philosophus dicit in IV Ethic., quod 'mendacium est per se pravum et fugiendum; verum autem est bonum et laudabile.' Unde omne mendacium est peccatum" (II-II, a. 110, a. 3; likewise Scriptum super Sententiis, t. 3, dist. 38, a. 3). The rational proof of Thomas Aquinas for the intrinsic sinfulness of lying limits itself to these few lines.

intrinsic sinfulness of lying. To this argument the other can be reduced which proves the sinfulness of lying from the disorder it carries in man and in the use of his faculties.

Nevertheless lying is not in itself a grievous sin. This is the universal teaching of theologians. The harm usually caused by a lie is not so grave that it would constitute a grave matter, nor is the disorder carried in the faculties of man by the misuse of speech considered to be a grievous one. The lie is a grave sin only if it is gravely detrimental to one's fellowman or causes great dishonour to God. The jocose lie is commonly not considered a sin. Its purpose is not that of serious information but of entertainment only.

The sinfulness of lying admitted, the difficult problem arises of how the truth can be defended against indiscreet inquirers or ruthless intruders who intend to abuse it. All theologians are aware that in these cases the truth cannot simply be given away, but as much as possible must be concealed. Often there is also an obligation in justice or charity to guard secrets. Ordinarily an unwarranted inquirer should not be answered at all, or he may be diverted by a counter-inquiry, or simply be rebuffed. But in many instances silence or a rebuff may betray the very secret they should protect. In consequence quite frequently there is no other way left open except to give an answer which does not reveal the truth.

Many philosophers and Protestant theologians, but also a number of Catholic authors as has been shown, permit the false speech or lie as an ultimate resort. The majority of Catholic theologians however reject this solution for the reason that lying is intrinsically evil. The way out proposed by them is the mental reservation. Both positions require further explanation and discussion in the following.

4. *Mental reservation*

The mental reservation is an equivocal use of the speech. It is also called veiled speech. In order to hide a truth, the speaker chooses words which have a double meaning: one is the usual meaning which the words ordinarily have when used in the conversation; the other is a less usual, though still possible meaning which is less readily perceived by the hearer. In order not to be simply a lie, the veiled speech must always have a discernible, secondary meaning. Some content of the exterior word must correspond to the interior knowledge or judgment of the speaker. If for example somebody is asked: "Were you in a movie yesterday?" and he answers: "Yes, I have seen a movie yesterday", this answer is not unequivocal. He may have seen the movie also in television. Customary usage can likewise give certain words a second meaning, such as in the conventional polite phrase: "The mistress is not at home," meaning "not at home to receive visitors." This is perceptible, broad mental reservation.

Distinguished from the broad is the strict or purely mental reservation. The latter is had when the actual meaning of the utterance can in no way be inferred from the words used or from the external circumstances. Thus it is a strict mental reservation if a thief asserts: "I have not stolen" and mentally adds the specification "today". This manner of speaking is not different from a lie.

For the legitimate use of the broad mental reservation two conditions must be fulfilled, first there must be a sufficiently good reason for permitting the deception of the hearer, and second, the hearer should have no right to the information which he seeks. Consequently mental reservation is not permitted when one is legitimately questioned in court or by a superior, when one enters into just onerous contracts, or when one is obliged in charity or justice to inform another regarding an error which may beset him.

A special problem is the question whether a broad mental reservation may be confirmed under oath for a proportionately grave reason. Very many moralists reply in the affirmative, since in itself the reservation is permissible. However this would require a very serious reason.

Common instances of broad mental reservation are the following: Ordinarily one may respond to unauthorized questions regarding professional secrets: "I do not know anything about it," with the mental reservation "that I am allowed to communicate to others." This applies in a special way to confessional matters. To an unjust demand in the courts one may answer: "I know nothing about it." The reservation "which I could be rightly interrogated about" is perceptible through the situation of illegality. According to many authors an accused criminal may plead "not guilty" in the courts, since this is a conventional way of declining information to the judge.[1] Nevertheless it seems

---

[1] Cf. Jone, 1963, nr. 370.

hard to maintain that this latter reservation should still agree with the ideal of Christian truthfulness.

5. *Concealment of truth through false speech*

The theory of mental reservation offers some help in the difficult situations where the truth must be concealed. But it is not without limitations and drawbacks. It is often not a safe means to conceal the truth, especially if the inquirer is intelligent. People who have little command of the language will frequently not find the appropriate reservation and be handicapped in its use. And finally the difference between mental reservation and false speech often seems actually not so great if it comes to the concrete applications, and looks to many like hairsplitting.

Hence time and again also Catholic theologians felt that the permission of false speech is a solution which does greater justice to the situations of emergency where the truth must be concealed and its abuse be prevented. The reasons advanced for this view are the following:

a) Truthfulness in speech is an important value, but it is not the only and not the highest value. There are other values which are still higher. A person has the right and, if need be, even the duty to sacrifice the good of truthfulness in order to protect the higher value. Such higher values are in principle the same as those which justify self-defence by violent resistance, namely, protection of innocent life, integrity of one's members, bodily integrity in attempts of rape, temporal goods of great value, national security, and in addition defence of important secrets. At all times the values defended must be more valuable and more urgent than those injured by the misleading speech.

Every person of reasonable mind who might happen to be the victim of a lie in such a situation will agree with this proceeding. Hence the usual evil consequence of the lie will not come about, the poisoning of mutual confidence. Moreover the damage caused to the person deceived in such conditions is usually not great, if any damage is caused at all. If however significant damage is caused, then the value which is the reason for the deception must be so high that the person deceived could not reasonably object against the action. One will also have to demand that at least the person who has been deceived without any fault on his part must be clarified about the true state of affairs after the threat has ceased and be indemnified if he has suffered harm, to the extent that the one and the other is possible.

b)   A second argument bases itself on the consideration that the right of the inquirer to know the truth is not absolute. The right to know the truth is limited by the right of a person to protection against unwarranted interference in his private, personal sphere and to defence against ill usage or abuse of the truth. Yet the right and not seldom even the duty to withhold the truth can in many instances not be safeguarded without the right to dismiss an importune or malevolent inquirer by a false speech or lie. Absolute proscription of the false speech leaves a person without sufficient means to defend his right to guard certain truths against interference by others and to defend still higher values against unjust attack.

Since however the right to the truth is itself an important privilege of every human being, it is unjust to deny it lightly to another person. The right to the truth must be presumed until the opposite is established with sufficient certainty. And even where the inquirer's right to the truth can rightly be contested, a false speech is only then justified when no other, less drastic means is available, e.g. silence, evasiveness or equivocal answers.

It is also possible that a person voluntarily renounces his right to the truth or that such a renunciation can be presupposed. Examples for this are the jocose lie or the sick person who might suffer serious harm if a certain truth were revealed to him as long as he is in a critical condition.

c)   The two preceding arguments may seem convincing to many. But so far most of the Catholic theologians do not consider them as conclusive. The reason is that these arguments do not refute the contrary arguments which are considered proof for the intrinsic sinfulness of lying. They only show that false speech in a situation of emergency does not necessarily undermine mutual confidence. But the arguments that every lie is a breach of promise and above all that it contradicts the nature of speech are not disproved. Hence the use of the lie in defence of a good which is supposed to be greater than the good of truthfulness is nevertheless the use of an evil means for a good end. And this is inadmissible.

In order to give an answer to this difficulty it is necessary to examine once more the nature of speech. The sciences of language can be of help in this. According to them the purpose of language is not only manifestation of a person's thought and information about facts. Language has a variety of functions.

593 Truth, Fidelity and Honour

Manifestation and information are two of them. There are still others, and among them the function of exercising influence on others is of special importance in the context here. Such influence is carried out by requests, questions, exhortations, threats, commands, etc. This function does not primarily and not necessarily have the purpose of information. Its primary purpose is to influence to a certain mode of action.[1] Thus, e.g., the purpose of a rhetoric question is not communication (the speaker does not intend to communicate a lack of knowledge), but to stir the hearer to reflection.

Applied to the problem of false speech, this permits the following conclusion. Even if the lie does not fulfill the functions of manifestation and information, it nevertheless fulfills the function of exercising influence. The lie wants to influence the hearer to desist from a certain way of action or also to perform an action which he otherwise would not perform. Accordingly the lie is not a use of the language for a purpose which is totally alien to it. This refutes the argument from the nature of speech which reasons that the lie absolutely contradicts the purpose of language.

d) As to the objection that every lie contains a breach of promise, it can indeed justly be pointed out that in the false speech the influence upon the other is brought about by statements which have the appearance of informations or manifestations. And it is the characteristic of these forms of speech that they implicitly contain the promise that the external statement agrees with the speakers internal knowledge or thought. This promise is not kept in the false speech. Hence, even though in the lie the language is used for a function which is not altogether alien to it, the lie is not a neutral means of influencing others. It operates with methods which are objectionable. The upright person has to abide by his promises and cannot break them at will.

Nevertheless promises do not bind unconditionally. They permit of exceptions, as is the common teaching of theologians. According to the principles of moral theology a promise ceases, either if its fulfillment should prove to be very harmful, immoral or impossible; or if the recipient of the promise voluntarily

---

[1] Cf. F. Kainz: Psychologie der Sprache, vol. 1: Grundlagen der allgemeinen Sprachpsychologie. — Stuttgart: F. Enke, 1954. Robert T. Harris and James L. Jarrett: Language and Informal Logic. — New York: Longmans, Green and Co., 1956, 158-165. John L. Austin: How To Do Things With Words. — New York: Oxford University Press, 1965.

renounces it or if such a renunciation can be presupposed; or if the preconditions upon which the promise was based underwent an essential change which was not foreseen. If one applies these principles to the promise of truthfulness of speech, one can draw the following conclusion: A person can be excused from the promise to truthfulness of speech if its fulfillment should prove to be very harmful or have immoral consequences; or if the recipient voluntarily renounces his right to the truth or if this can be presupposed. But here again it holds that the harm prevented by the lie must be greater than the harm which is caused by it. If this however is verified, a false speech would be justified.

The preceding reflections have repeatedly shown that truthfulness ultimately is faithfulness to a promise. This agrees with the understanding of Holy Scripture, for which truthfulness is closely related to faithfulness and is an expression of it. Truthfulness therefore is understood best in the light of the virtue of faithfulness.

IV.   The oath

Since man and society are often in need of the truth, and since the truth is all too frequently endangered by lies, men seek for a means to assure the truth. This assurance is especially sought in the oath. The oath calls God to witness for the truth of an assertion or the sincerity of a promise. It is accordingly divided in an assertory and a promissory oath.

Holy Scriptures[1] of the Old Testament contain many examples of oath taking. Even Yahweh swears by his own name (Gen 22:16; Ex 32:13; Jer 11:5). Naturally the only oath permitted is one sworn by Yahweh (Deut 6:13; 10:20). To swear by any other god is idolatry (Jer 5:7; 12:16; Amos 8:14; Zeph 1:4f). Whoever swears falsely or frivolously offends against God. "You shall not swear by my name falsely, and so profane the name of your God" (Lev 19:12; cf. Ps 24:4f; Sir 23:9-11). Divine punishment befalls the person who commits perjury (Num 5:21; 1 Kings 8:31f).

The attitude of the New Testament is more reserved. In the Sermon on the Mount Jesus even seems to forbid the taking of an oath. "Do not swear at all. . . Let what you say be simply 'Yes' or 'No'; anything more than this comes from evil"

---

[1] Cf. Karl Hermann Schelkle: Theology of the New Testament, vol. 3: Morality. — Collegeville, Minn.: Liturgical Press, 1973, 280-286.

(Mt 5:34.37; also Jas 5:12). The disciple's word should be so reliable that no oath is required to confirm it. Here as in many other instances Christ projects an ideal which should be aimed at. He challenges to a greater and more radical perfection. But these challenges are not to be taken after the manner of laws in the strict sense. (See the expositions on the style and literary character of Jesus' teaching in the first volume of this ethics.) That this is true of the oath can be seen from other passages of the New Testament.

Matthew 23:16-22 does not condemn the oath in principle; it only criticizes its misuse. Repeatedly and unhesitatingly the New Testament speaks of the oath with which God promised his mercy to the fathers (Lk 1:73; Acts 2:30; Heb 6:13-18; 7:20f). Paul, although he never formulates an express oath, frequently makes use of protestations similar to an oath (Rom 1:9; 2 Cor 1:18; Gal 1:20; 1 Thess 2:5.10). Nor is the use of an oath offensive to the Apocalypse. There an angel appears and swears a solemn oath by the eternal, living God that the final redemption is certain and close at hand (Rev 10:6). Since then the condemnation of the oath in the New Testament is not to be understood as an absolute rejection, Churches of every confession have at all times felt justified to allow the taking of an oath for sufficient reasons in the present, imperfect condition of the world.

For the *validity of an oath* it is required that the formula is appropriate and the intention of taking an oath is had. Sufficient formulae are: "I swear by God," "God is my witness," "So help me God," "I swear by the cross." Doubtful formulae are: "God knows," "I speak in the sight of God," "As God lives." In case of doubtful expressions an oath is taken if the person using them intends to swear; in doubt as to whether the intention was had or not, it is presumed that no oath was taken. Certainly insufficient are formulae which do not invoke God, such as "Upon my honour," "In honour and conscience," "As true as I live." Statutory declarations in lieu of oath are forceful and explicit attestations of one's truthfulness, but they are not oaths in the strict sense.

An oath taken without at least a virtual intention is not valid, e.g. the oath of a person who is drunk. An oath is called fictitious if a person deliberately swears without intention, while the bystanders believe that such intention exists. Even though this oath is not valid, it is nevertheless an abuse of God's name and a grave sin to confirm a lie by it. A fictitious, promissory oath would bind one to make good any loss accruing to another who entered into a contract in reliance on such an oath.

An oath extorted by fraud, violence or made under the pressure of grave fear has no binding force and is declared ipso iure void by the new code of canon law (CIC 1200 § 2).

For the *lawfulness of an oath* three things are required: truth, moral lawfulness, and sufficient reason. First, the one who swears must be convinced of the truth of his assertion or have the firm purpose to keep his promise. This excludes lying and reasonable doubt, but not invincible error or legitimate mental restriction. It is perjury and gravely sinful to invoke God as witness to a falsehood. It is likewise gravely sinful to swear to something as true which one seriously doubts. Second, the assertion or promise must be morally lawful. It is venially sinful if God is invoked to confirm sinful boasting or detraction. It would be seriously sinful, according to some authors, if the detraction were serious. To promise something evil under oath is gravely sinful, at least if the matter promised is gravely sinful. Third, the oath should be taken for a sufficient cause, since this is required by the reverence for God's name. Absence of this condition will ordinarily be a venial sin.

The *obligation of a promissory oath* is grave or light according as the object promised is grave or light. No obligation arises from an oath to do something that is forbidden or useless. The interpretation of a promissory oath depends chiefly on the intention of the person swearing. Otherwise the oath is to be interpreted strictly according to the law. If the oath is sworn with fraud, it is to be interpreted according to the intention of him in whose favour it is taken (CIC 1204).

The oath of allegiance or the oath of office means that one intends to be subject to the law of the land, fulfill his office according to the prescriptions of the law, and not to undertake anything contrary to rightful authority; but it does not mean that one thereby binds himself under oath to observe every civil law. The oath does not extend to such laws as are contrary to divine or ecclesiastical right.[1]

A promissory oath ceases to bind, if remitted by the promisee; if the object of the promise has substantially changed; if the object has become sinful or altogether indifferent, or an obstacle to a greater good; if the motive ceases to exist; if an essential condition under which the oath was pledged lapses; or

---

[1] Cf. Jone, 1963, nr. 188.

finally by legitimate suspension, dispensation or commutation. Whoever has the faculties to suspend, commute or dispense from a vow possesses the same power regarding the promissory oath. The dispensation must however not involve an injury to the acquired rights of others (CIC 1203).

B. Fidelity

I. Nature and foundation of fidelity

Fidelity is that virtue by which a person remains true to his conviction, word and promise. In a special way it obliges to fulfill the promises which a person explicitly or implicitly has made. Truthfulness and fidelity are closely related concepts in Holy Scripture, as has been shown. Truthful is the man who is faithful to God and to his neighbour. The two virtues are indeed cognate. Truthfulness of speech obliges a person to keep harmony between his words and thoughts. Faithfulness bids him to keep his deeds in harmony with his words. The reflections on truthfulness in conduct in the preceding section deal with this faithfulness. They may be recalled here.

Man's faithfulness towards God is a fundamental moral duty. All that man has received from the loving bounty of God constantly obliges him to loyal service of the Lord. The redemptive grace bestowed upon man by the salvific work of Christ is a further reason which calls man to faithful commitment to God, now in the particular form of the fellowship of Christ.

Faithfulness to God necessarily includes and demands faithfulness to men. The more intimate a personal relation, the more must it be characterized by fidelity, such as filial and parental fidelity, conjugal fidelity, fidelity in friendship. The Church values especially high the faithfulness to the promises of the marriage bond, the priestly office and the vows of the religious life.

The chief characteristic of fidelity is the element of stability and reliability in a person's actions. Fidelity in relation to others is an essential foundation of mutual trust and personal and social security. These are important preconditions for the happiness of life, the fruitfulness of common work and the safe development of the individual as well as the society. Also in this regard fidelity resembles truthfulness. Infidelity on the other hand undermines mutual trust, destroys solidarity and rends the bonds which assure mutual assistance and good will.

II. The promise

Fidelity proves itself most especially in the fulfillment of the promise a person has made. We distinguish between the mere resolve or resolution, the simple promise, and the contract of promise. The resolution is an express intention, not a real promise. Thus we may tell a person that we intend to visit him at Christmas time. This intention is not the basis of an obligation in fidelity towards the other. At best it is an obligation of fidelity towards oneself not to change the resolve without sound reason, if the intention was reasonable.

The simple promise is a gratuitous offer whereby a person binds himself to do something for the promisee. If accepted, it is the basis of an obligation in fidelity. Ordinarily the obligation to fulfill the promise is not a grave one. For in unilateral promises usually neither the promisor intends to bind himself gravely nor is the expectation of the promisee so great that it gives rise to a grave obligation. But if the promisor should give a firm assurance in a serious matter and the promisee, in reliance on this promise, undertakes a course of action which will be detrimental to him if the promise is not fulfilled, the obligation would be grave. Thus if the father of a family is given the firm assurance of a better job and in view of this terminates his former one, it would be a grave injustice not to keep the promise.

A contract of promise is had if a strict right to the matter promised is transferred to the promisee. In order to be effective, the offer must be accepted and the acceptance manifested to the promisor. It is the basis of an obligation in justice. A contract of promise is to be assumed not only in case of an express intention, but also if the circumstances are such that they argue for a real agreement. Thus the circumstances speak for a contract of promise if the promise is made in recompense for services rendered or if it is mutual. In order to prevent uncertainties, the law demands legal or notarial certification for legally binding promises, e.g. for the promise of a donation.

In doubt whether a contract of promise was had or only a simple promise, or whether merely a resolution was formed, the lesser obligation is to be presumed. If by sinful neglect to keep a promise one is the cause of loss to the promisee, even in the case of a simple promise, he is obliged to repair such damage insofar as he foresaw this at least indistinctly. Secret compensation may be resorted to in the case of non-fulfillment of a promise only in the event that the promise was made as a remuneration for rendering a special service.

A promise is invalid if the consent was imperfect, e.g. if made in a state of intoxication, or if it was obtained by fraud or extorted by grave and unjust fear, suppose the fear was inflicted in order to force the promise.

The obligation of a promise ceases (1) if the recipient of the promise voluntarily renounces it or if the renunciation can justly be presumed; (2) if the matter promised becomes impossible (e.g. because of impoverishment or sickness), harmful, immoral or useless; (3) if the conditions under which the promise was made undergo a substantial change which was not foreseen or if circumstances become known in which the promisor would never have made the promise; (4) by the death of either party. However a real promise, obliging in justice, passes on to the heirs, for example the promise of a legacy by a master to his servant for unpaid services. Likewise the obligation of a promise does not cease upon the death of the promisee if it was made not primarily as a favour to him, but principally for the sake of his family.

C. The secret

1. *Nature and foundation of the secret*

A secret is a hidden fact which may not be divulged. The hidden fact may be a defect or fault, e.g. the illegitimacy of a child or a financial embarrassment, or a good of high value which needs protection against abuse, e.g. an invention or secrets of national defence.

Three kinds of secrets are distinguished, the natural, the promised, and the entrusted secret. The natural secret is so called because its obligation arises immediately from natural law. No convention or agreement is required to make it binding. Fraternal concern and the nature of human fellowship demand secrecy. It includes all hidden facts whose revelation by the very nature of the case would injure or displease another.

A promised secret is one which one has promised to keep, after having received the knowledge thereof, even though apart from the promise there may be no obligation to secrecy. If the promise concerns a secret which at the same time is a natural secret, the obligation to secrecy is twofold, arising from charity or justice and from fidelity to the promise. A promise of secrecy in matters which are useless or unlawful does not bind.

An entrusted or committed secret is a secret the knowledge of which one obtains only upon the condition that one will keep it secret. Secrecy is assured before receiving the knowledge of the secret. The agreement may be explicit or implicit. To the latter class belongs the professional secret, to which one is obliged in virtue of one's profession, e.g. as a superior, magistrate, pastor, physician, lawyer, midwife, etc. The professional secret is the most binding of all. The strictest and most sacred secret is the confessional secret of the priestly office.

Secrecy is a stern imperative, arising from harsh and evil realities. We must always reckon with our own frailty and with that of others. Above all we must reckon with the war between good and evil in the world. Lack of discretion can cause very serious harm to ourselves, our neighbour and the various communities in which we live.

Reverence for values of a very personal, intimate and sacred nature likewise demands that they should be protected by discretion. In this sense Christ warns: "Do not give dogs what is holy; and do not throw your pearls before swine" (Mt 7:6). Reverence for truth "must caution us against manifesting it without reason where there is no preparation or disposition to receive or accept it fruitfully, where the right response to it will certainly not be given, or where we cannot actually bear witness to it."[1] In the most intimate and personal concerns of our life we can confide only in men who are discreetly silent. The same reverence forbids us to pry into the intimate life of our neighbour.

2.   *Revelation of secrets*

The great importance of secrecy for the good of the individual and the welfare of the community forbids to reveal secrets unless a sufficient reason is had for doing so. The more important the secret, the graver the reason must be.

Disclosure of a natural secret without sufficient reason is a grave or light offence against charity or justice according as another is seriously or lightly injured by such revelation. A fortiori it is a grave sin to violate a professional secret, unless the matter is trifling. If one has merely promised secrecy in instances where there is no natural or professional secret, such disclosure is usually no more than a venial sin.

---

[1] Häring III, 1966, 567.

The damage done by violation of the professional secret must always be repaired in justice. Other violations of secrecy as a rule oblige to restitution in charity, unless justice has also been violated by use of unjust means.

The obligation to keep a secret ceases (1) if the one concerned reasonably permits its disclosure; (2) if the matter has ceased to be secret because of disclosure by others; (3) if a sufficient reason justifies its revelation. A sufficient reason for revealing a natural secret is the avoidance of a relatively great inconvenience to oneself or a third, innocent party or the common good. A sufficient reason to reveal a promised secret which is not at the same time a natural or professional secret is any disproportionately great inconvenience. If a superior or a judge have a right to interrogate, the natural as well as the promised secret must be revealed. But the right to it must be certain.

The entrusted secret may not be divulged, not even to a superior, except for one of the following reasons: (a) in order to avert a grave danger to the common good. (b) in order to avert serious harm from a third, innocent party, the harm being unjustly caused by the person who entrusted the secret. For no entrusted secret can prevail against the right of the innocent person to be defended against unjust aggression. Therefore if a man who is sexually diseased cannot be dissuaded from marrying by his physician, the latter may reveal the matter to the bride. One may however not violate professional secrecy in order to testify against a criminal to save an innocent person from judicial condemnation, unless the criminal is the cause of the condemnation.[1] (c) in order to avert serious evil from him who has committed the secret, e.g. if he revealed the intention to commit suicide. (d) in order to avert a grave danger from him to whom the secret has been entrusted. The common good may however not be imperilled to avert personal danger.

It is permissible to discuss a secret matter with a prudent counsellor who will keep the secret, unless the person who entrusted the secret reasonably objects to it. At all times great caution must be used that public trust in professional secrecy and in the profession itself be not undermined, to the detriment of the common good.

3. *Probing into secrets*

It is unlawful and even punishable to pry into the secrets of

---

[1] Cf. Jone, 1963, nr. 384.

602   *Christian Ethics*

others. Therefore one may not acquire the knowledge of a hidden fact, e.g. an invention, a medical record or the private opinions of a person, by means of burglary, eavesdropping, opening of letters, secret taping of conversations, etc. Ordinarily this is a grave offence, unless the matter is trifling and no exploitation of the knowledge is sought.

Nevertheless for very serious reasons it may be permitted, and at times even required, to probe into the secrets of others, as long as the means employed are not unjust. Special questions are raised by the epistolary secret. Some of the norms elaborated for it are also applicable to the secret taping of conversations.

In general it is a violation of justice to read the letters of others without authorization. Such authorization exists if either the sender or the addressee give the permission to it. Parents have the right to read the letters of their children who are still under parental authority. Likewise educators have the right to read the letters of their charges, unless they contain family secrets or matters of conscience. In this case the reading of the letter must be discontinued. Custom at times gives certain rights to spouses or also to close relatives.

The letters of subjects in religious communities may be opened and read by superiors, if the rules permit this to be done, but not if the letters are written to higher superiors or contain matters of conscience.

Apart from this it is only lawful to read letters of others if this is necessary to avert grave damage to the common welfare, one's neighbour or oneself. The same reason would also justify the secret taping of a conversation. Civil authorities may open letters if this is necessary to protect the common welfare, e.g. in order to uncover or prevent crimes or the betrayal of state secrets. Naturally the officials may make use of the information only to the extent that it is required by the common good. As to the other contents of the letters, officials are bound by the professional secret. Also an individual person may be allowed to read another's letters if he has a right to assume that they contain matters which are seriously unjust and harmful to him. Thus a spouse may open the partner's letters in order to defend himself or the family against grave injustice and harm.

It is not unlawful to read letters that someone has discarded into some public litter bin. However where letters have been torn up into small fragments and thrown away in some open place, it will usually be an offence against charity to piece them together and read them. Letters that have been lost may not be read.

D.　The moral good of honour[1]

I.　Nature and foundation of honour

The good of honour consists in the acknowledgement of a person's value, not only by internal affirmation but also by external marks of respect. In a wider sense honour signifies a person's self-respect by which he is faithful to his convictions, word, and in general to his better self. This meaning is had if a person is characterized as "a man of honour".

The noblest form of honour is the moral honour. It adjudges moral probity to a person and respects it. Besides it, still other more restricted forms of honour exist, such as the scientific, civic or political honour of a person.

The basis of honour is the perfection, goodness and holiness which a person possesses. Since the highest perfection in every regard is found in God, the absolutely highest honour is due to him. God's holiness claims every man's unreserved worship and total dedication.

All creatures are radiations of God's perfection and beauty. As creations from God's hand they all merit reverence to a greater or lesser degree, depending on the values which they represent. The honour shown to them is ultimately an honour shown to God himself, their Creator.

The highest honour in the material creation is due to man, because he is the image of God. The more the image of God is realized in a person and the more he is a child of God, the greater honour is due to him. For this reason the saints deserve special honour, because they are especially close to God. Next to them are all the true followers of Christ who strive to live a holy life. The sincere dedication of a man to God merits greater honour than the natural qualities of beauty, intelligence, physical strength or the material wealth which he may possess. Nevertheless honour is also due to the person who has developed his natural talents and who has made good use

---

[1] The positive aspects of the moral good of honour have received little attention in the traditional handbooks. They limit themselves to the offences against honour. Moral value and responsible care for honour have been developed by Mausbach/Ermecke: Katholische Moraltheologie. vol. 3, 1961, 568-579, and B. Häring: The Law of Christ, vol. 3, 1966, 605-618.

of them, whether in the sciences or in economics, in the crafts or arts, etc.

Professions, religious communities, nations, etc. likewise have their honour and can claim it according to the measure in which they fulfill the tasks assigned to them and live up to their calling by God. Conversely every profession, community and nation must also look to its honour and endeavour to keep itself worthy of it.

Inasmuch as a man cannot renounce his being and his intrinsic value, he can also not renounce his honour. At times he may be permitted to relinquish his external honour, but he always retains his intrinsic honour and the external right to it. If honour is due to an office, it is not up to an individual to renounce it. Respect for another's honour is a duty of justice. Violation of another person's honour is accordingly violation of another's rights. It is unjust damage in the order of spiritual goods.

Honour is an important social good. The community whose members do not live in mutual respect lacks social coherence and is unable to call forth the best efforts of its members. Each individual needs honour in order to thrive in the community and to work fruitfully in it.

Honour is also of great pedagogical importance. Acknowledgement and respect for the good a man does or has achieved constitute an indispensable moral encouragement for him. Education may never disregard the sound sense of honour. Even where it makes use of reproach and punishment, it must ultimately invoke a person's self-esteem and so challenge him to better achievements. The person who is not honoured, who encounters nothing but indifference or disdain, all too readily is tempted to act in a corresponding way.

II. Principal duties of honour

1. *Regard for one's own honour*

According to the teaching of Holy Scripture the good name is a high good, among the temporal goods the highest. "A good name is to be chosen rather than great riches" (Prov 22:1). "Have regard for your name, since it will remain for you longer than a thousand great stores of gold" (Sir 41:12).

The good repute of the Christians promotes the cause of the gospel. "Give no offence to Jews or to Greeks or to the church of God, just as I try to please all men in everything I do, not seeking my own advantage, but that of many, that they may be saved" (1 Cor 10:32f). In a like manner their good example contributes to the glory of God. "Let your light so shine before men, that they may see your good works and give glory to your Father who is in heaven" (Mt 5:16).

Therefore the Christian, and every man who loves God, must care for his good name. "Brethren, whatever is true, whatever is honourable, whatever is just, whatever is pure, whatever is lovely, whatever is gracious, if there is any excellence, if there is anything worthy of praise, think about these things" (Phil 4:8). St. Paul is anxious to have a clear conscience towards God and towards men. He considers this his honour (Acts 24:16; 2 Cor 1:12). And he does not hesitate to defend it against those who downgrade it to the detriment of the good cause (1 Cor 9; 2 Cor 11f).

On the other hand the praise of men must not be sought for its own sake. If a person's good deeds are merely motivated by the desire for external honour, while the soul of genuine love for God and neighbour is lacking, no virtue is had at all. This is the pharisaical attitude so harshly condemned by Christ. "Beware of practising your piety before men in order to be seen by them; for then you will have no reward from your Father who is in heaven" (Mt 6:1; cf. Gal 1:10).

Responsible care for one's honour is lawful and often even an obligation. It is part of the well-ordered love of self. Very often it is also a duty towards those for whose moral and spiritual good a person is responsible. The obligation to care for one's honour is especially grave for parents, educators, priests, superiors and officials. Their effectiveness depends in a great measure on the good repute they enjoy. Regard for one's honour as a Christian is also an apostolic and missionary concern.

The duty to preserve one's honour does not imply that one must insist on it in petty ways. Minor defaults in respect which do not actually endanger one's honour should ordinarily be ignored. However a person has the right and often the duty to defend himself against unjust attacks which injure his honour seriously. In extreme cases he may be justified to take refuge to legal action in the courts in order to protect his good name. This holds above all if a person represents a community. The person unjustly attacked may resort to all lawful means in order to prove the charges unfounded and their author unworthy of credence.

Yet also in defending his rightful honour a person may not transgress the bounds of just self-defence and must limit himself to what is necessary and sufficient to repudiate the defamation. Under no circumstances is it permissible to use mendacious or sordid methods to defend oneself. Evidently the duel is in no way an acceptable means to restore a person's honour. Besides violating a person's duties towards his life and that of his neighbour, it is completely unsuited to guarantee justice to the offended party.

The proper sense of honour must forbid a person to seek recognition for pretended virtues which he does not really have, or for merits which are not his. Unmerited honour ought to be a source of shame rather than of joy. To seek honour excessively is the sin of inordinate ambition. If personal honour is pursued under serious disregard of the respect due to God, the rights of others and the good of the community, it is a grave sin. Offences in the opposite direction are indifference to one's honour and scorn for the opinion of others. Sins against due self-esteem are furthermore false humility, depreciation of the gifts received from God and self-disparagement. They are as much opposed to truthfulness as self-exaltation.

2. *Respect for one's neighbour*

Justice demands that the honour of others be respected. "Honour to whom honour is due" (Rom 13:7). Love urges that it also be promoted positively. "Love one another with brotherly affection; outdo one another in showing honour" (Rom 12:10). The man of a noble heart is generous in his praise. He does not wait until he receive honour himself, but readily and liberally bestows it upon others.

Special honour is due to those in office, since they represent the community and minister to its good. Therefore every lawful wordly authority is to be respected (Rom 13:7; 1 Pet 2:17). Even more worthy of respect are those in spiritual authority, most of all the bishops and priests (cf. Heb 13:17; 1 Pet 5:5). Respect for parents is enjoined by the fourth commandment of the decalogue and repeatedly stressed by Holy Scriptures (Ex 20: 12; Deut 27:16; Mt 15:4; 19:19). Old people are likewise worthy of special honour, because of their life experience and the toils with which they have served the younger generations (Lev 19:32; Prov 16:31; 1 Tim 5:1f).

Esteem for others can be manifested in various ways: by

reverential encounter in politeness, by praise and recognition of the neighbour when he is present, by good report and commendation of the absent. "The marks of honour must be evident from our entire conduct towards our neighbour. Even the giving of alms to the poor must reflect the esteem and honour which the poor man deserves as a brother in Christ."[1]

No man may be disregarded because of natural defects or poverty. The blind and crippled deserve as much honour as the healthy and strong, the poor as much as the rich, as long as they live an upright life. St. James strongly reproaches his Christians because they pay much attention to the rich in their assemblies, but dishonour the poor who receive the last places (Jas 2:2-6). Moral defects of course must diminish the esteem for the other. But everybody must be mindful of his own limitations. Weaknesses and faults often coexist with positive qualities which still merit respect and honour.

Since the honour shown to superiors is always also an expression of honour for the community which they represent, one may not simply refuse respect to the less worthy representatives of an office. However it is obvious that the superior who is dedicated to his duties and leads an honest life is worthy of greater respect than the one who does not live up to his obligations.

Not only the individual has a right to his good name, but also communities enjoy this right, e.g. religious orders, Church communities, nations, and every organized body of men. Even the dead retain their right to the good esteem of posterity, for every man wishes to live in the grateful memory of mankind.

III. Offences against the honour of others

More than in many other areas of the moral life a person can offend in the realm of honour by evil thoughts against his neighbour. Uncharitable thoughts are frequent sins, which are often not much attended to. Especially the rash judgment offends against the honour of the neighbour. Another person is judged guilty of some moral defect for no valid reasons. To this kind of judgment the warning of Christ applies: "Judge not, that you be not judged" (Mt 7:1). The neighbour has the right to our good esteem if he has merited it and is not guilty of an offence. It is an injustice to deny this esteem to him even merely in thoughts.

---

[1] Häring III, 1966, 609.

Rash judgment is a serious sin if the matter concerned is grave and if the judgment is made with full awareness that the reasons are not sufficient. Often however this awareness is lacking. Suspicions and doubts which are not determinate judgments are usually not grave sins.

To exercise caution in practical life is not sinful. Often it is a demand of prudence. The cautious man does not think evil of his neighbour, but merely reckons with the possibility that he may be deceived. Thus parents and educators have the obligation to watch prudently over their charges. That does not mean that they have to be distrustful, certainly not. But they must reckon with the reality of human weakness and prudently check on their children and charges in order to protect them from evil.

External sins against another's honour are contumely, calumny and detraction. They demand some closer attention.

1. *Contumely*

Contumely is had if another person is unjustly dishonoured in his presence. The contempt may be expressed in words, signs or omissions. It is not necessary that the person be actually present. He can also be dishonoured by contumelious treatment of his representative, picture, etc., suppose it is done in a way that it will come to his knowledge. To withhold honour that is due is negative contumely; positive contumely is the infliction of dishonour by word, writing or deed.

Dishonour deprives a man of what is due to him, and that is the sin of injustice. Serious contumely is a grave sin. Men generally value the good of honour even more highly than material goods. Christ's judgment on contumely is severe. "Whoever insults his brother shall be liable to the council, and whoever says, 'You fool!' shall be liable to the hell of fire" (Mt 5:22). Paul lists revilers among those who will not inherit the kingdom of God (1 Cor 6:10).

The gravity of the sin depends on the dignity of the person who is dishonoured and on the character of the words, actions and omissions by which the disrespect is expressed. Also common estimation must be taken into consideration. Some expressions which may be inoffensive and signs of familiarity among the less educated, may be a serious affront among the cultured people. The coarse language of certain rough characters is often not felt to be offensive, while the same words in the mouth of a person of a more serious nature may be a grave insult.

Reparation for an insult must be public or private according as the insult itself was public or private. It can be made either personally or by intermediary. The regrets may also be sent by letter if the guilty party cannot very well appear before the one offended. Reparation has to be made in a manner which unequivocally expresses regret and esteem for the injured person. Towards superiors reparation should be made by asking pardon, at least if the insult was serious. Towards equals or inferiors it generally suffices to show special signs of esteem and good will. But at times it might be necessary to ask for forgiveness for a grave insult even from an equal.

The obligation to reparation ceases if the injured person forgives the offence by saying or showing that he does not demand an apology or if such renunciation can reasonably be presumed; if he has taken revenge or if the insult was mutual and equally grave on both sides; if the offender has been punished by a judicial action; if the offence has been buried and forgotten so that it is more prudent not to revive the memory of it or if an excuse has become otherwise impossible.

2. *Detraction and calumny*

Detraction is the unjust violation of the good esteem of another by making known some true but hidden faults of his. Calumny is the imputation of false defects to another with the knowledge that they are false. A common form of calumny is a mixture of truth and falsehood. Talebearing is a similar offence. It consists in reporting to a person something unfavourable said of him by another. The reason often is the intention to sow the seeds of discord with the hope to profit therefrom in some way.

Defamation can also be committed in other ways than by plain words. Sinister interpretation which darkens the motives of the good actions of another, malicious silence, ambiguous insinuations, ironical praise, belittlement of the good done, they all are different forms of slander.

There is however no injury to reputation and hence no detraction if the faults mentioned are already publicly known or will soon be generally known. An offence publicly known in a closed community, e.g. a family group, boarding-school, seminary, convent, may not be reported to outsiders. A crime publicly known in one place but not known in another, or a fault formerly public but now forgotten, may not be revealed or brought to light again if he who was guilty has atoned for it and attempts to live a better life.

a) Sinfulness of defamation

A slanderous tongue is an abomination to Holy Scripture. Already the earliest books of the Bible bid: "You shall not go up and down as a slanderer among your people" (Lev 19:16). Whisperers and slanderers are cursed, because they have destroyed the peace of many. The virtuous man makes a door and a bolt for his mouth lest he err with his tongue (Sir 28: 13-26; Ps 101:5). Paul lists the gossips and slanderers among the evildoers who have strayed from God (Rom 1:29f; 2 Tim 3:3). "Do not speak evil against one another, brethren. . . Who are you that you judge your neighbour?" (Jas 4:11f; cf. Mt 7:1f).

It is obvious that calumny is a sin against justice and truth, since it deceitfully imputes faults to a man which he has not committed. The right to a true reputation is an unconditional and universal right. Truth and justice demand that one should not represent as evil a person who is really good.

Yet also detraction offends against justice and love, even though the faults reported are real. Civil law indeed does not punish slander if the slanderer can prove that his statements are true. But this does not make arbitrary defamation morally lawful. The good name is a social good which is based on the external conduct of a person. It may not lightly be prejudiced by the revelation of hidden faults, if the person has done nothing in public to forfeit it and if its possession by him is not harmful to anyone. Apart from the personal harm caused to the person detracted, this would also adversely affect the common good, because it will hamper him in his official business and social relations.

In a special way injustice is done by detraction if the fault in question is only an exceptional mistake or occasional weakness. The divulgation of defects usually tends to lead to their generalization and to attribute them to a person as characteristics. This exaggeration not only offends against justice but also against truth. Quite in general detraction is often accompanied by exaggerations. A frequent negative effect on its victims is the temptation to slacken in their moral striving and to abandon it, since they are not valued highly by the common opinion anyway.

Defamation is a more grievous sin than theft, since a good name is better than wealth. Its gravity depends on the foreseeable damage to a person's honour, the affliction caused to the person defamed, the detriment to his professional efficiency and the possible material loss (e.g. loss of position). The damage to a person's honour will usually be the greater the more serious the matter revealed, the more esteemed the position and office of the detractor and the detracted, and the greater the number of persons who hear the defamation. To reveal a fault to one person who will certainly not carry it further does not exceed a venial sin, unless there is a special reason why he who is guilty of it does not desire that particular person to know of his fault. Indirect defamation, which is defamation foreseen but not intended, is of the same moral character as defamation that is direct.

A man can still be entitled to the good esteem of others in one matter, even though he may have forfeited it in another. It would therefore be unjust to condemn a man altogether because he has transgressed in one point.

b) Reasons justifying the revelation of secret faults

For sufficient reasons the revelation of secret faults of others can be lawful and at times even obligatory. This is justified because "anyone who has acted dishonourably has now only a conditional right to his good name. He enjoys this right only insofar as, viewed as a whole, the preservation of his honour —which is inwardly undeserved— is for his own good and for the good of the community. But one who thinks he has the duty to reveal the secret fault of another must carefully weigh his motive and the danger of damage which is always to be anticipated."[1]

(1) The public good may justify the revelation of secret faults. It is right therefore to denounce criminals or conspirators to the proper authorities, or to testify against them. Students in a college should give information about companions who are depraving the morals of the student body. One may or even must reveal the secret faults of one who is seeking an office of which he is unworthy. In line with this, voters have a right to pertinent information about the qualification of candidates for

---

[1] Häring III, 1966, 621.

office. Hence they have a right to learn about the defects which make a candidate unfit or unworthy of the office he is running for. However it is a different matter regarding secret faults and past sins which have no bearing at all on his candidacy. This area of private honour is as inviolable for the office-seeker as it is for any other individual.

(2)   The private good of innocent parties may be preferred to the fame of one who is guilty of secret faults. One may reveal another's fault to anticipate unjust harm to oneself, as long as the harm caused to the other is not disproportionately great. A person who has been injured by his superior or another person may speak of this to a friend for the sake of obtaining consolation, or to a confessor or other adviser in order to seek counsel.

One may also reveal secret defects for the protection of others. Thus one should make known the true author of a crime for which an innocent person is about to suffer. One should put unsuspecting persons on their guard against seducers, impostors or quacks. In case of engaged parties one is permitted to reveal serious faults of the one party to the other if these faults constitute a serious threat to a happy marriage. One may caution an employer that a servant has "long fingers" or other defects that interfere with his business. However one must refrain from making the denunciation if the servant is threatened with much greater loss, material or moral.

(3)   The higher good of the person himself who has committed the fault may justify its revelation. Thus it is lawful to reveal the faults of children to their parents in order that they may be corrected. Or one may disclose failings of subjects to their superiors if this is necessary for their good.

For any good reason one may discuss publicly known matters which discredit others. Yet idle or frivolous gossip about these things is improper and easily a sin against charity, though not readily a grave one. Gossip is also dangerous insofar as it prepares the way for detraction.

c)   Cooperation in defamation

Not only the defamer sins, but also those who cooperate with him. The most ordinary form of participation in defamation is that of listening. Those who listen to detraction in such a way as to consent to what is said share in the guilt of the detraction.

The listener cooperates directly in defamation if he induces the speaker to detract or to calumniate or if he approves of what is said. To take pleasure in serious detraction out of hatred is a serious sin against charity. Mere curiosity or levity in a hearer would generally excuse from grave sin. The listener cooperates indirectly if he omits to stop the defamation or to protest against it when he could and should do so. Whoever acts thus sins against charity. Parents, pastors and superiors have a special obligation to prevent and check detraction by their subjects, but also to protect them from defamation by others.

Defamation may be opposed positively by a rebuke, a command to the defamer to be silent or by refutation of his words if they are false. This mode of correction is generally required of superiors, though at times it is suitable also for others. Defamation is opposed negatively by leaving the company, by having no share in the conversation, by changing the subject, etc.

One is freed from the obligation of preventing the detraction when interference will expose one to serious inconvenience, when one is unable to act with any success or when opposition will only make matters worse. "It is sometimes unwise to interrupt a defamatory story, for many such story seems to promise dire disclosures at its beginning, but when heard to the end is seen to be an affair of no importance or to contain little that is new or startling or credible."[1]

d) Restitution for defamation

Restitution for damages unjustly caused is a duty of justice and charity. Hence it is also required of the defamer. He must do what is in his power to repair the damage done to the injured person's reputation and also the possible material harm resulting therefrom. He incurs this duty to the extent that the harm was foreseen at least in a confused manner. The obligation to restitution is grave or light according as the injury inflicted was grave or light. The grave obligation binds even at the expense of serious inconvenience.

The calumniator must make restitution by withdrawing the false charges in a clear and unequivocal manner. False testimony in the courts must be revoked if the damage done cannot otherwise be repaired. The detractor cannot revoke his charges since they are true. Hence he must make reparation in some other

---

[1] J. McHugh/C. Callan: Moral Theology, vol. II. — New York: J. Wagner, 1960, 253.

way, e.g. by excusing the faults of the detracted person or by pointing out his good qualities.

The reparation must extend to all who were present when the defamer made his defamatory statements. As far as possible the defamation must also be undone before those to whom it was retailed. However the latter obligation primarily rests on the conscience of those who repeated the story, once they have become aware of its defamatory character. If one has defamed another in a newspaper, radio or TV, he can generally make restitution only through the same medium.

The obligation to restitution for injured reputation ceases if one can reasonably presume that the offended party renounces his right to it; if his good name has been restored in some other way; if the defamer was not given any credence; if the matter has been forgotten; if the faults reported in a detraction have become publicly known through sources other than the detraction itself; if the defamed has been guilty of the same offence towards his defamer (although a positive untruth will usually have to be corrected even in this case); if restitution is morally impossible. The latter obtains if the defamer in retracting had to suffer proportionately much greater harm than was the harm suffered by the defamed. As to voluntary condonation by the injured party, it is not admissible if such a renunciation is gravely injurious to one's relatives or to the common welfare. The latter especially holds if a defamation undermines the authority of a person in a public position, e.g. a pastor, superior or magistrate.

A

Abandoned goods 526.
Abdominal pregnancy 336f.
Abduction 429.
Abortion,
  excommunication for 358f;
  indications 357f;
  morality 357-364, 472;
  therapeutic 334-337 (indirect),
  359-364 (direct).
Abraham, example of faith 10f.
Abstinence, precept of the Church
  152-154.
Accession 523f.
Accidents, liability for 547, 564.
Accused, denial of accusation 590f.
Acedia 60.
Acrobatics, morality 342.
Adjuration 84f.
Admonition, fraternal 206-210.
Adultery 427-429;
  reason for denial of marriage
  debt 483.
Agape 65;
  integration of sexual love with
  408-412.
Aggression,
  defence against unjust 277, 365-
  367;
  war of 278f.
Alcoholism 312, 315;
  cause of traffic accidents 343.
Alms-giving 200f.
Ambition, inordinate 606.
*Amor complacentiae, concupiscen-
  tiae, benevolentiae* 64f.
Amplexus reservatus 469.
Amulets 100.
Angels, veneration of 86.
Animals,
  appropriation of wild or straying 526;
  love of 175;
  restitution for damages caused
  by domestic 564, 567.
Animation of the embryo,
  delayed animation and therapeutic abortion 359f;
  time of 353-356.

Annual confession 121.
Annulment of contracts of minors
  529, oaths 596, vows 159f.
Anointing of the sick,
  assistance for the sick and dy-
  ing through 369;
  duty to receive it 121f.
Anonymous denunciation 210.
Apostasy 48.
Apostolate,
  nature and duty 194f, 301;
  of the social mileu 205.
Appendix, incidental removal 321.
Artificial insemination 479-481.
Artificial means of birth control
  473-479.
Assensus religiosus 40-43.
Astrology 102f.
Atheism 46f.
Atomic warfare 276, 280f.
Authority,
  biblical teaching 228;
  concept 227;
  exercise in a spirit of service
  231f;
  functions 230f;
  necessity 229.
Autografts 326.
Avarice 544f.

B

Bankruptcy 549, 569f.
Baptism,
  duty to receive it 119;
  faith required in emergency 20.
Beauty culture 392.
Believers, duties towards the
  Church 299-301.
Bestiality 439.
Betrothal, see Engagement time.
Biphasic record 470.
Birth control,
  controverted means 471-479;
  justification 466-469;
  rhythm method 469-471.
Blasphemy 163f.
Blessed Sacrament, see Eucharist.
Blind obedience 240, 279.
Body, Christian view 307f.

Books, forbidden 27f.
Breviary, see Divine Office.
Bribery, to be penalized 266.
Burden attached to a contract 532.
Burglary 551.
Burial, ecclesiastical, loss of right
   for suicides 346f.
Buying and selling 532-535.

C

Calumny 609-614.
Cancer patients, nursing of incurable 322.
Canon law, function in the Church
   299.
Canonical form of marriage 426,
   460f, 462, 464.
Capital and labour, social partner
   forces 506f.
Capital punishment 272-274.
Caresses
   in premarital relations 412-416;
   in married life 483f.
Castration 329-333.
Cathartic method 338.
Celibacy,
   agape as its soul 412;
   commitment of priests to 296;
   need of vigilance in fantasy life
      in 400;
   recommendation by Scriptures
      376.
Cesareans 334;
   reason for sterilization 330f.
Charity,
   corporal and spiritual works of
      195-206;
   manner of charitable help and
      motivation 197;
   see also Love.
Chastity, virtue,
   imputability of offences against
      394-396;
   nature of 392-394.
Children,
   capacity of contracting 529;
   desirable number 469f;
   duties towards parents 256-258;
   protection against premature
      labour 501f;
   right to inheritance 537;
   rights 255.
Christ,
   followed in faith 11, 17;
   object of faith 12;
   object of worship 83, 86;
   pioneer of faith 17;

united with the Christian in
   love 70f.
Church,
   educational rights 247, 253-255,
      302;
   functions and duties 294-299;
   public teaching office in matters
      of morals 298, 303;
   teaching authority in faith and
      morals 39-42, 297f, 478f.
Church and state relation 301-304.
Citizens, duties 283-288.
Civic responsibility 287f.
Civil marriage 460f;
   dispensation from the canonical
      form in cases of 464.
Cleidotomy 335.
Clerics,
   duties and functions 295-299;
   exemption from combatant
      service 282;
   unworthy treatment and conduct
      164f.
Closed shop 507.
Clothing,
   hygiene in 311;
   modesty in 392.
Codetermination of workers
   510-513.
Co-education 377f.
Coercion,
   not incompatible with love 183f;
   right of authority to 230.
Cold war 276, 278.
Common good,
   duty of citizens to promote it
      265, 287;
   nature 223f;
   purpose of the state 264.
Communicatio in sacris 34-39.
Communion, Holy,
   admission of partners of invalid
      marriages to 457-459;
   duty to receive it 119f;
   duty to secure the state of grace
      125f, 407f.
Commutation of vows 161f.
Commutative justice 217.
Complicity in unjust damage and
   duty of restitution 565-568.
Concealment of truth 581f;
   through false speech 591-594;
   through mental reservation
      589-591.
Concubinage 426, 462.
Confession, duty to annual 121.
Confessional secret 600.

Confirmation, duty to receive it 119.

Conflict of duties in matters of birth control 477f.

Conjugal act, right to it and excuses 481-483.

Conjugal love,
agape as sustaining force 408f, 411;
expressed in the marital act 379-381;
fostered and protected by affectionate love 428f, 483f;
purpose of marriage 444f.

Conscience, ultimate norm in matters of birth control 467, 478f.

Conscientious objection against war 282.

Consecrated persons, reverence for 164f.

Consolation of the sorrowing, work of mercy 204.

Contraception, see Birth control.

Contracts,
capacity of contrating parties 529;
formal and informal 530;
object of 527-529;
obligations arising from 531f;
requirements for consent 529-531.

Contumely 608f.

Cooperation
in defamation 612f;
in illicit operations 324f;
in unjust damage and duty of restitution 565-568.

Copyright,
proprietary title 523f;
violation equivalent to theft 551.

Corporal works of charity 195-201.

Cosmetic surgery 325.

Creative discipleship 59f.

Credulity 44.

Crimes against humanity,
forced experimentation on prisoners 341;
immoral means of warfare 279.

Criminal jurisdiction of the state 271-274.

Criticism, see Fraternal correction 206-210.

Culture, care for it, task of the state 270.

Cursing 163f.

D

Dancing 391, 410.

Dating 409-411, 412-415;
role of erotic fantasies in 399.

Deacons, see Clerics.

Death,
Christian understanding of 321, 368-370;
desire of 370;
moment of 326.

Death duties 275.

Death penalty 272-274.

Debt, conjugal 481-483.

Debts,
prescription 540;
refusal to pay,
basis for the duty to restitution 559;
equivalent to theft 551;
ground for occult compensation 556f.

Defamation 609-614.

Democracy 263;
in trade unions 508;
supported by private ownership 519f.

Denial of faith 22.

Denunciation of faults to authorities 209f.

Desecration of sacred places 165f.

Desire, sinful, in matters of chastity 397f.

Despair 61f.

Detraction 609-614.

Development aid,
assistance in education, form of 204f;
obligation to 198f, 201, 544;
wage restraints on behalf of 501.

Directly willed evil effects, problematic of 332f, 362-364.

Disobedience
to immoral orders 240-242, 279, 281f;
to unjust state authority 288-294.

Disparity of cult, marriage impediment 463f.

Dispensation
from fast and abstinence 154;
from servile work on Sundays 151;
from Sunday Mass 145;
from vows 160f;
in mixed marriages 464.

Distractions
in prayer 114f;

in Sunday Mass 144.
Distributive justice 217.
Divination 101-104.
Divine Office,
  duty of clerics to pray it 112, 296;
  not invalid because of distractions 114f.
Divine virtues, see Theological virtues.
Divining rod 98.
Divorce,
  contrary to the nature of marriage 448-455;
  pastoral considerations 456-460;
  separation from bed and board 455f.
Domestic servants, rights and duties 258-260.
Domestic thefts 554.
Doubts against faith 49.
Drugs 312-318.
Dualism, religious 96.
Duel 606.

E

Easter Communion 120.
Eastern Churches,
  promotion of unity with 29-33;
  sharing in liturgical worship 35-38.
Economic policy,
  task of state authority 269;
  taxation as means of 274f.
Ectopic operations 336.
Ecumenical marriage 465.
Ecumenism,
  duty to promotion of Christian unity 29-34;
  ecumenical education 31f;
  guidelines on sharing of spiritual resources 34-39.
Education,
  apostolate of 204f;
  differentiation for the two sexes 377f;
  duty of parents 249-251;
  function of the family 244f;
  role of the Church 247, 253-255, 302;
  role of the state 247, 251, 253-255.
Employees, duties 259f, 496.
Employers, duties towards domestic servants 258-260.
Enemies, love of 174, 189-194.
Engagement time,
  expressions of affection in 411, 415, 441f;
  goals to be achieved 415f;
  nature, rights and duties of 440-443;
  role of fantasies in 399.
Epistolary secret 602f.
Equivocal speech 589-591.
Ergot, use during pregnancy 334f.
Eros 65.
Error
  in contracts 530f;
  in sales 534f;
  in vows 155f.
Eschatological approach in moral theology XIVf.
Eschatological mission of the Christian 59f, 62f.
Eucharist,
  duty to participation on Sundays 120, 130-145;
  duty to reverent treatment 166f;
  see also Communion, Holy.
Eucharistic fast 120f.
Eugenics, indication for abortion 357-359.
Euthanasia 351-353.
Evangelization, see Missionary activity.
Evasion of taxes 285f;
  duty to restitution for 562f.
Evil effects, directly willed, problematic 332f, 362-364.
Excursions and Sunday Mass 145.
Experimentation on human beings 340f.

F

Faith,
  condition for reception of sacraments 122f;
  duties of Christian faith 19-43;
  knowledge necessary for salvation 14-16, and for baptism of emergency 20;
  nature 7-14;
  necessity 2f;
  nourished by the liturgy 5f, 20, 140f, and by prayer 112;
  sins against 44-50;
  universal duty to 16-19.
Faith-healing 93f, 98, 105.
Fallopian tube, treatment of pregnancy in 336.
False speech 583, 591-594.
Family,
  duties and rights of parents 246-256;

duties in the wider family 258-260;
duties of children 256-258;
duties of spouses 245f;
economic duties of its members 243;
nature and functions 243-245.
Family planning 466-479.
Fashions 392.
Fasting,
eucharistic fast 120f;
means of self-discipline 130f;
precept of the Church 152-154, religious meaning 151f.
Fear, influence on contracts 531, oaths 596, vows 156.
Fellatio 432.
Fetichism 439.
Fictitious
consent to contract 529f;
oath 595f.
Fidelity 597.
Fiscal policy, requirements for just 274f.
Flight during persecution 23.
Food theft 555f.
Foods, clean and unclean 310.
Force, influence on contracts 531, oaths 596, vows 156.
Forgiveness 178, 191f.
Fornication 416-426.
Fortune-telling 101-104.
Fraternal correction 206-210.
Fraud 548f;
duty to restitution 559f.
Free market economy, limits 533.
Freedom of conscience 305f, 318.
Freedom of religion 302-306.
Freemasonry 29.
Friday abstinence 152-154.
Friendships dangerous to faith 28.

G

Gambling, duty not to waste in 243, 246.
Game, appropriation of 526.
Gay life 436.
Godparents in baptisms of children of different faith 38.
Good example, duty to 203f.
Government authorities, duties 265f.
Grace, state of,
condition for administration of the sacraments 129;
condition for reception of the sacraments of the living 125f.

Gratitude, duty of children towards parents 258.
Greed 544f.
Guerilla warfare 279f.

H

Hatred
against God 79f;
against the Church 80;
of repudiation and of enmity 190.
Health,
duty to care for 308-310, 318-320;
lawful and unlawful endangering of 341-344.
Heart transplants 326f.
Heresy 48f.
Heterografts 326.
Holy Communion, see Communion, Holy.
Holy days, sanctification 137, 143, 148.
Holy orders, duty of sacred ministers to receive them 122.
Homicide 348.
Hominization 353-356.
Homografts 326-329.
Homosexuality 431-439.
Honour,
nature and foundation 603f;
regard for one's own honour 604-606;
reparation for offences against 609, 613f;
respect for one's neighbour's 606f;
sins against 607-613.
Hope,
biblical teaching 52-55;
challenges of 58-60;
fruits 57-60;
nature 51-57;
necessity 2f;
nourished by prayer 112, and the liturgy 5f.
Housing, wholesome 311.
Humanae Vitae, teaching and echo 469-479.
Humility, false 606.
Hydrocephalic infant, aid for its delivery 335f.
Hygiene 309, 311.
Hypnoanalysis 338, 340.
Hypocrisy 580.
Hysterectomy 329-331.

I

Ideological misuse of faith 49f.
Idolatry 95-97.
Illegitimate children,
  adoption of, work of charity 248;
  duties of parents towards 248, 249, 442.
Immodest conversations 389f, fashions 392, looks 390f, touches 391.
Immoral contracts, obligation of 528.
Immunity of clerics 164f, 282.
Impure thoughts 396-400.
Incest 429-431.
Incurable patients, nursing of 321-324.
Index of forbidden books abrogated 27.
Indifference, sin against love of God 78f.
Indissolubility of marriage 448-456.
Indulgences, simoniac traffic in 168f.
Infidelity, sin against faith 48.
Inheritance,
  taxation of 275;
  title to private ownership 535f.
Insurance, social,
  duty of governments to provide for 270;
  means of social security 502f;
  sins of fraud against 549.
Intellectual property 514, 523f;
  violation equivalent to theft 551.
Intention, right,
  required for administration of sacraments 127f;
  required for reception of sacraments 123-125.
Interest,
  form of accession 524;
  permissibility 549f.
International politics, duty to responsible cooperation in 267.
Interrupted intercourse 473, 476.
Intestate succession 537f.
Inventory, benefit of, for heirs 537.
Invert 433.
Ipsation 401.
IUD 355, 471, 474;
  see Artificial means of birth control.

J

Judges, duties 268.
Juridical faults 564.
Jurisdiction for administration of sacraments 126f.
Justice,
  biblical teaching 210-212;
  classifications 216-219;
  nature 212-215;
  properties 215f;
  relation to love 198f, 219f.

K

Killing of the innocent,
  permissible indirect killing 350;
  sinful direct killing 348-350.
Kingship of divine right, not warrantable 263.
Kissing, morality 413.

L

Labour conditions,
  permission of dangers in 342;
  protection against inappropriate 269f, 501f;
  right to appropriate 503f;
  sinful negligence in 344.
Labour union 504-508.
Labourers, see Workers.
Laity,
  duties in the Church 299-301;
  promotion of its role in the Church 298;
  see also Apostolate.
Land reform 570, 572.
Landed property 525.
Last will 535-538.
Lawyers, duties 268.
Legal justice 217f.
Legislation, basic criteria for 267.
Legislative authorities, duties 268.
Lesbianism 432.
Lesser evil
  in conflicts of birth control 477;
  in therapeutic abortion, problematic 361-364.
Letters, reading of another person's 602f.
Liberalism (economic and political theory) 265, 269, 485f.
Life, bodily,
  Christian view 308;
  lawful and unlawful endangering 341-344, 347f, 350;
  responsibility for 308ff.

Life of man, meaning and purpose 490-494.
Literature,
duty of the state to protect against immoral 271;
duty to selective reading 27f, 390.
Liturgical prayer 111.
Liturgical worship,
duty to perform it properly 91f, 128f;
ecumenical sharing in 35-38;
nature 34, 85.
Loans at interest, justification and limits 549-551.
Lockout 508.
Lost objects 526, 551, 559.
Love,
integration of sexual love with agape 407-412;
nature and division in general 64f;
see also Conjugal love.
Love of enemy, 174, 189-194.
Love of God,
biblical teaching 65-71;
condition for reception of sacraments 125f;
nature 71-73;
necessity 3;
nourished by prayer 112, and liturgy 5f;
qualities 73-75;
realization in prayer and deed 75-78;
sins against 78-80.
Love of nature 73, 175, 178, 181f.
Love of neighbour,
biblical teaching 173-178;
manifestations 174, 178, 194-210;
nature 178-182;
necessary expression of divine love 75-78, 172;
order of 184-189;
qualities 182-184;
universality 176, 184.
Love of self 174f, 178, 181, 184-186.
LSD 312f.
Luxury 545f.
Lying,
biblical teaching 583-585;
concept 582f;
false speech 591-594;
historical background 585-587;
sinfulness, reasons 587-589.
Lynch law 348.

M

Magic 104-106.
Magic pendulum 98.
Magic practices of piety 93f.
Magisterium of the Church, duty of submission to its teachings 39-43, 49, 478f.
Malpractice of profession, duty to restitution for 564f.
Marijuana 313.
Marital act, right to it and excuses 481-483.
Marriage,
canonical form 426, 460f, 462, 464;
ends 443-446;
impediments 356f, 461;
indissolubility 448-456;
mixed marriages 463-465;
sacrament 461-463, duty to receive it 122.
Marriage witnesses of a faith different from that of the spouses 38.
Martyrdom,
supreme proof of love 74f;
supreme witness to the faith 21.
Marxist socialism 485f.
Mary,
example of faith 18;
duty of reverence for her name 163f;
image of the Christian woman 385f;
veneration of the Blessed Virgin 86f.
Mascots 100.
Masochism 439.
Mass media,
apostolic concern for good standards in 390;
duty of, to serve the cause of peace 282;
duty of the state to protect against immorality in 271.
Mass of precept, see Sunday Mass.
Masturbation,
causes and effects 401-403;
concept 401;
infant masturbation 394f;
moral evaluation 403-408.
Matrimony, sacrament 461-463;
duty to receive it 122.
Meditation, support of external prayer 110f.
Mental reservation 586f, 589-591.

Mercy killing 351-353.
Military service 281.
Minimum wage 499.
Minors,
   capacity of contracting 529;
   liability for damages 529.
Miracles, fruit of faith 18f.
Missionary activity,
   duty of spreading the faith
      through 24-27;
   dependent on God's grace 13.
Mixed marriages 463-465.
Mixed religion, marriage impedi-
   ment 463f.
Modesty 386-392;
   offences against by children 395.
Monarchy 263.
Monogamy 446-448.
Morality, public, duty of the state
   271.
Morning and evening prayer, ob-
   ligatory character 113.
Movies,
   apostolic concern for good
      standards in 390;
   duty to selectiveness in 27f,
      390;
   duty of the state to protect
      against immorality in 271.
Mucus method 470.
Murder 348-350.
Mutilation, criterion for its justi-
   fication 316.

N

Name of God,
   misuse of 163f;
   reverence for 162f.
Names, holy, reverence for 163,
   164.
Narcoanalysis 338, 340.
Narcotics 314f.
Nationalism 283.
Nationalization 570-573.
Natural family planning 469-471.
Natural law XIIIf.
Natural right, basis of justice 214.
Necessity, order of love in tem-
   poral and spiritual 187-189, 200f.
Necking 412-415.
Necromancy 104.
Neurosis,
   duty of parents to prevention
      of 251;
   result of human failure 309f;
   treatment 337-340.

Nourishment, care for healthy
   310f.
Nudity, morality 388, 390f.

O

Oath 84f, 594-597;
   confirmation of a mental reser-
      vation by 586, 590.
Oath of allegiance or office 596.
Obedience,
   biblical teaching 233-236;
   concept 232f;
   necessity 236-239;
   practice in responsibility 239-242;
   to civil authorities 283f;
   to God 9-11, 16-19, 236;
   to parents 257f;
   to the Church 300, and her
      teaching authority 39-43, 297;
   to the moral order, sufficient
      for salvation 14f.
Objects, sacred, reverence for 166f.
Occult compensation 556f.
Occultism 101-104.
Occupancy 525-527.
Officials, public, duties 265f.
Ogino-Knaus, method of family
   planning 469-471.
Onanism 401, 473.
Ontological approach in moral
   theology XIV.
Operations,
   cooperation in illicit 324f;
   in difficult pregnancy 334-337.
Ordeal 61.
Orientals, see Eastern Churches.
Ownership, private, see Property,
   private.

P

Parapsychological abilities, dis-
   tinguished from superstition 98f,
   101-106.
Parents, duties and rights 246-256.
Paresthesia, sexual 439.
Parliamentarians, duties 268.
Participation in worship of other
   Christian Communions 34-38.
Patent right,
   proprietary title 523f;
   violation equivalent to theft 551.
Patriotism 283.
Peace, duty to promote its cause
   282f.
Pederasty 432.

Penance, sacrament, duty to receive it 121.
Penitential works, meaning and duty 151f.
Perfection, duty of priests 296f.
Perfection of the world,
challenge of hope 58-60;
object of hope 55f.
Perjury 594.
Petition, prayer of 109f, 115f.
Petting 412-416.
Petty thefts, coalescence 554.
Pharisaism 580.
Physicians, rights and duties 317f.
Places, sacred, reverence for 165f.
Pleasure, morality 310, 378.
Poaching 526.
Political parties, duty to responsible choice of 29.
Politics,
Church involvement in 288, 303;
honourable art 266.
Pollution (masturbation) 401, 408.
Polyandry 448.
Polygamy 446-448.
Polytheism 96.
Pope, duty of submission to his teaching authority 39-43, 49, 478f.
Population control 466-479.
Pornography 390f.
Positive law theory 213.
Possessor in bad faith 559f, in good faith 560f, in doubtful faith 561f.
Prayer,
apostolic work of charity 202;
conditions 113-116;
ecumenical sharing in 33, 35;
fundamental expression of divine love 75-78;
nature 107-111;
necessity and duty 111-113;
precondition of a living faith 17.
Precepts of the Church 19 (see also footnote).
Preceremonial intercourse 425f.
Pregnancy,
duties during 248f, 244;
operations in difficult 334-337.
Premarital intercourse 416-426, 442.
Prescription 538-541.
Presumption 60f.
Preventive war 278.
Price, just 533f.

Pride, sin against faith 45.
Priests,
duties and functions 295-299;
right to material sustenance 300f;
unworthy treatment and conduct 164f.
Pinciple of totality 316f.
Private revelations 44 (see also footnote).
Prodigality 546.
Profanation of sacred places 165f.
Profanity 163.
Profession of faith, duty 21-24.
Professional duties,
liability for damages caused by negligence in 564, 566;
obligation to conscientious preparation 495f, and responsible performance 496;
sinful neglect 344.
Professional secret 600f.
Profiteering 533, 551.
Prolongation of life, duty and limits 321-324.
Promise 531, 598f.
Promotion of unworthy candidates 266.
Property, private,
biblical teaching 514-518;
concept 514;
duties of owners 199f, 541-546;
moral basis 518-521, 525;
sins against 546-555;
social character 521-523, 543f;
titles for acquisition 523-541.
Prostitution 426f:
obligations arising from contracts for 528.
Protestants,
promotion of unity with them 29-33;
sharing in liturgical worship 36-38.
Psychoanalysis 338-340.
Psychosomatic illnesses 337.
Psychotherapeutic treatments 337-340.
Public morality, duty of the state to care for 271.
Punishment of crime, right and duty of the state 271-274.

R

Racings, morality 342.
Radio,
duty of the state to protect

against immoral broadcasts 271;
duty to selective listening 27f, 390;
Mass attendance by 144.
Rape 429;
contraceptive measures in cases of 356;
instance of ethical indication 357-359.
Rash judgment 607f.
Reading, duty to selective 27f, 390.
Recreation 147f, 311f.
Relatives, order of charity among 186f.
Relics, sale of 168f.
Religion,
duty to seek the truth in religious matters 579;
virtue of 4f, 82;
see also Worship.
Religious assent 40-43.
Religious education,
duty of parents 250, and educators in general 21, 28;
right of parents 252;
right of the Church 254f.
Religious life, expression of love of God 75-78;
see Worship.
Reparation
for material damages, see Restitution;
for offences against another's honour 609, 613f.
Reporting to superiors 209f.
Representatives (congressmen), duties 268.
Reputation, see Honour.
Resignation, sin against hope 62f.
Resistance
against illegitimate rulers 289f;
against legitimate rulers 290-294.
Responsible parenthood, duty to 247f.
Restitution,
duty in cases of unjust possession 559-562, tax evasions 562f, unjust damage 563-565, culpable cooperation 565-568;
nature and duty in general 557-559;
recipient, manner and excuses 568-570;
right to claim it 192, 558f.
Reverence, duty
towards consecrated persons 164f, 299f;
towards God 162-164;
towards parents 256f;
towards sacred objects 166-169;
towards sacred places 165f;
towards the Church 299f.
Revolution 290f.
Rhythm method 469-471.
Riches,
biblical teaching 514-518;
not an end in themselves 521-523;
to be administered in the spirit of stewardship 541-543.
Robbery 551.
Rubrics, obligatory character 128f.

S

Sabbath 131-135.
Sacramental worship,
duty to observance of the rites 128f;
ecumenical sharing in 35-37.
Sacramentals, nature 117f.
Sacraments,
nature 116-118;
necessity and obligation 118-122;
requirements for administration 126-129;
requirements for reception 122-126.
Sacraments of the living 125.
Sacred objects and places, common use with the separated brethren 38.
Sacrifice,
basic act of worship 84;
holy Mass as sacrifice of Christians 137f.
Sacrilege,
local 165f;
personal 164f;
real 166f.
Sadism 439f.
Saints,
duty of reverence for their names 163f;
examples of living faith 18;
veneration of 86f, 179f.
Sale, contract of 532-535.
Sapphic love 432.
Schism 48.
Schools,
Christian concern for 28f;
rights and duties of the state concerning 253f, 270;

rights of parents to schools of their choice 252-254, 270;
right of private schools to public subsidies 252f;
right of the Church to Catholic schools 254f;
right to religious education in 28f, 270.

Secrets,
nature and foundation 599f;
probing into 601-603;
revelation of secrets 600f, and secret faults 611f.

Secularism and secularization 47.
Self-abasement 606.
Self-abuse 401.
Self-deception 578.
Self-defence 365-368;
against defamation 605f.

Separated Christians,
promotion of unity with them 29-33;
sharing in liturgical worship 35-38.

Separation from bed and board 455f.
Separation of Church and state 304.
Servile works 146f, 148f.
Sex plays of children 395.

Sexes,
encounter in adolescence 409-411, 412-415;
separate schooling during puberty 377f.

Sexual deviations 439f;
distinguished from sexual foreplays 400.

Sexual ethics, challenges and re-evaluation 371f, 382.
Sexual fantasies 396-400.

Sexuality,
biblical view 373-376;
chastity as ordering force 392-394;
constitutive part of man 376-378;
integration with agape 408-412;
nature and purpose 378-381;
social dependence 381f.

Shame,
education of children to 395;
nature of 386-389.

Sharing in worship and spiritual resources with separated Christians 34-38.

Sick persons,
eucharistic fast for 120f;

procurement of facilities for non-Catholic ministers to attend to their sick communicants 39;
visiting of the sick, work of charity 204.

Sickness, relation to sin 309f.
Simony 167-169.
Sin, repentance for it made possible by hope 58.
Sincerity, see Truthfulness.
Slander 609-614.
Social encyclicals 486.
Social justice 218f.

Social legislation,
OT instances of 488, 515f;
right of workers to protection by 501-504;
task of state authority 269f.

Social question 485f.
Socialism (economic and political theory) 265, 269, 485f.
Socialization 570-573.

Society,
concept 222f;
functions 223-227.

Sodomy 432.
Sorcery 99, 104-106.
Spiritism 101-104.
Spiritual works of charity 201-206.
Sponsors in baptisms of children of different faith 38.
Sports 312.
Spouses, mutual obligations 245f.

State,
duty to protect religious freedom 302-304;
educational role and rights 247, 251-256;
functions 264f;
nature 260-265;
origin (juridical) 262-264;
tasks and duties of state authority 265-275.

Statutes of descent and distribution 537f.
Sterilization 329-333, 472.
Sterilizing drugs 473-479;
therapeutic use 474.

Stolen property, duty to restitution 559-562.
Strike 508-510;
political strike 292, 510.
Subsidiarity, principle of 224-227.

Suffering,
Christian meaning 352, 368f;
endurance in it as fruit of hope 57f;

vicarious, work of charity 202f.
Suicide 345-347.
Sunday celebration,
   biblical origin 131-135;
   binding authority 135-137.
Sunday Mass,
   excuses 144f;
   gravity of the obligation 20,
      141-143;
   historical development 138f;
   meaning and reason of the pre-
      cept 139-141;
   specific requirements 143f.
Sunday rest,
   biblical origin 131-133;
   content of the obligation 148f;
   excuses 150f;
   gravity of the obligation 148-
      150;
   historical development 145-147;
   meaning and reason 147f.
Superfluities,
   duty to alms from one's 200f;
   duty to socially beneficial use of
      199f.
Supernatural virtues 4f.
Superstition,
   forms 93f, 99-106;
   nature 97-99.
Suspension of vows 160.
Symbols 97;
   importance for worship 90.

T

Talismans 100.
Taping of conversations, secret
   602.
Taxes,
   duty of citizens to pay 284-287;
   duty to restitution for evasions
      562f;
   right of the state to impose
      274f.
Television,
   duty of the state to protect
      against immoral telecasts 271;
   duty to selectiveness 27f, 390;
   Mass attendance by TV 144.
Temperance
   in nourishment 310;
   in stimulants 312.
Temptation of God 61.
Testament (last will) 535-538.
Theft,
   duty to restitution 559-562;
   nature and sinfulness 551f;

relative and absolute standard
   in 552-554;
special forms (domestic, petty,
   conspiratorial) 554f.
Theological virtues,
   necessity 2f;
   number 1f;
   relation to worship 5f, and to
      prayer 111f;
   supernatural character 4f.
Theonomous ethics XV.
Tolerance, religious 305f.
Totalitarian state,
   contrary to man's rights 263;
   right to resistance against 290-
      294.
Touches, immodest 391.
Trade union 504-508.
Traffic safety, duty to care for
   343f.
Transplantation of organs 325-329.
Treasure-troves 525f.
Treatments, medical,
   cooperation in illicit 324f;
   ordinary and extraordinary 318-
      320;
   unnecessary 320f.
Trust in God,
   condition of prayer 115;
   constituent of faith 8-11, 18;
   linked to hope 53.
Truthfulness,
   biblical teaching 574-577;
   concealment of truth 581f, 589-
      594;
   concept and basis 577f;
   duty to it in thought 578f, con-
      duct 579-581, words 581f.
Tubal pregnancy 336.
Tyrannicide 292-294.

U

Unbelief 45-47.
Unborn children, right to
   inheritance 538.
Unemployment,
   insurance against 502;
   right to assistance in 497.
Unity of Christians, see Ecumen-
   ism.
Unjust damage 547f;
   duty to restitution 563-565.
Usurpers 289f.
Usury 549-551.
Uterus, removal of sick 330f.

V

Vain observances 99-101.
Vain worship 94f.
Vasectomy 329.
Veneration of saints 86f.
Viaticum 120.
Violent resistance 292-294.
Virginity,
agape as soul of 412;
recommendation by Scriptures
376;
see also Celibacy.
Voting, right and duty to 287f.
Vows,
binding force 157f;
conditions for validity 155-157;
fulfillment 158f;
interpretation 158;
nature and meaning 154f;
release from 159-162.

W

Wage justice,
criteria 497-501;
denial of, basis for occult compensation 556f;
limits of wage claims 506-508;
right to family wage 253, 500.
War,
atomic warfare 276, 280f;
conditions of a just war 277-
279;
conscientious objection against
282;
means and methods 279f;
moral admissibility 276f;
participation of citizens in 281f.
Waste, sin against property 545f.
Witchcraft 99, 104-106.
Witness, non-Catholic, at a Catholic marriage and vice versa 38.
Woman,
Christian view of 382-386;
false egalitarianism 377f;
protection against inappropriate
work 501f;
right to equal wage 499.
Word of God, element of worship
84.
Work,
biblical teaching 487-490;
duty to work and to responsible
preparation 494-496;
meaning and purpose of 490-
494;
right to 496f;
title to property 523f.
Worker partnership 510-513.
Workers,
right to appropriate working
conditions 503f;
right to protection and social
security 501-503.
Works of charity,
corporal works 195-201;
spiritual works 201-206.
Worship,
forms 83-86;
nature 82f;
necessity and duty 75-78, 87-92;
relation to divine virtues 5f;
relation to involvement in the
world 75-78, 493f;
sins against 93-106.

Y

Youth,
encounter of sexes during adolescence 409-411, 412-416;
protection against immorality in
mass media 271.

BIBLIOGRAPHY

Part I

Faith
Bianchi, Eugene C. *Reconciliation. The Function of the Church.* New York: Sheed and Ward, 1969. (A study on secularization.)
Bosch, David J. *Witness to the World. The Christian mission in theological perspective.* Atlanta: John Knox Press, 1980.
Comblin, Joseph. *The Meaning of Mission. Jesus, Christians, and the Wayfaring Church.* Maryknoll, N.Y.: Orbis Books, 1977.
Curran, Charles E., and McCormick, Richard A., eds. *Readings in Moral Theology No. 3: The Magisterium and Morality.* New York: Paulist Press, 1982.
Danielou, Jean. *The Faith Eternal and the Man of Today.* Chicago: Franciscan Herald Press, 1970.
Ebeling, Gerhard. *The Nature of Faith.* London: Collins, Fontana Library, 1966.
"Faith", *Sacramentum Mundi,* vol. II, 1968, 310-325.
Fries, Heinrich, *Faith Under Challenge.* New York: Herder and Herder, 1969.
Heijke, S. J. *The Bible on Faith.* De Pere, Wisc.: St. Norbert Abbey Press, 1966.
Hermann, Ingo. *The Experience of Faith.* New York: P. J. Kenedy and Sons, 1966.
Hermission, Hans Jürgen, and Lohse, Edward. *Faith* (Biblical Encounter Series). Nashville: Abingdon, 1981.
Kasper, Walter. *An Introduction to Christian Faith.* London: Burns and Oates, 1980.
Macquarrie, John. *New Directions in Theology Today, vol. III: God and Secularity.* Philadelphia: Westminster Press, 1967.
Pieper, Josef. *Belief and Faith.* London: Faber and Faber, 1963.
Powell, John. *A Reason to Live! A Reason to Die!* Niles, Ill.: Argus Communications, 1972.
Rahner, Karl. "Theological Considerations on Secularization and Atheism", in *Theological Investigations XI.* London: Darton, Longman and Todd, 1974, 166-184.
idem. "The Foundation of Belief Today" and "Anonymous and Explicit Faith", in *Theological Investigations XVI.* London: Darton, Longman and Todd, 1979, 3-23; 52-59.
Sullivan, Francis A. *Magisterium: Teaching Authority in the Catholic Church.* Dublin: Gill and Macmillan, 1983.
Surlis, Paul, ed. *Faith: Its Nature and Meaning.* Dublin: Gill and Macmillan, 1972.
Trueblood, Elton. *The Validity of the Christian Mission.* New York: Harper and Row, 1972.

Hope
Alfaro, Juan. *Christian Hope and the Liberation of Man.* Rome/Sydney: E. J. Dwyer, 1978.
Capps, Walter H. *Time Invades the Cathedral: Tensions in the School of Hope.* Philadelphia: Fortress Press, 1972.
Häring, Bernard. *Hope is the Remedy.* Garden City, N.Y.: Image Books, 1972.
Hebblethwaite, Brian. *The Christian Hope.* Grand Rapids, Mi.: Eerdmans, 1985.
Macquarrie, John. *Christian Hope.* New York: Seabury Press, 1978.
Moltmann, Jürgen. *Theology of Hope.* London: SCM Press, 1967.
idem. *The Future of Hope.* New York: Herder and Herder, 1970.
Moule, C. F. D. *The Meaning of Hope.* Philadelphia: Fortress Press, 1963.

Pieper, Josef. *Hope and History*. New York: Herder and Herder, 1969.
Studia Moralia VII: Contributiones ad problema spei. Roma: Desclée, 1969.

Love of God
Barrosse, Thomas. *Christianity: Mystery of Love*. Notre Dame, Ind.: Fides Publ., 1964.
Colin, Louis. *Love the Lord Thy God*. Covent Garden/Glasgow: Sands and Co., 1956.
Deden, D. *The Bible on Love*. De Pere, Wisc.: St. Norbert Abbey Press, 1966.
Furnish, Victor Paul. *The Love Command in the New Testament*. Nashville/ New York: Abingdon Press, 1972.
Lussier, Ernest. *God is a Love According to Saint John*. New York: Alba House, 1977.
Rahner, Karl. "Reflections on the Unity of the Love of Neighbour and the Love of God", in *Theological Investigations VI*. London: Darton, Longman and Todd, 1969, 231-249.
idem. "Unity-Love-Mystery", in *Theological Investigations VIII*. 1971, 229-247.
Salet, Gaston. "Love of God, Love of Neighbour", in *Foundations of Biblical Spirituality,* translated by Joseph A. Grispino, Staten Island, N.Y.: Alba House, 1965, 37-64.
Spicq, Ceslaus. *Agape in the New Testament,* 3 vols. St. Louis/London: B. Herder Book Co., 1963-66.

Worship in general
Abba, Raymond. *Principles of Christian Worship*. New York/London: Oxford University Press, 1966.
Burkhart, John E. *Worship*. Philadelphia: Westminster Press, 1982.
Delling, Gerhard. *Worship in the New Testament*. Philadelphia: Westminster Press, 1962.
Horn, Henry E. *Worship in Crisis*. Philadelphia: Fortress Press, 1972.
Karrer, Otto. *Religions of Mankind*. New York: Sheed and Ward, 1945.
Panikkar, Raimundo. *Worship and Secular Man*. London: Darton, Longman and Todd (Orbis Books), 1973.
Parrinder, Geoffrey. *Worship in the World's Religions*. London: Sheldon Press, 1974, 2nd edition.
Schnackenburg, Rudolf. "Worship in Spirit and in Truth", in *Christian Existence in the New Testament, vol. II*. Notre Dame, Ind.: University of Notre Dame Press, 1969, 85-114.
Smart, Ninian. *The Concept of Worship*. London: Macmillan, 1972.
Vos, Wiebe, ed. *Worship and Secularization*. Bossum, Holland: Brand, 1970.
White, James F. *Introduction to Christian Worship*. Nashville: Abingdon Press, 1980.

Superstition, Magic, Parapsychology
Boelaars, H. "Riflessioni sulla Magia", *Studia Moralia* 10 (1972), 73-126.
Jahoda, Gustav. *The Psychology of Superstition*. London: The Penguin Press, 1971.
Koch, Kurt F. *Christian Counselling and Occultism*. Grand Rapids, Mich.: Kregel, 1973.
Ludwig, Jan, ed. *Philosophy and Parapsychology*. Buffalo, N.Y.: Prometheus Books, 1978.
Marwick, Max., ed. *Witchcraft and Sorcery. Selected Readings*. Harmondsworth: Penguin Books, 1982, 2nd edition.
Milingo, E. *The World in Between. Christian Healing and the Struggle for Spiritual Survival*. London: C. Hurst & Co., 1984.
Neff, H. Richard. *Psychic Phenomena and Religion*. Philadelphia: Westminster Press, 1971.
Reginald-Omez, Fr. *Psychical Phenomena* (Faith and Fact Books, 58). London: Burns and Oates, 1963.

Rhine, J. B., and Brier, R, eds. *Parapsychology Today*. New York: Citadel, 1968.
Watson, Lyall. *Supernature*. Garden City, N.Y.: Anchor Press, 1973.
White, Rhey A. *Surveys in Parapsychology: Reviews of the Literature, with Updated Bibliographies*. Metuchen, N.J.: The Scarecrow Press, 1976.
Wolman, Benjamin B., ed. *Handbook of Parapsychology*. New York: Van Nostrand Reinhold Co., 1977.

Specific manifestations of worship
a) *Prayer*

Gallen, John, ed. *Christians at Prayer*. Notre Dame/London: University of Notre Dame Press, 1977.
Green, Thomas H. *Opening to God. A Guide to Prayer*. Notre Dame, Ind.: Ave Maria Press, 1977.
idem. *Darkness in the Marketplace. The Christian at Prayer in the World*. Notre Dame, Ind.: Ave Maria Press, 1981.
Hamman, A. *Prayer: The New Testament*. Chicago: Franciscan Herald Press. 1971.
Hinnebusch, Paul. *Prayer: the Search for Authenticity*. New York: Sheed and Ward, 1969.
Howe, Leroy T. *Prayer in a Secular World*. Philadelphia: Pilgrim Press, 1973.
Nédoncelle, Maurice. *God's Encounter with Man: A contemporary Approach to Prayer*. New York: Sheed and Ward, 1964.
Wright, John H. *A Theology of Christian Prayer*. New York: Pueblo Publ. Co., 1979.

b) *Sunday observance*

Huber, Hans. *Geist und Buchstabe der Sonntagsruhe. Eine historisch-kritische Untersuchung bis auf Thomas von Aquin*. Salzburg: Otto Müller, 1958.
Hurley, Karen, ed. *Why Sunday Mass?* U.S.A.: St. Anthony Messenger Press, 1973.
Jewett, Paul K. *The Lord's Day. A Theological Guide to the Christian Day of Worship*. Grand Rapids: Eerdmans, 1972.
Jungmann, J. A. *The Meaning of Sunday*. Notre Dame, Ind.: Fides Publ., 1961.
Rordorf, Willy. *Sunday: The History of the Day of Rest and Worship in the Earliest Centuries of the Christian Church*. Philadelphia: Westminster Press, 1968.
Searle, Mark, ed. *Sunday Morning: A Time for Worship*. Collegeville, Minn.: Liturgical Press, 1982.
Strand, Kenneth A. *The Sabbath in Scripture and History*. Washington, DC: Review and Herald Publ. Association, 1984.
Troxler, Georg. *Das Kirchengebot der Sonntagsmesspflicht*. Universitätsverlag Freiburg, Schweiz, 1971.
Verheul, Ambrose, "From the Sabbath to the day of the Lord". *Theology Digest* 19 (1971), 58-66.

c) *Other manifestations*

Boelaars, Henri. "Riflessioni sul voto". *Studia Moralia* 16 (1978), 129-165.
idem. "La blasfemia". *Studia Moralia* 17 (1979), 189-229.
Cooke, Bernard J. *Christian Sacraments and Christian Personality*. Garden City, N.Y.: Image Books, 1968.
Davies, J. G. *The Secular Use of Church Buildings*. London: SCM Press, 1968.
Häring, Bernard. *The Sacraments and Your Everyday Life*. Liguori, Mo.: Liguori Publications, 1976.
Martos, Joseph. *The Catholic Sacraments* (Message of the Sacraments, no. 1). Wilmington, Del.: Michael Glazier, 1983.
McCauley, George. *Sacraments for Secular Man*. New York: Herder and Herder, 1969.

Prince, Derek. *Shaping history through prayer and fasting*. Old Tappan, N. J.: Fleming H. Revell Co., 1973.

Worgul, George S. *From Magic to Metaphor. A Validation of Christian Sacraments*. New York/Ramsey: Paulist Press, 1980.

Part II

Fraternal love

Andre, M. J. *As I Loved You*. St. Louis/London: B. Herder Book Co., 1969.

Cuttaz, Francois. *Fraternal Charity*. Staten Island, N.Y.: Alba House, 1962.

Kelsey, Morton T. *Caring: How Can We Love One Another*. New York/Ramsey: Paulist Press, 1981.

Oraison, Marc. *Being Together. Our Relationship with Other People*. New York: Doubleday, 1970.

Outka, Gene. *Agape: An Ethical Analysis*. New Haven/London: Yale Univ. Press, 1972.

Terbovich, John B. *The Faces of Love*. Garden City, N.Y.: Doubleday, 1966.

See also under "Love of God" in part I.

Justice and rights of man

Bird, Otto A. *The Idea of Justice*. New York/London: Frederick A. Praeger, 1967.

de Vecchio, Giorgio, *Justice: An Historical and Philosophical Essay*. Edinburgh: University Press, 1956.

Feinberg, Joel. *Social Philosophy*. Englewood Cliffes, N. J.: Prentice Hall, 1973 (contains much on justice and rights of man).

Haughey, John C., ed. *The Faith that Does Justice*. New York/Ramsey: Paulist Press, 1977.

Hollenbach, David. *Claims in Conflict. Retrieving and Renewing the Catholic Human Rights Tradition*. New York: Paulist Press, 1979.

"Justice" (7-item symposium). *The Way* 13 (1973), 171-228.

Maritain, Jacque. *The Rights of Man and Natural Law*. New York: Charles Scribner's Sons, 1951.

Marstin, Ronald. *Beyond Our Tribal Gods: The Maturing of Faith*. Maryknoll, N.Y.: Orbis, 1979.

Melden, A. I., ed. *Human Rights*. Belmont, Calif.: Wadsworth Publ. Co., 1970 (includes the Universal Declaration of Human Rights of 1948).

Miller, Allen O., ed. *A Christian Declaration on Human Rights*. Grand Rapids, Eerdmans, 1977.

Pontificial Commission "Justitia et Pax", ed. *Human Rights. Working Paper No. 1*. Vatican City: Pontificial Com. "Justitia et Pax", 1975.

Rawls, John. *A Theory of Justice*. Cambridge, Mass.: Belknap Press, 1971.

Stackhoube, Max L. *Creeds, Society and Human Rights. A Study in three Cultures*. Grand Rapids: Eerdmans, 1984.

Swidler, Arlene, ed. *Human Rights in Religious Traditions*. New York: Pilgrim Press, 1982.

Moral responsibility in community life

a) *Authority and obedience*

Duquoc, Christian, and Floristan, Casians, eds. *Christian Obedience* (Concilium 139, 9/1980). New York: Seabury Press, 1980.

Häring, Bernard. *The Liberty of the Children of God*. Staten Island, N.Y.: Alba House, 1966.

Shuster, George N., ed. *Freedom and Authority in the West*. Notre Dame/London: University of Notre Dame Press, 1967.

Simon, Yves R. *A General Theory of Authority*. Notre Dame: University of Notre Dame Press, 1962.

Todd, John M., ed. *Problems of Authority*. London: Darton, Longman and Todd, 1962.

Verghese, Paul. *The Freedom of Man. An Inquiry Into Some Roots of the Tension Between Freedom and Authority in Our Society*. Philadelphia: Westminster Press, 1972.

b) *The family*

Cox, F. D. *Human Intimacy, Marriage, the Family and its Meaning.* St. Paul, Minn.: West Publ. Co., 1984.

Cretney, Stephen M. *Principles of Family Law.* London: Sweet and Maxwell, 1984, 4th edition.

Feucht, Oscar E., ed. *Family Relationships and the Church.* Saint Louis/London: Concordia, 1970.

Finley, Mitch and Kathy. *Christian Families in the real World. Reflections on a Spirituality for the domestic Church.* Chicago, Ill.: Thomas More Press, 1984.

Grams, Armin. *Changes in Family Life.* St. Louis/London: Concordia, 1968.

Greely, Andrew, ed. *The Family in Crisis or in Transition* (Concilium 121, 1/1979). New York: Seabury Press, 1979.

Martin, Thomas M. *Christian Family Values.* Ramsey, N.J.: Paulist Press, 1984.

Messner, Johannes. "The Family", in *Social Ethics.* St. Louis/London: B. Herder Book Co., 1965, 397-427.

Shorter, Edward. *The Making of the Modern Family.* New York: Basic Books, 1977.

Spencer, Anita. *Mothers are People Too. A Contemporary Analysis of Motherhood.* Leonminster: Fowler Wright Books, 1984.

c) *The state, political morality*

Anderson, J. N. D. *Into the world: The need and limits of Christian involvement.* London: Falcon Books, 1968.

Boff, Leonardo and Clodovis. *Salvation and Liberation. In Search of a Balance between Faith and Politics.* Maryknoll, N.Y.: Orbis, 1984.

Clifford, Paul Rowntree, *Politics and the Christian Vision.* London: SCM, 1984.

Cullmann, Oscar. *The State in the New Testament.* New York: Charles Scribner's Sons, 1956.

Dumas, André. *Political Theology and the Life of the Church.* Philadelphia: Westminster Press, 1978.

Gutman, Amy, and Thompson, Dennis. *Ethics and Politics. Cases and Comments.* Chicago, Ill.: Nelson-Hall Publ., 1984.

Hampshire, Stuart, ed. *Public and Private Morality.* Cambridge: University Press, 1978.

Fierro, Alfredo. *The Militant Gospel. A Critical Introduction to Political Theologies.* Maryknoll, N.Y.: Orbis Books, 1977.

Hengel, Martin. *Christ and Power.* Philadelphia: Fortress Press, 1974.

Hertz, Karl H. *Politics Is a Way of Helping People.* Minneapolis: Augsberg Publ. House, 1974.

Hinchliff, Peter. *Holiness and Politics.* London: Darton, Longman and Todd, 1982.

Maritain, Jacque. *Man and the State.* Chicago: University of Chicago Press, 1951.

idem. *Scholasticism and Politics.* Garden City, N.Y.: Image Books, 1960.

idem. *The Person and the Common Good.* Notre Dame, Ind.: University of Notre Dame Press, 1966.

Messner, Johannes. "The Ethics of the Political Community", in *Social Ethics.* St. Louis/London: B. Herder Book Co., 1965, 541-744.

Moltmann, Jürgen. *On Human Dignity. Political Theology and Ethics.* London: SCM, 1984.

Neuhaus, Richard John. *Christian Faith and Public Policy.* Minneapolis, Minn.: Augsburg Publ. House, 1977.

Newman, Jeremiah. *Studies in Political Morality.* Dublin/London: Scepter, 1962.

Riga, Peter J. *Give Unto Caesar What Are God's: The Christian and Political Life.* New York: Exposition Press, 1973.

Schall, James V. *The Politics of Heaven and Hell. Christian Themes from Classical, Medieval and Modern Political Philosophy.* Lanhan, N.Y.: University Press of America, 1984.

d) *Criminal justice*

Böckle, Franz, and Pohier, Jacques, eds. *The Death Penalty and Torture* (Concilium 120, 10/1978). New York: Seabury Press, 1979.

Crowe, M. B. "Theology and Capital Punishment". *Irish Theol. Quarterly* 31 (1964), 24-61; 99-131.

Endres, Michael E. *The Morality of Capital Punishment. Equal Justice under the Law.* Mystic, CT: Twenty-Third Publications, 1984.

Gerber, Rudolph J., and McAnany, Patrick D. *Contemporary Punishment.* Notre Dame/London: Univ. of Notre Dame Press, 1972.

McHugh, Gerald Austin, *Christian Faith and Criminal Justice.* New York/Ramsey: Paulist Press, 1978.

Regan, A. "The Problem of Capital Punishment". *Studia Moralia* 14 (1976), 209-237.

e) *War and peace*

Barclay, Oliver R., ed. *Pacifism and War.* Downers Grove, Ill.: Inter-Varsity Press, 1984 (When Christians disagree).

Heyer, Robert, ed. *Nuclear Disarmament. Key Statements of Popes, Bishops, Councils and Churches.* New York/Ramsey: Paulist Press, 1982.

Hörmann, Karl. *Peace and Modern War in the Judgment of the Church.* Westminster, Md.: Newman Press, 1966.

Johnson, J. T. *Can Modern War Be Just?* New Haven: Yale Univ. Press, 1984.

Lawler, Justus George. *Nuclear War. A Catholic Assessment.* Westminster, Md.: Newman Press, 1966.

Lawler, Philip. *The Ultimate Weapon. Guide to the American Bishop's Pastoral Letter on War and Peace.* South Bend, Ind.: Regnery/Gateway, 1984.

Macquarrie, John. *The Concept of Peace.* New York: Harper and Row, 1973.

O'Brien, William V. *Nuclear War, Deterrence and Morality.* Westminster: Newman Press, 1967.

Pontifical Commission "Iustitia et Pax". *Peace and Disarmament. Documents of the World Council of Churches and the Roman Catholic Church.* Vatican City, 1982.

Potter, Ralph B. *War and Moral Discourse.* Richmond, Va.: John Knox, 1973.

Ramsey, Paul. *War and the Christian Conscience.* Durham, N.C.: Duke University Press, 1961.

idem. *The Limits of Nuclear War.* New York: The Council on Religion and International Affairs, 1968.

Russel, Frederick H. *The Just War in the Middle Ages.* Cambridge: University Press, 1977.

Schall, James B., ed. *Out of Justice, Peace. Winning the Peace.* Pastoral Letters of the West German and French Bishops. San Francisco: Ignatius Press, 1984.

Shannon, Thomas A., ed. *War or Peace? The Search for New Answers.* Maryknoll, N.Y.: Orbis Books, 1980.

Swaim, J. Carter. *War, Peace and the Bible.* Maryknoll, N.Y.: Orbis Books, 1982.

Swift, L. J. *The Early Fathers on War and Military Service.* London: Geoffrey Chapman, 1985.

Walzer, Michael. *Just and Unjust Wars. A Moral Argument with Historical Illustrations.* New York: Basic Books, 1977.

Wasserstrom, Richard A., ed. *War and Morality.* Belmont, Calif.: Wadsworth Publ. Co., 1970.

Yoder, J. H. *When War is Unjust.* Minneapolis: Augsburg, 1984.

f) *Civil disobedience, violence, revolution*

Bedau, Hugo Adam, ed. *Civil Disobedience: Theory and Practice.* New York: Pegasus, 1969.

Camera, Helder. *Spiral of Violence.* Denville, N.J.: Dimension Books, 1971.

Cullmann, Oscar. *Jesus and the Revolutionaries.* New York: Harper and Row, 1970.

Davies, J. G. *Christians, Politics and Violent Revolution.* Maryknoll, N.Y.: Orbis Books, 1976.

Eppstein, John. *The Cult of Revolution in the Church*. New Rochelle, N.Y.: Arlington House Publications, 1974.

Fortas, Abe. *Concerning Dissent and Civil Disobedience*. New York: World Publishing Co., 1969.

Hall, Robert T. *The Morality of Civil Disobedience*. New York: Harper and Row, 1971.

Langan, John. "Violence and Injustice in Society: Recent Catholic Teaching". *Theological Studies* 46 (1985), 685-699.

Marty, M. M., and Peerman, D. G., eds. *New Theology No. 6: On Revolution*. London: Macmillan Co., 1969.

Miller, William R. *Nonviolence. A Christian Interpretation*. New York: Shocken Books, 1966.

Shannon, Thomas A. *Render Unto God: A Theology of Selective Obedience*. New York/Ramsey: Paulist Press, 1974.

Sibley, Mulford O. *The Obligation to Disobey*. New York: The Council on Religion and International Affairs, 1970.

Zinn, Howard. *Disobedience and Democracy*. New York: Random House, 1968.

g) *The Church community*

Maritain, Jacque. *On the Church of Christ. The Person of the Church and Her Personnel*. Notre Dame/London: Univ. of Notre Dame Press, 1973.

McKenzie, John L. *Authority in the Church*. New York: Sheed and Ward, 1966; New York, Image Books, 1971.

Müller, Alois. *Obedience in the Church*. Westminster: Newman Press, 1966.

Nicodemus, Donald E. *The Democratic Church*. Milwaukee: Bruce, 1969.

Pelikan, Jaroslav. *Spirit versus Structure. Luther and the Institutions of the Church*. London: Collins, 1968.

Rahner, Karl. "The Function of the Church as a Critic of Society", in *Theological Investigations XII*. London: Darton, Longman and Todd, 1974, 229-249.

Suenens, Léon-Joseph. *Corresponsibility in the Church*. New York: Herder and Herder, 1968.

Bodily life and health

a) *Bioethics and medical ethics in general*

Ashley, Benedict M., and O'Rourke, Kevin. *Health Care Ethics*. St. Louis, Mo.: Catholic Health Association, 1982, revised edition.

Beauchamp, Tom L., and Childress, James F. *Principles of Biomedical Ethics*. New York/Oxford: Oxford Univ. Press, 1979.

Childress, James F. *Priorities in Biomedical Ethics*. Philadelphia: Westminster Press, 1981.

Dedek, John. *Human Life: Some Moral Issues*. New York: Sheed and Ward, 1972.

idem. *Contemporary Medical Ethics*. New York: Sheed and Ward, 1975.

Häring, Bernard. *Medical Ethics*. Slough, England: St. Paul Publ., 1973.

idem. *In Pursuit of Wholeness. Healing in Today's Church*. Ligouri, Mo.: Ligouri Publ., 1985. .

Illich, Ivan. *Limits to Medicine*. New York/Harmondsworth: Penguin Books, 1977.

Lobo, George V. *Current Problems in Medical Ethics. A Comprehensive Guide to Ethical Problems in Medical Practice*. Allahabad: St. Paul Publ., 1974.

Mahoney, John. *Bioethics and Belief. Religion and Medicine in Dialogue*. London: Sheed and Ward, 1984.

May, William E. *Human Existence, Medicine and Ethics*. Chicago: Franciscan Herald Press, 1977.

McFadden, Charles J. *Medical Ethics*. Philadelphia: F. A. Davis Co., 1967 6th edition.

idem. *The Dignity of Life: Moral Values in a Changing Society*. Noll Plaza, Huntington, Ind.: Our Sunday Visitor, 1976.

idem. *Challenge to Morality. Life Issues — Moral Answers*. Huntington, Ind.: Our Sunday Visitor, 1978.

Nelson, James B. *Human Medicine: Ethical Perspectives on New Medical Issues*. Minneapolis, Minn.: Augsburg Publ. House, 1973.

Nelson, John Robert. *Human Life. A Biblical Perspective for Bioethics*. Philadelphia: Fortress Press, 1984.

O'Donnel, Thomas J. *Medicine and Christian Morality*. New York: Alba House, 1976.

Ramsey, Paul. *The Patient as Person: Explorations in Medical Ethics*. New Haven/London: Yale Univ. Press, 1975.

Reich, Warren T., ed. *Encyclopedia of Bioethics,* 4 vols. New York: The Free Press, a Division of Macmillan, 1978.

Shannon, Thomas A., ed. *Bioethics: Basic Writings*. New York/Ramsey: Paulist Press, 1981, revised edition.

Shannon, Thomas A., and Manfra, Jo Ann, eds. *Law and Bioethics. Texts with commentary on major U.S. Court decisions*. New York: Paulist Press, 1982.

Shelp, Earl E. *Theology and Bioethics. Exploring the Foundations and Frontiers*. Dordrecht: D. Reidel, 1985.

Smith, Harmon L. *Ethics and the New Medicine*. Nashville: Abingdon Press, 1970.

Varga, Andrew C. *The Main Issues in Bioethics*. New York/Ramsey: Paulist Press, 1984, revised edition.

Vaux, Kenneth. *Biomedical Ethics: Morality for the New Medicine*. New York: Harper and Row, 1978.

Veatch, Robert M. *A Theory of Medical Ethics*. New York: Basic Books, 1981.

b) *Specific issues of medical ethics*

Atkinson, Gary M., and Moraszewski, Albert S., eds. *Genetic Counseling, the Church and the Law*. St. Louis, Mo.: The Pope John XXIII Medical-Moral Research and Education Center, 1980.

Block, S., and Chodoff, P., eds. *Psychiatric Ethics*. Oxford: Oxford Univ. Press, 1984.

Boyle, John P. *The Sterilization Controversy: A New Crisis for the Catholic Hospital?* New York/Ramsey: Paulist Press, 1977.

Connery, John R. "Prolonging Life: The Duty and its Limits". *Linacre Quarterly* 47 (1980), 151-165.

Flynn, E. P. *Human Fertilization in Vitro*. Landham, Md.: University Press of America, 1984.

Fuchs, Josef. "Christian Faith and the Disposing of Human Life". *Theological Studies* 46 (1985), 664-684.

Häring, Bernard. *Ethics of Manipulation: Issues in Medicine, Behavior Control and Genetics*. New York: Seabury Press, 1975.

Johnson, Paul R. "Selective Nontreatment of Defective Newborns". *Linacre Quarterly* 47 (1980), 39-53.

Jones, D. Gareth. *Brave new people. Ethical issues at the commencement of life*. Downers Grave, Ill.: Inter-Varsity, 1984.

McCormick, Richard A. "Notes on Moral Theology": On *in vitro* fertilization with embryo transfer. *Theol. Studies* 40 (1979), 99-112.

idem. "Notes on Moral Theology: Life and Its Preservation". *Theol. Studies* 42 (1981), 100-110.

Moskop, J. C., and Kopelmann, Loretta, eds. *Ethics and Critical Care Medicine*. Dordrecht-Boston-Lancaster: D. Reidel, 1985.

Rahner, Karl. "The Problems of Genetic Manipulation", in *Theological Investigations IX*, 1972, 225-252.

Ramsey, Paul. *Fabricated Man: The Ethics of Genetic Control*. New Haven/London: Yale Univ. Press, 1970.

Rosenfeld, Louis J., and Grosswirth, Marvin. *The Truth About Vasectomy*. Englewood Cliffs, N.J.: Prentice Hall, 1972.

Test Tube Babies — a Christian View. Papers from the Conference "In Vitro Fertilisation and the Quality of Life". London, 23 May 1983. London: Unity Press, 1985, 2nd edition.

Theological Studies. Developments in Genetics, Sept. issue of vol. 33 (1972), 401-552.

Walsh, James, and P. B. *Divine Providence and Human Suffering*. Wilmington, Del.: Michael Glazier, 1985.

For all issues consult also the general literature on bioethics and medical ethics.

c) *Euthanasia*

Behnke, John A., and Bok, Sissela, eds. *The Dilemmas of Euthanasia*. Garden City, N.Y.: Anchor Books, 1975.

Cahil, Liza Sowle. "A 'Natural Law' Reconsideration of Euthanasia". *Linacre Quarterly* 44 (1977), 47-63.

Dyck, Arthur J. "The Good Samaritan Ideal and Beneficent Euthanasia: Conflicting Views of Mercy". *Linacre Quarterly* 42 (1975), 176-188.

Grisez, Germain, and Boyle, Joseph M. *Life and Death with Liberty and Justice: A Contribution to the Euthanasia Debate*. Notre Dame/London: Univ. of Notre Dame Press, 1979.

Horan, Dennis J., and Mall, David, eds. *Death, Dying, and Euthanasia*. Washington: University Publications of America, 1977.

Maguire, Daniel C. *Death by Choice*. Garden City, N.Y.: Doubleday, 1974.

McCormick, Richard A. "Notes on Moral Theology: Care for the dying and euthanasia". *Theological Studies* 37 (1976), 87-107.

Reagan, Augustine. "Moral Argument on Self-Killing". *Studia Moralia* 18 (1980), 299-331.

Rizzo, Robert, and Yonder, Joseph. "Care of the Dying: The Doctor and Euthanasia". *Linacre Quarterly* 41 (1974), 253-268.

Weber, Leonard. *Who Shall Live: The dilemma of severely handicapped children and its meaning for other moral questions*. New York/Ramsey: Paulist Press, 1976.

d) *Abortion*

Brody, Baruch. *Abortion and the Sanctity of Human Life: A Philosophical View*. Cambridge, Mass.: MIT Press, 1976.

Burtchaell, J. T. *Rachel Weeping. The Case against Abortion*. San Francisco: Harper and Row, 1984.

Connery, John. *Abortion: The Development of the Roman Catholic Perspective*. Loyola University Press, 1977.

Curran, Charles E. "Civil Law and Christian Morality: Abortion and the Churches", in *Ongoing Revision: Studies in Moral Theology*. Notre Dame, Ind.: Fides Publ., 1975, 107-143.

Delahoyde, Linda. *Defending the Newborn's Right to Life*. Ann Arbor: Mich.: Servant Books, 1984.

Filice, Francis P. "Twinning and Recombination: A Review of the Data". *Linacre Quarterly* 48 (1981), 40-51.

Granfield, David. *The Abortion Decision*. Garden City, N.Y.: Doubleday, 1971.

Grisez, Germain. *Abortion: The Myths, the Realities, and the Arguments*. New York/Cleveland: Corpus Books, 1970.

Hilgers, Thomas W., and Horan, Dennis J., eds. *Abortion and Social Justice*. New York: Sheed and Ward, 1972.

Honings, Bonifacio. "L'aborto nella dottrina dei manualisti". *Studia Moralia* 12 (1974), 257-323.

Joyce, Robert E., and Joyce, Mary Rosera. *Let Us Be Born*. Chicago: Franciscan Herald Press, 1970.

Manney, James, and Blattner, John C. *Death in the Nursery. The Secret Crime of Infanticide*. Ann Arbor, Mich.: Servant Books, 1984.

Noonan, John T., Jr., ed. *The Morality of Abortion: Legal and Historical Perspectives*. Cambridge, Mass.: Harvard Press, 1970.

Pastrana, Gabriel. "Personhood and the Beginning of Human Life". *Thomist* 41 (1977), 247-294.

Regan, Augustine. "Abortion laws and fetal right of life". *Studia Moralia* 11 (1973), 265-313.

Schall, James V. *Human Dignity and Human Numbers*. Staten Island, N.Y.: Alba House, 1971.

Whitehead, K. D. *Respectable Killing: The New Abortion Imperative*. New Rochelle: Catholics United for the Faith, 1973.

Sexual morality

a) *Sexuality in general*

Adam, August. *The Sixth Commandment*. Cork: The Mercier Press, 1966.

Bird, Joseph W., and Bird, Lois F. *The Freedom of Sexual Love*. Garden City, N.Y.: Image Books, 1970.

Dedek, John. *Contemporary Sexual Morality*. New York: Sheed and Ward, 1971.

Doherty, Dennis, ed. *Dimensions of Human Sexuality*. Garden City, N.Y.: Doubleday, 1979.

Dominian, Jack. *The Growth of Love and Sex*. London: Darton, Longman and Todd, 1982.

Foucault, Michel. *The History of Sexuality. Vol. I: An Introduction*. New York: Vintage Books, 1980.

Gagern, Frederick von. *Marriage Partnership*. Westminster: Newman Press, 1966.

Grelot, Pierre. *Man and Wife in Scripture*. New York: Herder and Herder, 1964.

Hildebrand, Dietrich von. *Man and Woman*. Chicago: Franciscan Herald Press, 1965.

Hogan, Richard M., and Levoir, John M. *Covenant of Love. Pope John Paul II on Sexuality, Marriage and Family in the Modern World*. Garden City, N.Y.: Doubleday, 1985.

Human Sexuality and Personhood. Proceedings of the Workshop for the Hierarchies of the United States and Canada, Dallas, Tex., Feb. 2-6, 1981. St. Louis, Mo.: Pope John Center, 1981.

Jansen, Alphonsus. *The Meaning of Love and Marriage*. Techny, Ill.: Divine Word Publications, 1968.

Keane, Philip S. *Sexual Morality: A Catholic Perspective*. New York/Ramsey: Paulist Press, 1977.

Lawler, Ronald, Joseph Boyle and William E. May. *Catholic Sexual Ethics*. Huntington, Ind.: Our Sunday Visitor, 1985.

Liebard, Odile M., ed. *Love and Sexuality: Official Catholic Teaching* (A Consortium Book). Wilmington, N.C.: McGrath, 1978.

May, William E., and Harvey, John F. "On understanding human sexuality: a critique of the C.T.S.A. study". *Communio: Int. Cath. Review* 4 (1977), 195-225.

McCarthy, Donald G. *Handbook on Critical Sexual Issues*. Garden City, N.Y.: Doubleday, 1984.

Morrison, Eleanor S., and Borosage, Vera, eds. *Human Sexuality: Contemporary Perspectives*. Palo Alto, Calif.: National Press Books, 1973.

Nelson, James B. *Embodiment: An Approach to Sexuality and Christian Theology*. Minneapolis, Minn.: Augsburg Publ. House, 1979.

O'Neil, Robert P., and Donovan, Michael A. *Sexuality and Moral Responsibility*. Washington/Cleveland: Corpus Books, 1968.

Podimattam, Felix M. *A New Look at Chastity*. Bangalore: Asian Trading Corp., 1974.

Rinzema, J. *The Sexual Revolution: Challenge and Response*. Grand Rapids: Eerdmans, 1974.

Reuss, Josef M. *Modern Catholic Sex Instruction*. Baltimore/Dublin: Helicon, 1964.

Ryan, Mary Perkins, and Ryan, John Julian. *Love and Sexuality: A Christian Approach*. Garden City: Image Books, 1969.

Weber, Leonhard M. *On Marriage, Sex and Virginity* (Quaestiones Disputatae 16), New York: Herder and Herder, 1966.

Wynn, John C., ed. *Sexual Ethics and Christian Responsibility*. New York: Association Press, 1970.

b) *Woman in the Christian world*

Bouyer, Louis. *Woman in the Church*. San Francisco: Ignatius Press, 1979.

Daly, Mary. *The Church and the Second Sex*. London: G. Chapman, 1968.

Evans, Mary J. *Woman in the Bible. An Overview of all the crucial Passages on Woman's Roles*. Downers Grove, Ill.: Inter-Varsity Press, 1984.

Hebblethwaite, Margaret. *Motherhood and God*. London: Chapman, 1984.

Jewett, Paul K. *Man as male and female*. Grand Rapids: W. B. Eerdmans, 1975 (a biblical study).

LaPorte, Jean. *The Role of Women in Early Christianity*. New York/Toronto: Edwin Mellen Press, 1982.

Maertens, Thierry. *The Advancing Dignity of Woman in the Bible*. De Pere, Wis.: St. Norbert Abbey Press, 1969.

Ruether, Rosemary Radford, ed. *Religion and Sexism. Images of Woman in the Jewish and Christian Traditions*. New York: Simon and Schuster, 1979.

Ryrie, Charles Caldwell. *The Role of Women in the Church*. Chicago: Moody Press, 1978.

Schelkle, Karl Hermann. *The Spirit and the Bride: Woman in the Bible*. Collegeville, Minn.: The Liturgical Press, 1979.

Stagg, Evelyn and Frank. *Woman in the World of Jesus*. Philadelphia: Westminster Press, 1978.

Swidler, Leonard. *Biblical Affirmation of Woman*. Philadelphia: Westminster Press, 1979.

Taward, George H. *Woman in Christian Tradition*. Notre Dame/London: Univ. of Notre Dame Press, 1973.

Ulanov, Ann Belford. *Receiving Woman. Studies in the Psychology and Theology of the Feminine*. Philadelphia: Westminster Press, 1981.

c) *Premarital relations*

Duvall, Evelyn Millis. *Why Wait Till Marriage?* New York: Association Press, 1965.

Humbert, A. "Les péché de sexualité dans le Nouveau Testament". *Studia Moralia* 8 (1970), 149-183.

Manning, Francis V. "The Human Meaning of Sexual Pleasure and the Morality of Premarital Intercourse". *Am. Eccl. Review* 165 (1971), 18-28; 166 (1972), 3-21; 302-319.

McCormick, Richard A. "Notes on Moral Theology: Pre-marital Sexual Relations". *Theol. Studies* 34 (1973), 77-92.

Miles, Hervert J. *Sexual Understanding Before Marriage*. Grand Rapids, Mich.: Zondervan Publ. House, 1971.

Wright, H. Norman. *Premarital Counselling*. Chicago: Moody Press, 1978.

See also general literature.

d) *Homosexuality*

Boswell, John. *Christianity, Social Tolerance and Homosexuality. Gay People in Western Europe from the Beginning of the Christian Era to the Fourteenth Century*. University of Chicago Press, 1980.

Cahill, Lisa Sowle. "Moral Methodology: A Case Study". *Chicago Studies* 19 (1980), 171-187.

Cavanagh, John R. *Understanding the Homosexual*. Huntington, Ind.: Our Sunday Visitor, 1977.

Church Information Office. *Homosexual Relationships: A Contribution to Discussion*. London: Cio Publishing, 1979.

Hagmaier, George, and Gleason, Robert W. "Homosexuality", in *Counselling the Catholic*. New York: Sheed and Ward, 1964, 94-112; 228-238.

Harvey, John F. "The Controversy Concerning the Psychology and Morality of Homosexuality". *Am. Eccl. Review* 176 (1973), 602-629.

Lovelace, Richard F. *Homosexuality and the Church*. London: The Lamp Press, 1979.

Nugent, Robert, ed. *A Challenge to Love. Gay and Lesbian Catholics in the Church*. New York: Crossroad, 1983.

Martin, Del, and Lyon, Phyllis. *Lesbian Woman.* New York: Glide Publications (A Bantam Book), 1972.
Pittenger, Norman. *Time for Consent.* London: SCM Press, 1970.
Weinberg, Martin S., and Bell, Alan P., eds. *Homosexuality: An Annotated Bibliography.* New York: Harpers, 1972.
West, D. J. *Homosexuality.* Penguin Books, 1968.
See also general literature.

Marriage
a) *Marriage in general*
D'Souza, Anthony A. *Happiness in Marriage.* New Delhi: Usha Publications, 1979.
Gagern, Frederick von. *Marriage Partnership.* Westminster: Newman Press, 1966.
Häring, Bernard. *Love is the Answer.* Denville, N.J.: Dimension Books, 1970.
Harrington, Wilfrid J. *The Promise to Love. A Scriptural View of Marriage.* London: G. Chapman, 1968.
Hastings, Adrian. *Christian Marriage in Africa.* London: SPCK, 1973.
Kasper, Walter. *Theology of Christian Marriage.* New York: Seabury Press. A Crossroad Book, 1980.
Kindregan, Charles P. *A Theology of Marriage: A doctrinal, moral, and legal study.* Milwaukee: Bruce Publ. C., 1967.
Mackin, Theodore. *What Is Marriage? Marriage in the Catholic Church.* New York/Ramsey: Paulist Press, 1982.
Malone, Richard, and Connery, John, eds. *Contemporary Perspectives on Christian Marriage. Propositions and Papers from the International Theological Commission.* Chicago, Ill.: Loyola Univ., 1984.
Oraison, Marc. *Man and Wife: The Physical and Spiritual Foundations of Marriage.* New York: Macmillan, 1969.
Palmer, Paul F. "Christian Marriage: Contract or Covenant?" *Theol. Studies* 33 (1972), 617-665.
Thomas, David M. *Christian Marriage: A Journey Together.* Wilmington, Del.: Michael Glazier, 1983.
Vereecke, Louis. "Marriage et plaisir sexual chez les théologiens de l'époque moderne (1300-1789)". *Studia Moralia* 18 (1980), 245-267.
Vollebregt, G. N. *The Bible on Marriage.* London: Sheed and Ward, 1965.

b) *Monogamy, divorce and remarriage*
Basset, William W., ed. *The Bond of Marriage: An Ecumenical and Interdisciplinary Study.* University of Notre Dame Press, 1968.
Grib, P. J. *Divorce Laws and Morality.* Lanham, Md.: University Press of America, 1985.
Heth, William A., and Wenham, Gordon J. *Jesus and Divorce. Towards an Evangelical Understanding of New Testament Teaching.* London: Hodder and Stoughton, 1984.
Hillmann, E. *Polygamy Reconsidered: African Plural Marriage and the Christian Churches.* New York: Maryknoll, 1975.
Kelleher, Stephen J. *Divorce and Remarriage for Catholics?* Garden City, N.Y.: Douleday, 1973.
L'Abate, Luciano, and L'Abate, Bess. *How to avoid divorce.* Atlanta: John Knox Press, 1977.
Macking, Theodore. *Divorce and Remarriage. Marriage in the Catholic Church.* New York/Ramsey: Paulist, 1984.
Müller, Karl. "Die Taufe Polygamer, ein ungelöstes Problem". *Documenta missionalia 16: Prospettivi di missiologia, oggi.* Roma: Università Gregoriana, 1982, 217-240.
Noonan, John T., Jr. *Power to Dissolve: Lawyers and Marriages in the Courts of the Roman Curia.* Cambridge: Belknap Press, 1972.
Ripple, Paula. *The Pain and the Possibility: Divorce and Separation Among Catholics.* Notre Dame, Ind.: Ave Maria Press, 1984, 5th printing.
Robinson, Geoffry. *Marriage, Divorce and Nullity.* London: Chapman, 1984.
Tierney, Terence E. *Annulment: Do you have a case?* New York: Alba House, 1978.

Wrenn, Lawrence, G., ed. *Divorce and Remarriage in the Catholic Church.* New York: Newman Press, 1973.

idem. *Annulments.* Canon Law Society of America, 1972, revised edition.

Young, James J., ed. *Divorce Ministry and the Marriage Tribunal.* New York/Ramsey: Paulist Press, 1982.

c) *Birth control*

Billings, Evelyn, and Westmore, Ann. *The Billings Method: Controlling fertility without drugs or devices.* Richmond, Va.: Anne O'Donovan.

Dorairaj, Kathleen. *Teaching Natural Family Planning. A Guide For Fieldworkers.* New Delhi: Indian Social Institute, 1982.

Egner, G. *Contraception Vs. Tradition: A Catholique Critique.* New York: Herder and Herder, 1967.

Grisez, Germain G. *Contraception and the Natural Law.* Milwaukee: Bruce Publ. Co., 1964.

Hamel, Eduardus. "Conferentiae Episcipales et Encyclica 'Humanae Vitae'". *Periodica* 58 (1969), 243-349.

Horgan, John, ed. *"Humanae Vitae" and the Bishops.* Dublin: Irish University Press, 1972.

Joyce, Mary Rosera. *Love Responds to Life: The Challenge of Humanae Vitae.* Kenosha, Wis.: Prow, 1971.

Kippley, John F. *Birth Control and the Marriage Covenant.* Collegeville, Minn.: The Liturgical Press, 1976.

Kippley, John and Sheila. *The Art of Natural Family Planning.* Cincinnati, Oh.: The Couple to Couple League, 1979, 2nd edition.

Kloostermann, A. M. J. *Family Planning and Christian Marriage.* Fontana Books, 1970.

Noonan, John T., Jr. *Contraception: A History of Its Treatment by the Catholic Theologians and Canonists.* Cambridge, Mass.: Harvard Univ. Press, 1965.

Pyle, Leo, ed. *Pope and Pill: More documentation on the birth regulation debate.* London: Darton, Longman and Todd, 1968.

Rahner, Karl. "On the Encyclical 'Humanae Vitae'", in *Theological Investigations XI.* 1974, 263-287.

Roetzer, Josef. *Family Planning the Natural Way: A complete guide to the Sympto-Thermal Method.* Old Tappan, N.J.: Fleming H. Revell, 1981.

Santamaria, J. N., and Billings, John J., eds. *Human Love and Human Life: Papers on Humanae Vitae and the Ovulation Method.* Melbourne: The Polding Press, 1979.

Valsecchi, Ambrodgio. *Controversy: The birth control debate 1958-1968.* London: G. Chapman, 1968.

Work and property

a) *Christian social doctrine in general*

Bennett, John C. *Christian Social Ethics in a Changing World.* New York: Association Press, 1966.

Brockmann, Norbert, and Piediscalzi, Nicholas, eds. *Contemporary Religion and Social Responsibility.* Staten Island, N.Y.: Alba House, 1973.

Calvez, Jean-Yves, and Perrin, Jacque. *The Church and Social Justice: The Social Teaching of the Popes from Leo XIII to Pius XII (1878-1958).* Chicago: Henry Regnery, 1961.

Calvez, Jean-Yves. *The Social Thought of John XXIII: Mater et Magistra.* Chicago: Henry Regnery, 1964.

Clarke, Thomas E., ed. *Above Every Name: The Lordship of Christ and Social Systems.* New York/Ramsey: Paulist Press, 1980.

Cronin, John F. *Social Principles and Economic Life.* Milwaukee: Bruce Publ. Co., 1964, revised edition.

Curran, Charles E. *American Catholic Social Ethics. Twentieth-Century Approaches.* Notre Dame, Ind.: Univ. of Notre Dame, 1982.

De Santa Ana, Julio. *Towards a Church of the Poor: The Work of an Ecumenical Group on the Church and the Poor.* Maryknoll, N.Y.: Orbis, 1981.

Dorr, Donal. *Option for the Poor. A Hundred Years of Vatican Social Teaching.* Dublin: Gill and Macmillan, 1983.

Greeley, Andrew M. *No Bigger than Necessary: An Alternative to Socialism, Capitalism and Anarchism.* New York: American Library, 1977.

Green, Robert W., ed. *Protestantism, Capitalism, and Social Science: The Weber Thesis Controversy.* Lexington: D. D. Heath, 1973, second edition.

Gremillon, Joseph, ed. *The Gospel of Peace and Justice. Catholic Social Teaching since Pope John.* Maryknoll, N.Y.: Orbis, 1984.

Lane, Dermot A. *Foundations for a Social Theology. Praxis, Process and Salvation.* New York: Paulist Press, 1984.

Longenecker, R. N. *New Testament Social Ethics for Today.* Grand Rapids, Mich.: Eerdmans, 1984.

Mainelli, Vincent P., ed. *Social Justice: Official Catholic Teachings* (A Consortium Book). Wilmington, N.C.: McGrath, 1978.

Malherbe, Abraham J. *Social Aspects of Early Christianity.* Baton Rouge: Louisiana State Univ. Press, 1977.

McDonagh, Enda. *Social Ethics and the Christian.* Manchester: University Press, 1979.

Messner, Johannes. *Social Ethics.* St. Louis/London: B. Herder Book Co., 1965.

Mueller, Franz Hermann. *The Church and the Social Question.* Washington: American Enterprise Institute, 1984.

Novak, Michael. *Freedom with Justice. Catholic Social Thought and Liberal Institutions.* New York: Harper and Row, 1984.

O'Callahan, Denis. "A Just Society for Mankind: Recent Writing". *Irish Theol. Quarterly* 39 (1972), 79-87.

Seifert, Harvey. *Ethical Resources for Political and Economic Decision.* Philadelphia: Westminster Press, 1972.

Walsh, Michael, and Davies, Brian, eds. *Proclaiming Justice and Peace. Church Documents from John XXIII to John Paul II.* London: Collins, 1984.

b) *Moral order of work*

Argyle, Michael. *The Social Psychology of Work.* Harmondsworth, England: Penguin Books, 1972.

Baum, Gregory. *The Priority of Labor: A Commentary on 'Laborem exercens', Encyclical Letter of Pope John II.* New York/Ramsey: Paulist Press, 1982 (includes the text of the encyclical).

Cronin, John F., and Flannery, Harry W. *Labour and the Church* (Faith and Fact Books 50). London: Burns and Oates, 1965.

Jonas, H. *The Imperative of Responsibility. In Search of an Ethics for the Technological Age.* Chicago, Ill.: The University of Chicago Press, 1984.

Kwant, Remy C. *Philosophy of Labor* (Duquesne Studies). Louvain: E. Nauwelaerts, 1960.

Pohier, Jacqaue, and Mieth, Dietmar, eds. *Unemployment and the Right to Work.* (Concilium 160, 10/1982). Edinburgh: T & T Clark.

Preston, Ronald, ed. *Industrial Conflicts and Their Place in Modern Society.* London: SCM, 1974.

Redekop, John H., ed. *Labor Problems in Christian Perspective.* Grand Rapids, Mich.: W. B. Eerdmans, 1972.

Savary, Louis M. *Man, His World and His Work.* New York/Glen Rock: Paulist Press, 1967.

Schoonenberg, Peter. *God's World In The Making.* Dublin: Duquesne University Press, 1964.

Schumacher, E. F. *Good Work.* New York: Harper and Row, 1979.

Theilhard de Chardin, Pierre. *The Divine Milieu.* New York: Harper and Row, 1965.

Wyszynski, Stefan Cardinal. *Work.* Chicago/Dublin: Scepter, 1960.

c) *Property and social economy*

Boerma, Conrad. *The Rich, the Poor — and the Bible.* Philadelphia: Westminster Press, 1979.

Eagleson, John, ed. *Christians and Socialism. Documentation of the Christians For Socialism Movement in Latin America.* Maryknoll. N.Y.: Orbis Books, 1975.

Forell, George W., and Lazareth, William H., eds. *Corporation Ethics.* Philadelphia: Fortress Press, 1980.

Garrett, Thomas M. *Ethics in Business.* New York: Sheed and Ward, 1963.

Gnuse, Robert. *You shall not steal. Community and Property in the Biblical Tradition.* Maryknoll, N.Y.: Orbis, 1985.

Guinan, Michael D. *Gospel Poverty: Witness to the Risen Christ.* New York/Ramsey: Paulist Press, 1981.

Hengel, Martin. *Property and Riches in the Early Church.* Philadelphia: Fortress Press, 1974.

Hindery, Roderick. "Applying Comparative Ethics to Multinational Corporations", in *Essays in Morality and Ethics,* ed. by James Gaffney. New York/Ramsey: Paulist Press, 1980, 85-105.

Johnson, Luke T. *Sharing Possessions: Mandate and Symbol of Faith.* Philadelphia: Fortress Press, 1981.

Mullin, Redmond. *The Wealth of Christians.* Maryknoll, N.Y.: Orbis, 1984.

North, Gary. *An Introduction to Christian Economics.* Nutley, N. J.: Craig Press, 1973.

Novak, Michael. *The Spirit of Democratic Capitalism.* New York: Simon and Schuster, 1982.

Preston, Ronald, ed. *Technology and Social Justice.* Valley Forge: Judson Press, 1971.

Stevens, Edwards. *Business Ethics.* New York/Ramsey: Paulist Press, 1979.

Wirtenberger, Henry J. *Morality and Business.* Chicago: Loyola University Press, 1962.

Wogoman, J. Philip. *Christians and the Great Economic Debate.* London: SCM Press, 1977.

d) *Development ethics*

Adeney, Miriam. *God's Foreign Policy. Practical Ways to Help the World's Poor.* Grand Rapids, Mich.: Eerdmans, 1984.

Bauer, Gerhard. *Towards a Theology of Development: An Annotated Bibliography.* Geneva: Committee on Society, Development and Peace (SODEPAX), 1970.

Beckmann, David M. *Where Faith and Economics Meet: A Christian Critique.* Minneapolis: Augsburg Publ. House, 1981.

Block, Walter, and Shaw, Donald. *Theology, Third World Development and Economic Justice.* Vancouver: Fraser Institute, 1985.

Camara, Helder. *Church and Colonialism.* London: Sheed and Ward, 1969.

Dhavamony, Mariasusai, ed. *Evangelization, Dialogue and Development.* Rome: Gregorian University, 1972.

Dorr, Donal. *Spirituality and Justice.* Dublin: Gill and Macmillan, 1984.

Eagleson, John, and Scharper, Philip. *Puebla and Beyond.* Maryknoll, N.Y.: Orbis Books, 1979.

Elliott, Charles. *The Development Debate.* London: SCM Press, 1971.

Goulet, Denis. *The Cruel Choice: A New Concept in the Theory of Development.* New York: Atheneum, 1978.

idem. *A New Moral Order. Studies in Development Ethics and Liberation Theology.* Maryknoll, N.Y.: Orbis Books, 1974.

Land, Philip, ed. *Theology Meets Progress: Human Implications of Development.* Rome: Gregorian University, 1971.

Laurentin, René. *Liberation, Development and Salvation.* Maryknoll, N.Y.: Orbis Books, 1972.

McCormack, Arthur. *World Poverty and the Christian.* New York: Hawthorn Books, 1963.

McGinnis, James B. *Bread and Justice: Toward a New International Economic Order.* New York/Ramsey: Paulist Press, 1979.

Mooneyham, W. Stanley. *What do you say to a hungry world?* Waco, Texas: Word Books, 1975.

Munby, Denys, ed. *World Development: Challenge to the Churches.* Washington/Cleveland: Corpus Books, 1969.

Nelson, Jack A. *Hunger for Justice: The Politics of Food and Faith.* Maryknoll, N.Y.: Orbis Books, 1980.

O'Brien, David J., and Shannon, Thomas A., eds. *Renewing the Earth: Catholic Documents on Peace, Justice and Liberation.* Garden City, N.Y.: Image Books, 1977 (includes the documents of the Medellin Conference).

Vaughan, N. B. Y. *The Expectation of the Poor: The Church and the Third World.* London: SCM, 1972.

Ward, Barbara. *The Angry Seventies. The Second Development Decade: A Call to the Church.* Rome: Pontifical Commission Justice and Peace, 1970.

Truth and fidelity

Bok, Sissela. *Lying: Moral Choice in Public and Private Life.* New York: Vintage Books. A Division of Random House, 1979.

Brunner, Emil. *Truth as Encounter.* Philadelphia: Westminster Press, 1964.

Dorszynski, J. A. *Catholic Teaching about the Morality of Falsehood.* Washington: Catholic University of America, 1949.

MacKinnon, Edward M. *Truth and Expression.* New York: Newman Press, 1971.

Müller, Gregor. *Die Wahrhaftigkeitspflicht und die Problematik der Lüge.* Freiburg: Herder, 1962.

Rahner, Karl. "On Truthfulness", in *Theological Investigations* VII, 1971, 229-259.

Ecology

Auer, Alfons. *Umweltethik. Ein theologischer Beitrag zur ökologischen Diskussion.* Düsseldorf: Patmos, 1984.

Clarck, Stephen R. L. *The Moral Status of Animals.* Oxford: Oxford Univ. Press, 1984.

Cosmao, Vincent. *Changing the World. An Agenda for the Churches.* Maryknoll, N.Y.: Orbis, 1984.

Francis, Joh, ed. *Facing Up to Nuclear Power.* Edinburgh: St. Andrew Press, 1976.

Goodpaster, K. E., and Sayre, K. M. *Ethics and Problems of the 21st Century.* London: Univ. of Notre Dame Press, 1979.

Krolzik, Udo. *Umweltkrise — Folge des Christentums?* Stuttgart: Kreuz Verlag, 1980.

Hart, John. *The Spirit of the Earth. A Theology of the Land.* Leominster: Fowler Wright, 1984.

Kohak, Erazim. *The Embers and the Stars. A Philosophical Inquiry into the Moral Sense of Nature.* Chicago, Ill.: The Univ. of Chicago Press, 1984.

Santmire, H. Paul. *The Travail of Nature. The Ambiguous Ecological Promise of Christian Theology.* Philadelphia, Pa.: Fortress Press, 1985.

Steck, Odil Hannes. *World and Environment.* (Biblical Encounter Series). Nashville: Abingdon, 1978.

3 5282 00744 4238